Modern Theory of PUBLIC FINANCE

Raghbendra Jha
Faculty of Australia South Asia Research Centre
Department of Economics
College of Asia and the Pacific
Australian National University
Canberra

NEW AGE MANAGEMENT
An Imprint of

NEW AGE INTERNATIONAL (P) LIMITED, PUBLISHERS
LONDON • NEW DELHI • NAIROBI
Bangalore • Chennai • Cochin • Guwahati • Hyderabad • Kolkata • Lucknow • Mumbai
Visit us at **www.newagepublishers.com**

Published by New Age International (P) Ltd., Publishers
First Edition: 1987
Reprint: 2017

GLOBAL OFFICES

- **New Delhi** **NEW AGE INTERNATIONAL (P) LIMITED, PUBLISHERS**
  7/30 A, Daryaganj, New Delhi-110002, (INDIA)
  Tel.: (011) 23253771, 23253472, **Telefax:** 23267437, 43551305
  E-mail: contactus@newagepublishers.com • Visit us at www.newagepublishers.com
- **London** **NEW AGE INTERNATIONAL (UK) LTD.**
  27 Old Gloucester Street, London, WC1N 3AX, UK
  E-mail: info@newacademicscience.co.uk • Visit us at www.newacademicscience.co.uk
- **Nairobi** **NEW AGE GOLDEN (EAST AFRICA) LTD.**
  Ground Floor, Westlands Arcade, Chiromo Road (Next to Naivas Supermarket)
  Westlands, Nairobi, KENYA, **Tel.:** 00-254-713848772, 00-254-725700286
  E-mail: kenya@newagepublishers.com

BRANCHES

- **Bangalore** 37/10, 8th Cross (Near Hanuman Temple), Azad Nagar, Chamarajpet, Bangalore- 560 018
  Tel.: (080) 26756823, **Telefax:** 26756820, **E-mail: bangalore@newagepublishers.com**
- **Chennai** 26, Damodaran Street, T. Nagar, Chennai-600 017, **Tel.:** (044) 24353401
  Telefax: 24351463, **E-mail: chennai@newagepublishers.com**
- **Cochin** CC-39/1016, Carrier Station Road, Ernakulam South, Cochin-682 016
  Tel.: (0484) 2377303, **Telefax:** 4051304, **E-mail: cochin@newagepublishers.com**
- **Guwahati** Hemsen Complex, Mohd. Shah Road, Paltan Bazar, Near Starline Hotel
  Guwahati-781 008, **Tel.:** (0361) 2513881, **Telefax:** 2543669
  E-mail: guwahati@newagepublishers.com
- **Hyderabad** 105, 1st Floor, Madhiray Kaveri Tower, 3-2-19, Azam Jahi Road, Near Kumar Theater
  Nimboliadda Kachiguda, Hyderabad-500 027, **Tel.:** (040) 24652456, **Telefax:** 24652457
  E-mail: hyderabad@newagepublishers.com
- **Kolkata** RDB Chambers (Formerly Lotus Cinema) 106A, 1st Floor, S N Banerjee Road
  Kolkata-700 014, **Tel.:** (033) 22273773, **Telefax:** 22275247
  E-mail: kolkata@newagepublishers.com
- **Lucknow** 16-A, Jopling Road, Lucknow-226 001, **Tel.:** (0522) 2209578, 4045297, **Telefax:** 2204098
  E-mail: lucknow@newagepublishers.com
- **Mumbai** 142C, Victor House, Ground Floor, N.M. Joshi Marg, Lower Parel, Mumbai-400 013
  Tel.: (022) 24927869, **Telefax:** 24915415, **E-mail: mumbai@newagepublishers.com**
- **New Delhi** 22, Golden House, Daryaganj, New Delhi-110 002, **Tel.:** (011) 23262368, 23262370
  Telefax: 43551305, **E-mail: sales@newagepublishers.com**

ISBN: 978-81-224-2769-1
C-16-09-9672

Printed in India at Ajit Printing Press, Noida.

NEW AGE INTERNATIONAL (P) LIMITED, PUBLISHERS
7/30 A, Daryaganj, New Delhi-110002
Visit us at **www.newagepublishers.com**
(CIN: U74899DL1966PTC004618)

Preface

Public Finance, or Public Economics as it is more generally called these days, has virtually gone through a revolution in the past few years. Much of this literature is available only in highly specialized journals most of which are not easily accessible to a vast majority of our libraries and students. It is also useful to have an integrated and unified approach to the whole field. In this book I have made an attempt to introduce students to the exciting and fundamental changes that have occurred in Public Finance. However the new results are juxtaposed with the old so that students should not lose the sense of continuity.

For the past few years I have taught a course, broadly structured according to the subject matter of this book, at the Delhi School of Economics, University of Delhi. These students have patiently and diligently made their way through much of the material in this book. I am grateful to them for their frank appraisal of these lectures. My experience in the classroom has helped me arrive at a deeper understanding of some problems of public finance.

I would also like a thank Dr M.N. Murty of the Institute of Economic Growth for constantly encouraging me and providing absolutely critical help by giving me access to his several published and unpublished writings in this area. I also record, with happiness, my collaboration with him in research on the Indian public sector.

Mr Virender Singh and Mr Joginder Singh have done an excellent job in typing the manuscript under (occasionally) trying circumstances.

My greatest debt is to my family—my wife Alka and our son Abhay. I will, however, not be so presumptuous as to thank them.

AUTHOR

This book is dedicated to
Mataji

Contents

PART—I

MODERN WELFARE ECONOMICS

1. Introduction

This book is written as an advanced text on Public Finance. In recent times this subject has changed drastically and there seems to be a need for a book that will introduce our postgraduate and research students to these developments. This book has been written with this purpose in mind. At the same time some serious problems of the Indian public sector are also studied.

This book can be divided into four parts: (*i*) modern welfare economics; (*ii*) the economics of taxation; (*iii*) applied welfare problems; and (*iv*) Indian public finance.

In the first section we study the classical theorems of welfare economics under certainty and uncertainty. We then study the problem of external effects under uncertainty and certainty. The free rider problem and problems of incentive compatibility are discussed at length in the chapter on public goods. Local public goods are also studied. There is a chapter on social choice theory and notions of economic justice.

In the second section we study the incentive effects of taxation. Tax incidence is studied in static as well as dynamic models. We also explore problems of optimal taxation and the question of optimal mix of direct and indirect taxes.

In the third section we study theoretical models for the optimal (linear as well as non-linear) pricing of the output of a public sector commodity. The question of joint determination of public sector prices and indirect taxes is also studied. We review the new literature on the macro effects of fiscal deficits. Standard approaches to cost benefit analysis are also reviewed.

The last section of this book has three chapters. The first chapter gives an overview of the Indian public sector. The second chapter reviews the tax structure of the Indian economy and the last chapter reviews some problems of centre-state financial relations.

The level of mathematical sophistication required of the student is one standard course in analysis. Advanced ideas are developed in the text itself.

The following is a list of some symbols used in this book

Symbol	*Meaning*	*Example*
$\in$	element	$a \in A$ i.e. a belongs to set A.
$\subset$	Subset	$A \subset B$ i.e. A is a (proper) subject of set B.

Symbol	*Meaning*	*Example*
$\cup$	Set union	$A \cup B$ i.e. union of sets A and B.
$\cap$	set intersection	$A \cap B$ i.e. the set of common elements of sets A and B.
$\rightarrow$	implies	$a \rightarrow b$ i.e. a implies b.
$\not\rightarrow$	does not imply	$c \not\rightarrow d$ c does not imply d.

A variable with a subscript usually denotes a partial derivative e.g.

$$x_r = \frac{\partial x}{\partial r}$$

and

$$x_{rr} = \frac{\partial^2 x}{\partial r^2}.$$

2. Perfect Competition and Pareto Optimality

The notion of Pareto optimality has Occupied a central place in modern welfare economics. Paretian principles are guides to ordering (in terms of social welfare) of social states and do not necessarily have anything to do with the market mechanism. However, as we will see below, the correspondence between perfect competition and Pareto optimality is central to what are called the Classical Theorems of Welfare Economics.

PARETIAN RANKING OF SOCIAL STATES

Consider a two person world where utility is ordinally measureable and we are interested in discovering which allocations of utilities among these two people are "better" than others. The Paretian principle gives us one method

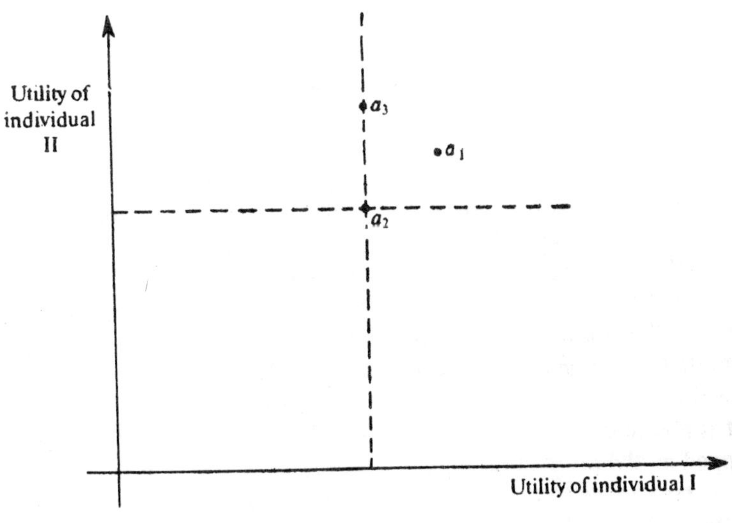

Fig. 2.1

of ranking these alternative distributions. On the x-axis of Fig. 2.1 we measure the utility of individual I and on the y-axis that of individual II.

The Weak Pareto Criterion (WPC) says that an allocation a_1 is superior to another allocation if and only if (iff) both individuals I and II are better off at a_1 than at a_2.

In Fig. 2.1 since a_1 lies to the north-east of east a_1 is weakly preferred (in the Pareto sense) to a_2.

According to the Strict Pareto Criterion (SPC) an allocation a_3 is preferred to an allocation a_2 iff everyone is at least well off at a_3 as they are at a_2 *and* at least one person is strictly better off. In Fig. 2.1 both a_1 and a_3 are strictly preferred to a_2. Note that a_3 is *not* weakly Pareto preferred to a_2.

The Pareto Criterion gives us one method of ranking social alternatives. However, this method is non-controversial and, when applicable, obviously quite satisfying. The major difficulty with the Paretian Criteria is that they are silent over vast ranges of social choices. In particular they give us no clue whatsoever about ranking social states in which, say, person I's utility has decreased and person II's increased.

Obviously many people have tried to get around this difficulty. The efforts have, however, not been very successful.[1]

PARETO OPTIMALITY

The Pareto Criterion as outlined above is concerned with ordering arbitrary social states. The notion of Pareto optimality focuses our attention on the "best" among those social states that are feasible. Let us study this concept in the simplest model of general equilibrium.

Consider a two person, two commodity, two factors of production economy. Each consumer in society has strictly quasi-concave, twice continuously differentiable utility functions. The production of the two commodities is carried on under conditions of constant returns to scale and diminishing returns to a factor. Both factors (say labour L and capital K) are substitutable for each other and full employment is continuously maintained.[2]

We can diagramatically show what is happening in this economy.

Figure 2.2(*a*) shows an Edgeworth box diagram depicting production of the two goods A (apples) and B (blankets) by capital and labour inputs. The availabilities of capital and labour define the size of the box and the south-west and the north-east corners of the box are the origins for measuring the outputs of A and B respectively. Plotted inside the box are the isoquants of A and B. The output A increases as we move towards O_B and vice versa. The points of tangencies of the two sets of isoquants (these points form a locus called the contract curve of production) map the maximum output of A that is possible given the output of B and vice versa. This contract curve is mapped as the production possibility frontier in Fig. 2.2(*b*).

Let us now move to the problem of distribution. Take any combination of outputs of A and B say point M in Fig. 2.2(*b*). This basket of goods can

[1]For a review of some attempts see Appendix I to this chapter.

[2]Note that we have consciously omitted making any statement about the presence of perfect competition.

be distributed in an infinite number of ways between individuals I and II. Let us chart the possibilities in Fig. 2.3.

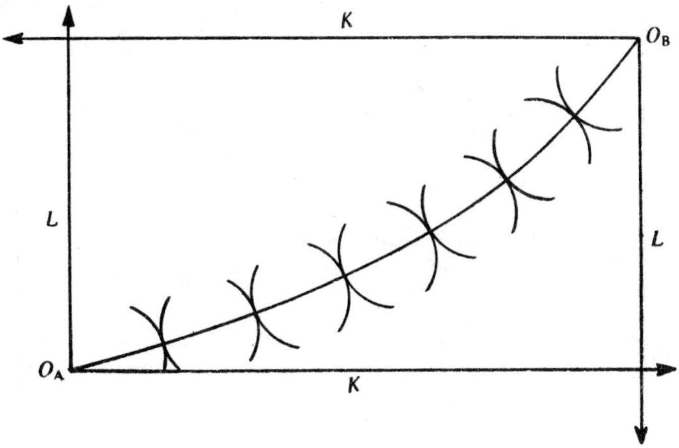

Fig. 2.2 (*a*)

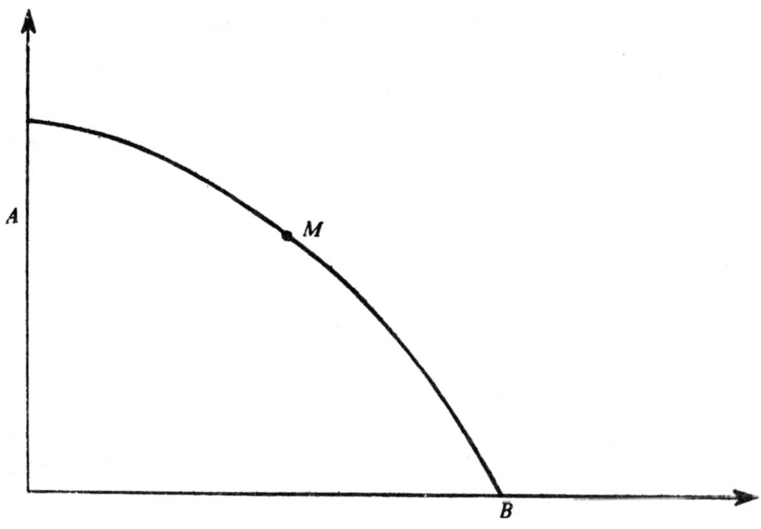

Fig. 2.2 (*b*)

Figure 2.3 depicts an Edgeworth box of consumption. The amounts of *A* and *B* available at point *M* in Fig. 2.2(*b*) define the size of this box. The origin of individual II is the north-east corner of the box and the south-west corner of this box is the origin for individual *I*. Plotted inside the box are indifference curves for individuals *I* and *II*. Individual *I*'s utility increases as we move towards O_B and *B*'s utility increases as we move towards O_I. The points of tangencies of the two sets of indifference curves (called the contract curve of consumption) gives the highest level of utility that I can attain *given* the level of utility of II.

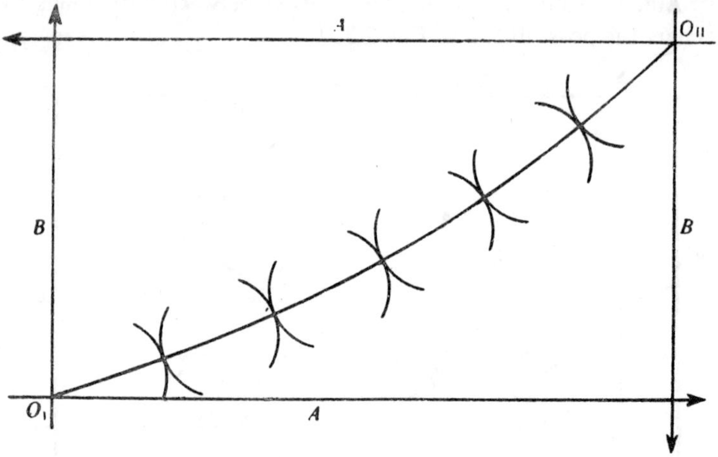

Fig. 2.3

In Fig. 2.4 we plot the utilities of the two individuals on the two axes. Line M_I M_I maps the contract curve of Fig. 2.3 onto utility space.

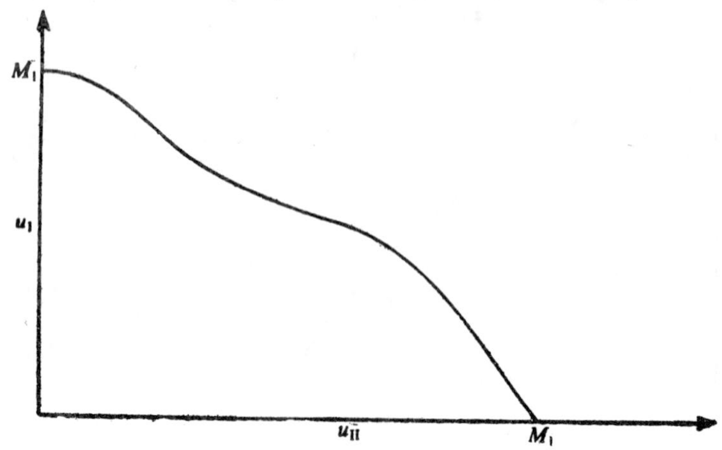

Fig. 2.4

However, there is nothing sacrosanct about the output combination denoted by *M* and indeed, it is possible to study the distribution of each basket of goods on the production possibility frontier. We may plot the resultant contract curves in Fig. 2.5.

Each line in the above diagram denotes distribution possibilities with a fixed basket of goods. Each such line is called a point utility possibility frontier (PUPF). There are clearly an infinite number of such frontiers. If we wish to summarise the utility tradeoffs for all points on the production possibility frontier we should take an outer envelope of all such PUPF.

The resulting frontier is sometimes called the situation utility possibility frontier (SUPF) and is depicted as dotted line in Fig. 2.6.

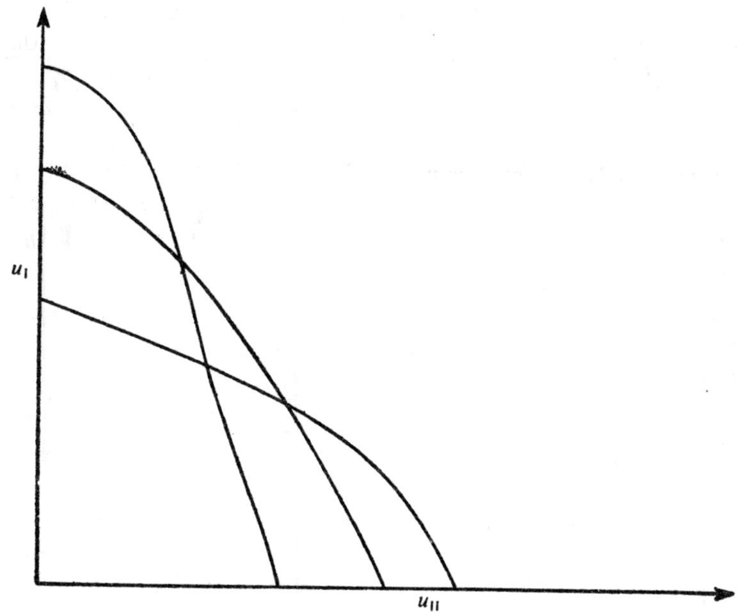

Fig. 2.5

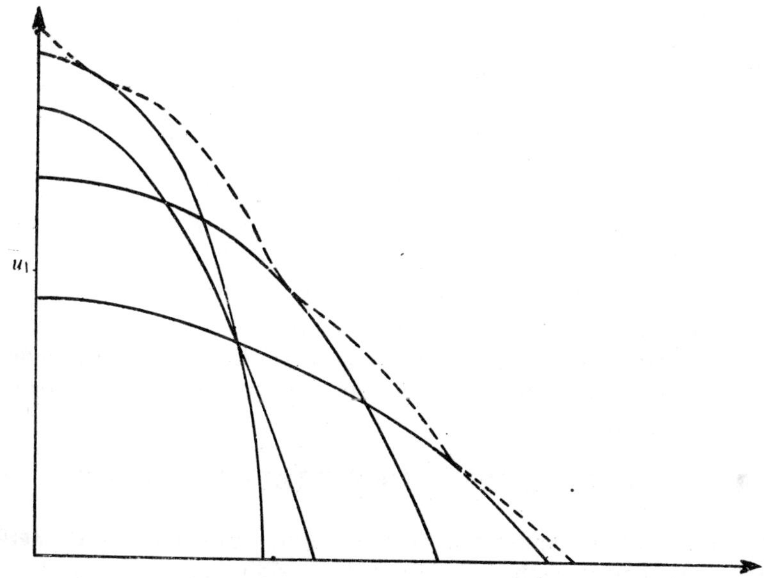

Fig. 2.6

By definition (or construction) every point on the SUPF has a PUPF tangent to it. This SUPF depicts the utility tradeoffs that are feasible given the fullest utilization of the society's resources. So any discussion of social choice must be restricted to points in this act.

In this social utility possibility set a feasible point b_1 is weakly Pareto optimal iff there does not exist a feasible point b_2 where both I and II are strictly better off, b_1 is strictly Pareto optimal if there does not exist another feasible allocation b_3 such that everyone is at least as well off at b_3 as he was at b_1 and at least one individual is strictly better off.

In Figs. 2.7(*a*) and 2.7(*b*) all points on both SUPF's are weakly pareto optimal. In Fig. 2.7(*a*) all points on the SUPF are also strictly Pareto optimal whereas in Fig. 2.7(*b*) only the points in dotted line are strictly Pareto optimal.

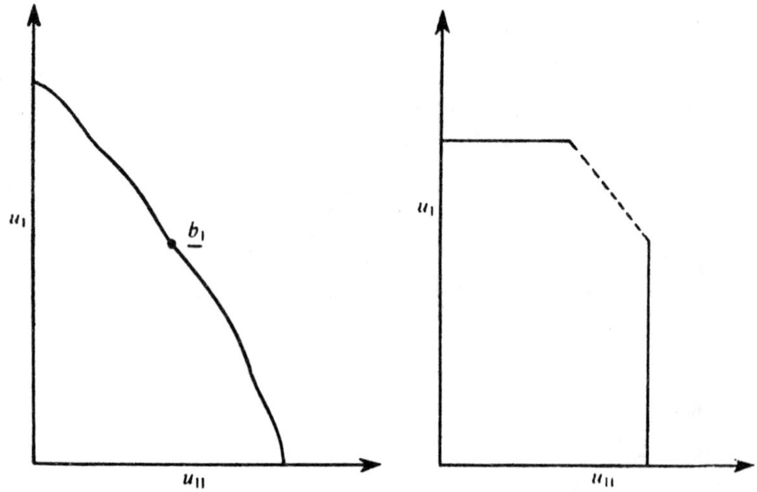

(*a*) (*b*)

Fig. 2.7

Some confusion has arisen with regard to the use of the Pareto criterion. Such confusion has arisen mainly because the Pareto criterion has been confused with common distributions. The trouble with the Pareto criterion is not that it says too much that it says too little. It does tell us to be on the SUPF but cannot narrow down the range any further. We will study efforts to narrow down the range at a later stage. In this chapter our concern is somewhat different.

THE CLASSICAL THEOREMS OF WELFARE ECONOMICS

These deal with the equivalence between Pareto optimality and the perfectly competitive market mechanism. We will give rather general proofs for these theorems (we don't use the calculus and do not presume the existence of utility or production functions). The standard calculus proofs are given in Appendix II. We first establish the context within which these theorems are operative.

Let our economy have N commodities amounts of which are to be designated by real numbers. R is the set of real numbers.

Definition. An economy E is characterized by

(*i*) N commodities.
(*ii*) m consumers (indexed by i) with consumption sets $X_i \in R^N$ for all i.
(*iii*) n producers (indexed by j) with production sets $Y_j \leqslant R^N$ for all j.
(*iv*) An initial endowment bundle $w \in R^N$.

This is a fairly general characterization of an economy.

A private enterprise economy $\hat{E}$ is E with the following additional specifications:

(*v*) for each consumer i a $w_i \in R^N(w_i \geqslant 0)$ $\sum_{i=1}^{m} w_i = w$.

(*vi*) for each consumer i and each producer j a fraction θ_{ij} such that

$$\sum_i \theta_{ij} = 1 \qquad \forall j.$$

Hence every firm is completely owned by the consumers. We have now explicitly brought in ownership.

An allocation a for this economy is an $(m + n)$ tuple of points in R^N specifying a consumption/production plan for each consumer/producer.

$$a = \{x_1, \ldots, x_m; y_1, \ldots, y_n\}.$$

This allocation is attainable if

(*i*) $x_i \in X_i$ for all i.
(*ii*) $y_j \in Y_j$ for all j.
(*iii*) $\sum_i x_i = w + \sum_j y_j$.

So each consumption plan must lie in the appropriate consumption set, each production plan lies in the appropriate production set and aggregate consumption cannot exceed aggregate production plus initial endowments.

This is a free enterprise economy or a market economy but not necessarily a perfectly competitive economy. A perfectly competitive equilibrium is an ordered pair $\langle \bar{a}, \bar{p} \rangle$ such that

(*i*) $\bar{a}$ is attainable.
(*ii*) for all i, $\bar{x}_i$ is R_i greatest bundle in

$$\{x_i \in X_i / \bar{p}x_i \leqslant \bar{p}w_i + \sum_j \bar{p}\theta_{ij}\bar{y}_j\}.$$

(*iii*) for all j, $\bar{p}\bar{y}_j \geqslant \bar{p}y_j$ for all $y_j \in Y_j$.

Condition (*ii*) merely states that each consumer maximizes his utility (in perfectly competitive equilibrium) subject to his budget constraint. $\bar{p}w_i$ is the values of his initial endownment and $\sum_j \bar{p}\theta_{ij}\bar{y}_i$ are the earnings of i from his ownership of shares. Condition (*iii*) states that each producer maximizes profits in perfectly competitive equilibrium $\bar{p}$ is the equilibrium vector of prices. Implicit in our discussion so far is the assumption that each producer and each consumer takes $\bar{p}$ to be parametrically (and exogenously) given. Also implicit is the assumption that producers and consumers do not cause external effects for each other.[3]

Two more definitions and we can tackle our theorem.

A consumer i satisfies the assumption of non-saturation iff $\exists\ x_i \in X_i$ such that $x_i' P_i x_i$ for all $x_i \in X_i$.

i satisfies local non-saturation iff $\exists\ x_i'$ such that $x_i' = x_i + \delta\ (\delta > 0$ and arbitrary small) such that $x_i' P_i x_i$, for all x_i.

It is immediately obvious that a consumer with the "usual" indifference map satisfies both these definitions.

We can now prove the first classical theorem of welfare economics.

THEOREM 1. Let $\hat{E}$ be a private enterprise economy where every consumer satisfies the property of local non-saturation. Let $\langle \bar{a}, \bar{p} \rangle$ be a perfectly competitive equilibrium for $\hat{E}$; then $\langle \bar{a}, \bar{p} \rangle$ is Pareto Optimal.

PROOF. Deny the theorem. Then there exists an allocation a such that a is attainable and $x_i R_i \bar{x}_i$ for all i and for some h $x_h P_h \bar{x}_h$.

This implies that either $xI\bar{x}$ or $xP\bar{x}$, We shall show that if $x_i I_i \bar{x}_i$ then $\bar{p}x_i \geqslant \bar{p}\bar{x}_i$. Deny this. Then $\bar{p}x_i < \bar{p}\bar{x}_i$ and $x_i I_i \bar{x}_i$.

Since the consumer satisfies the postulate of local non-saturation we can find a consumption bundle x_i' arbitrarily close to x_i (and hence below the budget line in Fig. 2.8) so that $x_i' P_i x_i$ and, by transitivity of R_i, $x_i' P_i \bar{x}_i$.

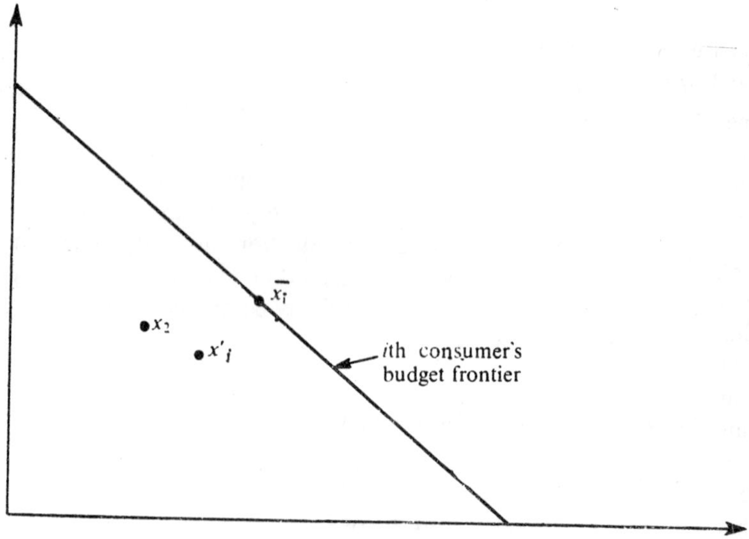

Fig. 2.8

But this is a contradiction since, by definition, $\bar{x}_i$ is R_i greatest bundle in the individualy's consumption set. Thus if $x_i I_i \bar{x}_i$ then $\bar{p}x_i \geqslant \bar{p}\bar{x}_i$. Analogously it is easy to show that if $\mu_h P_h \bar{x}_h$ then $\bar{p}x_h > \bar{p}\bar{x}_h$.

[3]This is dealt with in length in later chapters.

Adding these two results we obtain $\bar{p}x > \bar{p}\bar{x}$ which means

$$\Sigma\bar{p}y_j + \bar{p}w > \Sigma\bar{p}\bar{y}_j + \bar{p}w$$

which implies

$$\Sigma\bar{p}y_j > \Sigma\bar{p}\bar{y}_j$$

but this contradicts the statement for a perfectly competitive equilibrium which is that $\bar{p}\bar{y}_j \geqslant \bar{p}y_j$ for all $y_j \in Y_j$. Hence the theorem is proved.

We should clearly understand that the result we have proved is rather trivial since it says that if a perfectly competitive equilibrium exists then it is Pareto optimal. It thus sidesteps the question of existence of perfectly competitive equilibrium and the attendant problems *e.g.* external effects, non-convexities etc. Also it highlights the importance of the assumption of local non-saturation.

The second classical theorem—the central result—makes things more explicit.

THEOREM 2. Let $\bar{a}$ be a Pareto optimal allocation for economy E. Let

(*i*) for every i X_i be convex,
(*ii*) for every i R_i be convex,
(*iii*) for every j Y_j be convex,
(*iv*) for every i R_i satisfy continuity,
(*v*) For some i, $\bar{x}_i$ satisfies local non-saturation.

Then $\exists$ a price vector $\bar{p}$ (not all whose elements are zero) such that if $x_i R_i x_i'$ then $\bar{p}x_i \geqslant \bar{p}x_i'$.

Now if at this price vector $\bar{p}$ there exists a consumption bundle $x_i'' \in X_i$ (for all i) such that $\bar{p}x_i'' < \bar{p}\bar{x}_i$ then $\langle \bar{a}, \bar{p} \rangle$ constitutes a perfectly competitive equilibrium for some private enterprise economy $\hat{E}$ that can be constructed out of E.

This theorem states that under certain conditions any Pareto optimal allocation can be reached by a perfectly competitive market mechanism. (A calculus proof is given in the appendix). A simple illustration is given here for an exchange economy. Suppose that we have two consumers I and II and a fixed quantity of goods A and B to distribute between them. Hence there is only one PUPF. Let us study the Edgeworth box for this economy.

This economy is competitive. With initial endowment at T_1 the price ratio T_1Z_1 is established and the consumers willingly establish equilibrium at Z_1. We are, however, interested in establishing equilibrium at Z_2. The market mechanism allows us to attain this equilibrium if we redistribute initial endowments from T_1 to T_2 and establish the price ratio T_2Z_2. Once this is done consumers will arrive at the desired equilibrium voluntarily. This is the essence of Theorem 2 which we now proceed to prove.

PROOF. The proof of the theorem needs two lemmas. Suppose $\hat{x}_i \in X_i$ and with reference to $\hat{x}_i$ we define two sets.

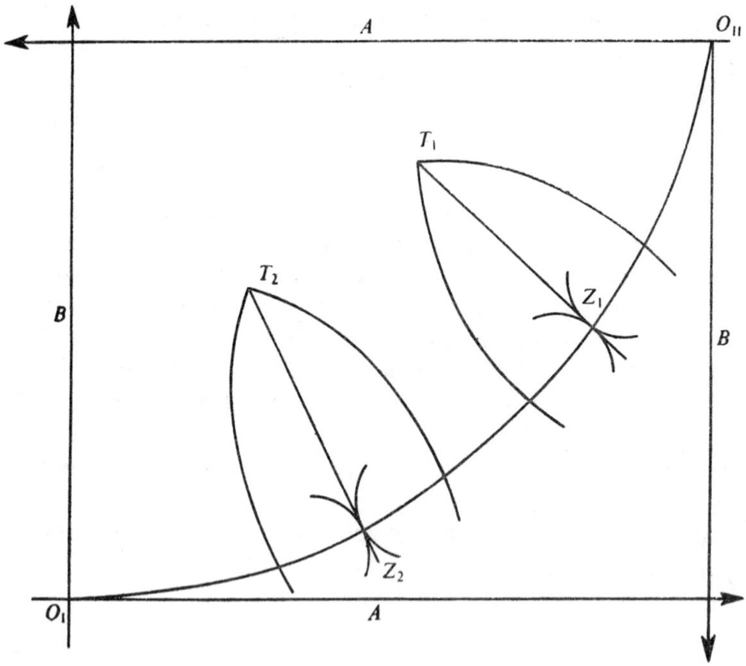

Fig. 2.9

Not worse than $\hat{x}_i$ set:

$NW(\hat{x}_i) = \{x_i \in X_i$ such that $x_i R_i \hat{x}_i\}$.

Better than $\hat{x}_i$ set:

$B(\hat{x}_i) = \{x_i \in X_i$ such that $x_i P_i \hat{x}_i\}$.
Then we have:

LEMMA 1.1. $NW(\hat{x}_i)$ and $B(\hat{x}_i)$ are convex sets for all $\hat{x}_i \in X_i$.

LEMMA 1.2. Let $x_i, x_i', x_i'' \in X_i$ and let $x_i' R_i x_i$ and $x_i'' P_i x_i$.
Then every consumption bundle in the closed interval (x_i', x_i'') is strictly preferred to x_i.

PROOF OF LEMMA 1.1. Take $NW(\hat{x}_i)$.

Let $x_i' R_i \hat{x}_i$ and $x_i'' R_i \hat{x}_i$) $(x_i', x_i'' \in X_i)$. We have to show that

$$\{\theta x_i' + (1 - \theta) x_i''\} R_i \hat{x}_i$$

$0 \leqslant \theta \leqslant 1$. Deny this. Then there exists some points along the closed interval (x_i', x_i'') such that x_i is preferred to them (*by* transitivity). Let there be just two such points $\bar{\bar{x}}_i$ and $\bar{x}_i$.

By implication we have

$$\hat{x}_i P_i \bar{x}_i \quad \text{and} \quad \hat{x}_i P_i \bar{\bar{x}}_i$$

By transitivity of R_i we have

$$x_i' P_i \bar{x}_i \quad \text{and} \quad x_i' P_i \bar{\bar{x}}_i$$

and

$$x_i'' P_i \bar{x}_i \quad \text{and} \quad x_i'' P_i \bar{\bar{x}}_i$$

Then by convexity and continuity of R_i all points along the segment x_i' to $\bar{\bar{x}}_i$ are preferred to $\bar{\bar{x}}_i$ and hence $\bar{x}_i P_i \bar{\bar{x}}_i$.
By an exactly similar arrangement
$\bar{\bar{x}}_i P_i \bar{x}_i$ (if we move in the opposite direction).
This gives us a contradiction.

Now consider the case when there is only one point along the segment x_i' to x_i'' such that $\hat{x}_i$ is strictly preferred to it. But this immediately violates the condition of continuity placed on R_i. Hence Lemma 1.1 is proved.

PROOF OF LEMMA 1.2. We have $x_i', x_i'' \in X_i$ and $x_i' P_i \hat{x}_i$ and $x_i'' P_i \hat{x}_i$. We have to prove

$$\hat{\hat{x}}_i = \{\theta x_i' + (1 - \theta) x_i''\} P_i \hat{x}_i.$$

If this was not true then either $\hat{x}_i P_i \hat{\hat{x}}_i$ or $\hat{x}_i I_i \hat{\hat{x}}_i$.

We know that both x_i' and x_i'' belongs to $NW(\hat{x}_i)$. Hence $\hat{x}_i P_i \hat{\hat{x}}_i$ is ruled out. By an argument exactly analogous to the proof of the first part of this lemma $\hat{x}_i I_i \hat{\hat{x}}_i$ is ruled out. So $B(\hat{x}_i)$ is convex.

LEMMA 1.2. Let $x_i, x_i', x_i'' \in X_i$ and $x_i' R_i x_i$ and $x_i'' P_i x_i$. We have to prove.

$$\hat{x}_i = [\theta x_i' + (1 - \theta) x_i''] P_i x_i.$$

Now since $x_i' R_i x_i$ we have either $x_i' P_i x_i$ or $x_i' I_i x_i$. If $x_i P_i x_i$ then since $B(x_i)$ is convex the result immediately follows. Let $x_i' I_i x_i$. Then, by transitivity $x_i'' P_i x_i'$. Then, all points along the segment x_i' to x_i'' are strictly preferred to x_i' (or x_i) by continuity. Hence $\hat{x}_i P_i x_i'$.

We will state the second lemma without proof. The interested reader can find the proof in a number of works. The classic reference is Debreu (1959).

LEMMA 2. Two non-empty, convex and non-intersecting sets in R^N can be separated by a hyperplane.

PROOF. The proof of this theorem is split up into five parts

(*a*) Define two sets G and H satisfying Lemma 2. The normal $\bar{p}$ is the price vector in Pareto theorem.

(*b*) Aggregate consumption bundle specified in Pareto optimal allocation $\bar{a}$ lies on the hyperplane itself.

(*c*) Given $\bar{p}$ every producer maximizes profits if he produces $\bar{a}$.

(*d*) Given $\bar{p}$ if $x_i R_i \bar{x}_i$ then $\bar{p}x_i \geqslant \bar{p}\bar{x}_i$ for every i.

(*e*) There exists another bundle $x_i \in X_i$ such that $\bar{p}x_i < \bar{p}\bar{x}_i$.

We will prove each part.

(*a*) Define $G = \{x/x = \Sigma x_i,\ x_i \in X_i$ for all i; $x_i R_i \bar{x}_i$ for all i and for some $x_h P_h \bar{x}_h\}$

$$H = \{h/h = w + \Sigma y_j;\ y_j \in Y_j \quad \text{for all } j\}.$$

To show G is non-empty.

We have assumed that in Pareto optimum at last one consumer is not fully saturated, without loss of generality let this be 1. Define a new aggregate consumption bundle

$$\hat{x} = x + \sum_{i=2}^{m} \bar{x}_i$$

where $x_1 P_1 \bar{x}_1$. Hence G is non-empty.

To show G is convex. Let $x', x'' \in G$.

To show $\hat{x} = \{\theta x' + (1 - \theta)x''\} \in G$.

$$\hat{x} = \theta(x_1' + x_2' + \ldots + x_m') + (1 - \theta)(x_1'' + \ldots + x_m'')$$

$$= \theta x_1' + (1 - \theta)x_1'' + \ldots + \theta x_m' + (1 - \theta)x_m''$$

$$= \hat{x}_1 + \hat{x}_2 + \ldots + \hat{x}_m$$

We know $\hat{x}_1 P_1 \bar{x}_1$ and $\hat{x}_i R_i \bar{x}_i$ for $i = 2, \ldots, m$. Hence by Lemma 1.2 G is convex.

To show H is non-empty.

$H = h = w + \Sigma\, y_j$. Now for all $j y_j \in Y_j$ and hence H is non-empty.

To show H is convex. Let $h', h'' \in H$.

To show $\hat{h} = \{\theta h' + (1 - \theta)h''\} \in H$

$$\hat{h} = \theta[w + \Sigma y_j'] + (1 - \theta)[w + \Sigma y_j'']$$

$$= \theta y_1' + (1 - \theta)y_1'' + \ldots + \theta y_n' + (1 - \theta)y_n''$$

$= \hat{y}_1 + \hat{y} + \ldots + \hat{y}_n$. By convexity of Y_j we have $\hat{y}_j \in Y_j$ for all . Hence H is convex.

(*a*) To show that G and H are non-intersecting. Let G and H intersect. Hence we have found a set of consumption and production plans that match and are, hence, attainable. Hence any element of this set is Pareto superior to $\bar{a}$ and hence $\bar{a}$ is not Pareto optimal—which gives us a contradiction. Hence G and H do not intersect.

Hence since all assumptions of Lemma 2 have been satisfied we have a hyperplane ($\bar{p}$) which separates G and H such that for all $x \in G$ and all $h \in H$ $\bar{p}x \geqslant \bar{p}h$.

(*b*) To show $\bar{a}$ lies on the hyperplane itself. Deny this that $\bar{a}$ can lie either above or below $\bar{p}$. Take the case where $\bar{a}$ lies above the hyperplane. Now since $\bar{a}$ is attainable it follows that $\bar{x} = (w + \Sigma\, \bar{y}_j) = h$ but $h \in H$; hence this is a contradiction. Let $\bar{x}$ lie below the hyperplane. Consider $x \in G$ and

$$\hat{x} = \theta\bar{x} + (1 - \theta)x$$

$$\hat{x} = \hat{x}_1 + \ldots + \hat{x}_m$$

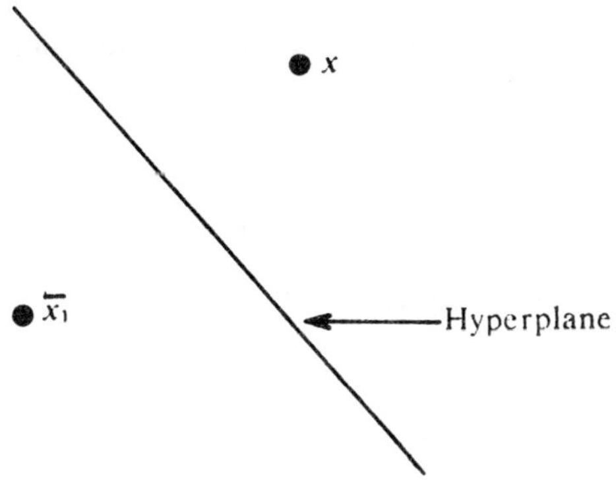

Now $\hat{x}_i \in X_i$ for all i. Furthermore $\hat{x}_i R_i \bar{x}_i$ for all i and $\hat{x}_h P_h \bar{x}_h$ for some h.

Hence $\hat{x} \in G$. Now if we let $\theta \rightarrow 1$, $\hat{x}$ will lie below the hyperplane. This gives us a contradiction. Hence $\bar{a}$ lies on the hyperplane itself.

(*c*) To show profit is maximized (relative to $\bar{p}$) if producers produce h.

Aggregate demand is $\bar{p}\bar{x}$.

Aggregate supply is $\bar{p}w + \sum_j \bar{p}\bar{y}_j$.

We also know $\bar{p}\bar{x}$ is greater in value than any bundle on hyperplane or below it. Hence $\bar{p}\bar{x} > \bar{p}h$ (for all $h \notin \bar{h}$).

Fix up $\bar{y}_2, \ldots, \bar{y}_n$.

Now

$$\bar{p}\bar{x} = \bar{p}w + \bar{p}\bar{y}_1 + \bar{p} \sum_{j=2}^{n} \bar{y}_j > \bar{p}w + \bar{p}y_1 + \bar{p} \sum_{j=2}^{n} \bar{y}_j.$$

Hence $\bar{p}\bar{y}_1 > \bar{p}y_1$. This is true for every producer so that profit is maximized by producing the Pareto optimal bundle.

(*d*) Given $\bar{p}$ if $x_i R_i \bar{x}_i$ then $\bar{p}x_i \geqslant \bar{p}\bar{x}_i$ for all i. Deny this then we have $\bar{p}x_i < \bar{p}\bar{x}_i$ and $x_i R_i \bar{x}_i$.

Fix up $\bar{x}_2, \ldots, \bar{x}_m$.

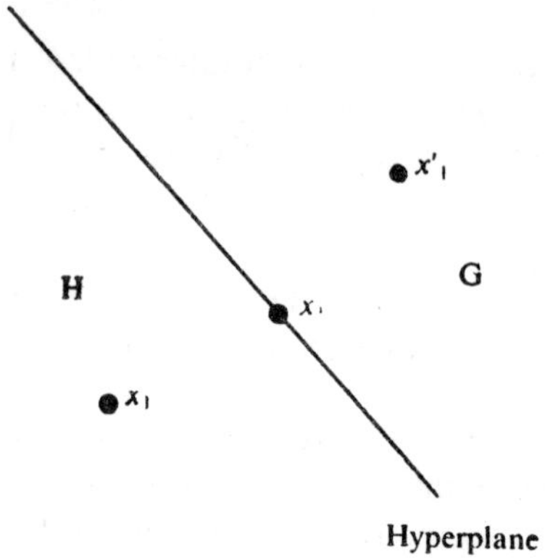

Now $\hat{x}_1 = \theta x_1 + (1 - \theta)x'_1$ where x_1 lies below the hyperplane and x'_1 lies above it. By Lemma 1.2 $\hat{x}_1 P_1 \bar{x}_1$.

Now let $\theta \to 1$ then $\hat{x}_1$ will lie below the hyperplane and $\hat{x}_1 P_1 \bar{x}_1$. Then $\bar{x}$ is clearly not Pareto optimal. Hence we get a contradiction.

(*e*) To show that $\bar{x}_i$ is R_i greatest bundle in each consumer's budget set.

We bring in the ownership of firms and fix up the initial endowment bundles such that

$$w_i = \bar{x}_i - \sum_{j=1}^{n} \theta_{ij}\bar{y}_j$$

Then we have to show that $\bar{x}_i$ is R_i greatest bundle in

$$\left\{x_i \in X_i / \bar{p}x_i \leqslant \bar{p}w_i + \bar{p} \sum_{j=1}^{n} \theta_{ij}\bar{y}_j\right\}$$

or in $\{x_i \in X_i / \bar{p}x_i \leqslant \bar{p}\bar{x}_i\}$.

Divide this set into two groups

$$\{x_i \in X_i / \bar{p}x_i < \bar{p}\bar{x}_i\} \quad \text{and} \quad \{x_i \in X_i / \bar{p}x_i = \bar{p}\bar{x}_i\}.$$

From stage (*d*) just proved it immediately follows that $\bar{x}_i$ is R_i greatest bundle in this set.

Now consider the set $\{x_i \in X_i / \bar{p}x_i = \bar{p}\bar{x}_i\}$

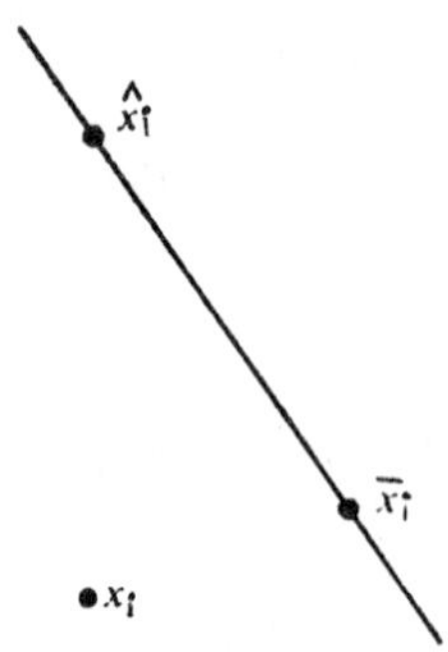

Consider x_i which lies below the hyperplane and $\hat{x}_i$ which is another point on the hyperplane.

We know $\bar{x}_i R_i \bar{x}_i$. Take a sequence $\theta x_i + (1 - \theta)\hat{x}_i$ with $0 \leqslant \theta \leqslant 1$, and let $\theta \to 0$. By continuity it immediately follows that $\bar{x}_i R_i x_i$.

Hence $\bar{x}_i$ is R_i greatest bundle in the set $\{x_i \in X_i / \bar{p}x_i \leqslant \bar{p}\bar{x}_i\}$. (If we had well defined utility functions we would have said that Pareto optimum is also individually optimum under the assumptions of Theorem 2).

This theorem is trully fundamental. It is saying several things simultaneously. Let us separate these.

1. Although it is not stated explicity, the theorem is supposed to drop a very strong hint to the effect that the question of reaching any Pareto optimal allocation can be separated from the question of deciding which Pareto optimal point society should attain. Thus the "normative" question of which distribution to aim for is separated from the "positive" question of how to reach such a distribution. This distinction is absolutely vital to a whole line of welfare theorists like Hayek, Buchanan and Milton Friedman (Maurice Dobb criticises this distinction as being artificial.[4]

2. To economists like Hayek it is particularly heartening that any Pareto optimal allocation can be reached with the help of the market mechanism. This, of course, means that a case can be made for non-interference by the government in the market. The market is efficient, indeed perfect, and an economical and proper user of information.

3. Stated this way one tends to become a little complacent about actually choosing a particular distribution. It is important to remember that the market cannot help us do that and the Pareto criterion is not going to be of much help either.

4. It is also important to emphasize that the market mechanism has no inherent informational advantage over other allocative mechanism. If we stick to the framework of Theorem 2 we need exchange ratios (which happen to be price ratios in a market economy) to support a Pareto optimal allocation. An exchange ratio established by a decentralized socialist economy would serve exactly the same function.

5. Moreover if we are also concerned about the distributional question we must realize that to pinpoint a desirable distribution (whether or not we use the market to attain it) we need information about production sets and consumption sets as well as preference relations etc. Thus in choosing the particular distribution we want to attain there is no special advantage that the market enjoys vis-a-vis even a centrally planned economy.

These comments should help put these theorems in perspective. For further discussion see Dobb (*Op. cit.*), Graaf (1956) and Koopmans (1957) for example.

In the next few chapters we will examine the implications for the allocative efficiency of the market of relaxing some of the assumptions of Theorem 2. We bring in uncertainty in the next chapter and then relax the assumption of non-interdependence.

---

[4]See Dobb (1960), (1969).

Appendix I

The Compensation Criteria

A fuller discussion of efforts to improve upon the ranking of social states provided by the Pareto criterion will come later. In this appendix we briefly discuss some compensation criteria of social choice.

Kaldor (1939) tried to say something about the vast ranges of the SUPF where the Pareto criterion is silent. Actually Kaldor himself announced this criterion solely for production efficiency but the "Kaldor Criterion" has been used as a welfare norm. The Kaldor Criterion says the following. Social state x is better than social state y if the gainers in the transition form y to x can more than adequately compensate the losers for their loss and still remain better off.

It ought to be pointed out that the criterion does not say that compensation actually takes place. The possibility of adequate compensation is sufficient. Dobb (*op. cit.*) discusses this point in detail and with his usual clarity. Moreover this criterion is two term inconsistent i.e. we can simultaneously have x being Kaldor preferred to y *and* y being Kaldor preferred to x.

In Fig. A.2.1, two PUPF are drawn and are labelled a_1a_1 and a_2a_2. According to the Kaldor mechanism individual I can "potentially" move along a_1a_1 from x and come to a point north-east of y. Hence x is Kaldor preferred to y. Individual II can however "potentially" move from y along a_2a_2 and come to a point that is north-east of x. Hence y is Kaldor preferred to x.

Hicks advocated the "dual" of the Kaldor compensation criterion and argued that social state x is preferred to social state y if the losers in the movement from y to x cannot adequately bribe the gainers (to not effect the change) and still remain better off. The Hicks criterion also talks of hypothetical not actual transfers and can, like the Kaldor criterion, be shown to be two-term inconsistent.

The Scitovsky criterion combines the Kaldor and Hicks criteria to say that social state x is better than social state y if the gainers in the movement from x to y can adequately compensate the losers and still remain better off and the losers cannot bribe the losers to not effect the change and still remain better off. This criterion again calls for hypothetical transfers. If actual transfers did take place there would be no need to use compensation criterion the Pareto criterion is sufficient. The Scitovsky criterion is also not free of contradictions.

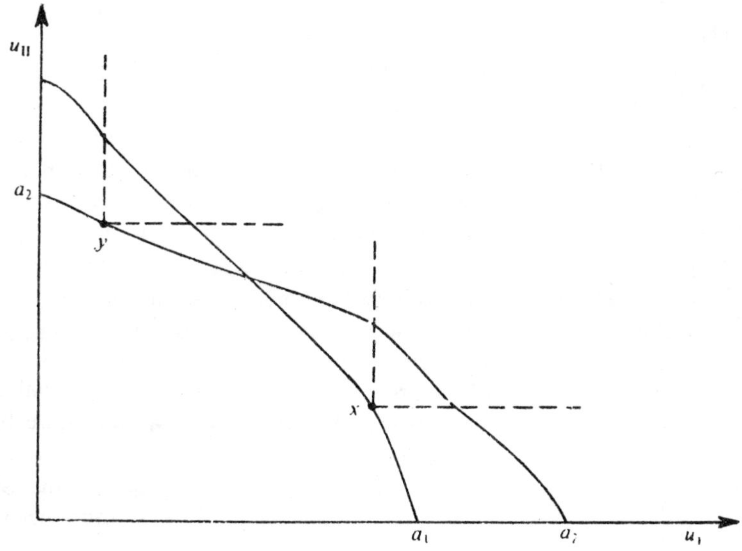

Fig. A 2.1

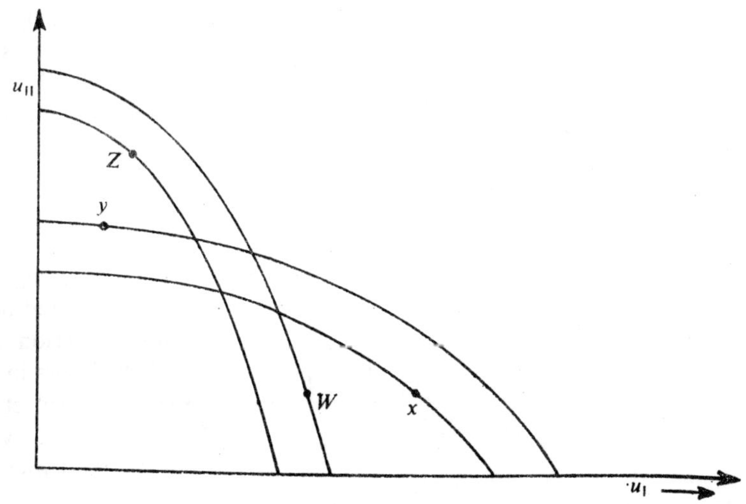

Fig. A.2.2

In Fig. A.2.2 four PUPF are drawn. In terms of the Scitovsky criterion the movement from x to y, y to z, z to w, w to x are all preferred. Thus we get our cycle.

Appendix II

The utility approach to Theorem 2.

Our consumer satisfies the basic rationality postulates of reflexivity (xR_ix, for all $x \in X_i$), connectedness (for all x, $x' \in X_i$ either xR_ix' or $x'R_ix$ or both) and transitivity (for all x, x', $x'' \in X_i$, xR_ix' and $x'R_ix'' \rightarrow xR_ix''$).

But just because xR_iy it does not follow that we can define a real valued utility function such that $U(x) \geqslant U(y)$. If X_i is a finite (or infinite but countable) set then it can be shown that the required U function always exists. But if X_i is uncountably infinite then we need some additional requirements. The standard illustration of an uncountable infinite consumption set is given by the lexicographic ordering. Suppose a consumer loves fish and indeed he loves it so much that given any amount of fish more rice makes him better off but if you give him just a little more fish he would be better off than with a consumption basket that contains the old amount of fish *irrespective* of the amount of rice in that basket. Thus an infinite number of real numbers is exhausted in calculating utility values associated with just one quantity of fish.

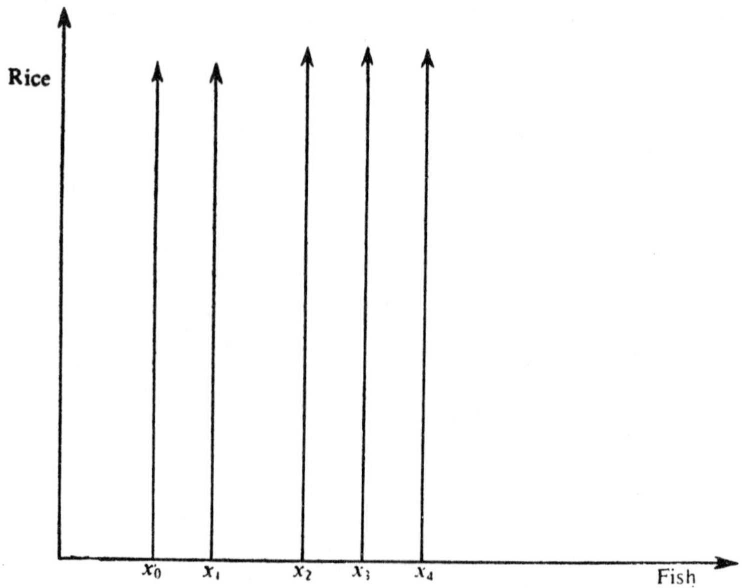

Fig. A.2.3

In the above diagram with x_0 level of fish utility increases along the vertical through x_0 but the very next highest amount of fish gives higher utility than any point on the vertical through x_0. So we run out of real numbers.

The additional requirement needed now is that of order denseness. With R as an ordering over X_i a subset J_i of X is P order dense in X iff xP_iz and x, $z \in X_i - J_i$ implies xR_iyR_iz for some $y \in J_i$. Then we can appeal to Cantor's theorem.

Cantor's Theorem. There is a real valued function U on X_i such that for all $x, x' \in X_i$, $x R_i x' \rightarrow U(x) \geqslant U(x')$ iff R is an ordering on X_i and there exists a countable subset of X_i that is P order dense in X_i (for a proof see for instance Luce and Suppes (1965)).

Having outlined the technical requirements let us assume that utility functions and productions functions exist and study the calculus proof of Theorem 2.

The utility of the ith individual is given by

$$U_i = U_i(x_{1i}, x_{2i}, \ldots, x_{Ni}), \qquad i = 1, \ldots, m.$$

where x_{ji} is the amount of the jth good consumed by individual i. (One can include, if one wishes, labour as a detractor from utility).

The production functions for the various goods can be written as

$$x_k = x_k(x_{1k}, x_{2k}, \ldots, x_{Nk}; l_{1k}, \ldots, l_{Sk}), \qquad k = 1, \ldots, N$$

where x_{wk} is the amount of the wth good used as input in the production of x_k. l_{tk} is an input of a natural resource or primary factor of production. There are S such natural resources or primary factor of production. The following accounting identities hold

$$x_k = \sum_{i=1}^{m} x_{ki} + \sum_{i=1}^{N} x_{ik}, \quad k = 1, \ldots, N$$

$$l_t = \sum_{k=1}^{N} l_{tk}, \qquad t = 1, \ldots, S.$$

To derive the conditions for Pareto optimality, we maximize the utility of one individual say 1 subject to the utilities of others being kept at a fixed level. So we write our Lagrangean as

$$L = U_1 + \sum_{i=2}^{m} \lambda_i(U_i - \bar{U}_i) + \sum_{k=1}^{N} \theta_k\left(x_k - \sum_{i=1}^{m} x_{ki} - \sum_{i=1}^{N} x_{ik} \right) + \sum_{t=1}^{S} \eta_t\left(l_t - \sum_{k=1}^{N} l_{tk}\right)$$

where λ_i, θ_k and η_t are appropriate Lagrange multipliers. Differentiating L with respect to the control variables we get

$$\lambda_i \frac{\partial U_i}{\partial x_{ki}} = \theta_k, \qquad i = 1, \ldots, m; \quad k = 1, \ldots, N$$

$$\theta_k \frac{\partial x_k}{\partial x_{ki}} = \theta_i \quad (i, k = 1, \ldots, N)$$

$$\theta_k \partial x_k / \partial l_{tk} = \eta_t \qquad (k = 1, \ldots, N, \; t = 1, \ldots, S)$$

where $\lambda = 1$.

Defining these results in proportionate terms now we get,

$$\frac{\partial U_i/\partial x_{ki}}{\partial U_i/\partial x_{Hi}} = \frac{\theta_k}{\theta_H}(i = 1, \ldots, m)$$

which simply states that the marginal rate of substitution (for any consumer) between any two goods is equal to the price ratio between these two goods. If the market mechanism is functioning perfectly every rational consumer would automatically satisfy this condition since this condition is also required for individual utility maximization.

Similarly the second condition can be written as:

$$\frac{\partial x_k/\partial x_{ki}}{\partial x_k/\partial x_{kj}} = \frac{\theta_i}{\theta_j}$$

which simply says that the rate of technical substitution between any two factors of production is equal to the ratio of the prices of these factors. Again this condition is automatically satisfied in perfectly competitive equilibrium since this condition implies constrained cost minimization or constrained revenue maximization.

Combining these two results we get,

$$\frac{\partial U_i/\partial x_{ki}}{\partial U_i/\partial x_{Hi}} = \frac{\partial x_k/\partial x_{kk}}{\partial x_k/\partial x_{kH}}$$

which requires that the marginal rate of substitution in consumption equal the rate of technical substitution in production.

Similarly we can interpret the second and third condition to give us marginal rate of substitution (between any two goods) equals marginal rate of transformation of production along the production possibility frontier. Again it is individually rational for firms and consumers to satisfy these conditions in perfectly competitive equilibrium.

For a two commodity, two individual, two factor case we can depict these results graphically:

On the basis of some welfare criterion we choose point *X* on the SUPF shown in Fig. A.2.4(*d*). This point is released by a PUPF that corresponds to an output basket given by *X* on the production possibility frontier shown in Fig. A2.4(*a*). The production of this basket is shown in the Edgeworth box of exchange shown in Fig. A2.4(*b*). Here the wage rental ratio is equal to the rate of technical substitution between capital and labour. The distribution of this basket between individuals *I* and *II* is shown in the Edgeworth box of exchange in Fig. A.2.4(*c*). Here the marginal rate of substitution between *A* and *B* is equal to the price ratio. This price ratio is also equal to the slope of the production possibility frontier (or the marginal rate of transformation between *A* and *B* in Fig. A 2.4(*d*).

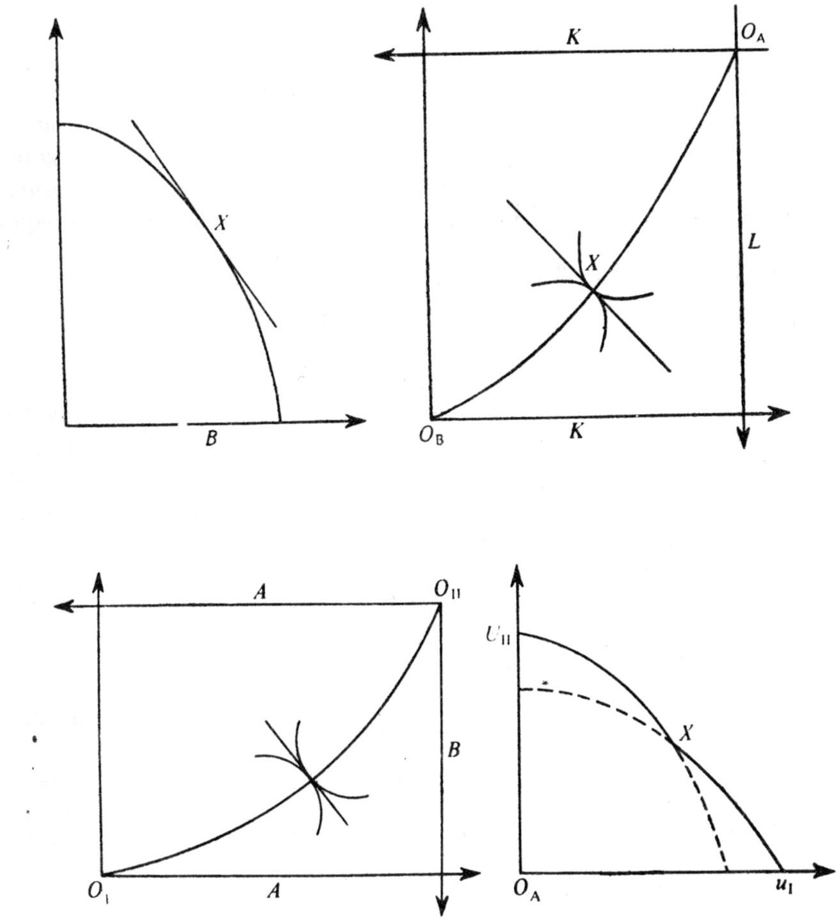

Fig. A.2.4

3. Uncertainty, Perfect Competition and Pareto Optimality

In the last chapter we discussed the classical theorems of welfare economies and studied the conditions under which they are valid. These conditions are rather rarefied and we wish to study the effects of relaxing some of these assumptions. In this chapter we bring in uncertainty and see what difference this makes.

The first formal effort in this direction was that of Debreu (1959). In a sense Debreu looks upon this problem as one of existence of markets. Usually a commodity is defined with respect to three characteristics—a certain pysical homogeneity, date and place. So red wheat from the 1984 rabi crop in Punjab is one commodity and different from white wheat from the 1983 rabi crop in Bihar. When dealing with uncertainty Debreu adds a fourth dimension—state of the world. The umbrella is one commodity if it rains and a different commodity if it does not rain. So the definition of a commodity (as usually articulated) is contingent upon the state of the world that obtains).

Debreu then proceeds to argue that the reason why the classical welfare theorems don't go through in the face of uncertainty is that there are no markets (or incomplete markets) for contingent commodities. If complete contingent markets can be made to exist then there will be no problems since the two classical theorems will go through. Let us formalize this a little.

In any time period l ($l > 1$) any of the following $E^* = (s_1, \ldots, s_n)$ states of the world is possible. We shall assume that E^* is finite. This is what is described as an event tree.

An event tree is a finite sequence $\langle \rho_0, \rho_1, \ldots, \rho_L \rangle$ satisfying the following conditions:

(*i*) $\rho_0 = E^*$

(*ii*) For every time period t ($1 \leqslant t \leqslant L$) there exists exactly one partition ρ_t in the sequence $\langle \rho_0, \ldots, \rho_L \rangle$; the non-empty elements of ρ_t are called events and are indexed by e_t going from 1_t to k_t.

(*iii*) Every element at L is a singleton.

(*iv*) Every event at $(t + 1)$ is a subset of some element at t (for all t; $1 \leqslant t \leqslant L$).

We can then define a *path*. Consider any event e_L at time period L. Let

$$\rho = \langle 1_1, 2_1, \ldots, k_1, \ldots, 1_L, \ldots, k_L \rangle$$

then the path from 1_0 to e_L is defined as $\rho(e_L)$ and is derived by dropping from ρ all events of which e_L is not a subset.

One Debreu's reinterpretation of the characteristics of a commodity we reinterprte consumption sets, production sets and ordering. Thus given e_L we can, for instance, define a production set $Y_j(e_L)$. A production plan $y_j(e_L)$ is feasible if $y_j(e_L) \in Y_j(e_L)$. The production set is one thing if it rains and quite another thing if it doesn't rain.

Similarly a consumption set is defined as $X_i(e_L)$ and a feasible consumption plan is $x_i(e_L)$ where $x_i(e_L) \in X_i(e_L)$.

Orderings are now defined over the redefined consumption set. But the convexity of R_i implies that the individual is risk averse. Let us take an example. Suppose there are two ordinary commodities (x_1, x_2) I give α value to a certain unit of x, and β value to a certain units of x_2. Suppose

$$(\alpha, \alpha) P_i \, (\beta, \beta)$$
$$(\alpha, \beta) I_i \, (\beta, \alpha).$$

Then by convexity of R_i any convex combination of (α, β) (β, α) is at least as good as (β, α) i.e., for instance,

$$\left\{\frac{1}{2}(\alpha, \beta) + \frac{1}{2}(\beta, \alpha)\right\} R_i(\beta, \alpha) I_i(\alpha, \beta)$$

i.e. the individual is risk averse in a weak sense. If R_i were strictly convex then

$$\left\{\frac{1}{2}(\alpha, \beta) + \frac{1}{2}(\beta, \alpha)\right\} P_i(\beta, \alpha) I_i(\alpha, \beta).$$

With such reinterpretation then it is quite clear that the formal results will go through. Some people have argued that this might land us below the SUPF. But Debreu is dealing with the problem of choice under uncertainty. Where this choice lands us after this uncertainty has been resolved is a different matter altogether. The usefulness of a method for making choice under uncertainty cannot be judged from the vantage point of expost consequences.

A more serious problem with the Debreu mechanism is that although formally the results go through it is impractical to suggest and unrealistic to expect complete contingent markets to exist. A method of dealing with uncertainty without resorting to the method of contingent commodities had to be found. Arrow in a path breaking work circumvented this difficulty somewhat. To study the Arrow mechanism we have to first study the expected utility theorem.

AXIOMS OF THE EXPECTED UTILITY THEOREM

Let $\Omega(\theta)$ be the (finite) set of all possible outcomes and let $\Omega(\alpha)$ be the (finite) set of all possible actions. Action can then be looked upon as a function of E^* from $\Omega(\theta)$ i.e. the outcome depends on action and state of the world i.e. $\theta_i = \alpha(s)$ i.e. if I take action α and state of the world s is realized then the outcome is θ_i. It also follows that any outcome that was not visualised does not affect my action. Suppose an event $e \subseteq E^*$ is given to me. Then if I take action α' then define a probability distribution over all the θ_i's. Let this probability distribution be designated by $\pi(e, \alpha')$. A special case of this is when there is no information whatsoever and we have to deal with the entire E^*.

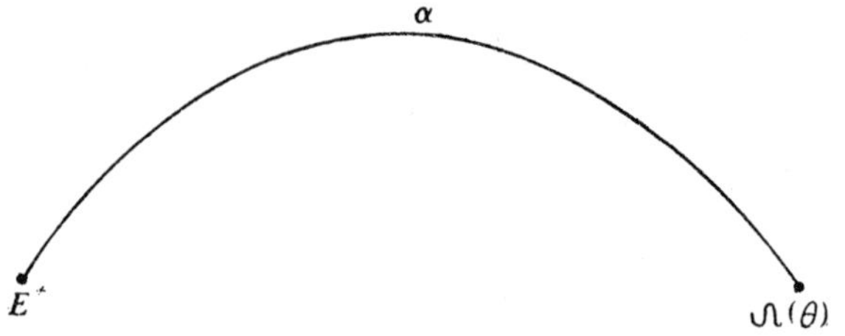

We can then state the axioms of the von-Neumann-Morgenstern expected utility theorem.

1. *Conditional Ordering*: Given any event e the agent has a conditional ordering R_e defined over $\Omega(\alpha)$ such that $\alpha, \alpha' \in \Omega(\alpha)$ if $\alpha'(s) = \alpha''(s)$ for all $s \in e$ then $\alpha' I_e \alpha''$.

2. *Probabilistic Belief*: Given any event e and any two actions α', α'' if $\pi(e, \alpha') = \pi(e, \alpha'')$ then $\alpha' I_e \alpha''$. This means that all that matters for choice is the probability distribution. As a counter example take the following case. One stage lottery.

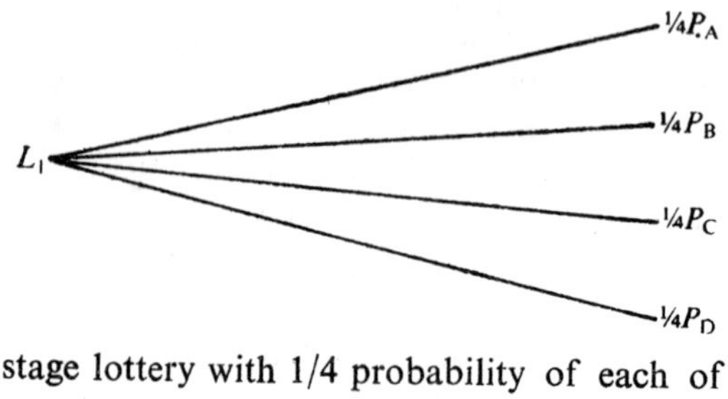

This is a one stage lottery with 1/4 probability of each of the outcomes A, B, C, D.

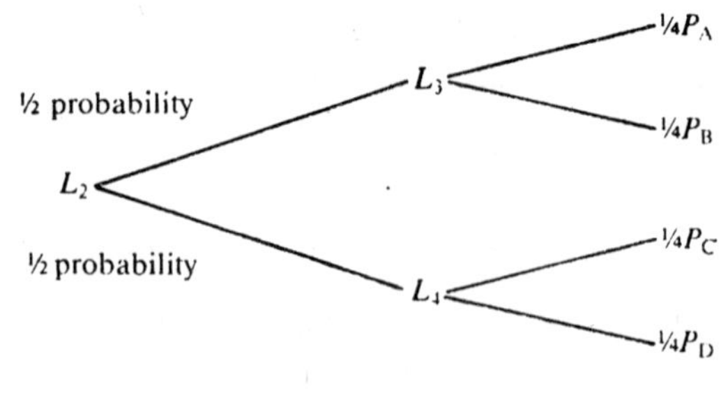

In this two stage lottery there is again 1/4 probability of each of the outcomes. The axiom of probabilistic belief says that the individual is indifferent between L_1 and L_2. However a gambler might prefer L_2 with 1/2 probability of L_3 and L_4 and then 1/4 probability of A, B, C or D.

Axiom of Continuity: Let α', α'', $\alpha''' \in \Omega(\alpha)$ and e be the given event such that $\alpha' P_e \alpha''$. Then there exists a neighbourhood of $\pi(e, \alpha')$ such that if $\pi(e, a''')$ lies in that neighbourhood then $\alpha''' P_e \alpha''$. Also there exists a neighbourhood of $\pi(e, \alpha'')$ such that if $\pi(e, \alpha''')$ lies in this then $\alpha' P_e \alpha'''$.

Axiom of Dominance: Suppose α' and α'' are any two actions in $\Omega(\alpha)$. Let ρ be a partition of E^*. Suppose $\alpha' R_e \alpha''$ for all e in ρ and $\alpha' P_e \alpha''$ for some e in ρ. Also suppose that $R_{E*-\rho} \neq R_{E*}$ that is the ordering in the event set is not the same as that in the event set less the partition, then $\alpha' P_e \alpha''$.

Expected Utility Theorem: Let the agent satisfy the axioms mentioned above then there exists a continuous real valued utility function U defined over $\Omega(\alpha)$ such that

(*a*) for all α', $\alpha'' \in \Omega(\alpha)$

$\alpha' R_e \alpha''$ iff $U(\alpha') \geqslant U(\alpha'')$

(*b*) for all $\alpha' \in \Omega(\alpha)$

$U(\alpha') = \sum_i t_i U(\theta_i)$ where t_i is the probability of θ_i given α' and $U(\theta_i)$ is the utility number assigned to θ_i per se irrespective of its being realized.

This utility function being cardinal, is unique upto a positive linear transformation i.e. suppose we have U' such that for all $\alpha' \in \Omega(\alpha)$, $U' = b + cU(\alpha')$ then U' also satisfies the theorem. Conversely if U and U' satisfy the theorem then they are positive linear transforms of each other. We know that this statement is not true of Hicksian ordinalist structure. We will now consider Arrow's treatment of the classical theorems under uncertainty. For the sake of simplicity we consider a pure exchange model (no production).

There are m consumers (indexed by i). N ordinarily defined goods (indexed by k) S states of the world (indexed by s), S unit securities (one for each state of the world), γ prices for goods (there are NS such prices).

Unlike in Debreu's where prices are paid and there is contingent delivery of the goods in Arrow's framework prices are contingent—to be paid when the state of the world is realized.

q_s is the price of the sth type of security—this is to be paid now. S such prices exist.

x_i is as before, the consumers' commodity bundle

x_{is} is the vector of x_i referring to state s.

d_{is} is the amount of securities corresponding to state of the world s that consumer i purchases. Thus consumer s's vector of securities is

$$(d_{i1}, d_{i2}, \ldots, d_{is}) = d_i.$$

We, moreover, define $(d_1, \ldots, d_m)$ as b, γ_{ks} is the price prevailing for physically defined good k in state of the world s.

The interpretations of allocation, economy etc. remain the same as in the previous chapter.

Definition. Let E_u be a private ownership, pure exchange economy where contingent markets for commodities do not exist but security markets exist. Suppose every consumer in this economy satisfies the assumption of conditional ordering. A Pareto optimal equilibrium for E_u is an ordered pain

$$\langle (\bar{a}, \bar{b}), (\bar{\gamma}, \bar{q}) \rangle \text{ such that}$$

(*i*) $\bar{a}$ is an attainable allocation

(*ii*) $\sum_{s=1}^{S} q_s = 1$ (cash is a composite unit consisting of one of each type of security). If $\sum_{s=1}^{S} \bar{q}_s > 1$ then people would move into securities and this certainly wouldn't be an equilibrium situation.

(*iii*) $\sum_{s=1}^{S} \bar{q}_s \bar{d}_{is} = w_i$ for all i. The agent has to, by definition, exhaust his cash. Even if he doesn't actually physically do so he has because cash is, by definition, nothing but a composite bundle of securities.

(*iv*) $\sum_{i=1}^{m} \bar{d}_{is} = \sum_{i=1}^{m} w_i = W$ for all s that is, when state of the world s has been realized then people get back the same amount of cash. This is just a market clearing equation.

(*v*) (*a*) $\bar{\gamma}_s \bar{x}_{is} \leqslant \bar{d}_{is}$ for all s and all i. This is the consumers' budget constraint.

(*b*) There does not exist d_i and $x_i \in X_i$ such that $\sum_s q_s \, d_{is} = w_i$ and for all s, $\bar{\gamma}_s x_{is} \leqslant d_{is}$ and $x_i P_i \bar{x}_i$.

(*vi*) For all i and all s, $\bar{x}_{is}$ is R_{is} greatest bundle in

$$\{x_{is} \in X_{is} / \bar{\gamma}_s \, x_{is} \leqslant \bar{d}_{is}\}.$$

We now address the central problem here. Can this Pareto optimal allocation be reached by a perfectly competitive mechanism. In other words can this Pareto optimal allocation be thought of as a perfectly competitive equilibrium for some private enterprise economy that can be constructed out of E?

Arrow's security market theorem states that under the following conditions this equivalence can be established.

Condition 1. X_i is convex for every i.

Condition 2. Every consumer satisfies the axioms of conditional ordering, probabilistic belief, continuity and dominance. Hence for each consumer i there exists a von Neumann-Morgenstern utility function U_i such that for all $x_i \in X_i$.

$U_i(x_i) = \sum_s \pi_{is} U_i(x_{is})$ where π_{is} is the probability i sets for state of the world s and $U_i(x_{is})$ is the utility number attached to a bundle where for each state of the world s the consumption bundle is x_{is}.

Condition 3. For every i, R_i is convex.

Condition 4. Non-Saturation (Strict Monotonicity). For every consumer if $x_i, x_i' \in X_i$ if $x_i' > x_i$ then $x_i' P_i x_i$. Then there exists $(\bar{\gamma}, \bar{q}) \neq 0$ such that for all $x_i \in X_i$ if $x_i R_i \bar{x}_i$ then

$$\sum_{s=1}^{S} \sum_{k=1}^{N} \bar{q}_s \bar{\gamma}_{ks} x_{iks} \geqslant \sum_{s=1}^{S} \sum_{k=1}^{N} \bar{q}_s \bar{\gamma}_{ks} \bar{x}_{iks}$$

and if at this $(\bar{\gamma}, \bar{q})$ there exists $\tilde{x}_i \in X_i$ such that

$$\sum_{s=1}^{S} \sum_{k=1}^{N} \bar{q}_s \bar{\gamma}_{ks} \tilde{x}_{iks} < \sum_{s=1}^{S} \sum_{k=1}^{N} \bar{q}_s \bar{\gamma}_{ks} \bar{x}_{iks}$$

then for some $\bar{b}$

$\langle (\bar{a}, \bar{b}), (\bar{\gamma}, \bar{q}) \rangle$ will be a perfectly competitive equilibrium for some $\bar{E}_u$ that can be constructed out of E_u.

PROOF STAGE I. For the Debreu type of framework we add a fourth dimension (contingency). No security markets nor securities exist but markets for contingent commodities does exist. Thus for this system we are assured that there exists a price vector $\bar{p} \neq 0$ such that if $x_i R_i \bar{x}_i (x_i \in X_i)$ then $\bar{p} x_i > \bar{p} \bar{x}_i$ and if at $\bar{p}$ there exists $\tilde{x}_i (\in X_i)$ such that $\bar{p} \tilde{x}_i < \bar{p} \bar{x}_i$ then $(\bar{a}, \bar{p})$ constitutes a perfectly competitive equilibrium for some $\hat{E}_u$ that can be constructed out of E_u.

In the remaining stages of the proof of the theorem we will construct a market for securities so that any Pareto optimal allocation can be reached as a result of the perfectly competitive process working through the goods and securities market.

STAGE II. Define

$$\bar{q}_s = \frac{\sum_{i=1}^{m} \bar{p}_s \bar{x}_{is}}{\bar{W}} \quad \text{for all } s \text{ and where}$$

$$\bar{w} = \Sigma w_i.$$

Also $\bar{\gamma}_{ks} = \dfrac{\bar{p}_{ks}}{\bar{q}_0}$ for all k and all s, and $\bar{d}_{is} = \bar{\gamma}_s \bar{x}_{is}$ for all s where $\bar{\gamma}_s = (\bar{\gamma}_{is}, \ldots, \bar{\gamma}_{Ns})$ is the vector of commodity prices in state of the world s.

Let us, to avoid triviality, suppose that $\bar{W} > 0$. Hence $\bar{x}_{is}$ is non-negative. Furthermore, since we have strict monotonicity $\bar{p}_s > 0$. Hence $\sum_{i=1}^{m} \bar{p}_s \bar{x}_{is}$ is non-negative for all s. Hence $\bar{q}_s \geqslant 0$. But since, obviously, $\bar{x}_{is} > 0$ for some i, $\bar{q}_s$ is strictly positive.

We have defined $\bar{\gamma}_{ks} = \dfrac{\bar{p}_{ks}}{\bar{q}_s}$ for all k and all s and hence we must have $\bar{\gamma}_{ks} > 0$.

Moreover, $\bar{d}_{is}$ $\{= \bar{\gamma}_s \bar{x}_{is}\}$ is strictly positive and hence $\bar{b}$ is strictly positive.

We have defined the characteristic of the "chosen". Pareto optimal allocation for a free enterprise economy with uncertainty in which markets for contingent commodities do not exist but security markets do exist to cover all states of the world. We will now show that $\langle (\bar{a}, \bar{b}) \rangle, (\bar{\gamma}, \bar{q}) \rangle$ is a competitive equilibrium for this free enterprise economy. Let us show, therefore, that $\langle (\bar{a}, \bar{b}), (\bar{\gamma}, \bar{q}) \rangle$ satisfies all the conditions for a competitive economy.

(*i*) To show that $\bar{a}$ is attainable. This is obvious since $\bar{a}$ is *a* Pareto optimal allocation.

(*ii*) To show $\sum_{s=1}^{S} \bar{q}_s = 1$

$$\sum_{s=1}^{S} \bar{q}_s \text{ (by definition)} = \sum_{s=1}^{S} \sum_{i} \frac{\bar{p}_s \bar{x}_{is}}{\bar{W}}$$

$$= \frac{1}{\bar{W}} \sum_{s} \sum_{i} \bar{p}_s \bar{x}_{is} = \frac{1}{\bar{W}} \cdot \sum_{i} \overline{px_i}.$$

($\bar{p}\bar{x}_i$ is total .penditure of the *i*th consumer in the Debreu model).

Now si..ce each consumer satisfies strict monotonicity he would exhaust his initial endowment in purchases.

$$\therefore \qquad \sum_{s} \bar{q}_s = \frac{1}{\bar{W}} \sum \bar{p}\bar{x}_i = \sum_{i} \frac{w_i}{\bar{W}} = \frac{\bar{W}}{\bar{W}} = 1.$$

(*iii*) To show $\sum_{s} \bar{q}_s \bar{d}_{is} = w_i$.

Substitute for $\bar{d}_{is}$ in the left hand side of the above expression to get $\sum_{s} \bar{q}_s \bar{\gamma}_s \bar{x}_{is}$ (remember that $\bar{\gamma}_s$ is a vector with $\bar{\gamma}_{ks}$ as a typical element and q_s is a scalar).

Now substitute for $\bar{\gamma}_{ks} = \dfrac{\bar{p}_{ks}}{\bar{q}_s}$

in the above expression to get

$$\sum_{s} \bar{p}_s \bar{x}_{is} = \bar{p}\bar{x}_i = w_i \quad \text{(by strict monotonity).}$$

(*iv*) To show that the securities market clears i.e. $\sum_{i} \bar{d}_{is} = \bar{W}$ for all s.

Now $$\sum_{i} \bar{d}_{is} = \sum_{i} \bar{\gamma}_s \bar{x}_{is}.$$

Moreover, $$\bar{\gamma}_{ks} = \frac{\bar{p}_{ks}}{\bar{q}_s} \quad \text{or} \quad \bar{\gamma}_s = \frac{\bar{p}_s}{\bar{q}_s}$$

Hence $$\sum_{i} \bar{d}_{is} = \sum_{i} \frac{\bar{p}_s}{\bar{q}_s} \bar{x}_{is}$$

$$= \frac{1}{\bar{q}_s} \sum_{i} \bar{p}_s \bar{x}_{is} = \frac{1}{\bar{q}_s} \bar{p}_s \sum_{i} \bar{x}_{is}$$

$$= \frac{1}{\bar{q}_s} \bar{W} \bar{q}_s = \bar{W}.$$

(*v*) This stage has two parts:

(*a*) In this part we have $\bar{d}_{is} \geqslant \bar{\gamma}_s\bar{x}_{is}$ for all i and all s. This we know to be true by definition.

(*b*) For no i does there exists a d_i and x_i such that $\sum_s \bar{q}_s d_{is} = w_i$ for all s and $x_i \in X_i$ and $\bar{\gamma}_s x_{is} \leqslant d_{is}$ for all s and $x_i P_i \bar{x}_i$. In other words no feasible bundle is preferred to the Pareto optimal bundle.

Deny this result then we have to show that this leads to a contradiction. Let $d_{is} \geqslant \bar{\gamma}_s x_{is}$ for all s. Multiply both sides of the inequality by $\bar{q}_s$

$$\bar{q}_s d_{is} \geqslant \bar{q}_s\bar{\gamma}_s x_{is} \text{ for all } s, \text{ so}$$

$$\sum_s \bar{q}_s d_{is} \geqslant \sum_s \bar{q}_s\bar{\gamma}_s\bar{x}_{is}.$$

By assumption, $$\sum_s \bar{q}_s d_{is} = w_i.$$

Hence $$w_i \geqslant \sum_s \bar{q}_s\bar{\gamma}_s x_{is}.$$

$$= \sum_s \bar{p}_s x_{is} = \bar{p}x_i.$$

Hence the budget constraint is satisfied. Now $x_i P_i \bar{x}_i$. Hence it is Pareto improving to move from x_i to $\bar{x}_i$. Hence $\bar{x}_i$ cannot be Pareto optimal. This gives us the required contradiction.

(*vi*) To show that for all i and all s $\bar{x}_{is}$ is R_{is} greatest element in

$$\{\hat{x}_{is} \in X_{is} / \bar{\gamma}_s \hat{x}_{is} \leqslant \bar{d}_{is}\}$$

that is if state of the world s is realized then the consumer finds it optimal to buy the bundle of goods $\bar{x}_{is}$.

Without loss of generality let us assume $s = 1$ so that we must prove that $\bar{x}_{i1}$ is R_{i1} greatest element in

$$\{\hat{x}_{i1} \in X_{i1} / \bar{\gamma}_1 \hat{x}_i \leqslant \bar{d}_{i1}\}.$$

If this was not true then there must exist a commodity bundle $x_{i1} \in X_{i1}$ such that $\bar{\gamma}_1 x_{i1} \leqslant \bar{d}_{i1}$, and $x_{i1} P_1 \bar{x}_{i1}$.

Construct $\tilde{x}_i \in X_i$ such that for all $s \neq 1$, $\tilde{x}_{is} = \bar{x}_{is}$ for all i and $\tilde{x}_{i1} = x_{i1}$ for $s = 1$.

Consider $U_i(\bar{x}_i) = \sum_s \pi_{is} U_i(\bar{x}_{is})$ and

$$U_i(\tilde{x}_i) = \sum_s \pi_{is} U_i(\tilde{x}_{is}).$$

Written more succinctly

$$U_i(\bar{x}_i) = \pi_{i1} U_i(\bar{x}_{i1}) + \sum_{s=2}^{S} \pi_{is} U_i(\bar{x}_{is})$$

and

$$U_i(\tilde{x}_i) = \pi_{i1} U_i(x_{i1}) + \sum_{s=2}^{S} \pi_{is} U_i(\bar{x}_{is}).$$

Hence whether $U_i(\bar{x}_i)$ is greater, equal to or less than $U_i(\tilde{x}_i)$ depends on whether

$$\pi_{i1}U_i(\bar{x}_{i1}) \gtreqless \pi_{i1}U_i(x_{i1}).$$

We must have $\pi_{i1} > 0$ to avoid triviality. Hence

$$\pi_{i1}U_i(x_{i1}) > \pi_{i1}U_i(\bar{x}_{i1})$$

which implies $$U_i(\tilde{x}_i) > U_i(\bar{x}_i).$$

For all $$s \neq 1 \bar{\gamma}_s\tilde{x}_{is} = \bar{\gamma}_s x_{is} \leqslant \bar{d}_{is}.$$

Thence $$\bar{\gamma}_1 x_{i1} \leqslant \bar{d}_{i1}.$$

Now combining $\bar{\gamma}_s\tilde{x}_{is} \leqslant \bar{d}_{is}$ and the fact that $\tilde{x}_i \in X_i$ and $U_i(\tilde{x}_i) > U_i(\bar{x}_i)$ we get $\tilde{x}_i P_i \bar{x}_i$. This contradicts condition (*v*).

Hence the original supposition was wrong. Hence x_{i1} is R_{i1} greatest element in

$$\{\hat{x}_{i1} \in X_{i1}/\bar{\gamma}_1\hat{x}_{i1} \leqslant \bar{d}_{i1}\}.$$

This completes the proof of the Arrow securities market theorem.

Some general comments on this theorem are warranted. We have assumed convexity for the weak preference relation R_i. This implies that consumers have weak risk aversion.

Moreover, even though we have demonstrated the theorem for a pure exchange economy it can be formally extended to a production economy. Moreover, this does not involve considerations of probabilistic profits etc. Take an example. Suppose a producer is planning for state of the world 1. The price vector in state of the world is given by $\gamma_1 = (2, 3)$. Output plan, y_{j1}, by producer j for state of the world 1 is to use 5 units of inputs to produce 6 units of output i.e. $y_{j1} = (-5, 6)$. Hence his profit is 8. Hence today he can sell 18 securities for $s = 1$. Hence now he gets $18q_1$ and he has net $8q_1$. Also $8q_1 = (\gamma_1 y_{j1})q_1$. Hence he has to choose his production plan in such a way that he gets maximum net cash flow. Hence the producer maximizes $\sum_{s=1}^{S} \bar{q}_s\bar{\gamma}_s y_{js}$ by choosing y_{js} subject to the condition that $y_j \in Y_j$ (the production set). This is a perfectly objective consideration and does not involve consideration of probabilistic profits at any stage.

However, although our theorem is formally going through we might occasionally encounter problems from some unexpected quarters. To take an example let us suppose that we have, in the absence of uncertainty, a fixed coefficients technology and hence constant returns to scale. This, of course, is essential for a perfectly competitive equilibrium. In the presence of uncertainty this fixed coefficients technology might show increasing returns.

Suppose 1 machine and one man hour of labour give us twenty four units of output. Now let us use 2 machines and two man hours of labour so that with certainty we would get 48 units of output. We introduce uncertainty by supposing that each machine has 1/2 probability of breaking down. Initially we have two machines and one man hour. Then we double both inputs.

Initially, thus, if no machines work we get zero output. If one or both machines work we get 24 units of output. Probability of both machines failing is 1/4. Hence expected output is

$$\frac{1}{4}\cdot 0+\frac{3}{4}\cdot 24=18.$$

In the new situation with no machines working we get zero output, one machines with one man hour produce 24 units of output, two machines and two man hours produce 48 units of output.

The probability that no machine works is $\frac{1}{16}$. The probability that 1 machine works is $4\times\frac{1}{2}\times\frac{1}{8}=1/4$. The probability that more than one machine works is

$$1-\frac{1}{16}-\frac{1}{4}=\frac{11}{16}.$$

Hence expected output is

$$\frac{1.0}{16}+\frac{1}{4}\cdot 24+\frac{11}{16}\cdot 48=39.$$

Hence doubling input use more than doubles output. The assumption of convex production sets becomes hard to defend.

Appendix

Measures of Consumer Surplus

Another way of looking at the second optimality theorem is that given the surplus of other consumers a perfectly competitive equilibrium maximizes the consumer's surplus of any particular consumer.

The idea of consumer's surplus is quite old and has its origins in the works of Dupuit and Marshall. Marshall defined it as "the excess of the price which he would be willing to pay rather than go without the thing, over that which he actually does pay." In Fig. A.3.1 shows consumer's surplus is the triangular area *ZAB* under the demand curve.

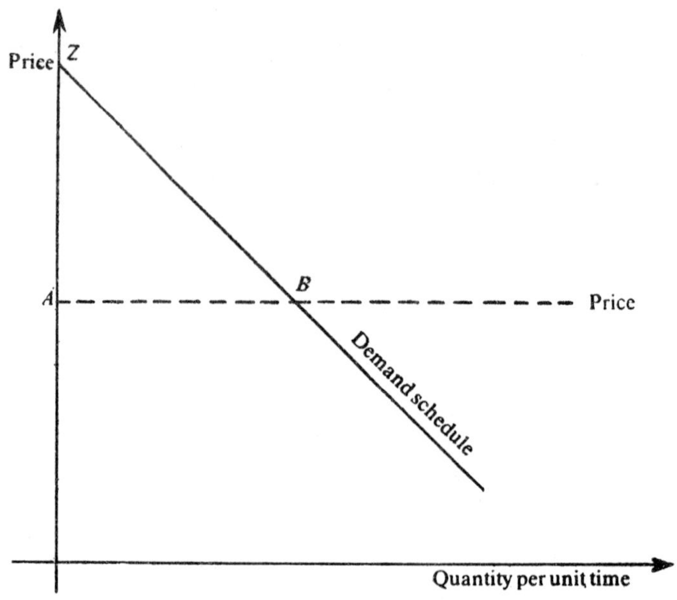

Fig. A.3.1

Modern economists have been less concerned with visualizing consumer's surplus as a utility measure and more with viewing it as a measure of the ability to pay.[1] Contemporary economic theory distinguishes between four measures.

1. When the price of a commodity changes the compensating variation (CV) is the amount of compensation in monetary terms that can be taken/given to the individual to leave him just as well off as before the change.
2. Suppose we could constrain the individual to buy at the new price the quantity of the commodity that he would buy without the compensation. Then compensating surplus (CS) is the amount of compensation that can be taken from the individual while leaving him just as well off as before the price change.
3. Equivalent variation (EV) is the amount of compensation that has to be given to the individual, in the absence of the change, to make him as well off as he would be without the change.
4. Equivalent surplus (ES) is the amount of compensation that has to be given to the individual, in the absence of the change, to make him as well off as he would be with the change if he were constrained to buy at the old price the quantity of the commodity he would buy in absence of compensation.

These measures can be depicted graphically as shown in Fig. A.3.2.

In the first part of Fig. A.3.2 we measure money or income on the y-axis and quantity of a commodity A along the x-axis. Initially the consumer faces price p_0 (for A) and comes to an equilibrium at K_0 along iddifference curve I_0. Then the price falls to p_1 and he moves to point K_1 on indifference curve I_1.

Now compensating variation (CV) is MOM', compensating surplus (CS) is K_1T_0, equivalent variation (EV) is M^0M^2, and equivalent surplus (ES) is K_0J_1.

In the second part of the diagram we draw a simple demand curve from the information in the first part. As the price falls from p_0 to p_1 purchases increase from A_0 to A_1. If the consumer pays CV he ends up at L_0 rather than K_1. Therefore UWk is the (Hicksian) compensated demand curve from u. Hence we can write in terms of this demand curve (in terms of areas now)

$$\text{CV} = p_0p_1wu.$$

Similarly we can calculate

$$\text{CS} = p_0p_1wu - wsl$$
$$\text{EV} = p_0p_1sk$$
$$\text{ES} = p_0p_1sk + uk_j.$$

We can, in addition define the Laspeyre cost difference of a price change as the amount of compensation that could be taken from the individual while

[1]In any case Marshall's measure involves the strong assumption of constant marginal utility of income. See Hicks (1940) or Ng (1979).

leaving him just able to buy the old bundle of goods. This is measured by the area p_0p_1yu. Similarly, we can define the Paasche index of cost difference as the amount the consumer would have to be paid a just be able to afford to buy the new bundle at the old prices. This is the area p_0p_1st.

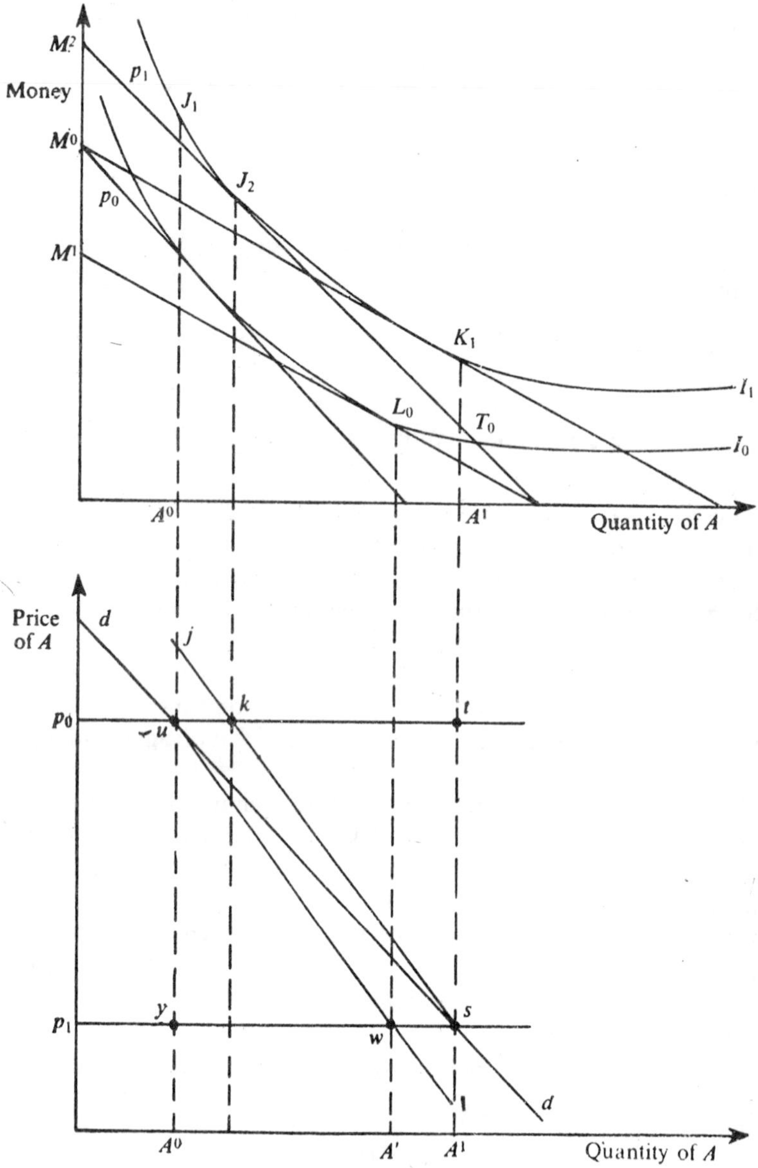

Fig. A.3.2

This gives us six different measures of consumer's surplus. Which measure is appropriate depends on, among other things, the purpose to which the measure is to be put, and the level of aggregation. See Ng (1979) for a detailed discussion.

4. External Effects and the Market

It has been implicit in our analysis so far that the ordering of any consumer is defined only over his own consumption set. Similarly, it has been implicit that the production set of any producer is independent of the production sets of other producers and of the consumption sets of consumers. When such narrow assumptions are relaxed we encounter interdependence of production and/or consumption sets and such external effects are often called externalities.

Externalities are really quite pervasive in the real world. Factories belch out smoke which affects our lungs, rivers are polluted, someone in the neighbourhood plays his television too loudly all night long or a lighthouse guides ships into the safety of the harbour. In each of these cases what any person is doing is directly affecting others. This notion can be made more precise. During the process of production of an ordinary commodity (say steel) the factory owner produces another commodity (smoke) which directly enters my utility function. Now although there is a well defined market for steel there is nothing automatic or obvious about a market for smoke. In this example smoke is an externality which can now be defined as a commodity that gets produced during the process of production or consumption of an ordinary good and for which it is hard to establish a market.

Why is it hard to establish a market for an externality? Three reasons can be advanced in general, specific cases will involve specific reasons in addition to these.

1. *Information Costs.* Suppose a honey producer keeps his bees next to an apple orchard. The bees take the nectar (the externality) from the apple flowers. The apple producer would find it almost impossible to ascertain how much nectar the bees have taken from the flowers. For an ordinary commodity this condition is necessarily satisfied. There is no problem in ascertaining how much food I consumed yesterday.

2. *Excludability.* Even if information costs are not a stumbling block excludability often is. How is the apple producer going to prevent the entry of bees into his orchard?

Even more difficult is regulating the entry of bees. In the case of ordinary goods this problem does not arise. It I cannot pay the price of sugar I can not buy sugar and that ends that story.

3. *Non-competitive Behaviour.* Even if excludability and information costs are not serious problems non-competitive behaviour almost always

obtains when one is dealing with externalities. In the market for apples and the market for honey there are a large number of buyers and sellers and competitive or "price taking" behaviour prevails. But no such statement can be made about the nectar from the apple flowers. This commodity is defined only between two people—one of whom is a buyer and the other a seller. Hence the large numbers assumption is not satisfied and hence there is no guarantee that competitive behaviour will prevail.

Externalities are, undoubtedly, a fundamental problem for the market economy.

Let us see in a simple set up the implications of the presence of external effects for the equivalence between Pareto optimality and perfect competition. Let us take a two person exchange economy with two goods. The utility functions are as follows:

$$u^1(x_{11}, x_{12}, x_{211}, x_{221})$$
$$u^2(x_{21}, x_{22}, x_{112}, x_{122})$$

where

x_{11} is 1's consumption of commodity 1.
x_{12} is 1's consumption of commodity 2.
x_{211} is 2's consumption of commodity 1 affecting individual 1
x_{221} is 2's consumption of commodity 2 affecting individual 1.
x_{21} is 2's consumption of commodity 1.
x_{22} is 2's consumption of commodity 2.
x_{112} is 1's consumption of commodity 1 affecting individual 2.
x_{122} is 1's consumption of commodity 2 affecting individual 2.

Now $x_{11} + x_{21} = x^1$ initial endowment of commodity 1.
$x_{12} + x_{22} = x^2$ initial endowment of commodity 2.

Also

$$x_{11} = x_{112}; \qquad x_{12} = x_{122}$$
$$x_{22} = x_{211} \quad \text{and} \quad x_{22} = x_{221}.$$

Now let us conduct the Pareto optimizing exercise of maximizing individual 1's utility subject to 2's utility being kept at a certain level $\bar{u}_2$. Letting up the Lagrangean we have

$$\begin{aligned} L = {} & u^1(x_{11}, x_{12}, x_{211}, x_{221}) \\ & +\lambda_1[u^2(x_{21}, x_{22}, x_{112}, x_{122}) - \bar{u}^2] \\ & +\lambda_2[x_{11} - x_{112}] + \lambda_3[x_{12} - x_{122}] \\ & +\lambda_4[x_{21} - x_{211}] + \lambda_5[x_{22} - x_{221}] \\ & +\lambda_6[x^1 - x_{11} - x_{21}] + \lambda_7[x^2 - x_{12} - x_{22}]. \end{aligned}$$

First order conditions are

$$\frac{\partial L}{\partial x_{11}} = \frac{\partial u^1}{\partial x_{11}} + \lambda_2 - \lambda_6 = 0$$

$$\frac{\partial L}{\partial x_{12}} = \frac{\partial u^1}{\partial x_{12}} + \lambda_3 - \lambda_7 = 0$$

$$\frac{\partial L}{\partial x_{211}} = \frac{\partial u^1}{\partial x_{211}} + \lambda_4 = 0$$

$$\frac{\partial L}{\partial x_{221}} = \frac{\partial u^1}{\partial x_{221}} - \lambda_5 = 0$$

$$\frac{\partial L}{\partial x_{21}} = \lambda_1 \frac{\partial u^2}{\partial x_{21}} + \lambda_4 - \lambda_6 = 0$$

$$\frac{\partial L}{\partial x_{22}} = \lambda_1 \frac{\partial u^2}{\partial x_{22}} + \lambda_5 - \lambda_7 = 0$$

$$\frac{\partial L}{\partial x_{112}} = \lambda_1 \frac{\partial u^2}{\partial x_{112}} - \lambda_2 = 0$$

$$\frac{\partial L}{\partial x_{122}} = \lambda_1 \frac{\partial u^2}{\partial x_{122}} - \lambda_3 = 0$$

and

$$\frac{\partial L}{\partial \lambda_i} = 0, \qquad i = 1, \ldots, 7.$$

If any allocative mechanism (including the market mechanism) wants to reach Pareto optimum it must satisfy these conditions. But can the market mechanism satisfy these conditions? If there are no external effects Lagrange multipliers λ_2 through λ_5 disappear and we get the straightforward condition that MRS between the two goods is the same for both individuals. In a competitive set up both consumers will look at the price ratio between the two goods and find it individually rational to equate their MRS with this price ratio. Thus through this price ratio the MRS's of the two individuals get equated. With externalities the individuals may still behave in the same manner but the difficulty is that the Pareto optimum conditions are different now. In fact the prices λ_2 through λ_5 which figure in the Pareto optimum conditions do not exist. So there is no point in talking about any automatic equivalence between the market mechanism and Pareto optimality.

So the market fails to allocate resources optimally. In the next two chapters we will study what can be done to restore this desirable property of the market mechanism. In fact we will discover that it may not always be possible to completely correct for external effects.

A problem related to externalities is that of public goods. Public goods in fact are an extreme form of externalities. The term "public" goods does not carry any implication that this commodity is necessarily produced in the public sector. A public good is simply a commodity whose consumption is non-competitive. You and I both consume the full amount of national defence. If expenditure on national defence goes up all of us get the full amount of the increase as your consumption does not conflict with mine. If, however, you go and buy some bread from the local store there is less bread left for the rest of us. Your consumption of bread (a private good) conflicts with mine; my consumption of defence (a public good) does not conflict with your consumption of defence. Thus in a two person would we may write the utility functions (with both public and private goods) as

$$u^1(x_{11}, x_G)$$

$$u^2(x_{21}, x_G)$$

where

x_{11} is 1's consumption of commodity 1.
x_{21} is 2's consumption of commodity 1.
x_G is the amount of the public good consumed by everyone.

What are the Pareto optimum conditions, under these circumstances? Let us maximize u^1 subject to u^2 being kept at certain level. Denoting $F(x_{11} + x_{21}, x_G) = 0$ as the (technological) transformation function we can write the Lagrangian as

$$L = u^1(x_{11}, x_G) + \lambda_1[u^2(x_{21}, x_G) - \bar{u}^2] + \lambda_2[F(x_{11} + x_{21}, x_G)].$$

We get as first order conditions

$$\frac{\partial L}{\partial x_{11}} = \frac{\partial u^1}{\partial x_{11}} + \lambda_2 F_1 = 0 \tag{1}$$

$$\frac{\partial L}{\partial x_{21}} = \lambda_1 \frac{\partial u_2}{\partial x_{21}} + \lambda_2 F_1 = 0 \tag{2}$$

$$\frac{\partial L}{\partial x_G} = \frac{\partial u^1}{\partial x_G} + \frac{\lambda_1 \partial u^2}{\partial x_G} + \lambda_2 F_2 = 0 \tag{3}$$

$$\frac{\partial L}{\partial \lambda_1} = \frac{\partial L}{\partial \lambda_2} = 0. \tag{4}$$

From (3) we get

$$\frac{\partial u^1}{\partial x_G} + \lambda_1 \frac{\partial u^2}{\partial x_G} = -\lambda_2 F_2$$

or

$$\left(\frac{\partial u^1}{\partial x_G} + \lambda_1 \frac{\partial u^2}{\partial x_G}\right) \Big/ F_2 = -\lambda_2.$$

From (1) and (2) then

$$\frac{\partial u^1}{\partial x_{11}} \Big/ F_1 = \lambda_1 \frac{\partial u_2}{\partial x_{21}} \Big/ F_1 = \left(\frac{\partial u_1}{\partial x_G} + \lambda_1 \frac{\partial u^2}{\partial x_G}\right) \Big/ F_2.$$

From which we get

$$\frac{\partial u^1}{\partial x_{11}} = \lambda_1 \frac{\partial u^2}{\partial x_{21}}.$$

Cross multiplying and using this fact we get:

$$\frac{F_2}{F_1} = \frac{\partial u^1}{\partial x_G}\bigg/\frac{\partial u^1}{\partial x_{11}} + \lambda_1 \frac{\partial u^2}{\partial x_G}\bigg/\lambda_1 \frac{\partial u^2}{\partial x_{21}}$$

$$= \frac{\partial u^1}{\partial x_G}\bigg/\frac{\partial u^1}{\partial x_{11}} + \frac{\partial u^2}{\partial x_G}\bigg/\frac{\partial u^2}{\partial x_{21}} \quad \text{or}$$

MRT between x^1 and x_G equals the sum of the MRS between x_1 and x_G for the two individuals. These are the famous Samuelsonian conditions for the optimal supply of a public good. A private enterprise economy will not be able to satisfy these conditions since it is still individually rational for each individual to equate his MRS with the price ratio and it is rational for every producer to equate the price ratio with the MRT. Thus in a competitive economy MRS = MRT the Samuelsonian conditions will not be satisfied. The market, left to itself, will not be able to satisfy the conditions for Pareto optimality.

With public goods there is another (still more fundamental) problem. Since you can not stop me from consuming the public good I will not have the incentive to pay for it. In fact if he is allowed this latitude no one will find it rational to pay for the public good. Consequently there will be inadequate resources for the public goods sector. Left to itself the market will not even produce public goods. From this vantage point the issue of Pareto optimal supply of the public good becomes secondary. We are faced with the *free-rider* problem. In Chapter 6 we will confront this problem in some of its manifestations.

Appendix

First, Second and Third Best Solution

A Pareto optimal allocation is often referred to as a first best solution. Consider an economy without uncertainty and external effects. We know that the Pareto optimum conditions simply are that ratio of any two prices equals the MRS in consumption between these goods and also the MRT in production between these two goods. Also the ratio of any two factor prices equals the rate of technical substitution between these factors in production. If all these conditions are simultaneously attained then we know that a Pareto optimum or a first best solution obtains.

What happens when all these conditions cannot be satisfied simultaneously. A natural temptation would be to suggest that these conditions should be satisfied in all the sectors where they can be satisfied. But as Lipsey and Lancaster (1957) have argued this need not get us to our second best optimum. The second best optimum is the next best solution given that the first best optimum or full Pareto.optimality cannot be attained.

This could arise because of a variety of reasons—say monopology in one sector, a union somewhere else or indivisibilities in the technology of some sector etc. Lipsey and Lancaster proved the following simple but powerful theorem.

The General Theorem of Second Best

(*i*) If all the conditions for Pareto optimality cannot be met it is not necessarily second best optimal to satisfy a subset of these conditions; (*ii*) in general to attain the second best optimum it is necessary to violate all the conditions of Pareto optimality.

Take a simple proof of this proposition. Suppose we are trying to maximize an objective function $F(x_1, \ldots, x_n)$ subject to the constraints $G(x_1, \ldots, x_n) = 0$. If we had no other restriction to worry about the first order conditions would simply be

$$\frac{F_i}{F_n} = \frac{G_i}{G_n} \quad (i = 1, \ldots, n - 1).$$

When the second optimality theorem is valid this would simply be equated to the price ratio between commodity i and commodity n and that would guarantee first best optimality.

But now let us say that in just one sector this condition cannot be met. To be more specific let us say that we have an additional constraint

$$\frac{F_1}{F_n} = k\frac{G_1}{G_n}, \quad k \neq 1.$$

If we now try to maximize $F(\quad)$, we will form the Lagrangean

$$L = F(x_1, \ldots x_n) + \lambda_1[G(x_1, \ldots, x_n)] + \lambda_2\left[\frac{F_1}{F_n} - k\frac{G_1}{G_n}\right]$$

and the first order conditions are

$$\frac{\partial L}{\partial x_i} = F_i + \lambda_1 G_i + \lambda_2 \left\{\frac{F_n F_{1i} - F_1 F_{ni}}{F_n^2} - k\left(\frac{G_n G_{1i} - G_1 G_{ni}}{G_n^2}\right)\right\} = 0$$

$$i = 1, \ldots, n - 1 \qquad (5)$$

$$\frac{\partial L}{\partial \lambda_1} = \frac{\partial L}{\partial \lambda_2} = 0,$$

where $F_{1i} = \dfrac{\partial F_1}{\partial x_i}$ etc.

We see that the single incongruity $\dfrac{F_1}{F_n} = k\dfrac{G_1}{G_n}$, $k \neq 1$ pervades all the first order condition. Unless F_{1i}, G_{ni} etc. are zero all the first order conditions are changed. All the conditions for Pareto optimality (or first best optimum) have to be violated. So unless separability of the above form obtains all the conditions for Pareto optimality have to be violated.

Now first best and second best policies place strong informational requirements. If such information is not easily available then first best or second best policies may not be operational and we are in the world of third best. Let us try to classify the informational availability.

Informational Poverty

Define $\dfrac{F_j}{F_n} - \dfrac{G_j}{G_n}$ as a relation curve and realize that under standard assumptions this difference will be concave.

Figure A. 4.1 depicts this schedule. Under first best conditions

$$\frac{F_j}{F_n} - \frac{G_j}{G_n} \text{ equals zero.}$$

With informational poverty we have two problems (*i*) we do not know the extent of distortion introduced by using first best solutions in a second best world and (*ii*) we do not know the shape and skewness of the

$$\frac{F_j}{F_n} - \frac{G_i}{G_n} \text{ schedule.}$$

Information Scarcity. Information is sufficient but it is not perfect.

Informational Abundance is a situation where there is no dearth of information.

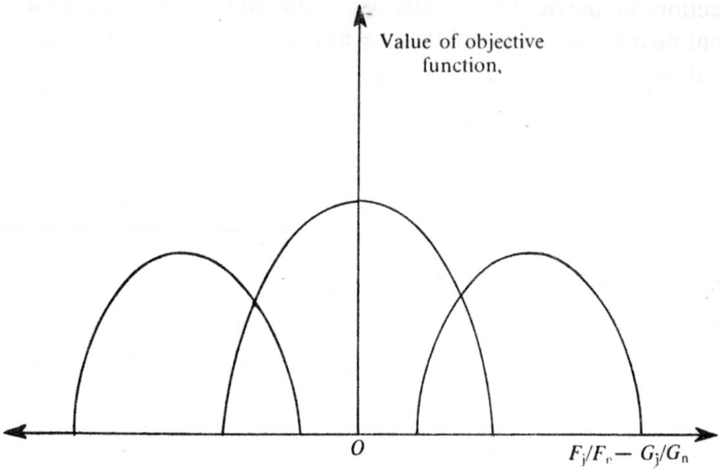

Fig. A.4 1

Clearly with informational abundance we use first best policies for first best situations and use second best policies for second best situations.

What do we do with the other two kinds of situations.

With informational poverty there is a real problem in deciding which

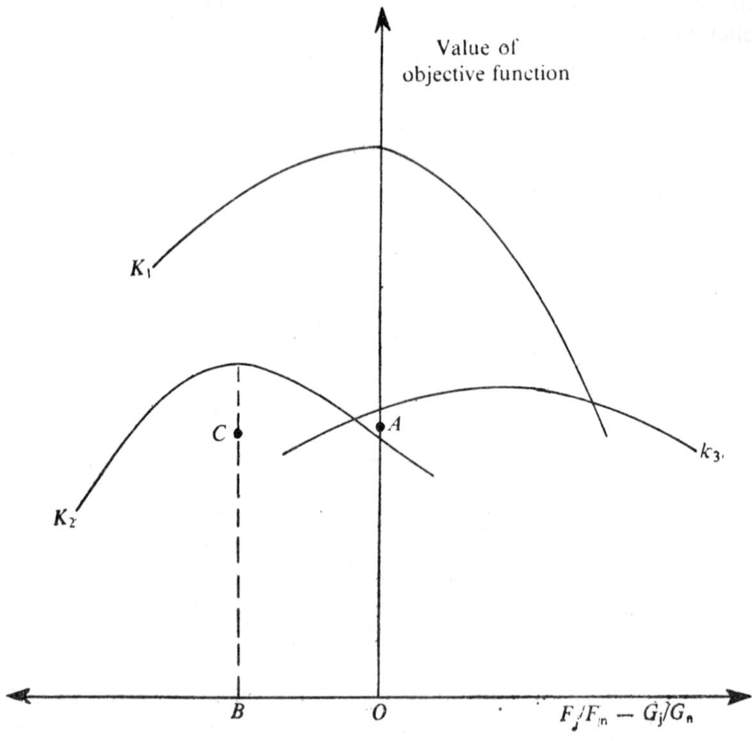

Fig. A.4.2

direction to move. In fact in a probabilistic framework given the informational poverty we are not even sure that we want to maximize expected value. But if we do then it is third best to use first best rules if the

$$\frac{F_j}{F_n} - \frac{G_j}{G_n} \text{ schedules are symmetric}$$

K_2 and K_3 are equally likely schedules. If we use first best rules the expected value of the objective function is OA which is as good *ex ante* as any other configuration. Hence, *ex ante* a first best policy in this kind of situation is at least as good as any other.

With informational scarcity we have much better information and the skewness and shape of these schedules can be fixed (probabilistically, but nonetheless much more accurately, than in the case of informational poverty). Hence in this kind of situation it will not be necessary to stick to first best solutions. A general proposition can then be advanced. With informational scarcity it is better to use third best policy. Now, unlike the first and second best situations we can not spell out simple and clear cut rules of thumb for third best policy. Every situation has to be evaluated for its own merits.

Economists like Ng have looked upon third best as a general policy framework with first and second best policies as extremes whose realization depends on the extent and quality of information that is available to the policy maker.

5. Correcting for Externalities Under Certainty

The policy problem of dealing with externalities varies considerably with the availability of information. In this chapter we will study the problem under conditions of full certainty.

To be more precise everybody (including the government) knows everybody elses' preference/production structure and the nature and characteristics of the external effect. Since such problems have very similar characteristics there is no harm in studying them in the simplest models and thus being able to concentrate on the essentials.

Let us take a partial equilibrium where what is happening in the sector producing external effects does not affect the rest of the economy. Also there is only one such sector and, further, what is happening in the rest of the economy does not affect this sector. Hence income effects are absent.

Individual I by indulging in activity *X* creates an external diseconomy (a bad) which affects individuals *II*. In Fig. 5.1, we depict this situation.

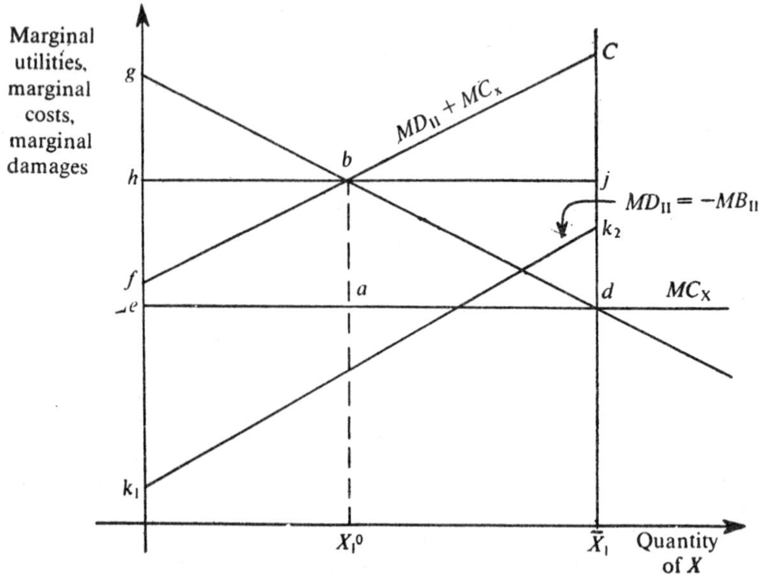

Fig. 5.1

In Fig. 5.1 *gd* is the marginal benefit (equal to marginal utility) from activity X to individual I. The marginal cost of X is constant and is depicted in the diagram by the line *ed*. Hence if the government does not intervene individual I would find it rational to consume $\bar{X}_I$ units. This would cause damage to the tune of $\bar{X}_I k_2$ to individual II. k_1k_2 is the marginal damage schedule which rises as I's consumption of X rises whereas MB_I falls with increases in X because of diminishing marginal utility. True social cost of X is therefore $(MD_{II} + MC_X)$ and is given by the schedule *fc*. So if we could completely correct for the externality we would equate the true marginal social cost with the marginal benefit to I and thus X_I^0 of X would be consumed.

How can we achieve this? Four different measures have been explained.

(1) *Pigovian Taxation.* We tax I's consumption at the rate *ab* thereby making his private marginal cost equal to the true social cost. Thus X_I^0 would be consumed. Here II gains by the amount of reduction in I's consumption. I loses because of the taxes he has to pay. Society gains tax revenue. The net social gain is the sum of all these.

(2) *Pigovian Subsidization.* With this method we evaluate MD_{II} at X_I^0 and offer this as a subsidy to individual I in exchange for his reduction of consumption of $\bar{X}$ from X_I to X_I^0. This raises the opportunity cost of consuming X from MC_X to $MD_{II} + MC_X$ and thereby I now finds it rational to consume X_I^0. Individual I gains the subsidy. Individual II gains by the amount of reduction of I's consumption of X whereas society loses to the extent that it subsidizes I. Net social gain can again similarly be calculated.

(3) *Liability Laws.* Yet another way out is to make I legally liable for the damage that he inflicts on II. Hence II is effectively given property rights on the activity X. He would again find it profitable to consume X_I^0. II's gain would be the amount of reduction in I's consumption of X while I's loss would be the increase in his cost. The state does not enter into this transaction except for fixing liability. Thus net social gain is calculated by adding II's gain to I's loss.

(4) *Property Rights.* This is the famous Coase solution. I is given property rights over activity X and if II wants his consumption of X reduced it is his business to offer I sufficient monetary incentives. So the two bargain for I's reduction in his consumption of X. So long as $MD_{II} > (MB_I - MC_X)$ this bargaining will be profitable. II will find it rational to bribe I. This process will come to an end when $MD_{II} = (MB_I - MC_X)$ that is, in other words where X_I^0 is being consumed. So the Coase method also attains Pareto optimality although it has vastly different distributional implications from the other measures. Loosely speaking, then, the problem of correcting for external effects is largely a matter of assigning property rights properly.

We will comment on these measures at greater length in the next chapter but one property of the solutions reached so far needs to be singled out. In Chapter 2 when we were studying the (Pareto) optimal properties of perfectly competitive equilibrium we talked of the allocative efficiency of the market mechanism *without any reference* to the particular point on the SUPF we wanted to reach. The efficiency of the market mechanism is thus *independent* of the distributive question of which point on the SUPF we want to attain. Hence the advocates of the market mechanism claim let moral philosophers or normative economists tell you which point on the SUPF is desirable. But we, as positive economists, know that no matter what their recommendation is it can always be attained with the help of the market mechanism. This distinction between normative and positive economics is critical to the supporters of the market mechanism.

But our study in this chapter finds a fundamental flaw with the market logic. When we try to correct for (or internalize) externalities we necessarily disturb the distribution of resources. Thus we can no longer conceive of distribution and allocative efficiency as *distinct* questions. Distribution is being changed to attain allocative efficiency. The "positive" economist cannot now be content with allocative efficiency. He must now also worry about the distribution of income and resources associated with this equilibrium.

An externality does create severe problems in the presence of uncertainty. This is the proper context in which to study many of these problems and we spend some time on it in the next chapter. In this chapter we attempt a review of the literature on the methods (already outlined above) to correct for external effects. In this we closely follow the work of Murty and Nayak. We attempt this in the context of a straightforward example.

Suppose there is a firm producing electricity (a normal good) but the production process of electricity also involves the production of a joint product (smoke). If the electricity producer attempts to reduce the output of smoke he can only do so by adopting a costly process.

Now let us confine ourselves to the case of a production externality and assume that the smoke does not affect any individuals. However, the smoke does affect a number of laundries who are in that area and raises their cost of production. If the electricity producer tries to control the smoke he raises his own cost of production but lowers that of the laundries. So here we have an externality problem that is amenable for analysis in terms of any of the methods outlined above.

Two possible solutions of this problem are the following. One is for the factory to relocate itself the other is for the laundries to relocate themselves. In either case the externality ceases to exist. But these are rather extreme solutions—in fact they are the *two* extreme solutions. There are a whole range of intermediate solutions which one could try and if one views the problem in this manner then the problem of correcting for this external effect is tantamount to the general problem of finding a Pareto optimal allocation in the presence of externalities.

Consider this problem then. In an n individual world there are $m + 1$ commodities. Commodity 1 is electricity which produces smoke, $2, \ldots, m$ are ordinary commodities, commodity $m + 1$ is leisure and R is the total supply of labour. x_{ij} is the quantity of the ith commodity consumed by individual j, $i = 1, \ldots, m + 1$, $j = 1 \ldots, n$. E_1 is the (yet unpriced) external effect

$$c_1(x_1, E_1), \left(\frac{\partial c_1}{\partial x_1} > 0, \frac{\partial c_1}{\partial E_1} < 0\right)$$

is the cost function of the electricity producer and $c_i(x_i, E_1)$

$$\frac{\partial c_i}{\partial x_i} > 0, \qquad \frac{\partial c_i}{\partial E_1} > 0$$

are the cost functions of the firms receiving the external effect. We set $P_{m+1} = 1$ and define the prices P_i of the various commodities.

The Pareto optimal problem is to max $u_1(x_{11}, \ldots, x_{m+1})$

subject to $u_j(x_{1j}, \ldots, x_{m+1j}) = \bar{u}_j, \qquad i = i, \ldots, n$

$$\sum_{j=1}^{n} x_{ij} = x_i, \qquad (i = 1, \ldots, m + 1)$$

and the production function

$$\sum_{i=1}^{m} c_i(x_i, E_1) + x_{m+1} = R.$$

Labour is the only primary input into the production process of the industries. We can then define the Lagrangean as:

$$L = u_1(x_{11}, \ldots, x_{m+1}) + \sum_{j=2}^{n} \lambda_j[u_j(x_{ij}, \ldots, x_{m+1j}) - \bar{u}_j]$$
$$+ \sum_{i=1}^{m+1} r_i \left[x_i - \sum_{j=1}^{n} x_{ij}\right] + \mu\left[R - \sum_{i=1}^{m} c_i(x_{ij}, E_1) - x_{m+1}\right].$$

From the first order conditions Murty and Nayak derive

$$P_i = c_{ii}\left(c_{ii} = \frac{\partial c_i}{\partial x_i}\right), \qquad i = 2, \ldots, m$$

$$P_{m+1} = 1.$$

and

$$\sum_{i=2}^{m} c_{iE} = - c_{1E}\left(c_{iE} = \frac{\partial c_i}{\partial E}\right).$$

These conditions define Pareto optimum. The first condition merely equates price with marginal cost, the second states that all prices are expressed in terms of hours of labour. The last condition answers a problem like the following: How much pollution abatement should go on? The answer is till the marginal damage to the externality producing firm equals the sum of the marginal gains to the externality receiving firms. These are the conditions for Pareto optimality.

If we confine correcting external effects to the case where the polluter is encouraged to adopt pollution abatement methods it can be shown that Pigovian taxes are the only measure that can control external effects. To see this suppose that we impose a per unit tax equivalent to

$$\overset{*}{t_1} = -\overset{*}{c}_{1E} = \sum_{i=2}^{m} \overset{*}{c}_{iE}$$

on E_1.

The electricity producer then maximizes

$$\phi_1 = p_1 x_1 - c_1(x_1, E_1) - \overset{*}{t}_1 E_1.$$

The first order conditions are

$$P_1 - c_{11} = 0$$

and

$$\frac{-\partial c_1}{\partial E_1} - \overset{*}{t}_1 = 0$$

so that

$$P_1 = c_{11} - \frac{\partial c_1}{\partial E_1} = \overset{*}{t}_1.$$

But $$\overset{*}{t}_1 = \overset{*}{c}_{1E}(\overset{*}{x}_1, \overset{*}{E}_1).$$

Thus with imposition of Pigovian tax the external effect is completely internalized and the polluter produces the Pareto optimal amount of x_1 and E_1. The firms affected by the pollution are already producing their optimal amounts.

A few facts about this result ought to be noted. First if the cost function is not convex then the equivalence breaks down. Second there has been some debate in the literature as to whether Pigovian taxes can, by themselves, fully internalize an external effect. Some authors (e.g. Davis and Whinston (1962)) have argued that only if cost functions are separable in x and E can Pigovian taxes, by themselves, completely internalize an external effect. But Murty and Nayak show that so long as the cost function is convex separability is unimportant. Whether or not the cost function is separable, Pigovian taxes succeed.

Murty and Nayak further show that the Coase solution will not work under these circumstances. Let us try to structure this argument. In the case of undefined liability that is when it is not clearly spelt out as to who is responsible for the consequences of the pollution the firm affected by the pollution has an incentive to bribe the polluter to lower the level of pollution so that by not reducing pollution the polluter will be incurring an opportunity cost to the extent of the bribe. We can show that in this case the outcome is necessarily Pareto non-optimal. An algebraic proof is given in Murty and Nayak. We will give a geometric illustration here.

In Fig. 5.2 we plot the electricity producer's cost function (as a function of E_1) as well as the cost function of a representative firm that is affected by the pollution. With Pigovian taxation (at the rate given by slope of S_1S_1 or S_2S_2) $\overset{*}{E}_1$ units of smoke is generated. This is the rational solution along the lines suggested earlier. With undefined liability if the electricity producer were to produce the same output as before his realized costs will be lower because of the bribe. These costs are minimized by producing $\hat{E}_1$ amount of the externality. The Pareto optimal output of x is associated with a Pareto non-optimal output of E_1. Thus we are not at Pareto optimum. We can show that neither x nor E are optimal.

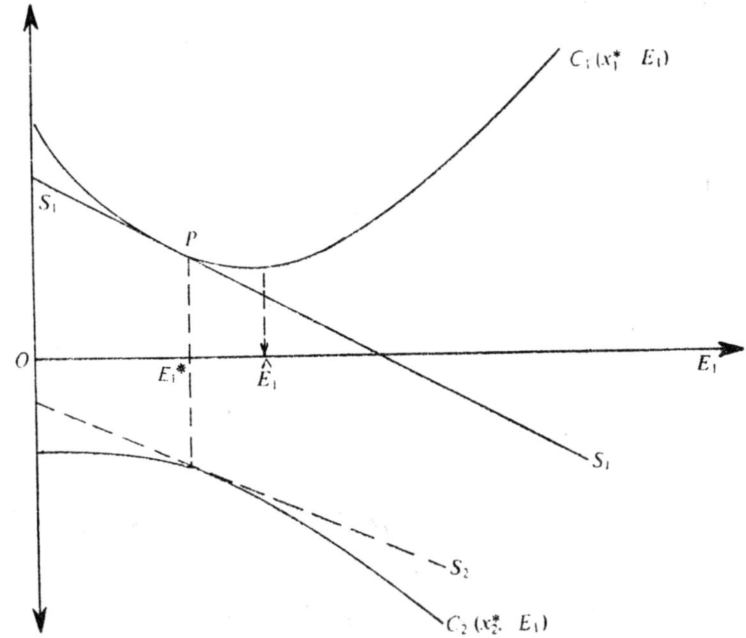

Fig. 5.2

The Case of Defined Liability

In this case the law declares that the externality generating firm is liable for the damage. Thus the liability is L where

$$L = C_2(x_2, E_1) - C_2(x_2, 0)$$

that is the liability is equal to the difference in cost for the externality receiving firm (assuming, for the sake of simplicity, that there is only one such firm) with the profit maximizing E_1 of firm 1 and zero production of E. One can define the cost function of firm 1, now, to include this liability and firm 2's cost is lower by the amount of the liability.

Under the property rights doctrine we can view firm 1 getting a bribe from two sources. It gets a bribe from the government to adopt abatement technology (in the liability case this corresponds to the additional cost imposed on firm 1). Similarly there is a second bribe (a negative bribe) from the second individual (which in the liability case corresponds to the reduction in cost of firm 2). Minimization of cost by firm 1 is, then, tantamount to maximizing this net bribe. We can depict this problem diagramatically as in Fig. 5.3.

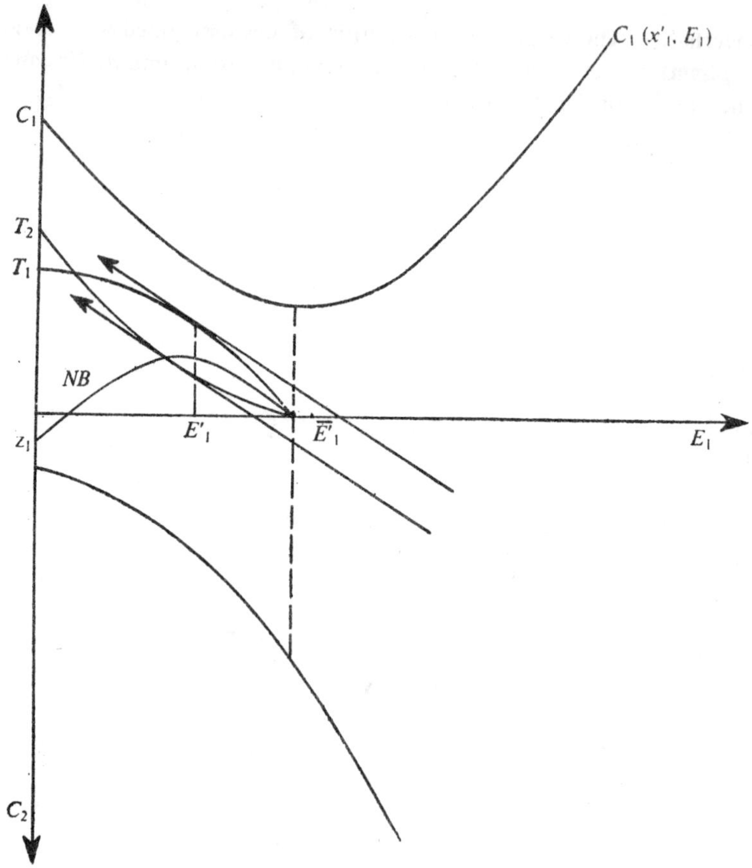

Fig. 5.3

As the level of pollution rises the levels of bribes fall. $T_1\bar{E}_1'$ is the schedule for the bribe society pays whereas $T_2\bar{E}_1'$ is the schedule for the bribe firm 2 pays firm 1. The net barter schedule is labelled *NB* and is given by $Z_1\bar{E}_1'$. For output level x_1' ordinary cost minimization gives rise to pollution level $\bar{E}_1'$. Maximization of net benefit means equating the marginal bribe from each source so that the firm generates pollution to the extent E_1'. Now E_1' is not equal to E_1^* which is the Pareto optimal amount of the externality. The reason for this is the following. Assume, for a moment, that the polluter is producing the Pareto optimal amount of electricity i.e. x_1^*. With Pigovian taxation (which we already know attains Pareto optimality) the tax rate is equated to the marginal cost of reducing the externality by one unit. In the present case, however, the net opportunity cost of reducing the externality is marginal cost of reducing the externality (along 1's cost schedule) less the marginal cost because of the external effect to 2. Pigovian taxation takes only the first factor into account. The Coase solution or the liability laws solution takes the second factor also into account and hence the amount of externality produced will be different from the Pareto optimal amount.

In general it can be shown that under the bargaining solution neither the Pareto optimal amount of x_1 nor the Pareto optimal amount of E_1 will be produced. Thus under conditions of convex non-separable costs Pigovian taxation is the best method to internalize externalities.

Murty and Nayak also show that with separable cost this result does not necessarily hold. With separable costs the cost functions are to be written as

$$C_1(x_1, E_1) = d_1(x_1) + d_2(E_1)$$

$$C_2(x_2, E_1) = d_3(x_1) + d_3(E_1).$$

With such a cost function and no specific assumption made about the curvature of the cost function it can be shown that the Davis-Whinston propositions are right i.e. unless the cost function is separable Pigovian taxes are not enough to attain full Pareto optimality. Similarly, the necessarily sub-optimal nature of the Coase solution cannot be accepted.

6. Incentives, External Effects and the Market Mechanism

Subject to the caveat that the distribution of resources can no longer be separated from the allocation of resources there does seem to be ample room to internalize external effects. But it must be clearly understood that the solutions we have been pondering over so far refer to a world with certainty. Our troubles multiply astronomically once we leave the safety of certainty and move to the more realistic scenario of uncertainty.

Let us take an example to pin things down somewhat. Suppose a factory which is in the middle of a residential locality belches smoke. If we could get true information from the residents about the extent of harm caused by the smoke we could start working towards a solution along the lines of one of the methods discussed in the previous chapter. But now suppose that such information is not forthcoming in an accurate form. Not only does the policy planner have to face the objective fact of uncertainty but also a wholly different problem raises its head. This is the problem of strategic behaviour on the part of individuals. Since I know that neither the policy planner nor the factory owner accurately knows my preferences it might pay me-depending on the policy in use—to misrepresent my preferences. To put it more precisely, let us suppose that the factory owner wants to purchase the land around the factory. Under normal circumstances if the land owner was offered a price above his reservation price the deal would be clinched and the story would end right there. But since nobody (except myself) knows my reservation price, I might refuse an offer which was higher than my (true) reservation price. Thus by misrepresenting my preferences (in this case my reservation price) I could get a higher price for the land.

A huge literature in the theory of public finance deals with this kind of question. It is obviously individually rational to misrepresent one's preferences. It is also collectively rational to internalize the external effect or supply an optimal amount of the public good. In modern terminology the idea is to evolve an incentive compatible mechanism for deciding the amount of the public good. If this mechanism also assures a Pareto optimal supply of the public good then so much the better. An incentive compatible mechanism is one where when the policy planner announces a decision say x and expects certain response from the public; the rules of the game are such that people find it individually rational to respond in exactly the same manner as anticipated by the policy planner. The meaning of this very important concept will become clearer as we study a few examples. Suffice it to say here that we have to devise a non-cooperative game whose equilibrium point in the sense of Nash is also an efficient allocation of resources.

We will study this problem from a number of angles. The first one is purely hypothetical. Suppose we have found an incentive compatible mechanism. What are its characteristics?

Since we wish to concentrate on the problem of incentive compatibility we will keep the model and its underlying structure as simple as possible. The method we describe here is due to Arrow (1977). Take a two person exchange economy. There are two goods (a private good x and a public good y). It is costless to transfer one good into the other so that the marginal (and average) rate of transformation between the two goods is one. The two persons are E and V. The initial endowment of the economy is W so that

$$x_E + x_V + y = W \tag{1}$$

where $x_i (i = E, V)$ is the amount of the private good with agent i. The two individuals are free to choose any allocation they like (in particular without any outside intervention), but if they fail to reach an agreement then there is zero production of the public good and each individual consumes his initial endowment (W_E, W_V) as the private good.

The Samuelsonian condition for the optimal supply of the public good is

$$MRS^E_{x_E, y} + MRS^V_{x_V, y} = 1 \tag{2a}$$

that is the marginal rate of substitution between x and y for E plus the MRS between x and y for V equals the MRT that is 1.

Both x and y are normal goods in the preference structures of the two individuals. Moreover an allocation with positive y is preferred, ceteris paribus, by both individuals to an allocation with zero y. Thus

$$u^i(x^i, y) \geqslant u^i(W_i, 0), \qquad i = E, V. \tag{2b}$$

Suppose E makes V an offer which V can either accept or reject. If we are operating in the world of certainty so that utility functions are known E's optimal strategy to maximize his utility subject to the constraints

$$x_E + x_V + y = W; \qquad u^V(x^V, y) \geqslant u^V(W_V, 0). \tag{3}$$

Now recall our Pareto optimization exercise. There we maximized one person's utility subject to the other person's utility being kept at a certain level and also subject to the resource constraint. This is precisely what E is doing. He is maximizing his utility subject to the resource constraint and the constraint that V's utility is kept at a certain level. Thus the solution to (3) gives us a Pareto optimal supply of the public good. Also clearly it is not rational for E to make an offer that V would reject. However we know that this happy state of affairs is not the result of a perfectly competitive process.

Now let us bring in uncertainty into the picture. To still keep things tractable and simple let us suppose that uncertainty enters this structure in a very simple manner. E does not know V's utility function but he knows that it is either u_a^V with probability p_a or u_b^V with probability p_b. What are the feasible offers that E can make now?

Offer 1.

$$E \text{ offers } A^* = (x_E^* x_V^*, y^*) \text{ to maximize}$$

$$u^E(x_E, y) \quad \text{subject to } x_E + x_V + gy = W$$

and

$$u_a^V(x_V, y) \geqslant u_a^V(W_V, 0)$$

$$u_b^V(x_V, y) \geqslant u_b^V(W_V, 0). \tag{4}$$

Now since V's utility function is either u_a^V or u_b^V (but not both) it follows that the solution to this problem can never give us a Pareto optimal allocation (although the probability of acceptance by V is 1).

Offer 2.

E assumes that V has utility function u_a^V

and offers $A^a = (x_E, x_V, y)$

to maximize $u^E(x_E, y)$

subject to $x_E + x_V + y = W$ and $u_a^V(x_V, y) \geqslant u_a^V(W_V, 0)$. (5)

This offer has probability p_a of acceptance and a probability $p_b (= 1 - p_a)$ of rejection. Hence the expected pay off is

$$p_a u^E(x_E, y) + p_b u^E(W_E, 0). \tag{6}$$

Offer 3.

E assumes that V has utility function u_b^V and offers $A^b = (x_E, x_V, y)$ to maximize

$$u^E(x_E, y) \text{ subject to}$$

$$x_E + x_V + y = W \quad \text{and} \quad u_b^V(x_V, y) \geqslant u_b^V(W_V, 0) \tag{7}$$

This offer has probability p_a of being rejected and a probability p_b of acceptance so that the expected pay off is

$$p_a u^E(W_E, 0) + p_b u^E(x_E, y). \tag{8}$$

Now expost offer 2 or offer 3 could turn out to be Pareto optimal depending on whether V's utility function was u_a^V or u_b^V. But *exante* all these measures are Pareto non-optimal since they all have a non-zero probability of failing. And it is exante optimality that matters, expost optimality here is largely a matter of chance.

Now let us introduce learning into the model. Does this very negative result change if, people can learn, about each other's utility functions? Arrow illustrates this with a very succinct example. We take a very simple form of this story. If the mechanism succeeds then, as we have stated above, we have been able to make it rational for individuals to tell the truth. Honesty would, then, be the best strategy.

The game is conceived in the following manner. Each individual follows the axioms of the von Neumann Morgestern expected utility theorem. Furthermore we can postulate utility as being separable in the public good and other goods. Also the utility function is linear in income. Thus *I* can write person *i*'s utility function (from the public good *X*) as

$$u^i(x) + \text{other income.}$$

We thus talk of the allocation of the public good distinctly from the allocation of other goods in the economy. Moreover the utility function is linear[1].

The amount of the public good is decided on the basis of certain announcements made by the public. Let us suppose that the form of the utility functions are known upto a certain parameter. Thus I may know that your utility function is of the form x^α + other income, but I don't know the value of α. People are asked to make announcements about this parameter. The decision on how much of the public good to supply depends upon these parameters. People might find it strategically advantageous to lie. A successful preference solicitation game is one where people find it rational to tell the truth. It is not our purpose here to prove existence of such an equilibrium. Our purpose is more modest. Assuming that such an equilibrium exists we want to find out how individuals behave in this equilibrium.

Suppose there are *n* people in society and the announced parameter of person *i* is γ_i so that the public goods supply rule is[2]

$$x = x(\gamma_1, \ldots, \gamma_n).$$

As we know these γ_i's may or may not equal the true parameters, which for person *i* is ρ_i. Let us also call ρ^i the vector of true parameters of everybody except person *i* i.e.

$$\rho^i = (\rho_1, \rho_2, \ldots, \rho_{i-1}, \rho_{i+1}, \ldots, \rho_n).$$

Similarly we define $\gamma^i = (\gamma_1, \gamma_2, \ldots, \gamma_{i-1}, \gamma_{i+1}, \gamma_n)$ as the vector of announced parameters of everyone except agent *i*.

Let us now suppose that each individual in his decision making is a Nash Cournot bargainer which means that he assumes that his decision will not affect anyone else's decision. We further assume that each agent assumes that everyone else is telling the truth. He however, uses his own announcement as a strategic variable to maximize his utility which is

$$E_{\rho^i} \{u^i[x(\gamma_i, \rho^i)], \rho_i]\} \tag{9}$$

[1]This set of assumptions is common to almost the entire literature on incentive comparability with public goods. Results are almost impossible to prove without them.

[2]Arrow calls this a responsive collective decision rule. More precisely, a responsive collective decision rule is one which changes the marginal utility of the public good and the amount of the public good in the same direction.

Person i is assuming that everyone else is telling the truth so that x gets determined by the rule $x(\gamma_i, \rho^i)$. However, how much utility he gets from x depends on the true value of his parameter so that his utility is

$$u^i[x(\gamma_i, \rho^i), \rho_i].$$

Although person i assumes (with certainty) that everyone else is telling the truth *ex-ante* he does not know the value of ρ^i. So his utility is uncertain and we take the expected value of u_i over the distribution of ρ^i. This fixes i's utility.

We would like to see $\gamma_i = \rho_i$ for all i. To repeat what we have said earlier we are not trying to discover when this would be the case. Rather, at this stage, we are interested only in characterizing individual behaviour in truth telling equilibrium that is an equilibrium in which truth telling is rational.

Suppose we prescribe a function $T_i(\gamma_i)$ for agent i which says that if agent i makes an announcement γ_i he has to pay an amount $T_i(\gamma_i)$ to the others. Thus we define $T_{ij}(\gamma_j)$ as the amount that agent j pays to agent i if he (i.e. agent j) makes the announcement γ_j. These payments may be positive, negative, or zero. Obviously

$$\sum_{i \neq j} T_{ij}(\gamma_j) = T_j(\gamma_j) \tag{10}$$

that is whatever agent j pays out is the sum of his payments to everyone else.

We can now define agent i's expected utility as (remember that his utility is assumed to be linear in income).

$$E_{\rho_i}\{u^i[x(\gamma_i(\rho_i), \gamma^i(\rho^i), \rho_i] - T_i[\gamma_i(\rho_i)] + E_\rho \{\sum_{j \neq i} T_{ij}[\gamma_j(\rho_j)]\} \tag{11}$$

where I have used the fact that i's announcement is a function of his true parameter. Everyone else's announcement is also a function of his true parameter. However, since so far as agent i is concerned everybody else is telling the truth it follows that we can write i's utility function as

$$E_{\rho^i}\{u^i[x(\gamma_j, \rho^i), \rho_i] - T_i(\gamma_i) + E_{\rho^i}[\sum_{j \neq i} T_{ij}(\rho_j)]\} \tag{12}$$

Agent i chooses γ_i to maximize (12). Differentiating (12) with respect to γ_i and setting the derivative equal to zero we get as first order condition for utility maximization

$$E_{\rho^i}\{u^i_x[x[\gamma_i, \rho^i], \rho_i]X_{\gamma_i}(\gamma_i, \rho^i)\} - T'_i(\gamma_i) = 0. \tag{13}$$

To have a truth telling equilibrium the solution of (13) for γ_i should be ρ_i for each i that is,

$$T'_i(\rho_i) = E_{\rho^i}\{u^i_x[x(\rho_i, \rho^i), \rho_i]X_{\gamma_i}(\rho_i, \rho^i)\}$$

for all i. (14)

The "truth telling transfer" for i can be easily obtained by integrating both sides of (14). If I have a truth telling equilibrium then (14) is satisfied for each agent[3].

So we have been able to characterize "truth telling equilibrium" in a fairly simple framework. Of course there is nothing automatic about its existence nor have we proved existence.

THE DEMAND REVELATION GAME OR CONFRONTING THE FREE RIDER PROBLEM

Revealing true demand for public goods is a problem hence financing the public good is a problem. So what can be done about it? Ideally we would like to devise a non-cooperative game such that the Nash solution is one where (*a*) the supply of the public good is Pareto optimal; (*b*) everyone finds it in his self-interest to tell the truth and, given that we do not want allocative repercussions on the rest of the economy; (*c*) the public goods budget is balanced.

We will discuss here three important attempts to solve the free rider problem. Unfortunately none of them is completely satisfactory. Indeed there is good reason to believe that the free rider problem cannot ever be satisfactorily solved. Let us discuss these attempts seriatim.

The Lindahl-Wicksell Mechanism

The Lindahl-Wicksell mechanism may-at only marginal risk of simplification—be called the market's solution to the problem of public goods. We will study this and other mechanism within a very simple context since our aim is to focus on the incentive structure rather than complication for the sake of complication.

We have an n person exchange economy in which there is one commodity which can be used either as a private good or (costlessly transformed) into a public good. Hence the marginal rate of transformation between the private and the public good is 1 and hence the Pareto optimal condition of supply of the public good is that the sum of the *MRS* between the private and public good must be one. We once again assume that the individual's utility function is separable in the public good (x) and the private good (y) and it takes the form

$$u_i(x, y_i) = V_i(x) + y_i$$

Each individual's $V_i(\ )$ function is assumed concave so that we can graphically depict it as in Fig. 6.1.

Now if the individuals were to act on their own the free rider problem will ensure that the public good does not get produced. Now let us suppose that

[3]The reader can easily check that under standard assumptions about the utility function second order conditions are satisfied.

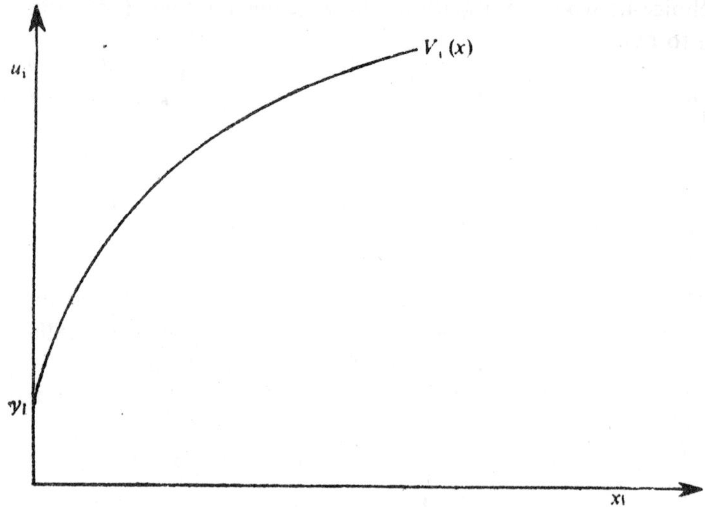

Fig. 6.1

each individual has to pay for the public good so that the ith individual's budget constraint is

$$y_i + T_i = w_i \qquad i = 1, \ldots, n \tag{15}$$

w_i is the initial endowment.

Along with Lindahl and Wickself we suppose that this tax is linear so that

$$T_i = t_i x; \qquad i = 1, \ldots, n \tag{16}$$

and, naturally,

$$\sum_{i=1}^{n} t_i = 1. \tag{17}$$

Let us look at the individual's maximization problem under these conditions Individual i maximizes

$$V_i(x) + y_i \quad \text{subject to } y_i + T_i = w_i.$$

In other words he wants to maximize

$$V_i(x) + w_i - T_i \qquad (\text{since } y_i = w_i - T_i).$$

The first order condition is

$$\frac{dV_i(x)}{dx} - \frac{dT_i}{dx} = 0.$$

Or that marginal utility from the public good equals the marginal (and average) tax rate. Diagrammatically, in Fig. 6.2 below the consumers optimum occurs when the slope of the $V_i(\;)$ schedule equals t_i or, in other words, when the gap between V_i and T_i is the largest.

In Fig. 6.2 the line OA with slope t_i measures tax liability. To find i's tax liability for any x we just have to refer to the schedule OA. If the individual had a choice he would x^* amount of the public good. The line Z_1Z_2 is parallel to OA.

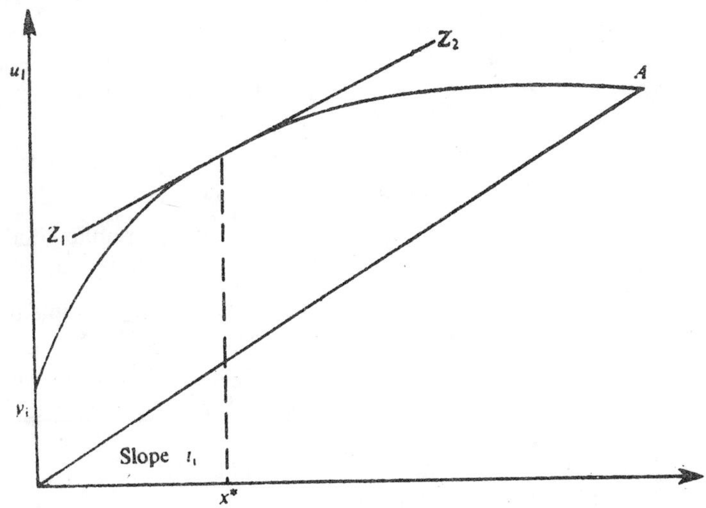

Fig. 6.2

Lindahl and Wicksell are after such a tax structure but with the following additional specifications.

(*a*) The public goods' supply must be Pareto optimal, that is,

$$\sum_{i=1}^{n} V_i' = 1$$

where V_i' is the first derivative of V_i with respect to x.

(*b*) The tax liability of any person should be linked, in interest of fairness, to the amount of benefits he receives from the public good.

By the individual's optimization condition

$$V_i' = T_i' = t_i$$

so $\Sigma V_i' = \Sigma t_i = 1$ so the Lindahl-Wicksell mechanism automatically satisfies stipulation (*a*).

In satisfying stipulation (*b*) we have the following problem *I*, with a strong preference for the public good might want x^* units while you with a weaker preference for the public good might want x^{**} units where $x^* > x^{**}$. But by the very nature of a public good both you and I consume all of the public good.

Lindahl and Wicksell propose an iterative algorithm to solve this problem and link this method with stipulation (*b*). The tax shares (t_i's) are interpreted as "prices". Let us start the situation say in an n person world where $t_i = 1/n$. for all i. Some people want less and some people want more of the public good depending upon their preference structure. Increase the tax shares of those who want more of the public good and decrease t_i for those who want less of the public good. Given the shape of the V_i schedule those who wanted less of the public good will, after adjustment, ask for more whereas those who wanted more will now ask for less. Assume this iteration converges than we have a set of "personalized" tax shares $t_1, t_2, \ldots, t_n$ such that each individual asks for the same amount of the public good. We already know that the Pareto optimality conditions are satisfied. This is the famous Lindahl equilibrium.

Formally, then, the Lindahl equilibrium is a set of personalized tax rates $t_1. \ldots, t_n$ and a public good output say x such that

(*i*) Each individual wants the same amount ($\hat{x}$) of the public good and

(*ii*) x is a Pareto optimal supply of the public good.

But although the Lindahl-Wicksell logic is powerful and simple there are a couple of very serious flaws with it.

(*i*) There is nothing to guarantee the convergence of the iterative algorithm. If this convergence does not occur then, clearly, the Lindahl-Wicksell mechanism collapses.

(*ii*) Logically prior to the aforementioned difficulty is the fact that the Lindahl-Wicksell method is not solving the free rider problem—it is merely wishing it away. It is supposing that individual faced with a tax rate t_i will honestly reveal his 'true' preference for the public good. But the crux of the free rider difficulty is that the individual finds it strategically proper to misrepresent his preference for the public good. In fact he finds it individually rational to say (in the extreme case) that he does not want any amount of the public good. Thus by supposing that each individual in society correctly reveals his preference for the public good the Lindahl Wicksell mechanism does not address the central difficulty posed by the free rider problem.

In 1970 Duncan Foley proved that if the Lindahl equilibrium exists it belongs to the core of the economy. Fig. 6.3 illustrates the notion of the core for a two person, two commodity exchange economy.

Initial endowment is at C so that voluntary trade can occur in the area bounded by the two indifference curves (one each for individuals I and II) that pass through C. The set of feasible competitive solutions is then given by the stretch L_1L_2 on the contract curve. This stretch (L_1L_2) is also the core of the economy. Foley's result is important because it gives the Lindahl equilibrium an intuitively appealing interpretation.

But as Ellickson (1974) has shown the problem lies in the existence of the Lindahl equilibrium. Without assuming essentially all the conditions of the second fundamental theorem of welfare economics it is not possible to prove Foley's result. Ellickson gives us a number of interesting counter examples to prove his point. Ellickson objects particularly to the assumption of divisibility of a public good. This assumption needless to say, is required if we are to use the second optimality theorem. A bridge is a bridge. A quarter of a bridge is no bridge at all Public goods by their very nature are indivisible and so a result that requires their divisibility is not taking us very far.

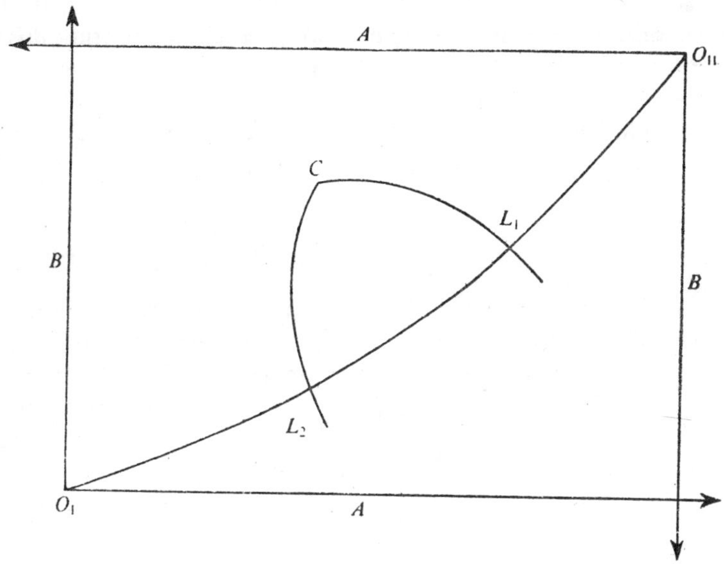

Fig. 6.3

In short, then, the Lindahl-Wicksell mechanism is simple and powerful but it does not really address the free rider problem. It is, of course, somewhat of a sacrosanct concept for reasons of intellectual history, its elegance, and more.

We now turn to a discussion of some recent suggestions for dealing with the free rider problem.

The Groves-Loeb Mechanism

Groves and Loeb have in a number of articles talked of a very different method of dealing with the free rider problem. Below we discuss the main features of their arrangement. There are points of detail which we have purposely avoided.

We study the Groves-Loeb mechanism within the same structure as that for the Lindahl-Wicksell mechanism. There is however the important difference that there is a serious attempt to confront the free rider problem.

In the Groves-Loeb mechanism a public goods board is entrusted with the task of supplying the public good. This board asks the people for their V_i schedules. At this stage there is no supposition that this V_i is true or false. The public goods board also lets it be known that person i's tax liability will be decided by

$$T_i = \hat{x} - \sum_{j \neq i} V_j(\hat{x})$$

where $\hat{x}$ is the amount of the public good. Thus my tax liability is the amount of the public good supplied less the sum of the utilities (from the public good) of everyone except me.

Let us for a moment suppose that people are telling the truth about their preferences. We will see that under the Groves-Loeb tax mechanism no one will have an incentive to lie.

On obtaining information about the V_i schedules the public goods board decides on the optimal supply of the public good by solving for that $\hat{x}$ for which

$$V_1'(\hat{x}) + V_2'(\hat{x}) + \ldots + V_n'(\hat{x}) = 1.$$

Since this is one equation in one variable it can easily be solved. We are also assumed that if people tell the truth about their V_i schedules then the public goods board is insuring a Pareto optimal supply of the public good:

How does any individual i decide which V_i schedule to report to the board? This, of course, is the product of a rational utility maximizing exercise. The consumer i maximizes $u_i = V_i(\hat{x}) + y_i$ subject to $Y_i + T_i = W_i$. Substitute $Y_i = W_i - T_i$ in the utility function to realise that the consumer is maximizing

$$V_i(\hat{x}) + W_i - T_i \text{ or, since, } W_i$$

is predetermined i is maximizing $V_i(\hat{x}) - T_i$.

But since

$$T_i = \hat{x} - \sum_{j \neq i} V_j(\hat{x})$$

it follows that i is trying to maximize

$$V_i(\hat{x}) - [\hat{x} - \sum_{j \neq i} V_j(\hat{x})]$$

Now since the public goods board supplies a Pareto optimal quantity of the public good ($V_1'(\hat{x}) + \ldots + V_n'(\hat{x}) = 1$) it follows that if we were to interpret the board's decision as a maximizing problem we would say that the board is maximizing aggregate net benefit that is it is maximizing

$$\sum_{i=1}^{n} V_i(\hat{x}) - \hat{x}$$

(differentiate this expression with respect to $\hat{x}$ to get back our Pareto optimum conditions).

The individual in maximizing his personal utility that is

$$V_i(\hat{x}) - [\hat{x} - \sum_{j \neq i} V_j(\hat{x})] = V_i(\hat{x}) + \sum_{j \neq i} V_j(\hat{x}) - \hat{x}$$

$$= \sum_{i=1}^{n} V_i(\hat{x}) - \hat{x}$$

He is doing precisely what the public goods board is doing. Hence under the Groves-Loeb demand revelation or tax mechanism the interest of the public goods board and each individual member of society coincide. It will therefore reduce i's utility if i gives the board a wrong message about V_i, his utility. Since the government is acting in your interest it will never be (truly) beneficial to be dishonest with the government. Hence no individual will have any incentive to cheat or lie.

This seems like an ingenious mechanism and it is. But unfortunately, this does not mean that the free rider problem has been solved. Although we have an incentive compatible structure and a Pareto optimal supply of the public good there is still one basic problem that is potentially extremely damaging for the Groves-Loeb mechanism.

In the Groves-Loeb mechanism nothing assures us that the public good board's budget will be balanced. Nothing in this set up ensures that $\sum_{i=1}^{n} T_i = \hat{x}$. Remember we are doing a partial equilibrium exercise so we cannot appeal to the rest of the economy to bail us out. That equilibrium cannot be upset without causing incalculable demage. The solution to this problem must, somehow, come from the public goods sector itself.

If $\hat{x} > \sum_{i=1}^{n} T_i$ we have a deficit in the budget. Now if we add an amount to everyone's tax liability where this amount does not depend upon $\hat{x}$ or V_i we clearly do nothing to make it profitable for i to lie. In other words we can always change tax liabilities to ensure

$$\sum_{i=1}^{n} T_i \geqslant \hat{x}.$$

To see this more clearly let us define

$$Z_i = \max_{x} \sum_{j \neq i} \left[V_j(x) - \frac{x}{n} \right].$$

Let us suppose that everyone is asked to pay for $1/n$ th of the cost. Then the net benefit to person j is $V_j(x) - \frac{x}{n}$ and the sum of such net benefits is

$$\sum_{j \neq i} \left(V_j(x) - \frac{x}{n} \right).$$

Z_i is then simply the maximum of this function. Now define a new tax for i

$$T_i = \hat{x} - \sum_{j \neq i} V_j(\hat{x}) + Z_i$$

we can rewrite this as

$$T_i = \frac{\hat{x}}{n} + Z_i - \sum_{j \neq i}\left[V_j(\hat{x}) - \frac{\hat{x}}{n}\right].$$

Since Z_i does not depend on i's reported V_i or on $\hat{x}$ it follows that truth telling is still the dominant strategy for i (and everyone else).

Given the definition of Z_i, however, it follows that

$$T_i \geqslant \frac{\hat{x}}{n} \quad \text{and hence} \sum_{j \neq 1}^{n} T_i \geqslant \hat{x}.$$

So there is no deficit. But how about a surplus that is $\sum_{i=1}^{n} T_i > \hat{x}$. What do we do with this surplus? We cannot throw it away since waste would imply that we are operating at a Pareto inferior solution—whether or not the Pareto optimal marginal conditions are satisfied. Suppose we give it back to the people as a transfer—lump sum or otherwise. In either case this is going to alter the problem in a fundamental manner. People now know that there is the possibility of a rebate and the rebate, F, can be accommodated in the tax function of individual i as

$$T_i = F(i, \hat{x}, V_1, \ldots, V_n).$$

The incentive structure for the problem is now fundamentally altered. People are now going to make the announcement keeping in view the possibility of a rebate. The powerful conclusions of the Groves-Loeb mechanism are now quite weak.

This leads us to a slightly deeper question. Is it possible to construct a demand revelation mechanism, which has the following three characteristics, (*i*) it is incentive compatible, (*ii*) it ensures a Pareto optimal supply of the public good, and (*iii*) the public good board's budget is balanced. Hurwicz considers this problem in an important recent contribution and comes to the disturbing conclusion that it is not possible to construct a demand revelation mechanism that simultaneously satisfies all three conditions mentioned above.

The Groves-Ledyard Mechanism

We finally look at another recent attempt to address the free rider problem. This scheme is quite similar in many ways to the Groves-Loeb mechanism but differs from it in several important respects. In the Groves-Ledyard approach people are not asked to express their V_i schedules but only their desired increment (Δ_i) in the quantity of the public good. Hence people might express their views about the nation's air force (a public good) by saying that they want three more planes or five less.

For this mechanism to work it is clear that initially we must have mutually consistent desired increments or there must be an iterative procedure (which converges fairly quickly) to make consistent initially inconsistent proposal by members of the public. This is a problem with the Groves-Ledyard mechanism.

Turning now to the operational side of the story the public goods board decides on the amount of the public good, by summing up the desired increments of various people, i.e.

$$\hat{x} = \sum_{i=1}^{n} \Delta_i .$$

We should realize at this stage that we may start from a position of no public goods and ask for desired increments. The natural thing to do with increments is to add them upto arrive at the absolute level of supply of the public good. We will see that this scheme of Groves and Ledyard bears good fruit. The natural thing to do is also the right thing to do.

The board sets taxes according to the rule

$$T_i = \frac{\hat{x}}{n} + \frac{r}{2}\left\{\frac{n-1}{n}(\Delta_i - A_i)^2 - \sum_{j\neq i} \frac{1}{n-2}(\Delta_j - A_i)^2\right\}$$

where

$$A_i - \frac{1}{n-1} \sum_{j\neq i} \Delta_j = \frac{1}{n-1}(\hat{x} - \Delta_i)$$

and r is some positive number. The tax liability is now more complicated than the Groves-Loeb but this, of course, is not without reason.

The first term of $T_i \left(\frac{\hat{x}}{n}\right)$ allocates an equal share of the cost of the public good to everyone. This, of course, can easily be generalized to an arbitrary fixed share i.e. $\frac{\hat{x}}{n}$ can be replaced with $\infty\ t_i$ so long as

$$\sum_{j\neq i}^{n} t_i = 1$$

and i's share could then be expressed as $1/n$th of the cost of the public good plus an adjustment factor. A_i is the mean of the desired increments of the other $n - 1$ people and so long as Δ_j $(j \neq i)$ does not depend on Δ_i, A_i does not depend on Δ_i. This is where the Cournot-Nash assumption referred to earlier in this chapter becomes extremely important. Everybody is assumed to make his decision in isolation and, furthermore, assume that his decision does not affect anyone else nor does anybody else's decision affect him except as a parameter. Thus i takes Δ_j $(j \neq i)$ as a parameter when announcing Δ_i.

Having discussed the decision making process of the public goods board we proceed to a discussion of how individuals decide upon the Δ_i message to send to the public goods board. A representative individual i, chooses his Δ_i to maximize

$$u_i = V_i(x) + y_i \text{ s.t. } y_i + T_i = w_i$$

or

$$V_i(\ ) - T_i.$$

Given the way decision on public goods supply is reached at and substituting for T_i we get as i's problem

$$\max_{\Delta_i} V_i(\Delta_i + \sum_{j \neq i} \Delta_j) - \frac{1}{n}(\Delta_i + \sum_{j \neq i} \Delta_i)$$

$$-\frac{r}{2}\left\{\frac{n-1}{n}(\Delta_i - A_i)^2 - \sum_{j \neq i} \frac{1}{n-2}(\Delta_j - A_i)^2\right\}.$$

The first order condition for an internal optimum gives us

$$V_i'(\Delta_i + \sum_{j \neq i} \Delta_j) - \frac{1}{n} - \frac{r(n-1)}{n}(\Delta_i - A_i) = 0$$

or

$$V_i'(\Delta_i + \sum_{j \neq i} \Delta_j) = \frac{1}{n} + \frac{r(n-1)}{n}(\Delta_i - A_i).$$

Thus person i choose the Δ_i that solves this equation.

Hence we can now define a Groves-Ledyard equilibrium. A Groves-Ledyard equilibrium is a list of desired increments $\Delta_1, \ldots, \Delta_n$ and a level of public good output

$$\hat{x} = \sum_{i=1}^{n} \Delta_i$$

such that Δ_i maximizes person i's after tax utility given $\Delta_1, \ldots, \Delta_{i-1}, \Delta_{i+1}, \ldots, \Delta_n$.

This equilibrium has certain very desirable properties. Summing up the right hand side and the left hand side of individual i's first order condition we get

$$\sum_{i=1}^{n} V_i'(\Delta_i + \sum_{j=i} \Delta_j) = \sum_{i=1}^{n}\left[\frac{1}{n} + \frac{r(n-1)}{n}(\Delta_i - A_i)\right]$$

which yields

$$\sum_{i=1}^{n} V_i'(\hat{x}) = 1 + \frac{r(n-1)}{n}\sum_{i=1}^{n}(\Delta_i - A_i)$$

$$= 1 + 0 = 1.$$

Hence in Groves Ledyard equilibrium the supply of the public goods is Pareto optimal.

Secondly it can be shown that

$$T_i = \frac{\hat{x}}{n} + \frac{r}{2n(n-2)}\left[n^2\Delta_i^2 - n\sum_{j=1}^{n}\Delta_j^2 + 2\hat{x}^2 - 2n\hat{x}\,\Delta_i\right].$$

If we sum this over all the individuals we get

$$\sum_{i=1}^{n} T_i = \Sigma \frac{\hat{x}}{n} + \frac{r}{2n(n-2)} [0] = \hat{x}.$$

Thus, unlike the Groves-Loeb demand revelation game, the Groves-Ledyard mechanism produces no budgetary surplus or deficit.

Hence the Groves-Ledyard mechanism produces a Pareto optimal supply of public goods, is incentive compatible and invariably manages to balance the budget. Thus if all goes well then the Groves-Ledyard mechanism performs very well indeed.

However, we must necessarily temper our enthusiasm for the Groves-Ledyard mechanism. The apparent success of this mechanism rests on the particular Cournot-Nash assumption that Δ_i does not affect Δ_j. But suppose that individual *i* (or a proper subset of individuals forming a coalition) decides to exploit the fact that he knows the public goods supply rule. Thus Δ_i will depend on Δ_j and the same first order condition does not obtain (for individual *i*). This means, of course, that we are not assured of a Pareto optimal supply of the public good. However, it can be seen that if the problem takes the simple form of only one person behaving strategically we are still able to balance the budget without any deficit or surplus. However, if others also realize their mutual interdependence the model will break down. Certain equilibria may exist but there is no reason whatsoever why they should involve a Pareto optimal supply of the public good, or that they should be incentive compatible equilibria. In the face of enlightened strategic behaviour the Groves-Ledyard scheme breaks down. This scheme requires people to be rational in a very narrow sense.

Appendix I

Accident, Liability and Uncertainty

In this appendix we want to study accidents as a form of an externality and the associated problem of assigning liability and penalty for an accident in the presence of uncertainty. An accident, apart from being unfortunate, is also a rather complex economic phenomenon.

An injurer causes damage to a victim. But the story just about begins there. There might be more than one injurer and/or more than one victim with varying degrees of injury. Public or private property may be destroyed in the process. An accident is an external effect but evaluating the effects of the externalities involved is a very difficult job. What is usually done in most countries is to define a law that makes one or more parties liable for an accident and then assign costs. But before we go into the details of the ---fulness or otherwise of liability laws we must inquire as to whether liability laws are the best means to internalize this particular externality.

Ideally if we could pinpoint precisely the cost of an accident we would make it mandatory for people to choose levels of care that would minimize the cost of an accident. As an illustration let us suppose that in an n individual society i chooses level of care x_i. If i is a victim we would suppose that this cost involves crossing the road only with a green signal, observing pedestrian or, in general, traffic rules. These costs are monetized and expressed as $g(x_i)$. If persons i and j could potentially be involved in an accident (and we will deal solely with accidents involving two parties) we describe the probability of an accident by $\pi(x_i, x_j)$. If C is the cost of an accident then total expected costs to society are

$$\sum_{i=1}^{n} \sum_{\substack{j=1 \\ j>1}}^{n} C\pi(x_i, x_j) + \sum_{i=1}^{n} g(x_i). \tag{1}$$

We are using the von Neumann-Morgenstern assumptions to add certain and probabilistic costs. Ideally, then, if care levels could be monitored continuously the first best policy would be to make it mandatory for people to observe the levels of care $(x_1, \ldots, x_n)$ that minimize (1). Hence liability laws do not constitute first best policy.

However, it is going to be impossible for a court to monitor care levels continuously and it is going to be very easy for the parties to an accident to lie. Hence, while the aforementioned policy is first best it is not practical. What the courts need are simple rules that clearly assign liability for an accident. Once this is done the courts can fix damages. This is where liability laws become operational and hence meaningful. Given that this is the case we would like to see liability laws that are close to the first best solution that is we want to define liability laws that internalize the external effects of accidents in the best possible way.

We will consider here only those accidents that involve just two parties—one injurer and one victim. The injurers exercise level of care x whereas the victims exercise y level of care. The probability of an accident is then given by $\pi(x, y)$. This, of course, involves a number of simplifying assumptions viz. the two groups (of injurers and victims) are of equal size. We further assume that accidents between different pairs of individuals are independent random events. In this sense we treat $\pi(x, y)$ as the parameter of a Poisson process[1]. We further confine our analysis to one time period.

Wherever an accident occurs there are two kinds of costs--recognized costs C involving, say, hospital bills, foregone earnings for the time hospitalized, car repairs etc. and unrecognized (or psychic costs) D_x for injuries and D_y for victims. This includes phenomena like being "shaken up by the accident", anguish of family etc. The courts can shift C but it is going to be very difficult to shift D_x or D_y.

A number of authors have considered the problem of internalizing the external effects of an accident under these conditions. Prominent among these authors are Brown, Diamond and Green. Since the analysis gets extremely complicated very fast we will confine ourselves to a study of liability laws under the assumptions mentioned above. The interested reader can look up some extensions of these ideas particularly in the work of Green.

Let us suppose that at the time of the accident the courts can assess care levels exercised by both victims and injurers and they have to decide how to distribute the recognized costs of the accident between injurer and victim. The entire cost of the accident is borne by the two parties involved and no shifting to, say, society in general is possible.

Hence the court wishes to find a fraction $V(x, y)$ such that $CV(x,y)$ is the injurers share of the cost whereas the victim pays $C(1 - V(x, y))$. We do not stipulate anything else at this stage about the nature of V. We will realise presently that the form of V depends on the particular type of liability law adopted by the courts.

Let us interject here a dose of reality $V(x, y)$ cannot be conceived of as a continuous function. It will be impossible for the courts to monitor care precisely. Usually all they are able to do is to determine whether the injurer

[1]The Poisson distribution defines the probability of an event k as

$$\frac{e^{-\lambda}\lambda^k}{k!}$$

where λ is the sole parameter of the distribution.

or victim has met certain due care standards. If, say, the victim has met "due care" standards the injurer could, conceivably, he asked to incur all the recognized costs. These "due care" standards may be fixed by experience or convention and may involve stipulations like a motor vehicle having good brakes that are checked every quarter etc. Thus $V(x, y)$ is restricted to have values of either zero or one and be constant in over the regions

$$\{(x, y)/x < x^*, y < y^*\}$$
$$\{(x, y)/x < x^*, y \geqslant y^*\}$$
$$\{(x, y)/x \geqslant x^*, y < y^*\}$$
$$\{(x, y)/x \geqslant x^*, y \geqslant y^*\}$$

where $x^*(y)^*$ are the due care standards for injurer (victim).

DESCRIPTION OF LEGAL RULES

If $y < y^*$ (victim exercises less than due care) we have the following possible legal rules:

(1) injurer is not liable independent of x.
(2) injurer is liable if $x < x^*$ and not otherwise.
For $y \geqslant y^*$ (victim exercises due care or more).
(3) injurer is liable if $x < x^*$, not otherwise.
(4) injurer is always liable, independent of x.

A legal rule is a choice of one from the pairs (1-3), (2-3), (1-4) and (2-4). Four other legal rules are possible

(*a*) strict liability of injurer.
(*b*) injurer not liable.
(*c*) injurer liable if $x \geqslant x^*$ and $y < y^*$.
(*d*) injurer liable if $x \geqslant x^*$ or $y < y.^*$

(*a*) and (*b*) are interesting policy alternatives but there is nothing much to say after these rules are adopted. (*c*) and (*d*) are meaningless. Hence we confine ourselves to the above rules.

Individual Behaviour under Alternative Legal Rules

We assume that each individual has linear von Neumann Mongenstern utility functions. Thus we can write the injurer's utility function as

$$-x - D_x\pi(x, y) \quad \text{(when not liable)}$$
$$-x - (D_x + C)\pi(x, y) \quad \text{(when liable).}$$

For victims the utility function is

$$-y - D_y\pi(x, y) \quad \text{(when not liable)}$$
$$-y - (D_y + C)\pi(x, y) \quad \text{(when liable)}$$

when liable an injurer has to incur recognized and unrecognized costs when not liable he incurs only unrecognized costs.

For an injurer if we keep y fixed and add a large enough constant to the utility function we can depict, it in Fig. A.6.1.

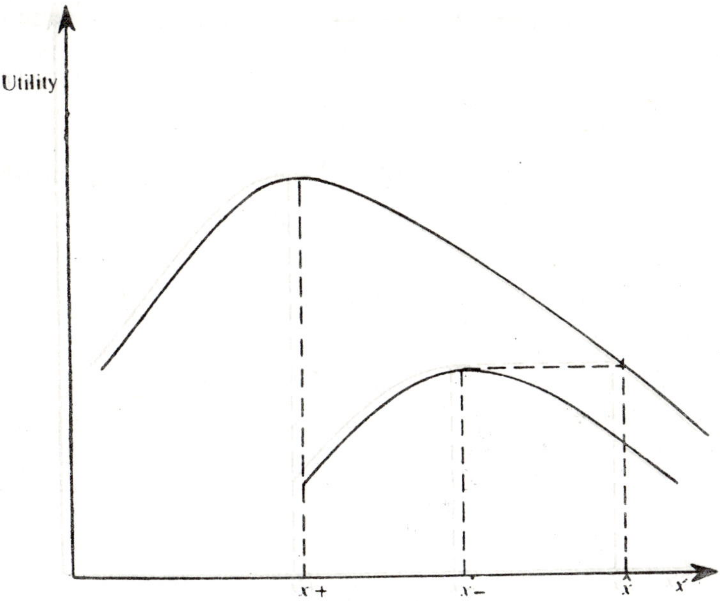

Fig. A.6.1.

The higher of the two utility schedules depicts the injurer's utility when he is not liable and x_+ is the utility maximizing level of care in this case. The lower schedule depicts the injurer's utility when he is liable. x_- is the corresponding utility maximizing utility. $\hat{x}$ is the level of care that gives the same utility as x-does (when the individual is liable) when the individual is not liable. These schedules are parameterized by y. When y changes the probability of an accident changes and the utility schedules shift. Now we can depict the behaviour patterns of injurers and victims. In legal system (1) $y < y^*$ and the injurer is not liable independent of x thus the injurer will choose $x = x_+$.

In case (2) the individual will choose

$$x = x_+ \qquad \text{if } x^* \leqslant x_+$$

$$x = x^* \qquad \text{if } x_+ < x^* \leqslant \hat{x}$$

$$x = x_- \qquad \text{if } \hat{x} \leqslant x^*.$$

Here in the first case the individual is allowed the freedom to choose x_+. In the second case with legal system (2) the injurer avoids liability by choosing x^*. In the last case since $x^* \leqslant \hat{x}$ the injurer maximizes utility by choosing $\hat{x}$. We can easily check that for legal rule (3) as well the same behavioural responses as this case are optimal.

In case (4) since the injurer is necessarily liable he chooses x_- to maximize utility.

In a similar manner we define the utility of the victim and describe his behaviour in various legal regimes. The victim's behaviour is entirely symmetric and there is no point in repeating it.

For the injurer we know that x^+, x_- and $\hat{x}$ are all functions of y. For larger y each of these care levels will be lower. We know that three broad classes of responses are possible from the injurer depending on whether x^* is:

(A) below $x_+(y)$

(B) between $x_+(y)$ and $\hat{x}(y)$

(C) above $\hat{x}(y)$.

We know that $x = x_+$ and $x = x_-$ are the solutions for the no liability and strict liability rules, respectively. Thus there are twelve cases to be analyzed. For the injurer we can depict the behaviour pattern as in Table A.6.1.

TABLE A.6.1

Mode of Behaviour	*Legal Rule*			
	1 – 3	1 – 4	2 – 3	2 – 4
x_+	$x \geqslant x^*$ or $y < y^*$	$y < y^*$	$x \geqslant x^*$	$x \geqslant x^*$ and $y < y^*$
x^*	$\max(\bar{\bar{y}}, y^*) < \bar{y}$	ϕ	$\bar{\bar{y}} < y < \bar{y}$	$\bar{\bar{y}} < y <$ min $\cdot$ $(y^*, \bar{y})$
x_-	$x < x^*$ and $y \geqslant y^*$	$y \geqslant y^*$	$x < x^*$	$x < x^*$ or $y \geqslant y^*$

where

$$\hat{x}^{-1}(x^*) = \bar{y}$$
$$x_-^{-1}(x^*) = \bar{\bar{y}}.$$

Let us first describe these two terms and then discuss the table itself. $\hat{x}^{-1}(\hat{x}^*) = \bar{y}$ is to be read in the following manner. When the due care standard is x^* the injurer will choose level of care $\hat{x}$ if the level of care by the victim is $\bar{y}$. Similarly, if the level of care by the victim is $\bar{\bar{y}}$ and the due care standard is x^* the injurer will choose level of care x_-.

A word explaining the entires in Table A.6.1. Legal rules are represented as columns whereas modes of behaviour are read along the rows. Thus under legal rule (1) — (3) if $y < y^*$ the injurer is not liable independently of his x and if $y \geqslant y^*$ the injurer is liable only if $x < x^*$. Thus if $x > x^*$ it is optimal to choose x_+ or if $y < y^*$ then it is safe to assume that the injurer is not liable and he chooses x_+ to maximize his utility. Similarly under legal rule (1) — (4) if $y < y^*$ the injurer is not liable independent of his x so he maximizes utility by choosing x_+. Again if $y \geqslant y^*$ the injurer is always liable so x_+ is a non-viable mode of action. The reader should work through each entry in the matrix.

In a completely analogous manner we portray the victim's behaviour pattern in Table A.6.2.

TABLE A.6.2

Mode of Behaviour	*Legal Rule* 1 – 3	1 – 4	2 – 3	2 – 4
y_+	$x < x^*$ and $y \geqslant y^*$	$y \geqslant y^*$	$x < x^*$	$x < x^*$ or $y \geqslant y^*$
y^*	$\bar{\bar{x}} < x < \min(\bar{x}, x^*)$	$\bar{\bar{x}} < x < \bar{x}$	ϕ	$\max(\bar{\bar{x}}, x^*) < x < \bar{x}$
y_-	$x \geqslant x^*$ or $y < y^*$	$y < y^*$	$x \geqslant x^*$	$x \geqslant x^*$ and $y < y^*$

where

$$\hat{y}^{-1}(y^*) = \bar{x}$$

and

$$\hat{y}_-^{-1}(y^*) = \bar{\bar{x}}.$$

$\bar{x}$ and $\bar{\bar{y}}$ are interpreted in a completely analogous manner to the interpretation of $\bar{y}$ and $\bar{\bar{y}}$ in Table A.6.1. The interpretation of the elements in the matrix should also be carried out analogously.

We next combine Tables A.6.1 and A.6.2 to define the various equilibria for this system in Table A.6.3.

As one can see under legal system (1) — (3) with $x \geqslant x^*$ or $y < y^*$ the injurer would choose x_+ while the victim would opt for y_-. Thus we explain this term in the above matrix. Similar explanations are to be given for each term in the above matrix.

In Fig. A.6.2 we plot the broad contours of these solutions. Rules 1-3 and 2-4 can attain points on the segment in dotted. The point $(x_- y_-)$ is of particular interest both because it is the most prevalent legal system and because Diamond and Brown concentrate on it. This is the legal system in which one person is held liable but the other is threatened with full liability if his care falls below the due care standard. Thus both persons

TABLE A.6.3

Legal system / *Possible equilibria*	1 − 3	1 − 4	2 − 3	2 − 4
x_+y_-	$x \geqslant x^*$ or $y < y^*$	$y < y^*$	$x \geqslant x^*$	$x \geqslant x^*$ and $y < y^*$
x^*y_-	$\max(\bar{\bar{y}}, y^*) < y < \bar{y}$	ϕ	$\bar{\bar{y}} < y < \bar{y}$	$\bar{\bar{y}} < y < \min(y^*, \bar{y})$
x_-y^*	$\bar{\bar{x}} < x < \min(\bar{x}, x^*)$	$\bar{\bar{x}} < x < \bar{x}$	ϕ	$\max(\bar{\bar{x}}, x^*) < x < \bar{x}$
x_-y_+	$x < x^*$ and $y \geqslant y^*$	$y \geqslant y^*$	$x < x^*$	$y \geqslant y$ or $x < x^*$

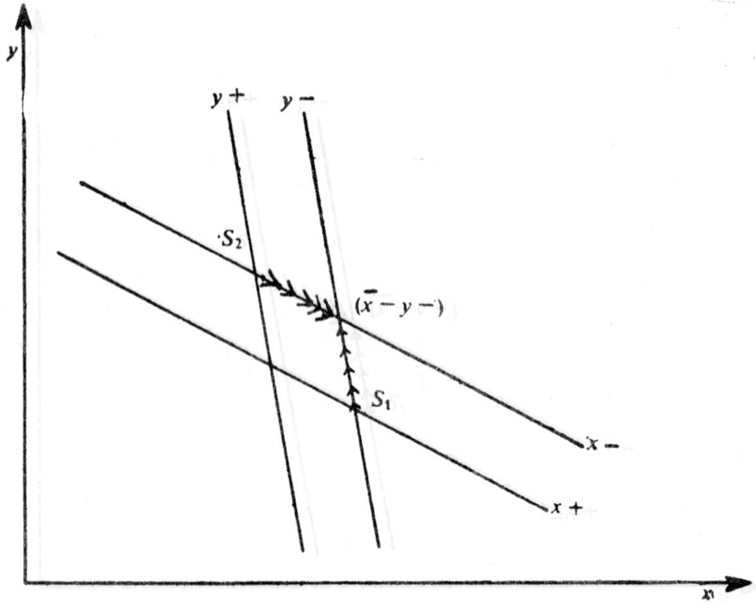

Fig. A.6.2

act as if they are liable and the probability of an accident is minimized. The point x_-y_- is to be interpreted as the limit of a sequence from S_1 or from S_2. As we move from S_1 to (x_-y_-) we move from a point of full liability of the victim and no liability for the injurer to increasing possibility of liability of injurer. Thus x_-y_- is a limit of this sequence. If we from S_2 to x_-y_- we describe the reverse sequence i.e. we move from a position of full liability of injurer and no liability for victim to increasing probability of liability for victim. Both injurer and victim do not bear the full cost of the accident. But if we interpret $(x_{-}y_{-})$ as the limit of these sequences we can see a rationale for it. $(x_{-}y_{-})$ by eliciting maximal care minimizes the probability of an accident.

Hence if we articulate the problem of internalizing the external effects of an accident in this manner then this particular legal rule does seem best (remember it is second best). But we must be quite clear that this conclusion is valid only within the very limited conditions described here. An accident even just its economic aspects—is a complex phenomenon and we must be wary of applying solutions out of context.

Appendix II

Uncertainty, Externalities and Non-Strategic Behaviour

In this chapter we have attempted to discuss the strategic aspects of the theory of public goods. But uncertainty, of course, means much more than just that—even for the theory of public goods. Even if there is no strategic behaviour, as such, there is still the problem of optimal allocation of resources in the presence of external effects and uncertainty. The policy problems are quite serious. Thus we may not know how well a malaria eradication programme is working because we do not know how much (privately) better off individual beneficiaries from the eradication problem are. In fact even the beneficiaries themselves may not know how well off they are. Despite all this malaria eradication remains an important policy problem and the economist has to devise standards and ways by which this policy can be evaluated. The programme is generating private benefits and external effects but the policy authorities and/or the individuals themselves are imperfectly informed. There is non-strategic behaviour on the part of the individuals but still the practical (and theoretical) problem of how to deal with the external effect remains.

In an important recent article Ordover and Willig have analyzed this problem in a relatively simple model. The answers they give are, almost necessarily, of relevance primarily to the model they have considered. Nonetheless, their paper is a decisive effort and will pave the way for more applied work in this area. Looking at this difficulty in another way, the results of this chapter were derived under quite specific assumptions so Ordover and Willig's contribution by considering an important policy issue is a path breaking one for the theory of externalities.

Let us make some simplifying assumptions. Assume that we can carry out a partial equilibrium exercise i e. the externality producing activity we are considering has no implications for allocation in the rest of the economy. Similarly what is happening in the rest of the economy does not affect this section. In some instances we will assume that we know the (joint) distribution of people over benefits and external affects. Also we will assume that (private) benefits, external effects and costs to society can be measured in the same units. We will adopt a welfare maximization approach and the relationship of this to Pareto optimality may, at times, be tenuous.

A person by engaging in an activity derives private benefits B and generates external effects E. This activity is available at a constant marginal cost, C, to society. B, E and C are all measured in the same units. Society (and sometimes the individual as well) is imperfectly informed about the B's and E's of various individuals but $h(B, E)$, the distribution of people over B's and E's is common knowledge. Thus high school education may mean different things to different people. A poor student may seek a job immediately after graduation whereas his richer classmate may opt for more education. However, the poor boy also comes from a poor neighbourhood where his success is a source of inspiration to his disadvantaged friends. He, therefore, generates very strong external effects. The rich student lives in a society where higher education is very common so that the external effect that his education generates is very limited. The important policy question, in the context of this example, then is how should education be priced? Ordover and Willig discuss a number of policy options which we discuss here.

Pure Price Subsidy

Suppose there is a common fee for all students. Now, each individual will have a reservation price for education i.e. if education costs more than that amount it won't be worthwhile for the consumer. In particular if the price exceeds the private benefit then it won't be worthwhile for the individual to participate in the education programme.

The government realizes this and it also realizes that the individuals are generating external effects which benefit society but which the individuals themselves are in no position to realize as personal gain. It is in the society's collective interest to encourage education. Suppose the government decides to do this by introducing a uniform subsidy for everybody. What is the effect of this policy and what are the merits and demerits of this policy? To these questions we now turn.

The optimal uniform subsidy is given by maximizing

$$W = \int_{p}^{\infty} \int_{0}^{\infty} (B + E - C)\, h(B, E)\, dB\, dE \tag{1}$$

p is the price of education.

We think of $h(\ )$ as a continuous distribution $B + E - C$ is the gain to society from education of one person. W is, then, aggregate social welfare from education.

Performing the maximization, then,

$$\frac{\partial W}{\partial p} = -\int_{0}^{\infty} (p + E - C) h(p, E)\, dE = 0$$

which implies

$$p^{*} + m(E/p^{*}) = C.$$

Given the price p^*, $m(E/p^*)$ measures the average external effect generated. When the government announces the price p^* some people buy this commodity and certain external effects are generated. The amount of external effect generated depends on p^* since only those people whose B's are greater than p^* buy the commodity. $m(E/p^*)$ is then the subsidy available to everyone. As a single price rule this policy makes eminent sense. Society's gains also include the external effect whose average value is given by the $m(\ )$ function. Thus if society is to maximize welfare it must equate marginal gain with marginal cost. The marginal gain is the private gain (at the margin this is p^*), since only those people for whom $B \geqslant p^*$ buy the commodity, plus the external effect ($m(\ )$). The sum of these two is then equated with the marginal cost C. Thus $m(\ )$ is the amount of the subsidy. This, then, is the optimal single price rule.[1]

But a single price rule is not necessarily the best policy available to the government. We can see this in Fig. A.6.3.

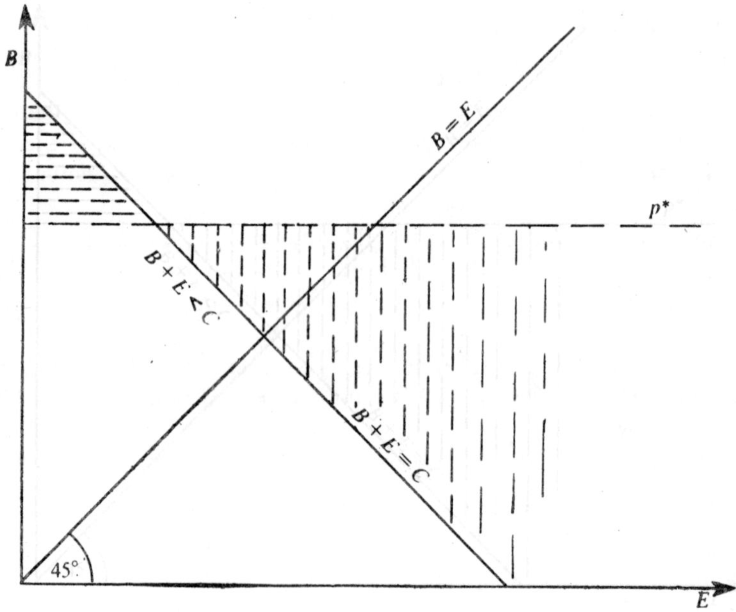

Fig. A.6.3

In Fig. A.6.3, we have the $B + E = C$ line which shows various combination of B and E which give the same marginal cost C. We have also drawn the optimal price line p^* and a 45° line along which $B = E$. Above the

[1]The second order condition is that

$$\frac{d[B + m(E/B)]}{dB} > 0$$

at

$$B = p^*.$$

$B + E = C$ line we have $B + E > C$ and below it $B + E < C$. The p^* line divides the population into two interesting sets. One labelled 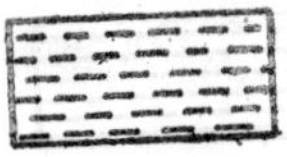 is the set of people for whom $B + E < C$ but since their B is higher than p^* they buy the commodity. The other set labelled  is the set of people for whom $B + E > C$ but since their B is less than p^* they don't buy the commodity. A single price rule, therefore, errs in both directions by excluding people with high social benefits and including those with low social benefits. There is need, therefore, for improving upon the single price scheme.[2] This naturally leads us to consider screening mechanisms that depend on self selection.

Screening Mechanisms

Instead of a single price let us suppose that we can adopt a double price system. Suppose that we can distinguish between two broad classes of people —one has a characteristic α and the other does not have that characteristic. In the education example suppose we divide prospective students into two categories—one that has annual parental income of Rs 5,000 or less (group α) and the other whose annual parental income is greater than Rs 5,000 (group $\bar{\alpha}$). We know the distribution $h^{\bar{\alpha}}(B, E)$ of the people with characteristic α over B and E. Similarly, the distribution $h^{\bar{\alpha}}(B, E)$ of people without the characteristic α over B and E is also known. We can now define aggregate social welfare as the sum of that arising from groups α and $\bar{\alpha}$:

$$W = \int_{p}^{\infty} \int_{0}^{\infty} (B + E - C)\, h^{\bar{\alpha}}(B, E)\, dB\, dE$$

$$+ \int_{p_\alpha}^{\infty} \int_{0}^{\infty} (B + E - C - s)\, h^{\bar{\alpha}}(B, E)\, dB\, dE.$$

People with characteristics α face a special price p_α. s is the cost of verifying that a given individual has characteristic α. Anybody who wants to pay the special price has to subject himself to a test that costs s. There is no fear of adverse selection here since if somebody lies and stakes a claim on p_α he has to pay s any way and then pay the higher price once it is found out that he belongs to group $\bar{\alpha}$ and not α. Hence only those people who genuinely have the characteristic α will take the test. Once the programme goes through has optimal price equation for group $\bar{\alpha}$ is

$$p^* + m^{\bar{\alpha}}(E/p^*) = C$$

[2]We need to state explicitly that p^* might be zero in which case this problem might be eliminated. But this, of course, is purely a matter of chance. Similarly, p^* might be so high that it excludes everyone so that we err only in one direction.

where p^* is the optimal price and $m^{\bar{\alpha}}$ is the average external effect generated from group $\bar{\alpha}$ when its members face the price p^*.

For group α we have

$$\overset{*}{p_\alpha} + m^\alpha(E/\overset{*}{p_\alpha}) = C + s$$

where m^α is the average external effect generated by members of group α when they face the price $\overset{*}{p_\alpha}$.

This set of prices now clearly improves upon the earlier single price policy. The higher price for the $\bar{\alpha}$ group excludes some people (above the p^* line in Fig. A.6.3) who were being excluded and p_α includes some people (below the p^* line in Fig. A.6.3, who were being excluded. This mechanism, then, improves upon the single price policy espoused earlier. The fact that there is no adverse selection makes this policy particularly attractive.

It is now possible to think of classification of the population by more than one characteristic. Thus in the education example apart from parental income being above or below Rs 5,000 per year one could use, for instance, whether the student lives within five miles of a major urban centre. Additional examples could be if he belonged to a backward community, if he had good transport facilities to get to school etc. Thus, in principle, we could segment the population into finer and finer categories and have a real multiplicity of prices. But imagine the administrative difficulties. This policy retains its attractiveness only if the number of criteria by which we classify the population is relatively small.

Thus we should look at other methods if we want to improve or supplement the performance of the pricing system. To these we now turn.

Conditional Perfect Price Discrimination

This is a policy which can usefully be appended to any program. Suppose agents know their own B's and E's but the government doesn't. The government announces a program of conditional perfect price discrimination (*cppd*). Under this programme agents can get their B's and E's tested for a small application fee. t is the screening cost and the government will test an agent only if his $B + E \geqslant C + t$. If this criterion is met the agent gets back his application fee and is offered a price just below his measured B. Once again there is no room for adverse selection. An agent may want to cheat. But $B + E$ is measured by the government which, given the assumptions, is able to measure this accurately. Thus he cannot get a cheaper price. Adverse selection is ruled out—by assumption practically.

This system of personalized prices is clearly a desirable improvement. In fact $E + B \geqslant C + t$ is the first best standard for allocating the input and *cppd* thus has all round advantages. Obviously with a large population it would be administratively impossible to institute *cppd* as the only pricing mechanism. It is more likely that once say a policy of pure price subsidy or a two tier pricing system is adopted *cppd* can probably be used in the neighbourhood of such prices.

It is useful to compare *cppd* with classical personalized pricing. This is the case of third degree price discrimination. Here agents are also screened according to their B's. In this case one can add to E to the menu but in classical price discrimination there are no information or screening costs so that t is not recognised. If $t > 0$ then *cppd* clearly outperforms classical price discrimination.[3]

Conditional Perfect Internalization (*cpi*)

This is another useful policy measure to appened to some other more gener al policy. This is based on a screening of people solely according to their E's.

The *cppd* with its condition that $B + E \geqslant C + t$ is a good programme but it might not be very appealing to individuals with high E's but very low B's. An example might help. Let us compare two hypothetical adult education groups. One group is a bunch of well motivated social workers with low salaries. The other is sponsored by a large business house which gets tax write-offs for the amount it spends on this group. Both groups have high E's but the second group has large B's as well. The problem before the government is how to supply additional educational material to these two groups. Here we may want to screen people only by their E's.

The government, then, announces an E verification test for people with E's equal to some prespecified value. The cost of verifying E is less than t, the cost of verifying both B and E. We call this cost e. People with this

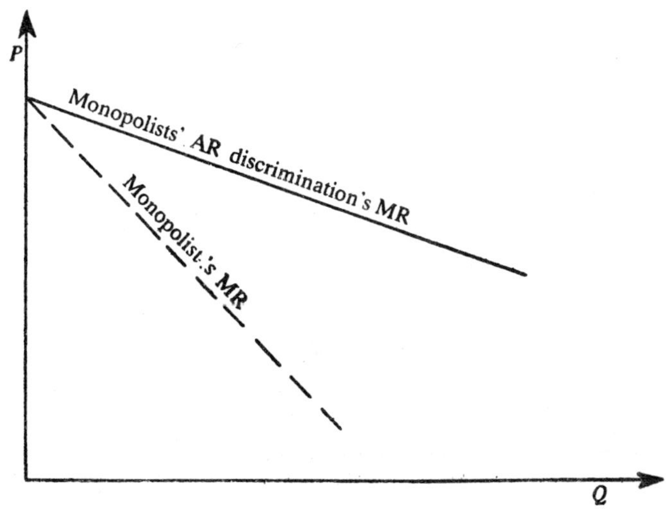

[3]The standard example of third degree price discrimination is a doctor (the only doctor) in a village. His patients don't know that all of them have the same problem but the doctor does. He misleads everyone charges everyone a different price and extracts the full consumers surplus. Thus what would have been a monopolist demand or average revenue schedule becomes his marginal revenue schedule.

particular value of E are then offered a special price $p(E)$. Social welfare from this group is

$$W(t) = \int_{p(E)}^{\infty} (B + E - C - e)h(B, E)\, dB.$$

Maximization with respect to $p(E)$ yields

$$p^*(E) = \begin{cases} (C + e) - E & \text{if } E < C + e \\ 0 & \text{if } E \geqslant C + e. \end{cases}$$

People with this E will now participate in the programme if their B is larger than $p^*(E)$. Thus the surplus to an individual will be

$$0 \leqslant B - p^*(E) = \begin{cases} B + E - (C + e) & \text{if } E < C + e \\ B & \text{if } E \geqslant C + e. \end{cases}$$

Once again it should be clear that there cannot be any problem of adverse selection here. Since the E of an individual can be measured accurately adverse selection is ruled out—almost, once again, by assumption.

This process yields a perfect allocation relative to the information cost e. If $E \geqslant C + e$ then the agents are all desirable and it is only appropriate that they face a zero price. For those with $B \geqslant C + e - E$, the imposition of price $p^*(E)$ means that $B + E \geqslant C + e$ and this is only appropriate.

One can visualize the consequences of *cpi* more completely with the help of a simple diagram.

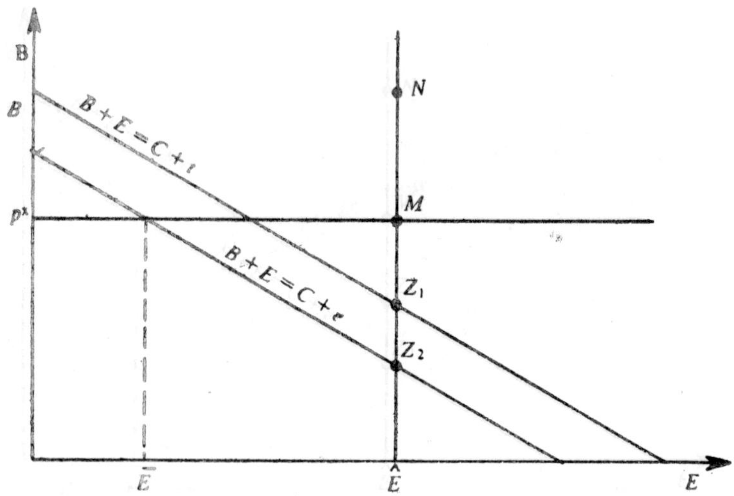

Fig. A.6.4

In Fig. A.6.4, we are screening (under *cpi*) on the externality level $\hat{E}$. The line $B + E = C + t$ is drawn parallel to and above the line $B + E = C + e$ since screening costs under *cppd* are larger than those under *cpi*.

p^* is the optimal price under the pure price subsidy scheme (drawn for purposes of reference).

People having E levels equal to $\hat{E}$ have B levels ranging from O to N. People who lie on the segment MZ_1 will switch from *cppd* to *cpi* (since they will now have to pay a lower price) and save society $t - e$ in screening cost (per person). People who lie on the segment Z_1Z_2 were excluded from *cppd* (because their $B + E < C + t$) but can now participate in the programme and thus generate positive external effects. People on the segment $Z_2\hat{E}$ are excluded even from *cpi*. These are the plus points of *cpi*. However, with *cpi* people on the segment MN (who would willingly have paid p^*) get a lower price. Remember that in *cpi* everybody with the same E pays the same price—irrespective of their B's. The net usefulness of the *cpi* then depends on which effects are stronger, that is on the distribution of agents along $\hat{E}N$.

Moreover, for *cpi* to be useful E levels have to be quite high. It would be wasteful, for instance, to try *cpi* at (or in the neighbourhood of) $\bar{E}$.

These are the broad policy options studied by Ordover and Willig. Their contribution also has some useful discussion about information structure. Their work is useful in that it forces a cogent discussion of neglected and important issues. The main drawback of the analysis seems to be the wishing away almost of questions of strategic behaviour. However, it is a good beginning.

7. Local Public Goods

The public goods that we have been discussing so far are pure public goods. Pure public goods satisfy two important criteria: (*i*) there is no congestion or crowding out in the sense that no matter what the population a public good caters to, everybody enjoys all of it. If, on the other hand, we think of a neighbourhood park as a public good one *c* can't realistically, make the same kind of assumption, (*ii*) the population that the public good is catering to is not variable. These two criteria place "pure" public goods in a very different class from local public goods.

Local public goods, loosely speaking, are meant for collective consumption but they don't satisfy the two criteria mentioned above. A local beach gets crowded and the population enjoying it is variable. Grassland for grazing becomes crowded and messy if too many cows are let loose on it. If a community is protected in the sense that "outsiders" are not allowed to live there it might decide to increase educational and recreational facilities for children. With too many children around these facilities would get "crowded."

These are all examples of local public goods. The last example is particularly important in western societies where stringent zoning laws define the minimum sized house that someone can build in a locality. These laws fall mostly in the jurisdiction of local government. The more affluent sections of society often use zoning laws to make sure that only 'their' kind of people live in their localities. The ghettoes don't have such zoning restrictions. In our country as well such problems arise. Witness for instance the displacement of jhuggi dwellers in large urban centres like Bombay and Delhi.

Local public goods have the characteristics of public goods but have some additional complications as well. The policy questions of importance here are twofold: (*i*) how to we decide on the optimal provision of local public goods, and a prior question, (*ii*) how do we decide on the optimal degree of decentralization (among levels of government) in the provision of public goods. Should all decisions on public goods be made by a national government? If not what is the appropriate delegation of authority? What are the types of public goods over which state governments or local governments (city corporations etc.) have jurisdiction? How are conflicts between levels of government to be resolved? The theory of local public goods, which started taking serious shape in the early 1950's, is addressed to such questions. We will attempt a survey of the state of art here.

BUCHANAN'S THEORY OF CLUBS

What considerations are relevant in determining the degree of decentralization in the structure of government? An economist, of course, would recommend the cheapest and most efficient manner. By cheapest one understands least costly and most efficient means confirming to (or responsive to) individuals' preferences. We can study the forces determining the degree of centralization with a simple example.

A person's utility depends on two things—a private good Y and a crowdable public good x. His own consumption of the public good is x^* where $x^* = (1/\alpha(N))^x$. N is the size of the society α is an increasing function of N. So that as the population enjoying the public good gets larger the person's effective claim over x diminishes. The individual's utility function is written as

$$u(y, x^*) \qquad \text{where} \quad y = Y - T(x).$$

$T(\ )$ is a tax function that specifies tax liability as a function of the amount of the public good. To keep things simple let us suppose that an equal sharing arrangement is in effect that is

$$t = \frac{px}{N} = \frac{\alpha(N)px^*}{N}.$$

N is the size of the population and p is the (constant) marginal cost of supplying x. Using $t = \dfrac{\alpha px^*}{N}$ we maximize u with respect to x^* to get

$$u_x^*/uy = \frac{\alpha(N)p}{N} \quad \text{as the consumer's}$$

first order condition for utility maximization. This is known in the literature as the adapted Samuelson condition (for Pareto optimal supply of the "crowdable" public good).

Denote the tax price, $\alpha(N)p/N$, by p^* and differentiate p^* with respect to N to get

$$\frac{dp^*}{dN} = \frac{p}{N}\frac{\partial\alpha}{\partial N} - \frac{\alpha p}{N^2}.$$

The community wants to do two things. It, first, wants to supply a Pareto optimal amount of the public good. Thus it achieves because each consumer satisfies the amended Samuelson conditions. Secondly, and given that the Pareto optimum quantity of the public good has been supplied, the community wants to minimize the tax ability of its members. We achieve this by setting $dp^*/dN = 0$, *i.e.*

$$\frac{p}{N}\frac{\partial\alpha}{\partial N} - \frac{\alpha p}{N^2} = 0.$$

Rewrite this as

$$\frac{\alpha}{N}\frac{p}{N}\frac{N}{\alpha}\frac{\partial\alpha}{\partial N} - \frac{\alpha p}{N^2} = 0$$

or $$\frac{\alpha p}{N^2}(r - 1) = 0$$

where $r = \dfrac{N}{\alpha}\dfrac{\partial \alpha}{\partial N}$ is the elasticity of α with respect to N.

Since $\alpha p/N^2 \neq 0$ society achieves maximum tax liability if it choose a population of size N such that $r = 1$.

This is Buchanan's fundamental result. We could state it somewhat differently. There is some fixed factor say land. People have to share this. It is, therefore, not possible to meet the amended Samuelson condition and define an optimal community size of 1. The community has to be larger than one. Every new entrant into the community automatically satisfies the amended Samuelson condition. He reduces the tax burden of everybody in the community which is a plus point. The negative point, of course, is that he also adds to congestion. Buchanan defines the optimum size of the community (he calls it club) by allowing community size to grow until the marginal decrease in tax liability is just balanced by the marginal increase to congestion. This occurs when $r = 1$ that is the elasticity of α with respect to N equals unity.[1]

One should note a few facts about this result.

1. Since individuals are identical in this conceptualization and lump sum taxes are being used it follows that there are no distortions and everybody shares the cost of the public good equally. If people are non-identical and/or taxes are distortionary (we have an income tax, say) then optimum club size need not be defined by this relation.

2. Since N is a determinant of tax obligation the same public service can be priced differently in different communities. Tax obligations are minimized when p^* takes its optimal value. If a public good that is optimally supplied for N individuals is suddenly supplied centrally tax obligations will rise and hence x^* will be lower unless price elasticity of demand is zero. If this is the case then everybody consumes the same x^* but aggregate expenditure is higher than J times (where J is the number of jurisdictions) the expenditure in a single jurisdiction.

3. Implicit in our discussion so far is the assumption that the benefits of the public good are confined to the members of the club. But no club is necessarily an island and there might be external effects from one club to another.

The analysis so far has concerned itself with a club that is a mutual benefit club. As an illustration let us take the case where the club is profit maximizing. This analysis draws on the work of Hillman. Suppose that a public good x is provided to a club membership N from a club facility of capacity

[1]With no crowding that is when α is identically equals to 1 it follows from an examination of the expression for dP/dN that pure public goods should only be supplied centrally.

$\bar{X}$. Thus we define $x = x(\bar{X}, N)$. Let us suppose that facilities are provided at a fee of π per unit of time.

We posit
$$\frac{\partial x}{\partial N} < 0, \qquad \frac{\partial x}{\partial \bar{X}} > 0$$
$$N \geqslant 1, \qquad x, \bar{X} \geqslant 0.$$

We further assume the $x(\ )$ function to be strictly convex so that we can invert and write

$$\bar{X} = \bar{X}(N\ x),$$

and
$$\frac{\partial \bar{X}}{\partial N} > 0, \qquad \frac{\partial^2 \bar{X}}{\partial N^2} > 0.$$

Further posit a demand function for this good of the form

$$x = D(p) \qquad \text{where } p \text{ is a price}$$

The revenue for the club is

$$R(x, N) = Npx = N \cdot D^{-1}(x) \cdot x$$

and cost is

$$C(x, N, \pi) = \pi \bar{X} = \pi \bar{X}(x, N).$$

Profit is, therefore,

$$\begin{aligned}\phi(x, N, \pi) &= R(\ ) - C(\ ) \\ &= N \cdot D^{-1}(x) \cdot x - \pi \bar{X}(x, N).\end{aligned}$$

Maximizing profits we get

$$\begin{aligned}\frac{\partial \phi}{\partial x} &= NP + x\frac{N\partial P}{\partial x} - \frac{\pi \partial \bar{X}}{\partial x} = 0 \\ &= NP\left(1 + \frac{1}{\beta}\right) - \frac{\bar{X}\pi}{x} \frac{\partial \bar{X}}{\partial x} \cdot \frac{x}{\bar{X}} = 0 \\ &= NP\left(1 + \frac{1}{\beta}\right) - a_c \xi = 0.\end{aligned}$$

where β is elasticity of demand $a_c = \bar{X}\pi/x$ is average cost whereas ξ is the elasticity of $\bar{X}$ with respect to x.

The second first order condition for profit maximization yields

$$\frac{\partial \phi}{\partial N} = Px - \pi \frac{\partial \bar{X}}{\partial N} = 0.$$

The first order condition simply says that $NMR = MC$*.

*Remember that for a profit maximizing monopolist $MR = P\left(1 + \frac{1}{\beta}\right)$ where β is the elasticity of demand.

Rewrite the second first order condition in the following manner

$$NPx - \pi\frac{N}{\bar{X}}\frac{\partial \bar{X}}{\partial N}\bar{X} = 0$$

Now this can be rephrased as

$$R(\ \ ) - \pi\bar{X}\eta(\ \ ) = 0$$

where η is the elasticity of $\bar{X}$ with respect to N.

In profit maximizing equilibrium

$$\eta = \frac{R}{C} \gtreqless 1 \text{ as } \phi \gtreqless 0$$

is the ratio of revenue to costs and as per the standard monopoly kind of interpretation this elasticity is greater than equal to or less than one as profits are positive, zero or negative. This relates the club's choice of N to this elasticity. Realize immediately that if $\gamma = \phi/C$ is the average rate of profit then $\gamma = \eta - 1$. This defines N size.

Hillman also shows that it is not easy to establish a clear cut one to one relationship between the monopolist club's N and the N of the former type of club.

Tiebout Hypothesis

The theory of clubs has implicitly assumed that individuals are identical in every respect. It then proceeds to solve for the optimal size of a club when this choice is constrained only by the beneficial aspects of the public good in question and by the possibility of congestion. However an important reason why people live in different towns or neighbourhoods is because they have different tastes. Thus we find middle income people averse to living in poor neighbourhoods. In the West where zoning laws are very rigid and elaborate one will handly find any poor black families in the affluent suburbs of Chicago or New York. Hence while there is some point to a line of reasoning that says that an individual has the choice of area he wants to live in and the decisions of such individuals defines a club or a neighbourhood this idea does not exhaust all possibilities. Whereas Buchanan in 1965 emphasized the discretionary powers of groups Tiebout had, nine years earlier, emphasized the role of the individual in defining a neighbourhood. His intriguing results popularly known as the Tiebout hypothesis is a central result in the theory of local public goods.

Tiebout starts by noting that most public goods are local (and not national) in character. Most of these local public goods (sanitation, police etc.) are provided by local governments. Let us suppose that these local governments are small in size but large in number. Moreover, any individual who is contemplating settling down, knows (costlessly) the public goods package offered by each government as well as the tax liabilities associated with this public goods package.

Individuals are mobile and there are zero transportation and relocation costs. Hence just as in a large vegetable market I can move from shop to shop to buy the basket of vegetables I need I can also move with my feet and settle down in a place where the public goods/tax packet most suits my preferences. There are no external effects between jurisdictions. There are fixed factors or production (say land) and each jurisdiction has a U-shaped cost curve. Zoning laws prevent population from exceeding that given by the minimum point on the average cost schedule. Tiebout does not consider employment difficulties. His world is populated by rentiers alone. Now the greater the number of jurisdictions and the greater the variance among their characteristics the greater is the chance that any individual will be able to settle down in the jurisdiction of his choice. Thus the rich can live with the rich, people who like pets live with people who like pets and so on. In Tiebout's scheme of things a community gets defined by its members and not (loosely speaking) the other way around. As in private markets the mobile individual is a price taker and a quantity adjuster. It is also implicit that taxes are lump sum (or non-distortionary) otherwise we should have to worry a fresh about the welfare properties of the Tiebout equilibrium.

The Tiebout model is very important because of the intriguing nature of the solution offered. Samuelson thought that people like variety and are willing to incur some welfare costs to live in heterogeneous communities.

Mueller raised a more practical issue. Tiebout claims that the larger the number of communities and the greater the variance of the attributes of communities the greater is the chance that individuals will be satisfied. Mueller argues that the number of clubs or communities would have to be very large if all preferences have to be satisfied. He considers the case where a town has an open space which can be filled with tulip plants and trees. Some people may not want tulips at all, some may want 100% tulips and so on. Once we add trees the problem becomes much more complicated. Mueller shows, for this example, that 101^2 clubs would be required. Theoretically, this would be okay except for the fact that in the case of say, produced public goods such heterogeneity may not be able to sustain production at minimum cost. In other words if the cost conditions for the public good are summarized by a U shaped average cost schedule it is implied that a certain minimum rate of production must take place in order to ensure that production is carried out most cheaply. If, on the other hand, the requirements of the Tiebout process are such that very few people belong to this community then it follows that there is a very good chance that these people will not be able to exercise enough demand to make production at minimum cost a meaningful operation.

Oates has launched another fundamental attack on the Tiebout process. Individuals, he argues, are members of two communities at the same time. One is the local community and the other is the larger national community. The national government is, clearly, the legislatively superior one and has the authority to create and curtail powers of local governments. Suppose the national government functions according to a simple majority rule. Then the majortiy may find it necessary, in order to maximize its benefits, to curtail the public goods activities of local government. A major national highway may go through land earmarked for a park for children living in a particular community. Hence there is no good reason to suppose that, automatically, homogeneous communities will emerge. The national government working in the interest of the majority may find it necessary to curtail the powers of local government to set upper and lower limits for taxes, for instance.

Another serious attack on the Tiebout process comes from a number of sources: Buchanan and Wagner (1970), Buchanan and Goetz (1972), Flatters, Henderson and Mieszkowski (1974), Boadway (1979), Atkinson and Stiglitz (1980). These contributions argue that free movement between Communities may not be Pareto optimal. The argument is put in the following manner. There are two communities, A and B both producing a local public good. Region A is larger in area than B—otherwise the two regions are identical. Initially the population is the same in both regions. Migration is costless. Since labour has more land to work with in region A its marginal product (and under competitive conditions, its remuneration) is higher in A than B. This induces a migration from B to A. This migration will go on till factor rewards per head are equalized. However, because of larger population size, total income is higher in A.

Now realize that total tax collection is also higher in A. Moreover, recall that with local public goods tax liability of an individual varies inversely with population size. For both these reasons tax liability (for the same public good) is lower for a representative family in region A than in region B. So people in region A have larger consumer's surpluses than the people in region B. This will then induce a second round of migration which is Pareto non-optimal.

This is a powerful criticism of the Tiebout process. However, under one condition this criticism losses much, if not all, its force. Suppose as is the case above, that A involves distinctly lower tax liabilities. Then in the long run, if land and property constitute the tax base and capital is mobile, this fact would be reflected in land prices. Because land in A is associated with lower tax liabilities its price will be bid up relative to land price in region B and the consumers' surplus gain associated with lower tax liability will be capitalized. Any individual would then, in the long run, attempt to optimize the joint price of land and public goods. Once this joint price is equalized across regions A and B the Pareto non-optimal migration will automatically stop.

Despite all this the important criticisms against the Tiebout hypothesis remain. Some have tried to gather empirical evidence in support of the Tiebout hypothesis. These attempts have, at best, been only partially successful. This although no one is suggesting that people are not sensitive to fiscal variables the Tiebout process does seem to be a rather extreme proposition.

An important deficiency of the Tiebout equilibrium is that it cannot ex-

explain the presence of communities with heterogeneous individuals. People with different tastes, backgrounds, skills and vocations often live in the same community. One has to, therefore, discuss a theory of heterogeneous communities. In a pioneering contribution Berglas (1976) has made such an effort.

In Berglas' model people have different tastes (as in Tiebout) as well as different skills. We can illustrate Berglas' method with his example. In a society we have two types of individuals type a and b. Each group is homogeneous within itself with respect to both tastes and skills. There are N individuals of type a and M individuals of type b. There is a public good x and a private good y and individuals have utility functions of the form

$$u^a = u^a(y^a, x)$$

and

$$u^b = u^b(y^b, x)$$

y^a and y^b are the private good consumption of individuals of types a and b, $y = y^a + y^b$ and production conditions for y are defined by

$$y = y(n, m)$$

where n and m are the numbers of type a and b individuals working to produce y. We assume

$$y_1, y_2 > 0, \qquad y_{11}, y_{22} < 0$$
$$y(n, O) = y(O, m) = 0.$$

Hence marginal products are positive and diminishing and each type of labour is essential for the production of y.

In the production of the public good the private good and labour are inputs. Here, however, it does not matter whether labour is of type a or b or both. The production function is

$$x = x(y^x, n + m)$$

where y^x is the amount of y used in the production of x. Here production of x by labour is to be understood in the sense of crowding, that is the larger the population the less, *ceteris paribus*, is the amount of the public good. Thus $x_2 < 0$. However $x_1 > 0$. For a given level of production of x an increase in population requires more of y to maintain the level of x that is

$$\left.\frac{\partial y^x}{\partial(n + m)}\right|_{x \text{ constant}} > 0.$$

Apart from the congestion argument advanced above one can interpret the production relation as saying that as the population increases the costs of servicing it increase as would reasonably be the case with, say, police protection and fire services.

Let us first look at the Pareto optimum for this economy. We maximize a's utility subject to b's utility being maintained at a certain level and the production relations for goods x and y. Setting up the Lagrangean we get

$$L = u^a(y^a, x) + \lambda_1(\bar{u}^b - u^b(y^b, x))$$
$$+ \lambda_2[y^x + my^b + ny^a - x(n, m)] + \lambda_3[x(y^x, n + m) - x].$$

The first order conditions are

$$n\frac{u_2^a}{u_1^a} + m\frac{u_2^b}{u_1^b} = \frac{1}{x_1}$$

$$y_1 - y^a = -x_2/x_1$$

$$y_2 - y^b = -x_2/x_1.$$

The first order condition reiterates the Samuelsonian condition for Pareto optimality that is the sum of the marginal rates of substitution equals the marginal rate of transformation. In interpreting the other first order conditions one can define $-x_2/x_1$ as the marginal social cost per individual whereas $y_1 - y^a$ (marginal product minus personal consumption) is the net contribution of an individual of type *a*. At the margin, then, the marginal net contribution of an individual of type *a* is equated with the marginal social cost. This is the second equation. The third equation does the same thing for individuals of type *b*.

The Pareto optimum defined here is relative to $\bar{u}^b$. As we parametrically increase u^b, u^a will fall. As a consequence the mix of the community, its size, and consumption by the two groups will change. The direction of change will depend on the relative preferences for the public good by the two types of individuals. But that we need heterogeneous communities is clear from the very specification of the production relations.

Suppose there exists a u^{b*} for which the optimal population mix is n^* and m^* such that $n^*/m^* = N/M$. Then a Pareto optimal solution for the population is a whole is to divide the total population into N/n^* identical communities composed of n^*, m^* people of the two types with identical production and consumption.

Let us suppose that with such a population one community starts taxing people of type a more heavily. Then $u^a < u^{a*}$ and $u^b > u^{b*}$. Thus there will be migration. But since both types of labour are needed for production this community must either return to the optimal tax rule or be empty.

Hence no matter how people shop for communities, heterogeneity is inevitable. In this stipulation there are two opposing forces. The crowding of public goods might make for homogeneity whereas the fact that both types of labour are required for the production of the private good, means that heterogeneity is a must. This line of reasoning appeals to common sense. No matter how rich a community (so that its members don't like poor children playing in their parks) the poor are still needed for so many chores and this would tend to make heterogeneity for the community desirable.

Appendix

Voting Models of Public Goods

In this appendix we concentrate on explicitly political solutions to the free rider problem. This has been a development in the literature parallel to (but independent of) the literature on incentive compatible demand revelation mechanisms. In a sense this voting literature is at least as relevant since democratic governments are, in general, coercive and may decide on public goods without showing much patience for designing elaborate tax/subsidy mechanisms.

Voting theory is sophisticated and complicated. What we present below is a summary of some of the simpler models.

The Optimal Constitution

A public good requires people to cooperate. Without mutual cooperation either formally through a representative government or otherwise the free rider problem overwhelms any allocative mechanism. Thus by cooperating with each other people make arrangements to exploit the gains from trade associated with a public good.

Buchanan and Tullock conceive of the voting process (for a public good) as a method of exploiting the gains from such trade. The natural question that rises, then, is what is the best way to exploit the gains from trade. The answer to this, of course, depends on the precise way in which the problem is posed.

Buchanan and Tullock pose the problem in the following manner. Every voting rule has associated with its two cost functions for the representative individual. The external cost associated with a voting rule is the following. If the supply of the public good is different from the Pareto optimal one the individual experiences a loss in utility or will, potentially, face a loss of utility in the future. This external cost C, rises as n (the proportion) of the population that must vote for the proposal for it to pass) falls, because if fewer people are required to agree the chance that an individual will be faced with a decision that doesn't suit him rises. Similarly one can define a decision making cost function which is the cost that society incurs for taking a decision through the political process. As the proportion of people required to vote for a proposal in order for it to pass rises these administrative and other costs also rise. Under any distributive rule, then, the cost D, to the representative individual also rises. For Buchanan and Tullock the optimum constitution (in other words the determination of the optimum proportion required to vote for a proposal in order for it to pass) is one which minimizes the sum, $C + D$, of these costs. We depict the solution diagrammatically in Fig. A.7.1.

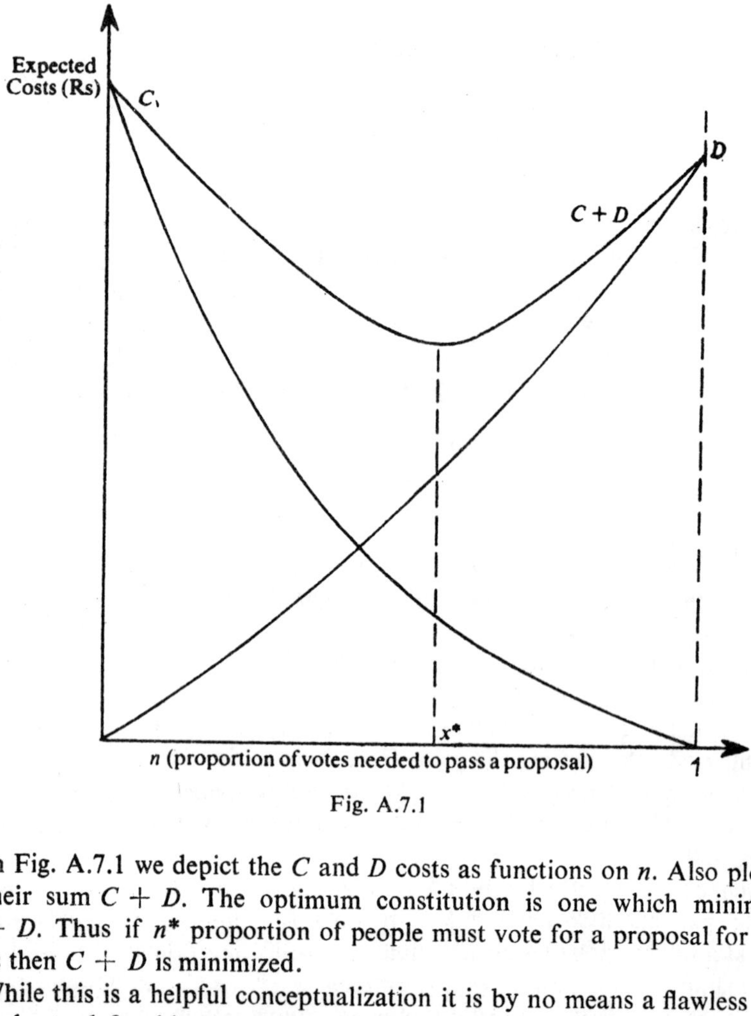

Fig. A.7.1

In Fig. A.7.1 we depict the C and D costs as functions on n. Also plotted is their sum $C + D$. The optimum constitution is one which minimizes $C + D$. Thus if n^* proportion of people must vote for a proposal for it to pass then $C + D$ is minimized.

While this is a helpful conceptualization it is by no means a flawless one. In order to define his external cost function C, an individual must know his utility in Pareto optimum. But as we know there is an infinite multiplicity of Pareto optimum allocations. Hence the definition of C becomes very ambiguous. In this situation how should the individual select the benchmark against which to measure the cost of less than unanimity rules—particularly because one of those costs is likely to result from pure redistribution? Another serious problem with this method of choosing the optimum constitution is that x^* may not be the same for everyone. If that is the case how are we to establish a uniform rule for vote counting?

While these problems are potentially very damaging to the Buchanan—Tullock mechanism there still is the consideration that it opens up the question of the best method of counting votes to economic analysis.

The Bowen-Black Majority Voting Model

This method tries to show that if tax shares are given, the output of public goods which would be preferred by a majority would be uniquely determined and, under certain conditions, would even be optimal. We can show this in a simple model. Let us think of a partial equilibrium framework for the public good. This good is produced at constant marginal cost. We also specify that each individual bears MC/N of the cost (that is there is equal sharing among the N members of society). Samuelsonian conditions for Pareto optimality are

$$\sum_{i=1}^{N} MRS_i = MC$$

or

$$\frac{\sum_{i=1}^{N} MRS_i}{N} = \frac{MC}{N}$$

that is if the marginal benefit to the mean individual equals his share of the marginal cost.

Under the payment agreement visualized here suppose we select the quantity of the public good which satisfies

$$\frac{\Sigma MRS_i}{N} = \frac{MC}{N}.$$

We know that such a supply is Pareto optimal. The question Bowen and Black pose is the following. Under what conditions does a recommendation that we supply the above mentioned quantity of public goods pass under majority voting. We depict this problem in Fig. A.7.2.

In Fig. A.7.2 we have drawn the constant marginal cost schedule MC/N. We have also depicted the distribution of demands (MRS_i schedules) through six schedules a, b, c, e, f and g. The mean individuals' demand ($\Sigma MRS_i/N$) is also shown in the Fig. A.7.2. Thus x^* is the optimal supply of the public good. Persons with demand schedules e, f and g want more than x^* while the rest want less. Now suppose that demand is normally distributed around x^* (as mean). If x^* were put to vote and a majority was needed to turn it down, x^* would not lose. The essential reason why x^* would not lose is because x^* also happens to be median demand. If that were not so then only the mediam demand would win. However, with such a supply, the Pareto optimum conditions would not be satisfied. Thus the Pareto optimality of the allocation rests critically on the assumption that demand is distributed normally around mean demand.

Black showed that if individuals had single peaked preferences the median would always win under majority voting. Single peaked preferences are depicted in Fig. A.7.3.

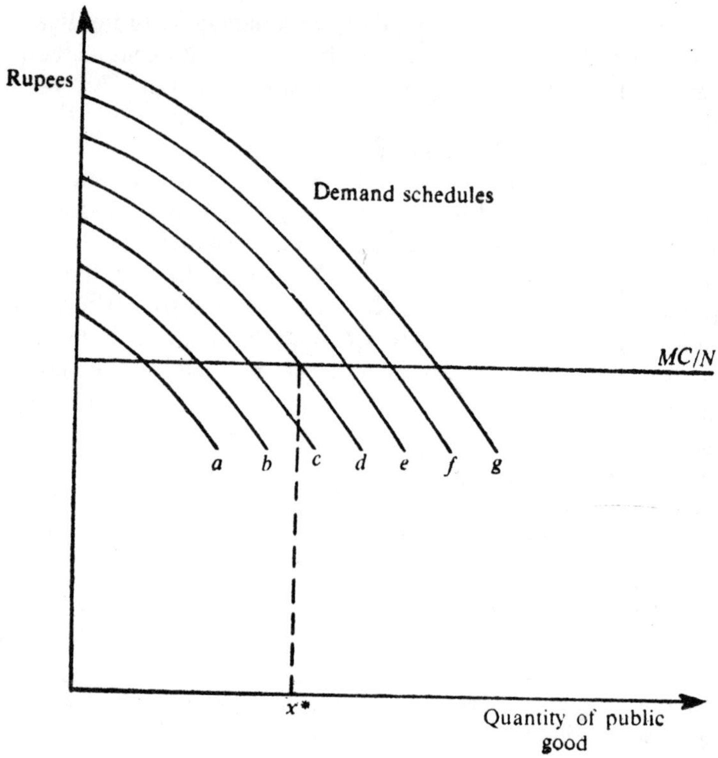

Fig. A.7.2

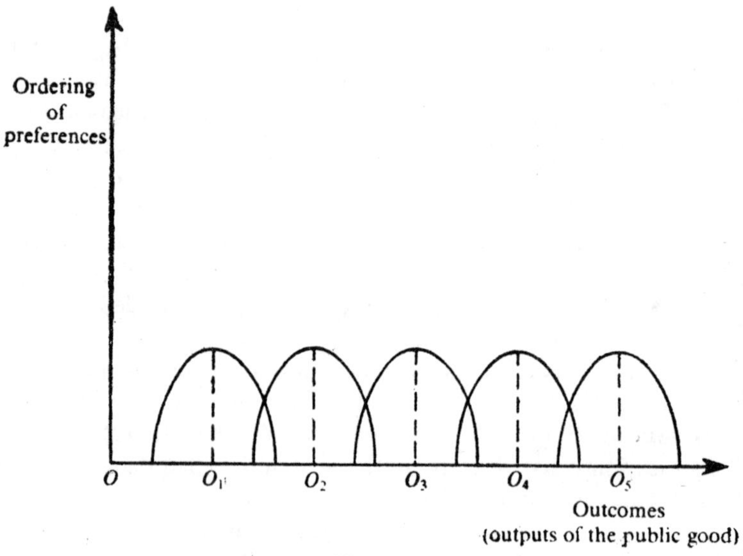

Fig. A.7.3

Preferences of five persons over various outcomes (outputs of the public good) are shown in Fig. A.7.3. Each individuals' preferences peak out at only one output of the public good (i.e. for individual 1, O_1 is the most preferred output, for individual 5, O_5 is the most preferred output). Such preferences are single peaked. Four individuals would want more than O_1 units of the public good. Similarly four people would want less than O_5 units of the public good. The only output level which would win under majority voting is O_3.

The absence of single peaked preferences may give rise to a well known problem in voting theory. This problem is that of cyclical majorities or the intransitivity of social preferences under majority voting. Consider a three individual society with three choices put to vote. Social decisions are made through majority voting rule. The preferences of the three individuals (1, 2, 3) over the three outcomes (x, y, z) are as follows:

$$xP_1yP_1z$$

$$yP_2zP_2x$$

$$zP_3xP_3y.$$

Now two individuals prefer x to y hence xPy. Similarly two individuals prefer y to z hence yPz. We would then, under a transitive social decision rule expect xPz. But two individuals prefer z to x hence zPx.

This problem of intransitive social preferences under majority voting is a small facet of a deep problem arising when we try to define social preferences by aggregating individual preferences. This problem was first studied by Arrow and its many manifestations form the core of what is called social choice theory. We will study some aspects of this theory in the next chapter.

The Phenomenon of Log Rolling

An important contribution of Buchanan and Tullock explores two aspects of the political decision process which are particularly important in the majority voting rule. One is the fact that irrespective of how much anyone pays for the public good he has only one vote which is exactly alike every other vote. The second is that issues are not decided independently. Thus if an individual doesn't particularly care for an issue he might be persuaded to vote for it by some other individual in exchange for a promise that the latter individual will support, at some time in the future, a proposal that the former individual does care about. Thus vote trading or logrolling is a viable option.

We highlight the phenomenon of logrolling through a few examples.

As a first step suppose that each individual has the same intensity of preferences (expressed in terms of the amount he is willing to pay) for the option which has been put to vote. In this case the results are bound to be Pareto optimal. In terms of the example used by Buchanan and Tullock, suppose that Re1 has to be spent on road improvement and three people are going to use the roads. Suppose each individual gets Re1 benefit from improvement in the roads. The most likely outcome is that two people will vote to pay fifty paisa each for improving their roads while the dissenter pays nothing and doesn't get his road repaired. Benefits are equal to Re1 and the resulting allocation is Pareto optimal.

But if the individuals have different preferences then the automatic attainment of Pareto optimality is no longer guaranteed. As an example let us suppose that individual 1 stands to gain rupees ten individual 2 rupees five and individual 3 rupee one from repairs to their respective roads. The possible allocations representing payoffs to the individuals are (5, $2\frac{1}{2}$, 0), (0, $2\frac{1}{2}$, 1), (5, 0, 1) representing three alternative situations in which winning coalitions can be formed. But none of these situations is Pareto optimal since the maximum possible gain to individual 1 is rupees ten.

But now suppose that vote trading is possible that is, it is possible to bribe to get the outcome you want. Then likely outcomes are

$$(5, 5, 0), \quad (5, 0, 5), \quad (0, 5, 5).$$

In the first case individual 1 has bribed individual 2. All these allocations are Pareto optimal.

Buchanan and Tullock argue that logrolling is efficient to the extent that it makes arrangements like the ones above possible. Full vote trading is not possible. As a formal practice vote trading is probably illegal in most democracies. But partial vote trading that is logrolling is often practiced. What are the implications of logrolling?

Clearly logrolling moves us in the direction of Pareto optimality. To that extent it is desirable. However, some people have argued that logrolling involves wastage. It is best to study this in the context of a simple, example. Suppose there are 200 farmers each of whom wants a road to be built to his farm. To achieve this, however, he has to be in a majority which means having to support 100 other farmers who also want roads built. Each farmer is doing this. Ultimately each farmer will have secured agreement to have his road built. But in determining the costs to the 101 who get the roads are considered. The costs to the 99 who do not get the roads are not considered. Each farmer wants 100 more votes hence logrolling arrangements are likely to lead to overspending and hence waste.

Downs, however, has argued that public expenditure is notoriously hard to value. Infact the benefits are grossly undervalued whereas the costs (i.e. taxes) are easy to see. Thus the fact that logrolling may involve waste shouln't worry us much.

This process of logrolling involves redistribution among people and the fact that this occurs through the political process means that this redistribution is occurring through the state. Is this desirable? Or rather is it something that individuals would willingly submit to. Remember that people may be losers. Buchanan and Tullock give the following answer to this question. At the time of entering into an agreement about voting rules people do not know their future income with certainty. There may be periods when income is abnormally high or low. If individuals have diminishing marginal utility the losses of one year cannot be compensated by the gains in another year. Hence people would like to carry out an insurance policy. Private insurers would not be able to provide such insurance partly because of imperfections in the capital market (people are not able to borrow against their human capital) and partly because of moral hazard in the insurance market. Hence individuals might find it better to hand over insurance responsibilities to the state. Thus individuals might willingly entrust redistributive responsibilities through the voting mechanism to the state.

One last problem remains. How are we sure that a majority would not systematically use the voting mechanism to redistribute income from a minority to itself. The catch in this line of reasoning is that this kind of arrangement cannot be sustained over the long run. This is because coalitions change over time and some of those who are in the majority today may find themselves in the minority tomorrow. Hence over the long run this policy cannot be sustained. It is common in modern societies to entrust systematic redistributive mechanisms to impersonal policies e.g. progressive income taxation.

The Downs Model

In the Buchanan and Tullocks model the problem is characterized as one of designing appropriate voting mechanisms to internalize the gains from trade. Downs proceeds along different lines. He takes as given the political system with two or more political parties that compete with each other (periodically) for power. This system, therefore, rules out logrolling explicitly but there is an explicit form of vote trading. Each party comes with a set of proposals on fiscal measures as well as other things.

In the simplest form of the Downs story there are two political parties. Voters attempt to maximize their expected utility so that voters at election time vote for the party which, given its policy announcements, will give them the highest value for a their expected utility. If there is a multiplicity of political parties people may have subpreferences among parties and people may not vote for the party they like most simply because "it has no chance of winning." In this kind of system how are we sure that the same political party will not always receive the majority voters. Downs advances the following reasons.

Matching of Policies

Suppose individuals have single peaked preferences and also that the distribution of voters according to their most preferred political party or policy is unimodal. It is then clear that the ruling party has tended to cater to the median voter. It is optimal for the opposition party (in a two party system) to also be close to the median. If people at the ends of the distribution abstain from voting then there might be greater difference between the two parties. If the distribution of people according to their political preferences has more than one mode then there is every incentive for other parties to come up and the system will not be stable.

Along the lines of the voting paradox discussed above we know that the outcome of the majority voting process may exhibit cyclical majority or intransitivity of social preferences. Suppose, for instance, that we are in a two party system where there are three kinds of voters 1, 2, 3 and they categorize the policies of the two parties as x, y or z. Then following the voting paradox discussed earlier it is straightforward to show intransitive social preferences. To the extent that there exists a multiplicity of parties, this problem is eliminated.

Coalition of Minorities

When issues are multidimensional there are some circumstances in which the opposition parties can defeat the party in power. This is accomplished when the opposition parties (acting jointly) take a strong stand on different issues in favour of minority groups that feel strongly about these issues. Under the following conditions this is possible. More than half the voters must be in the minority on at least one issue and they must hold stronger preferences for those views when in a minority than those for which they are with the majority. Furthermore, the party in power must reveal its position before the other parties do at least on those issues which have minorities with strong views.

But these are strong requirements. Furthermore in the real world both voters and political parties are greatly uncertain so that political parties may be reluctant to drastically change their policies from election to election. This adds to stability and puts a question mark on the success of the coalition of minorities.

Does the Downs mechanism give us a Pareto optimal supply of public goods? In a world of certainty the answer is yes because a non-Pareto optimal supply would be defeated. In the real world there is tremendous uncertainty about the future. People are thus unclear about the effects of state policies on their utilities. This would be exaggerated by the fact that private sector advertizing does tell people how private goods affect utilities. Thus, according to Downs, public goods would be under supplied. Contrast this result with that of Buchanan and Tullock where logrolling led to an over-expenditure on public goods.

8. The Problem of Social Choice

Let us go back to the theme of chapter 2. There we had conceived of the problem of the economy as being twofold. One question was deciding which (Pareto optimal) allocation we want. The second was finding out methods of reaching such an allocation. In chapter 2 and subsequent chapters we have been dealing only with the second question. It is time to consider the first.

This question turns out no less difficult (and in some ways more exacting) than the one we have been talking about. Our plan for this chapter is the following. We first discuss the democratic system's ability to solve the problem of social choice. We will realize soon that not much headway can be made here so that an imposition of a social welfare function may be necessary. We will discuss a few social welfare functions that have been discussed in the literature. In the appendix to this chapter we discuss some earlier attempts to formalize the problem of social choice.

In their classic formulations Bergson and Samuelson had given some coherence to the idea of social choice. Their approach is that of a social welfare function (SWF). Suppose we have a set of social alternatives x, y, z, w, etc. They may be different rates of unemployment and inflation and/or various distributions of income in society, and the like. This set of social alternatives may be infinite but the more important aspects may be captured in a set of variables $\alpha_1, \ldots, \alpha_n$ etc. Social welfare $W(\alpha_1, \ldots, \alpha_n)$ is a function of these variables. The domain of this SWF is the α's whereas the range of this function is the set of real numbers. In this manner we articulate the notion of social welfare.

But to fix a form of $W(\quad)$ we need to weight the α's but to weight the α's we need value judgements. We need to express clearly how society values different alternatives and this cannot be done except by explicitly introducing value judgements. Bergson and Samuelson are not keen to commit themselves to value judgements.

In one of the truly fundamental pieces of work in modern welfare economics Kenneth Arrow confronted this problem. He first did away with real valued welfare functions. We know that a ranking will suffice. Having dealt with this relatively minor problem he started out by asking himself the following question. Suppose I start by imposing value judgements on the social ranking. How for can I go without running into an absurd kind of situation The answer, unfortunately, is not very far at all. Before we detail Arrow's result we need some notation. To this we now turn.

Notations

We have the set of all conceivable alternatives S. There are N individuals in society. At any point in time a non-empty subset of S is feasible and is called the issue A. The basic value judgement that arrow makes is that social choice is based on individual preference relations.

Each individual, i, is supposed to have a binary weak preference relation R_i defined over S (or A if we so please).

Any given N tuple of individual weak preference relations $(R_1, \ldots, R_N)$ is called a situation s. We then define.

A group decision rule (GDR) is a functional relation f which for every possible situation s specifies exactly one social weak preference relation R defined over S: $R = f(s)$. We define a preference relation P as

$$xPy \text{ iff } xRy \text{ and not } yRx.$$

Moreover the indifference relation is defined as

$$xIy \text{ if } xRy \text{ and } yRx.$$

Our weightage of individual R_i's will fix the form of $f(\;)$ and hence determine R.

We will call R a *binary* GDR if when considering the preference between two alternatives x and y we don't have to appeal to other alternatives z, w etc. We now define other properties of R. R is *transitive* iff xRy and $yRz \rightarrow xRz$, for all $x, y, z \in S$.

R is *quasi-transitive* iff

$$xPy \text{ and } yPz \rightarrow xPz, \text{ for all } x, y, z \in S.$$

This does not say anything about weak preference.

P is *acyclic* over S iff there does not exist an integer m such that for some $x_1, \ldots, x_m \in S$

$$x_1Px_2 \text{ and } x_2Px_3 \text{ and } \ldots \text{ and } x_{m-1}Px_m \text{ and } x_mPx_1$$

P is *founded* over S iff there does not exist any long descending P chain of the type

$$\infty \ldots, \text{ and } x_3Px_2 \text{ and } x_2Px_1$$

where $x_1, \ldots, \infty \in S$.

We can then prove.

LEMMA 1(a). If R is transitive it is also quasi-transitive but the converse is not necessarily true.

(*b*) if R is quasi-transitive P is acyclic but the converse is not necessarily true.

(*c*) If P is founded it is also acyclic but the converse is not necessarily true.

(*d*) If S is finite then foundedness of P and acyclicity of P are identical statements.

PROOF. (*a*) Suppose R is transitive and not quasi-transitive. This means xPy and yPz and not xPz.

Now $xPy \rightarrow xRy$ and $yPz \rightarrow yRz$. By transitivity xRy and $yRz \rightarrow xRz$. But R is not quasi-transitive so that not xPz. But not xPz means not xRz. But this contradicts the transitivity of R. Hence transitivity of R implies quasi-transitivity of R.

To show that quasi-transitivity of R does not necessarily imply transitivity consider the following example

$$aIb \text{ and } xPy \text{ and } xIa \text{ and } yIa.$$

This clearly violates transitivity of R but quasi-transitivity of R is not violated since the preference relation is defined only over two elements.

(*b*) Suppose quasi-transitivity of R does not imply acyclicity of P. Then there exists an m such that

$$x_1Px_2 \text{ and } x_2Px_3 \text{ and } \dots \text{ and } x_{m-1}Px_m \text{ and } x_mPx_1.$$

If R is quasi-transitive then x_1Px_m.

Hence if x_1Px_m and x_mPx_1 then x_1Px_1 which means x_1Rx_1 and not x_1Rx_1. This, of course, is a contradiction. To show that acyclicity of P does not necessarily imply quasi-transitivity of R consider the following example xPy and yPz and xIz. P is acyclic but R is not quasi-transitive.

(*c*) To show that foundedness of P implies acyclicity of P. Deny this then there exists an m such that

$$x_1Px_2 \text{ and } \dots \text{ and } x_{m-1}Px_m \text{ and } x_mPx_1.$$

Extend this chain indefinitely. Here we immediately violate foundedness of P.

To show that acyclicity of P does not necessarily imply foundedness of P consider an infinite number of alternatives in the interval $]x, y[$

$$x \text{———————} y$$

We stipulate for all $a, b \in]x, y[$

$$aRb \text{ iff } \geqslant b.$$

Here R is an ordering but there is an infinite number of points in $]x, y[$ so P is not founded.

(*d*) We have already shown that foundedness of P means that P is acyclic. Now suppose S is finite and acyclicity of P does not imply foundedness of P. We show now that P violates acyclicity.

If P is not founded then there exists an infinite chain

$$\infty \dots \text{ and } x_3Px_2 \text{ and } x_2Px_1.$$

If $x_1 \equiv x_2$ then the result is proved.

If $x_1 \not\equiv x_2$ but $x_2 \equiv x_3$ then again there is a P cyclic.

Hence x_1, x_2, x_3 etc. must all be distinct to avoid cyclicity.

Hence the preference chain consists of distinct elements to avoid violation of acyclicity of P. But since S is finite a cycle is established.

Let f be any GDR. Let s and s' be any two situations. Let $R = f(s)$ and $R' = f(s')$. We define the following properties of R.

(*i*) *Rationality condition* [RC(1)].

R is an ordering for every possible situation i.e. R is reflexive, connected and transitive.

(*ii*) *Rationality condition* 2[RC(2)].

R is reflexive, connected and quasi-transitive.

(*iii*) *Rationality condition* 3 [RC(3)].

R is reflexive and connected and P is acyclic.

(*iv*) Binariness (B): For all $x, y \in S$ if

$$[xR_iy \text{ iff } xR'_iy) \quad \text{and} \quad (yR'_ix \text{ iff } yR'_ix)] \quad \text{for all } i \text{ then}$$

$$[(xRy \text{ iff } xR'y) \quad \text{and} \quad (yRx \text{ iff } yR'x)]$$

that is when we are comparing x and y we don't have to appeal to Z, W etc. This is sometimes known as the axiom of independence of irrelevant alternatives.

(*v*) Weak Pareto Criterion (WP): For all $x, y \in S$ if xP_iy for all i then xPy.

(*vi*) Strict Pareto Criterion (SP): For all $x, y \in S$ if xR_iy for al! i and xP_iy for some i then xPy.

(*vii*) Non-Dictatorship (ND): There does not exist any individual i such that for all $x, y \in S$ and for all situations s,

$$xP_iy \rightarrow xPy.$$

We can now state and prove Arrow's fundamental result.

Arrow's General Possibility Theorem

Let S have at least three distinct alternatives x, y, z then there does not exist a GDR satisfying B, WP, RC(1) and ND. These absolutely innocuous looking value judgements are inconsistent with each other.

The proof of this theorem needs a lemma. We need some notation for this lemma.

Let L be the set of individuals in society and let L' be a non-empty subset of it. Define two such subsets D'_L (nearly decisive set) is defined as the set such that for all $x, y \in S$ and all $L' \subseteq L$.

xD'_Ly iff $x \neq y$ and for every situation s if xP_iy for all i in L' and yP_jx for all j in L-L' then xPy. Hence if everyone in L' prefers x to y and every body else prefers y to x then the GDR is such that xPy. Near decisiveness does not work if some members of L-L' do not prefer y to x.

We also define the fully decisive set $\bar{D}_{L'}$. L' is fully decisive if for all distinct $x, y \in S$ and every situation s if xP_iy for all i in L' then xPy. We then write $x\bar{D}_{L'}y$. Hence L' is fully decisive if everyone in L' prefers x to y then, irrespective of the preferences of everyone else in society, the GDR is such that xPy. Now, our lemma.

LEMMA 2. Let S have at least three distinct alternatives and the GDR satisfy B, WP and RC(2) (these conditions are weaker than those in Arrow's

General Possibility Theorem). Let $L' \subseteq L$. Then if $xD_{L'}y$ for some $x, y \in S$ then $a\bar{D}_{L'}b$ for all a, b in S.

In other words if L' is nearly decisive over some pair of alternatives and the GDR satisfies the above conditions then that set (L') is fully decisive over every pair of alternatives.

PROOF. We are given $xD_{L'}y$. Let z be an alternative distinct from x and y. We prove the lemma in two stages.

I. We first prove it for $a, b \in \{x, y, z\}$.

II. We next generalize it for all $a, b \in S$.

I. Consider a situation s such that for all $i \in L'$,

$$xP_iyP_iz; \quad \text{for all} \quad i \in (L - L')yP_ix \quad \text{and} \quad yP_iz.$$

This does not imply, yet, anything about the relation between x and z.

Now we know xP_iy for all i in L' and yP_ix for all i in $L - L'$. Since $xD_{L'}y$ it follows that xPy. Moreover by WP we have yPz. Hence by RC(2) we must have xPz. Hence, using binaries, we have

$$xD_{L'} \rightarrow x\bar{D}_{L'}z.$$

II. Consider a situation s such that for all i in L',

$$zP_ixP_iy$$

for all i in $(L - L')\,yP_ix$ and zP_ix.

Now given $xD_{L'}y$ we have xPy.

By WP we have zPx. Hence by RC(2) we have zPy. By using binariness we have

$$xD_{L'}y \rightarrow z\bar{D}_{L'}y.$$

Now there is nothing special about x, y, z and we can interchange them. We write two purely hypothetical relations and interchange y and z in them. These relations are:

$$xD_{L'}y \rightarrow x\bar{D}_{L'}z \qquad (1)$$

$$xD_{L'}y \rightarrow z\bar{D}_{L'}y. \qquad (2)$$

Interchanging y and z in (1) and (2) we get

$$xD_{L'}z \rightarrow x\bar{D}_{L'}y \qquad (1')$$

and

$$xD_{L'}z \rightarrow y\bar{D}_{L'}z. \qquad (2')$$

Combine (1′) and (1) to get

$$xD_{L'}y \rightarrow x\bar{D}_{L'}y. \qquad (3)$$

Combine (2′) and (1) to get

$$xD_{L'}y \rightarrow y\bar{D}_{L'}z. \qquad (4)$$

In (1) we interchange x and z to get

$$zD_{L'}y \rightarrow z\bar{D}_{L'}x. \qquad (1'')$$

Combine (2) and (1″) to get

$$xD_{L'}y \rightarrow z\bar{D}_{L'}x. \qquad (5)$$

In (5) interchange y and z to get

$$xD_{L'}z \rightarrow y\bar{D}_{L'}x. \tag{5'}$$

Combine (5′) and (1) to get

$$xD_{L'}y \rightarrow x\bar{D}_{L'}z \rightarrow xD_{L'}z \rightarrow y\bar{D}_{L'}x$$

and hence

$$xD_{L'}y \rightarrow y\bar{D}_{L'}x. \tag{6}$$

All of these statements are "if then" statements. Now assert what we know to be true that is $xD_{L'}y$ from which we get

$$x\bar{D}_{L'}z$$
$$z\bar{D}_{L'}y$$
$$x\bar{D}_{L'}y$$
$$y\bar{D}_{L'}z$$
$$z\bar{D}_{L'}x$$
$$y\bar{D}_{L'}x.$$

Hence the first part of the lemma is proved. Let us have a generalization i.e. to show $a\bar{D}_{L'}b$ for all a, b in S. We have the following possibilities of choosing a and b

(1) $a \in \{x, y, z\}$
  $b \in \{x, y, z\}$. This we have already done.

(2) $a \notin \{x, y, z\}$
  $b \in \{x, y, z\}$.

(3) $a \in \{x, y, z\}$
  $b \notin \{x, y, z\}$.

Cases (2) and (3) are entirely symmetric hence we need to consider only one.

(4) $a \notin \{x, y, z\}$
  $b \notin \{x, y, z\}$.

Consider case (2). Since x, y, z are all distinct there must be two alternatives in x, y, z distinct from b. Suppose $b = x$. Hence $b\,\bar{D}_{L'}\,z$ (by first step). Consider $a = y$ that is, the triple (b, a, z). We know $bD_{L'}z \rightarrow b\bar{D}_{L'}z$ and the entire proof of the first part is entirely valid for the triple (b, a, z).

Consider case 4. We know $y\bar{D}_{L'}z$. Consider $\{a, y, z\}$. We know $a\bar{D}_{L'}y$. Consider $\{a, y, b\}$. L' is fully decisive for a against y. Hence it is nearly decisive for a against y and hence fully decisive for any alternative against any other alternative. Hence $a\bar{D}_{L'}b$. This proves the lemma.

With this lemma behind us the proof of Arrow's theorem is a relatively simple matter.

Proof of Arrow's General Possibility Theorem

The conditions of Arrow's theorem are stronger than those of the lemma we have just proved. Hence the lemma is valid.

Since WP is satisfied there exists a set which is nearly decisive for some alternative against some other alternative. In other words given WP for all x, y in S if $x \neq y$ then there exists a set of people L' such that $xD_{L'}y$. Consider distinct $x, y, z \in S$. There exists at least one L' such that $xD_{L'}y$. In general we cannot rule out the possibility of more than one such set existing. Similarly for y and z. Out of these nearly decisive sets pick up the smallest (with fewest members) nearly decisive set L'. Assume without loss of generality, that L' is nearly decisive for x against y.

Now consider an individual k who belongs to this nearly decisive set L'. Construct a situations s such that

$$xP_kyP_kz$$

$$yP_izP_ix \qquad \text{for all } i \text{ in } L - L'$$

$$zP_jxP_jy \qquad \text{for all } j \text{ in } L' - k$$

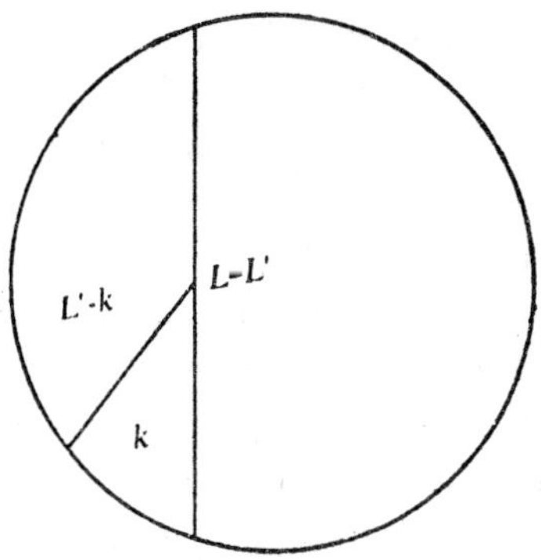

Consider the choice between x and y. We know $xD_{L'}y$. We see from the situation constructed that all members of L' prefer x to y while everybody else prefers y to x. Thus xPy by near decisiveness of the set L'.

Now consider the choice between y and z. k prefers y to z but everybody else in L' prefers z to y. L' is the smallest nearly decisive set hence we must have not zPy. By connectedness we must have yRz. Combining xPy and yRz by transitixity of R we get xPz.

Now k is the only person who prefers x to z. Everybody else (whether or not he is a member of L') prefers z to x. Hence k is nearly decisive in the choice between x and z. By the lemma just proved k is fully decisive in all choices that is,

$$xD_kz \rightarrow a\bar{D}_kb \text{ for all } a, b \in S.$$

Thus k is a dictator. Since the GDR satisfies B, WP and RC(1) it violates ND.[1]

[1]There is another condition which we have not explicitly stated. This is that R is defined for every n tuple $(R_1, \ldots, R_n)$ of individual orderings. This is the axiom of universality of Domain.

This, of course, is an eminently important as well as a profoundly disturbing result. Unfortunately, again, it is not easy to get around this difficulty in a simple way. A whole new area of welfare economics (social chice theory) has developed around Arrow's result. People have tried every conceivable method to get around Arrow's difficulty. But so long they stuck to the basic Arrowian framework they found that all they managed to do was to come up with new impossibility results.[2] Thus people relaxed *B*, then RC(1), then universality of domain and so on but the impasse remains. Just to give readers an idea of such results we present two important theorems. Gibbard's Oligarchy Theorem and Sen's Impossibility of a Paretian Liberal Theorem.

Gibbard's Oligarchy Theorem

Gibbard relaxed RC(1) to RC(2) and came us with a powerful oligarchy instead of a dictator. Before we prove his theorem we need a lemma.

LEMMA 3. Let *S* have at least three distinct alternatives and let the GDR satisfy RC(2), WP and *B*. If for some $a, b, a', b' \in S$ and for some subsets $\bar{L}$ and $\bar{L}'$ of $\bar{L}$ we have,

$$aD_{\bar{L}}b' \quad \text{and} \quad a'D_{\bar{L}'}b' \quad \text{then}$$

for all distinct $a'', b'' \in S$

$a''\bar{D}_{\bar{L}\cap\bar{L}'}b''$. Thus if one set of people is nearly decisive over two alternatives and another set is nearly decisive over two alternatives then the intersection of these two sets is fully decisive over all alternatives.

PROOF OF LEMMA. $a, b, a', b', \bar{L}, \bar{L}'$ exist.

Then by the previous lemma we must have

$$a\bar{D}_{\bar{L}}b \quad \text{and} \quad a'\bar{D}_{\bar{L}'}b'$$

for all distinct *a*, *b* in *S*. Partition the set of individuals into four subsets.

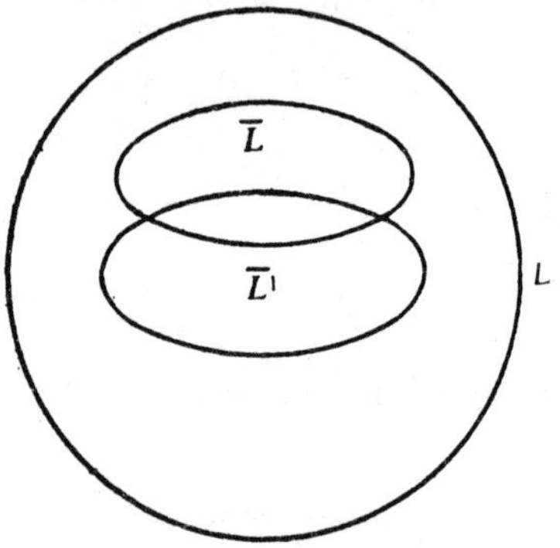

These subsets are,

$$\bar{L}\cap\bar{L}'; \qquad \bar{L}-\bar{L}'; \qquad \bar{L}'-\bar{L}; \qquad L-(\bar{L}\cup\bar{L}')$$

[2]Below we will sse how one can get around Arrow's problem by simply abandoning his framework altogether.

Consider three distinct alternatives x, y, z in S. Assign preference orderings as

$$\begin{array}{ll} xP_iyP_iz & \text{for all } i \text{ in } \bar{L}\cap\bar{L}' \\ yP_izP_ix & \text{for all } i \text{ in } \bar{L}' - \bar{L} \\ zP_ixP_iy & \text{for all } i \text{ in } \bar{L} - \bar{L}' \\ zP_iyP_ix & \text{for all } i \text{ in } \{L - (\bar{L}\cup\bar{L}')\}. \end{array}$$

Now consider the rankings of x and y.

Every person in the set $\bar{L}$ prefers x to y. Also everybody else prefers y to x. Since $\bar{L}$ is nearly decisive between x and y we have xPy.

Now consider the choice between y and z. Everybody in the set $\bar{L}'$ prefers y to z while everybody else opposes it. By near decisiveness we must have yPz.

Now combine xPy with yPz to get xPz by RC(2). But only people in the set $\bar{L}\cap\bar{L}'$ prefer x to z. Everybody else prefers z to x. Hence

$$xD_{\bar{L}\cap\bar{L}'}z\cdot$$

By the previous lemma

$$a\bar{D}_{\bar{L}\cap\bar{L}'}b \qquad \text{for all distinct } a, b \text{ in } S.$$

Statement and Proof of Gibbard's Oligarchy Theorem

Let S have at least three distinct alternatives and let the GDR satisfy RC(2). WP, and B. Then there exists a unique non-empty subset $L^* \subseteq L$ such that for all x, y in S.

(*i*) if xP_iy for all i in L^* then xPy.

(*ii*) if yP_ix for some i in L^* then yRx.

Hence there exists a strong oligarchy.

With consensus within the oligarchy society's views do not matter at all. If even one person, prefers one option to another society, irrespective of the preferences of others, considers the first option at least as good as the other.

Since the GDR satisfies WP there exists some group of individuals which is nearly decisive for some alternative x against some other alternative y. Pick out the smallest such set L^*. We now show that L^* is the group we are interested in.

Hence we have to show that

(1) For all x, y in S if xP_iy for all i in L^* then xPy. There are two cases:

(*a*) if $x = y$ then the proposition is trivially true since the antecedent is false.

(*b*) x and y are distinct. We know that $aD_{L^*}b$ implies that for

$$a', b' \in S\ a'\bar{D}_{L^*}b'.$$

(2) For all x, y in S if yP_kx for some $k \in L^*$ then yRx. If $x = y$ then this is trivially true. Take $x \neq y$ suppose yP_kx and not yRx.

We can now show a contradiction. By connectedness not $yRx \rightarrow xRy$. Putting these two together we get xPy. Now partition L into three groups:

$$L_1 = \{i \in L / xP_iy\}$$

$$L_2 = \{i \in L/xI_iy\}$$
$$L_3 = \{i \in L/yP_ix\}$$

k belongs to L_3.
Construct a situation s' such that

$$zP_i' \, xP_i' \, y \qquad \text{for all } i \text{ in } L_1.$$

$$zP_i' \, xI_i' \, y \qquad \text{for all } i \text{ in } L_2.$$

$$yP_i' \, zP_i' \, x \qquad \text{for all } i \text{ in } L_3.$$

Compare s and s'. Between x and y the individual preferences have remained unchanged. Thus by binariness social weak preference relation should have remained unchange that is, we must have $xP'y$. Now compare z and x. Everyone prefers z to x. Hence by WP zPx. By quasitransitivity $zP'y$.

Now everyone in L_1 prefers z to y. Everyone in L_2 prefers z to y whereas everyone in L_2 prefers z to y whereas everyone in L_3 prefers y to z. Hence $L_1 \cup L_2$ is nearly decisive between z and y, that is

$$zD_{L_1 \cup L_2}y.$$

L^* is also nearly decisive for some alternative against some other alternative. Hence by the lemma just proved $\{L_1 \cup L_2\} \cap L^*$ must be fully decisive for every alternative a' against every other b', that is

$$a'\bar{D}_{\{L_1 \cup L_2\} \cap L^*}b'$$

for all $a', b' \in S. \; a' \neq b'$.

This leads to a contradiction. The intersection of two sets has to be a subset. We know $k \in L^*$ and also that $k \in L_3$ that is, $k \notin L_1 \cup L_2$.

Hence $L^* \cap \{L_1 \cup L_2\}$ is a proper subset of L^*. But L^* is the smallest nearly decisive set. Hence we have the contradiction. Hence if yP_kx then we must have yRx.

To show that L^* is unique. Suppose L^* is not unique. Let $\hat{L}$ be another such set. By assumption $L^* \neq \hat{L}$. Then we must have either

(*i*) there is some j in L^* who is not a member of $\hat{L}$,

or

(*ii*) there is some j in $\hat{L}$ who is not a member of L^*.

Consider (*i*). Construct a situation s'' such that

$$xP_i''y \quad \text{for all } i \text{ in } \hat{L}$$

and $$yP_j''x \quad \text{for } j \in L^* \text{ and } j \notin \hat{L}.$$

The first relation gives us xPy whereas the second gives us yRx. This, of course, is a contradiction. The proof for case (*ii*) is entirely symmetric. Hence L^* must be unique. This completes the proof of Gibbard's theorem.

Sen's Impossibility of a Paretian Liberal

In this story we give up both binariness as well as RC(2) but we realize that the Pareto criterion conflicts with some basic principles of liberalism. In a society that claims to be liberal people are allowed certain basic freedoms. Thus if some people want to sleep with their feet to the south society should not deny them this. It is in this spirit that we define.

Minimal Federalism (MF)

There exists two non-empty disjoint subsets L_1 and L_2 such that for some pairs (a, b), (c, d) of distinct alternatives if aP_jb for all j in L_1 then aPb and if bP_ja for all j in L_1 then bPa, and if cP_kd for all k in L_2 then cPd and if dP_kc for all k in L_2 then dPc.

One cannot object to this because different groups stay in society only if they can retain a certain individuality of their own. Then the consequence is.

Sen's Theorem. There does not exist any GDR which satisfies RC(3), WP and MF. No binariness is involved here.

PROOF. Since MF is being satisfied there exists two non-empty disjoint subsets L_1 and L_2.

Now if $a = c$ and $b = d$ then each of these sets is decisive over the same pair of alternatives. Consider a situation s such that

$aPjb$ for all j in L_1. Hence aPb and bP_ka for all k in L_2. Hence bPa.

This is of course a contradiction. Thus (a, b) and (c, d) have to be distinct.

There are two possibilities now:

(*i*) a, b, c, d are all distinct.

(*ii*) $(a, b) \cap (c, d)$ is a singleton.

Consider (*i*). Partition L in into L_1, L_2, $L - (L_1 \cup L_2)$. Construct a situation s such that

$dP_jaP_jbP_jc$	for all j in L_1
$bP_kcP_kdP_ka$	for all k in L_2
dP_ia and bP_ic	for all i in $L - (L_1 \cup L_2)$.

By MF we get a Pb and cPd.

By WP we get bPc (everyone prefers b to c).

Again by WP we get dPa (everyone prefers d to a).

Thus we have aPb, bPc, cPd, and dPa. Hence RC(3) is violated and we have a P cycle.

Now consider (*ii*) that is, $(a, b) \cap (c, d)$ is a singleton. Without loss of generality assume $b = c$. Construct a situation such that

dP_jaP_jb	for all j in L_1
$bP_kd\ P_ka$	for all k in L_2
dP_ia	for all i in $L - (L_1 \cup L_2)$.

Now by MF we get aPb. Also by MF bPd. But by WP we have dPa (everyone prefers d to a). Thus we get aPb, bPd and dPa. RC(3) is violated and we get a P cycle.

Sen accepts RC(3) so we have a conflict between MF and WP. Hence the impossibility of a Paretian Liberal.

Beyond the Arrow Framework

There is no easy escape from the Arrow dilemma. Various methods have been tried but without any success. The list of impossibility theorems is very long. The interested reader is referred to Kelley (1976) for an exhaustive analysis of the results.

Just when the string of impossibility theorems made it appear that the death knell had been sounded for social choice theory a completely different line of inquiry began. Some people began wondering whether the Arrow dilemma had been made inevitable by posing the question in the manner that it had been posed. This point needs quite a lot of amplification. To this we now turn.

Welfare economics, in the classical tradition, always postulated individual utility as being cardinal and further stipulated that it was possible to compare the utilities of different people. This was done both for expounding the theory of consumer behaviour as well as for making pronouncements on social welfare. This methodology was perceived as being archaic and a monumental early attack on this line of reasoning was Hicks' (1939) masterpiece. Hicks convincingly showed that for, among other things, demand theory and welfare theory (as the classical theory was interested in) we needed neither cardinal utility nor interpersonal comparison of utility. Ordinal ranking expressed in the form of consumer indifference maps was sufficient for demand theory and Paretian welfare economics. So in the interest of scientific refinement, the "cumbersome" and value loaded notions of cardinality and interpersonal comparison of utility were abandoned. Later refinements, as we know, realised that even an ordinal utility function was too demanding. An ordering was all that was required to obtain the results.

Some, however, linked the Arrowian paradoxes to this advancement. Cardinality was not really important since cardinal utility functions do not rescue us from the dilemmas. Strasnick and Hammond in separate papers showed that if interpersonal comparison of utility was allowed then the Rawlsian maximin criterion satisfies all of Arrow's original conditions and more. Interpersonal comparison of utility is visualized in the following manner. A person, i, compares his well being in state x with that of another person j, in state y. Thus an individual's ordering is defined over the ordered pair (x, i). Hence $(x, i)R_i(y, j)$ is read person i considers himself in state x to be at least as well off as person j is in state y. The Group Decision Rule is an aggregation of such R_i. Hammond shows that the maximin criterion satisfies all of Arrow's conditions and more.[2] This is a major possibility result for a change. Strasnick achieved the same result. Ng showed that with

[2]The maximin criterion is discussed later in this chapter.

what he calls "finite sensibility" assumed for individuals the utilitarian criterion also satisfies Arrow's conditions.[3]

As such results began to trickle in the suspicion began to grow that the Arrowian framework really starves itself of information and thereby paves the way for dilemmas and pandoxes ad infinitum. Sen's 1978 contribution formally proved that these suspicions are right.

Sen's Interpretation of Information in the Arrowian Framework

Sen shows that within the Arrow framework a GDR which satisfies B, WP, RC(1) and universality of Domain is *necessarily* dictatorial. In other words the restriction on information is so severe that a GDR that satisfies the other conditions has to be dictatorial. One can prove this proposition in a fairly straightforward manner.

Recall the lemma proved just before Arrow's theorem. This lemma said that if the GDR satisfied B, WP and RC(2) any group that is nearly decisive between any two alternatives is fully decisive between any pair of alternatives. Thus, for this group, opposition is irrelevant. Along the same line we can prove a stronger lemma.

Irrelevance of Support

This lemma enables one to continuously reduce the size of the nearly decisive (or decisive) set. Suppose there are three distinct alternatives x, y, z and suppose that a set L_1 is decisive between alternatives x and y. Partition L_1 into two subsets L_1' and L_1''. Construct a situation s as

$$xP_iyP_iz \quad \text{for all } i \text{ in } L_1'$$

$$yP_izP_ix \quad \text{for all } i \text{ in } L_2'$$

$$zP_ixP_iy \quad \text{for all in } L - (L_1 \cup L_2).$$

By the previous lemma L_1 is decisive between y and z as well so yPz. Now given universality of domain and RC(1) we must have either yPx (in which case L_2' is nearly decisive between y and x and hence by the previous lemma L_2' is fully decisive between every pair of alternatives) or xRy. In this case since yPz we must have by RC(1), xPz. Now this makes L_1' nearly decisive between x and z and hence it is fully decisive, by the previous lemma, over every pair of alternatives. Thus no matter what the size of decisive set it is always possible to reduce it. The logical conclusion is the Arrowian dictator.

Hence a reconstruction of the proof of Arrow's theorem would read like the following. By WP the entire population (at least) is nearly decisive between some pair of alternatives. By the lemma on irrelevance of opposition it is also fully decisive. By the lemma on irrelevance of support it is always possible to keep cutting down the size of this set. Since the number of people is finite we have the lone dictator as the logical outcome of restricting the information set. The Arrowian dictator is, after all, inevitable.

[3]We discuss the utilitarian criterion later in this chapter.

When Sen's results are juxtaposed with those of Hammond and Strasnick one starts interpreting GDR's in a different manner. By confining ourselves to individual orderings we also neglect or discard information, say on interpersonal comparison of utility, which is really a waste. The restrictions on the GDR constructed by aggregating individual orderings makes the Arrowian dilemma a logical inevitability. The only way to escape such problems is to expand the information set.

Forms of the Social Welfare Function (SWF)

From some time *before* the advent of social choice theory economists have tried to get a straightforward and acceptable measure of social welfare. Hence while Bergson and Samuelson were hesitant to make value judgements to fix a form of their SWF, writers in this earlier tradition have never hesitated to make the requisite value judgements to justify their measure of social welfare. There are three major varieties of social welfare functions. We discuss each of these in turn.

Classical Utilitarianism

This is the oldest of the three schools and its proponents can be traced to John Stuart Mill and, indeed, before him. To utilitarians individual utility is measured in cardinal terms and society's welfare is measured as the sum of the utilities of everyone in society. Thus if $u_1, \ldots, u_n$ are individual utility functions and these individuals get consumption baskets $x_1, \ldots, x_n$ so that individual i's utility is $u_i(x_i)$, society's welfare is simply

$$\sum_{i=1}^{n} u_i(x_i).$$

Social policy should be geared to maximize this welfare. This means that optimal policy equates marginal utility across the population, that is resources are distributed in such a way that everyone's marginal utility is the same. If everyone has the same utility function then this amounts to a perfectly egalitarian distribution. But if this is not the case then application of the utilitarian criterion can exacerbate existing inequalities. Take the case of dividing a fixed income Y between two persons. One is an invalid and the other is a jet setting enjoyer of life. The resulting optimal allocation is shown in Fig. 8.1.

The jet setter's marginal utility schedule is K_1PK_2 whereas that of the invalid is K_3PK_4. On the horizontal axis the distance O_jO_I is Y. As we move rightwards from O_j the jet setter's share rises (that of the invalid falls). Optimal allocation is at P^* with the inequality in the distribution of resources adding to the differences in capacities to enjoy.

Some authors have, therefore, thought of the utilitarian social welfare function as a concave function of individual utilities

$$W = W(u_1, \ldots, u_n)$$

where $W(\quad)$ is a concave function.

Thus lower utility levels would be given greater weight in the social welfare function. But as Sen (1973) has pointed out this is really an effort (and quite recent at that) to arrest the distinctly inegalitarian prescription of the utili-

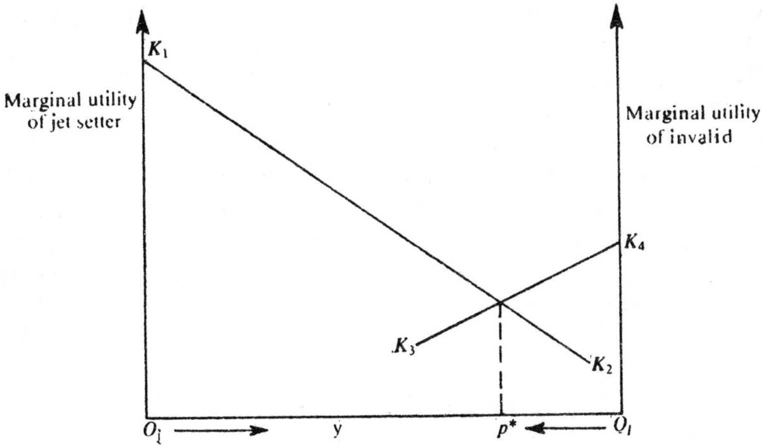

Fig. 8.1

tarian approach. Moreover, reasonable people may disagree about the degree of concavity to be given to the W function. Sen has proposed an axiom to reduce the inegalitarian nature of utilitarianism.

Sen's Weak Equity Axiom

Suppose individual i always has lower utility than individual j for every distribution of income between them. Then every distribution of income between them must give i a larger income than individual j.

The weak equity axiom has not proved very popular although the utilitarian SWF has often been made concave.

Neo-Utilitarianism

This theme is developed in papers by Vickrey and Harsanyi. The basic idea here is that people are uncertain about what they are going to be in the next time period. If society is to be fair people must be ethically impartial between alternative social states between who they are going to be in the next time period. This can be accomplished only if we had an equal chance of being each person in society. So I have the same chance of being a Rockefeller or a beggar. I derive utility from each of these possibilities but these utilities are uncertain. We assume that the probability of being in different states is known so that I define a von-Neumann Morgenstern utility function by adding up the products of different utilities and the associated probability. As a rational agent I maximize

$$\sum_i \pi_i u_i$$

where u_i is the utility from being an i person and π_i is the probability. Thus each possibility gets an adequate weightage in my maximand and in this sense I am impartial between different alternatives.

There are three quite serious problems with this approach. Firstly, let us suppose that both you and I have 1/2 probability of getting a prize of Rs 100. Now suppose that it is certain that person j is going to get this prize and that you and I have 1/2 probability of being person j. Are these two schemes equivalent? Morally they clearly aren't but according to the neo-utilitarians they are.

Secondly people with different degrees of risk aversion will not rank social states in a similar manner. Moreover, quite apart from risk aversion, different people may have different ethical perceptions about different states of the world. Such differences have nothing to do with risk aversion.

Rawls raises another point. The π_i that I assign to state i depends upon the number of people in that state. Thus solely the number of people in a particular state determine the weight given to that particular state of the world. This is morally rather arbitrary.

Maximin. The major exposition of this approach is Rawls. In this conception of justice people make choices behind "a veil of ignorance." They do not know who they are going to be. They are also risk averters. Rawls argues that such a society would opt for the following two part constitution.

(*a*) the same amount of basic liberty is available to all that is no matter whose shoes you land yourself in you still get, say, protected from murderers.

(*b*) since each individual is risk-averse he would like very much to protect himself in case he lands in the shoes of the least well off person. He would like social arrangements to maximize the welfare of the least well off person. Hence this criterion of justice is called maximin justice or Rawlsian justice.

Rawls orders social states according to the lexical difference principle. Hence state x is better than state y only if the least well off person in the former is better off than the least well off person in the latter. State z is maximin optimal or Rawls optimal if the least well off person in state z is at least as well as off the least well off person in any other state.

Several objections hence been raised against the Rawlsian society. Some people have argued that if there is a non-zero probability of my not being the least well off person I would not act so conservatively. Similarly others have asked how the maximin criterion would be used across federal units. If states or provinces within a federal set up are such that there is considerable inequality among them then if the national (maximin) calls for equalizing the welfare of the least well off person(s) across states then does this directive not interfere with the federal principle? Arrow has raised another objection. Suppose we apply the maximin criterion across time then do we not get a directive to arrest economic growth? If the welfare of people is going to rise over time (because of economic growth) then do we not discriminate against the least well off person who belongs to the first generation? Arrow supposes, later, that people derive utility from their own consumption and the consumption of their children. Then clearly growth can be allowed but it cannot be continuous growth. This is because people of the first (or any) generation do not have the consumption of their grandchildren in their utility functions. Thus, starting from generation one capital accumulation is allowed to benefit their children. But as soon as the first generation is dead if we are to be maximin just we should lower the capital stock to what was available to the first generation when it was young. Thus capital follows the see-saw path shown in Fig. 8.2.

Fig. 8.2

Along the x-axis we measure time. From 0 to 1 generation 1 works and hence capital k_t is accumulated since the children of this generation enjoy this higher capital stock. Once generation 1 is dead it becomes the least well off group and capital must now be depleted. This see-saw pattern of capital accumulation apart from being prejudiced against growth is also wasteful.

This is however a somewhat unfair criticism. Calvo has provided a framework in which the application of maximin criterion is perfectly consistent with continuous growth. Suppose every generations utility depends on its own consumption and the utility of its children. Thus the utility of generation 1 can be written as

$$\begin{aligned} u_1 &= u_1(C_1, u_2) \\ &= u_1(C_1, C_2, \ldots) \end{aligned}$$

since u_2 depends on u_3 and u_3 on u_4 and so on. So rising consumption levels make the "least well off" generation happier. Continuous growth and the maximin criterion are reconciled.

Conclusions

These welfare criterion are by no means the only ones available. Radicals would talk of very different social welfare functions. Several thinkners don't like the very idea of a social welfare function. Foley and Varian would consider an allocation as fair if it was free of envy that is I should not feel envious of Amitabh Bachan's money if I can't match his skill in histrionics. An ideal social state for them would be one that is free of envy in the above sense. But the three criteria discussed above are the major ones used in the applied welfare literature. We will see some applications in the taxation section of this study.

Appendix

In this appendix we describe an attempt that has been made to portray the Bergson social welfare function in commodity space. These contours are called Scitovsky indifference curves. They have been used for welfare analysis particularly in the theory of international trade. We will take a particularly simple example.

Take a two person two commodity economy in which individual utilities are fixed at prespecified levels and the supply of one good is fixed. We ask the following question what is the minimum amount of the other commodity that is needed to sustain utilities at the prespecified levels. This, clearly, is a Pareto optimizing exercise. The problem can formally be defined as

$$\text{minimize} \qquad x_1^1 + x_2^1$$

$$\text{subject to} \qquad u_1(x_1^1 + x_1^2) - u_1^0 = 0$$

$$u_2(x_2^1 + x_2^2) - u_2^0 = 0$$

$$x_1^2 + x_2^2 = \bar{x}^2$$

where x_j^i is the amount of the ith commodity going to individual j and $\bar{x}^2$ is the fixed supply of commodity 2. Setting up the Lagrangean we have

$$L = x_1^1 + x_2^1 + \lambda_1[u_1(x_1^1 + x_1^2) - u_1^0] + \lambda_2[u_2(x_2^1 + x_2^2) - u_2^0] + \lambda_3[\bar{x}^2 - x_1^2 - x_2^2].$$

The minimum quantity of x^1 is determinate. For each value of $\bar{x}^2$ a different optimal value (x^{1*}) of x^1 can be found. The locus of all such $(x^{1*}, \bar{x}^2)$ points for given values of u_1 and u_2 forms a Scitovsky indifference curve.

If the individual indifference curves are convex to the origin the Scitovsky contours will also be convex. But it is immediately obvious that if we change the specified values of u_1 and u_2 we will get a different Scitovsky indifference curve. To realize this look at point P in the Fig. A.8.1. P belongs to the Scitovsky indifference curve S_1 and corresponds to utility levels u_1^0 and u_2^0 for the two individuals. But the quantities of x^1 and x^2 at P could also be distributed differently and that would result in different utility levels u_1^1 and u_2^1. The Scitovsky indifference curve S_2, for these utility levels will pass through P but there is no reason whatsoever why S_1 and S_2 should coincide.

Thus social indifference curves are very sensitive to distribution and can intersect even though individual indifference curves do not intersect.

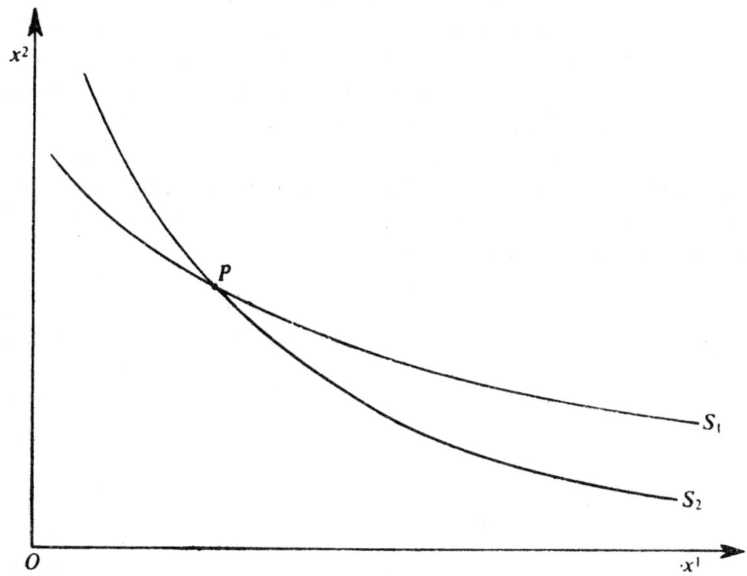

Fig. A.8.1

We can eliminate intersecting social indifference curves in the manner depicted in Fig. A.8.2.

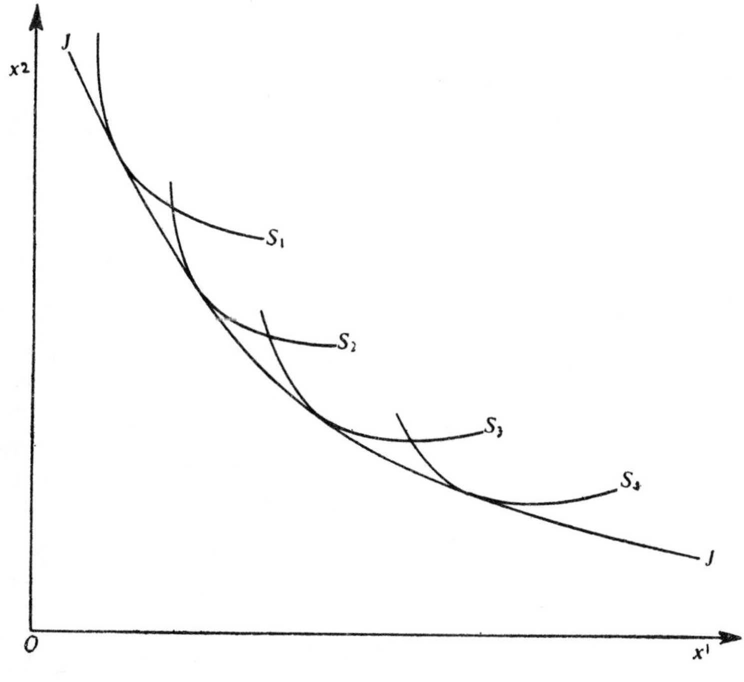

Fig. A.8.2

Suppose we define a Bergson social welfare function $W(u_1, u_2)$ and consider the various u_1, u_2 combinations which give a prespecified value W^0 of the Bergson social welfare function. Four such Scitovsky indifference curves are depicted as S_1, S_2, S_3 and S_4 as in the Fig. A.8.2. Now take the lower envelope JJ of all such Scitovsky indifference curves. JJ is called a Bergson contour and depicts the minimum x^2 (x^1) needed to sustain Bergson welfare level W^0 given the value of $x^1(x^2)$. Formal optimization gives us this leeway but we do know that we need value judgements to fix the form of the Bergson social welfare function.

PART-II

ASPECTS OF THE ECONOMICS OF TAXATION

9. Taxation and Household Behaviour

We have to study taxation in steps. There are, broadly speaking, two methods of studying incidence of tax. First, we have the calculus based general equilibrium approach (the partial equilibrium approach of undergraduate textbooks is a special case of this) and the relatively new general equilibrium computational approach. We will study the first approach in some detail but we will take time out to comment on the computational approach as well.

Before we can study the incidence of taxation we must detail how the individual actors—firms and households—behave in the presence of taxation. In this chapter we detail household behaviour. We first sketch household behaviour without taxation and then detail consumer behaviour with various types of taxes. We use "individual" and "household" interchangeably. Hence we sidestep a whole branch of the literature dealing with the composition of the household and the production of satisfaction through the household production function. Introducing these would constitute useful refinements but we are not interested in considering them in the present work nor has much work done in this area of tax theory.

A Recapitulation of the Theory of Household Behaviour

This is by no means meant to be an exhaustive treatment of the theory of household behaviour. Rather what we are interested in is to merely develop those results that are necessary for tax incidence theory.

Consider the case where the consumer is buying two goods X_1 and X_2 and the amounts of the two goods consumed are x_1 and x_2. We define his ordinal utility function as

$$u = u(x_1, x_2). \tag{1}$$

We assume that $u(\ )$ is a continuous twice continuously differentiable, regular strictly quasi-concave function. This assumption makes certain derivations easier. We assume u_1 and u_2 (the partial derivatives of u with respect to x_1 and x_2 respectively) are both strictly positive although this can be changed to accommodate special cases.

The utility function is ordinal it is unique upto a monotonic transformation. A monotonic transformation is a rank preserving transformation that is if the distance from Delhi to Calcutta is greater than the distance from Delhi to Chandigarh this relationship is preserved whether distance is measured in miles or kilometres. The transformation scale is a monotonic transformation.

The utility function is defined with respect to the time period over which consumption takes place. Consumption as well as utility, as defined here, are flow concepts.

We now define an indifference curve as the combination of x_1 and x_2 giving a prespecified level of utility u^0. Thus the combination x_1, x_2, for which $u^0 = u(x_1, x_2)$ is an indifference curve. An indifference map is a collection of indifference curves with a higher indifference curve denoting a higher level of utility than a lower curve (Fig. 9.1).

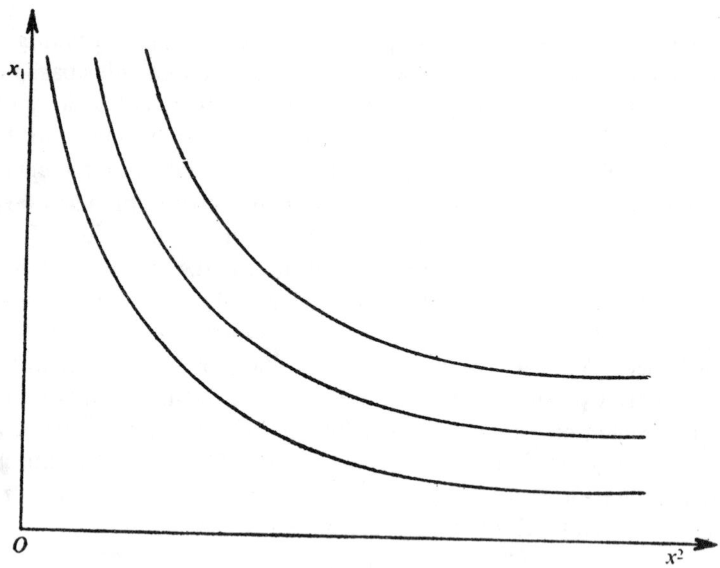

Fig. 9.1

Two indifference curves cannot cross each other. Why? The assumption that the utility function is strictly quasi-concave restricts the shape of the indifference curves. Consider two points on a given indifference curves where

$$u^0 = u(x_1^0, x_2^0) = u(x_1^1, x_2^1) \tag{2}$$

By strict quasi-concavity, for all λ such that for $0 < \lambda < 1$

$$u(\lambda x_1^0 + (1 - \lambda)x_1^1, \lambda x_2^0 + (1 - \lambda)x_2^1) > u^0.$$

Thus all linear combinations of A and B give a higher utility than u^0 and hence lie on a higher indifference curve.

Now totally indifferentiate the utility function to get

$$du = u_1\, dx_1 + u_2\, dx_2. \tag{3}$$

Along on an indifference curve $du = 0$ so that the slope of the indifference curve is

$$-\frac{dx_2}{dx_1} = \frac{u_1}{u_2}. \tag{4}$$

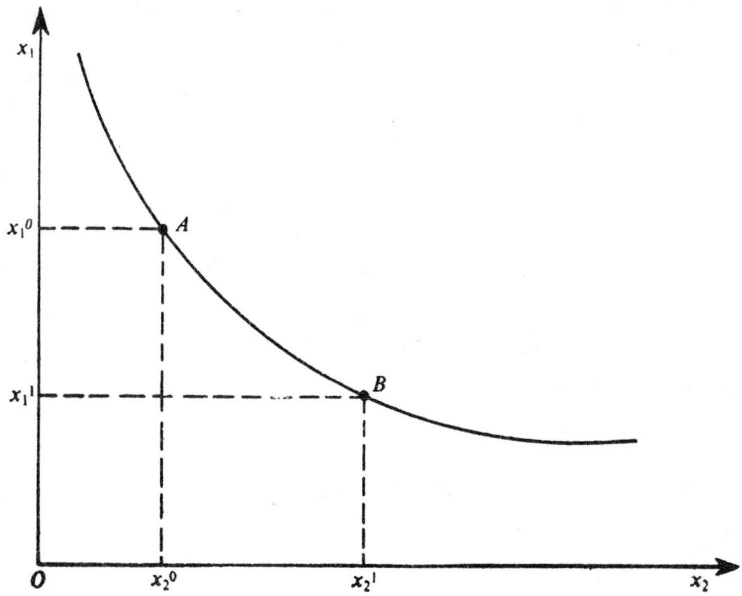

Fig. 9.2

This is also called the marginal rate of substitution between x_1 and x_2. Since the utility functions is regularly strictly quasi-concave we have

$$2u_{12}u_1u_2 - u_{11}u_2^2 - u_{22}u_1^2 > 0. \tag{5}$$

Totally differentiating (4) we get

$$\frac{d^2x_2}{dx_1^2} = -\frac{1}{u_2^3}(u_{11}u_2^2 - 2u_{12}u_1u_2 + u_{22}u_1^2). \tag{6}$$

By (5) and the assumption that $u_2 > 0$ it follows that

$$\frac{d^2x_2}{dx_1^2} < 0.$$

This is often known as diminishing marginal rate of substitution.

Consumer's Optimal Purchase Programme

Our consumer is perfectly competitive in the markets for X^1 and X^2. Hence the prices (p_1 and p_2) of these goods are parametrically given to him. For the time period under consideration the consumer's money income is given as Rs y.

The consumer thus faces the budget constraint

$$y - p_1x_1 - p_2x_2 = 0 \tag{7}$$

assuming that income is exhausted in the purchase of x_1 and x_2. The consumer controls his consumption to maximize his utility subject to the budget constraint. To do this he sets up and maximizes the following Lagrangean with respect to x_1, x_2 and the Lagrange multiplier μ.

$$L = u(x_1, x_2) + \mu[y - p_1x_1 - p_2x_2].$$

The first order conditions are

$$\frac{\partial L}{\partial x_1} = u_1 - \mu p_1 = 0 \tag{8}$$

$$\frac{\partial L}{\partial x_2} = u_2 - \mu p_2 = 0 \tag{9}$$

$$\frac{\partial L}{\partial \mu} = y - p_1x_1 - p_2x_2 = 0. \tag{10}$$

Combining (8) and (9) we get

$\dfrac{u_1}{u_2} = \dfrac{p_1}{p_2} \rightarrow$ the marginal rate of substitution equals the price ratio.

Thus the consumer's optimum is described by point C in Fig. 9.3.

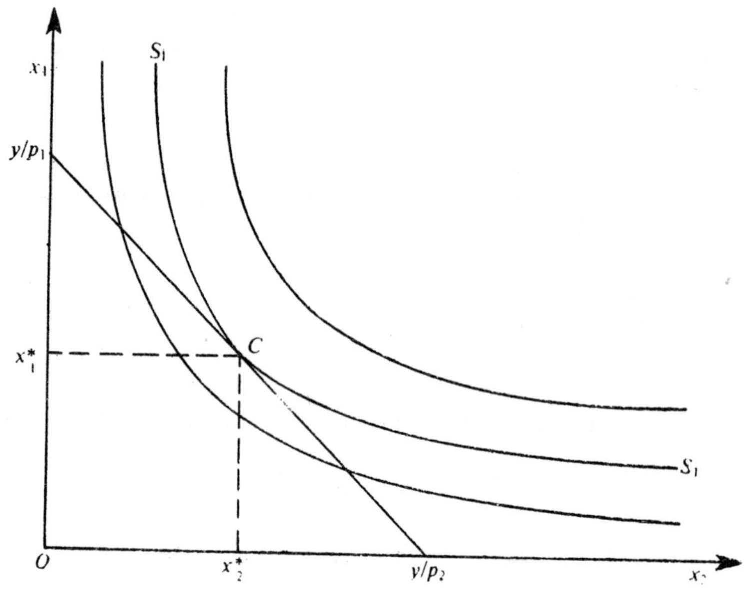

Fig. 9.3

The maximum x_1 that is obtainable is y/p_1 and the maximum x_2 is y/p_2.

Given the budget line the highest indifference curve that is attainable is S_1CS_1. The consumer buys $x_1^*(x_2^*)$ units of $x_1(x_2)$.

The second order condition for a maximum is that the following Hessian determinant

$$\begin{vmatrix} u_{11} & u_{12} & -p_1 \\ u_{21} & u_{22} & -p_2 \\ -p_1 & -p_2 & 0 \end{vmatrix} > 0.$$

Replace p_1 by u_1/μ and p_2 by u_2/μ and the above condition can be written as

$$2u_{12}u_1u_2 - u_{11}u_2^2 - u_{22}u_1^2 > 0$$

which is true by regular strict quasi concavity of u.

The above exercise solves the consumers' choice problem. We can now obtain demand functions for x_1 and x_2 from the first order conditions and write the demand functions for x_1 and x_2 as functions p_1, p_2 and y. Thus

$$x_1 = x_1(p_1, p_2, y) \tag{11}$$

$$x_2 = x_2(p_1, p_2, y). \tag{12}$$

These demand functions have two important characteristics (i) the demand functions are single valued functions of prices and income, (ii) the demand functions are homogeneous of degree zero in prices and income i.e. if *I* double p_1, p_2 and y the demands for x_1 and x_2 do not change. This can easily be seen by multiplying the first order conditions by 2.

Compensated Demand Functions

These are demand functions that isolate the substitution effect of a price change. There are two ways of articulating this substitution effect. These (for a fall in p_1) are depicted in Fig. 9.4.

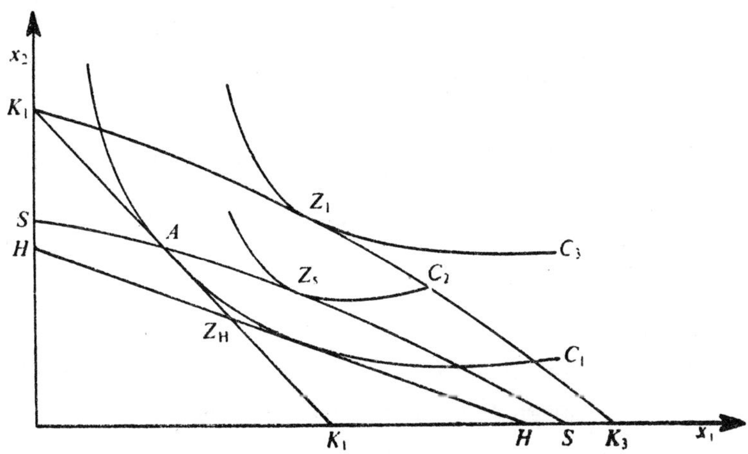

Fig. 9.4

The budget line before the price fall is K_1K_1 and the consumer comes to an equilibrium at A on indifference curve C_1 with the price fall the budget line rotates to K_1K_3 and the consumer now attain his equilibrium at Z_1 on indifference curve C_3. This move has been visualized by Hicks and Slutsky as a sequence of two steps. According to Hicks, if we have to force the consumer to remain on his old indifference curve C_1 but face the new price ratio HH(HH and SS are parallel to K_1K_3) the resulting move from A to Z_H

is the result of a pure price change devoid of any income or utility connotations. This is called the substitution effect and is always in the right direction i.e., for a fall in the price of x_1 more of x_1 will be consumed. The movement from Z_H to Z_1 is the income effect. This will imply that, when its price falls, more of x_1 will be bought (if x_1 is a normal good). If x_1 is an inferior good the income effect reduces the purchase of x_1 whereas if x_1 is a Giffen good then this reduction overwhelms the substitution effect.

For Slutsky the substitution and income effects are measured differently. He makes it possible for the consumer to buy the old commodity bundle at the new price ratio. The consumer, then, faces the budget constraint SS and the substitution effect is from A to Z_S. For Slutsky normal, inferior and Giffen goods are defined in a manner exactly analogous to Hicks.

Formally, then, we can compute the (Hicks) compensated demand curves by minimizing total expenditure subject to a utility constraint. Hence we form the Lagrangean

$$L = p_1x_1 + p_2x_2 + \mu[u^0 - u(x_1, x_2)] \tag{13}$$

and set its partial derivatives equal to zero. Thus

$$\frac{\partial L}{\partial x_1} = p_1 - \frac{\mu \partial u}{\partial x_1} = 0 \tag{14}$$

$$\frac{\partial L}{\partial x_2} = p_2 - \frac{\mu \partial u}{\partial x_2} = 0 \tag{15}$$

$$\frac{\partial L}{\partial \mu} = u^0 - u(x_1, x_2) = 0. \tag{16}$$

The demand functions computed from (14), (15) and (16) are compensated demand functions:

$$x_1' = x_1'(p_1, p_2, u^0) \tag{17}$$

$$x_2' = x_2'(p_1, p_2, u^0). \tag{18}$$

Elasticities of Demand

Consider the demand functions

$$x_1 = x_1(p_1, p_2, y) \quad \text{and} \quad x_2 = x_2(p_1, p_2, y)$$

and the compensated demand functions

$$x_1' = x_1'(p_1, p_2, u^0) \quad \text{and} \quad x_2' = x_2'(p_1, p_2\ u^0).$$

We define the following elasticities:

1. Own price elasticity of demand

(*i*) for x_1: $\dfrac{d \log x_1(\ )}{d \log p_1} = \epsilon_{11}$

(*ii*) for x_2: $\dfrac{d \log x_2(\ )}{d \log p_2} = \epsilon_{22}.$

2. Cross price elasticity of demand

(*i*) for x_1: $\dfrac{d \log x_1(\ \ )}{d \log p_2} = \epsilon_{12}$

(*ii*) for x_2: $\dfrac{d \log x_2(\ \ )}{d \log p_2} = \epsilon_{21}$.

3. Income elasticity of demand

(*i*) for x_1: $\dfrac{d \log x_1(\ \ )}{d \log y} = \eta_1$

(*ii*) for x_2: $\dfrac{d \log x_2(\ \ )}{d \log y} = \eta_2$.

4. Compensated own price elasticity of demand

(*i*) for x_1: $\dfrac{d \log x_2'(\ \ )}{d \log p_1} = \epsilon_{11}'$

(*ii*) for x_2: $\dfrac{d \log x_1'(\ \ )}{d \log p_2} = \epsilon_{22}'$.

5. Compensated cross price elasticity of demand

(*i*) for x_1: $\dfrac{d \log x_1'(\ \ )}{d \log p_2} = \epsilon_{12}'$

(*ii*) for x_2: $\dfrac{d \log x_2'(\ \ )}{d \log p_1} = \epsilon_{21}'$.

There are certain well defined relationship between these elasticities which we now proceed to note.

First totally differentiate the budget constraint to get

$$dy = x_1\, dp_1 + p_1\, dx_1 + x_2\, dp_2 + p_2\, dx_2. \tag{19}$$

Set

$$dy = dp_2 = 0 \text{ to get}$$

$$0 - x_1\, dp_1 + p_1\, dx_1 + p_2\, dx_2.$$

Multiply through by $\dfrac{p_1 x_1 x_2}{y x_1 x_2\, dp_1}$ to get

$$0 = \frac{p_1 x_1}{y} + \frac{p_1 x_1}{y}\epsilon_{11} + \frac{p_2 x_2}{y}\epsilon_{21}$$

or

$$\alpha_1\epsilon_{11} + \alpha_2\epsilon_{21} = -\alpha_1 \tag{20}$$

where $\alpha_i (i = 1, i)$ is the share of x_i in total expenditure.

Similarly totally differentiate the utility function to get

$$du = u_1\, dx_1 + u_2\, dx_2 \quad \text{and set} \quad du = 0, \quad \text{to get}$$

$u_1\,dx_1 + u_2\,dx_2 = 0$. Remembering the first order conditions $\frac{u_1}{u_2} = \frac{p_1}{p_2}$, multiply through by

$$\frac{p_1 x_1 x_2}{y x_1 x_2\, dp_1} \text{ to get}$$

$$\alpha_1 \epsilon'_{11} + \alpha_2 \epsilon'_{21} = 0. \tag{21}$$

From the income elasticities of demand we can get the Engel aggregation condition.

Totally differentiate the budget constraint and set $dp_1 = dp_2 = 0$ to get

$$p_1\,dx_1 + p_2\,dx_2 = dy. \tag{22}$$

Multiply through by y/y to get

$$\frac{yp_1}{y}\,dx_1 + \frac{yp_2}{y}\,dx_2 = \frac{dy}{y}\,y.$$

Now multiply the first term on the left hand side by $\frac{x_1}{x_2}$ and the second term by $\frac{x_2}{x_2}$. Now divide through by dy to get

$$\alpha_1 \eta_1 + \alpha_2 \eta_2 = 1. \tag{23}$$

The Labour Leisure Choice Problem

An important choice problem in public finance theory is the labour-leisure decision taken by a household. Both consumption goods and leisure are desirable. But more consumption (at a fixed wage) can only be had by working more i.e. reducing leisure. The consumer then maximizes $u(x, L)$ where x is consumption and L is leisure. He faces two constraints: (i) an income constraint which says $(T - L)W - px = 0$ where T is total time available so that $(T - L)$ is the amount of time worked, W is the wage rate and p is the price of x, (ii) a time constraint i.e.

$T = L + K$ where $K(= T - L)$ is the amount of time worked.

This optimization would release a supply curve of labour (and hence the implied demand for income) and the demand for x. It is clear that in the demand curve for income the substitution and income effects will be working in opposite directions.

The Slutsky Equation

The Slutsky equation is a very useful summary statement of the effects of a price change. To derive it recall the first order conditions for utility maximization

$$u_1 - \mu p_1 = 0 \tag{8}$$

$$u_2 - \mu p_2 = 0 \tag{9}$$

$$y - p_1 x_1 - p_2 x_2 = 0. \tag{10}$$

Totally differentiate these equations to write

$$u_{11}\,dx_1 + u_{12}\,dx_2 - \mu\,dp_1 - p_1\,d\mu = 0 \tag{8'}$$

$$u_{21}\,dx_1 + u_{22}\,dx_2 - \mu\,dp_2 - p_1\,d\mu = 0 \tag{9'}$$

$$dy - p_1\,dx_1 - x_1\,dp_1 - p_2\,dx_2 - x_2\,dp_2 = 0. \tag{10'}$$

We can write these equations compactly in matrix form:

$$\begin{pmatrix} u_{11} & u_{12} & -p_1 \\ u_{21} & u_{22} & -p_2 \\ -p_1 & -p_2 & 0 \end{pmatrix} \begin{pmatrix} dx_1 \\ dx_2 \\ d\mu \end{pmatrix} = \begin{pmatrix} \mu\,dp_1 \\ \mu\,dp_2 \\ C \end{pmatrix} \tag{24}$$

where $C = -dy + x_1\,dp_1 + x_2\,dp_2$.
Thus by Cramer' rule

$$dx_1 = \frac{\mu\,dp_1\,D_{11} + \mu\,dp_2\,D_{21} + CD_{31}}{D} \tag{25}$$

and

$$dx_2 = \frac{\mu\,dp_1\,D_{12} + \mu\,dp_2\,D_{22} + CD_{32}}{D}$$

where D_{ij} is the cofactor of the ijth element of the 3×3 matrix on the left hand side of (24) and D is the determinant of this matrix.

The price effect of p_1 on x_1 i.e. $\frac{\partial x_1}{\partial p_1}$ is obtained by setting $dp_2 = dy = 0$ in (25) to get

$$\frac{\partial x_1}{\partial p_1} = \mu\,\frac{D_{11}}{D} + x_1\,\frac{D_{31}}{D}. \tag{26}$$

Now, we know $\frac{\partial x_1}{\partial y} = -\frac{D_{31}}{D}.$

Now when $du = 0$ we find that $u_1\,dx_1 + u_2\,dx_2 = 0$.
But we also know from (8) and (9) that

$$\frac{u_1}{u_2} = \frac{p_1}{p_2}.$$

Hence $p_1\,dx_1 + p_2\,dx_2 = 0$. Thence from (10′) we get

$-dy + x_1\,dp_1 + x_2\,dp_2 = 0$ from which

$$\left(\frac{\partial x_1}{\partial p_1}\right)_{du=0} = \frac{D_{11}}{D}\,\mu.$$

Thus the first term in (26) measures the substitution effect and the second term the income effect of a change in p_1 on the demand for x_1. Thus we can rewrite (26) as

$$\frac{\partial x_1}{\partial p_1} = \left(\frac{\partial x_1}{\partial p_1}\right)_{\text{u constant}} - x_1\left(\frac{\partial x_1}{\partial y}\right)_{\text{prices constant}}. \tag{27}$$

This is known as the Slutsky equation.

The Slutsky equation can be used to derive useful relations between ordinary and compensated elasticites of demand. Multiply (27) by p_1/x_1 and multiply the last term on the right by y/y to get

$$\epsilon_{11} = \epsilon'_{11} - \alpha_1\eta_1. \tag{28}$$

We can use (25) and (26) to get Slutsky equations for $\frac{\partial x_1}{\partial p_2}$, $\frac{\partial x_2}{\partial p_1}$, and $\frac{\partial x_2}{\partial p_2}$. The generalized Slutsky relation is

$$\frac{\partial x_i}{\partial p_j} = \frac{D_{ji}\mu}{D} + x_j \frac{D_{3i}}{D} \tag{29}$$

$$= \left(\frac{\partial x_i}{\partial p_j}\right)_{\text{u constant}} - x_j\left(\frac{\partial x_i}{\partial y}\right)_{\text{prices constrant}}$$

from which we find

$$\epsilon_{ij} = \epsilon'_{ij} - \alpha_j\eta_i \qquad i = 1, 2. \tag{30}$$

Moreover we find

$$\epsilon'_{11} + \epsilon'_{12} = \frac{p_1D_{11}\mu}{x_1D} + \frac{p_2D_{21}\mu}{x_1D}$$

$$= \frac{\mu(p_1D_{11} + p_2D_{21})}{x_1D} = 0 \tag{31}$$

since the term in the parentheses equals zero since it is an expansion of the determinant of (24) in terms of alien cofactors.

From (30), (31) and the fact that $\alpha_1 + \alpha_2 = 1$ we find

$$-(\epsilon_{11} + \epsilon_{12}) = -(\epsilon'_{11} + \epsilon'_{12}) + (\alpha_1 + \alpha_2)\eta_1$$

$$= \eta_1. \tag{32}$$

One last result and we will have our necessary tools for the analysis of consumer behaviour under taxation. Not all goods can be complements. Thus in our two good story here these goods have to be substitute. This can be shown very easily. Multiply (26) by p_1, $\frac{\partial x_1}{\partial y} = -\frac{D_{31}}{D}$ by y and (29) (for $i = 1$ and $j = 2$) by p_2 and add

$$\frac{D_{11}}{D}\mu p_1 + x_1\frac{D_{31}}{D}p_1 + \frac{D_{21}\mu}{D}p_2$$

$$+ x_2\frac{D_{31}}{D}p_2 - \frac{D_{31}}{D}y$$

$$= \frac{1}{D}[D_{11}\mu p_1 + D_{21}\mu p_2 - D_{31}(y - p_1x_1 - p_2x_2)]$$

$$= \frac{1}{D}[D_{11}\mu p_1 + D_{21}\mu p_2 - 0)] = 0, \tag{33}$$

since we are expanding by alien cofactors. Now substituting $S_{ij} = \frac{D_{ji}\mu}{D}$, we find

$$S_{11}p_{11} + S_{12}p_2 = 0.$$

We know $S_{11} < 0$. Hence $S_{12} > 0$.
Thus x_1 and x_2 are substitutes.

Household Behaviour Under Taxation

In this chapter we study the effect of taxation—income taxation, conceived in different ways,—on individual households. Taxation, affects several aspects of a households' life. It affects labour leisure choice as well as the allocation of resources overtime i.e. savings. It may affect the type of job the individual might want to do and whether he wants to work as someone's employee or incorporate himself (with or without others) as a firm. It might affect the form in which individuals hold savings as well as the types of assets to bequeath to their inheritors or, indeed, the decision whether to bequeath. This list could easily be extended and it should be very clear that a tax as it impinges on an individual household has a whole range of effects.

This variety raises two very important issues. Firstly given this variety of effects how do we compare different taxes? Second, how do we formulate a framework for the analysis of the effects of taxes?

We take up the second issue first. What we are interested in at this stage is the development of a framework for the static, atemporal general equilibrium incidence of taxes. Hence we explicitly suppress those considerations that call for a study of the intertemporal allocation of resources by the household. Moreover we rule out contemporarneous external effects between consumers/producers, consumers/consumers and producers/producers. All uncertainty is ruled out as is every type of non-competitive and strategic behaviour. What we have, then, is a three way classification of the effects of a tax.

(1) *Income Effect*

When a tax is imposed an individual is poorer than before the tax was imposed. This may prompt an individual to work harder, postpone retirement etc.

(2) *Substitution Effect*

The imposition of a tax will tend to divert activity, ceteris paribus, from taxed to untaxed areas. Thus if we have an expenditure tax we would expect people to save more. An income tax would encourage people to retire early or work less hard. A substitution effect would make people spend money ceteris paribus, on less taxed commodities.

(3) *Financial Effect*

A tax also has a financial effect. A doctor making Rs 5,000 a month in government service could save some taxes by becoming a private practitioner.

A private practitioner and a government doctor perform the same function but they are treated differently for tax purposes. The tax system may encourage people to make such shifts.

Income Taxation and Labour Supply

One of the most important effects of the tax system is on labour supply. Particular attention has been given to the effects of an income tax on labour supply. We have already seen the labour leisure choice problem and have also come to learn that for a rational consumer the labour supply curve (as a function of the wage rate) could be upward sloping or downward sloping. Income taxes impinge critically on this labour leisure choice. The precise nature of this imposition depends on the type of tax that we have in mind. A purely lump sum tax (where everyone pays a fixed amount say Rs 100 per year) simply has an income effect i.e. it does not alter the terms of trade (i.e. the wage rate) between income and leisure. Hence if the utility function defined over income and leisure is homothetic (indifference curves have the same slope along any straight line drawn from the origin) the ratio between income and leisure is kept unchanged.

To alter the terms of trade between income and leisure one has to affect the consumer's decision at the margin. A proportionate tax can do this. Let us suppose that the consumer has non-wage income M so that his total income is $WL + M$ where L is the amount of time worked. This is before tax. If the consumer is taxed at the proportionate rate t his net income is $(l - t)(WL + M)$. The effect of this tax is depicted in Fig. 9.5 through Fig. 9.8.

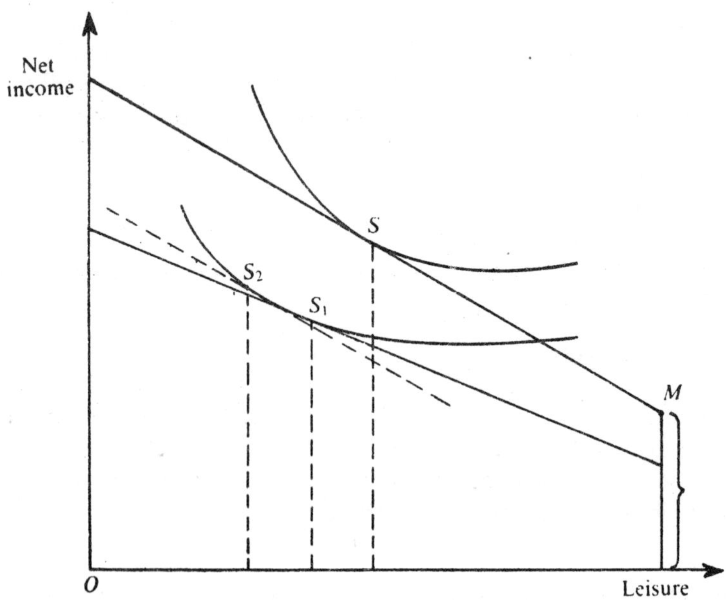

Fig. 9.5

Before tax the individual comes to his equilibrium at point S. After the proportionate tax he comes to his equilibrium at S_1. If we draw a line tangent to the new indifference curve but with the slope of the old budget line the equilibrium would be at S_2. Thus the movement from S to S_2 is the income effect whereas the movement from S_2 to S_1 is a pure substitution effect. In this case the income effect reduces leisure whereas the substitution effect increases leisure. The net effect is to increase work. The opposite happens in Fig. 9.6.

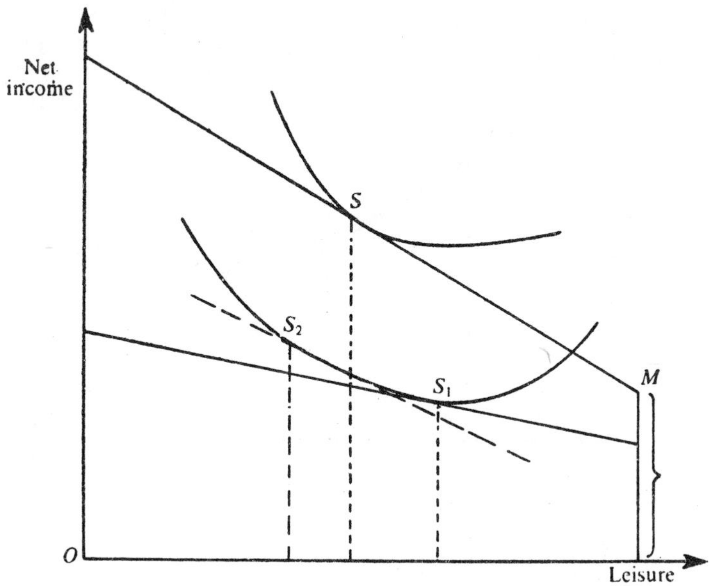

Fig. 9.6

Figures 9.7 and 9.8 plot these same effects when M is zero. Figure 9.7 shows the situation corresponding to that in Fig. 9.5 whereas Fig. 9.8 shows the situation paralleled to Fig. 9.6.

In Figs. 9.5 and 9.7 the income effect dominates whereas in Figs. 9.6 and 9.8 the substitution effect dominates, which case obtains in a given situation is an empirical question and, unfortunately, for our country empirical work along these lines in scarce and tangential.

With progressive taxation the story becomes still more different. With progressive taxation the marginal tax rate varies with income i.e. if $T(y)$ is the tax liability of a person with income y, $T'(y) = dT/dy$ is constant with proportional or linear taxation but with progressive (or more generally non-linear taxation) T' varies with income.

In Fig. 9.9 above we have called a tax progressive if T' rises with y. The tax is called regressive if T' falls with y and it is called linear if $T'(y)$ does not change with y.

Each of these taxes could be accompanied by an exemption limit and, indeed, any non-linear tax could be approximated by a set of linear taxes with appropriate exemption limits.

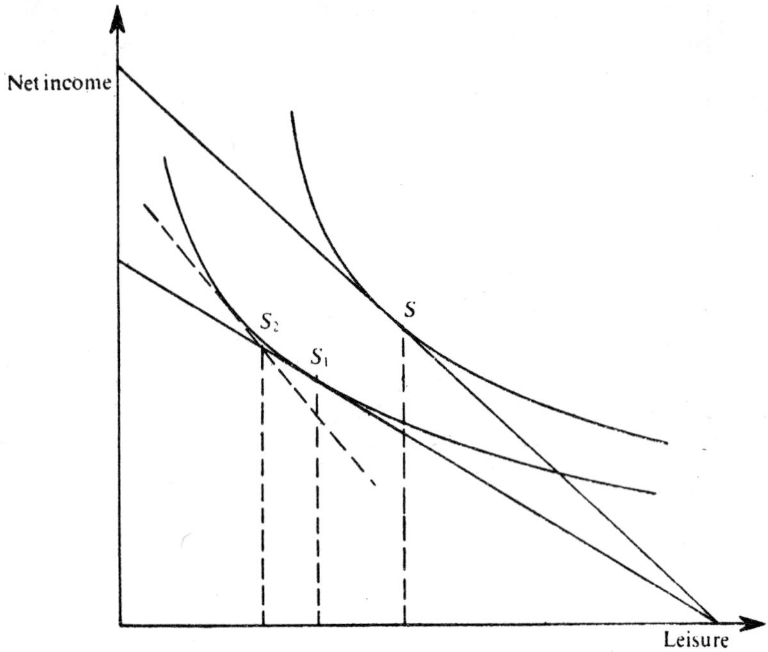

Fig. 9.7

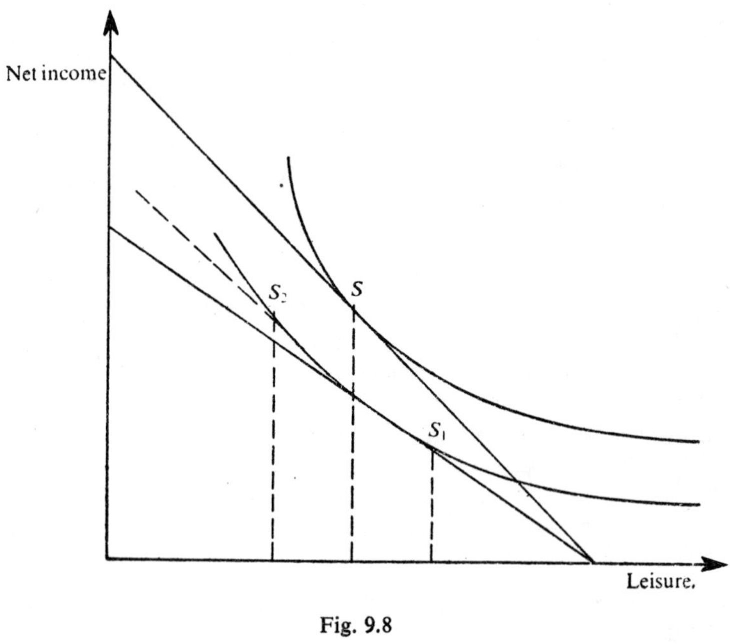

Fig. 9.8

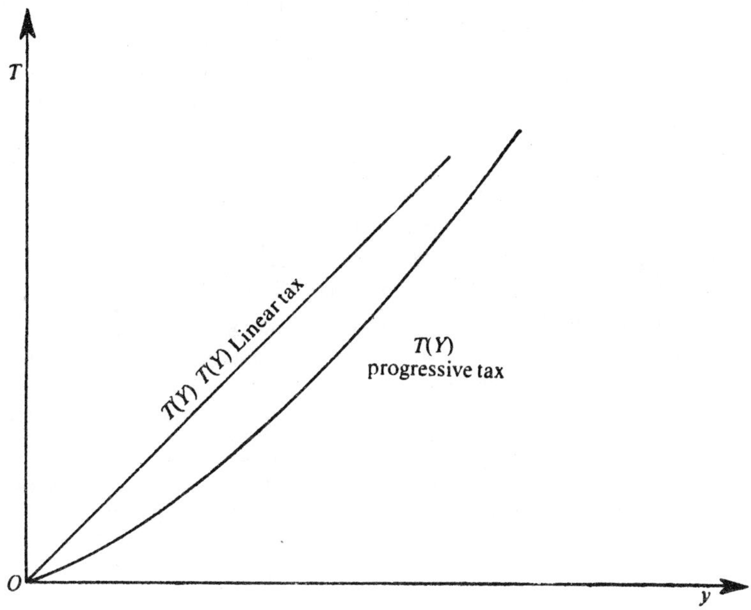

Fig. 9.9

The definition of progression adopted here is rather special. In fact Musgrave and Thin (1948) have suggested four different measures of the degree of progression of a tax. Let Y be gross income and let $a\left(=\frac{T}{y}\right)$ and $m(=T'(y))$ be the average and marginal tax rates respectively. The Musgrave and thin measures are:

(*i*) average rate progression $\frac{da}{dY}$

(*ii*) marginal rate progression $\frac{dm}{dy}$

(*iii*) liability progression $\frac{m}{a}$

(*iv*) residual income progression $\frac{(1-m)}{(1-a)}$.

As should be immediately relevant these measures give different answers even with relatively simple tax functions. Hence which measures one uses must depend on the purpose of measuring tax progression.

A priori it is fairly hard to say anything about the relative incentive effects of linear and non-linear taxes. Musgrave has stated that for linear and progressive taxes that yield the same revenue if the progressive tax involves a higher marginal tax rate then it must discourage work effort more than the linear tax does. If we are not concerned about distributional issues then it can be shown that if revenue is a declining function of the tax rate then we can conceive of a lower (linear) tax rate yielding the same revenue as the non-linear tax and able to induce more work effort. In this case, however, the non-linear tax would be ruled out on grounds of efficiency. Furthermore whether a progressive tax which yields as much revenue as a proportional tax necessarily has greater disincentive effects if it involves a higher marginal tax rate then the proportional tax depends critically on what we assume about exemption limits. If the exemption limit with a progressive tax is higher the disincentive effects need not necessarily be greater.

How do we compare different taxes for their effect on labour supply? Some have suggested that we compare taxes that give same post tax utility. But this standard has the disadvantage that it makes a non-observable such as utility the basis of comparison. Nevertheless a standard for comparison has to be found. Some authors have used equal yield the basis of comparison. One could think of still other criteria such as equal distortion in the allocation of resources or equal deadweight loss[1] but the idea of using equal yield has found much favour recently.[2] In Fig. 9.10 we use this criterion to compare a lump sum tax with a proportional tax.

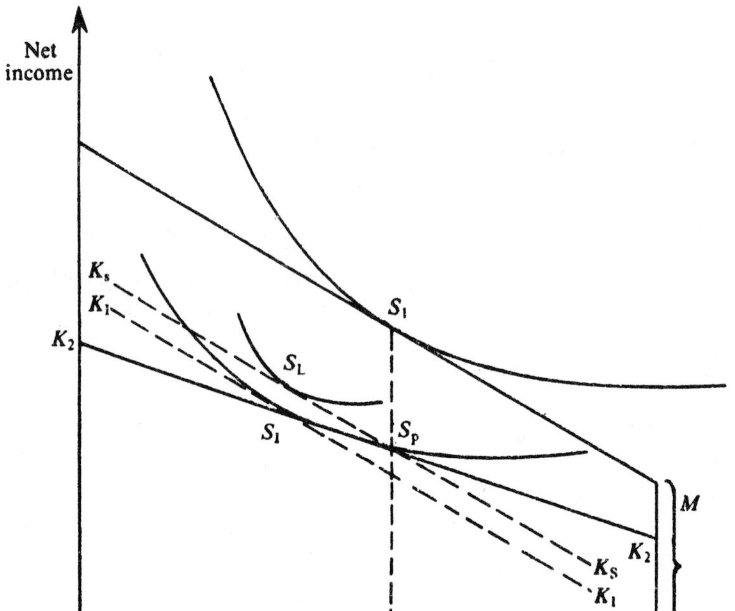

Fig. 9.10

[1]The concepts of a tax induced misallocation of resources and deadweight loss are explained in a later chapter.

[2]See, for example, Atkinson and Stiglitz (1980).

Before the tax is imposed the consumer faces the budget line K_1K_1 and comes to equilibrium at point S_1. With proportional tax the budget line is K_2K_2 and the consumer comes to an equilibrium at S_p. The movement from S_1 to S_I is the income effect (K_1K_1 is parallel to K_sK_s) and that from S_I to S_p is the substitution effect.

An equal yield lump sum tax (government revenue is the vertical distance between pre and post tax budget lines) displaces the budget line to K_SK_S and the consumer's equilibrium is at S_L. In this example, the proportional tax has no effect on work while the lump sum tax increases work but this need not always be the case. Moreover, the lump sum tax (since it does not alter the terms of trade between leisure and income) gives a higher utility to the household than the proportional tax does.

How important, empirically, is the disincentive effect of an income tax? It is important here to pose the question properly. Obviously we are not talking about a situation in which the tax structure prompts workers to leave the labour market. This kind of supposition is simply unsustainable in the Indian context. More appropriately, the issue is whether the tax structure discourages people from working longer hours or whether people prefer leisure to working overtime.

Unfortunately there is not much empirical work on this issue in India. Surveys conducted in the US and UK have covered professionals of different types. The consensus from such surveys seems to be that professionals work for self respect and for the social dignity of their families is important. Idleness is a sign of waste and is hence taboo. Monetary rewards (gross or net of taxes) are of secondary importance. The direct tax structure has far greater implications for entrepreneurship and risk taking than for labour supply. We will study these factors in later chapters. Another way to interpret the weak influence of direct taxes on working hours is, of course, to suggest that the income and substitution effects are of equal or near equal magnitude. Notwithstanding this, however, we must understand that the theoretical model for analyzing the effect of direct taxes on labour supply needs to be enriched.

This is a promising area for research. Some people have used Becker's theory of the allocation of time as a point of departure. Still others have used his theory of the household production function. Still others have analyzed the labour supply decision of the household as a joint decision problem for husband and wife. At the time of writing of this book these development remain interesting extensions. They have yet to be integrated in the general theory of tax incidence.

10. Taxation and Savings

Taxation has profound effects on savings and hence on the allocation on resources. In this chapter we study these effects at the level of individual agents—firms and households. The allocative effects are better studied in a general equilibrium model of tax incidence and this is described at length in later chapters.

Broadly speaking one can think of taxes affecting savings, risk taking and investment behaviour in a profound manner. We will take up the first two in this chapter and take up investment in the next chapter.

The effect of taxation on savings has to be studied differently depending on whether we are working with a world of certainty or uncertainty. We concentrate on the model with certainty first and later study the effects of taxation on saving decisions taken under conditions of uncertainty.

Savings Under Certainty

People save for a variety of reasons. Some people save in order to buy something which they couldn't with their monthly salaries. Thus a housewife may save in order to buy an expensive kitchen gadget or a sewing machine. This is a target savings model. Other people save for precautionary purposes i.e. they might save to meet an unforeseen contingency—a prolonged illness or a disability. Most people save in order to have positive consumption when they are retired or to leave behind bequests for their children.[1] This is often referred to as the life cycle model of savings. A related idea is that people save in order to earn a rate of return. Another related notion is that people save in order to speculate. This set constitutes what might loosely be called the "mainstream" motives for saving. Radical authors have always had very different notions about savings. Kaldor and Passinetti in their respective growth models talk of savings being determined by class membership. Workers as a class have a lower propensity to save than the capitalists. In other Marxian models only capitalists save and in still other articulations only capitalists save and they save all their income. In most of these articulations the long run of growth rate of the economy depends only on

[1]It can be argued that a beuqest is more or less a byproduct of this decision. A bequest is more of an accident, it has been argued, than the product of a conscious decision.

the savings propensity of capitalists.[2] Thus the long run equilibrium effects of a tax on savings depend on how it affects the income and/or the saving propensities of capitalists. This chapter will cover mainly the mainstream models.

We realize immediately that the effects of taxation on saving will depend upon the particular motive for saving we adduce to individual economic agents and the time horizon involved. A person with a targeted saving is going to be less affected by an interest tax than a person who is saving for profit. This is going to be particularly true if the time horizon to attain targeted savings is long.

Hence it is important to develop a common framework in terms of which we can analyze the effects of different types of taxes on savings. We develop this framework in two stages. We first consider a life-cycle model without bequests and then consider an intertemporal model that extends the time horizon still further and specifically allows for bequests.

The basic life cycle model of savings is the following. Any individual lives for two time periods. During the first period he works and earns a wage. In the second time period he is retired and lives off the savings he accumulated during his working days. The consumer faces competitive labour and capital markets so that the wage rate W and the rate of interest r are parametrically given to him. The consumer maximise his utility $U(C_1, C_2)$ where C_1 is first period consumption and C_2 is second period consumption.[3] This utility function is strictly quasi concave, twice continuously differentiable and has regular smooth indifference curves associated with it. Hence we can depict consumer's utility maximization problem as:

$$\max_{C_1, C_2} U(C_1, C_2) \text{ subject to}$$

$$C_1 + \frac{C_2}{1 + r} = W.$$

Graphically, the situation is depicted in Fig. 10.1.

Maximum consumption possible in period 1 is W. Maximum consumption in period 2 is $W(1 + r)$ since saved wage earns interest at the rate of r. Utility is maximized by consuming the combination (C_1^*, C_2^*) where the MRS in consumption is equal to $(1 + r)$. How does a change in the rate of interest affect C_1^*, C_2^*? Realize that the relative price of next period's consumption is $\frac{1}{1 + r}$ since this is the at which one unit of C_2 can be transformed into C_1. Define $\frac{1}{1 + r} = p$ as this relative price.

[2]For further discussion of these problems the reader is referred to a number of texts in economic growth e.g. Sen (1965), Burmeister and Dobell (1970), Stiglitz and Uzawa (1967), and Marglin (1984).

[3]The ommission of labour supply may seem incongruous. It is somewhat limiting to omit labour supply decisions when dealing with savings and omit savings when dealing with labour supply. The standard received theory makes this bifurcation. For an integrated treatment see, for instance, Jha (1986).

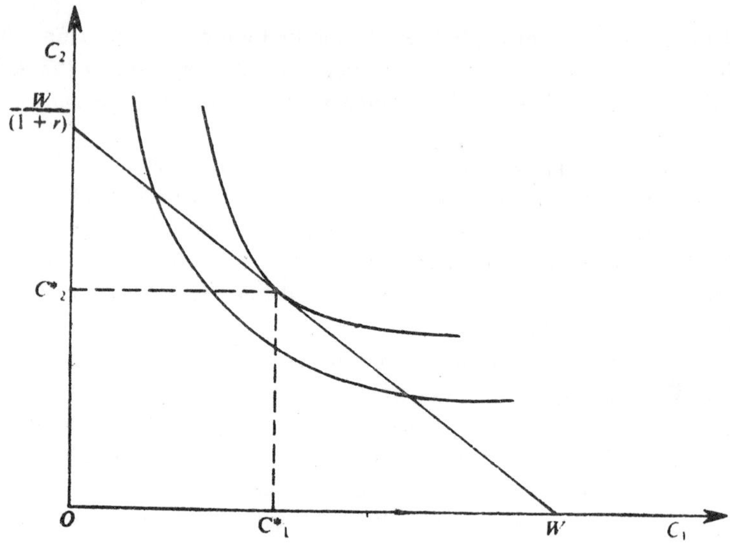

Fig. 10.1

Define the elasticity of substitution:

$$\sigma = \frac{d \log C_2/C_1}{d \log 1 + r}\bigg|_{\bar{u}} = \frac{\partial \log C_1}{\partial \cdot \log p}\bigg|_{\bar{u}} - \frac{\partial \log C_2}{\partial \log p}\bigg|_{\bar{u}}.$$

The sensitivity of the combination C_1^*, C_2^* to a change in r depends on this elasticity of substitution. With a rise in r if σ is high C_2^* wili go up substantially. The situation is depicted in Figs. 10.2(a & b).

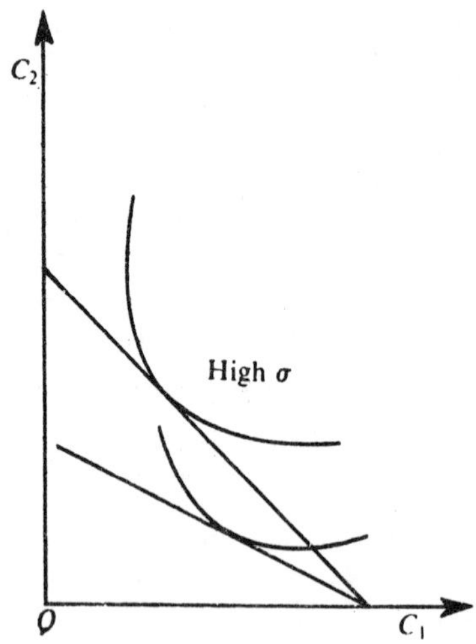

Fig. 10.2(a)

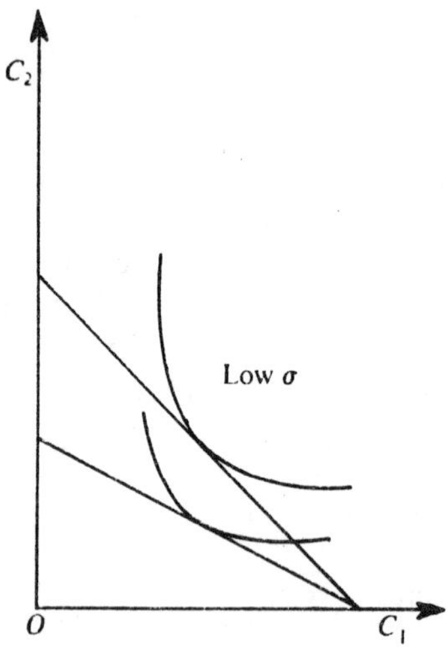

Fig. 10.2(b)

An increase in the rate of interest twists the budget line up along the C_2 axis. With a high σ savings hence C_2 go up substantially in Fig. 10.2(a).

With a low σ the income effect is dominant and the change is not substantial. (Fig. 10.2(b)). Hence any tax that alters the relative price between C_1 and C_2 will have its effects (at least partly) determined by the value of σ.

In this context let us study the effect of a proportional tax t_r on interest income and a proportional tax, t_w, on wage income. The first tax changes the slope of the budget line. (The effective interest rate is $r(1 - t_r)$), whereas the second tax changes the position of the budget line on the C_1 axis. Let us calculate the effect of the imposition of these two taxes on savings. With the imposition of t_w savings are given by

$$C_2 = W(1 - t_w) - C_1.$$

Totally differentiating this expressing, realizing that C_1 is a function of $W(1 - t_w)$ we get

$$dC_2 = dW - Wdt_w - t_w\,dW$$
$$- \frac{\partial C_1}{\partial W(1 - t_w)}(-W\,dt_w).$$

But $dW = 0$,

so that $$dC_2 = -Wdt_w\left(1 - \frac{\partial C_1}{\partial W(1 - t_w)}\right).$$

With an interest tax the change in savings is

$$\frac{\partial C_1}{\partial p}\frac{\partial p}{\partial t_r}\,dt_r$$

so that the total effect of the two taxes is

$$-Wdt_w\left(1 - \frac{\partial C_1}{\partial W(1 - t_w)}\right) - \frac{\partial C_1}{\partial p}\frac{\partial p}{\partial t_r}\,dt_r. \tag{1}$$

To see the effect of σ divide (1) by $\dfrac{dt_r}{1 - t_r}$ to get

$$-W(1 - t_r)\frac{dt_w}{dt_r}\left(1 - \frac{\partial C_1}{\partial W(1 - t_w)}\right)$$
$$-\left(\frac{1 - t_r}{dt_r}\right)\frac{\partial C_1}{\partial p}\frac{\partial p}{\partial t_r}\,dt_r. \tag{2}$$

Now realize that $\dfrac{\partial p}{\partial t_r} = rp^2$.

Substituting in (2) we have

$$-W(1 - t_r)\frac{dt_w}{dt_r}\left(1 - \frac{\partial C_1}{\partial W(1 - t_w)}\right)$$
$$-(1 - t_r)\frac{p}{C_1}\frac{\partial C_1}{\partial p}C_1 rp\,dt_r. \tag{3}$$

Now recall the definition of σ that is,

$$\sigma = \left.\frac{d \log C_2/C_1}{d \log (1 + r)}\right|_{\bar{u}}$$

$$= \left.\frac{\partial \log C_1}{\partial \log p}\right|_{\bar{u}} - \left.\frac{\partial \log C_2}{\partial \log p}\right|_{\bar{u}}.$$

But from the Slutsky relation

$$\left.\frac{\partial C_1}{\partial \log p}\right|_{\bar{u}} + p \left.\frac{\partial C_2}{\partial \log p}\right|_{\bar{u}} = 0.$$

Hence

$$\left.\frac{\partial \log C_1}{\partial \log p}\right|_{\bar{u}} = \frac{pC^2}{C_1 + pC_2}\, \sigma = s\sigma$$

where s is the savings rate.
Hence

$$\frac{\partial \log C_1}{\partial \log p} = s(\sigma - \eta) \text{ where}$$

$$\eta = \frac{\partial \log C_1}{\partial \log W(1 - t_w)}.$$

Thus we can rewrite equation (3) as

$$-W(1 - t_r) \frac{dW}{dt_r}\left(1 - \frac{\partial C_1}{\partial W(1 - t_w)}\right)$$

$$- (1 - t_r)\, s(\sigma - \eta)\, C_1 rpdt_r$$

and the effect of σ is transparent.

Thus the effect of these taxes on savings depends on the above expression. With explicit functional forms for $U(\;\;)$ and specific assumptions about the ratio $\frac{1 - t_r}{1 - t_w}$ more can be said but these results would not generally be true.

Within this framework it is straightforward to study pensions. Suppose the government pays pension as a lump sum — to the individual in the second time period. If the individual is able to shift this payment to the first period (by borrowing against it, say) them the entire budget line shifts out as in Fig. 10.3.

In the situation as depicted in Fig. 10.3 savings decline. But this is one of the simplest and least ambiguous cases. Feldstein has argued that the timing of retirement is itself a function of the pension policy. We can't capture that effect here both because we have fixed time periods and because labour supply is not variable in this story. Moreover, complete borrowing against pensions may not be possible. Furthermore, some jobs do not necessarily involve pension in old age and, quite often, only those people who get less than a certain income as wages are eligible for pension. Thus the relationship between pensions and saving is quite complex and varies from individual to individual.

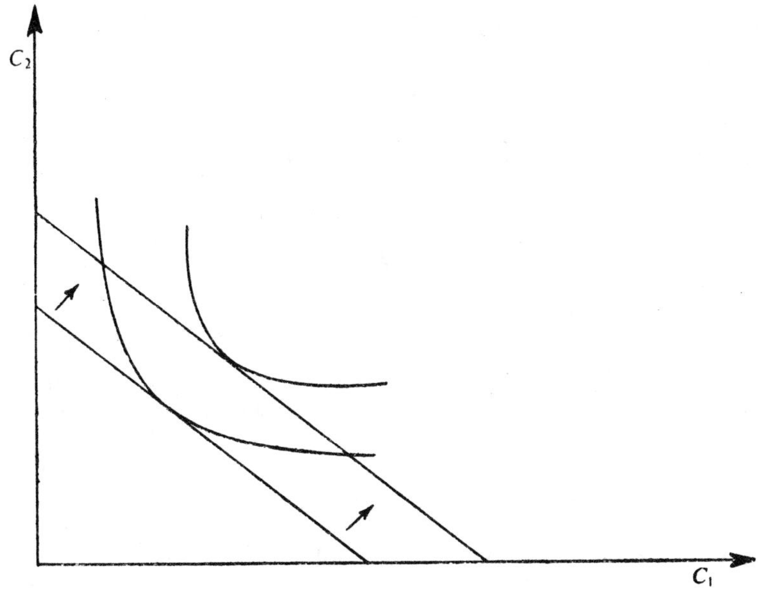

Fig. 10.3

A Broader Model of Savings and Taxation

The life cycle model discussed above has served as a framework for analyzing the effects of taxes on savings. It is straightforward to extend the analysis —if one wants to—to a multiperiod framework.

Suppose that an individual expects—with confidence—to live for T time periods.[4] Thus he is interested in maximizing his utility $U(C_1, \ldots, C_T)$ where C_i is his consumption in period i. The wage income is W_t in period t. He faces a perfect capital market where he can lend or borrow freely at the fixed rate of interest r. Thus if we are considering utility maximization at time period l his budget constraint would be

$$\sum_{i=1}^{T} \frac{W_t}{(1+r)^{t-1}} = \sum_{i=1}^{T} \frac{C_t}{(1+r)^{t-1}}.$$

This simple framework can easily be extended to include bequests received (B_0) and bequests left behind (B_T). Both get included in the budget constraint whereas the latter will have to figure in the consumer's utility function as well. The problem can then be rewritten as

$$\underset{C_1, \ldots, C_T, B_T}{\text{maximize}} \quad U(C_1, \ldots, C_T, B_T).$$

[4]Yaari (1964) considers the continuous time analogue of this problem where T is stochastic i.e. the individual is uncertain about his longevity. He proves the following important result. Suppose the probability of death causing events is given by a poisson process with parameter λ. If the consumer is maximizing a utility function with stochastic T and discount rate δ then the individual is actually maximizing utility over an infinite horizon with discount rate $\delta + \lambda$. This assumption of death causing events being described by a poisson process is, realistically speaking, valid only for young people.

Subject to

$$\sum_{t=1}^{T} \frac{W_t}{(1 + r)^{t-1}} + B_0 = \sum_{t=1}^{T} \frac{C_t}{(1 + r)^{t-1}} + \frac{B_T}{(1 + r)^T}.$$

Hence any pair of taxes (t_1, t_2) that affect the left hand side and right hand side of the budget constraint in the same manner are equivalent in their effects on consumer choice. Thus a proportional tax t_1 on wage income plus inheritance reduces net resources and alters the budget constraint to read

$$\left(\sum_{t=1}^{T} \frac{W_t}{(1 + r)^{t-1}} + B_0\right)(1 - t_1) = \sum_{t=1}^{T} \frac{C_t}{(1 + r)^{t-1}} + \frac{B_T}{(1 + r)^T}.$$

A proportional tax at rate t_2 on consumption plus bequests would increase gross expenditure and the budget constraint would read

$$\sum_{t=1}^{T} \frac{W_t}{(1 + r)^{t-1}} + B_0 = \left(\sum_{t=1}^{T} \frac{C_t}{(1 + r)^{t-1}} + \frac{B^T}{(1 + r)^T}\right)(1 + t_2).$$

If the nominal effects of the two axes are the same (i.e. if the imposition of t_1 recues receipts by the same amount as the imposition of t_2 increases gross expenditure) then the two sets of taxes have, equivalent effects on the consumer's equilibrium. In a completely analogous manner one can talk of other pairs of equivalent taxes e.g. taxes only on bequests and inheritances or only on wage income and consumption etc.[5]

Concluding Note on Taxation and Savings

Above we have detailed a simple framework for the analysis of the effects of taxes on savings. At a broader level one can think of taxes as having four broad classes of effects. First we have a substitutions effect. Taxation of savings makes future consumption more expensive. Hence if utility is held constant present consumption is increased and savings fall. The income or wealth effect is slightly more complicated. If the net rate of return to capital is reduced debtors stand to gain whereas creditors lose. Hence there is an asymmetry in the income effect. The case analyzed in this chapter is clearly the case when the individual—over his lifetime—is neither a debtor nor a creditor. Hence we clearly sidestepped this question. There is no reason, whatsoever, why the income effect for debtors should cancel out the income effect for creditors. There is a further financial effect. Savings by households might be treated differently under the tax laws from the retained earnings by corporations. Thus the savings of a government doctor might be treated differently than the savings of a doctor who is part of a nursing home. Moreover, there is a capitalization effect. Suppose there are two assets—one is an asset fixed in supply and the other is variable is supply e.g. a government bond. Suppose that we begin with a situation without any tax. Then the

[5]The assumption of perfect capital markets is central to this whole story. Imperfect capital markets disturb this equilibrium in a profound manner. See, for instance, Hu (1980), or Jha (1986).

rates of return on the fixed and variable asset would reflect a situation in which any investor would be indifferent between holding the fixed and variable asset i.e. the flow rates of return are equalized. Now suppose the asset in fixed supply is taxed a higher rate but the rate of return of the variable asset is fixed—say at an international level. Then the flow rates of return are still equalized but the price of the fixed asset—as a stock—will decline to reflect the difference in tax burdens. Thus the capitalized value of the asset will be altered. This is the capitalization effect and is likely to be quite important in economies with fixed and variable assets.

In this chapter we have been concentrating on the simpler stories with perfect markets. We will consider some complications in a later chapter. In this chapter we are interested in extending the story told here to a world with uncertainty.

Taxation and the Taking of Risk

Savings are kept in the form of assets. Only a fraction of savings are kept in the form of "absolutely safe" assets like a government bond or plain cash and coins. The availability and riskness of various types of assets affect the volume of savings. Furthermore attitudes toward risk affect the rate of investment. The tax structure, particularly but not exclusively the structure of direct taxes—effects the riskness of various projects.

A recurring question has been does the direct tax structure necessarily reduce risk-taking. This is somehow regarded as a "bad" and hence needs to be discouraged. This is not necessarily true since a society does not and should not take all risks. There is an optimal amount of risk taking as well as an optimal volume of savings and investment.

Apart from the above paragraph we will say nothing more in this chapter about the normative theory of risk taking. Our concern here is the positive theory of risk taking. We are also interested in discovering how risk taking is affected by taxation.

There are, broadly speaking, two approaches to the study of the effects of a tax on risk taking. One is the liquidity preference as behaviour towards risk approach pioneered by Tobin (1958) and the other is the portfolio allocation model of Markovitz, Stiglitz, Modigliani, Miller and others.[6] We will study each of these approaches for the simplest case where the choice is between a safe asset S (say cash amounts of which are denoted by s) and a risky asset (a security amounts of which are denoted by r). We will study equilibrium for various types of savers-risk lovers, risk averters and those that are risk neutral.

Liquidity Preference as Behaviour Towards Risk

Suppose we live in an inflation free world with two assets. Cash, S carries zero yield but, by definition, the distribution of returns has zero variance.

[6]The reader may find it useful to review the theory of consumer behaviour under uncertainty outline in Chapter 3.

The security, R, on the other hand has a mean return of μ and standard deviation σ. We think of this standard deviation as a measure of the risk of holding R. The individual saver has a utility function defined over risk and return with risk "normally" being a bad and return a good.[7] What do we expect the individuals indifference curves over risks and returns to look like. The possibilities are plotted in Fig. 10.4.

In Fig. 10.4 (a & b) we plot the indifference curves of a risk averter. The saver can be made to undertake greater risk only if the mean return goes up. The individual in Fig. 10.4(a) is a diversifier because at low absolute risk levels a one percent increase in risk requires less than one percent increase in mean return to keep the saver on the same indifference curve whereas at high risk levels a one percent increase in risk requires larger than one percent increase in mean return to compensate the saver. Thus he diversifies. Equivalently the indifference curves are concave. For the opposite reasons the saver in Fig. 10.4(b) is a plunger. The saver in Fig. 10.4(c) is a risk lover since he will trade off return, for higher risk (to increase his chances of a capital gain).

Let us analyze the choice problem in this situation. Suppose, to begin with, we are dealing with a risk averter who is a diversifier. He can put all his savings in cash earn zero return and incur zero risk or he can invest some in the risky asset. Figure 10.5 visualizes the possibilities for this individual.

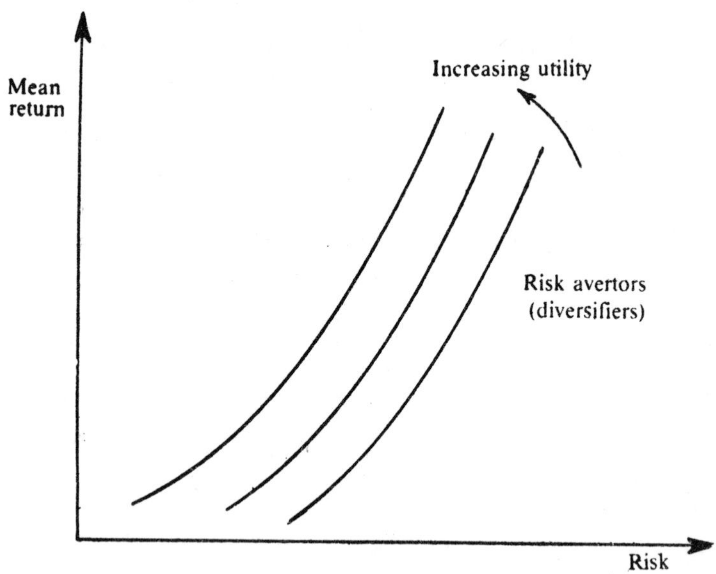

Fig. 10.4(a)

[7]This is a fairly restrictive assumption. The conditions which it is valid are detailed in Tobin (1958).

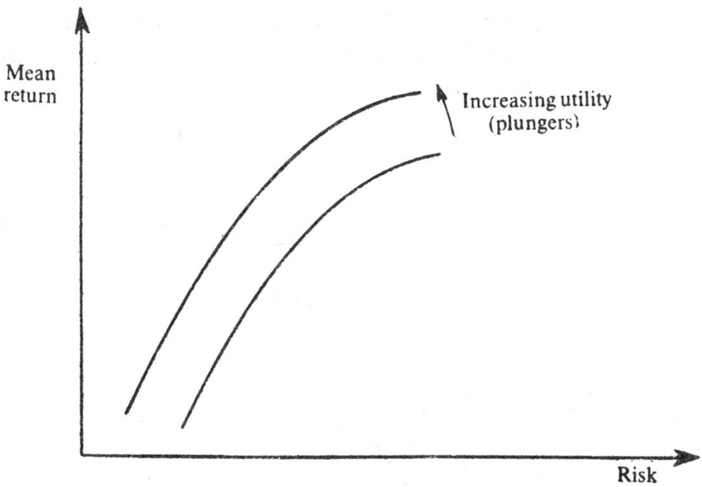

Fig. 10.4(b)

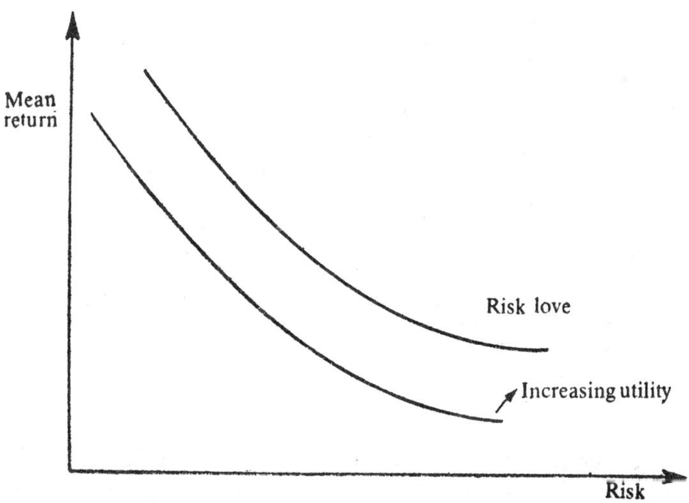

Fig. 10.4(c)

In the first half of Fig. 10.5 we plot the risk/return combination afforded by the individual's portfolio. With cash he gets zero of risk and return. As he increases the proportion of risky asset, R, in his portfolio he gets higher μ and higher σ. With the interest payment on the risky asset at r_1%, OA_1 shows the investment opportunities available to this individual. As the proportion of assets held in R increases the mean return increase as well as the risk. Hence OA_1 is upward sloping. With a higher interest, r_2, this opportunity locus shifts to OA_2. With r_1 the consumer comes to an equilibrium at D_1 and with r_2 the equilibrium is at D_2. The proportions in R can be read off from the line OB in the lower half of Fig. 10.5. An increase in the rate of interest has a substitution effect that should encourage the saver to take greater risks. The income effect could make the person want more security and this would mean a reduction in risk. In Fig. 10.5 we have assumed that the substitution effect dominates.

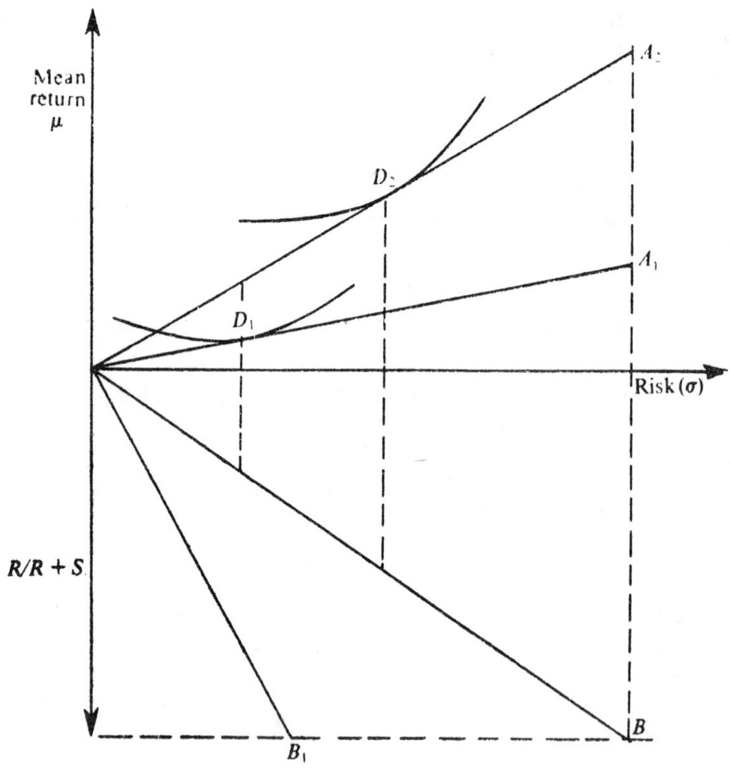

Fig. 10.5

It is straightforward within this context to analyze the effect of an interest tax. Suppose there is a proportional tax on all capital income with full loss offsets. Hence, the same proportion of the risky asset in the saver's portfolio now carries less risk. Thus the relation between $R/R + S$ and σ in Fig. 10.5 shifts from OB to OB_1. With full loss offset, however, the investment opportunity locus remains unchanged and the saver would, hence, want the same (μ, σ) combination. But to attain this now he has to increase the proportion of R in his portfolio. With no loss offset or less than complete loss offset the investment opportunity locus itself would shift closer to the σ axis in the upper closer to the σ axis in the upper half of Fig. 10.5. This is because with incomplete loss offset the government lowers the yield without sharing the risk. With full loss offset the government shares the risk and if there is an equal chance of there being a loss or a profit the net yield from R is unaltered.

One can repeat this analysis for the case of risk lovers and risk averters' But this is left as an exercise for the reader. It is important to note that in these cases the chance of getting corner solutions (zero S or zero R) is much higher.

The Portfolio Allocation Model

In the portfolio allocation model we allow the safe asset to carry a fixed rate of return say r percent. The individual invests $R/R + S(= \alpha)$ fraction of his wealth in the risky asset. Now the individual has wealth W_0 to invest and wants to maximize the expected utility from wealth in the terminal period (assumed to be period 2). We denote by k the (uncertain) return per rupee invested in the risky asset. Let $F(k)$ denote the cumulative probability distribution of k with $k > -1$. Hence the individuals expected utility is

$$E(U(W)) = \int U\{W_0[(1 + \alpha k) + (1 - \alpha)r]\} \, dF.$$

$W_0(1 + \alpha k)$ is the return from the risky asset whereas $W_0(1 - \alpha)r$ is the return from the safe asset. We will assume $U' > 0$, $U'' < 0$. The saver choses $\alpha(0 \leqslant \alpha \leqslant 1)$ to maximize his expected utility. The first order conditions are

$$\frac{\partial}{\partial \alpha} E(U(W)) = 0 \qquad \rightarrow$$

$$E[U'(k - r)] = 0 \qquad \alpha > 0$$

or $$E[U'(k - r)] < 0 \quad \text{and} \quad \alpha = 0.$$

Thus a corner solution occurs when the expected return from the risky asset is less than the return from the safe asset. Otherwise for an interior solution these two returns are equated. It is straightforward to check that if $U'' < 0$ (the individual is risk averse) the second order conditions are satisfied.

The Effects of Taxation

We study here the effects (*i*) a lump sum tax, (*ii*) a proportional tax on wealth, and (*iii*) a proportional tax on income from wealth.

With a lump sum tax the effect on the composition of the portfolio depends on the wealth elasticity of demand for the asset R. If the wealth elasticity of demand for R equals unity then the same portfolio composition holds for all levels of wealth. If this elasticity is less than one then there is a less than proportionate decline in the demand for the risky asset. If the elasticity is zero then there would be no decline in the demand for R.

Now suppose that there is a proportional wealth tax t_w and a proportional income tax, t_y. What the government does with tax is of no immediate concern to us. In any case this analysis would be valid if the revenue was used to finance government expenditure which enters the individuals' utility in an additive separable manner so that the first order conditions for maximization of expected utility with respect to α, remain unchanged. With these two taxes terminal wealth becomes

$$W = (1 - t_w)\{1 + [r + \alpha(k - r)](1 - t_y)\}W_0.$$

So that the first order condition for maximizing $E(u(W))$ with respect to α become

$$(1 - t_w)(1 - t_y)E[U'(k - r)] = 0$$

for an internal solution and

$$(1 - t_w)(1 - t_y)E[U'(k - r)] < 0$$

for a corner solution. Now since $(1 - t_w)$ and $(1 - t_y)$ are positive it follows that the first order conditions are the same as before. However, this does not mean that the taxes do not affect the individual's optimal plan. The taxes determine W and hence the level of expected utility but not the choice at the margin. Hence whether risk taking is increased or not depends solely on the value of the wealth elasticity of demand of the risky asset R. We know that, by assumption, how the government spends this tax revenue does not affect the individuals' optimum condition, hence this result is fairly robust.

Notice another facet of this interpretation; t_w acts in the W equation to reduce terminal wealth. Hence the wealth elasticity of demand is enough to determine the effect of t_w on portfolio composition t_y however, enters the W equation in a more complicated manner. Let us analyze its effect.

To do this we need two intermediate results. First we must show that the wealth elasticity of demand of the risky asset is positive or negative as $E(u''(k - r))$ is positive or negative. The second is that $E(-u''(k - r))$ is positive. Taking the second proposition first. This follows immediately if $u'' < 0$ and at least one k is not equal to r. Assume that this is the case. Take the first result now. Differentiate with respect to W_0 the first order condition assuming the demand for R to be given by $R = \alpha W_0$.

$$E\left[u''(k - r)\left\{[1 + r(1 - t_y)] + (1 - t_y)(k - r)\frac{\partial R}{\partial W_0}\right\}\right] = 0$$

where we have set $t_w = 0$ and, since it is positive, removed the term $1 - t_y$. Thus we get

$$\frac{W_0}{R}\frac{\partial R}{\partial W_0} = \frac{E[u''(k - r)]}{E[-u''(k - r)^2]}\,\frac{[1 + r(1 - t_y)]}{\alpha(1 - t_r)}.$$

Since, by the first result, the denominator is strictly positive it follows that wealth elasticity of demand has the sign of $E(u''(k - r)]$.

We can now proceed with our analysis of the effect of t_y. Differentiating the first order condition with respect to t_y we get

$$E\left(u''(k - r)\left\{(k - r)(1 - t_y)\frac{\partial\alpha}{\partial t_y} - [\alpha(k - r) + r]\right\}\right) = 0.$$

The literature has spoken of a private as well as a public risk. See, for instance, Domar and Musgrave (1944). If the saver invests α proportion of his wealth in the risky asset he bears only $(1 - t_y)\alpha$ proportion of the risk. The rest of the risk social risk is borne by the government since the realization or otherwise of the gains from R affect, among other things, tax receipts. Now

$$\left[(1 - t_y)\frac{\partial}{\partial t_y} - \alpha\right] = \frac{-rE(u''(k - r)]}{E(-u''(k - r)^2)}.$$

The left hand side is simply the derivative of private risk with respect to t_y. Thus private risk taking decreases (increases) if the wealth elasticity of demand for the risky asset is positive (negative). Let us take social risk taking now. Differentiate it with respect to t_y to get

$$\frac{(1 - t_y)}{\alpha}\frac{\partial\alpha}{\partial t_y} = \frac{1 - \text{rate} - rE[u''(k - r)]}{\alpha E[-u''(k-r^2)]}$$

$$= 1 - \left(\frac{W_0}{R}\frac{\partial R}{\partial W_0}\right)\frac{r(1 - t_y)}{1 + r(1 - t_y)}.$$

Thus for a critical value of the terms on the right hand side

$$\left(1 = \frac{W_0}{R}\frac{\partial R}{\partial W_0}\frac{r(1 - t_y)}{1 + r(1 - t_y)}\right)$$

there is no effect on social risk taking.

We know $0 < \frac{r(1 - t_y)}{1 + r(1 - t_y)} < 1$. Hence we can say that the higher is wealth elasticity of demand for R the higher is the chance that social risk taking will be reduced and vice versa. These results hold with $r > 0$. With $r = 0$ the derivative of the first order condition with respect to t_y simplifies considerably but the analysis, necessarily, has limited applicability.

A Comparison of Income and Wealth Taxes

We have analyzed separately the effects of the wealth and income taxes. We now address the question of the relative effects of the two taxes. There is first the problem of basis of comparison. We can adopt here, the following basis for comparison. We compare those taxes that involve the same reduction in utility. We know that with the wealth tax the effect on the allocation of portfolio depends upon the wealth elasticity of demand for R. We have also analyzed the effect of an income tax on portfolio allocation. What can we say about, the relative effects of the two taxes? With an income tax the government becomes a party to the flow return from the risky asset as the terms affect government revenue. In the case of the wealth tax no such commitment exists. Hence although private risk taking is the same in both cases (remember the allocative effects of the income effect also depend on the wealth elasticity of demand for R) social risk taking is higher with the income tax and hence total risk is higher.

For an equal reduction in utility which tax nets higher revenue? The revenue from the wealth tax is simply equal to t_w multiplied by the final wealth. The value of the final wealth depends upon the wealth elasticity of demand for R. An income tax that reduces the utility to the same extent also reduces the individuals' risk (by the amount of the social risk) and hence fetches higher revenue.

Special Cases of the Analysis

In keeping with our analysis of "the liquidity preference as behaviour towards risk" model we now ask what the portfolio allocation predicts when less than complete offseting of loss is allowed. To see this let us take the extreme case where zero loss offset is allowed. Let us suppose that in the terminal period return from R is zero. We now have an imposition of an income tax without loss offset. The no less offset clause alters the terms of trade between R and S and the substitution effect would increase the proportion of R. The wealth effect however works in the opposite direction so that the net result is qualitatively ambiguous. Similar conclusion can be had for partial offset of loss.

Similar conclusions obtain for the case where capital gains are either completely or partially exempted from taxation. It is often argued, even here, that exemption of capital gains from taxation encourages risk taking. In a weaker form the argument is that a reduction in capital gains taxes would encourage risk taking. We might do well to remember that not all increase in risk taking is an unqualified good. Leaving aside this normative argument we realize that the claim is not necessarily true. Let us take the case most favourable to the argument above. We suppose that capital gains are completely exempt from tax and that only the certain income from the safe asset is taxed. Does this mean that risk taking rises? This stipulation means that terminal wealth is now given by

$$W = W_0[1 + \alpha k + (1 - \alpha)r(1 - t_y)].$$

The substitution effect of the tax would encourage risk taking. But the wealth effect works in the opposite direction. Thus if the wealth elasticity of demand for R is greater than zero the wealth effect would reduce the demand for R. Thus the net effect is ambiguous. Thus whether exemption of capital gains from taxation leads to an increase in risk taking depends on the form of the demand function for R.

Conclusions

In this chapter we have investigated some of the effects that taxes have on savings. We chose particularly simple models to address these questions to. Some of the results obtained here extend to the multiperiod multiasset case; several don't, Atkincon and Stiglitz (1980) discuss some of these extensions.

Many people would argue that in a country like India savings are largely contractually determined. The importance of fiscal policy is the effect it has on investment. In the next chapter we study this issue in detail.

11. Taxation and Investment

Just as not all increases in risk taking are socially desirable a higher rate of investment is not necessarily "better" than a lower rate. Every society has to solve the vexed economic (and political) problem of determining its optimal rate of investment.

In this chapter we are not concerned with this normative question although we shall touch upon these issues in later chapters. We are interested here primarily in describing how investment is determined and assessing the impact that different kinds of taxes have on the rate of investment.

In doing so we have to make a number of assumptions. Certain assumptions are specific to the particular model being studied and they are best listed there. The more general assumptions are enumerated here. Throughout we work within a partial equilibrium framework. We assume that firms are perfectly competitive and, therefore, that when studying the problem of investment in this industry we will find it sufficient to analyze the investment decisions of a "representative" firm. Moreover we will by and large, concentrate on a world with certainty. Again we will study a world with zero inflation. Inflation has profound impacts on the incentive to invest and this issue has been the subject of lengthy and involved debates. We will consider the issue at a later stage in this volume. We make the standard neoclassical assumptions about a frictionless world. Armed even with this kit of assumptions, the going is tough.

Alternative Views on the Determinants of Investment

What determines the rate of investment? A coherent modern answer to this question goes back to the *General Theory* of J.M. Keynes. It is worth doing so even here because textbook (and scholarly) articulations of the Keynesian theory of investment often misinterpret him. To Keynes the fundamental determinant of investment is, what he calls, the marginal efficiency of capital, MEC. The marginal efficiency of capital is that rate of discount which when applied to the stream of returns from an investment makes the present value just equal to the present value of the costs. Keynes then argues that the MEC is a declining function of the rate of investment. Moreover, optimizing the rate of investment calls for equating the MEC with the rate of interest. Hence the rate of investment is a declining function of the rate of interest.[1] Keynes explained this relationship in terms of a rising supply curve of capital goods. As the rate of investment rises the price of capital goods rises since the capital goods industry has an upward sloping supply schedule. Hence cost of investment rises. But given the nominal stream of returns from the investment the MEC must be lower to equate the present value of returns to the present value of costs. Since the MEC is set equal to the rate of interest the rate of investment is a declining function of the rate of interest.

This, by way of an opening remark, helps keep a potential source of confusion at bay. We will do well to remember this when we start thinking of the channels of effects of taxes on investment.

Broadly speaking there are two different theories of investment behaviour. One is the market valuation approach pioneered by Tobin and the other is the structural adjustment approach of Jorgenson and others. These approaches are basically the same and differ only in emphasis. When analyzing the effects of a tax, therefore, it will be safe and prudent to take an eclectic view.

The structural adjustment approach (SA) or the standard neoclassical approach adopted by Jorgenson and others is very briefly the following. The demand for capital is determined via an aggregate production function.[2] The production function itself is taken to be of the Cobb Douglas variety. At any point in time given the production function (and hence output) and relative prices there is a desired capital stock or capital demand K_t^*. If the current capital stock (K_t) is less than K_t^* then investment takes place. Since there are delivery lags and other rigidities in the system the gap ($K_t^* - K_t$) cannot be filled in one time period. Current investment is a flow—a partial adjustment to this gap. As K_t^* varies from period to period investment never tapers down to zero. An estimable investment function would then express current investment depending on a distributed lag of past capital stocks.[3] Thus the flow of current investment is purely a response to a quantity signal the magnitude of which depends on the gap between desired and actual capital stocks. The reader should notice that the partial adjustment to the gap that Jorgenson talks of is essentially an arbitrary process. However, a substantial empirical and theoretical literature has developed around Jorgenson result.

Tobin's approach to investment is different. He proceeds not from considerations of an optimal capital stock but from considerations of the market

[1]Recall that in standard textbook exposition the MEC is a declining function of the rate of investment because the marginal product of capital falls with addition to the capital stock; while the marginal product of capital does fall with additions to the capital stock current investment is too miniscule a fraction of the capital stock for this reason to serve as an adequate explanation for the aforementioned relation.

[2]The analysis of this chapter could be described as one of partial equilibrium or an aggregative/macro one.

[3]The basic structure of the Jorgenson model is expounded in the Appendix I to this chapter.

valuation of new capital goods. For Tobin the crucial variable determining investment is q. q is defined as the ratio of the market's valuation of new capital goods to their replacement costs. If $q > 1$ firms will obviously find it profitable to invest. Now, investment is available only along an upward sloping supply schedule so that optimal investment is given by equating the marginal cost of new capacity to q. Investment is an increasing function of q. This approach also has some arbitrariness because an upward sloping schedule for additions to capacity is quite as arbitrary as the fixed structure of delivery lags posited in Jorgenson's approach. Tobin's approach does not explicitly introduce an aggregate production function on other constructs used by Jorgenson, but clearly they are all there in the background.

We have two purposes in this chapter. First we want to study the equivalence between the two approaches, Secondly we want to use the "model of equivalence" to address certain important questions of tax policy. In particular we want to see what kinds of taxes could, potentially, stimulate investment.

A Unified Approach to Investment Theory

Investment is a complex phenomenon. So complex indeed that Keynes often preferred to treat it simply as an exogenous variable. The difficulties are both at the level of predicting the future and that of adjusting to new capital.[4] The firm must predict the future stream of costs and returns associated with an investment. Investment thus invariably involves prediction of future events—or at least intelligent guesses about them. What we assume about the telescopic faculty of the entrepreneur has an important bearing on the type of investment function we end up with. Usually the assumption of long run perfect foresight has been made but recently there have been some attempts to introduce rational expectations into the picture.[5] We will confine ourselves to the case of long run perfect foresight and thus avoid dealing with the problems thrown up by uncertainty.

Moreover, even within the relatively simple framework that we are working in here the nature of investment matters for the results we get. Thus we could have investment with zero or positive installation costs. Investment could involve adjustment within the firm and it matters whether these costs of adjustment are convex or concave, separable or non-separable from cost of output.[6] It matters whether investment is of the putty-putty, putty-clay or clay-clay type.[7] In this chapter we will concentrate exclusively on investment of the putty-putty type. Various assumption about the costs can be accommodated within this framework.

[4]For excellent reviews see Hellivel (1976) or Abel (1978).

[5]See for instance Merton (1978), Lucas (1976) and Harris and Townsend (1978).

[6]See Soderstrom (1976) or Rothschild (1976) for instance.

[7]Putty-putty means capital/labour ratio can be changed before and after investment. Putty clay means the capital/labour ratio is alterable before investment but not after it. Clay-clay means capital/labour ratio is alterable before or after investment.

Our first task is to show that the q approach and the SA approach are essentially equivalent. To this we now turn.

To avoid unnecessary detail we concentrate on the simplest version of the story. We study the investment decision of the representative firm. Output at time i is given by a Cobb Douglas production function:

$$Q_i = AL_i^{\alpha}K_i^{1-\alpha} \tag{1}$$

where Q_i output, L_i and K_i are labour and capital inputs respectively and $0 < \alpha < 1$. A is a term denoting technical progress.

The firm is contemplating its investment plans today (time t) and takes as given and predetermined[8] the time path of output Q_i for $i > t$. The real wage rate is fixed at W_0 for all time. Assuming competition in the labour market this means that the marginal product of labour is predetermined. The firm discounts the future at a fixed rate of r per time period. We consider a continuous time version of the story and for simplicity keep depreciation at zero so that there is no distinction between gross and net investment. We also assume that there are no taxes.

When a firm invests the marginal unit of investment makes a contribution toward the reducing the wage bill. For constant output, Q_i, this saving in the wage bill can be obtained directly from equation (1). Totally differentiate equation (1) and set $dQ_i = 0$ to get

$$dQ_i = \alpha L_i^{\alpha-1}\, dL + (1 - \alpha)^{(1-\alpha-1)} K_i\, dK_i = 0 \tag{2}$$

since $\quad dA = 0.$

From equation (2) the saving in the wage bill is $-W_0\dfrac{dL_i}{dK_i}\Big|_{Q_i}$ constant which is equal to

$$W_0\left(\frac{1-\alpha}{\alpha}\right)\left(\frac{Q_i}{AK_i}\right)^{1/\alpha}$$

since

$$\frac{\partial Q_i}{\partial L_i} = \alpha\frac{Q_i}{L_i} = \alpha L_i^{\alpha-1}$$

and

$$\frac{\partial Q_i}{\partial K_i} = (1-\alpha)K_i^{(1-\alpha-1)} = (1-\alpha)\frac{Q_i}{K_i}.$$

We are at time period t and this saving in the wage bill has just begun at t. Given the assumption of zero depreciation the discounted value of this stream of returns is given by

$$Z_t = \int_t^{\infty} \frac{1-\alpha}{\alpha} W_0\left(\frac{Q_i}{AK_i}\right)^{1/\alpha} e^{-r(i-t)} d_i. \tag{3}$$

[8]This is the essence of the assumption of long run perfect foresight in this case.

This is the market value of a unit of installed capital. We use output as numeraire so that the replacement cost of this unit of the capital good. Hence Z_t is also Tobin's q_t.

Realize that even with this simple articulation we still have to predict the path of output and that of the capital stock. To keep things simple we assume that the firm expects its output to grow at the constant exponential rate g and it neglects its own investment in the future.

Hence $$Q_i = AL_t^{\alpha} K_t^{1-\alpha} e^{g(i-t)}$$

for $$i > t \quad \text{and} \quad K_i = K_t.$$

Making these substitutions in (3) we get

$$Z_t = q_t = \frac{1-\alpha}{\alpha} W_0 \frac{L_t}{K_t} \frac{1}{r - g/\alpha}. \tag{4}$$

We can easily see that the S.A. approach of Jorgenson gives us the same result.

To do this we suppose along with Jorgenson that the supply of capital services is proportional to the existing stock of installed capital. Hence the stock of capital and the supply of capital services are both fixed at any point in time. How about the demand for capital? If the rental rate on capital is C_t at time t then profit maximizing firms will find it optimal to equate the marginal gain from an additional unit of investment (this under our assumptions, is equal to the reduction in wage cost occasioned by the installation of this unit) to the marginal cost. Thus in equilibrium

$$C_t = \frac{1-\alpha}{\alpha}\left(\frac{Q_t}{AK_t}\right)^{1/\alpha} W_0. \tag{5}$$

Now in equation (3) all we have done is to sum up the discounted value of C_i $(i = t, \ldots \infty)$.

Hence the two approaches give identical results. We can see this equivalence in another way. In Tobin's model if $q_t > 1$ there is positive investment. At time t, $g = 0$ and hence

$$q_t = \frac{1-\alpha}{\alpha} \frac{W_0 L_t}{rK_t}.$$

Thus $q_t > 1$ implies

$$\frac{1-\alpha}{\alpha} \frac{W_0 L_t}{r} > K_t.$$

With this condition satisfied there is positive investment in Tobin's model. With the S.A. approach we get identical results. The desired level of capital is that which satisfies equation (5). Solving for K_t^* we get

$$K_t^* = \frac{(1-\alpha)Q}{C} \tag{6}$$

where C is the long run value of C_t. In the long run $C = rp$ where p is the long run price[9] of capital goods. Here $p = 1$, hence $c = r$. Substituting in (6) we get

$$K_t^* = \frac{(1-\alpha)Q}{r} = \frac{1-\alpha}{\alpha}\frac{WL}{r}$$

and there will be investment so long as $K_t < K_t^*$. This is the same criterion as derived by Tobin.

It is possible to show the equivalence between Tobin's method and that of Jorgenson in more complicated models e.g. those that involve depreciation, installation costs etc. but the basic point has been made. Tobin and Jorgenson are emphasizing different aspects of the decision to invest but are arriving at identical conclusions. For analysis of the effects of a tax, therefore, it would not matter which version we chose.

Fiscal Policy and the Rate of Investment

Assuming that it is desirable to do so, what are the fiscal measures available to the government to encourage investment? We obviously rule out here direct investment by the public sector itself and confine ourselves to the case where incentives are to be given to competitive, profit maximizing firms to improve the rate of investment. In a sense this issue has a certain empirical validity. A recent study[11] has lamented the fact that the private corporate sector's share of investment has remained virtually constant. In US the policy issue of stimulating private investment was one of the central economic questions in the 1980 and 1984 presidential elections. Similar stories could be told from the experience of other countries.

When one talks of incentives to stimulate private investment two issues assume critical importance. The first is that when we talk about stimulating private investment we are talking about making it more profitable for the private sector firms to invest. Thus a tax policy would make it more profitable to invest in plant, machinery and the like rather than hold speculative capital or inventories etc. The second important point is that a decision to invest is a commitment that spans time i.e. the costs and benefits of the investment are going to last for more than one time period. By its very nature investment is a dynamic activity not an atemporal one.

The literature has spoken of various measures to stimulate private investment. We briefly outline a subset below and then analyze the effects of some of them in the context of a specific intertemporal optimization problem for a firm.

One of the most widely practised measures is a depreciation allowance i.e. the firms are allowed to write off a certain percentage of the value of

[9]See the appendix to this chapter for details.

[10]Inflation particularly unanticipated inflation can disturb this equivalence. See Feldstein, Green and Shesinski (1978).

[11]See Gupta and Gupta (1985).

their capital assets for tax purposes. When confronted with a heterogenous capital stock one is never sure whether a common rate of depreciation allowance for all types of capital equipment is good policy. On the other hand it is clearly impractical to have several different rates of depreciation allowance. Yet another difficulty is that although this measure is geared towards physical depreciation economic depreciation—or obsolescence as it is more usually called—is extremely important as well. New technology makes machines obsolete even if they have not physically depreciated. It is clearly infeasible to compensate for the effects of economic obsolescence with the help only of a tax rebate based an physical depreciation.

In many instances corporate profits that are ploughed back as investment are taxed at a different (lower) rate than corporate profits in general. A related measure is a tax holiday. Under the arrangements announced in the 1984-85 union budget, for instance, twenty-five percent of profits from new industrial undertakings and ships are eligible for a deduction from taxable income for a period of eight years.[12]

Whereas these measures adjust the tax liability of either the firm as a corporate entity or the shareholders as individual tax payers, an investment tax credit is immediately paid back to the firm.

Thus when we talk of a fiscal stimulus to promote investment we talk of an increase in the investment tax credit, or an increase in depreciation allowance or a cut in the corporate profit tax rate etc. We should realize that any of these (and other) measures could be permanent or temporary. The temporal character of these stimuli has a profound impact on the incentive to invest.

We now study some of these propositions in somewhat greater detail and more formally.

A Neoclassical Approach to the Incentive to Invest

In this section we build up a relatively straightforward model of investment decision by a firm. Within this context we explore the incentive effects of some of the measures discussed above. This effort is merely for exposition and no claim to originality is made. The analysis involves some results from the theory of optimal control. This is a fairly difficult proposition—mathematically—and an exposition of this theory is provided in a mathematical appendix.

Apart from the assumptions we have already made so far we will also assume that our perfectly competitive firm is a price taker i.e. it faces a horizontal demand schedule.[13] The firm attempts to maximize the present

[12]There are some coveats though. The rebate is available to undertakings not engaged in the production of any one or more non-priority articles listed in the Eleventh Schedule of the Income Tax Act. There are other caveats as well.

[13]The results derived here can be shown to be for the fixed output flexible price case as well. This is left as an exercise for the leader. Indeed Abel shows that these conclusions are broadly true of models in which both price and quantity vary.

value of its cash flow defined over an infinite horizon. The firm's production function is Cobb Douglas $Q = L^{\alpha}K^{1-\alpha}$ where Q is output. If P is the price of output revenue is $PL^{\alpha}K^{1-\alpha}$. The wage rate of labour is W_0 and the corporate (proportional) profit tax rate is t_{π}. Hence before we take capital into account the first element of the cash flow is

$$(PL^{\alpha}K^{1-\alpha} - W_0L)(l - t_{\pi}).$$

Now let us take up capital costs. Capital equipment once bought are visualized to have two types of installation costs. One is an external cost i.e. alien to the firm's operation. The second is an internal cost and we assume that the higher the volume of investment the greater is this internal cost of adjustment. We thus visualize the existence of a function $C(I)$ that describes the total cost of purchasing and internal adjustment cost of level of investment. We suppose that $C'(I) > 0$ and $C''(I) > 0$ with the stipulation that $C(0) = 0$ we can think of the $C(I)$ function as describing a cash outflow associated with rate of investment I.

Before tax and tax related credits, $C(I)$ describes capital expenditures. We now bring in the tax related adjustments. Let us suppose that a fraction α' of $C(I)$ is paid back to the firm as investment tax credit.[14] Suppose now that for one unit of capital of age n the government allows $D(n)$ as depreciation allowance. The firm is visualized as having capital of different ages and they fetch depreciation allowance as per the form of the function $D(n)$. The present value of such deduction is

$$x = \int_0^{\infty} D(n)e^{-rn}\, dx.$$

Hence the total cash inflow due to depreciation is $xt_{\pi}C(I)$. Hence there is a net outflow because of capital cost which is equal to total investment cost less investment tax credit and depreciation allowance i.e. the net cash outflow for the firm is $(1 - \alpha' - t_{\pi}x)C(I)$.

Hence the firm's optimal programme can be written as[15]

$$\max_{I,\, L} \cdot V = \int_0^{\infty} \{(PL^{\alpha}K^{1-\alpha} - W_0L)(1 - t_{\pi}) - (1 - \alpha' - t_{\pi}x)C(I)\}e^{-rt}\, dt \tag{7}$$

subject to $\dot{K} = I - \delta K$ (8)

where r is the after tax rate of discount, and δ is the fixed exponential rate of decay of capital. The Hamiltonian for this probem is

$$H = (PL^{\alpha}K^{1-\alpha} - W_0L)(1 - t_{\pi}) - (1 - \alpha' - t_{\pi}x)C(I)\} + \theta(I - K) \tag{9}$$

[14]It is an easy step to alter this to accommodate the "tax holiday" we spoke of in the text. In that case there is a commensurate decrease in t_{π} rather than a writing off of some of the capital related expenses.

[15]For convenience we are omitting time subscripts.

where θ is the costate variable for this problem. The first order conditions for an internal maximum and their interpretations are jotted below. The first order condition is

$$\frac{\delta H}{\partial I} = -(1 - \alpha' - t_\pi x)C'(I) + \theta = 0. \tag{9'}$$

This means

$$C'(I) = \frac{\theta}{(1 - \alpha' - t_\pi x)}\cdot \tag{10}$$

The right hand side of equation (10) is Tobin's q — the ratio of the shadow price of installed capital to the tax adjusted cost of replacement. Hence marginal cost of investment is equated in the optimum to q. Furthermore since $C''(I) > 0$ it follows that investment is an increasing function of q.

We then proceed to get

$$\frac{\partial H}{\partial L} = (\alpha P L^{\alpha-1} K^{1-\alpha} - W_0)(1 - t_\pi) = 0.$$

Hence since $t_\pi \neq 0$, we have

$$\frac{L}{K} = \left(\frac{W_0}{\alpha P}\right)^{1/\alpha-1}. \tag{11}$$

This gives us a relation between L and K along the optimal path. Notice that all terms on the right hand side of equation (11) are exogenously determined.

The canonical equation for θ is

$$\begin{aligned} \dot{\theta} &= r\theta - \frac{\partial H}{\partial K} \\ &= r\theta - \{(PL^\alpha(1 - \alpha)K^{-\alpha})(1 - t_\pi) - \theta\delta\} \\ &= (r + \delta)\theta - (1 - t_\pi)(1 - \alpha)P(W_0/\alpha P)^{\alpha/\alpha-1}. \end{aligned} \tag{12}$$

(using (11)).

This equation expresses the equality of the realized and required return from capital. The required return is $(r + \delta)\theta$ whereas the realized return is capital gain (i.e. $\dot{\theta}$)plus the after tax value of marginal product of capital (i.e. $(1 - t_\pi)(1 - \alpha)P(W_0/\alpha P)^{\alpha/\alpha-1}$.

The canonical equation is one of two basic equations governing the dynamics of the system. The second is the optimized value of investment i.e.

$$\dot{K} = I - \delta K = C'^{-1}\left(\frac{\theta}{1 - \alpha' - t_\pi x}\right) - \delta K \tag{13}$$

from (6).

In steady state both $\dot{\theta}$ and $\dot{K}$ are zero. From (12) we have (for $\dot{\theta} = 0$) that in steady state θ is independent of K

$$\theta = \frac{(1 - t_\pi)(1 - \alpha)P(W_0/\alpha P)^{\alpha/\alpha-1}}{r + \delta}. \tag{14}$$

From equation (13) however we get for $\dot{K} = 0$

$$K = \frac{C'^{-1}}{\delta}\left(\frac{\theta}{1 - \alpha' - t_{\pi}x}\right). \tag{15}$$

Under our assumptions in steady state K depends positively on θ.

We obtain behaviour in the neighbourhood of steady state (θ^*, K^*) by linearizing equations (12) and (13) around the steady state values θ^* and K^* respectively. We get

$$\begin{pmatrix} \dot{\theta} \\ \dot{K} \end{pmatrix} = \begin{pmatrix} r + \delta & 0 \\ \dfrac{1}{(1 - \alpha' + t_{\pi}x)C''} & -\delta \end{pmatrix} \begin{pmatrix} \theta - \theta^* \\ K - K^* \end{pmatrix}. \tag{16}$$

The matrix on the right hand side of equation (16) has one positive root and one negative root so that the steady state is a saddle path equilibrium. In Fig. 11.1 below the saddle path is along the $\dot{\theta} = 0$ locus.

Optimal policy hence calls for an immediate jump to the $\dot{\theta} = 0$ schedule. We then proceed to steady state. Now since θ is constant, the rate of investment is constant (at its steady state level) and hence is a proportion of the existing capital stock.[16]

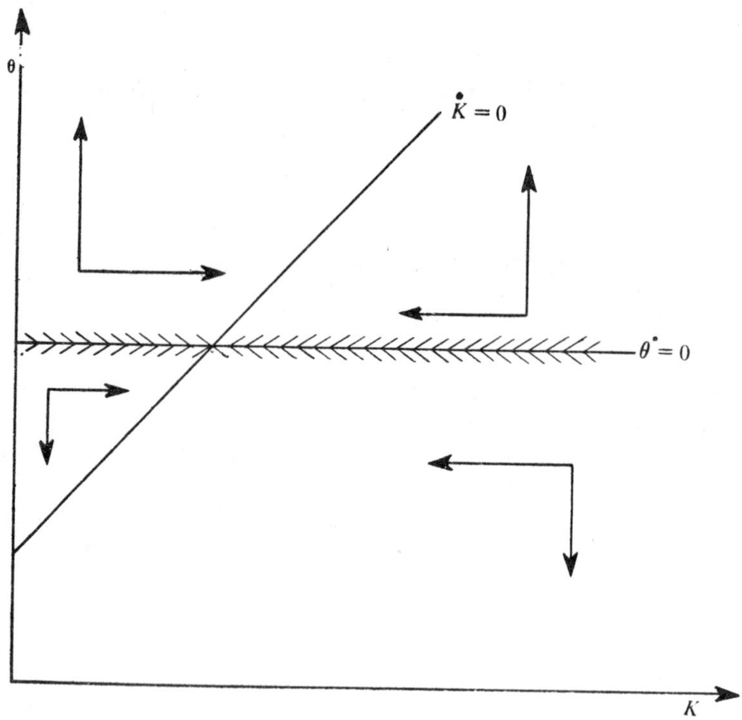

Fig. 11.1

[16]Recall that this stipulation is important to the Jorgenson version of investment behaviour.

Policy analysis must take place at and in the neighbourhood of steady state.[17] We conceive of the effects of policy in the following. Our two dynamic equations contain all the fiscal instruments in the governments kit. We analyze the effect of a change in any of these instruments on the steady state of the model. A policy that calls for a higher K^* is more stimulative of investment, ceteris paribus, than a policy that calls for a lower steady state value of the capital stock.

We still have one difficulty to clear. How are we to ensure comparability of fiscal policies? How are we to compare a ten percent investment tax credit with a twenty percent upward revision of depreciation allowance? We compare fiscal policies that have the same effect on K^* for their effects on government revenue.

Permanent Policies[18]

We compare two fiscal measures here—one is a permanent cut in the corporate tax rate and the other is an increase in the investment tax credit. We choose a new value of t_π say t'_π and a new value of α' say α''. Each of these is chosen so that the increment in K^* in each case is identical. Thus the incentive effects of the two measures are identical. We then compare the drop in government revenue in the two cases.

We now compute changes in tax revenue in the two cases. With the investment tax credit government revenue T^{ITC} can be written as the government revenue before the credit less the amount paid out as tax credit. This can be written as

$$T^{\text{ITC}} = t_\pi \int_0^\infty (1-\alpha)P\left(\frac{W_0}{\alpha P}\right)^{\alpha/\alpha-1} K_t e^{-rt}\, dt$$

$$-(\alpha'' + t_\pi x)\int_0^\infty C(I^*)e^{-rt}\, dt. \tag{17}$$

The rate of investment tax credit is α''. We recall that $(1-\alpha)P\left(\frac{W_0}{\alpha P}\right)^{\alpha/\alpha-1}$ is the value of marginal product of capital. Thus the first term on the right hand side of equation (17) gives us corporate tax collections before tax credits. The second term gives the refund paid to corporations.

Similarly we can define government revenue with a drop in the corporate tax rate as corporate tax collections with the new corporate tax rate less the investment tax credit paid out under the *old* tax credit rules. Thus government revenue with a cut in the corporate tax rate can be written as T^π where

$$T^\pi = t'_\pi \int_0^\infty (1-\alpha)P\left(\frac{W_0}{\alpha P}\right)^{\alpha/\alpha-1} K_t e^{-rt}\, dt$$

$$-(\alpha' + t'_\pi x)\int_0^\infty C(I^*)e^{-rt}\, dt. \tag{18}$$

[17]If we eschew this stipulation the problems get mathematically onerous see Chapter 13.
[18]Readers should realize that the case of a tax holidday can easily be accommodated.

Thus

$$T^{\text{ITC}} - T^{\pi} = (t_{\pi} - t'_{\pi}) \int_0^{\infty} (1 - \alpha)P\left(\frac{W_0}{\alpha P}\right)^{\alpha/\alpha-1} K_t e^{-rt}\, dt$$

$$-\{(\alpha'' + t_{\pi}x) - (\alpha' + t'_{\pi}x)\} \int_0^{\infty} C(I^*)e^{-rt}\, dt. \tag{19}$$

It is easy to check[19] that

$$(\alpha'' + t_{\pi}x) - (\alpha' + t'_{\pi}x) = \frac{t_{\pi} - t'_{\pi}}{1 - t_{\pi}}(1 - (\alpha'' + t_{\pi}x)). \tag{20}$$

Substituting (20) into (19) we get

$$T^{\text{ITC}} - T^{\pi} = \frac{t_{\pi} - t'_{\pi}}{1 - t_{\pi}}\left\{\int_0^{\infty} (1 - t_{\pi})(1 - \alpha)P\left(\frac{W_0}{\alpha P}\right)^{\alpha/\alpha-1} K_t\, e^{-rt}\, dt\right.$$

$$\left. -(1 - (\alpha'' + t_{\pi}x)) \int_0^{\infty} C(I^*)e^{-rt}\, dt\right\}. \tag{21}$$

Notice that the expression inside curly brackets ({ }) is nothing but the maximized present value of cash flow to the firm under investment tax credit (we call it V^{ITC})

$$T^{\text{ITC}} - T^{\pi} = \frac{t_{\pi} - t'_{\pi}}{1 - t_{\pi}} V^{\text{ITC}}.$$

Since $V^{\text{ITC}} > 0$ and $t_{\pi} > t'_{\pi}$ and $1 - t_{\pi} > 0$ it follows that

$$T^{\text{ITC}} - T^{\pi} > 0.$$

The government loses more revenue with a corporate tax cut than with an equivalent investment tax credit. Thus a permanent investment tax credit is unambiguously superior to a permanent cut in the rate of corporate profit taxation.

The results are some whatless clear with only a temporary policy. It can be shown that if we are relatively close to K^* then a temporary investment tax credit is less costly (again in terms of foregone government revenue) than a temporary reduction in the rate of corporate tax. This is the same result as the case considered above. However, these results do not carry over (in the case of temporary fiscal changes) generally. Hence the results are less clear in the case of temporary policy changes.

Conclusions

In this chapter we have studied some of the fiscal channels through which the incentive to invest may be affected. A permanent fiscal policy has un-

[19]To see this obtain a value for K^* from the optimization problem. This is Equation (15). Realize from it that equivalent policies are such that

$$\frac{1 - t_{\pi}}{1 - (\alpha'' + t_{\pi}x)} = \frac{1 - t'_{\pi}}{1 - (\alpha' + t'_{\pi}x)}.$$

Rearrange this to get equation (20).

ambiguous results whereas the results of a temporary policy are uncertain.

Throughout this chapter we have made the simplifying assumption of perfect foresight. Changing this assumption would really change the character of the analysis as the work of Jordan (1977) and others suggest.

Another important characteristic of the analysis of this chapter has been that we have dealt exclusively with real variables. Inflation or monetary variables have had no say in the story told so far. Stated differently, we have been assuming that any inflation that may be occurring has been fully anticipated and, therefore, that it is sufficient to concentrate exclusively on real variables. Recently, however, there has been a burgeoning of the literature which suggests that inflation has been profoundly affecting the incentive to invest. We will survey some of this literature in a later chapter.

The investment model that has been studied in this chapter is very special and valid only under the assumptions listed. The reader is encouraged to read the more recent literature that has tended to expand the horizons of the analysis presented here.

Appendix I

The Jorgenson Model of Investment

We first briefly sketch Jorgenson's model of investment behaviour.

We consider the decision problem for an investing firm which is identical to the firm whose behaviour was discussed in Chapter XI. We define the cash flow (without taxation) of a firm at time t as

$$R(t) = pQ(t) - W_0L(t) - Z'(t)I(t)$$

where p is the fixed price of output and $Z'(t)$ is the price of the investment good. The firm wishes to maximize the discounted sum of $R(t)$ i.e. the firm wishes to maximize

$$Z = \int_0^\infty R(t)e^{-rt}\,dt \tag{A.11.1}$$

where r is the (exogenously determined) fixed rate of discount. The constraints on this optimization problem are as follows

Net investment is given by

$$\dot{K} = I - \delta K \tag{A.11.2}$$

and output is given by an implicit production function

$$F(Q, L, K) = 0. \tag{A.11.2'}$$

The Hamiltonian-Lagrange expression for this problem can be written as

$$H = e^{-rt}\{R(t) + \theta[I - \delta K]\} + \lambda F(Q, L, K) \tag{A.11.3}$$

where θ is a costate variable and λ is a Lagrange multiplier. The first order conditions for an internal maximum are

$$\frac{\partial H}{\partial Q} = e^{-rt}p + \lambda\frac{\partial F}{\partial Q} = 0 \tag{A.11.4}$$

$$\frac{\partial H}{\partial L} = e^{-rt}W_0 + \lambda\frac{\partial F}{\partial L} = 0 \tag{A.11.5}$$

$$\frac{\partial H}{\partial I} = e^{-rt}Z' + \theta = 0 \tag{A.11.6}$$

$$\frac{d}{dt}(e^{-rt}\theta) = -\frac{\partial H}{\partial K} = -\left\{e^{-rt}\left(\frac{p\partial Q}{\partial K} - \theta\delta\right) + \lambda\frac{\partial F}{\partial K}\right\} \tag{A11.7}$$

$$\frac{\partial H}{\partial \lambda} = 0. \tag{A.11.8}$$

Combining equations A.11.4 and A.11.5 we get

$$\frac{\partial Q}{\partial L} = \frac{W_0}{p}, \tag{A.11.9}$$

i.e. the marginal product of labour equals the real wage in optimum. From equation A.11.6 we get

$$\theta = -e^{-rt}Z'. \tag{A.11.10}$$

From equation A.11.7 we have

$$-re^{-rt}\dot{\theta} = -e^{-rt}p\frac{\partial Q}{\partial K} - e^{-rt}\theta\delta + \lambda\frac{\partial F}{\partial K}. \tag{A.11.11}$$

But we know from A.11.10 that

$$\dot{\theta} = re^{-rt}\dot{Z}'.$$

Using this and equations A.11.4 in A.11.11 we get

$$\frac{\partial Q}{\partial K} = \frac{Z'(r+\delta) - \dot{Z}'}{p} = \frac{C}{p} \tag{A.11.12}$$

where

$$C = Z'(r+\delta) - \dot{Z}'.$$

C is the implicit rental value of capital services supplied by the firm to itself. Jorgenson justifies this interpretation in the following manner. The flow of capital services over an interval of length dt beginning at time t from a unit of investment good acquired at time i is

$$e^{-\delta(t-i)}\,dt.$$

If $c(t)$ is the price of capital services at time t then the discounted price of capital services will be $e^{-rt}c(t)$ so that the value of the stream of capital services during dt is

$$e^{-rt}c(t)e^{-\delta(t-i)}\,dt.$$

Similarly if $Z'(i)$ is the price of capital goods at time i, then the discounted price is $e^{-ri}Z'(i)$ so that the value of a unit of investment goods acquired at time i is:

$$e^{-ri}Z'(i).$$

But the value of investment goods acquired at time i is equal to the integral of the discounted value of all future capital services derived from these investment goods

$$e^{-ri}Z'(i) = \int_i^\infty e^{-ri}c(t)e^{-\delta(t=i)}\,dt$$

$$= e^{\delta i}\int_i^\infty e^{-(r+\delta)t}c(t)\,dt.$$

Thus,

$$Z'(i) = e^{(r+\delta)i} \int_i^{\infty} e^{-(r+\delta)t} c(t)\, dt$$

$$= \int_i^{\infty} e^{-(r+\delta)(t-i)} c(t)\, dt.$$

Differentiating with respect to time we get

$$\dot{Z}'(i) = [r(i) + \delta]Z'(i) - c(i).$$

Hence $$c = Z'(r+) - \dot{Z}'$$

which is the expression derived above.

The expression $\frac{\partial Q}{\partial K} = c/p$ defines the optimal capital stock that is desired by the firm. Now, Jorgenson says that this optimal capital stock cannot be reached in one time period because of production and other lags. Hence, Jorgenson conceives of the idea of an investment function that depends on the distribution lag of past capital stocks.

Appendix II

Some Results in Optimal Control Theory

In this chapter we have encountered optimal control theory as a mathematical tool to solve for the firm's optimal investment programme. The theory of optimal control is an immensely large and important one and all we are interested in here is establishing some of the basic results that we need in this chapter and the chapters to follow. There are a number of excellent textbooks on the subject of optimal control and the interested reader is referred to Bryson and Ho (1973) or Arrow and Kurz (1968) for excellent exposition of the theory.

Suppose I have a set of n variables $x_1, \ldots, x_n$ describing the problem we are considering. $x_1, \ldots, x_n$ for instance might be the levels of consumption of the n persons in a society. We may also have n first order differential equations telling us how these variables move across time. Thus we may write

$$\dot{x}_1 = f_1(x_1, \ldots, x_n, u(t))$$
$$\vdots$$
$$\dot{x}_n = f_n(x_1, \ldots, x_n, u(t))$$

where $u(t)$ is a vector of variables which can be controlled to affect $x_1, \ldots,$ x_n. The vector $u(t)$ is to be chosen to maximize a performance function

$$\int_0^T \phi(x_1, \ldots, x_n; u(t))dt.$$

Thus $\phi(\ )$ might be some kind of aggregate measure of welfare. The variables $x_1, \ldots, x_n$ are called the state variables of the system whereas the variables $u(t)$ are called the control variables of the system.

Then the famous Maximum Principle of Portryagin states that we form the Hamiltonian function

$$H = \phi(\ ) + \sum_{i=1}^{n} \theta_i f_i$$

and maximize this function by choice of $u(t)$. The first order conditions for an optimum are given by

(i) $\frac{\partial H}{\partial u} = 0,$

or

(ii) $\dot{\theta}_i = -\frac{\partial H}{\partial x_i}$ (this is called the canonical equation for θ_i. θ_i itself is called a costate variable.

In the previous appendix as well as in the text of Chapter XI we have encountered optimal control problems. In particular they have been discounted infinite time optimal control problems with one state variable. Let us concentrate on this problem for a while. We have one state variable say C and one dynamic equation governing the flow of c say $c = f(c, u)$ where u is a control variable. (It is not necessary that the number of state variables equal the number of control variables). Our objective function is

$$\int_0^\infty e^{-rt}(V(c, u))\, dt.$$

We form the Hamiltonian

$$H = e^{-rt}[V(c, u) + \theta f]$$

or equivalently

$$H = V(c, u) + \theta f.$$

The necessary conditions for the latter formulation are:

$$\frac{\partial H}{\partial u} = 0$$

$$\dot{\theta} = r\theta - \frac{\partial H}{\partial c}$$

$\left[\text{In the first formulation this would be } \theta = -\frac{\partial H}{\partial C}\right].$

Now a steady state for this problem is characterized by a situation where the state and costate variable are unchanging over time i.e. $\dot{c} = \dot{\theta} = 0$.

But an "optimal" steady state is one which satisfies the first order condition for optimality i.e. $\partial H/\partial u = 0$. Under the assumptions we have been making in this chapter given the parameters of the system this "optimal" steady state is unique.

We next come to the idea of a phase diagram. We substitute the optimal value of u in the c and θ equations and set them equal to zero. We plot these loci in the (c, θ) plane. We analyze local stability either diagrammatically by seeing how c and θ behave in the phase diagram if $\dot{c}$ and/or $\dot{\theta}$ are/is not zero. Alternatively, we take a Taylor expansion of the c, θ equation around the steady state values c^*, θ^* and examine the roots of the matrix of Taylor series expansion i.e.

$$\begin{pmatrix} \dot{c} \\ \dot{\theta} \end{pmatrix} = \begin{pmatrix} \frac{\partial \dot{c}}{\partial \dot{c}} & \frac{\partial \dot{c}}{\partial \dot{\theta}} \\ \frac{\partial \dot{\theta}}{\partial \dot{c}} & \frac{\partial \dot{\theta}}{\partial \theta} \end{pmatrix} \begin{pmatrix} c - c^* \\ \theta - \theta^* \end{pmatrix}$$

Stability then depends on the characteristic roots of the 2×2 matrix on the right hand side of the above expression. If both roots are negative the system is stable. If both roots are positive then the system is unstable. If one root is positive and the other negative then the system manifests saddlepath stability.

Transversality Conditions

Apart from the above mentioned necessary conditions the system must satisfy two transversality conditions viz. $\theta(t) \geqslant 0$ for all t

$$\text{and } \lim_{t \to \infty} \theta(t)c(t) = 0.$$

These are necessary to ensure the asymptotic optimality of the policy chosen.

We will encounter more optimal control problems in later chapters. At that stage we will also have to delve more deeply into the theory of multistate optimal control problems. For an example of such problems see Jha (1986).

12. The Incidence of Taxes in Static Equilibrium

The study of the effects of various types of taxes is one of the oldest branches of economics. The problem of discovering who bears the burden of a tax has occupied the interest of economists for some generations now. Indeed even the interpretation of the term "incidence of a tax" has been the subject of intense debate among economists.

In this chapter we study this problem within the context of static or atemporal equilibrium. We begin by enumerating some of the principles of taxation and then catalogue some important types of taxes in a modern mixed economy like ours. We then study incidence of taxes in partial equilibrium. Realizing the limitations of partial equilibrium incidence we study incidence in a general equilibrium model. We first consider a competitive model and then consider the impact of various types of imperfections. Finally we consider recent attempts to assess incidence of a tax by computational methods.

Principles of Taxation

In general there are two criteria (but by no means the only two) by which taxes are judged. The efficiency criterion and the equity criterion.

Efficiency Criterion. Let us go back to the world of equivalence between perfect competition and Pareto optimality. We see that in this world unless they are lump sum, taxes are going to introduce welfare losses. These welfare losses are also sometimes called a deadweight loss as they involve departures from Pareto optimality. The efficiency criterion ranks taxes by deadweight loss per rupee revenue collected. Those taxes that involve a smaller deadweight loss per unit revenue collected are said to be more efficient than those taxes that involve a higher deadweight loss per unit revenue collected.[1]

[1]Readers must realize that a tax need not necessarily involve a deadweight loss. Infact to the extent that some taxes (at least partially) correct for some distortions or external effects they may actually cause an improvement in welfare. Thus a tax on cigarettes is a partial correction for the external diseconomy caused by smokers. Similarly a tax on petrol could both conserve energy as well as partially compensate for the environmental poltution caused by cars.

For a simple one person, two commodity, two factor of production world we can fairly simply illustrate the idea of deadweight loss.

This is done in Fig. 12.1 below

In Fig. 12.1 *ZZ* is society's aggregate production possibility curve for goods *A* and *B*. In the absence of government the single individual[2] would

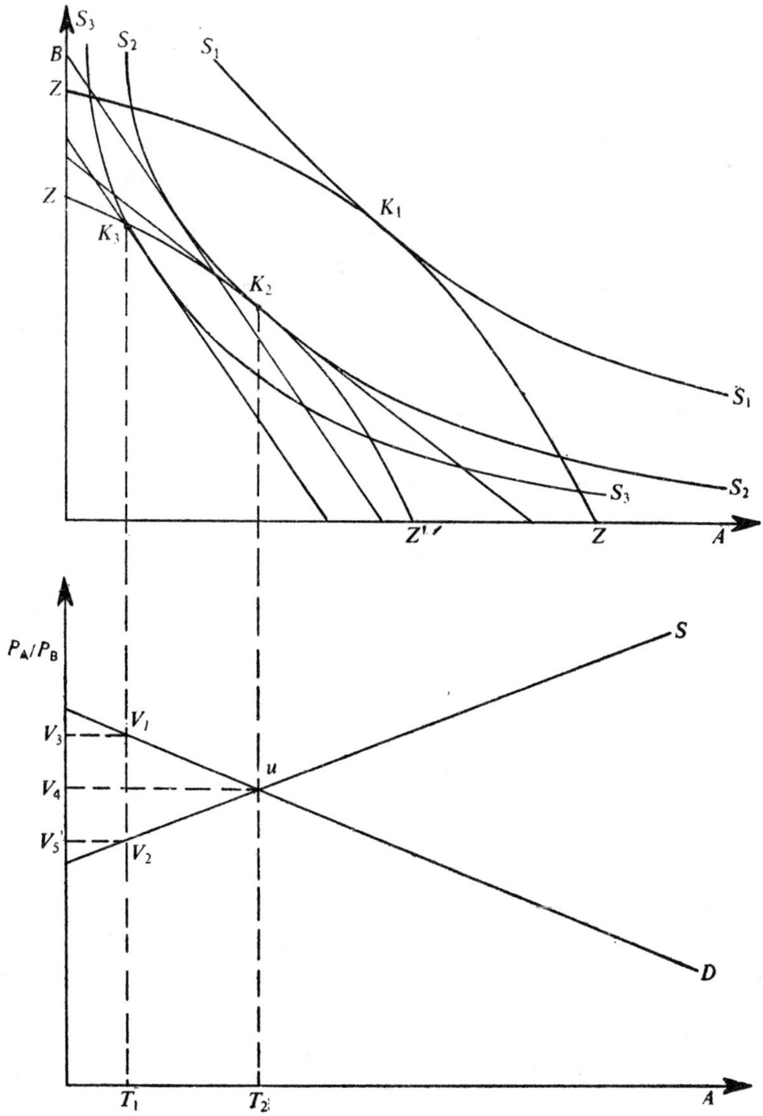

Fig. 12.1

[2]This analysis need not be restricted to the case of a single individual. We can think of a multiperson society with the indifference curves representing social indifference curves.

choose point K_1 on indifference curve S_1S_1. Here $MRS_{A,B} = MRT_{A,B}$ and the situation is Pareto optimal. The government now enters the picture and takes away some resources from the private sector. This shrinks the production possibility frontier to $Z'Z'$. Presumably, however the goverment spends the resources for the benefit of public. Hence although resources at the command of the private sector are, fewer the public also has a different indifference map now and S_2S_2 and S_3S_3 come from the new indifference map.

Now let us compare two taxes, an income tax and an excise tax on A. With an income tax the remuneration paid to a factor is different from the remuneration received by the factor. But in the simple world we have been studying, income taxes (irrespective of whether they are on wage income or capital income or both) do not affect the supply of factors. By assumption, factors of production are inelastically supplied. Hence the deadweight loss is zero and society comes to an equilibrium at point K_2. Hence Pareto optimality are satisfied.

With an excise tax on A a wedge is established between $MRS_{A,B}$ and $MRT_{A,B}$. Equilibrium is established at K_3 on indifference curve S_3S_3. The difference in the utility $S_2S_2 - S_3S_3$ measures the deadweight loss or excess burden of the tax system.

The same idea is established in the lower part of Figure I. There we plot the supply and demand for A. In moving from K_3 to K_2 the gain in consumer's surplus is $V_3V_1uV_4$. The gain in producer's surplus is $V_4uV_2V_5$. These gains are partly offset by the loss in tax revenue $V_3V_1V_2V_5$ which must now be made up from the income tax. The net gain to society by abandoning the excise tax and moving to an income tax is $V_1U_2V_2$. This is also the deadweight loss associated with the excise tax.

Equity. In the literature on principles of taxation two notions of equity have been distinguished. Horizontal equity calls for people in similar situations to be treated similarly. Vertical equity on the other hand calls for people in different situations to be treated differently. These concepts are, however, not always easy to apply in practice.

To illustrate some of the problems let us take the case of an income tax. Suppose we follow a practice that economists generally eschew and compare the utility levels of two individuals and declare that their utility levels are the same. However suppose that the tastes of the two persons differ in that one of them has a stronger preference for leisure than the other. An income tax would then be inequitable since it would discriminate against the person with the weaker preference for leisure. Hence although as per the dictates of horizontal equity these two persons should be treated similarly we realize that in practice doing this runs the risk of running up against some other difficulties.

Similar problems arise when we are dealing with vertical equity. In this case we are faced with the onerous task of deciding which individuals are in different utility situations and then treating them differently for tax purposes. Most countries follow the practice of using comprehensive income as tax base i.e. income from all sources (e.g. wage income, interest income, income from property, capital gains etc.) is lumped together to provide the comprehensive base for the tax. Most tax laws also allow for some deductions. Thus one set of potential differences is swept under the rug. It does not matter if person earns an annual salary of Rs 30,000 whereas person two also earns Rs 30,000 a year albeit solely from the ownership of property. Both pay the same tax. This is of course a problem but most economists seem to agree that devising tax structure by source of income would be a really difficult task and the benefits of using the comprehensive income as base outweigh the costs. Nonetheless some difficulties remain which need to be mentioned.

Firstly there is the problem of taxing capital gains. Some people feel that since the beneficiary "didn't really do very much" to get it this income should be treated differently. Again there is the problem of timing the tax on capital gain. Should it be taxed on accrual or on realization. If it is taxed only on realization then some people might leave the asset (which earned the capital gain) in investment so as to postpone paying the tax. Infact if they do this long enough their inheritors might pay an inheritance tax on the asset rather than the original owner paying a capital tax. One way out of this difficulty, of course, is to impute a certain fraction of capital gains as current income if the capital gain is not realized but only accrued. This has problems of its own. An advantage of collecting capital gains tax only on realization is that people do not face severe problems of liquidity when paying the tax i.e. they do not sell the asset to pay the tax.

Another source of difficulty is fluctuating incomes. Suppose we have a progressive tax structure with the marginal tax rate rising with income. Compare two people one who earns Rs 30,000 a year every year and another person whose income fluctuates from year to year but averages to Rs 30,000 a year over, say, five years. Over a five year period these two people will end up paying different amounts as taxes. Hence there is the need to average incomes rather than strictly following the dictum of computing tax solely on the basis of income earned in one calendar (or financial) year.

Many problems in determining tax amounts (and hence problems of vertical equity) are common to the problems of measuring income, one such problem is that of imputing income. In one household the wife works outside and hires help for household chores. In another household the wife is a housewife and no outside help is hired for chores. How are we to apply the principle of vertical equity in this case? Then, of course, there is the well known problem of distinguishing between persons who live in their own homes and those who have rented accommodation. How are we to impute rent to owner occupied housing? Usually the practice is to assume that the owner is paying a rent (equal to the market rent) to himself and this amount then gets included in the owner's income. But what if the rental market is not perfect? Or if the house owner gets extra satisfaction from staying in his own house?

These are fairly old and well known problems with operationalizing the principles of taxation. There is no easy way of getting round them. Taxes have to be paid and every society (or tax authority) must detect its own problems and try to solve them as best as they can and approach some kind of satisfactory solution.

We have so far spoken of the principles of efficiency and equity as if we could treat them as separable and non-conflicting goals. This is, of course, not true. A tax levied on grounds of efficiency will have consequences for equity and vice versa. Thus, for instance, a tax on commodities with low elasticities of demand (e.g. tobacco or alcohl) has little damaging effect on allocation and hence is preferred on grounds of efficiency. However, these commodities are also consumed in disproportionately large amounts by the poor. Hence the tax might be inequitable.

Of course we realize that the government imposes a wide variety of taxes. Thus it would be better to discuss the properties of a tax in the context of the tax structure of which it is a part. We now discuss some of the taxes that form part of the overall tax structure in most countries.

Apart from the income tax already discussed above some countries charge a surcharge or super tax on the tax amount. Till very recently our own tax laws called for the payment of a surcharge on the amount paid as tax. Similarly tax payers were obliged to advance a certain portion of the taxable amount of their income as low interest loans to the government. This was the compulsory deposit scheme operative in India till very recently. This practice has now been discontinued.

In addition to income taxes most countries also have some form of *wealth tax* whereas a certain fraction of an individuals' wealth is taxed. Two reasons are advanced in favour of the wealth tax. Firstly wealth should be taxed for its own sake. If two persons have the same income the one with the higher wealth should pay more taxes since he has greater "ability to pay". Moreover wealth, in the view of some, gives a surer base for taxation than income. In many countries wealth taxation has been resorted to after a war when the government has felt an urgency to repay war debts. In such instances some governments have taxed large parts of all increases to wealth during a war since such increases are deemed "undeserved", by many people.

Property Tax

There are two forms of property taxes. One is tax levied almost exclusively on the holding of land. The second is levied across the broad on almost all forms of property with a sale value.

In our country tax on the holding of agricultural land is very important and as we know this tax has had a long and unenviable history. In contemporary times the argument for taxing agricultural land holding is simply that in a situation (like ours) where there is no tax on agricultural income this property tax is best and, given that agricultural incomes are (loosely) associated with holding of land, it is also a fair tax as it taxes according to "ability to pay".

In the urban sector, however, this argument is not very tenable and it is much more common to see income and net wealth taxes.

In most countries a death duty is also imposed. It is often described as the testators's last tax and the first tax of the inheritor. There are two forms of the death duty. In one case tax is assessed on the value of the inheritance. In the second case the wealth of the inheritor is also taken into account. Two kinds of questions have been raised about the death duty. The first is its effect on savings and the second is its implications for continuity in corporate life.

So far as the first question is concerned theorists like Stiglitz[3] feel that death duties by reducing the value of bequests reduces savings. One can argue, however, that this very fact can stimulate savings. People may wish to ensure a certain minimum as bequest for their children and hence, under taxation, save more.

So far as continuity in corporate life is concerned some people feel that the continuity implicit in the passing of a business from father to son is a good thing for reasons of stability. In modern societies, however, a son may not like to follow in the footsteps of his father. Moreover, there is something to be said for injecting some young blood into business.

Another tax much discussed in the literature is an expenditure tax to replace the income tax. Kaldor[4] was one of the most fervent advocates of this tax. Recently it has become popular once again.[5] In India we have this tax to some extent since certain categories of expenditure (e.g. saving in the form of national saving certificates) are, at least partially, exempt from income taxation. The main advantages of the expenditure tax seems to be that it might stimulate savings. While this is a desirable goal the question remains as to whether the expenditure tax is the best method to do this.[6] An expenditure tax alters the marginal rate of substitution between present and future consumption and this may distort the allocation of resources. Moreover some people have the feeling that the cost of administering an expenditure is going to be quite high compared to the cost of administering an income tax.

These are some of the major direct taxes (taxes that directly reduce earnings) that have been discussed in the literature. Apart from these we have the entire set of indirect taxes that the government uses. An indirect tax decreases earnings indirectly (usually via commodities).

[3]See Stiglitz (1976) or Atkinson and Stiglitz (1980).

[4]See Kaldor (1955).

[5]See for instance, Feldstein (1983).

[6]We need to remind readers that sometimes it is necessary to use fiscal policy to reduce rather than increase the rate of savings e.g. to pull an economy out of a recession.

In India indirect taxes are levied at three levels: local government, state government and the government of India.[7] Thus the government of India imposes central excise duties usually on an ad valorem item by item basis. Sometimes subsidies are also granted. Thus in cotton textiles the production of handlooms is subsidized whereas there is a positive excise tax on millspun high grade cotton textile. The union government also imposes licence fees, export and import taxes, custom duties and the like. The state governments also have some excise duties particularly on certain types of commodities which are taxable by the state e.g. some states change entry fee for trucks laden with goods. Some taxes on alcohol, agricultural implements etc. also fall in this category. State and local governments also have the freedom to set rates of sales tax. Local governments set municipal dues, sewage and water rates. Thus while direct taxes are almost entirely controlled by the central government, the state and local governments have considerable leeway in the matter of indirect taxes.[8]

An indirect tax raises prices uniformly for everybody and treats rich and poor alike.[9] In this sense it is regressive. Moreover by altering managerial rates of transformation (in production) and marginal rates of substitution (in consumption) indirect taxes have a profound effect on the allocation of resources in society.[10]

In a country like ours indirect taxes are immensely important as a source of revenue to the government. Given that incomes are so low the government has to finance much of its expenditure from revenues from indirect taxation. In developed countries the reverse is often true. It has been increasingly felt, however, that high rates of indirect taxation often stifle industrial growth by choking off demand. But this is the kind of unhappy and unenviable situation in which we have found ourselves. The potential for raising revenues from direct taxation are extremely limited in an economy like ours.

Incidence of Tax in Partial Equilibrium

Tax incidence in partial equilibrium is not taken very seriously nowadays so this section will be brief. By tax incidence we will simply understand the effect of a tax on the static equilibrium of the market under study.

[7]In India where public sector production is so important the price of a public sector product is very much like an indirect tax i.e. it reduces earnings indirectly. We will see this equivalence more succinctly in a later chapter when we consider formulae for optimal mix of public sector price/indirect tax.

[8]The Indian indirect tax structure is fairly complex and in urgent need of harmonization. We will discuss this and related issues in a later chapter.

[9]For a sophisticated treatment of this problem see Murty (1985).

[10]One must here distinguish between the nominal and effective rate of tax on a commodity. A steel chair may face an excise duty of 10 percent. But the effective tax on this chair depends on the taxes on the inputs used the chair and the technology by which these inputs have been combined to produce the chair. See Ahmed and Stern (1983).

Let us suppose as in Fig. 12.2 below that we have a competitive market and an ad valorem tax at the rate t is imposed. Hence the supply curve shifts from S to S'.

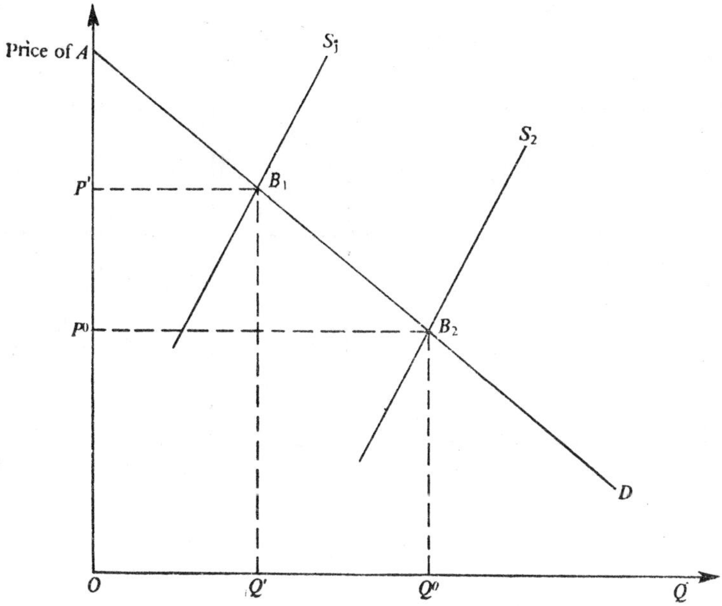

Fig. 12.2

The new equilibrium is P^1, Q^1.

In this diagram the reader should immediately be able to realize that the entire price increase has not been passed on to the consumer. Infact how much of the tax is passed on to consumers depends on the elasticities of supply and demand. We portray some cases in Figs. 12.3 to 12.4

In Fig. 12.3 the supply curve does not shift and the producer bears the full burden of the tax. In Fig. 12.4 the supply curve shifts by the amount of the tax and the consumer bears the full burden of the tax.

In Fig. 12.5 the supplier will bear the full burden of the tax and in Fig. 12.6 the consumers bear the full burden of the tax. The perceptive reader will have realized that the extent and distribution of the deadweight loss is different in the various cases. Thus elasticities of supply and demand are important.

We can easily study tax incidence in non-competitive markets as well. Let us take the case of a monopolist. Remember that price equals average revenue for the monopolist so that average revenue after tax (AR′) is related to that before the tax (AR) by the relation AR $=$ AR′$(1 + t)$. The net price (to the monopolist) is reduced by the amount of the tax. The situation is depicted in Fig. 12.5.

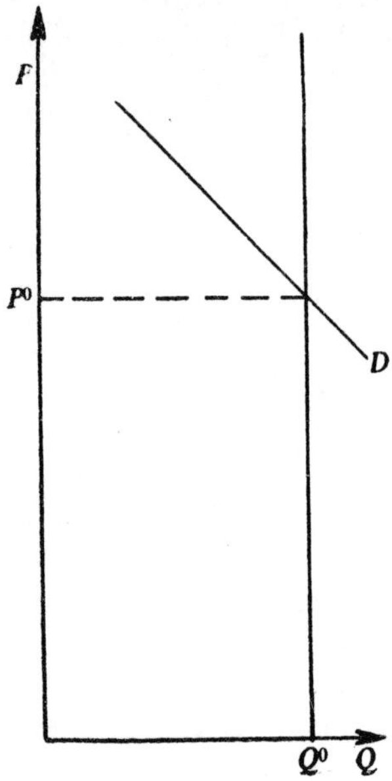

Fig. 12.3

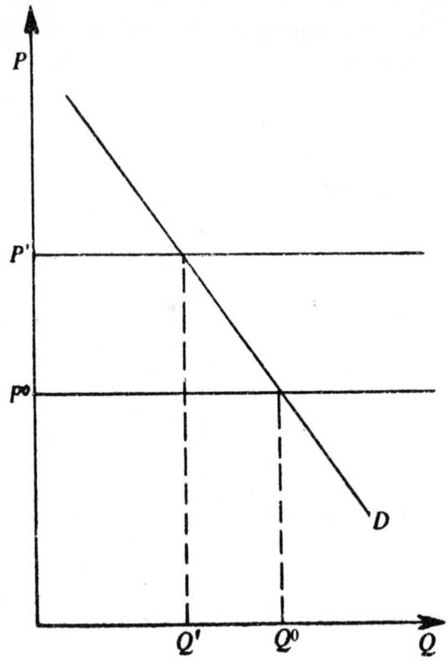

Fig. 12.4

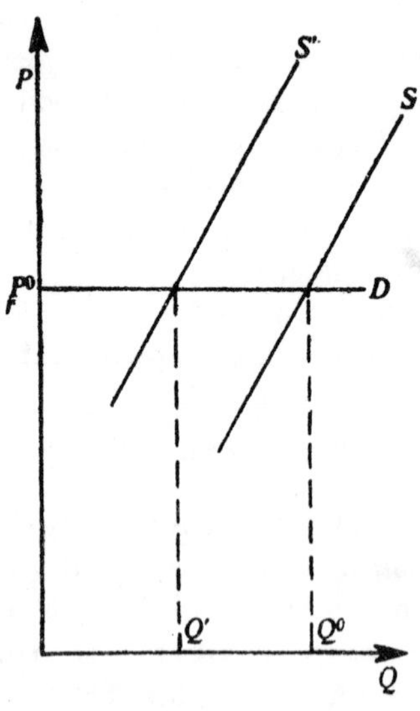

Fig. 12.5

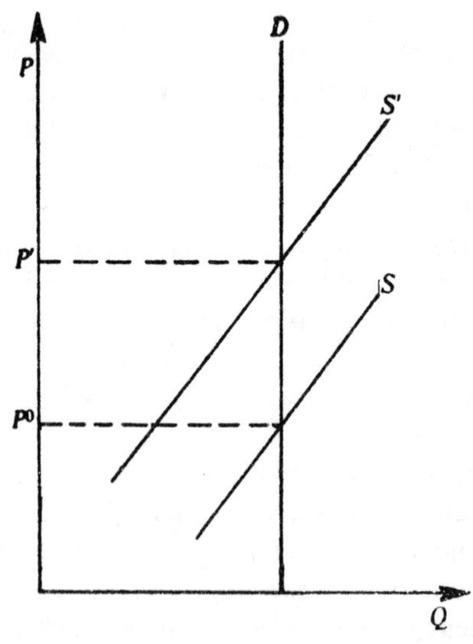

Fig. 12.6

In Fig. 12.7 we have drawn the "usual" U-shaped average cost and marginal cost schedules. The average revenue and marginal revenue schedules before and after the tax have also been drawn. Before tax equilibrium is P^0Q^0. After tax equilibrium is $P'Q'$. The price to the consumer after the tax is P''.

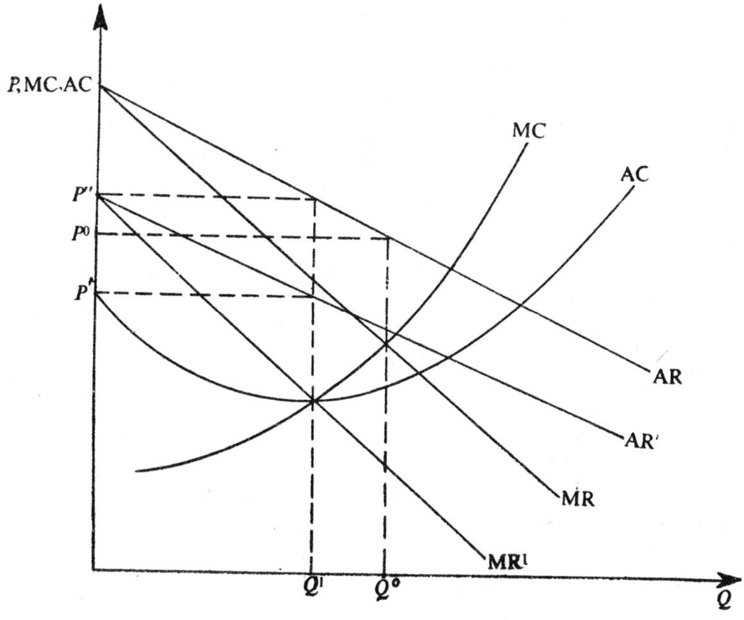

Fig. 12.7

In a similar vein one can analyze the effect of a tax on a factor. A tax on a factor, say capital, will increase the long run AC and MC schedules from AC^0, MC^0 to AC', MC' respectively. Output and price will accordingly also change. This is depicted in Fig. 12.8.

As a consequence of the tax the equilibrium price quality configuration shifts from (P^0, Q^0) to (P', Q').

But this is all partial equilibrium. And partial equilibrium analysis has many limitations—in fact so many limitations that modern public finance theorists do not take incidence studies in partial equilibrium very seriously. We list below some of the major difficulties with partial equilibrium incidence studies.

First, is the very nature of partial equilibrium analysis. It assumes that the sector or market under study is unaffected by the rest of the economy. This may be a singularly untenable assumption. Think, for instance, of the effect on factor markets if factor rewards in this sector differ from those prevalent in the rest of the economy.

A corollary of this is the fact that income effects are obviously neglected. Similarly the revenue that the government collects from the tax is simply

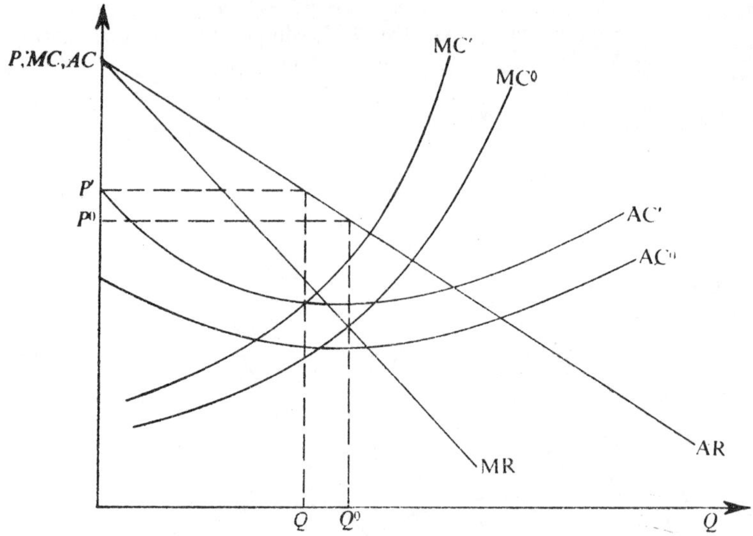

Fig. 12.8

ignored. It matters very much how the government spends the revenue from taxation.

Furthermore, the analysis of tax incidence in partial equilibrium cannot accomodate forms of industrial organization in the rest of the economy. Thus all we could do is to talk of perfect or imperfect competition only in the market under study not in other sectors—not even the markets closely related to the market under study.

For these and other reasons we now turn to a study of tax incidence in general equilibrium.

Tax Incidence in General Equilibrium

In this chapter we are dealing with tax incidence in static equilibrium. Nevertheless, the time has now come to be more specific and list clearly the conditions under which we propose to study tax incidence.

By a static setting we obviously mean a situation in which factor supplies are unchanging. Hence we shelve, for the time being, all results on the incentive effects of taxation which we collected earlier. Moreover, we assume that tastes and technology do not change.

Even so the sheer diversity of an economy makes it necessary to trim down the size of the general equilibrium model being considered. We reduce the level of disaggregation to consider a two commodity, two factor of production world. This is the simple set up that we adopted in a number of examples in earlier chapters.[11]

[11]An alternative to the analysis here is the computational general equilibrium approach of Scarf, Shoven, Whalley, Fullerton and others. We will consider some of their results later in this chapter.

The analysis done here follows in the tradition of Jones (1965), Johnson (1977) and Atkinson and Stiglitz (1980) and the numerous expositions of the simple two sector model (partially) in trade theory and growth theory. There are two goods (final goods) A, B. Both are produced by constant returns to scale technology characterized by smooth substitution possibilities between the two factors of production capital and labour. Both A and B are normal goods and one can express social preferences by a Bergson type social welfare function to be specified below. The economy is characterized by perfect competition, full information and full price flexibility in all markets.

Production conditions are given by the production functions

$$A = A(K, L) \tag{1}$$

$$B = B(K, L) \tag{2}$$

with $\frac{\partial A}{\partial K}, \frac{\partial A}{\partial L}, \frac{\partial B}{\partial K}, \frac{\partial B}{\partial L}$ all positive.

$$A(0, K) = A(K, 0) = B(0, L) = B(K, 0) = 0$$

i.e. each factor is necessary for production.

Second order derivatives $\partial^2 A/\partial K^2$ etc. are all negative.

Since both A and B are produced competitively their prices equal the respective marginal costs i.e. if p_A and p_B are the respective prices then

$$p_A = C_A(r, W) \tag{3}$$

$$p_B = C_B(r, W) \tag{4}$$

where C_A and C_B are, respectively, the marginal costs of producing A and B. These marginal costs depend on the rate of rental r and the wage rate which are themselves established in competitive markets. Given constant returns total costs of producing A and B are respectively

$$C_A = C_A A \tag{5}$$

$$C_B = C_B B \tag{6}$$

i.e. total cost is marginal cost multiplied by output. Let us define the terms

$$C_{LA} = \frac{\partial C_A}{\partial W}, \quad C_{KA} = \frac{\partial C_A}{\partial r},$$

$$C_{LB} = \frac{\partial C_B}{\partial W}, \quad C_{KB} = \frac{\partial C_B}{\partial r}.$$

Demand for labour in industries A and B are simply

$$L_A = C_{LA} \cdot A, \quad L_B = C_{LB} \cdot B.$$

Similarly demands for capital are

$$K_A = C_{KA} \cdot A, \quad K_B = C_{KB} \cdot B.$$

If K_0 and L_0 are the fixed quantities of capital and labour available full employment requires that

$$C_{LA} \cdot A + C_{LB} \cdot B = L_0 \tag{7}$$

$$C_{KA} \cdot A + C_{KB} \cdot B = K_0. \tag{8}$$

We will first develop the supply side of the model and then consider demand. What we are interested in discovering at this stage is if there is an exogenous change (say because of a tax) how does the static equilibrium of the economy change. Part of the answer to the question lies in discovering how supply changes. The rest is reckoning how demand changes. We concentrate on the supply side to begin with. We denote rates of change by a hat ($\wedge$) i.e. for any variable X, $\hat{X} = \frac{dX}{X}$.

First totally differentiate equations (3) and (4) to get

$$dp_A = C_{KA}\, dr + C_{LA}\, dw \tag{9}$$

$$dp_B = C_{KB}\, dr + C_{LB}\, dw. \tag{10}$$

Divide equation (9) by $p_A = c_A$ and multiply and divide appropriately by r and W to get

$$\frac{dp_A}{pA} = r\frac{C_{KA}}{C_A}\frac{dr}{r} + W\frac{C_{LA}}{C_A}\frac{dW}{W}$$

or

$$\hat{p}_A = r\frac{C_{KA}}{C_A}\hat{r} + W\frac{C_{LA}}{C_A}\hat{W}. \tag{9'}$$

Similarly,

$$\hat{p}_B = r\frac{C_{KB}}{C_B}\hat{r} + W\frac{C_{LB}}{C_B}\hat{W}. \tag{10'}$$

We now use the notation

$$\beta_{Li} = \frac{WC_{Li}}{C_i} \text{ (share of labour in industry } i, i = A, B)$$

$$\beta_{Ki} = \frac{rC_{Ki}}{C_i} \text{ (share of capital in industry } i, i = A, B).$$

By Euler's theorem

$$\beta_{Li} + \beta_{Ki} = 1.$$

Subtract (10′) from (9′) to get

$$\hat{p}_A - \hat{p}_B = (\beta_{KA} - \beta_{KB})\hat{r} + (\beta_{LA} - \beta_{LB})\hat{W}. \tag{11}$$

This gives us a basic relation between changes in factor prices and changes in output prices. Now

$$C_{LA} = C_{LA}(r, w) \tag{12}$$

$$C_{KA} = C_{KA}(r, w) \tag{13}$$

$$C_{LB} = C_{LB}(r, w) \tag{14}$$

$$C_{KB} = C_{KB}(r, w). \tag{15}$$

Now totally differentiate (12) to get

$$dC_{LA} = \frac{\partial C_{LA}}{\partial r} dr + \frac{\partial C_{LA}}{\partial W} dW. \tag{12'}$$

Divide by C_{LA} and divide and multiply conformably to get

$$\frac{dC_{LA}}{C_{LA}} = r\frac{C_{LKA}}{C_{LA}}\frac{dr}{r} + \frac{WC_{LLA}}{C_{LA}}\frac{dW}{W}$$

where $C_{LKA} = \frac{\partial C_{LA}}{\partial r}$ and $C_{LLA} = \frac{\partial C_{LA}}{\partial W}$.

Thus,

$$\hat{C}_{LA} = r\frac{C_{LKA}}{C_{LA}}\hat{r} + W\frac{C_{LLA}}{C_{LA}}\hat{W}. \tag{16}$$

Now since the production function is homogeneous of degree 1 factor demand functions are homogeneous of degree zero. Thus

$$WC_{LLA} + rC_{LKA} = WC_{KLA} + rC_{KKA} = 0$$

whence $$C_{LKA} = -\frac{W}{r}C_{LLA}.$$

Substitute this into (16) to get

$$\begin{aligned}\hat{C}_{LA} &= r\left(-\frac{W}{r}\frac{C_{LLA}}{C_{LA}}\right)\hat{r} + W\frac{C_{LLA}}{C_{LA}}\hat{W} \\ &= -W\frac{C_{LLA}}{C_{LA}}\hat{r} + W\frac{C_{LLA}}{C_{LA}}\hat{W} \\ &= (\hat{W} - \hat{r})\left(W\frac{C_{LLA}}{C_{LA}}\right).\end{aligned}$$

Multiplying and divide the right hand side by $-\frac{rC_{KA}}{C_A}$ to get

$$\begin{aligned}\hat{C}_{LA} &= -\left(\frac{rC_{KA}}{C_A}\right)\left(\frac{-WC_{LLA}C_A}{rC_{LA}C_{KA}A}\right)(\hat{W} - \hat{r}) \\ &= -\beta_{KA}\sigma_A(\hat{W} - \hat{r})\end{aligned} \tag{17}$$

where σ_A is the elasticity of substitution[12] between K and L in industry A.

This is a very convenient expression relating changes in labour's contribution to marginal cost to changes in factor prices, the elasticity of substitution and share of capital.

In a completely analogous manner we can derive

$$\hat{C}_{LB} = -\beta_{KB}\,\sigma_B(\hat{W} - \hat{r}) \tag{18}$$

$$\hat{C}_{KA} = \beta_{LA}\,\sigma_A(\hat{W} - \hat{r}) \tag{19}$$

$$\hat{C}_{KB} = \beta_{LB}\,\sigma_B(\hat{W} - \hat{r}). \tag{20}$$

[12]The elasticity of substitution is formally defined as

$$\frac{d\log K/L}{d\log RTS_{K,L}} = \frac{d\log K/L}{d\log W/r} \text{ (in competition).}$$

Now totally dfferentiate the factor availability equations (7) and (8). Consider (7) first

$$C_{LA}dA + AdC_{LA} + C_{LB}dB + BdC_{LB} = dL_0 = 0$$

or

$$AC_{LA}\frac{dA}{A} + AC_{LA}\frac{dC_{LA}}{C_{LA}} + BC_{LB}\frac{dB}{B} + BC_{LB}\frac{dC_{LB}}{C_{LB}} = 0$$

or

$$AC_{LA}\hat{A} + AC_{LA}\hat{C}_{LA} + B_{CLB}\hat{B} + BC_{LB}\hat{C}_{LB} = 0$$

i.e.

$$AC_{LA}(\hat{A} + \hat{C}_{LA}) + BC_{LB}(\hat{B} + \hat{C}_{LB}) = 0. \tag{21}$$

Now, divide (21) by L_0 to get

$$\lambda_{LA}(\hat{A} + \hat{C}_{LA}) + \lambda_{LB}(\hat{B} + \hat{C}_{LB}) = 0,$$

where λ_{LA} is share of industry A in total employment. Similarly λ_{LB} is B's share in total employment.

Finally substitute for C_{LA} and C_{LB} from equations (17) and (18) to get

$$\lambda_{LA}\hat{A} + \lambda_{LB}\hat{B} = (\hat{W} - \hat{r})(\lambda_{LA}\beta_{KA}\sigma_A + \lambda_{LB}\beta_{KB}\sigma_B). \tag{22}$$

If we now repeat this process for equation (8) we will get

$$\lambda_{KA}\hat{A} + \lambda_{KB}\hat{B} = -(\hat{W} - \hat{r})(\lambda_{KA}\beta_{LA}\sigma_A + \lambda_{KB}\beta_{LB}\sigma_B). \tag{23}$$

Equations (22) and (23) are our fundamental equations from the supply side. They relate output movements to movements in factor prices, technology and the shares of A and B in total employment of labour and capital.

Now let us look at the demand side of the story. Again we will make drastically simplifying assumptions. We will assume that preferences of society can be represented[13] by an aggregate utility function $U(A, B)$. National income is $M = WL_0 + rK_0$. $U(\ )$ is maximized subject to M and p_A, p_B. Thus we get aggregate demand functions for commodities A and B.

$$A = A(p_A, p_B, M) \tag{24}$$
$$B = B(p_A, p_B, M). \tag{25}$$

Differentiating equation (24) totally to get

$$dA = \frac{\partial A}{\partial p}dp_A + \frac{\partial A}{\partial p_B}dp_B + \frac{\partial e}{\partial_B}\frac{\partial A}{\partial M}dU \tag{24'}$$

where $e = e(p_A, p_B, U)$ is the aggregate expenditure function. Divide equation (24′) by A to get (after a little manipulation).

$$\frac{dA}{A} = \frac{p_A}{A}\frac{\partial A}{\partial p_A}\frac{dp_A}{p_A} + \frac{p_B}{A}\frac{\partial A}{\partial p_B}\frac{dp_B}{p_B} + \frac{M}{A}\frac{\partial A}{\partial M}\frac{du}{M}e_u$$

[13]The circumstances under which such representation is possible have been discussed in an earlier chapter.

or

$$\hat{A} = E'_{AA}\,\hat{p}_A + E'_{AB}\,\hat{p}_B + \eta_A \frac{du}{M}\,e_u \tag{26}$$

where the E's are compensated elasticities and η_A is income elasticity of demand.

Similarly we can write

$$\hat{B} = E'_A\,\hat{p}_{AB} + E'_{BB}\,\hat{p}_B + \eta_B \frac{du}{M}\,eu. \tag{27}$$

We can then write

$$\eta_B\hat{A} - \eta_A\hat{B} = (\eta_B E'_{AA} - \eta_A E'_{BA})\,\hat{p}_A$$
$$-(\eta_A E'_{BB} - \eta_B E'_{AB})\,\hat{p}_B. \tag{28}$$

Now since

$$E'_{AB} = -E'_{AA}$$

we can reduce (28) to

$$\eta_B\hat{A} - \eta_A\hat{B} = (\eta_B E'_{AA} + \eta_A E'_{BB})(\hat{p}_A - \hat{p}_B)$$
$$= -\Delta_D(\hat{p}_A - \hat{p}_B). \tag{28'}$$

We will suppose that $\Delta_D > 0$, a sufficient condition for which is that both goods are normal. Throughout this chapter we assume demands to be homothetic.

We are now in a position to discuss incidence of taxation in our simple set up here. To study the (static) general equilibrium incidence of a tax three factors are crucial:

(*a*) the specific model in which we are studying the effect of the tax. This we have already done.

(*b*) the state of taxes before we impose the tax we wish to study. Are we starting from scratch and imposing an infinitesimal tax? Or are we functioning in a system where there are other taxes and subsidies and the tax imposed is discrete rather than infinitesimal? These questions are really quite important.

(*c*) what does the government do with the tax revenue it collects? How the government spends its revenue will affect post tax equilibrium and hence the final effect of the tax.

We will consider questions (*b*) and (*c*) as we go along.

In deciding upon incidence of tax we will consider general equilibrium before and after tax and adduce the difference to the tax. To do this it will perhaps be best to consider incidence pictorally first and then move on to consider tax incidence in the structure developed above.

In this case we will simply assume that the tax revenues collected by the government are not spent on commodities A and B. CC is the production possibility frontier after the government has taken away its revenue. If this is collected by a lump sum tax equilibrium would be attained at S_1. Suppose instead that this revenue was raised not by a lump sum tax but a propor-

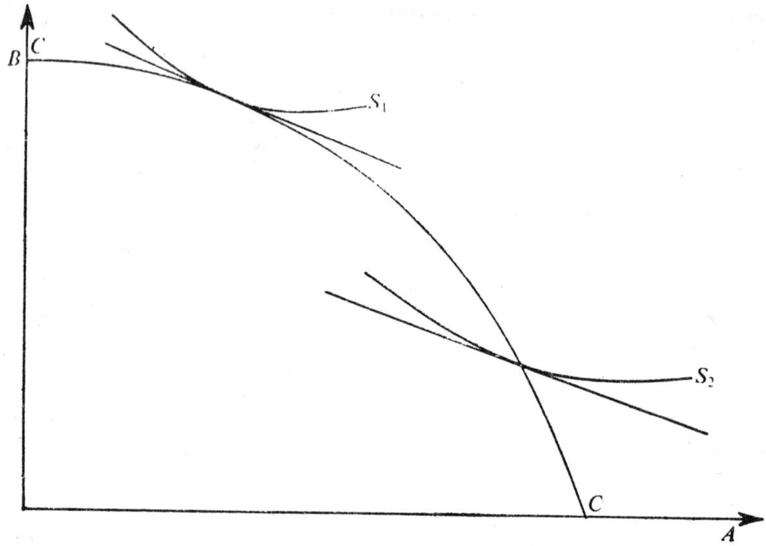

Fig. 12.9

tional (at rate t_A) ad valorem tax on commodity A. This will change the marginal rate of substitution between goods A and B. However the MRT remains unchanged. Equilibrium occurs at point S_2 were

$$\text{MRS}_{A,B} = \frac{p_A(1 + t_A)}{p_B} = (1 + t_A)\,\text{MRT}_{A,B}.$$

How does this affect factor markets and consumption? Let us consider factor market first.

In Fig. 12.10 equilibrium before the tax occurs at point S_1' with capital labour ratios as plotted. After the tax the equilibrium moves to point S_2'. The wage rental ratio is different in post tax equilibrium and the capital labour ratio has increased in both sectors.

What more can we say about the incidence of the tax? First since the price of A has gone up there has heen a shift in demand from A to B. How much of a shift that is depends on the elasticity of substitution in consumption between A and B. (Δ_D in our analysis). Secondly the greater is the difference in factor proportions (the β's) the greater is going to be the potential impact on the wage rental ratio. Related to this is the first point already made. The greater the shift in differences in factor proportions the greater will be the impact on the wage rental ratio. How much of this is really possible depends upon the elasticity of substitution in production (the σ's) between K and L.

In terms of factor rewards in Fig. 12.10 we have drawn A the relatively capital intensive industry. The excise tax on A will hurt capital more than labour.

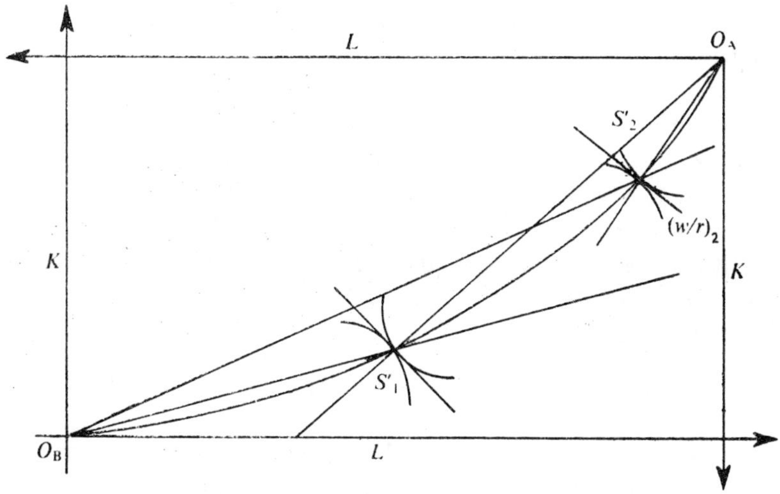

Fig. 12.10

In a similar vein we can analyze the incidence of other taxes.

In the analysis above we had implicitly assumed that when the excise tax was imposed no other taxes were present and the excise tax imposed was an infinitesimal one. Since we are working with calculus the second assumption has to be retained but the first is not essential. We will now use our framework developed above to understand incidence with a multiplicity of taxes.

Let us extend the analysis first by introducing excise taxes on both commodities. The rate of ad valorem tax is t_A on A and t_B on B. Thus producer prices p_A and p_B will differ from consumer prices q_A and q_B where

$$q_A = p_A(1 + t_A) = p_A\tau_A$$

$$q_B = p_B(1 + t_B) = p_B\tau_B.$$

Thus the effect on the demand side is (on rewriting equation (28)).

$$\eta_B\hat{A} - \eta_A\hat{B} = -\Delta_D(\hat{q}_A - \hat{q}_B). \qquad (28')$$

From the supply side we will get (on rewriting equation (11))

$$\hat{q}_A - \hat{q}_B = (\beta_{KA} - \beta_{KB})\hat{r} + (\beta_{LA} - \beta_{LB})\hat{W} + (\hat{\tau}_A - \hat{\tau}_B). \qquad (11')$$

Equations (22) and (23) remain unchanged. Equation (28′) measures the change in demand as a result of change in consumer prices. Equation (11′) is obtained simply by realizing that the change in consumer prices (from the supply side) depends on the pure supply side effects (from equation (11)) and the net change in taxes.

We complicate the analysis one step further by introducing factor taxes. Now there are factor taxes on capital and labour in the two sectors. Thus gross rewards to the two factors are

$$\left.\begin{aligned} r(1+t_K^A) &= r\tau_K^A \\ r(1+t_K^B) &= r\tau_K^B \end{aligned}\right\} \text{ for capital.}$$

for labour we have

$$w(1+t_L^A) = w\tau_L^A$$

$$w(1+t_L^B) = w\tau_L^B.$$

The demand equation remains the same as (28′) but the supply equations will now be altered to reflect the new taxes.

Equation (22) will now read

$$\lambda_{LA}\hat{A} + \lambda_{LB}\hat{B} = (\hat{W} - \hat{r})(\lambda_{LA}\beta_{KA}\sigma_A + \lambda_{LB}\beta_{KB}\sigma_B) + \lambda_{LA}\beta_{KA}\hat{\tau}_L^A + \lambda_{LB}\beta_{KB}\hat{\tau}_L^B \qquad (22')$$

and equation (23) becomes

$$\lambda_{KA}\hat{A} + \lambda_{KB}\hat{B} = -(\hat{W} - \hat{r})(\lambda_{KA}\beta_{LA}\sigma_A + \lambda_{KB}\beta_{LB}\sigma_B) + \lambda_{KA}\beta_{LA}\sigma_A\hat{\tau}_K^A + \lambda_{KB}\beta_{LB}\sigma_B\hat{\tau}_K^B. \qquad (23')$$

Equation (11′) changes to

$$\hat{q}_A - \hat{q}_B = (\beta_{KA} - \beta_{KB})\hat{r} + (\beta_{LA} - \beta_{LB})\hat{W} + (\hat{\tau}_A - \hat{\tau}_B) + \beta_{LA}\hat{\tau}_L^A - \beta_{LB}\hat{\tau}_L^B + \beta_{KA}\hat{\tau}_K^A - \beta_{KB}\hat{\tau}_K^B. \qquad (11'')$$

These equations are easily derived by substituting the new values for the wage rate and rental rate and differentiating appropriately.

From this we can see the following results very easily.

If capital is taxed at rate τ_K^A in sector *A* and at the same rate (τ_K^B) in sector *B* then the two together are equivalent to a general tax of the same rate on capital. Similarly if labour is taxed at rate τ_L^A in sector *A* and at the same rate τ_L^B (in sector *B*) then the two together are equivalent to a general tax of the same rate on labour. *A* tax at rate τ_K^A on capital and at equivalent rate τ_L^A on labour in sector *A* amounts to an excise tax (at the same rate) on sector *A*. Similarly if capital is taxed at rate τ_K^B in sector *B* and labour in sector *B* is taxed at equivalent rate τ_L^B then the two together are equivalent to a general excise tax (at the same rate) on sector *B*. In the same vein a tax on *A* and *B* is equivalent to a general lump sum tax since this is a tax on both factors and the factors are in fixed supply. Hence this kind of tax would be non-distortionary. However, if factors were not in fixed supply then the factor supplies would change in response to the tax and hence non-neutrality would be unavoidable.

From the above results on equivalences we immediately realize that only three of these taxes need to be considered. They, however, have to be independent. We have already considered one of them in the preceding paragraph. One other is discussed below. The third is extremely straightforward and is left as an exercise for the reader.

The case that we want to consider is a particularly complicated one and has been often been discussed in the literature. (See for instance Harberger (1962)). This is the case of a partial factor tax i.e. a tax that applies to one factor in one industry. Let us study the example used by Harberger by considering a capital tax on industry A. Since in the multi tax case the demand and supply equations would be a special case of the example studied above we concentrate on the factor tax in the absence of all other taxes.

Since this is a factor tax the demand equation remains unchanged in that

$$\hat{A} - \hat{B} = -\Delta_D(\hat{p}_A - \hat{p}_B).$$

On the supply side, however, now

$$\hat{C}_{LA} = -\beta_{KA}\sigma_A(\hat{W} - \hat{r}) + \beta_{KA}\sigma_A\hat{\tau}_K^A$$

and

$$\hat{c}_{KA} = \beta_{LA}\sigma_A(W - r) - \beta_{LA}\sigma_A\hat{\tau}_K^A.$$

Hence, equation (22) changes to

$$\lambda_{LA}\hat{A} + \lambda_{LB}\hat{B} = (\hat{W} - \hat{r})(\lambda_{LA}\beta_{KA}\sigma_A + \lambda_{LB}\beta_{KB}\sigma_B) - \lambda_{LA}\beta_{KA}\sigma_A\hat{\tau}_K^A \qquad (22'')$$

and equation (23) changes to

$$\lambda_{KA}\hat{A} + \lambda_{KB}\hat{B} = -(\hat{W} - \hat{r})(\lambda_{KA}\beta_{LA}\sigma_A + \lambda_{KB}\beta_{LB}\sigma_B) + \lambda_{KA}\beta_{LA}\sigma_A\hat{\tau}_K^A. \qquad (23'')$$

Hence the price equation (11) changes to

$$\hat{p}_A - \hat{p}_B = (\beta_{KA} - \beta_{KB})\hat{r} + (\beta_{LA} - \beta_{LB})\hat{W} + \beta_{KA}\hat{\tau}_K^A. \qquad (11'')$$

Combining equation (11″) with the demand equation (28′) we can deduce the following conclusions:

(i) If $\lambda_{LA} < \lambda_{KA}$ then the net rate of profit will fall relative to wages

(ii) If $\lambda_{LA} > \lambda_{KA}$ and we have fixed coefficients in production in sector A then the rate of profit will rise relative to the wage rate.

(iii) Combining (i) and (ii) then if $\lambda_{LA} > \lambda_{KA}$ then, ceteris paribus, the greater is the likelihood of profits rising relative to wages the (*a*) smaller is σ_A; (*b*) larger is Δ_D and (*c*) the larger the difference $\beta_{KA} - \beta_{KB}$ or $\beta_{LA} - \beta_{LB}$.

We can view the incidence of this capital tax diagrammatically in the Fig. 12.11. It is also possible to make a rather useful distinction between an output effect and a factor substitution effect. This distinction was first articulated by Miszekowski (1974).

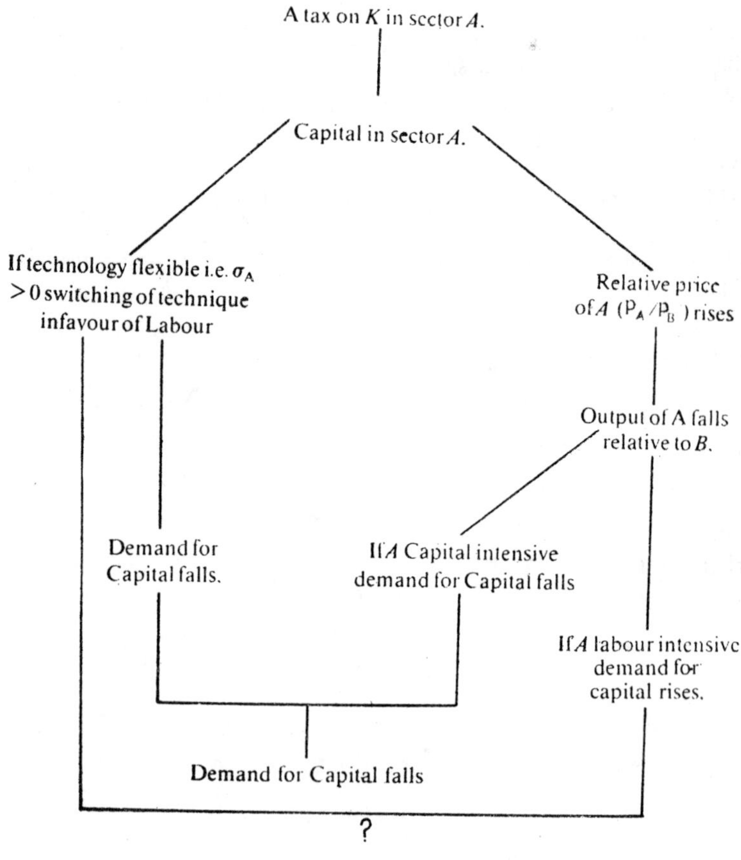

Fig. 12.11

The imposition of a capital tax on industry A raises the cost of capital in industry A. Via equation (11″) the price of A rises relative to P_B which means that via the output effect (equation (28′)) the output of A falls relative to B. Thus if A is labour intensive it will release more labour per unit capital than B can absorb (at the existing wage rental ratio). Demand for capital must, therefore, rise. If A is more capital intensive then more capital per unit labour is released than which industry B can absorb. The demand for capital would then fall.

For the factor substitution effect we realize that if technology permits it (i.e. $\sigma_A > 0$) there will be a substitution of labour for capital in industry A. Hence this effect would tend to reduce the demand for capital.

Some Extensions of Tax Incidence Theory

The basic model of tax incidence studied above is the simplest general equilibrium model in terms of which we describe tax incidence. This model has been extended in a number of important directions. We consider some of these now.

Factor Immobility

We have been implicitly assuming that both factors of production are perfectly mobile between sectors A and B. It is straightforward to amend the analysis to allow for complete immobility of one of the factors. If, for instance; capital is immobile its return may diverge in its two uses. Thus a tax on capital in sector A becomes a tax on capital in general and is borne entirely by capital. If the tax levied was an excise tax or industry A the mobile factor (labour) would move and thus reduce its wage in B. By the same token returns to capital in industry B would increase.

Distortions in Factor Markets

Suppose that workers in industry A get unionized and secure a premium over the return to workers in industry B i.e.

$$W_A = kw,\ W_B = w,\ k > 1. \tag{29}$$

This mark up over wages is considered to be exogenous. We are not, for the time being, concerned about its implications for employment or the earnings of workers in general, with the wage structure implied by equation (29) the factor employment equations can be written as

$$C_{LA}(r, W_A)A + C_{LB}(r, W)B = L_0 \tag{7''}$$

$$C_{KA}(r, W_A)A + C_{KB}(r, W)B = K_0. \tag{8''}$$

Since perfect competition is still assumed to prevail in the product market we must have

$$p_A = C_A(r, W_A)$$
$$p_B = C_B(r, W).$$

Thus price equals marginal cost in both markets.

Nothing happens to the demand side of the model and these are the only changes in the supply side.

If we now compare this set up with the one derived earlier for the no distortion case we realize immediately that the presence of the difference between W_A and W acts simply like a tax or labour in sector. If we look back at our earlier analysis we realize immediately that it does not matter whether we write the distortion as in equation (29) or simply as $W(1 + t_L^A) = W\tau_L^A$; $W_B = W$. The distortion is merely a tax on labour in industry A. The previous analysis is completely applicable.

We must realize however that we have visualized unionization in a rather simple minded manner. Perhaps the most important power of a union stems from its ability to restrict entry (into jobs as well as the union). If (as we have implicitly done above) we allow free migration from one sector to another we are really missing the essence of union activity. However, this is a useful beginning that enables us to make a direct link between taxes and distortion. A distortion in the capital market can be similarly analyzed.

Monopoly Power

Suppose industry A is controlled exclusively by one firm. We follow Harberger (1962) in assuming that the monopolist follows a simple mark up pricing rule

$$p_A = (1 + m)C_A(r, W). \tag{30}$$

No other distortions are present in the economy m is a mark up over costs exercised by the monopolist in industry A. It is quite clear then that the presence of the monopoly is equivalent to an excise tax on A in the competitive economy. This analogy is strictly valid only if m is arbitrarily close to zero i.e. the mark up is an infinitesimally small one. If that is not the case then we have to be realize first that β_{LA} and β_{KA} will now refer to share of labour and capital in industry A's cost not in the value of output of industry A. The divergence between the two (which didn't exist in the competitive case) is accounted for by the mark up. Thus

$$\tilde{\beta}_{LA} = \frac{\beta_{LA}}{1+m}; \quad \tilde{\beta}_{KA} = \frac{\beta_{KA}}{1+m}$$

where the tildas ($\sim$) refer to share in value. Thus the equations relating factor price changes to product output changes equations (22) and (23) will have to be altered. The rest of the analysis stays the same.

A number of other interesting extensions of the static general equilibrium model of tax incidence have been made but the short list above should suffice to give us an idea of the types of problems that have been considered. We will now consider our last chore in this chapter i.e. computable models of tax incidence.

Computable Models of Tax Incidence

In recent years an important alternative to the standard calculus oriented method of assessing tax incidence has developed. This uses an algorithm perfected by Scarf (1973) to compute general equilibrium. Modern proofs of the existence[14] of general equilibrium usually use a fixed point argument.[15] Scarf's algorithm uses the idea that if the general equilibrium model being studied is empirically computable then if we can define a process of iteration (the algorithm) that converges to the fixed point then we have essentially proved existence of general equilibrium.

Shoven, Whalley and some others have made very innovative use of Scarf's algorithm to measure tax incidence. In a given empirical setting they

[14]For an example see the appendix to this chapter.

[15]For a lucid discussion see Arrow and Hahn (1971).

compute the fixed point before and after the tax(es) is (are) imposed and adduce the difference to tax incidence. This method has the advantage that it circumvents the cumbersome equations of the calculus approach, is more general because of signs that may be ambiguous in the calculus case are explicit here and also gives us precise numerical values for tax incidence. Also the comparison of tax incidence is global rather than infinitesimal, around equilibrium.

We briefly describe the approach used in this analysis. The basic point is to compute general equilibrium with and without taxes i.e. we define two continuous mappings on closed, bounded convex sets with one mapping corresponding to the no tax case and the other mapping corresponding to the tax case. The respective fixed points define the equilibria for the economy in the two cases. The differences between them constitute the incidence of the tax.

The basic equations of our system are

$$C_{LA}(r, W)A + C_{LB}(r, W)B = 0$$
$$C_{KA}(r, W)A + C_{KB}(r, W)B = K_0.$$

These are the supply equations. Since product prices are equal to the respective marginal costs there is no need to consider product prices separtately. The demand equations are

$$A = A[C_A(r, W), C_B(r, W), rK_0 + WL_0]$$
$$B = B[C_A(r, W), C_B(r, W), rK_0 + WL_0].$$

Now suppose we have a tax on labour in industry B. These equations will now have to be rewritten as

$$C_{LA}(r, W)A + C_{LB}(r, W_L^{\tau B})B = L_0$$
$$C_{KA}(r, W)A + C_{KB}(r, W_L^{\tau B})B = K_0$$

and

$$A = A[C_A(r, W), C_B(r, W_L^{\tau B}), WL_0 + rK_0]$$
$$B = B[C_A(r, W), C_B(r, W_L^{\tau B}), WL_0 + rK_0].$$

It is possible now to compute the two equilibria and compare them if resource endowments and parametric values are pre-specified. Shoven and Whalley assume the elasticities of substitution in production (σ_A and σ_B) to be fixed. We can then take different values of the resource endowments and incorporate different assumptions about the demand functions for A and B.

Shoven and Whalley have in an example designed to study the taxation of r taken resource endowment values first used by Harberger (1962). They also assume that there are two classes of consumers with constant propensities to purchase the goods A and B. Resource endoments and elasticities of substitution and demand are varied parametically to study the effect that such variations may have on tax incidence.

In later works the level of disaggregation has been quite impressive. A large number of sectors with different values of elasticities of substitution have been considered. Resource endowments have been varied parametrically. Different types of consumes (i.e. with different incomes) have been considered and various assumptions have been made about their price and income elasticities of demand.

The amount of work that can be done in this area is really mindboggling.[16] One can reasonably expect that over time the parametric values chosen in such studies would be econometrically estimated. Moreover, one can even visualize a single approach—an integrated approach to tax incidence that uses econometric estimation and general equilibrium computation together. Since Scarf's algorithm is so handy and has been further developed and simplified such advances are not really far off.

Concluding Remarks

In this chapter we discussed different approaches to assessing incidence of tax in static general equilibrium. Some elements have been critical to the story we had to tell. To mention just a few we have the static nature of the problem, fixed supplies of factors etc.

In subsequent chapters we will try to get around some of these shortcomings. Dynamic models are considered in the next chapters. We will also study mixes of direct and indirect taxes.

The problem of variable factor supplies is taken up at length in the chapter on optimal taxation.

[16]For instance variable factor supplies and comparison of income and expenditure taxes have already been done. See Shoven and Whalley (1976) and Fullerton, Shoven and Whalley (1983).

Appendix

Proof of Existence of General Equilibrium

In this appendix we briefly sketch, the proof of the existence of general equilibrium using a fixed point argument. Shoven and Whalley compute the fixed point before and after tax and adduce the difference to tax incidence.

Consider a general equilibrium system with n markets. We assume that regular excess demand functions exist for these markets and general equilibrium implies zero excess demand in all markets.

Consider a normalized price point such that

$$X_j = 0 \quad \text{for} \quad p_j > 0 \quad \text{and} \quad X_j \leqslant 0 \quad \text{for} \quad p_j = 0, \qquad j = 1, \ldots, n$$

where X_j is the excess demand and p_j is the price prevailing in this market. Let us consider the system now such that

$$\sum_{j=1}^{n} p_j = 1, \quad p_j \geqslant 0,$$

so that prices are never negative and have been normalized to sum to unity.

Now let us define excess demands in terms of these normalized prices as

$$\bar{X}_j(p_1, \ldots, p_n); \quad j = 1, \ldots, n.$$

Define n functions by

$$H_j(p_1, \ldots, p_n) = \max\,[p_j + \bar{X}_j;\ 0.5p_j] > 0.$$

Since prices are never negative and *a* zero price implies a positive excess demand it follows that all functions H_j are strictly positive.

Let

$$T(p_1, \ldots, p_n) = \sum_{j=1}^{n} H_j > 0.$$

Now define n new functions as

$$S_j(p_1, \ldots, p_n) = \frac{H_j}{T} > 0, \quad j = 1, \ldots, n.$$

Obviously the S_j's form a continuous mapping of prices. Now

$$\sum_{j=1}^{n} S_j = \sum_{j=1}^{n} H_j/T = 1,$$

we have a normalized set and S_j maps this normalized set onto itself.

Now we are in a position to use Brouwer's fixed point theorem. Brouwer's fixed point theorem says that a continuous mapping of a closed bounded, convex set into itself has a fixed point i.e. if $F(x)$ is the function then there exists a point x^* such that

$$x^* = F(x^*).$$

This theorem is clearly usable in our case and from this we have the existence of a set of prices $\overset{*}{p}_1, \ldots, \overset{*}{p}_n$ such that

$$p_j^* = S_j(p_1^*, \ldots, p_n^*) = \frac{H_j(\overset{*}{p}_1, \ldots, \overset{*}{p}_n)}{T} > 0$$

$$j = 1, \ldots, n.$$

Now all that remains to be shown is that at this vector of prices all excess demands are zero.

Now $H_j(\overset{*}{p}_1, \overset{*}{p}_2, \ldots, \overset{*}{p}_n)$ is at least as great as $0.5\overset{*}{p}_j$. If each $H_j(\ )$ were equal to $0.5\overset{*}{p}_j$ the sum, T, would equal 0.5. If any $H_j(\ )$ exceeds $0.5\overset{*}{p}_j$, $T(\ ) > 0.5$. If all $H_j(\ ) = 0.5\overset{*}{p}_j$ then it is clear that all $\bar{X}_j(p_j^*, \ldots, p_n^*) < 0$. This implies that $\sum_{j=1}^{n} \overset{*}{p}_j\bar{X}_j < 0$ which contradicts Walra's law. Hence not all $H_j = 0.5\overset{*}{p}_j$. Assume that it is true for some j. Then

$$p_j^* = \frac{H_j(\ )}{T} = \frac{0.5\overset{*}{p}_j}{T} < p_j^*, \quad \text{since } T > 0.$$

But this is a contradiction.
Hence

$$p_j^* = \frac{\overset{*}{p}_j + \bar{X}_j}{T}; \quad j = 1, \ldots, n.$$

This cannot be true unless $\bar{X}_j = 0$ for all j. Thus the price vector $\overset{*}{p}_1, \ldots, \overset{*}{p}_n$ is associated with zero excess demand in each market and hence with general equilibrium.

13. Tax Incidence in a Growing Economy

The analysis so far has been static. It has given us some insight into how taxation affects the static equilibrium of an economy. But clearly it does not tell us how taxation affects the movement of an economy through time. The time has come to confront this question.

The effect of fiscal variables on the growth path of an economy is a complex matter. A basic framework of analysis has to be chosen. We choose the simplest one sector neoclassical model of growth as expounded by Solow (1956). Tax incidence in multi-sector or general equilibrium models of growth is a difficult matter and not much work has been done in this area. Once the model becomes dynamic, however, we realize that the government has fiscal instruments other than taxation at its disposal. In particular the public debt policy of the government is important. The government can borrow from the private sector and finance its expenses without taking recourse to taxation. Recently there has been some concern voiced in some countries over the large and increasing magnitude of the national debts in these countries. In view of such controversy the study of national debt becomes important.

Yet another topic which has recently dominated growth theory is the recent concern over rapidly depleting exhaustible resources. We will amend the Solow model suitably to study the tax incidence in a growing economy with exhaustible resources.

A framework which has sometimes been used as an alternative to but mostly as a supplement to the basic Solow model is the life cycle model of saving and consumption. We will study some problems of tax incidence within such a framework as well.

The plan of this chapter is as follows. We first detail the simple Solow model without taxation and study the incidence of some taxes in such a model. We then move on to the life cycle or overlapping generations model of saving and consumption and study incidence. We then start bringing in financial variables. We first study tax incidence in a monetary growth model with exhaustible resources. Then we move on to consider fiscal policy in general. The chapter closes with an example to show distorting effects of inflation. In the appendix to this chapter we discuss some results from the relatively new area of dynamic tax incidence.

The Basic One Sector Growth Model

The neoclassical theory of economic growth originated in a classic paper by Robert Solow. Solow wrote this paper partly as an answer to the pessimisitic[1] conslusions of Harrod and Domar and partly as an independent way of visualizing the growth process.

While writing the introduction to a famous text on growth theory[2] Solow stated"... The choice at the moment seems to be between exponential steady states and paths that depart even further from steady states. Given this choice the steady state seems the better approximation so the facts of economic growth." This is ample reason, then, to study stable growth models.

In Solow's model aggregate output, Q, is produced by capital and labour inputs. Production is described by a smooth, twice continuously differentiable, strictly quasi-concave production with constant returns. Thus we write

$$Q = F(K, L) \tag{1}$$

with

$$\frac{\partial F}{\partial K} > 0; \ \frac{\partial F}{\partial L} > 0; \ \frac{\partial^2 F}{\partial K^2} < 0, \ \frac{\partial^2 F}{\partial L^2} < 0.$$

Clearly capital and labour are smoothly substituable in the production process.

From linear homogeneity of the production function we can write

$$\frac{Q}{L} = q = F(K/L, 1) = f(k). \tag{2}$$

Given our assumptions $f'(\ \ ) > 0$ and $f''(\ \ ) < 0$. We assume factor markets to be competitive. Thus the wage rate (w) equals the marginal product of labour and the rate of rental (r) equals the marginal product of capital. From equation (2) we have

$$w = f - kf'$$

and

$$r = f'.$$

Thus labour force is assumed to grow exogenously at the fixed exponential rate n so that

$$\frac{\dot{L}}{L} = n. \tag{3}$$

A constant fraction, s of output is saved. Savings are automatically transformed into investment.

Thus

$$\mathring{K} = sQ. \tag{4}$$

[1]Harrod, far instance, argued that if the rate of growth of the economy was not equal to the "warranted" rate of growth the economy would either experience every increasing inflation or ever increasing depression.

[2]See E. Burmeister and R. Dobell (1970).

Now the rate of grwth ($\mathring{k}/k$) of the capital labour ratio is

$$\frac{\mathring{k}}{k} = \frac{\mathring{K}}{K} - \frac{\mathring{L}}{L}. \tag{5}$$

Substituting from (3) and (4) we get

$$\dot{k} = sf(k) - nk = \phi(k). \tag{6}$$

This is the fundamental equation of Solow's growth model. If capital and labour both grow at the rate n, output itself will also grow at rate n and the capital labour ratio will be constant. If k is constant w and r will remain unchanged since they are both functions of k alone. We can plot equation (6) to better study the dynamics of the model

In Fig. 13.1 we plot the $sf(k)$ and nk schedules against k. Our assumptions about technology are sufficient to guarantee the shape of $sf(k)$. At k^* $\mathring{k} = 0$ and steady state is achieved. To the left of k^*, $\mathring{k} > 0$ so we move toward k^*. To the right of k^*, $\mathring{k} < 0$ and, once again, we move toward k^*. The k^* equilibrium is locally stable. In fact we can show that this equilibrium is globally stable.[3]

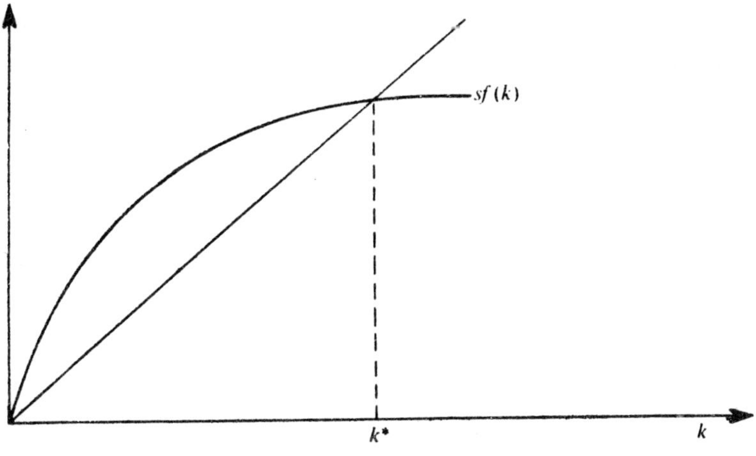

Fig. 13.1

We know that there exists k_1 such that $\phi(k) > 0$ for $0 < k < k_1$ and $\lim_{k \to \infty} \cdot \phi(k) < 0$.

Take some capital labour ratio k_2. If $\phi(k_2) > 0$ then there exists (by the intermediate value theorem of calculus) an equilibrium point $k > k_2$. Define

[3]The satisfaction of the Inada conditions is necessary for the existence of steady state equilibrium. These conditions are

$$f(0) = 0, f(\infty) = \infty;$$
$$f'(0) = \infty, f'(\infty) = 0.$$

$k^* = \inf \{k/\phi(k)\} = 0, k > k_2$, we see immediately that $\phi(k^*) = 0$. Similarly if $\phi(k_2) < 0$ an analogous argument applies. Thus from any initial value k_2, $0 < k_2 < \infty$ the solution approaches some equilibrium point and hence the system is globally stable.

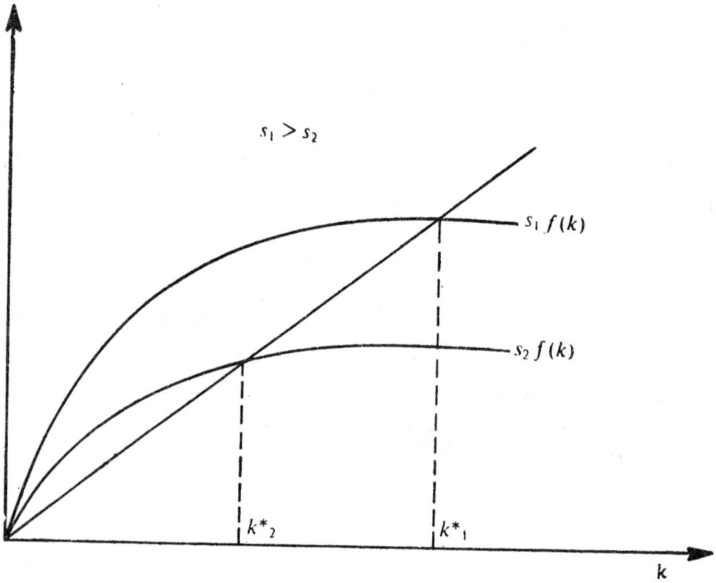

Fig. 13.2(a) The effect of an increase in the propensity to save.

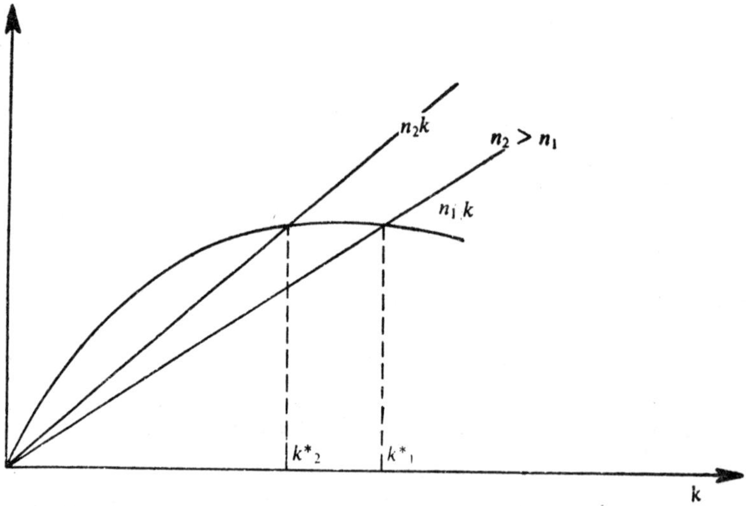

Fig. 13.2(b) The effect of an increase in the rate of growth of labour.

A lot of criticisms can be made against the model. Some of them have to do with the simple nature of the exercise e.g. it is a highly aggregative model, the labour force and population growth rates are the same. These assumptions can and have been relaxed in later work. Some other criticisms are more fundamental and have to do with the neoclassical nature of the excise. These include the assumption of continuous full employment, the presence of perfect competition, the automatic transformation of savings into investment.[4] However, this is a long term model where all these problems should not carry much significant. In any case this remains thefundamental neoclassical growth model and, more importantly, the fundamental model in terms of which analyses of incidence of taxes in growing economies have been carried out.

Tax Incidence in the Solow Model of Economic Growth

Just because a steady state equilibrium exists at k^* does not mean that we are always at steady state. A tax will alter the steady state equilibrium of the economy. Moreover, it will also affect the path that the economy takes to reach the steady state equilibrium. Hence there are two different methods of calculating tax incidence in a growing economy. One would be to see how the steady state equilibrium is affected by the tax. Thus we compare pre and post tax steady states. However this analysis implicitly assumes that adjustment to steady state is infinitely fast. Alternatively we can calculate incidence of the tax without reference to steady state. We will study the first method and consider an example of the second method in the appendix.

Let us consider a tax on capital and let us suppose that the government intends this tax to be redistributive so that the proceeds from the tax are paid to workers as a lump sum payment. This would require us to make a formal distinction between workers and capitalists.[5]

We suppose that capitalists save a fraction s_r of their income and workers save a fraction s_w. Clearly $s_r > s_w$. Let us suppose that workers get a fraction λ of national income. By Euler's theorem $(1 - \lambda)$ goes to capitalists. We also suppose that capitalists do not work. Capitalists pay the tax τ_k which the workers receive as transfer payment. We can hence write

$$sf(k) = s_r[(1 - \lambda) f - \tau_k] + s_w(\lambda f + \tau_k).$$

The condition for steady state growth now reads

$$s_r[(1 - \lambda)f - \tau_k] + s_w(\lambda f + \tau_k) = nk. \tag{7}$$

To find the effect of the tax on steady state k we differentiate equation (7) with respect to τ_k to get

$$(s_r f' - \lambda' s_r f - s_r \lambda f') \frac{dk}{d_k} - s_r$$
$$+(s_w \lambda f' + s_w f \lambda') \frac{dk}{d\tau_k} + s_w = n \frac{dk}{d\tau_k}.$$

[4]Readers will recall that the difficulties associated with transforming savings into investment lie at the root of Keyne's theory of unemployment.

[5]Building a growth model with a formal distinction between workers and capitalists is a tradition that goes back to the writings of Kaldor (1955) and Passinetti (1962). For a recent statement see Marglin (1983).

Rearranging terms we get

$$(s^0 f' + (s_w - s_r)\lambda' f - n)\frac{dk}{d\tau_k} = s_r - s_w \tag{8}$$

where $s^0 = s_w\lambda + s_r(1 - \lambda)$ is the average saving rate.

Thus

$$\frac{dk}{d\tau_k} = \frac{s_r - s_w}{\Delta}. \tag{9}$$

Now it can be shown that if the steady state is stable $\Delta < 0$ and hence $dk/d_k < 0$ (since $s_r > s_w$).

Hence the tax lowers the capital labour ratio in steady state equilibrium.

Are workers better off? Ceteris paribus a lowering of k will reduce w but there is also the transfer to contend with. To see the effect on worker's income differentiate it with respect to τ_k

$$\frac{d[\lambda f + \tau_k]}{d\tau_k} = (\lambda f' + f\lambda')\frac{dk}{d\tau_k} + 1. \tag{10}$$

Substituting directly for $\lambda f' + f\lambda'$ we get

$$\frac{d(\lambda f + \tau_k)}{d\tau_k} = \frac{s^0 f' - n + (s_r - s_w)\lambda f'}{\Delta}$$

$$= \frac{s_r f' - n}{\Delta}. \tag{11}$$

Now $\Delta < 0$, if $s_r f' < n$, then worker's income does indeed go up. Otherwise the drop in k overwhelms the transfer and worker's income goes down. Even in the case it does go up the magnitude of this increase may be relatively small.

Let us now study a case in which the government taxes capital not to redistribute income but merely to finance its own consumption. In this case it will not be necessary to distinguish between workers and capitalists. We can, however, make the savings rate a function of k and the tax rate t_k on capital.

The condition for steady state equilibrium now becomes

$$s(k, t_k)\, f(k) = nk. \tag{12}$$

Differentiating with respect to t_k we have

$$\left(s_k \frac{dk}{d_k} + s_{t_k}\right) f + s(k, t_k) f' \frac{dk}{dt_k} = n\frac{dk}{dt_k}.$$

Or rearranging terms we have

$$(sf' + s_k - n)\frac{dk}{dt_k} = - s_{t_k} f. \tag{13}$$

Again local stability requires that $\Delta(=sf' + s_k - n)$ be negative. Thus

$$\frac{dk}{dt_k} = -\frac{s_{tk}f}{\Delta} < 0 \tag{14}$$

as $$s_{tk} < 0.$$

Suppose $s_{t_k} < 0$ then $dk/dt_k < 0$ so that the imposition of the tax leads to a fall in equilibrium k. This fall will lower the return to labour. To that extent the tax will have been shifted.

It is natural here to ask whether the fall in k will be so severe that the rental rate actually rises. The net return to capital is

$$\rho = (1 - t_k)f'. \tag{15}$$

Differentiating with respect to t_k we have

$$\frac{d\rho}{dt_k} = (1 - t_k)f''\frac{dk}{dt_k} - f'. \tag{16}$$

It is possible for this expression to be positive.

As an exercise the reader can try to show that if we adopted a two class framework with $s_r > 0$ and $s_w = 0$, $d\rho/dt_k = 0$ and hence the tax is fully shifted to labour.

In a similar vein it is possible to analyze a tax on labour.

It is a relatively straightforward matter to extend the model to accommodate "neutral" technical. There are three types of neutral technical progress as described below.

In the Table 13.1, we have defined three types of neutral technical progress at rate α and given Cobb-Douglas examples. Hicks neutral technical progress augments both capital and labour. Solow neutral technical progress

Table 13.1

Type of technical progress	*Form of production function/example*
Hicks neutral	$Q = e^{\alpha t}F(K, L)$ Cobb Douglas example $Q = e^{\alpha t}K^{1-\lambda} L^{\lambda}$
Solow neutral	$Q = F(e^{\alpha t}K, L)$ Cobb Douglas example $Q = e^{\alpha t}K^{1-\lambda} L^{\lambda}$
Harrod neutral	$Q = F(K, e^{\alpha t}L)$ Cobb Douglas example $Q = K^{1-\lambda} e^{\alpha t}L^{\lambda}$

augments only capital whereas Harrod neutral technical progress augments only labour. As is evident for the Cobb-Douglas case all three types of neutral progress amount to the same thing. In essence for this case we can consider, say, labour growing at rate $n + \alpha$ where n is the biological rate of growth and α is the rate of technical progress. Hence the fundamental dynamic equation of Solow's model becomes

$$\dot{k} = sf(k) - (n + \alpha)k. \tag{17}$$

The rest of the analysis remains the same.

Neutral technical progress as an idea is hard to defend but not much work has been done in the theory of tax incidence although the theory of technical progress is itself fairly well developed.

Tax Incidence in a Life Cycle Model of Savings

The analysis in the previous section can be criticized for making an arbitrary assumption about savings. Usually, it may be argued, savings are the result of conscious choice by people. The natural framework to study the incidence of taxation when savings are the product of conscious choice is the life cycle model of savings already detailed in a previous chapter.

We stick to the simplifying assumptions made in the previous section i.e. that we live in a world without technical progress and that the tax we study is imposed on an economy with no other taxes and that there is no public debt.

Let us consider the choice problem of a typical consumer of generation g. c_1^g is his first period consumption, c_2^g his second period consumption. His wage is w^g and the rate of interest is r^{g+1}. He maximizes utility $u(c_1^g, c_2^g)$ subject to the budget constraint

$$c_2^g = (w^g - c_1^g)(1 + r^{g+1}). \tag{18}$$

Hence one can write savings of generation g as (all individuals are assumed identical)

$$S^g(w^g, r^{g+1}) = w^g - c_1^g(w^g, r^{g+1}) \tag{19}$$

People of generation g have the savings of generation $g - 1$ as capital whereas they leave behind their savings as capital for generation $g + 1$. Thus

$$K^{g+1} = S^g(\ \ )\cdot L^g. \tag{20}$$

We assume that labour grows exogenously at rate n so that

$$k_{g+1} = \frac{K^{g+1}}{L^{g+1}} = S^g(\ \ )\,\frac{L^g}{L^{g+1}} = \frac{S^g}{1 + n}. \tag{21}$$

We once again define steady state as a situation where the capital labour ratio does not change from one generation to another i.e. when

$$k^1 = k^2 = \ldots\ldots = k^{g-1} = k^g = k^{g+1} = \ldots\ldots$$

Hence in this situation for generation g we must have

$$c_1^g = w^g - (1 + n)k^g \tag{22}$$

and similarly

$$c_2^g = (1 + r^{g+1})(1 + n)k^g. \tag{23}$$

Here the value of k^g is arbitrary and it would be natural to vary k^g to see how steady state c_1 and c_2 depend on k^g. From equation (22) we have

$$\frac{\partial c_1^g}{\partial k^g} = f' - k^g f'' - f' - (1 + n)$$

since $$w = f - k^g f'.$$

Similarly from equation (23) we get

$$\frac{\partial c_2^g}{\partial k^g} = (1 + f')(1 + n) + k^g(1 + n)f''$$

$$= (1 + n)\,[(1 + r^{g+1}) + k^g f'']$$

since $$r^{g+1} = f'.$$

Hence the envelope defining how steady state consumption changes when the capital labour ratio changes has slope

$$\frac{dc_2^g}{dc_1^g} = \frac{\partial c_2^g/\partial k^g}{\partial c_1^g/\partial k^g} = \frac{(1 + n)[(1 + r) + k^g f'']}{-k^g f'' - (1 + n)}.$$

This envelope has been plotted in Fig. 13.3.

For a competitive consumer the marginal rate of substitution between first and second period consumption would be $(1 + r^g)$. Hence he would come to an equilibrium at point N. We have also drawn the point N^* which is the so called golden rule.[6]

We now bring taxation into the picture. Suppose now that we have a tax at the rate t_k and this tax is used to give a lump sum grant to the old.

[6]This idea is due to Phelps who asked the following question: What is the maximum sustainable per capita consumption in the Solow model? As an illustration take the model of the previous section where in steady state $sf(k) - nk = 0$ so that

$$s = \frac{nk}{f(k)}.$$

Per capita consumption is, then

$$c = (1 - s)f(k)$$

$$= \left(1 - \frac{nk}{f(k)}\right) f(k) = f(k) - nk.$$

Maximizing this with respect to s we have

$$\frac{dc}{ds} = (f' - n)\frac{dk^*}{ds} = 0,$$

where k^* is now the "optimum" steady state capital labour ratio. Now since

$$\frac{dk^*}{ds} > 0$$

we must have in optimum. $f' = n$ i.e. the "optimum" rate of interest equals the rate of growth of population. Samuelson has called this the "biological" rate of interest.

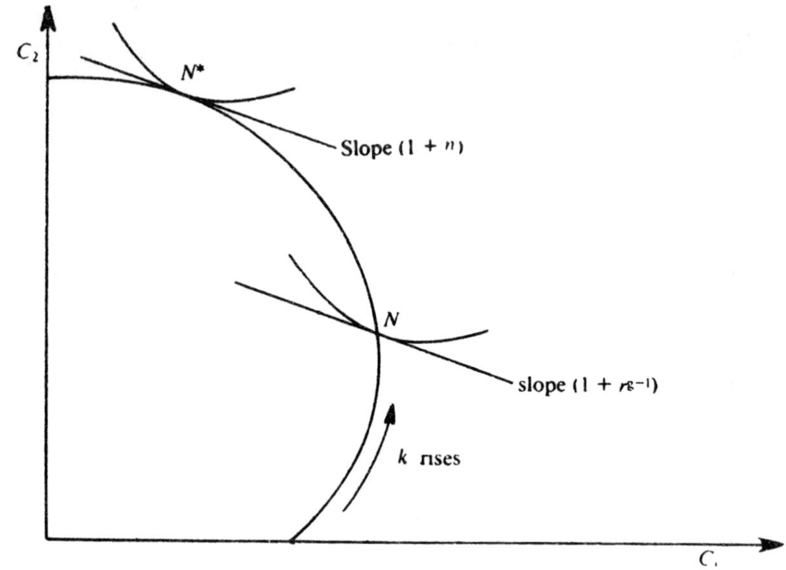

Fig. 13.3

The individual's budget constraint is now[7]

$$c_1^g + \frac{c_2^g}{1 + r^{g+1}} = w^g + \frac{T}{1 + r^{g+1}} \tag{24}$$

where $r^{g+1} = (1 - t_k)f'$ and T is the transfer.

Hence the c_1^g, c_2^g frontier is given by

$$c_1^g = w^g - (1 + n)k^g$$

$$c_2^g = [1 + f'(1 - t_k)](1 + n)k^g + T.$$

We calculate the proceeds from the tax to be

$$T = t_k f'(1 + n)k^g \text{ so that}$$

$$c_2^g = (1 + r^{g+1})(1 + n)k^g.$$

Hence the c_1, c_2 frontier remains the same as before. However, since the net interest rate has altered the marginal rate of substitution between first and second period consumption is altered.

In Fig. 13.4 pre-tax equilibrium is at N where the solid line represents the consumer's budget line before the tax. After the imposition of the tax the tax the budget line rotates to become the dashed line. If consumption is a normal good then k will not rise.

In the analysis so far we have analyzed taxes seriatim. Suppose we wanted to compare the incidence of two taxes. What basis should we have for comparing taxes. Stiglitz (1978) has suggested that we choose balanced

[7]It is time to make explicit an assumption we have been making throughout i.e. there is perfect foresight. In other words r^{g+1}, k^{g+2} can be predicted with complete accuracy.

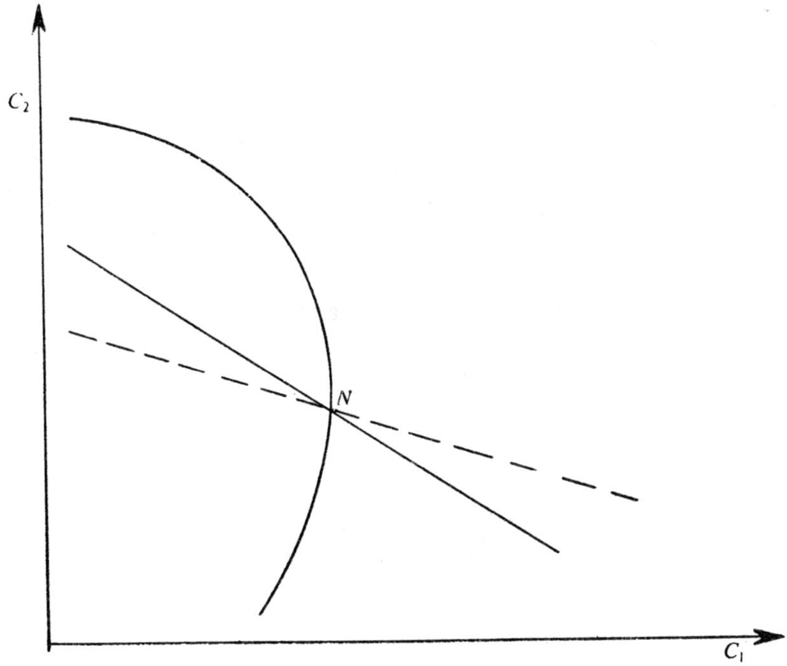

Fig. 13.4

growth path incidence. Suppose that the government can issue bonds to finance any government deficit. In this situation the effect of a tax on k is neutralized through appropriate government debt policy. Thus debt is changed to return the economy to the same steady state capital labour ratio that existed in pre tax equilibrium. This is the idea behind balanced growth path incidence.

It is clear that government debt is essentially a transfer between generations. A tax has to be paid by members of the current generation. But government debt is repaid from the earnings of future generations by taxing them or by some other measure. Thus current government debt is a transfer from future generations to present generations.

Barro (1974) has argued that government bonds should not be counted as net wealth. If people consider their offsprings' welfare important and do not discount the future this result would automatically hold. However, these are rather extreme assumptions and the members of any generation would consider government bonds to be net wealth on par with bonds issued by corporations. However, there is some fear now in some western countries that the extent of the national debt is staggering and one which compromises future plans in some important directions. Thus if the national debt is very high the ability of future generations to follow expansionary monetary and fiscal policies (without unleashing severe inflation) is restricted. For instance in the US some people are worried about the fact that large Federal deficits (mainly because of the expenses on armaments) has increased national debt to such a large amount that just interest payment on this debt runs into millions of dollars annually.

Tax Policy in a Growth Model with Exhaustible Resources

One important and recent development in growth theory has been the inclusion of exhaustible natural resources in the analysis. This interest has clearly been sparked off by the difficulties that the western world faced in reaction to the sharp increase in the price of fuel and quantitative restrictions first imposed in 1973. Fiscal policy has just started to be incorporated in the literature and the implications of such policy are not yet clearly understood. We will study here a paper which was the first to analyse tax policy in a monetary economy that has exhaustible resources. This theme was developed by Jha and Lachler (1983).

This paper provides us with a framework to study the interplay of monetary and fiscal forces. The paper generalizes the original contribution of Stiglitz (1974) and has important comments to make on inflationary finance as first studied by Phelps (1973).

Consider an economy with an aggregate production function[8]

$$Q = K^{\alpha_1} R^{\alpha_2} e^{\lambda t}, \ \alpha_1 + \alpha_2 = 1 \tag{25}$$

where R is the rate of utilization of the natural resource and λ is the rate of exogenous technical progress. Population is assumed constant.

We write disposable national income Y^D as

$$Y^D = Q + (\theta - \pi)M/p + [(\pi_R - \pi) - \gamma](p_R/p)S \tag{26}$$

with M = nominal outside money supply

p = money price of output

S = total stock of the natural resource so that $R = -\dot{S}$

p_R = money price of the natural resource

π_R = expected rate of change of p_R

π = expected rate of change of p

$\gamma = R/S = -\dot{S}/S$ (rate of resource depletion)

$\theta = \dot{M}/M$ = rate of growth of money supply.

Private savings behaviour is modelled as follows. Private savings, Z, are given by

$$Z = s(r)Y^D \tag{27}$$

with $0 < s < 1$ and $s' > 0$. r is the real rate of return (equal in equilibrium for all assets) which is equal to the marginal product of capital. All three real assets—human capital, physical capital and the natural resource—are perfect substitutes in the investor's portfolio. The government uses tax

[8]As explained in Jha and Lachler this production function can be obtained by assuming that labour and capital are perfect substitutes in the production process.

revenue merely for redistributive purposes and does not on its own finance any public expenditure.

Savings are costlessly transformed into net additions to wealth i.e.

$$Z = s(r)Y^{D} = \dot{K} + (\theta - \pi)\frac{M}{P} + (\pi_{R} - \pi - \gamma)\frac{p_{R}S}{p}. \qquad (27)$$

The first term on the right hand side is addition to capital stock (we assume zero depreciation), the second term is addition to holdings of real cash balances, and the last term is addition to R.

Thus $$\dot{K} = sQ - (1 - s)(\theta - \pi)M/p - (1 - s)(\pi_{R} - \pi - \gamma)\frac{P_{R}S}{p}.$$

Factor markets are assumed competitive and hence the marginal product of each factor is its reward i.e.

$$\partial Q/\partial R = \alpha_{2}Q/R = (1 + t_{p})(P_{R}/p) \qquad (28)$$

and $$\partial Q/\partial K = \alpha_{1}Q/K = r = \alpha_{1}\beta \qquad (29)$$

where t_{p} is a linear tax on the use of the natural resource and β is the output/capital ratio.

Since wealth holders regard capital and the natural resource as perfect substitutes the rates of return must be equalized i.e.

$$(1 - t_{c})(\pi_{R} - \pi) = \alpha_{1}\beta \qquad (30)$$

t_{c} is visualized as a tax on the value appreciation of the natural resource due to the price of the natural resource inflating at a higher rate than the general price level.

We will use two assumptions about the formation of expectations. We will assume alternatively that inflationary expectations are formed by perfect foresight and that expectation of inflation follows and adaptive expectations mechanism i.e.

$$\dot{\pi} = \epsilon(g_{p} - \pi), \qquad \pi_{R} = \epsilon(g_{pR} - \pi_{R}) \qquad (31)$$

where $0 < \epsilon < 1$ is the speed of adjustment whereas g_{p} is the actual rate of price inflation and g_{pR} is the actual rate of inflation of price of natural resource.

Since money carries no interest it is held only for transactions purposes. The opportunity cost of holding money is $r + \pi$ and there is only a transactions motive and no wealth motive or speculative motive for holding money. We model demand for money as per a very famous specification suggested by Cagan (1956)

$$\frac{M^{D}}{p} = Qe^{-a(r+\pi)}. \qquad (32)$$

We assume that the money market clears instantly and is always in equilibrium.

Using equations (31), (30), (29), (28) in the expression for $\dot{K}$ we get (upon dividing by K)

$$\frac{\dot{K}}{K} = g_K = s\beta - (1 - s)(\theta - \pi)\beta e^{-a(r+\pi)}$$

$$- (1 - s)\left(\frac{\alpha_1\beta}{1 - t_c} - \gamma\right)\frac{\alpha_2}{1 + t_p}\frac{\beta}{\gamma} \tag{33}$$

which is the rate of growth of capital with adaptive expectations. We will write everything in terms of rates of growth. Now we know

$$g_\beta = g_Q - g_K \quad \text{and} \quad g_\gamma = \gamma + g_R.$$

Differentiate (25) logarithmically to get

$$g_Q = \alpha_1 g_K + \alpha_2 g_R + \lambda. \tag{34}$$

Logarithmically differentiating equation (28), using equations (30) and (31) we have

$$g_Q = g_R + \alpha_1\beta/(1 - t_c) + \alpha_1\dot{\beta}/\epsilon(1 - t_c). \tag{35}$$

From equations (34) and (35) we solve simultaneously for g_Q and g_R to get

$$g_Q = \frac{\lambda}{\alpha_1} + g_K - \alpha_2\beta/(1 - t_c) - \alpha_2\beta g\beta/\epsilon(1 - t_c)$$

$$g_R = \frac{\lambda}{\alpha_1} + g_K - \beta/(1 - t_c) - \dot{\beta}/\epsilon(1 - t_c).$$

Substituting these values into the expressions for g_β and g_γ yields

$$g_\beta = [\lambda/\alpha_1 - \alpha_2\beta/(1 - t_c)]/(1 + \alpha_2\beta/\epsilon(1 - t_c)) \tag{36}$$

$$g_\gamma = \gamma + \lambda/\alpha_1 + g_K - \dot{\beta})/(1 - t_c) - \dot{\beta}/\epsilon(1 - t_c). \tag{37}$$

These are two equations in three variables γ, β and π. Hence we need an expression for the formation of π. To get this logarithmically differentiate the money demand function to note

$$\theta - g_p = g_Q - a(\dot{r} + \dot{\pi}). \tag{37'}$$

Notice from equation (39) that β is independent of γ and π. Hence we can solve for the steady state β as

$$\beta^* = \lambda(1 - t)/\alpha_1/\alpha_2 \tag{38}$$

by simply setting $g_\beta = 0$. We assume that we are always at the steady state value of β. Hence $r = \alpha_1\beta$ and $\dot{r} = 0$. Hence from (equation (37′) we have

$$g_p = \theta - g_Q + a\dot{\pi}. \tag{39}$$

Substituting equation (39) into (31) we finally get

$$\dot{\pi} = \frac{\epsilon}{1 - \epsilon a}[A + B + C] \tag{40}$$

where

$$A = (1 - s) - \frac{\alpha_1\alpha_2}{(1 - t_c)} \cdot \frac{\beta^{*2}}{(1 + t_p)} \cdot \frac{1}{\gamma}$$

$$B = (\theta - \pi)[1 + (1 - s)\beta^* e^{-a(r+\pi)}]$$

$$C = -\left(s + (1 - s)\frac{\alpha_2}{1 + t_p}\right)\beta^*.$$

Hence equation (37) can now be rewritten as

$$g_\gamma = \gamma - A + (\theta - \pi) - B - \left[C + \frac{\alpha_1\beta^*}{1 - t_c}\right]. \tag{41}$$

From equations (36), (40) and (41) form the basic dynamic structure of the economy. Moreover we have made a simplifying assumption that β always equals β^*. We may concentrate hence on equations (40) and (41).

Now the steady state solution to equations (40) and (41) is given by

$$A + B + C = 0 \tag{42}$$

$$\gamma + (\theta - \pi) - \alpha_1\beta^*/(1 - t_c) = 0. \tag{43}$$

Realize immediately that

(i) $A > 0$, $A_\gamma < 0$, $\lim\limits_{\gamma\to 0}. A = \infty$, $\lim\limits_{\gamma\to\infty}. A = 0$.

(ii) $C < 0$.

(iii) $B < 0$ as $\pi > \theta$ and

$$B_\pi = -[1 + (1 - s)\beta^*(1 + a(\theta - \pi)e^{-a(r+\pi)}] < 0$$

$$\text{for} \quad \pi < \theta + \frac{1}{a}.$$

Totally differentiate (42) and rearrange terms to get

$$\left.\frac{d\gamma}{d\pi}\right|\dot{\pi} = 0 = \frac{-B_\pi}{A_\gamma}$$

which is negative for $\gamma > 0$ and $\pi < \theta + 1/a$. Moreover, there exists a value for $\pi < \theta$ called $\hat{\pi}(\theta)$ so that $B + C = 0$. So the schedule $\dot{\pi} = 0$ for $\hat{\pi} \leqslant \pi \leqslant \theta + 1/a$ is downward sloping in the γ, π plane as drawn in Fig. 13.5. Similarly the schedule $g_\gamma = 0$ is upward sloping in the same plane so that steady state (described as a situation where $g_\beta = g_\pi = g_\beta = 0$) is unique.

Realize that steady state is characterized by $\gamma > 0$ so that the solution is non-trivial.

We now analyze stability. Take a linearizing Taylor expansion of equations (40) and (41) around γ^*, π^* and study the characteristic matrix

$$X = \begin{pmatrix} \frac{\epsilon}{1 - a\epsilon} B_\pi & \frac{\epsilon}{1 - a\epsilon} A_\gamma \\ -(1 + B_\pi) & (1 - A_\gamma) \end{pmatrix}.$$

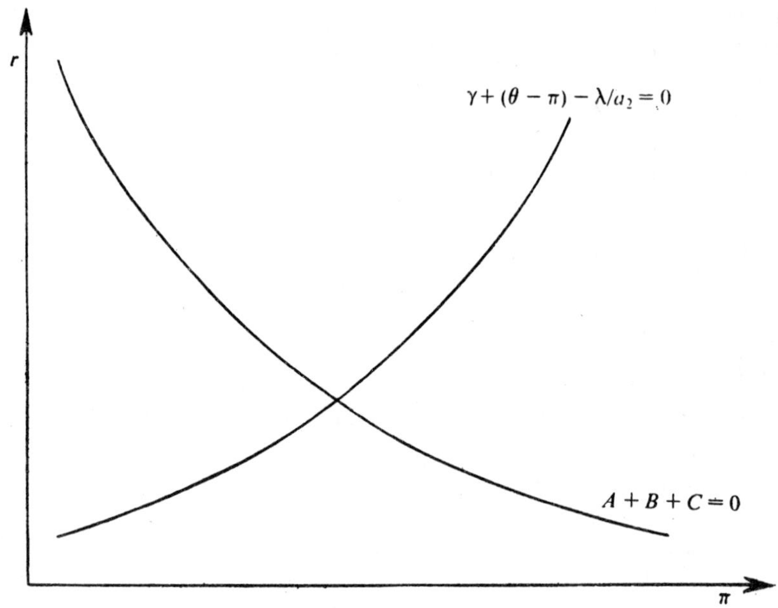

Fig. 13.5

Now if $\epsilon/1 - a\epsilon > 0$ the roots are of opposite sign so that the system is saddlepoint stable i.e. if the initial conditions happen to be just right the economy will converge to γ^*, π^*. If the initial conditions are not just right then the market system, left to itself, will never attain γ^*, π^*.

If $\epsilon \to \infty$, i.e. we have perfect foresight both roots are positive so that the system is necessarily unstable. In this case if we are not at γ^*, π^* to begin with, we will never get there.

In both cases the market system is functioning in an unsatisfactory manner so that there is need for government to intervene. We will now conceptualize how the government can intervene with its policy instruments t_c, t_p and θ to attain steady state. We first study the case of long run perfect foresight and then study adaptive expectations.

With long run perfect foresight we realize that initial conditions have to be just right otherwise since the roots of the characteristic matrix are both positive we will either deplete the resource too fast or perpetually underexploit it, in other words we will never get to steady state.

Since we have perfect foresight we need not take $\gamma(0)$ or $\eta(0)$ parametrically. Indeed we will realize the instability of the system and allow $\gamma(0)$ and $\pi(0)$ to adjust discontinuously so that we are at γ^*, π^* at time 0. The reader should realize that this is possible only because of the assumption of perfect foresight and will not be true in the adaptive expectation case where $\gamma(0)$ and $\pi(0)$ will have to be treated parametrically. Once the perfect foresight equilibrium gets disturbed the inherent dynamic instability of the system takes over.

Since this system is unstable we should not be doing comparative static exercises. Howerer, we realize that any steady state equilibrium is parametrized by t_c, t_p and θ. Moreover these policy variables are linearly independent. So one can visualize a series of steady state equilibria for different values of t_c, t_p and π so that were a certain equilibrium relevant (i.e. those values of t_c, t_p and θ obtained) we could work our way back to time 0.

In that spirit, then, we totally differentiate equations (42) and (43) to get

$$\begin{pmatrix} A_\gamma & B_\pi \\ 1 & -1 \end{pmatrix}\begin{pmatrix} d_\gamma^* \\ d\pi^* \end{pmatrix}$$

$$= \begin{bmatrix} -B_\theta\, d\theta - (A_{t_p} + C_{t_p})\, dt_p - (A_{t_c} + B_{t_c} + C_{t_c})\, dt_c \\ -d\theta \end{bmatrix}. \tag{44}$$

We can then compute

$$\frac{d\gamma^*}{d\theta} = \frac{1}{\Delta}(B_\theta + B_\pi) < 0 \tag{45}$$

$$\frac{d\pi^*}{d\theta} = (A_\gamma - B_\theta)/(A_\gamma + B_\pi) > 0 \tag{46}$$

$$\frac{d\gamma^*}{dt_p} - \frac{d\pi^*}{dt_p} = \frac{1}{\Delta}(A_{t_p} + C_{t_p}) < 0 \tag{47}$$

$$\frac{d\gamma^*}{dt_c} = \frac{d\pi^*}{dt_c} = \frac{1}{\Delta}(A_{t_c} + B_{t_c} + C_{t_c}) > 0 \tag{48}$$

where $\Delta = -(A_r + B_\pi) > 0$ is the determinant of the matrix on the left hand side of equation (44).

From this set of results we note that an increase in the rate of growth of the money supply or a higher tax on the use of R would reduce the steady state rate of exploitation of the natural resource. We also note that an increase in θ or t_p raises the equilibrium rate of growth of output. An increases in θ raises π but less than proportionately. Thus even in the world of perfect foresight there is no proportional correspondence between the rate of monetary growth and inflationary expectations. The difference between θ and π stimulates real economic growth. A higher t_c raises the rate of resource depletion and reduces the rate of economic growth. Also a higher t_c raises the capital intensity of the economy.

Thus the existence of the inflation tax (the ability to raise θ) gives policy makers an additional degree of freedom in attaining γ^*, π^*. The fact that θ is linearly independence of t_c and t_p is important. In a seminal article Phelps (1973) had noted the effect of θ on controlling the steady state rate of growth of the economy in a growth model without exhaustible resources. The same result holds in the case of our model which has exhaustible resources.

The welfare effects of an increase in θ are, however, ambiguous. A higher θ means a higher rate of growth of θ. However a higher θ also means a lower R which reduces (and hence k since β is constant) in the initial phase. The time path of steady state output with two different θ's is plotted in Fig. 13.6.

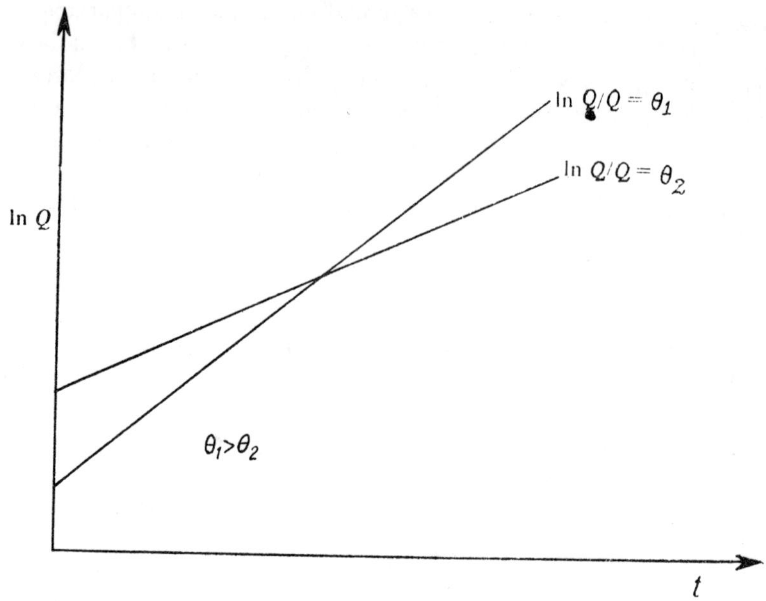

Fig. 13.6

So no single θ completely dominates other values of θ. It depends on the horizon of the monetary authorities.

This is as much as one can say for the model with perfect foresight. We now turn to a study of the model with adaptive expectations. Readers will recall that the adaptive expectations case displays saddlepath stability, whereas the perfect foresight case displays complete instability.

We already know how t_p, t_c and θ affect γ and π. With saddlepath instability and three policy tools we might be interested in choosing that combination of θ, t_c and t_p that, for a given steady state, puts us on the saddlepath to steady state equilibrium. In asking this question we clearly sidestep another important questions. Which of these steady states would we want to attain. This is the first best question. What we are addressing is the second best question.

Once again we write the $\dot{\pi}$ and $\dot{r}$ equation as.

$$\begin{pmatrix} \dot{\pi} \\ \dot{\gamma} \end{pmatrix} = \begin{pmatrix} \frac{\epsilon}{1 - a\epsilon} B_\pi & \frac{\epsilon}{1 - a\epsilon} A_\gamma \\ -(1 + B_\pi) & (1 - A_\gamma) \end{pmatrix} \begin{pmatrix} \pi \\ \gamma \end{pmatrix} \tag{49}$$

$$+ \text{ constants involving } \theta \text{ and } t_p.$$

Solving these differential equations we have

$$\pi = G_0 e^{\rho t} + G_1 e^{\mu t} + \pi^*(\theta, t_p)$$

$$\gamma = \frac{\left(\frac{\rho(1 - a\epsilon)}{\epsilon} - B_\pi\right)}{A_\gamma} G_0 e^{\rho t} + \frac{\left(\frac{\mu(1 - a\epsilon)}{\epsilon} - B_\pi\right)}{A_\gamma} G_1 e^{\mu t} + \gamma^*(\theta, t_p)$$

where μ and ρ are the characteristic roots of the matrix on the right hand side of (49) and G_0 and G_1 are initial conditions.

The question now is can we choose G_0 and G_1 such that we traverse the saddlepath to steady state equilibrium? The answer to this is yes. To see this realize that if ϵ is finite, $\pi(t)$ and $\gamma(t)$ are predetermined variable and hence

$$\begin{pmatrix} G_0 \\ \\ G_1 \end{pmatrix} = \frac{1}{\Delta} \begin{pmatrix} e^{-\rho t} & 0 \\ \\ 0 & e^{-\mu t} \end{pmatrix} \begin{pmatrix} \dfrac{\dfrac{\mu(1 - a\epsilon)}{\epsilon}}{A_\gamma} - B_\pi - 1 \\ \\ B_\pi - \dfrac{\dfrac{\rho(1 - a\epsilon)}{\epsilon}}{A_\gamma} - 1 \end{pmatrix} \begin{pmatrix} \pi - \pi^* \\ \\ \gamma - \gamma^* \end{pmatrix} \tag{50}$$

where $\Delta = \dfrac{\mu - \rho}{A_\gamma}$.

Thus
$$G_0 = G_0(\pi(t), \gamma(t), \pi^*(\theta, t_p), \gamma^*(\theta, \dot{t}_p))$$
$$G_1 = G_1(\pi(t), \gamma(t), \pi^*(\theta, t_p), \gamma^*(\theta, t_p)).$$

Suppose $\rho > 0$ then G_0 must be zero for stability. Hence when the policy maker observes $\pi(t)$ and $\gamma(t)$ he can alter θ or t_p or both to get $G_0 = 0$ and hence ensure stability.

This simple model serves to highlight the point that by influencing different asset returns through its monetary and fiscal policy parameters the policymaker is able to induce a readjustment in the relative values of assets in private portfolios. This affects the allocation of savings and hence the rate of capital accumulation and the rate of resource depletion. The fact that all of this occurs in a monetarist model only adds strength to the results.

Taxation, Inflation and the Incentive to Invest

We have realized that even in a monetarist world with perfect foresight, inflation profoundly affects the real sector and moreover that increases in the rate of growth of the money stock affect the real sector.

At the aggregate level one question remains unanswered. How does inflation affect the interest rate? In the standard macroeconomic literature that excludes fiscal variables an increase in the supply of money increases the proportion of real assets and decreases that of money in the individual's portfolio. The inflation that follows the increase in the rate of monetary expansion is the difference between the real and the nominal rate of interest.[8]

The existence of direct taxes fundamentally alters this result. We first study a simple example of how this happens.

Secondly, at the micro level, tax laws treat debt and equity finance differently. During inflation this difference gets distorted. In particular the incentive to invest (in bonds vis a vis equities) gets seriously altered and this

[8]This literature is well reviewed in Burmeister and Dobell (1970) Ch. 6.

then, has important implications for investment. We will study some results in this area as well.

To study the effects of inflation on the real rate of interest we utilize results from a study of Feldstein (1976). Consider the simple Solow one sector neoclassical growth model with the following additional specifications. The steady state of the economy[9] is characterized by an inflation[10] rate of λ. The nominal interest rate is i and the real rate is r such that $i = r + \pi$. Consider a simple two part interest tax system. Suppose that real interest payment are taxed at rate t_r and that the inflation component is taxed at rate t_i. The net nominal rate of return is thus $i_N = (1 - t_r)r + (1 - t_i)\pi$. With complete inflation adjustment $t_i = 0$ so that $i_N = (1 - t_r)r + \pi$. The production structure is the same as in Solow's model. As was the case there labour force is assumed to grow exogenously at rate n.

Firms face the following fiscal structure. They finance all investment by issuing debt and the interest paid is deducted for tax purposes. τ_r is the tax rate at which the real component of interest payments is deducted and τ_i is the tax rate at which the inflation component can by deducted. The net rate of interest paid by firms is then

$$(1 - \tau_r)r + (1 - \tau_i)\pi.$$

If there was no corporate tax then the marginal product of capital would equal the real rate of interest. The presence of the corporation tax changes this fundamentally.

To see this consider a rupee invested at the margin. Suppose that this marginal rupee produces a constant stream of output for T years with no additional labour requirement. Suppose that currently the value of this stream is m. Hence the value in year t would be $me^{\pi t}$. Since real output is constant economic depreciation for tax purposes would require that all depreciation should occur at the end of the economic life of the investment. With original cost depreciation of the one rupee investment, this implies that at the end of investment other tax liabilities are reduced by τ_r. We can then define the time path of the loan as

$$\begin{aligned} \dot{B}(t) = (r + \pi)B(t) - \{me^{\pi t} - \tau_r(me^{\pi t} - rB(t)) \\ - \tau_i\pi B(t)\} \end{aligned} \tag{51}$$

where $B(t)$ is loan at time t. $(r + \pi)B(t)$ is the gross payment on the loan. The value of the stream of output at time t is $me^{\pi t}$. This would in itself reduce the value of the increase in loan. From this, however, we must deduct the amount $\tau_r(me^{\pi t} - rB(t))$ on account of tax deductions on real interest payments and $\tau_i\pi B(t)$ on nominal payments.

[9]How this comes about is explained later in a full blown model of the effects of infiation on the incentive to invest.

[10]Inflation is fully anticipated.

The solution to equation (51) is

$$B(t) = \exp[\{(1-\tau_r)r + (1-\tau_i)\pi\}t]$$
$$\left\{(1-\tau_r)m\int_0^t \exp\{-[(1-\tau_r)r - \tau_i\pi]s\}\,ds + J\right\} \quad (52)$$

where J is an arbitrary constant. We know $B(0) = 1$ i.e. the initial investment is $1Re$. Hence $J = 1$. We also have the terminal condition $B(T) = \tau_r$ and hence

$$\tau_r \exp\{-[(1-\tau_r)r + (1-\tau_i)\pi]T\}$$
$$= 1 - \frac{(1-\tau_r)m[1-\exp(-[(1-\tau_r)r - \tau_i\pi]T])}{(1-\tau_r)r - \tau_i\pi}. \quad (53)$$

If $\tau_r = \tau_i = 0$ then equation (53) reduces to

$$m = \frac{r}{1-e^{-\gamma T}}. \quad (54)$$

If $T = \infty$, $m = r$. This is the traditional result that the product of a marginal unit of investment equals the rate of interest. This result would still hold if $T = \infty$ and there are taxes but no inflation or if there is inflation and there is full indexing.

In general the marginal product of capital does not equal the rate of interest. From equation (53) for $T = \infty$ we can calculate

$$m = r - \left(\frac{\tau_i}{1-\tau_r}\right)\pi. \quad (55)$$

Moreover we already know the relationship between r and i_N so that we have the full set of effects of taxes on the interest rate. Collecting them we have

(*a*) In the traditional model

$$m = r \text{ and } i = r + \pi.$$

(*b*) In the model with explicit recognition of taxes

$$m = r - \left(\frac{\tau_i}{1-\tau_r}\right)\pi$$

and $$i_N = (1-t_r)r + (1-t_i)\pi.$$

Equation (55) however should not be construed to mean that inflation lower the marginal product of capital. In fact as we will see in the case of the more general model described below the real rate of interest is itself affected by taxation.

The results discussed below are those of Feldstein, Green and Sheshinski (1978) who generalize Feldstein's (1976) study, discussed above, to the case of debt and equity finance by firms. It turns out that in the presence of taxation inflation has profound effects on the incentive to invest. Moreover the measures that Feldstein thought would make the system inflation proof i.e. $\tau_i = t_i = 0$) are no longer sufficient. This is an important advancement and the empirical results presented amply support the theoretical results derived by the authors. Let us dwell on these results.

Consider a Solow type neoclassical model of economic growth with money. The production structure of the model is identical i.e. output is produced by a twice continuously differentiable linear homogeneous production function with competitive factor markets. Labour grows exogenously at rate n.

Only households demand cash and the demand for real cash balances per capita is written as

$$m = Ak \tag{56}$$

where m is real cash per capita, k (as before the capital labour ratio) is related to money demand. A should depend on the relative rates of return to various assets but it is assumed that A is constant. Hence the demand for money is purely a transactions demand.

The government demands a constant fraction, α, of output. We assume that the governments' budget is continuously balanced. Attention is centred on the steady state of the model.

Since m is real cash per capita and n is the rate of growth of population it follows that if the government issues money at the rate mn the price level will be stable.

Disposable income per capita can now be written as

$$y^D = (1 - \alpha)y + mn \tag{57}$$

where y^D is disposable income and $y\{= f(k)\}$ is national output.

A fraction s of y^D is saved. Savings are allocated between real cash balances and capital stock i.e.

$$sy^D = n(1 + A)k. \tag{58}$$

One might generally suppose that s might depend on the relative rates of return to various assets. But s is assumed fixed for stability. This is not really a very outlandish assumption because a host of writers from Friedman to Modigliani have demonstrated the long run constancy of average propensity to save.

We now go to the heart of the analysis i.e. to the determinants of corporate financial policy.

All firms are identical in this story. They finance investment by issuing debt or equity. Given that labour is inelastically supplied the only real choice that the firm has is of deciding upon the "optimal" mix of debt and equity with which to finance investment. Optimality here will be defined with reference to minimizing the cost of one unit of capital. What are the components of this cost of capital to the firm.

Let us suppose that the firm faces three constraints; (*i*) a corporate income tax of rate τ. The base for this is corporate income net of interest payments on debt issued by the firm and net of depreciation which itself is based on historical costs, (*ii*) capital income from the holding of bonds and equities is taxed at rate t. (*iii*) the cost of depreciation based on historical costs is deducted from corporate income for tax purposes.

Hence, C, the cost of a unit of capital to the firm can be written as

$$C = j(1 - \tau)i + (1 - j)e - j\pi \tag{59}$$

j is the proportion of capital financed by debt. i is the interest payment on debt. Since interest payment on debt is eligible for deduction from corporate income tax (which rate is τ), in a non-inflationary world the cost of a unit of capital financed entirely by debt is $(1 - \tau)i$. However if inflation (fully anticipated) occurs at rate π the real value of debt goes down at this rate. Since only a fraction j is financed by debt the effective cost is $j(1 - \tau)i - j\pi$. e is the dividends paid by firms (plus retained earnings) on equities. Since this rises with inflation the cost of one unit of capital financed entirely by equity is e. Since only a fraction $(1 - j)$ is financed by equity the cost is $(1 - j)e$. The firm chooses j to minimize C.

In principle, then, it is possible to make a distinction between the market and the firm in three areas. The firm may finance fraction j of its investment by debt whereas the market average might be $\hat{j}$. The firm may pay i_N and e_N return on debt and equity holdings whereas the market pays $\hat{i}_N$ and $\hat{e}_N$ respectively we could then write the firms' supply functions of debts and equity as inverse functions from

$$e_N = e_N(j, \hat{j}, \hat{e}_N, \hat{i}_N) \tag{60}$$

$$i_N = i_N(j, \hat{j}, \hat{e}_N, \hat{j}_N). \tag{61}$$

Since all firms are identical in equilibrium we must have

$$j = \hat{j} \tag{62}$$

$$e_N = \hat{e}_N \tag{63}$$

$$i_N = \hat{i}_N. \tag{64}$$

Let us now consider the real rates of return as actually received by debt and equity holders. So far as bond holders are concerned they are taxed at rate t on their nominal earnings and the real value of their wealth declines with inflation. Hence

$$i_N = (1 - t)i - \pi \tag{65}$$

from which

$$i = \frac{i_N + \pi}{1 - t}. \tag{66}$$

For equities we have the return from them also being taxed at rate t. Moreover, since dividends go up with inflation equity holders experience capital gains. Let us suppose that γ is the rate of capital gains taxation. Hence we must have

$$e_N = (1 - t)e - \gamma\pi \tag{67}$$

so that

$$e = \frac{e_N}{1-t} + \frac{\gamma\pi}{1-t}. \tag{68}$$

Hence the firm in addition to satisfying equations (60) to (64) must also satisfy equations (65) to (68) in equilibrium.

But this does not mean yet that the firm is a perfect competitor. To ensure that we must have the firm earning zero net profits i.e. payment obligations completely exhaust profits. Now the firms' gross profit is f' which is taxed at rate τ. Moreover inflation increases the nominal value of the firm's assets at rate π. This, of course, means that the firm can borrow $j\pi$ without changing its debt equity ratio. Hence the total funds available with the firm are

$$(1-\tau)f' + \pi + j\pi. \tag{69}$$

Now let us look at the disbursal of funds. The firm has to meet its commitment to bond holders (to whom the payment is $j(1-\tau)i$). Equity holders are paid $(1-j)e$ and the nominal value of equity payments goes up at rate π. δ is the fixed rate of depreciation. So nominal depreciation allowance with inflation occuring at rate π is $\delta\pi$. Thus total payments are

$$j(1-\tau)i + (1-j)\,e + \pi + \delta\pi. \tag{70}$$

For zero net profit we equate (69) with (70) to get another equilibrium condition

$$(1-\tau)f' = j(1-\tau)i + (1-j)e + (\delta - j)\pi. \tag{71}$$

Finally if the real return on debt is higher than that on equities then j must rise. Hence we must have

$$\dot{j} = \eta(\hat{i}_N - \hat{e}_N) \tag{72}$$

with $\eta' > 0$.

In summary, then, the fixity of savings fixes capital per head. j, $\hat{j}$, e_N, $\hat{e}_N$, i_N, $\hat{i}_N$ are determined by minimizing equations (59) and (62) through equations (64) and (71). i and e can then be computed from equations (66) and (68).

This completes the discription of the equilibrium of the system. We can now address questions of comparative status to this system. We can change say one of the tax rates or the rate of growth or money supply. However what is of particular interest here is the effect that a change in the rate of inflation has on steady state equilibrium.

To do this we must first reduce the number of equilibrium conditions in this system to a manageable level. In fact we need to have linearly independent equations.

First in equation (71) substitute for i and e from equations (66) and (68) and multiply throughout by $(1-t)$ to get

$$(1-t)(1-\tau)f' = j(1-\tau)i_N + (1-j)e_N + \pi[j(t-\tau) + \gamma(1-j) + \delta(1-t)]. \tag{73}$$

Now in equation (59) substitute for i and e to get

$$(1 - t)C = j(1 - \tau)i_N + (1 - j)e_N + \pi[(t - \tau)j + (1 - j)\gamma]. \quad (74)$$

The firm selects j to minimize this cost. This gives us

$$(1 - \tau)i_N - e_N + \pi(t - \tau - \gamma) + j(1 - \tau)\frac{\partial iN}{\partial j} + (1 - j)\frac{\partial eN}{\partial j} = 0. \quad (75)$$

We also know that since $j = \hat{j}$, $i_N = \hat{i}_N$ and $e_N = \hat{e}_N$ in equilibrium we must have

$$\dot{j} = \eta(i_N - e_N). \quad (76)$$

Equations (73), (75) and (76) for fixed values of the parameters completely describe a single steady state. To get the comparative static propositions with respect to changes in the rate of inflation we totally differentiate equations (73), (75) and (76) with respect to j, e_N, i_N and π and rearrange terms to get

$$\begin{pmatrix} E & (1 - j) & j(1 - \tau) \\ F & -1 & (1 - \tau) \\ 1 & \eta' & -\eta' \end{pmatrix} \begin{pmatrix} dj \\ de_N \\ di_N \end{pmatrix} = -\begin{pmatrix} j(t - \tau) + (1 - j)\gamma + \delta(1 - t) \\ t - \tau - \gamma \\ 0 \end{pmatrix} d\pi \quad (77)$$

where $E = (1 - \tau)i_N - e_N + \pi(t - \tau - \gamma)$

$$F = \frac{\partial^2(1 - \tau)C}{\partial j^2} \cdot E < 0 \text{ and } F > 0.$$

We can solve for the effect of inflation on the debt equity ratio, and the real rates of return on equity and bonds from equation (77).

Thus by Cramer's Rule we have

$$\frac{dj}{d\pi} = \frac{\eta'[(\tau - t) + \gamma(1 - \tau) - \tau\delta(1 - t)]}{\Delta} \quad (78)$$

$$\frac{di_N}{d\pi} = \frac{1}{\Delta}[(\tau - t) - \delta(1 - t) + \eta'\{E(t - \tau - \gamma) - F[j(t - \tau) + (1 - j)\gamma + \delta(1 - t)] \quad (79)$$

$$\frac{de_N}{d\pi} = \frac{1}{\Delta}\{-(1 - \tau)[\gamma + \delta(1 - t)] + \eta'\{E(t - \tau - \gamma) - F[j(t - \tau) + (1 - j)\gamma + (1 - \delta)t]\}\} \quad (80)$$

where Δ is the determinant of the matrix on the left hand side of equation (77). We can analyze these effects separately now.

The Effect of Inflation on j

We first notice that if $\eta' = 0, \Delta > 0$ but with $\eta' > 0$ the sign of Δ is ambiguous. We assume throughout that $\Delta > 0$. If capital gains taxation and depreciation are both zero $\gamma = \delta = 0$) then $dj/d\pi$ has the sign of $\tau - t$. This is really the only clear cut case theoretically. With γ and δ different from zero we can calculate $dj/d\pi$ only by assigning numerical values.

It should also be evident that $\gamma = \delta = 0$ does not mean that the tax system is inflation proof. There are two reasons for this. Firstly nominal and not real interest costs are tax deductible. Secondly at the individual level it is nominal interest income rather than real interest income which is taxed. With full idexing we would have

$i_N = (1 - t)(i - \pi)$ whereas in this analysis we have $(1 - t)i - \pi$. Hence when $\gamma = 0$ pure inflationary gains of equity holders are not taxed, bond holders are not treated symmetrically.

The Effect of Inflation on i_N (The Real Rate of Interest)

Consider (79) with $\gamma = \delta = 0$ then

$$\frac{di_N}{d\pi} \gtreqless 0 \quad \text{as} \quad \tau \gtreqless t.$$

When $\tau > t$ the firm can increase the nominal rate of interest by $\pi/(1 - \tau)$ and keep the some i_N for any j. This would, then, increase the net yield to households. In addition if $\tau > t$ firms have an incentive to substitute debt for equity thus raising i_N. The opposite conclusions hold for $\tau < t$.

Again with γ and/or δ different from zero not much can be said qualitatively about $\frac{di_N}{d\pi}$. One can, however, compute its value for specific empirical settings.

The Effect of Inflation on e_N (The Net Real Return on Equity)

With $\gamma = \delta = 0$ equation (80) reduces to

$\frac{de_N}{d\pi} = (jF - E)\frac{dj}{d\pi}$ equation (81) so that $de_N/d\pi$ has the same sign as $dj/d\pi$. Once again only with $\gamma = \delta = 0$ can unambiguous qualitative conclusions be advanced.

Policy implications. The Feldstein-Green-Sheshinski paper describes very clearly the fact that equilibrium real rates of return on debt and equity and the debt/equity ratio vary with the rate of inflation. This is undesirable since inflation a factor that should be exogenous to investment profoundly affects the incentive to invest as well as the form (debt or equity) in which investments are held. The tax system should correct this anomaly.

Four different measures are advanced as solutions. First set $\gamma = \delta = 0$. This will go part of the way in making the system inflation proof. However, as we have seen above this will not suffice. Second firms must be taxed on their real interest receipts $j(i - \pi)$. Thirdly firms are allowed tax deductions on real rather than nominal interest costs. Hence firm's taxable profits would be $f' - j(i - \pi)$ so that tax is $\tau[f' - j(i - \pi)]$. When such changes are made the equations (73), (75) and (76) describing the steady state equilibrium of the economy are independent of the rate of inflation. If such changes are made in the rate of inflation would not distort the incentive to invest.

Whereas these results are strong theoretically and are well supported by empirical findings there is the problem that it may be inadequate to think of direct taxation solely from the point of view of efficiency of allocation of resources. In general in Western societies direct taxes are levied for reasons of redistribution. While one acknowledges the incentive effects of the tax structure in the presence of inflation it needs to be pointed out that government expenditure policy in general and redistributive policy in particularly have not been modeled adequately. Nor has the analysis made an effort to make explicit the preferences of government in this matter.

Conclusions. In this chapter we have studied several different efforts to study the effects of taxation in a growing economy. While some of the results are very strong we have necessarily to make strong assumptions to get them. One also cannot escape the important conclusion that much needs to be done in this area particularly in trying to integrate some of the approaches studied.

Since the models will, as a result, necessarily get more complicated empirical results will be more important than purely qualitative ones. We will study some such attempts in a later chapter.

Appendix

The tax incidence we have studied in this chapter has consistently referred to steady state. In other words we compared the steady state equilibria in pre and post tax situations. While such analysis is reasonable if the tax imposed is an infinitesimal one (so that the post tax equilibrium is very close to the pre tax equilibrium) and the speed of adjustment to the new equilibrium is very fast, this method may not be so useful if the tax causes a large jump in steady state equilibrium, or the speed of adjustment to the new equilibrium is low, or, indeed, the steady state is unstable. In such cases we should study the effect of the tax independently of steady state. We will study an example of this study an example of this problem as developed by Boadway (1977).

Consider the simplest Solow growth model as studied in this chapter with the basic dynamic equation $\overset{\circ}{k} = sf(k) - nk$ if we have a fixed propensity to save. Into this framework we introduce a wage tax at rate t_w and a capital tax at rate t_r. Let w be the net of tax wage rate whereas r is the net of tax rental rate. s_w and s_r are the saving propensities out of wage and interest income respectively. The government requires revenue to the tune of g per capita. Capital and labour are both inelastically supplied. Also define σ, the local elasticity of substitution, as

$$\frac{-\alpha f'(k)}{kf''(k)} \quad \text{where } \alpha = w(1 + t_w)/f \text{ is labour's share of output.}$$

Now
$$g = t_w w + t_r rk \tag{A.13.1}$$

so that the government's budget is balanced. In equation (A.13.1) only one of t_r, t_w or g is endogenous. Thus if t_r and g are parametrically given t_w will be automatically determined as

$$t_w = \frac{(g - t_r rk)}{w}. \tag{A.13.2}$$

Let us make this assumption.

Now from the fact that factor markets are perfectly competitive we have that gross factor payments equal the respective marginal products i.e.

$$w(1 + t_w) = f - kf' \tag{A.13.3}$$

$$r(1 + t_r) = f' \tag{A.13.4}$$

Thus
$$\overset{\circ}{k} = s_w w + s_r rk - nk. \tag{A.13.5}$$

In equation (A.13.5) substitute equations (A.13.3) and (A.13.4) for w and r and eliminate t_w using equation (A.13.2) to get

$$\overset{\circ}{k} = s_W\left[f - kf' - g + \frac{t_r kf'}{1 + t_r}\right] + \frac{s_r kf'}{1 + t_r} - nk \qquad \text{(A.13.6)}$$
$$= h(k, t_r, t).$$

This is a non-linear differential equation in k. For given paths of g, s_W, s_r and $k(0)$ (A.13.6) determines k for any t_r.

Consider now the following problem in tax incidence. Start with an arbitarily growing economy and increase t_r infinitesimally from zero and allow the exogenous path of g to be financed by endogenous changes in t_w i.e. t_w adjusts to keep g on its path. Let

$$\hat{k}(t) = \frac{\partial k(t)}{\partial t_r} \quad \text{then}$$

$$\overset{\circ}{\hat{k}}(t) = h_k(t)\hat{k}(t) + h_{t_r}(t) \qquad \text{(A.13.7)}$$

with

$$\hat{k}(0) = 0. \qquad \text{(A.13.8)}$$

Equation (A.13.7) is a non-homogenous linear differential equation in $k(t)$. The solution is

$$\hat{k}(t) = \exp\left(\int_0^t h_k(s)\, ds\left[\int_0^t h_{t_r}(s)\right]\right) \exp\left(-\int_0^a h_s(x)\, dx\right) ds \qquad \text{(A.13.9)}$$

Notice an important property of equation (A.13.9) namely that

$$\hat{k}(t) \gtreqless 0 \quad \text{if} \quad h_{t_r}(s) \gtreqless 0 \quad \text{for} \quad 0 \leqslant s \leqslant t.$$

Now we know

$$h_{t_r} = \frac{-rk(s_r - s_W)}{1 + t_r}. \qquad \text{(A.13.10)}$$

Thus equation (A.13.9) tells us that

$$\hat{k} \lesseqgtr 0 \quad \text{as} \quad s_r \lesseqgtr s_W \quad \text{for} \quad t > 0. \qquad \text{(A.13.11)}$$

This holds regardless of whether we start in steady state.

We now inquire into the implication of this for factor earnings. Let us first look at the wage rate. Let $\hat{w} = dw/dt_r$. Eliminating t_w from equation (A.13.3) and using equation (A.13.2) we totally differentiate the result to get

$$\hat{w} = \frac{-kf''}{1 + t_r}\hat{k}\frac{+kf'}{(1 + t_r)^2} + \frac{t_r f'}{1 + t_r}k$$
$$= \frac{\alpha}{\sigma}r\hat{k}\frac{+rk}{1 + t_r} + t_r r\hat{k} \qquad \text{(A.13.12)}$$

so that

$$\frac{\hat{w}}{w} = \left(\frac{(1 - \alpha)}{\sigma} + t_r\frac{(1 - \alpha)}{\alpha}\right)\frac{\hat{k}}{k} + \frac{(1 - \alpha)}{\alpha(1 + t_r)}. \qquad \text{(A.13.12')}$$

We know $s_r > s_w$ and hence $\hat{k} < 0$ so that the effect on after tax wage is ambiguous. At $t = 0$ the first expression on the right hand side of equation (A.13.12′) is zero since $\hat{k}(0) = 0$ and hence labour gains. However this is only a static gain—As time, goes by k starts falling and labour's gains get reduced. In the long run w might actually fall. This possibility is greater the smaller is σ and the larger is capital's share in output i.e. $1 - \alpha$.

We now examine the impact on r. In equation (A.13.4) r is a function of t_r and k. We define $\hat{r} = dr/dt_r$ and totally differentiate equation (A.13.4) to get

$$\hat{r} = \frac{f''}{1 + t_r}\hat{k} - \frac{f'}{(1 + t_r)^2} \tag{A.13.13}$$

so that

$$\frac{\hat{r}}{r} = \frac{-\alpha}{\sigma}\frac{\hat{k}}{k} - \frac{1}{(1 + t_r)}. \tag{A.13.13′}$$

Again since $s_r > s_w$, $\hat{k}(t) < 0$ and the effect on r is ambiguous. At time zero, however, $\hat{k} = 0$ so that r falls. But at time goes by k starts falling and hence r rises. This may now settle at a higher value than originally. This is more likely the smaller is σ and the larger is α.

Despite the ambiguity noted it can be shown that no where along the path can both r and w, rise to a level higher than originally. Only one of them can do so. From equation (A.13.12′) we have

$$\hat{w} > 0 \quad \text{if} \quad \frac{(1 - \alpha)/(\alpha(1 + t_r))}{((1 - \alpha)/\sigma + t_r(1 - \alpha)/\alpha)} > \frac{\hat{k}}{k}.$$

From equation (A.13.13′) $\hat{r} > 0$ if

$$\frac{1/(1 + t_r)}{\alpha/\sigma} < \frac{\hat{k}}{k}.$$

Both these conditions can hold simultaneously only if

$$\frac{(1 - \alpha)/(\alpha(1 + t_r))}{((1 - \alpha)/\sigma + t_r(1 - \alpha)/\alpha)} > \frac{1/(1 + t_r)}{\alpha/\sigma}$$

which reduces to

$$\frac{\alpha}{(\alpha + t_r\sigma)} > 1.$$

Since $t_r, \sigma > 0$ this is not possible. Hence both w and r cannot rise above the levels in the original path. Hence any gain that say labour might get must be accompanied by a fall in the remuneration of capital. However a tax on labour by raising k could promise higher returns to both wage earners and capital income earners than an equivalent capital tax. In that sense a wage tax may be Pareto superior to an interest tax.

Let us now look at the effect on the total earning of capital. We know $r\tilde{k} = kf'/(1 + t_r)$. Denote $\frac{d(rk)}{dt_r}$ by $\tilde{rk}$ and realise that

$$\tilde{rk} = \frac{f'k}{1 + t_r} + \frac{kf''}{1 + t_r}\hat{k}$$

or

$$\tilde{rk} = \left(1 - \frac{\alpha}{\sigma}\right)\frac{\hat{k}}{k} - \frac{1}{1 + t_r}. \qquad \text{(A.13.14)}$$

Since $s_r > s_w$, $\hat{k} < 0$ and hence capital income will decline unambiguously all along the path if $\sigma \geqslant \alpha$.

Readers should realise that the above results do not have anything to do with keeping t_w endogenous and t_r exogenous. To see this let us twist the analysis and make t_w exogenous and t_r endogenous so that we must have

$$t_r = (g - t_w w)/rk. \qquad \text{(A.13.15)}$$

With this change the capital accumulation equation would now be written as

$$\begin{aligned} \overset{\circ}{k} &= s_w\frac{(f - kf')}{1 + t_w} + s_r\left[kf' - g + t_w\frac{(f - kf')}{1 + t_w}\right] - nk \\ &= z(k, t_w, t). \end{aligned} \qquad \text{(A.13.16)}$$

We now find

$$\overset{\circ}{\hat{k}} = z_k\hat{k} + \frac{w(s_r - s_w)}{1 + t_w}; \quad \hat{k}(0) = 0 \qquad \text{(A.13.17)}$$

Again $\hat{k} \gtreqless 0$ as $s_r \gtreqless s_w$ for $t > 0$.

Now totally differentiate equations (A.13.3) and (A.13.4) treating k as a function of t_w. We get

(*i*) for the effect on the wage rate

$$\frac{\hat{w}}{w} = \frac{(1 - \alpha)}{\sigma}\frac{\hat{k}}{k} - \frac{1}{1 + t_w} \qquad \text{(A.13.18)}$$

(*ii*) for the effect on the rate of rental

$$\frac{\hat{r}}{r} = \left(t_r - \frac{\alpha}{\sigma}\frac{(1 + t_r)}{(1 + t_w)}\right)\frac{\hat{k}}{k} + \frac{\alpha}{(1 - \alpha)}\frac{(1 + t_r)}{(1 + t_w)^2} \qquad \text{(A.13.19)}$$

(*iii*) for the effect on the earnings of capital

$$-\frac{\tilde{rk}}{rk} = \left(1 - \frac{\alpha}{\sigma(1 + t_w)}\right)(1 + t_r)\frac{\hat{k}}{k} + \frac{\alpha}{(1 - \alpha)}\frac{(1 + t_r)}{(1 + t_w)^2}. \qquad \text{(A.13.20)}$$

As before the effects on w and r are ambiguous if $s_r > s_w$. At time zero since $\hat{k}(0) = 0$ capital gains and labour loses by the full amount of the tax change. However as time passes these initial changes are offset at least partially. They may be totally offset if the elasticity of substitution is low enough. We can say the same thing for capital income. However when $\sigma(1 + t_w) > \alpha$, rk will unambiguously fall.

We can now prove that an increase in t_w can cause both w and r to rise but cannot cause both to fall.

14. Taxation—Direct and Indirect

The optimal mix of direct and indirect taxes is an important and difficult question that every economy must solve. Indeed this question has been posed in different ways over the years. Taxes have been raised over the years for several reasons. State expenses, particularly wars, have always been financed by taxation. In more modern times taxes have been looked upon as more than revenue gathering devices. The government has used taxes to allocate resources efficiently (recall our discussion of external effects and the markets) to protect industries, to stimulate investment in some areas and discourage it in others, to bring out redistribution or approximate the position of a just society and so on. The role of taxation is fundamental to the health of an economy.

It is, hence, quite simply imperative that we study the normative properties of different sets of taxes. How do we decide which tax is normatively superior to some other taxes? How do we formalize the notion of optimal taxation?

Several approaches have been discussed in the literature. Among them three have been considered particularly important. Firstly one has the argument that taxes should be evaluated according to their implications for justice or fairness.[1] Secondly one could argue that taxes should be judged according to their implications for economic efficiency. Thus if the resource allocation in an economy is not Pareto optimal for some reasons a good set of taxes should take us to Pareto optimum. In a growth context, a good tax would allocate resources optimally in the intertemporal sense. Thirdly if we do not worry about resource allocation in the economy as a whole or about justice, as such, then a good tax is one that simply minimizes the cost of assessing, collecting and paying the tax.

In previous chapters we have studied, at length, the role of taxation in restoring an economy to Pareto optimality. The problem of administrative and other costs associated with taxation is yet to be completely integrated into the formal literature. Optimal taxation in the sense of maximizing a social welfare function will be dealt with in the next chapter.

In this chapter we will be concerned mainly with the efficiency aspect of taxation with the specific understanding that taxation is not meant for res-

[1]One form of this argument is to suggest that what set of taxes should be levied should be formally derived from the maximization of a social welfare function. We will consider this problem in detail in the next chapter.

toring Pareto optimality in the economy. In fact modern tax literature starts by assuming that we already are in a first best or a Pareto optimum kind of situation. Hence unless the tax being introduced is a poll or a lump sum tax the imposition of the tax will necessarily distort the allocation of resources. The government needs the revenue, however. Hence the tax has to be imposed. The question, then, is: which taxes should we impose.

Posed in this manner the problem seems to be a second best one. This problem—without being called a second best problem—was attempted by Ramsey, as far back as 1927. Recently the solution given by Ramsey has been generalized in a number of important directions by Diamond and Mirrlees (1971a, b) Baumol and Bradford (1970), Lerner (1970); Dixit (1970) and Atkinson and Stiglitz (1972, 1976, 1980).

We begin this chapter by discussing various variants of the Ramsey approach. Next we consider the problem of optimal mix of direct and indirect taxes. An important issue in this area is the direct tax versus indirect tax controversy. We also consider some distributional issues here. Finally we look at the relatively new area of tax reform or tax improvement.

The Ramsey Problem. Ramsey was set the following problem by Pigou. Suppose the government wants to raise a certain amount as revenue. Suppose we allow linear or proportional taxes on all commodities including labour. What is the best set of taxes to use to maximize some measure of social welfare. To make the problem more succinct let us consider the following version of it.

Let us suppose that there are $n + 1$ goods; $x_1, \ldots, x_n, x_{n+1}$, in an economy. $x_i (i = 1, \ldots, n)$ are ordinarily defined goods whereas x_{n+1} is labour. Suppose the economy is inhabited by just one person[2,3] and we can visualise his utility as

$$u(x_1, \ldots x_n, x_{n+1}).$$

Linear taxes (not necessarily all non-zero) at rates $t_1, \ldots, t_n, t_{n+1}$ are imposed on these commodities so that tax revenue is

$$\sum_{i=1}^{n+1} t_i x_i.$$

The government requires an amount T in taxes so that we must have

$$\sum_{i=1}^{n+1} t_i x_i = T.$$

The problem of the fiscal planner is then to maximize $u(\ )$ subject to $\Sigma\, t_i x_i = T$. Setting up the Lagrangean we have

$$L = u(x_1, \ldots, x_n, x_{n+1}) + \lambda_1[\Sigma t_i x_i - T]. \tag{1}$$

[2]Relaxing this assumption is one of the major contributions of the papers by Diamond and Mirrlees mentioned above.

[3]Another way to look at this problem is to presume the existence of a social welfare function with no redistributional objectives.

The first order conditions for an internal solution are

$$\frac{\partial L}{\partial P_j} = \sum_{i=1}^{n+1} \frac{\partial u}{\partial x_i} \frac{\partial x_i}{\delta P_j} + \lambda_1 \left\{ \sum_{i=1}^{n+1} t_i \frac{\partial x_i}{\partial P_j} + x_j \right\} = 0 \tag{2}$$

$$j = 1, \ldots, n + 1$$

where P_j are consumer prices.

This is the society's problem. The equivalent problem from the point of view of the single consumer we are taking about is:

$$\max u(x_1, \ldots, x_n, x_{n+1}) \text{ subject to}$$

$$P_{n+1}x_{n+1} = \sum_{i=1}^{n} P_i x_i. \tag{3}$$

The consumer's budget constraint simply tells us that earnings from work are exhausted on consumption of the goods. If we measure labour supply negatively then we can rewrite equation (3) as

$$\sum_{i=1}^{n+1} P_i x_i = 0. \tag{3'}$$

The consumer's Lagrangean can now be written as

$$L' = u(x_1, \ldots, x_{n+1}) - \lambda_2 [\sum_{i=1}^{n+1} P_i x_i].$$

From which we have

$$\frac{\partial L'}{\partial x_i} = u_i - \lambda_2 P_i = 0 \tag{4}$$

where $$u_i = \frac{\partial u}{\partial x_i}.$$

Substituting from equations (4) into (2) we have

$$\lambda_2 \sum_{i=1}^{n+1} P_i \frac{\partial x_i}{\partial P_j} + \lambda_1 (\sum_{i=1}^{n} t_i \frac{\partial x_i}{\partial P_j} + x_j) = 0 \tag{4'}$$

$$j = 1, \ldots, n + 1.$$

From the individual's budget constraint (3′) we have

$$\sum_{i=1}^{n+1} P_i \frac{\partial x_i}{\partial P_j} + x_j = 0. \tag{5}$$

Substituting equation (5) into (4′) we get

$$-\lambda_2 x_j + \lambda_1 \left(\sum_{i=1}^{n} t_i \frac{\partial x_i}{\partial P_j} + x_j \right) = 0$$

and hence

$$\sum_{i=1}^{n} t_i \frac{\partial x_i}{\partial P_j} = \frac{\lambda_2 - \lambda_1}{\lambda_1} x_j = \tau x_j \tag{6}$$

$$j = 1, \ldots, n.$$

Equation (6) can now be used to discuss Ramsey's rule for taxation. The Slutsky equation for x_i for a change in P_j is

$$\frac{\partial x_i}{\partial P_j} = -x_j \frac{\partial x_i}{\partial M} + S_{ij} \qquad (7)$$

$$i, j = 1, \ldots, n$$

where M, as before, is total earnings and S_{ij} is the substitution term.

Substitute this into equation (6) to get

$$\sum_{i=1}^{n} t_i S_{ij} = \tau x_j + x_j \sum_{i=1}^{n} t_i \frac{\partial x_i}{\partial M}. \qquad (8)$$

Now since the Slutsky substitution terms are symmetric i.e. $S_{ij} = S_{ji}$ we write S_{ji} for S_{ij} in equation (8) to finally get

$$\sum_{i=1}^{n} t_i S_{ji}/x_j = \tau + \sum_{i=1}^{n} t_i \frac{\partial x_i}{\partial M} \qquad (9)$$

$$j = 1, \ldots, n.$$

We can now interpret equation (7) to get the Ramsey rule. The left hand side of equation (9) measures the proportionate decrease in the demand for commodity j if the individual is compensated so that he can stay on the same indifference curve. The right hand side, however, is independent of j. Hence it follows that taxes are optimal when the proportionate decrease in consumption of every commodity is the same.

If we make another assumption we will make transparent another form of the Ramsey rule. Suppose

$$\frac{\partial x_i}{\partial P_j} = \frac{\partial x_j}{\partial P_i} \; i, j = 1, \ldots, n. \qquad (10)$$

When is this true? Going back to Slutsky equation we have

$$\frac{\partial x_i}{\partial P_j} = -x_j \frac{\partial x_i}{\partial M} + S_{ij}.$$

From the fact that $S_{ij} = S_{ji}$ we realize that equation (10) can be ture only if

$$\frac{M}{x_i} \frac{\partial x_i}{\partial M} = \frac{M}{x_j} \frac{\partial x_j}{\partial M} \; i, j = 1, \ldots, n$$

i.e. all goods have the same income elasticity of demand. If this is true then we get from equation (6) on rewriting (9).

$$\left(\sum_{i=1}^{n} t_i \frac{\partial x_j}{\partial P_i} \right) / x_j = \tau \quad j = 1, \ldots, n \qquad (11)$$

which means that the Ramsey rule of equi proportionate decrease in the demands for all goods would obtain even if we did not have the restrictive assumption of zero tax revenue.

With this stipulation then we can say that if indifference map between two goods is homothetic (i.e. the Engel curve is linear) Ramsey optimal taxation would require an equiproportionate decline in consumption of both goods so that relative prices remain unchanged. This is illustrated in Fig. 14.1.

In Fig. 14.1, K_1K_1 is the pre-tax budget line whereas K_2K_2 (which is parallel to K_1K_1) is the post-tax budget line. There is an equiproportionate decline in the consumption of x_1 and x_2.

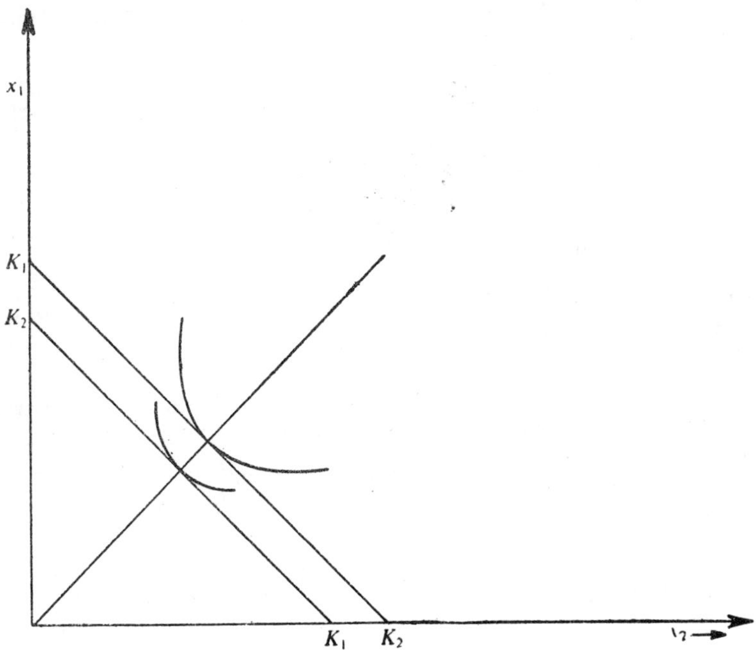

Fig. 14.1

It is time now to make explicit an assumption that we have made in deriving the Ramsey rule. We have implicitly assumed that labour supply does not change in response to commodity taxation. But the utility function that we assumed had ordinary goods and labour as arguments. Hence the argument we have been making is strictly speaking valid only if the utility function is separable between all other goods and labour i.e.

$$u(x_1, \ldots, x_n, x_{n+1}) = u_1(x_1, \ldots, x_n) + u_2(x_{n+1}) \tag{12}$$

so that the maximization of $u_1(\ )$ can take place independently of x_{n+1}.

Another way to rationalize this argument is the following. Suppose that labour is inelastically supplied with respect not only to the wage rate but also other prices. Hence if the government had to raise revenue the ideal thing to do would be to tax labour. But now suppose that labour cannot be taxed then exactly the same result can be obtained by taxing all commodities at a uniform rate.

It follows by implication that if the utility function is not separable between labour and other goods and/or labour supply is variable then uniform taxation may not be the best thing to do. However, not much work has been directed in this direction.

If labour cannot be taxed the only reason for non-uniform taxation of commodities must be in the fact that different commodities have different income elasticities of demand. One can derive on interesting result in this connection. From the Slutsky equation and the symmetry of the Slutsky substitution term $S_{ij} = S_{ji}$ we must have

$$\frac{\partial x_i}{\partial P_j} = \frac{\partial x_j}{\partial P_i} + x_i \frac{\partial x_j}{\partial M} - x_j \frac{\partial x_i}{\partial M}.$$

Substituting into equation (6) we finally get (after rearranging terms).

$$\left(\sum_{i=1}^{n} t_i \frac{\partial x_i}{\partial P_j}\right) \Big/ x_j = \tau - \sum_{i=1}^{n} t_i x_i \left(\frac{1}{j} \frac{\partial x_j}{\partial M} - \frac{1}{x_i} \frac{\partial x_i}{\partial M}\right). \tag{13}$$

This equation has a very appealing interpretation. Taxes have income and well as substitution effects.

The income effect is similar to the effect of a lump sum tax which we know to be non-distortionary. Substitution effects bring in the distortions of taxation. Hence we must tax those commodities that have a larger income effect of tax (i.e. larger values of the income elasticity of demand) at a higher rate than those commodities for which the substitution effect is more important.

Yet another form of the Ramsey rule of taxation is the so called inverse elasticity formula. This can easily be derived from equation (6). In equation (6) suppose that all cross derivatives in the demand function vanish so that

$$t_j/P_j = \frac{\tau}{\epsilon_{jj}} \qquad j = 1, \ldots, n \tag{14}$$

where ϵ_{jj} is the own price elasticity of demand. This is the famous inverse price elasticity formula. Its justification is the following. The pre-tax situation is the non distributionary or the first best solution.If rule (14) is followed goods with low price elasticity of demand are taxed at a higher rate than those with high price elasticity. This ensures minimum departure from the pre-tax first best situation. This argument is, clearly, a partial equilibrium one. The inverse elasticity formula becomes very complicated and, indeed, hard to defend in the general equilibrium case.

The analysis so far has made several restrictive assumptions. We seek to highlight a few major ones here. One is the neglect of production activities. Secondly the analysis is, strictly speaking, applicable only to an infinitesimal tax. Third the structure of preferences assumed in this model is particularly stringent. We have assumed just one consumer or, what is as limiting, a number of identical consumers so that aggregate utility can be expressed in the relatively simple form outlined above.

As Diamond (1975) has noted it is a relatively simple matter to extend the one person Ramsey rule to a many person world. To focus on the issue let us suppose that the incomes of all consumers are given and are unalterable. We further suppose that each consumer has the same income M. Moreover we explicitly bring production into the picture.

Suppose there are H individuals in society and we index them by h. Their indirect utility functions can be written as:

$$V^h(P_1, \ldots, P_n, M) \qquad h = 1, \ldots, H$$

where $P_1. \ldots, P_n$ are, as before, the consumer prices of the n goods. Society maximizes a social welfare function

$$W(V^1, V^2, \ldots, V^H) \tag{15}$$

subject to the production relation written in implicit form i.e.

$$F(x_1(P_1, \ldots, P_n; M); x_2(\quad); \ldots, x_n(\quad)) = 0. \tag{16}$$

In equation (16) the output of each good is a function of the consumer prices and money income.

Producers, however, face the prices $q_1, \ldots, q_n$. The difference between the two is excise taxes i.e.

$$t_i = P_i - q_i \tag{17}$$

is the excise tax on the ith commodity $i = 1, \ldots, n$.

Setting up the Lagrangean for the maximization we have

$$L = W(V^1, V^2, \ldots, V^H) + \lambda[F(x_1, x_2, \ldots x_n)]. \tag{18}$$

The first order conditions are

$$\sum_h \frac{\partial W}{\partial V^h} \frac{\partial V^h}{\partial P_j} = \lambda \sum_i F_i \frac{\partial x_i}{\partial P_j} \qquad j = 1, \ldots, n. \tag{19}$$

We choose commodity 1 as numeraire

so that $$P_1 = F_1 = q_1 = 1.$$

From the property of indirect utility functions[4] we have

[4]The indirect utility function for individual h is obtained from his direct utility function u^h

$$\begin{aligned} u^h &= u^h[D_1(P_1, \ldots, P_n, M), \ldots, D_n(P_1, \ldots, P_n, M)] \\ &= V^h(P_1, \ldots, P_n) \end{aligned}$$

where D_i is demand for ith good and, in writing the last equality, we have assumed that M is constant. From the composite function rule we must have

$$\begin{aligned} \frac{\partial V^h}{\partial P_j} &= \sum_i \frac{\partial u^h}{\partial D_i} \frac{\partial P_i}{\partial P_j} \\ &= \mu \sum_i P_i \frac{\partial P_i}{\partial P_j}; \qquad j = 1, \ldots, n \end{aligned}$$

where μ is the Lagrange multiplier associated with the utility maximization problem faced by the individual.

$$-\sum_h \beta^h x_j^h = \lambda \sum_h \sum_i q_i \frac{\partial x_i^h}{\partial P_k} \tag{20}$$

where
$$\beta^h = \frac{\partial W}{\partial V^h} \frac{\partial V^h}{\partial M}$$

is the social marginal utility of consumption with $\alpha^h = \partial V^h/\partial M$ being the private marginal utility of consumption. To arrive at β^h we weigh the private marginal utility (α^h) with the weight given to α^h in the social welfare function. x_i^h is the consumption of the ith good by individual h.

In equation (20) we replace q_i by $P_i - t_i$. Note also from the individual's budget constraint that

$$\sum_i P_i(\partial x_i^h/\delta P_i) = -x_j^h.$$

We substitute appropriately into equation (20) to get

$$\sum_h \beta^h x_j^h = \lambda \sum_h \left(x_j^h + \sum_i t_i \left(S_{ij}^h - x_j^h \frac{\partial x_i^h}{\partial M} \right) \right) \tag{21}$$

where S_{ij}^h is the substitution effect in individual h's Slutsky equation.

Now define the social marginal utility of income δ^h as the gain to society from an extra rupee being given to individual h. This gain consists of two parts. The first is, β^h, the social evaluation of the higher utility made possible to individual h because of the income. The second part is the increased tax revenue that is possible because of the higher income to h.
This amount is

$$\sum_i t_i \frac{\partial x_i^h}{\partial M}.$$

Hence

$$\delta^h = \beta^h + \lambda \sum t_i(\partial x_i^h/\partial M). \tag{22}$$

The first order condition for social optimum can now be written as (on substituting for β^h from (22))

$$\sum_h (\delta^h - \lambda) x_j^h = \lambda \sum_i \sum_h t_i S_{ij}^h. \tag{23}$$

This is one form of the many person Ramsey rule. This result becomes still more interesting if we also introduce an optimal lump sum tax i.e. we introduce variable M. Now from the maximization of $W(\ \ )$ subject to the production constraint $F(\ \ )$ with M as the control variable we have

$$\sum_h \beta^h = \lambda \sum_i F_i(\partial x_i/\partial M). \tag{24}$$

Following the same sequence of steps as in the case for optimal excise taxes we have

$$\sum_h \beta^h = \lambda \sum_i \sum_h q_i \frac{\partial x_i^h}{\partial M} = \lambda \sum_h \sum_i (P_i - t_i) \frac{\partial x_i^h}{\partial M}$$

$$= \lambda \sum_h \left(1 - \sum_i t_i \frac{\partial x_i^h}{\partial M}\right) \tag{25}$$

whence from (22) we have $\sum_h \delta^h = \lambda H$ (where H is the total number of individuals in society).

The general formulation of the many person Ramsey rule is

$$\frac{\Delta x_i}{x_j} = \frac{\sum_h (\delta^h - \lambda) x_i^h}{\lambda x_i}. \tag{26}$$

Now since λ is equal to the average of the δ^h we can interpret equation (26) as a covariance formula. From the left hand side of (26) we subtract $\sum_h (\delta^h - \lambda)\bar{x}_i$ where $\bar{x}_i$ is the average of x_i^h. Hence for each commodity i the change in aggregate compensated quantity demand must be proportional to the covariance between individual quantities demanded and social marginal utilities of income.

Let us return for a while to the simplicity of the one person Ramsey rule and look at an alternative derivation of it. This form, which is due to Atkinson and Stightz (1972), will be helpful to us in our discussion of the direct versus indirect tax.

In this stipulation we make fuller use of the fact that commodity x_{n+1} is labour which is variable in supply. Now if the individual's utility function is $u(x_1, \ldots, x_{n+1})$ it must be true that a characteristic of the individuals optimal plan must be that

$$\sum_{i=1}^{n} u_i x_i + \frac{\partial u}{\partial x_{n+1}} x_{n+1} = 0. \tag{27}$$

Suppose that government's tax revenue requirement is T. Also suppose that the government can directly control the x_i so that prices are obtained as a function of the x_i's. The problem before society, then, is to maximize.

$u(x_1, \ldots, x_n, x_{n+1})$ subject to

(*i*) $W x_{n+1} - \Sigma x_i - T = 0$ and (W is the wage rate)

(*ii*) $\sum_{i=1}^{n} u_i x_i + \frac{\partial u}{\partial x_{n+1}} x_{n+1} = 0.$

The appropriate Lagrangean is

$$L = u(\ \ ) + \mu_1 (W x_{n+1} - \Sigma x_i - T) + \mu_2 \left(\Sigma u_i x_i + \frac{\partial u}{\partial x_{n+1}} x_{n+1} \right). \tag{28}$$

The first order conditions are

$$\frac{\partial L}{\partial x_j} = u_j - \mu_1 + \mu_2 \left(\sum_{i+1}^{n} u_{ij} + \frac{\partial}{\partial x_j} \frac{\partial u}{\partial x_{n+1}} x_{n+1} \right) = 0$$

or on multiplying through by -1 and rearranging (29)

$$\mu_1 - \mu_2 u_j \left(1 + \frac{\sum_1 u_{ij}}{u_j} + \frac{\partial}{\partial x_j} \frac{\partial u}{\partial x_{n+1}} \frac{x_{n+1}}{u_j} \right) = 0$$

$j = 1, \ldots, n.$

Now let us suppose that all producer prices are equal to one. Hence consumer price for the ith good is simply $(1 + t_i) = P_i$. Realize that from the individual maximizing condition.[5]

$$u_i = \alpha P_i \qquad i = 1, \ldots, n \tag{30}$$
$$-u_{x_{n+1}} = \alpha W.$$

Hence
$$u_j = \alpha(1 + t_j) \text{ for } j = 1, \ldots, n.$$

Define a term

$$N^j = -\left(\Sigma' \frac{u_{ij}x_i}{u_j} + \frac{\partial}{\partial x_{n+1}} \frac{\partial u}{\partial x_{n+1}} / u_j\right)$$

for
$$j = 1, \ldots, n. \tag{31}$$

Hence using equations (30) and (31) in (29) we have

$$(1 + t_j)\,[1 - \mu_2(N^j - 1)] = \frac{\mu_1}{\alpha} \tag{32}$$

for
$$j = 1, \ldots, n$$

With respect to x_{n+1} we can similarly derive

$$\frac{\partial u}{\partial \mu_{n+1}} = -\mu_1 W - \mu_2 \frac{\partial u}{\partial x_{n+1}} \frac{\left(1 + \Sigma \frac{\partial}{\partial x_i} \frac{\partial \mu}{\partial x_{n+1}} x_i + \frac{\partial^2 u}{\partial x_{n+1}^2} x_{n+1}\right)}{\frac{\partial u}{\partial x_{n+1}}} \tag{33}$$

Once again define

$$N^{x_{n+1}} = -\frac{\left(\Sigma \frac{\partial}{\partial x_i} \frac{\partial u}{\partial x_{n+1}} x_i + \frac{\partial^2 u}{\partial x_{n+1}{}^2} x_{n+1}\right)}{\partial u / \partial x_{n+1}}.$$

Now substitute

$$\frac{\partial u}{\partial x_{n+1}} = -\alpha w \text{ to get}$$

$$\mu_2(1 - N^{x_{n+1}}) = \frac{\mu_1 - \alpha}{\alpha}. \tag{34}$$

Between equations (32) and (34) we can eliminate μ_2 to finally get the Ramsey formula

$$\frac{t_j}{1 + t_j} = \frac{\mu_1 - \alpha}{\mu_1}\left(\frac{N^j - N^{x_{n+1}}}{1 - N^{x_{n+1}}}\right). \tag{35}$$

[5]The problem is max $u(x_1, \ldots, x_{n+1})$ subject to

$$W x_{n+1} = \sum_{i=1}^{n} P_i x^i.$$

The first order conditions give us terms like

$$u_i - \alpha P_i = 0 \qquad i = 1, \ldots, n.$$

where α is the Lagrange multiplier for this problem. Remember that α is the marginal utility of money.

This is not a complete statement in the sense that N^j and $N^{x_{n+1}}$ themselves depend on t_j. However, some interesting conclusions can be drawn from equation (35). First let us suppose that $\frac{\partial^2 u}{\partial x_{n+1}{}^2} \rightarrow -\infty$ which means that $-N^{x_{n+1}} \rightarrow \infty$ then from equation (35) we have

$$\frac{t_j}{1 + t_j} = \frac{\mu_1 - \alpha}{\alpha}$$

i.e. there is a uniform tax on all goods. From our discussion above it would follow that if labour is completely inelastically supplied this would correspond to the case of a tax on labour and no tax on the other commodities. Similarly if $N^{x_{n+1}} \rightarrow 0$ we have a completely elastic supply of labour because the marginal utility of income is constant. From this if

$$u_{ij} = 0 \text{ for } i \neq j,\ i,\ \ j = 1, \ldots, n$$

we have

$$u_{jj} \frac{\partial x_j}{\partial P_j} = \alpha \text{ which means}$$

$$\frac{t_j}{1 + t_j} = \frac{\mu_1 - \alpha}{\alpha} \frac{1}{\epsilon_{jj}} \text{ because } N^{x_j} = \frac{1}{\epsilon_{jj}}$$

where ϵ_{jj} is the own price elasticity of demand for commodity j. This is the inverse elasticity formula already derived above.

Similarly if the utility function is separable i.e.

$$u(x_1, \ldots, x_n, x_{n+1}) = u^1(x_1) + u^2(x_2) + \ldots + u^{n+1}(x_{n+1})$$

$$u_{ij} = 0 \qquad \text{and} \qquad N^{x_j} = -\frac{u_{jj} x_j}{u_j}.$$

Now recall the individual's first order condition for utility maximization

$$u_j - \alpha P_j = 0 \qquad j = 1, \ldots, n.$$

Differentiate this with respect to M to get

$$u_{jj} \frac{\partial x_j}{\partial M} - \alpha \frac{\partial P_j}{\partial M} - P_j \frac{\partial \alpha}{\partial M} = 0.$$

But P_j is constant once the tax is imposed so that

$$u_{jj} \frac{\partial x_j}{\partial M} = P_j \frac{\partial \alpha}{\partial M}. \qquad \text{But } P_j = \frac{u_j}{\alpha}$$

so

$$u_{jj} \frac{\partial x_j}{\partial M} = u_j \frac{1}{\alpha} \frac{\partial \alpha}{\partial M} = P_j \frac{\partial \alpha}{\partial M}$$

or

$$N^{x_j} \frac{1}{x_j} \frac{\partial x_j}{\partial M} = \frac{1}{\alpha} \frac{\partial \alpha}{\partial M}.$$

Hence when the utility function is additive separable the optimal tax rate depends inversely on the income elasticity of demand. Thus means that necessities are optimally taxed at a higher rate than luxuries. This result, however, is true only with separability. Clearly the optimality of the tax draws simply on static efficiency of the type outlined above. This result should not, however, lead one to believe that efficiency necessarily calls for penalizing the less well off.

The Direct versus Indirect Tax Controversy

An important debate in the tax literature has centered on the question of whether a direct or an indirect tax is "best" suited for an economy. How we choose to define "best" has an important bearing on the answer to this question. This question has been approached in one way in the modern Anglo-American literature. Thus it has been stated that there are two different approaches to this problem. One approach states that an economy must arrive at a judicious mix of direct and indirect taxes. The second states that, almost unequivocally, a direct tax is superior to an indi rect tax. We shall inquire into this standard wisdom and realize that both these statements can be true under different conditions. Having analyzed this for different sets of taxes we will briefly consider the applicability of this wisdom to a developing economy like ours. In India no more than one percent of the population pays direct taxes.

Let us first consider a case where this government has no redistributive objectives. This facilitates our reverting to the one person case or the equivalent case in which all individuals are identical.

There are $n + 1$ goods in the economy. There are n ordinarily defined private goods and the $n + 1$st good is labour. The government spends an amount G on these individuals. The government chooses G and the tax rates $t_1, \ldots, t_n$ to maximize the utility of a representative individual subject to a revenue requirement of R. We represent the utility of the individual by an indirect utility function

$$V(P_1, \ldots, P_n; W, G).$$

Hence the problem is max $V(\ )$ subject to $\sum_i t_i x_i - G - R = 0$. Setting up the Lagrangean we have

$$L = V(P_1, \ldots, P_n, W, G) + \lambda[\Sigma t_i x_i - G - R]. \tag{36}$$

The first order conditions are

$$\frac{\partial L}{\partial t_j} = \frac{\partial V}{\partial t_j} + \lambda\left(x_j + \Sigma t_i \frac{\partial x_i}{\partial P_j}\right) = 0 \tag{37}$$

$$\frac{\partial L}{\partial G} = \frac{\partial V}{\partial G} + \lambda\left(\Sigma t_i \frac{\partial x}{\partial M} - 1\right) = 0. \tag{38}$$

We can easily derive from footnote 4 an important property of the indirect utility function namely that

$$\frac{\partial V}{\partial P_j} = -\alpha x_j \qquad \text{and} \qquad \frac{\partial V}{\partial G} = \alpha$$

where α is the private marginal utility of money. Using this fact and the Slutsky equation

$$\left(\frac{\partial x_i}{\partial P_j} = S_{ij} - x_j \frac{\partial x_i}{\partial M}\right)$$

in[6] (37) and (38) we have

$$\sum_i \frac{t_i S_{ji}}{x_j} = -\left(1 - \frac{\alpha}{\lambda} - \sum_i t_i \frac{\partial x_i}{\partial M}\right)$$

and

$$1 - \frac{\alpha}{\lambda} - \sum_i t_i \frac{\partial x_i}{\partial M} = 0.$$

Since S_{ji} and x_j are non-zero it follows that in the optimal solution each $t_i = 0$. The government, however, is free to vary G which can be positive or negative. But the important point to note is that optimal G is the same for everyone. Thus in this framework with identical individuals and hence no redistributive goals a direct tax/subsidy is entirely superior to an indirect tax. Thus if the government has only efficiency considerations in mind it should not go in for indirect taxation.

How does this result change if we bring in redistributive objectives. Let us suppose that individuals are identical in tastes so that they have the same (direct and indirect) utility function. Individuals, however, differ with regard to the wage that they get.[7] Individual h's budget constraint is

$$\sum_i P_i x_i^h = w^h x_{n+1}^h + G,$$
$$h = 1, \ldots, H. \tag{39}$$

Social welfare function is now defined as a function of the individual indirect utilities. Thus we have

$$W(V^1(P_1, \ldots, P_n; W^1, G), \ldots, V^H(P_1, \ldots, P_n; W^H, G)). \tag{40}$$

The budget constraint for the government now takes explicit recognition of the fact that different individuals now consume different amounts of the various goods. Thus the government's budget constraint is

$$\sum_i t_i \sum_h x_i^h - HG - R = 0. \tag{41}$$

Setting up the Lagrangean we have

$$L = W(\;) + \lambda(\sum_i t_i \sum_h x_i^h - HG - R). \tag{42}$$

We again introduce the term $\beta^h = \frac{\partial W}{\partial V^h} \frac{\partial V^h}{\partial W}$ as the social marginal utility of additional consumption by individual h. The first order conditions for the maximization of equation (42) are:

[6]We also use the usual symmetry of the Slutsky substitution term.

[7]The results here are only a part of a long story. We concentrate on this issue in the next chapter.

$$\frac{\partial L}{\partial t_j} = \underset{h}{\Sigma}\left[(\lambda - \beta^h)x_j^h + \lambda\underset{i}{\Sigma}t_i \frac{\partial x_i^h}{\partial t_j}\right] = 0 \tag{43}$$

$j = 1, \ldots, n$

$$-\frac{\partial L}{\partial G} = \underset{h}{\Sigma}\left[(\lambda - \beta^h) - \lambda\Sigma t \frac{\partial x_i^h}{\partial G}\right] = 0. \tag{44}$$

To interpret equations (43) and (44) reintroduce δ^h (the gain to society from an extra rupee being given to individual h). Using the definition of δ^h, the Slutsky equation, and the symmetry of the Slutsky substitution term we can write equations (43) and (44) as

$$\frac{\underset{i\ h}{\Sigma\Sigma} t_i S_{ij}^h}{H\bar{x}_j} = -\left[1 - \underset{h}{\Sigma}\left(\delta^h \frac{x_j^h}{H\bar{x}_j}\right)\right], \tag{45}$$

$j = 1, \ldots, n$

and

$$\bar{\delta} = \underset{h}{\Sigma}\delta^h/H = 1, \tag{46}$$

with $\bar{x}_j = \Sigma x_j^h/H$ (the average consumption of commodity j).

Now if the government had no distributional objective then $\delta^h = \bar{\delta}$ and we would be back to the case of the previous example in which a lump sum tax/subsidy and zero indirect taxation was the best solution. Hence the only reason we would have indirect taxes is if the government did indeed have redistributional objectives i.e. if δ^h varied with h.

If δ^h did vary with h indirect tax rates would vary with the distributional characteristics of commodities. The distributional characteristic ϕ_j of a commodity j is defined as

$$\phi_j = \underset{h}{\Sigma} \frac{1}{H}\left(\frac{x_i^h}{\bar{x}_j}\right)\left(\frac{\delta^h}{\bar{\delta}}\right) - 1 \tag{47}$$

$x_j^h/\bar{x}_j$ is the consumption of commodity j by individual h as a proportion of the average consumption of commodity j whereas $\delta^h/\bar{\delta}$ measures the ratio of the social worth of a rupee going to individual h as a proportion of the social worth of a rupee going to the average individual. From equations (45) and (46) then

$$\underset{i\ h}{\Sigma\Sigma} t_i \frac{S_{ij}^h}{H\bar{x}_j} = \bar{\delta}\phi_j - (1 - ij), \qquad j = 1, \ldots, n \tag{48}$$

with no redistributive objectives $\bar{\delta} = 1$, $\phi_j = 0$ and $t_i = 0$. Otherwise t_i defines optimal excise tax for commodity i.

The result that indirect taxes should be used for redistributive purposes alone is in direct conflict with the popular view that indirect taxes should be used for purposes of efficiency rather than equity.

In this section we have been using only linear direct and indirect taxes. This was for two reasons. First is the simple and powerful one that non-linear taxes are hand to deal with. Secondly we have been able to substantiate the proposition that under certain circumstances direct taxes are unambiguously superior to indirect taxes whereas in other circumstances a judicious mix of the two can be applied.

What does this debate have to say about tax structure in a country like ours? In India hardly one per cent of the population pays income tax so any talk of using direct taxes to redistributive income is clearly of extremely limited applicability. As a matter of fact the last exercise above seems more applicable. It would make eminent sense to use indirect taxes for redistributive purposes whereas direct taxes can be used for reasons of allocative efficiency or collecting revenue. Precisely the opposite is happening though. The proponents of this approach sound extremely unconvincing,[8] when they talk of direct taxes being used for redistributive purposes. Such considerations are useful only in developed countries where a much larger proportion of the population pays taxes. Also direct taxes form a much larger fraction of total tax revenue in these countries than in India. Unfortunately there seems to be no empirical work on the redistributive effects of indirect taxes in India.

The Theory of Tax Reform

The analysis in this chapter has primarily concerned itself with finding out tax structures that maximize a certain well defined objective function. Hence these optimal taxes presume that the policy maker has the freedom to write the tax laws on a clear slate. It is possible to take exception to this line of reasoning and suggest that at any point of time the policy maker can only make limited changes in the neighbourhood of existing tax rates. The question then is how optimally should these tax changes be made.

Two different approaches have been followed in the literature on this topic which is quite new, really. On the one hand authors like Dixit, Feldstein and Stiglitz have argued that we are dealing essentially with a second best situation. Hence only the uncertaintities associated with second best rules can be an appropriate guide for the policy maker. To make this situation more transparent consider an economy where the allocation of resources is already distorted by the existence of some indirect taxes. Suppose now that the marginal adjustment that is possible around the existing fiscal structure allows for the partial reduction in the rates of some of the indirect taxes in exchange for the imposition of a poll tax. We know that the theory of second best would tell us that this is not necessarily superior to the old situation. To really assess whether the potential fiscal situation is superior to the existing one we will, of necessity, have to compare the values of the objective function in the two situations.

The second approach to marginal changes in fiscal structure is the "optimal tax perturbation" approach[9] associated with Diewert, Gusenerie and

[8] As an example consider Chelliah (1978).

[9] An excellent analysis of this approach is Diewert (1978).

others. The idea here is to not worry about the overall second best optimality or otherwise of the fiscal equilibrium. This approach is interested in delineating Pareto optimal improvements from the others. This a marginal change in the tax structure (or a tax perturbation) is desirable so long as it leads us in a Pareto superior direction. But then the problem does remain of comparing two tax perturbations that are both Pareto superior to the initial fiscal equilibrium. The argument that Diewert and others would then advance is that, this objection notwithstanding, we do get a clear cut guide for framing policy. Diewert's 1978 paper goes into great details about this approach.

Conclusions

In this chapter we studied some problems in devising a good mix of direct and indirect taxes. The qualitative answers that we could give were not terribly general. Indeed some of our conclusions hold under very specific conditions.

In the next chapter we will explore the new area of optimal non-linear taxation and see whether our conclusions can be made more general or more precise.

15. Optimal Taxation

In this chapter we undertake an indepth study of those taxes that are derived from an explicit maximization of some index of social welfare. Readers will remember from the last chapter, that this was just one of the criteria of optimality that has been discussed in the literature.

The basic setting for most of this literature is a first best situation so that the introduction of the tax necessarily makes us depart from the first best solution. An economy would want to do this for purposes of redistribution. We know that the Pareto criterion, by itself, is silent on questions of redistribution. Thus the theory of optimal taxation chooses explicit social welfare maximization as its basis.[1] Two important reasons why the government would opt for non-lump sum taxation are (*a*) if lump sum taxation is simply infeasible; and (*b*) if the labour force is heterogenous.

Mirrlees in a seminal paper in 1971 first broke the stranglehold of lump sum taxation on public economics. Lum sum taxation is impractical and infeasible in the real world and there is no reason why economists should continue to give lump sum taxation so much importance. Mirrlees visualized the labour force as being homogenous in every respect except ability to work. Thus individuals have identical utility functions but a high ability person can, for instance, do twice as much work per hour as a low ability person. Mirrlees arranges the population along an ordinal and continuous distribution of abilities.

The vast literature on optimal taxation that has followed Mirrlees' work has used this basic structure. This is true of models focusing exclusively on income taxes and those that consider direct and indirect taxes simultaneously. This consideration applies to models of optimal taxation in both static and growing economies.

The plan of this chapter is as follows. Using Mirrlees framework we first consider a model of optimal linear taxation. We then discuss the basic Mirrlees model of optimal non-linear taxation. We then extend the analysis to cover commodity taxation. The analysis then considers the problem of optimal Mirrlees taxation in growing economies.

[1]A relatively new approach calculates the loss to society from an "inoptimal" degree of inequality. It then tries to minimize this loss subject to some constraints. See Ray (1985) for example.

Optimal Linear Taxation of Income

Consider a static economy in which every individual has the same utility function $u(y, L)$ defined over net income and L is labour. This utility function is, as usual, strictly quasi concave, twice continuously differentiable, strictly increasing in y and strictly decreasing in L. Thus $y = (1 - t_y)wL + G$ where t_y is the union tax on income and G is the government demogrant that is given to everyone. w is the wage paid to a person with standard ability, m, equal to one. Thus the budget constraint above applies to a person with ability $m = 1$. The first order[2] conditions for utility maximization are

$$(1 - t_y)wu_y + u_L = 0 \quad \text{for} \quad L > 0 \tag{1}$$

and

$$(1 - t_y)wu_y(G, 0) + u_L(G, 0) \leqslant 0 \quad \text{for} \quad L = 0.$$

With this stipulation it follows that for a critical wage say w^* we must have

$$L(w) > 0 \quad \text{for} \quad w > w^* \tag{2}$$
$$L(w) = 0 \quad \text{for} \quad w \leqslant w^*$$

We can see this by noting that the second expression in equation (1) is strictly negative for $L = 0$ and is strictly increasing in w.

Let us suppose that production is carried on under conditions of perfect competition so that there are no profits. Thus total net income plus government revenue must add upto total income generated by society so that we must have

$$\int_{w}^{\infty} y d\Phi + \bar{R} = \int_{w^*}^{\infty} wL\, d\Phi \tag{3}$$

where Φ is the distribution of people over ability levels and $\bar{R}$ is the fixed government revenue requirement. We now normalize so that

$\int_{w}^{\infty} d\Phi = 1$ and see that we can rewrite equation (3) as

$$G + \bar{R} = t_y \int_{w^*}^{\infty} wL\, d\Phi. \tag{4}$$

The government maximizes a social welfare function[3] $W(u)$. We maximize W subject to equation (4). Write the Lagrangean as

$$L = \int_{w}^{\infty} [w + \lambda(t_y wL - G - \bar{R}]d\Phi. \tag{5}$$

[2]In this section we take a particularly simple form of the Mirrlees articulation. The implications of the strict Mirrlees stipulation are developed later in this chapter.

[3]Different forms of W yield, for instance, the utilitarian or the Rawkian social welfare function.

The first order conditions are

$$\int_{w}^{\infty} [W_u u_G + \lambda(t_y W L_G - 1)] d\Phi = 0 \tag{6a}$$

$$\int_{w}^{\infty} [W_u u_{t_y} + \lambda(wL + LwL_{t_y})] d\Phi = 0. \tag{6b}$$

From the context it should be clear that or $w < w^*$ we have

$$L = 0 \quad \text{and} \quad L_G = L_{t_y} = 0.$$

We may write the Slutsky equation for the consumer as

$$\frac{\partial L}{\partial t_y} = - wS_{LL} - wL\frac{\partial L}{\partial M} \tag{7}$$

where S_{LL} is the substitution term and is, therefore, non-negative. Also recall that $\partial u/\partial t_y = u_{t_y} = -\alpha wL$ where α is the private marginal utility of income. Using these two results we can rewrite equations (6a) and (6b) as

$$\int \left(w_u \frac{\alpha}{\lambda} + t_y w \frac{\partial L}{\partial M} - 1 \right) d\Phi = 0 \tag{8a}$$

$$\int wL \left(W_u \frac{\alpha}{\lambda} + t_y w \frac{\partial L}{\partial M} - 1 + t_y w - \frac{SLL}{L} \right) d\Phi = 0. \tag{8b}$$

Now define
$$W_u \frac{\alpha}{\lambda} + t_y w \frac{\partial L}{\partial M} = b \tag{9}$$

so that these conditions can be reduced to

$$\bar{b} = 1 \tag{10a}$$

$$\frac{t_y}{1 - t_y} = - \frac{\text{cov}\,(b, M)}{\int M \epsilon_{LL}\, d\Phi} \tag{10b}$$

where $\bar{b}$ is the mean value of b.

These two conditions have a very straightforward and intuitively appealing interpertation, equation (10a) says that the lump sum demogrant should be so adjusted that the net social valuation of the transfer of Re 1 should on average equal the cost, which is Rel. Equation (10b) indicates that the tax depends on the compensated labour supply elasticity, ϵ_{LL}, and the way in which marginal social valuation, b, varies with M that is, the wage.

This is all that can usefully be said about the optimal linear tax. We now move to the Mirrlees analysis proper and explore the properties of the optimal non-linear tax. We will first study the optimal non-linear income tax and then bring in optimal commodity taxation as well. In this analysis we will follow closely the work of Mirrlees (1971, 1976) Seade (1977) and Cooter (1978). We will also briefly examine the optimal non-linear Rawlsian tax first studied by Phelps (1973).

The basic structure common to all purely income tax models is the following. People are identical in their tastes etc. but differ in their ability to work.

A person with ability m equal to one is only half as efficient as a person with ability $m = 2$. There exists a continuous distribution of people along this ordinal scale of ability. The distribution function is denoted by $\Phi(m)$. The highest and lowest ability levels are denoted by m_2 and m_1 respectively.

Apart from these efficiency differences workers are substitutable for each other in the production process. The labour market is perfectly competitive so that a person with ability m has a gross wage of mw where w is the wage rate of a standard ($m = 1$) unit of labour. Each person has an m independent utility function

$$u = u(-1^a, c) \tag{11}$$

where 1^a is labour and c is consumption. Leisure and consumption are both desirable goods but one can only be had by sacrificing the other. This utility function is assumed to be strictly quasi-concave and twice continuously differentiable.

The individual's budget constraint is dependent upon his m. We choose units so that the wage rate for a person of ability $m = 1$ is equal to 1. Thus the earnings of an m person are, simply,

$$Z = 1^a m. \tag{12}$$

The budget constraint is, therefore,

$$Z - T(Z) - c \geqslant 0 \tag{13}$$

where $T(Z)$ is the tax schedule that the individual faces. We have normalized the price of the consumption good to equal one. Setting up the Lagrangean we have

$$L = u(-1^a, c) + \mu[Z - T(Z) - c]. \tag{14}$$

The first order conditions are

$$u_1' = m(1 - T'(\ ))\mu \tag{15a}$$

$$u_2 = \mu \tag{15b}$$

$$Z - T(Z) - c = 0. \tag{15c}$$

In this simple story the government has a fixed revenue requirement R_0 that is independent of the tax system. Tax receipts must therefore, add up to R_0 that is,

$$\int_{m_1}^{m_2} T(Z)\Phi(m)\, dm = R_0 \tag{16}$$

where, clearly $$T(Z) = Z - c. \tag{17}$$

Along with Mirrlees we suppose that the government wishes to maximize a utilitarian social welfare function. The governments' problem can hence be written as

$$\max_{Z,\, c,\, T} \int_{m_1}^{m_2} W(u(-Z/m, c)\Phi(m)\, dm \tag{18}$$

subject to

$$\int_{m_1}^{m_2} T(Z)\Phi(m)\,dm = R_0$$

$$T(Z) = Z - c$$

where W is the social welfare function.

We would like to convert the constraints of equation (18) into differential equations so that we could use the methods of optimal control to solve this problem. We have already used the maximum principle in our study of taxation and Investment behaviour.

We first substitute equation (17) into (16) and differentiate with respect to m to get

$$\frac{dR}{dm} = (Z - c)\Phi(m) \tag{19}$$

$$R_{m_2} = R_0 \tag{20}$$

where R_{m_2} is cumulative tax revenue upto ability level m_2. We will now use equations (19) and (20) in the maximization programme.

Now define the utility of a m person when Z and c are optimally chosen to satisfy the individual's first order conditions for an internal solution equations (15a, 15b and 15c):

$$V_m = \max u(-Z/m,\ c) \tag{21}$$

Differentiating this with respect to m we have

$$\frac{dVm}{dm} = -u_1 \frac{d}{dm}(Z/m) + u_2 \frac{dc}{dm} + u_1 Z/m^2. \tag{22}$$

Now if we differentiate equation (13) with respect to m and substitute equations (15a) and (15b) into this expression for u_1 and u_c respectively we will get

$$-u_1 \frac{d}{dm}\left(\frac{Z}{m}\right) + u_2 \frac{dc}{dm} = 0 \tag{23}$$

so that

$$\frac{dVm}{dm} = u_1 Z/m^2. \tag{24}$$

Equation (24) and equations (15) are equivalent statements. Equation (15) describe V_m by enunciating the first order conditions for a maximum. Equation (24) tells us how this maximized utility varies across people with different levels of ability. This is, then, a simple envelope argument.

Now in Equation (21) since u monotonically declines in 1 inversion is possible. We write $Z = z(V,\ c,\ m)$. We are thus able to eliminate Z as a control variable and include V as a state variable. The final form of the problem is

$$\max \int_{m_1}^{m_2} W(V)\Phi(m)\,dm$$

subject to $$\frac{dV}{dm} = u_1(-Z(V, c, m)/m, c)z(v, c, m)/m^2$$

$$\frac{dR}{dm} = (Z(V, c, m) - c)\Phi(m)$$

with the terminal conditions

$$R_{m_2} = R_0 \quad \text{and} \quad R_{m_1} = 0.$$

We write the Hamiltonian for this problem as

$$H = W(V)\Phi(m) + \theta_1 u_1(\ )Z(\ )/m^2 + \theta_2(z(\ ) - c)\Phi(m) \tag{25}$$

where θ_1 and θ_2 are costate variables for this problem. The necessary conditions are:

(i) $\dfrac{\partial H}{\partial c} = 0 = \theta_1\left\{\dfrac{\partial}{\partial c}(u_1 Z(\ )/m^2)\right\} + \theta_2\left(\dfrac{\partial Z}{\partial c} - 1\right)\Phi(m)$

(ii) $\dfrac{\partial H}{\partial V} = -\dfrac{d}{dm}\theta_1$ (canonical equation)

(iii) $\dfrac{\partial H}{\partial R} = -\dfrac{d}{dm}\theta_2$ (canonical equation)

(iv) $\theta_{1m_1} = \theta_{1m_2} = 0$ (transversality conditions)

(v) $R_{m_1} = 0$ and $R_{m_2} = R_0$.

The strand results in optimal tax theory are all derived by interpreting these conditions. Let us first note that

$$\frac{dVm}{dm} = u_1 Z(\ )/m^2 \geqslant 0.$$

A person with a high ability can work less than a person with less ability and yet have the same consumption and, of course, higher leisure. Thus dVm/dm cannot be negative. A person with high ability has at least as much utility as a person with low utility.

In a similar vein we can prove that $T' < 1$. To see this let us suppose that in some interval of gross income $T' > 1$. In this interval a person who gives up leisure to work ends up paying more than 100 percent of the incremental income in taxes. No rational consumer would target an income in this range of Z.

We now show an important result i.e. that the marginal tax rate at the top and the bottom ends of the ability distribution is equal to zero. From the condition $\partial H/\partial c = 0$ we have

$$\theta_1\left\{\frac{\partial}{\partial c} u_1 Z(\ )/m^2)\right\} + \theta_2\left\{\frac{\partial Z}{\partial c} - 1\right\}\Phi(m).$$

Now

$\partial Z/\partial c = dZ/dc =$ marginal rate of substitution between income and consumption. From the individual's first order conditions for utility maximization (equation (15)) we have

$$\frac{dZ}{dc} = \frac{1}{1-T'} \quad \text{whence}$$

$$T' = \frac{-\theta_1 \left\{ \frac{\partial}{\partial c} u_1 Z(\ )/m^2 \right\}}{\theta_2 \Phi \frac{dZ}{dc}}.$$

Now from the transversality conditions we have

$$\theta_{1_{m_2}} = \theta_{1_{m_2}} = 0 \quad \text{that is,}$$

$T' = 0$ at m_1 and m_2. Thus the person with the highest ability and the person with the lowest ability face a zero marginal tax rate.

A related result is that under certain conditions the tax schedule is non-decreasing i.e. $T' \geqslant 0$. There are two such conditions

(*i*) that the cross partial is non-negative i.e. $u_{12} \geqslant 0$

(*ii*) that the marginal social value of leisure declines with ability i,e.

$$\frac{d(W_u u_1)}{dm} \leqslant 0.$$

We first show that if condition (*ii*) obtain then $\theta_1 \leqslant 0$.

Now from the canonical equation for θ_1 we have

$$\frac{-d}{dm}\theta_1 = \left[W_u + \theta_2 \frac{\partial Z}{\partial V}\Phi\right] + \left[\frac{\partial}{\partial V}\frac{\partial u}{\partial m}\right]\theta_1$$

$$= \alpha(m) + (\beta(m))\theta_2. \tag{26}$$

This is a linear differential equation in θ_1 we solve it to get

$$-\theta_1(m^*) = \int_{m_1}^{m^*} \alpha(j) \exp\left(\int_{m^*}^{j} \beta(\hat{j})\, d\hat{j}\right) dj. \tag{27}$$

Since the exponential function is non-negative the sign of equation (27) is given solely by $\alpha(j)$

Now $$\frac{\partial Z}{\partial V} = -m/u_1$$

where $$\alpha(j) = \left(W_u \frac{u_1}{j} - \theta_2\right)\frac{\Phi j}{u_1}$$

so that $\alpha(j) \geqslant 0$ whenever $W_u \frac{u_1}{j} \geqslant \theta_2$ and vice versa.

Now since $W_u u_1$ is monotonically decreasing by assumption and θ_2 is constant we must have $\alpha(j)$ changing sign at most once and that from $+$ to $-$. Now from the transversality conditions $\theta_{1_{m_1}} = \theta_{2_{m_2}} = 0$. Thus $\theta_1 \leqslant 0$.

Now from the first order condition we have

$$0 = \frac{\partial H}{\partial c} = \theta_1 \frac{\partial}{\partial c}\{u_1 z/m^2\} + \theta_2\left(\frac{\delta z}{\delta c} - 1\right)\Phi.$$

We also know that $\frac{\partial Z}{\partial c} = \frac{1}{1 - T'}$ so that

$$\frac{1}{1 - T'} - 1 = \left(-\frac{\theta_1}{\theta_2 \Phi}\right) \frac{\partial}{\partial c} [u_1 \cdot z/m^2].$$

We know $\theta_1 \leqslant 0$ and θ_2 is a positive constant (It is positive because $\theta_1 \leqslant 0$ and it is constant because of the canonical equation in θ_2). To prove that $T' \geqslant 0$ we have to show that $\frac{\partial}{\partial c} [u_1 z/m^2] > 0$. But this derivative equals $\left(-Z \frac{\partial Z}{\partial c} u_{11}/\text{m} + Zu_{12} + \frac{\partial Z}{\partial c} u_1\right)/m^2$ $u_{11} < 0$ by concavity of u, $u_{12} > 0$ and $\frac{\partial Z}{\partial c} > 0$ so that $\frac{\partial}{\partial c} u_1 Z/m^2 > 0$ and hence $T' \geqslant 0$.

If we combine this result with the result that T' is zero at m_1 and m_2 we realize that the marginal tax rate will rise in some ranges of income and it will fall in others. Between the two extremes of m_1 and m_2 the tax schedule behaves in this manner whereas at these and points the marginal tax rate is zero.

At the qualitative level not much more can be said about the optimal non-linear tax. To get more precise results we must do some numerical calculations. Mirrlees himself did some calculations using a Cobb Douglas example. His main conclusions are threefold (*a*) the optimal tax schedule is approximately linear, (*b*) the marginal tax rates are rather low, and, therefore, that (*c*) the income tax is optimally not a very redistributive tax[4].

Phelps in his articulation of the optimal tax problem with a Rawlsian social welfare function came to almost the same conclusions as Mirrless. As would be expected, however, the Rawls Optimum tax schedule is more redistributive.

Why is the optimal marginal tax rate zero at m_1 and m_2? The transversality conditions say so but it is possible to advance a heuristic explanation. Take the case of the person with the highest level of ability. If he faces a positive marginal tax rate it would be rational for him to supply less labour so that his effective labour is equal to that provided by a person with ability just below m_2. At the lower end of the ability scale a positive marginal tax rate might induce withdrawal from the labour force.

Optimal Taxation with Many Goods

We have already encountered optimal taxation with many goods in the linear case. In the case of commodity taxation we had analysed various forms of the Ramsey rule and within the Diamond-Mirrlees framework we had analysed the mix of direct and indirect taxes.

[4]This goes back to the tax assignment problem. In a real world situation if we are in position where indirect taxes are ideally non-uniform then there is no harm in using indirect taxes for redistributive purposes and the income tax to raise revenue.

In this section we plan to use the Maximum Principle to see how far we can go (qualitatively) in the case of optimal non-linear taxation of many goods and labour. We pose the problem strictly within the framework of the previous section. Necessarily, therefore, the analysis gets a bit unrealistic. At the level of aggregation of the previous section having people identical except for their levels of ability is passable. But when it comes to the many commodity case this does become indefensible. In addition to their levels of ability people might differ with respect particularly to their tastes for various commodities, preference for leisure, access to various markets etc. In addition since we are generalizing it makes some sense to unveil the mystery around differences in innate ability. Part of the difference in ability may be acquired through differential access to good education. Moreover what may be a perceived difference in innate ability may actually only be differences in class membership. Good scientists may not be able to make a living wage whereas a mediocre management consultant may average Rs 10,000 a month. Notwithstanding all these difficulties we will persist with our tried and tested formulation in the many good case. If nothing else it might provide us with a benchmark case.

Labour, apart from efficiency differences, is still substitutable. There are n goods for whom tax rates have to be chosen. The individual's utility function is written as

$$u(-Z/m; c_1, \ldots, c_n) \tag{27'}$$

where $c_1, \ldots, c_n$ are the goods for which tax rates have to be found. The individual's budget constraint is

$$T(Z) + \sum_j p_j c_j = Z \tag{28}$$

where q_i is the producer price for c_i and p_i is the consumer price such that $p_i = q_i + t_i$ where t_i is the tax rate.

By following the same steps as in the previous section we can define maximized utility as a function of optimally chosen leisure and consumption goods i.e.

$$V = \max u(-Z/m; c_1, \ldots, c_n). \tag{29}$$

Again we arrive at our familiar envelope condition

$$\begin{aligned} \frac{dV}{dm} &= \frac{\partial}{\partial m} u(-Z/m; c_1, \ldots, c_n) \\ &= u_1 Z/m^2. \end{aligned} \tag{30}$$

Mirrlees (1971, 1976) has focused on an optimal derivation of the $T(\ )$ and the optimal linear tax rates t_i. Since this is added up in the price this is tantamount to choosing p_i. For this case since we are choosing prices and not quantities it is better to work in terms of minimized expenditure functions instead of maximized utility functions. We know that maximization of utility subject to a budget constraint is equivalent to minimization of expenditure subject to a utility constraint.

The expenditure minimization problem can be written as

$$\min_{c_1, \ldots, c_n} \quad -z + T(Z) + \sum_i p_j c_j$$

subject to $$u(-Z/m, c_1, \ldots, c_n) \geqslant V \tag{31}$$

where V is the maximized utility just defined. The solution to this is a minimized expenditure function e which is such that

$$e = e(p_1, \ldots, p_n! \ V; \ -Z/m) \tag{32}$$

Now $e_{p_j} = \dfrac{\partial e}{\partial p_j} = c_j$ are the demand functions.

In equation (30) we substitute $c_1, \ldots, c_n$ to arrive at the final form of the envelope equation.

$$\frac{\partial V}{\partial m} = (Z/m^2)\, u_1(-Z/m, e_{p_1}, \ldots, e_{p_n}). \tag{33}$$

The final form of the optimal tax problem can now be written as

$$\max \int_{m_1}^{m_2} W(V)\Phi(m)\, dm$$

subject to

$$\frac{dV}{dm} = \left(\frac{Z}{m^2}\right) u_1(-Z/m; \ e_{p_1}, \ldots, e_{p_n})$$

and

$$\frac{dR}{dm} = (Z - \Sigma p_j e_{p_j})\, \Phi(m) \tag{34}$$

$$R_{m_1} = 0 \text{ and } R_{m_2} = R_0.$$

The Hamiltonian for this problem can be written as

$$H = W(V)\, \Phi(m) + \theta_1(Z/m^2)\, u_1(-Z/m; \ e_{p_1}, \ldots, e_{p_n})$$
$$+ \theta_2(Z - \sum_i p_j e_{p_j})\, \Phi(m). \tag{35}$$

Once again θ_1 is a function of m whereas θ_2 is independent of m.

The first order conditions for an internal maximum are

$$\frac{\partial H}{\partial Z} = 0 \tag{36}$$

$$\frac{-d}{dm}\theta_1 = \frac{\partial H}{\partial V} \quad \text{canonical equation}$$

$$\frac{-d}{dm}\theta_2 = \frac{\partial H}{\partial R} \quad \text{canonical equation}$$

$$\theta_{1m_1} = 0 = \theta_{1m_2} \quad \text{transversality conditions}$$

$$R_{m_1} = 0, \ R_{m_2} = R_0.$$

The results from this problem are, on the whole, straightforward extensions of the problem considered in the previous section. It is trivial to show that post tax utility is a non-decreasing function of ability. Similarly the result that $T' < 1$ follows easily. The end point conditions get amended somewhat. The individual's tax liability can be written as

$$\tau = T(Z) + \sum_{i} t_j e_{p_j} \tag{37}$$

where t_j is the tax rate imposed on the jth commodity so that $p_j = q_j + t_j$ where q_j is the producer's price of the jth commodity $j = 1, \ldots, n$.

Now increase labour income, Z, by a small amount for some m person on the optimal path. The controls are held constant-in particular c_i is constant.

Then $$\frac{\partial \tau}{\partial z} = 1 - \sum_{j} q_j \frac{\partial e_{p_j}}{\partial Z}.$$

Now from the first order conditions for the maximization of the Hamiltonian we have

$$0 = \frac{\partial H}{\partial Z} = \theta_1 \frac{\partial}{\partial Z}\left(\frac{\partial u}{\partial m}\right) + \theta_2 \left(1 - \Sigma q_j \frac{\partial e_{p_j}}{\partial Z}\right) \Phi.$$

Combining these two we get

$$\frac{\partial \tau}{\partial Z} = \frac{-\theta_1}{\theta_2 \Phi} \left\{\frac{\partial}{\partial Z}\left(\frac{\partial u}{\partial m}\right)\right\}.$$

At m_1 and m_2 we have $\theta_1 = 0$.

Thus we have the result that at the end points of the ability distribution total (i.e. direct and indirect) marginal tax liability is zero.

The intuitive explanation that one can advance for this result is similar to that advanced in the previous section. The tax rate relevant now is the direct plus indirect tax. Thus at m_2 having a positive total marginal tax rate would induce these people to supply less labour and thus move, in terms of effective labour supply, to the position of persons with ability level just below m_2. The result that the total marginal tax rate should be zero does not, of course, mean that the marginal direct and indirect tax rates should each be zero. One of them could be positive and the other negative.

In a similar vein we could establish that $\frac{\partial \tau}{\partial Z} \geqslant 0$ so long as (*i*) goods subject to taxation and leisure have non-negative cross partials that is,

$$u_{lc_j} \geqslant 0; \qquad j = 1, \ldots, n.$$

(*ii*) the marginal social utility of a rupee is a non-increasing function of utility i.e. $dW_v\lambda/dv \leqslant 0$ (where λ is the Lagrange multiplier associated with the consumer utility maximization problem).

This result which is left as an exercise for the interested reader is the exact analogue of a result provide in the earlier section. The required proof is a simple extension of the proof developed earlier.

In the Mirrlees framework, then, the existence of several goods is tackled in a very simple manner. Leisure and all other taxed commodities are treated as if they could be aggregated such that we could make a distinction between taxed commodities (including leisure) and other commodities (non taxed). Thus some of the propositions deal with taxed commodities considered as a group.

It is possible to extend the analysis to cover tax schedules for some commodities and tax rates for other commodities. But the qualitative results are very specialized. A non-linear income tax schedule is a reality but a non-linear excise schedule is not yet quite operational. In any case it is perhaps best to study this in the context of non-linear prices for public services. So we postpone this discussion.

Optimal Taxation in a Growing Economy

An important limitation of the analysis in this chapter is that it is static. This is evident from both the atemporal nature of the optimal tax problem and from the (implicit) specification of a production function with only labour as input so that all questions of capital accumulation and the effects of the tax structure on it can be ignored. It is now time to confront this question.

How the optimal tax problem is specified is crucial to the answer we can give. Two similar approaches have traditionally been followed in the literature. One is to use the Solow growth model as the framework to which the question of optimal taxation is addressed. Usually we think of an immortal representative consumer whose utility is described as the discounted integral of lifetime consumption. This is maximized subject to the Solow growth model (suitably modified to accommodate taxation) type of specification of the real sector. This specification has an important drawback. Capital investment decisions have implications for more than one generation. Thus there is room for intergenerational conflict. The current generation realizes that future generations are not yet born so it can deplete natural resources too quickly or save too little. Hence there is need for a concept of justice that embraces more than one generation.

The second approach—that of the life cycle model of saving and consumption—makes the intergenerational differences explicit. We will hence develop our arguments in terms of the life cycle model. At one end we will see the implications of intragenerational justice being captured in the standard utilitarian or Rawlsian manner whereas the intergenerational problems are solved in an ad hoc manner. Other works particularly that of Atkinson and Stiglitz (1976) explicitly require[5] Pareto optimality across generations. At the other end there are some works which explicitly extend the same concept of justice to cover both intergenerational and intragenerational justice.

In this section we will follow the classic paper of Ordover and Phelps (1979) and there will be some reference to the numerical simulations carried out by Jha (1978).

Recall the overlapping generations model of saving and consumption. Each generation lives for two time periods. During the first period it works

[5]Thif was clarified in Ordover and Phelps (1979)

and saves. During the second period it is retired and consumes its savings. At any time two generations are alive—the "young" and the "old". Suppose further that we are in the two good case.[6] One good is labour (or leisure). The other is produced with the help of capital and labour. Capital, itself, is indistinguishable from this commodity. The production function for this commodity is of the constant returns to scale variety. Each consumer has utility defined over consumption and leisure.

Let us look at the problem from the vantage point of members of generation g. Apart from the taxation of savings and wage income the government has two other policy tools available. Each person gets a demogrant G_g when they are young and H_g upon retirement. 1^m is the labour supply of a person with ability m. A person with ability m is assumed to supply $m1^m$ units of effective labour. The wage of a standard unit of labour is w per hour. First period consumption is c_1^m and second period consumption is c_2^m. An individual of ability m solves the following optimization problem.

$$\max u \{c_1^m, c_2^m, 1^m\} \tag{38}$$

subject to

$$wm1^m + G_g + \frac{H_g}{F_k} - c_1^m - \frac{c_2^m}{F_k}$$
$$-T_1(wm1^m) - T_s(c_2^m - H_g) = s^m \geqslant 0.$$

The budget constraint needs a little explanation. $wm1^m$ is wage earnings. G_g is the value of the demogrant received when young. Thus $wm1^m + G_g$ is first period earnings by the young of generation g. C_2^m is second period consumption. To obtain its worth today we discount it at the rate $1 + r_g$ where r_g is the real rate of interest for generation g. Since factor markets are assumed to be competitive $1 + r_g$ must equal the marginal product of capital[7] $F_k(k_g, 1_{g+1}) \geqslant 0$. Similarly the second period is discounted. $T_1(\ )$ and $T_s(\ )$ are, respectively, the (possibility) non-linear) tax schedules for wage income and savings. s^m is savings

We write down the Lagrangean for this problem as

$$L = u(\ ) + \lambda(wm1^m + G_g + \frac{H_g}{F_k} - c_1^m - \frac{c_2^m}{F_k}$$
$$-T_1(\ ) - T_s(\ )) \tag{39}$$

[6]Our results with the many commodity case should convince us that this is not very restrictive.

[7]$F(\ )$ is the production function. When calculating the discount rate for the young generation g we must realize that when they are old 1_{g+1} (the labour from generation $g + 1$) will work with the capital that they (generation g) leave after retirement. The wage of a standard unit of labour equals the marginal product of labour: thus $w = F_{1_g}(k_{g-1}, 1_g)$. Clearly

$$1_g = \int_{m_1}^{m_2} m1^m \, d\Phi(m)$$

The first order conditions are

$$u_{c_1}m - \lambda = 0$$

$$u_l m + \lambda[wm - T_l' wm] = 0$$

whence $$u c_1^m = -\frac{u_l m}{um(1 - T_l')}$$

and $$u c_2^m + \lambda\left[-\frac{1}{F_k} - T_s'\right] = 0 \tag{40}$$

or $$u_{c_2}m - \lambda\left(\frac{1}{F_k} + T_s'\right) = 0$$

or $$u_{c_2}m = u_{c_1}m\left(\frac{1}{F_k} + T_s'\right) = -\frac{u_l m}{wm(1 - T_l')}$$

and $$wm1^m + G_g + H_g/F_k - c_1^m - (c_2^2/F_k) - T_l(\ ) - T_s(\ ) = 0.$$

In this set up it has been assumed that savings are taxed only once (in the second period). Thus first period consumer price is the same as producer price and we have set both equal to one thereby choosing our numeraire. From the way we have set up the budget constraint. It is clear that

$$c_2^m \equiv H_g + (1 + r_g)s^m$$

$$c_1^m = G_g + wm1^m - T_l(\ ) - T_s(\ ) - s^m.$$

Now write the maximized utility for a person with ability m as

$$V^*(m) \equiv \max u(wm1^m + G_g + \left(\frac{H_g - c_2^m}{F_k}\right) - T_l(\ )$$

$$-T_s(\ );\ c_2^m,\ 1^m) \tag{41}$$

In a manner completely analogous to the static model we define the envelope as

$$\frac{dV^*(m)}{dm} = -\frac{u_l m 1^m}{m^2} \geqslant 0. \tag{42}$$

We now invert equation (41) to get

$$c_1^m = Z(V^*(m),\ c_2^m,\ 1^m). \tag{43}$$

These are the utility envelope conditions to be satisfied by the government of generation g. We could impose a revenue requirement condition for the government g and soive for the optimal taxes. In fact Ordover and Phelps (1976) do precisely this. In the intergenerational context, however, it makes more sense to think of generation g inheriting the debts of the government of generation $g - 1$. Moreover the government of generation g may borrow in the market to finance its expense so that it passes on its debts to generation $g + 1$.

The full problem of intra and intergenerational justice can be looked upon as a two step exercise. In the first step each generation solves its own problem of intragenerational justice according to some well specified norm of justice e.g. the utilitarian or Rawlsian criterion. In the next step these plans are coordinated and amended to make them conform to society's notion of intergenerational justice.

The government budget constraint for generation g is, therefore,

$$G_g + \frac{H_g}{F_k(k_g, l_{g+1})} = \int_{m_1}^{m_2} [T_l(w_g m l_g^m + T_s(c_{2,g}^m - H_g)] \, d\Phi(m) + (\Delta_g - d_{g-1}) + F_k k_{g-1} - (c_{2,g-1} - d_{g-1}) \quad (44)$$

where l_{g+1} is total labour supply from workers in generation $g + 1$. $c_{2,g}^m$ is second period consumption of a person of type m of generation g. Δ_g is the market value of debt issued by generation g and d_{g-1} is the face value of the debt of generation $g - 1$ that has to be retired.[8] Equation (44) can now be interpreted in the following manner. The left hand side of the equation is the present value of the demogrant payments. On the right hand side we have government receipts. The first term represents tax collection. $(\Delta_g - d_{g-1})$ represents net borrowing by the government. The government also gets interest on capital. $c_{2,g-1} - d_{g-1}$ represents net claims of the old of generation $g - 1$.

Let us now consider the problem of optimal taxation. The government of generation g maximizes the welfare functional

$$W^g = \int_{m_1}^{m_2} W^g(u(c_{1,g}^m, c_{2,g}^m, l_g^m)) \, d\Phi(m) \quad (45)$$

subject to the production and individual preference conditions outlined above and the intergenerational constraints to be discussed below.

Ordover and Phelps place the following intergenerational constraints on the maximization of W^g. First there is the question of intergenerational trust. The government of generation g must meet the second period consumption of the old of generation $g - 1$. In other words if, as part of their own maximization plan, generation $g - 1$ gave themselves $c_{2,g-1}$ as second period consumption then the government of generation g is ethically bound to supply them with this much consumption.

Moreover the future path of capital and second period consumption is predetermined i.e. k_{g+i}, $c_{2,g+i}$; $i = 1, 2, \ldots$ is a datum. Why is this justified? Taking $c_{2,g+i}$ first. The current generation can always increase its utility by leaving less for future generations second period consumption. Intergenerational justice requires that generation g should not be permitted to do so. This would also, of course, imply that the capital stocks for future generations are also predetermined. Thus generation g can choose its capital stock k_g, its second period consumption $c_{1,g}$ and its labour supply l_g. Maximized utility V^* is a state variable and c_1, g is a function of V^*. However, notice that since k_{g+i} and $c_{2,g+i}(i = 1, 2, \ldots,)$ are given it follows that l_{g+i} is

[8]It is assumed that only one period bonds can be issued.

already predetermined. Given the capital stock for any generation and consumption obligations the labour required to produce this is also predetermined if the labour supply in generation 1 is known. Thus we need to concentrate on the optimal tax programme of generation 1.

For generation $g = 1$. $c_{2,1}^{m}$, 1_1^m are control variables. V^* is a state variable and $c_{1,1}^{m}$ is a function of V^* from equation (43). Apart from the differential equation (42) two other constrains exist for generation 1. First the second period consumption of its citizens cannot be arbitrarily large. In other words generation 1 cannot issue an indefinitely large debt (which will have to be paid by generation 2). Thus second period consumption of generation 1 cannot be larger than some $\bar{c}_{2,1}$:

$$\bar{c}_{2,1} - \int_{m_1}^{m_2} c_{2,1}^{m} \, d\Phi(m) \geqslant 0. \tag{46}$$

Moreover, as discussed earlier, generation 1 must leave a certain minimum capital stock, say $\bar{k}_1$, for the young of the next generation that is.

$$F(k_0, 1_1) - \int_{m_1}^{m_2} c_1^{m} \, d\Phi(m) - c_{2,0} \geqslant \bar{k}_1. \tag{47}$$

The problem of the government of generation $g = 1$ is to maximize equation (45) subject to the envelope condition equation (42) and the intergenerational constraints equations (46) and (47). The Hamiltonian for this problem can be written as

$$H_1(m) = V^*(m) \, d\Phi(m) + \lambda_1' \left(\bar{c}_{2,1} - \int_{m_1}^{m_2} c_{2,1}^{m} \, d\Phi(m) \right. \tag{48}$$

$$+ \lambda_2' \left(-\bar{k}_1 + F(k_0, 1_1) - c_{2,0} - \int_{m_1}^{m_2} c_1^{m} \, d\Phi(m) \right)$$

$$+ \theta(m) \left(- \frac{u_1^m 1_1^m}{m^2} \right)$$

where λ_1' and λ_2' are Lagrange multipliers. In particular they are both independent of m. $\theta(m)$ is a costate variable. Now if $W_1^*(k_1, C_{2,1})$ is the maximum welfare that generation 1 can attain given its target $\bar{k}_1$, $\bar{C}_{2,1}$ it follows that

$$\frac{\partial W_1^*}{\partial \bar{c}_{2,1}} = -\lambda_1'; \text{ and } \frac{\partial W_2^*}{\partial k_1} = -\lambda_2'.$$

If we have an internal maximum for W_1 then $\lambda_1' < 0$ and $\lambda_2' < 0$ so that along the locus where W_1^* is constant we must have

$$\left(\frac{dk_1}{dc_{2,1}} \right) = - \frac{\partial W_1^* / \partial \bar{c}_{2,1}}{\partial W_1^* / \partial k_1} = \frac{\lambda_1'}{\lambda_2'} > 0. \tag{49}$$

This is the marginal rate of substitution between capital and second period consumption for generation 1.

Generation 2 inherits k_1 from generation 1 which it (generation 2) can invest at the going rate of interest. Thus along a contour where W_2^* is constant.

$$\left(\frac{dk_1}{dc_{2,1}}\right) = \frac{1}{F_k(k_1,\ l_2(k_1,\ c_{2,1}))} \tag{50}$$

where $l_2(\ \ )$ is the predetermined amount of labour supply of generation 2. Equation (50) is the marginal rate of substitution between k_1 and $c_{2,1}$ for generation 2.

If there is Pareto optimality across generations then the marginal rates of substitution for generations 1 and 2 must be the same i.e.

$$\frac{\lambda_1'}{\lambda_2'} = \frac{1}{F_k(k_1,\ l_2(k_1,\ c_{2,1}))} \tag{51}$$

It should be realized that the criterion for intergenerational justice adopted here in no way requires Pareto optimality across generations.[9]

However, we can proceed with this additional specification to derive some results of a qualitative nature.

From equation (51) we write

$$\lambda_1' = \frac{\lambda_2'}{F_k(k_1,\ l_2(k_1,\ c_{2,1}))}$$

Also define r_1^* and Δ_1^* by

$$1 + r_1^* = F_k(k_1^*,\ l_2(k_1^*,\ c_{2,1*})) \tag{52}$$

and

$$(1 + r_1^*)^{-1}c_{2,1*} - k_1^* = \Delta_1^* \tag{53}$$

Throughout, the stars (*) refer to optimal values. Thus, equation (52) defines the relationship between the rate of interest and the marginal product of capital. The discounted value of second period consumption for the old of generation 1 must equal the sum of the capital stock and the face value of debt. This is stated by equation (53).

Substitute equations (52) and (53) into the Hamiltorian and use the value for λ_2' derived for situations with Pareto optimality across generations. Thus we get

$$\begin{aligned} H_1(m) = {} & V_*(m)\,d\Phi(m) + \lambda_2'[\Delta_1^* - (1 + r_1^*)^{-1}c_{2,1}^m \\ & + F(k_0,\ l_1) - c_1^m - c_{2,0}^m]\,d\Phi(m) \\ & + \theta(m)\left(-\frac{l_1^m u_{l_1}^m}{m^2}\right). \end{aligned} \tag{54}$$

[9]The results of Jha (1978) discussed later in this chapter bear ample testimony of this.

The first order conditions for the maximization of the Hamiltonian yield

$$\frac{\partial H_1}{\partial c_{2,1}(m)} = \lambda_2' \left[-(1+\overset{*}{r}_1)^{-1} - \left(\frac{\partial c_1^m}{\partial c_{2,1}^m}\right)_{V^*(m)} \right] d\Phi(m)$$

$$+ \theta(m) \left\{ -\frac{1}{m}\overset{m}{} \left[u_{1,1} m_{c_1} \left(\frac{\partial c_1^m}{\partial c_{2,1}^m} \right)_{V^*(m)} \right] + u_{1,1} m_{c_{2,1}} \right] \right\}$$

$$= 0 \qquad (55)$$

In practice little can be said about equation (55). However the transversality condition requires that θ be zero for m_1 and m_2 ability levels. At these ability levels since $\lambda_2 \neq 0$ we must have

$$\left(\frac{\partial c_1^m}{\partial c_{2,1}}\right)_{V^*(m)} = -(1+\overset{*}{r}_1)^{-1}.$$

But we know that $\dfrac{\partial c_1^m}{\partial c_{2,1}}$ is marginal rate of substitution between c_1 and c_2 and that $(1+\overset{*}{r}_1) = F_k(\ )$. Hence the marginal rate of transforming c_1 and c_2 is the same in production as well as consumption. Thus the marginal tax on savings must equal zero at ability levels m_1 and m_2. By analogous reasoning it is easy to show that the tax rate on wage income also equals zero at m_1 and m_2.

It is time now to put another result in perspective. Atkinson and Stiglitz (1976) had said that if the utility function is weekly separable in consumption and leisure then the marginal tax rate on savings is zero irrespective of the level of ability. This result holds only if we require Pareto optimality across generations. Consider the first order condition equation (55) and recall that weak separability of the utility function means that the partial derivatives $u_{1,1}m_{c_1}$ and $u_{1,1}m_{c_{2,1}}$ are both zero. From equation (55) then $T_s'(\ )$ must be zero. It is important to realize that this result holds only when we require Pareto optimality across generations. Ordover and Phelps emphasize that this result is true whether one uses the Rawlsian on the utilitarian Bengson—Samuelson criterion of welfare.

Jha (1978) studied a numerical simulation of a modified and simplified version of this problem. In a two factor would he considered linear taxation of wages and wealth. He also did not require Pareto optimality across generations. Moreover his model was static not only in the sense of the absence of a secular rising trend of utility, but also in the sense that each generation was constrained to leave behind the same capital stock for its descendents as it itself inherited. Society is Rawlsian just both intra and intergenerationally so that minimum utility is maximized in any generation. Society is further constrained to not let the minimum utility of any generation rise above the minimum utility of any other generation. Jha uses a Stone Geary utility function (so separability is satisfied) defined over first and second period consumption and leisure. The production function is of the constant elasticity of substitution variety. Different values of the rate of interest and the standard wage rate are assumed. The distribution of abilities is defined alternatively by a logistic, lognormal and Pareto distributions.

Jha is able to calculate the optimal mix of taxes for each case chosen. The most important result of this exercise is that the tax rate on savings income is very high—nearly 100 percent. Of course Jha's model is not as general as that of Ordover and Phelps but it does pinpoint the central importance of the stipulation of Pareto optimality to the results of Atkinson and Stiglitz.

In the Ordover and Phelps framework not much more can be said at the qualitative level. To get more concrete results one has to undertake numerical simulati ons.

Optimal Taxation in the Non-Overlapping Generation Model

A relatively small literature has departed somewhat from the Mirrlees-Phelps tradition. These authors have chosen to define social welfare not a sum of individual utilities but as directly the result of production and disitribution activities in the economy. For example Pestieau and Possen (1978) consider a two class version of the Solow growth model where workers work and save whereas capitalists do not work. The wage income of workers and the capital income of workers and capitalists are both taxed (linearly). Social welfare is defined as the discounted integrate of instantaneous social utility which, in turn, is a function of the extent of production of the economy and some index of the inequality of income between capitalists and workers. Tax rates are chosen to maximize social welfare.

In the first application of optimal tax theory to problems of economic development, Jha and Lachler (1981) consider a dynamic version of the Harris Todaro model[10]. The economy has two sectors. The rural sector produces food with capital, unskilled labour and land as inputs. The urban sector produces manufactured goods with the help of capital, skilled and unskilled labour. The labour force in the urban sector is heterogenous precisely in the Mirrlees-Phelps sense. Only unskilled workers work in the rural sector. The skilled labour force owns the private capital as well as agricultural land. The minimum wage in the urban sector is higher than the marginal product (and hence the wage) of labour in the rural sector. Labour migrates from the rural sector to the urban sector till the expected urban wage (the minimum wage multiplied by the rate of employment in the urban sector) is equal to the rural wage. The government taxes wages and capital income and also invests in the two sector. Instantaneous social utility is a function of the outputs of the rural and urban sectors and an index of inequality between the average skilled worker and the rural worker. Social welfare is a discounted integral of these instantaneous utilities. Optimal tax and investment policies are discussed.

[10]See Harris and Todaro (1971).

Concluding Remarks. In this chapter we have presented the salient features of the vast and rapidly expanding literature on optimal taxation. Particularly in the case of developing countries the work to be done is trully immense. Much of the optimal tax literature remains inapplicable to developing countries because of the rarefied assumptions of the theory. But the insights are important and good work can and should be done to improve tax design in developing countries.

PART—III

APPLIED PROBLEMS IN WELFARE ECONOMICS

16. Fiscal Policy and the National Debt

In this chapter we revert back to some macro concerns. We have been looking at aggregative models off and on. Our principal concern here is fiscal policy. We wish to study the effects of government tax, expenditure and debt policy on the macro-economic equilibrium and the growth path of the economy.

The standard textbook presentation of this problem is usually cast within the IS-LM framework.

Figure 16.1 plots the standard IS-LM diagram. The IS curve is the locus of interest rate (r) and national income (Y) combinations which give equilibrium in the goods market i.e. where investment equals saving.[1] The LM schedule[2] plots the (r, y) combination which yield an equilibrium in the money market. Simultaneous equilibrium is achieved where the IS and LM schedules interest each other. Stimulative fiscal policy (a decrease in income tax or increased government expenditure) shifts the IS curve to the right (the dashed line in Fig. 16.1). If we had a simple Keynesian system where monetary influences did not affect y the increase in income would have been AB. BC is then the monetary feedback—with a fixed money supply increased expenditure increases the rate of interest which restricts the expansion of investment.

This simple but powerful framework has been used to frame answers to a number of important policy questions. But there are some fundamental shortcomings in this apparatus. To mention just a few. It is difficult to accomodate government debt and corporate financial policy in the analysis. It is also rather difficult to use this apparatus in a growth context or when the price level is changing.

[1]The equation of the IS curve is

$$I(r) = S(r, \underset{+}{y}).$$

Totally differentiating we calculate

$$I_r\, dr = S_r\, dr + S_y\, dy.$$

So dr/dy along the IS schedule is negative.

[2]The equation of the LM curve is $L(\underset{+}{y}, \underset{-}{r}) = \frac{M}{P}$. Totally differentiating for fixed M, P we have $L_y\, dy + L_r\, dr = 0$ so $\frac{dr}{dy}$ along the LM schedule is positive.

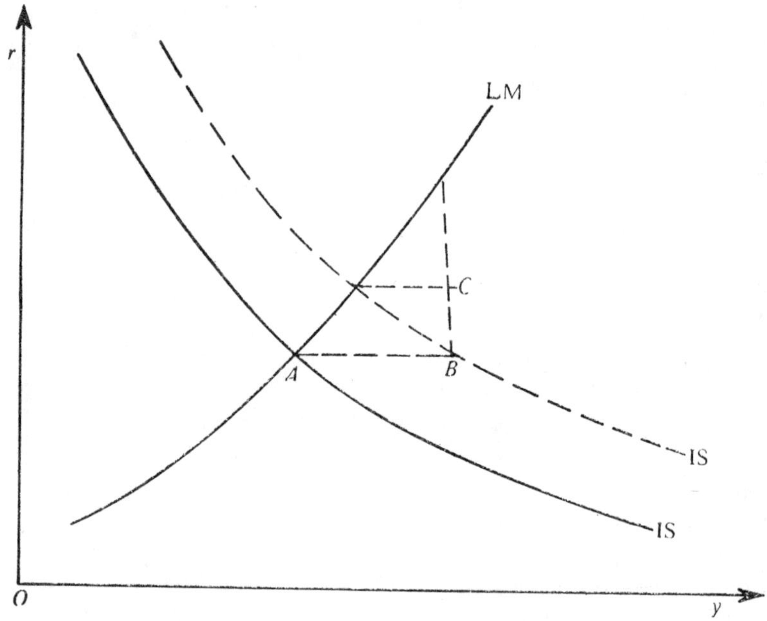

Fig. 16.1

Our concern in this chapter is the development of a cogent framework for the analysis of fiscal policy in a growth context. Recently there has been considerable research in this area. Some of the most important works in this area are Blinder and Solow (1972, 1974), Turnovsky (1977, 1978, 1980) and Brems (1983). This chapter is meant to be an introduction to this literature. The plan of this chapter is as follows. In the first section we detail the behaviour of economic agents—firms, households and government. In the second section we study the long run steady state of the system and try to discover the effects that government fiscal policy has on long run values of some key variables like the real rate of interest, In the last section we concentrate our attention on some aspects of non-steady state behaviour.

A Framework for the Analysis of Fiscal Policy

Government's fiscal policy has profound effects on among other things—the rate of employment and inflation, prospects for growth and a host of real variables e.g. the real rate of interest. Such effects differ depending on whether policy is short or long run, anticipated or unanticipated among other things. In this chapter we wish to develop a framework for analyzing the long term effects of fiscal policy. We will also assume that policy is anticipated and hence that there are no surprises.

In India a quantitative study along the lines of the theoretical model presented here is urgently needed. Whenever we have talked of and debated fiscal policy in this country the extent of ad hocism has been, quite simply, unsatisfactory. To this day even, "distinguished" economists talk of a budgetary deficit as having only one effect—on the rate of inflation. Even this simple exercise advanced here shows, quite unambiguously, that a fiscal deficit has profound effects on the a-temporal as well as the inter-temporal allocation of resources.

The model developed here draws upon the works of Blinder, Solow, Brems and Turnovsky. We consider the basic Solow growth model already discussed in earlier chapters and append to it a financial sector as well as an inflationary potential. We first describe the behavioural roles of households, firms and the government.

The economy being considered is perfectly competitive so that households as well as firms take the values of some key variables e.g. the price level, the wage rate, the rate of discount etc. as exogenously determined and parametrically given to them. To keep matters simple we suppose that government imposes a uniform linear tax on wage and property (or more generally non-wage income). Since there are no surprises there are no capital gains. There is a single composite commodity which can be consumed or saved (and invested). There are three financial assets-money and bonds (issued solely by the government) and shares (issued solely by firms). Only households save so that they can run a current account surplus whercas firms and the government can have a deficit which they cover by issuing shares and money/bonds respectively. Let us look at activities of each of these agents in turn.

Firms. Firms employ labour, issue shares, invest and produce output. If the money price of output (or capital) is P then the firm's nominal wealth is

$$V_f = PK - P_S Q_S \tag{1}$$

where V_f is nominal wealth. P_S is the price of a share issued by the firm and Q_S is the quantity of shares issued. By assumption firms do not issue bonds nor do they hold money or bonds for financial purposes. Hence capital K, is their only asset and shares their only liability.

We can then define the rate of change of real wealth of the firm. Divide (1) by P to get real wealth and differentiate with respect to time to get

$$\frac{d(V_f/P)}{dt} = \frac{dK}{dt} - \frac{d(P_s Q_s/P)}{dt}$$

$$= I - (g_{P_s} + g_{Q_s} - g_P) P_s Q_s / P \tag{2}$$

where I is real investment and for any variable x g_x denotes rate of growth that is, $\frac{dx}{dt}\Big/x$.

We can now define I. For any sector the net excess supply on goods and claims accounts taken together must be zero. Firms issue claims on themselves but do not themselves hold any claims. Thus their excess demand from the goods account (nominal investment IP) must equal the excess supply on claims account (nominal value of additional shares issued). Thus we have

$$IP = P_s \frac{dQ_s}{dt} = P_s g_{Q_s} Q_s. \tag{3}$$

Multiply equation (3) by $-1/P$ and insert into equation (2) to get

$$\frac{dV_f/P}{dt} = (g_P - g_{P_s}) \frac{P_s Q_s}{P}. \tag{4}$$

Equation (4) has a very straightforward interpretation, $P_s Q_s/P$ is the real value of shares outstanding. To the extent that inflation in the price of goods is higher than inflation in the price of shares ($g_P - g_{P_s} > 0$) the firm experiences an increase in real wealth.

We now move to a discussion of the production activities of the firm. We will suppose that output X is given by a Cobb Douglas production function

$$X = aL^\alpha K^\beta, \qquad \alpha + \beta = 1 \quad \alpha, \beta > 0 \tag{5}$$

where a is a neutral technical progress term and L is labour utilization.

If w is the nominal wage rate then profit maximization would imply that

$$\frac{w}{P} = \frac{\alpha X}{L}. \tag{6}$$

Hence the wage bill

$$W = wL = \alpha PX. \tag{7}$$

From equation (6) we have that the parametrically given price is an implicit mark up over labour costs that is,

$$P = \frac{WL}{\alpha X}.$$

Differentiate this with respect to time to get

$$g_P = g_w + g_L - g_X. \tag{8}$$

In a similar vein we can define capital's share of output, S, as

$$S = \frac{\partial X}{\partial K} = \beta \frac{X}{K}. \tag{9}$$

Hence nominal capital income before tax is

$$Z = SPK = \beta PX. \tag{10}$$

Now, we have assumed that all income is taxed at the constant linear rate T. We further assume that all capital income (after tax) is given to shareholders as dividends. Dividends are not taxed again so that we must have

$$(1 - T)SPK = \delta Q_S \tag{11}$$

where δ is the dividend payment per share. Without loss of generality we assume that one dividend entitles you to one unit of the capital stock whence $Q_S = K$ and equation (11) reduces to

$$(1 - T)SP = \delta. \tag{12}$$

We now discuss the investment activities of the firm.

Let N be the present net worth of the capital stock K. The firm would like to choose K such that this present net worth is maximized. However since the firm is a perfect competititor it must be true that this net worth must equal zero.

Let us now find the desired capital stock. At time t after tax value of marginal product of capital is $(1 - T)S(t)P(t)$. In the money market we assume that money can be lent or borrowed at the constant nominal interest i. We will suppose that interest income is taxed whereas interest expenses are tax deductible. Hence tax the after tax rate of interest is $(1 - T)i$. We will use this as the discount rate on all future cash flows. If the current time period is 0 then the after tax value of marginal product of capital is

$$(1 - T)S(t)P(t)e^{-(1-T)i(t)}.$$

Define present gross worth of another physical unit of capital as the present worth of all future after tax values of marginal product over the entire useful life of capital (assume) to be infinity. This is then

$$k(0) = \int_0^\infty (1 - T)S(t)P(t)e^{-(1-T)i(t)}\, dt. \tag{13}$$

Let entrepreneurs expect physical marginal productivity of capital to grow at the stationary rate g_s. Thus

$$S(t) = S(0) \exp^{g_s t}. \tag{14}$$

They are also assumed to expect the price level to grow at the stationary rate g_P so that

$$P(t) = P(0) \exp^{g_p(t)}. \tag{15}$$

We substitute equations (14) and (15) into (13) and write

$$k(0) = \int_0^\infty (1 - T)S(0)P(0)\, e^{-\rho(t)}\, dt \tag{16}$$

where
$$\rho = (1 - T)\, i - (g_s + g_P) \tag{17}$$

is the after tax real rate of interest. Now since $(1 - T)S(0)P(0)$ is independent of t we can write equation (16) as

$$k(0) = (1 - T)S/\rho. \tag{18}$$

Net present worth of a unit of capital is the gross worth minus P. Thus

$$n = k(0) - P = [(1 - T)S/\rho - 1]P \tag{19}$$

is the net present worth. Now $n = 0$ in equilibrium so

$$(1 - T)S = \rho. \tag{20}$$

Insert equation (18) into equation (20) and divide by $(1 - T)$ to get

$$S = i - (gs + g_P)/(1 - T). \tag{21}$$

Now since $0 < T < 1$ then

$$(gs + g_P)/(1 - T) > gs + g_P.$$

Ceteris paribus, then desired physical marginal product of capital is higher with the tax. Thus taxation raises the desired stock of capital. This is not correct, mutatis mutandis, since taxation affects the real rate of interest.

From equations (9) and equation (20) we have

$$K = (1 - T)\,\beta X/\rho \tag{22}$$

so that

$$I = \frac{dK}{dt} = (1 - T)\,\beta g_x X/\rho. \tag{23}$$

Equation (22) defines the desired capital stock and equation (23) the implied rate of investment.[3]

We now describe the behaviour of households.

Households

Households work, consume, and hold the three financial assets. Let P_b be the price of a bond and D_m, D_b and D_s be respectively the household demand for money, bonds and shares respectively. Household's nominal wealth is, therefore,

$$V_h = D_m + P_b D_b + P_s D_s. \tag{24}$$

In a manner analogous to that of the firm, we now look at the households' current budget constraint (in flow terms). Now nominal national income Y is given by

$$Y = PX. \tag{25}$$

Disposable income, therefore, is

$$y = rQ_b + Y - R \tag{26}$$

where r is the rate of interest on bonds. R is total tax revenue which is a deduction from all kinds of household income (wage or non-wage). Let nominal consumption be C so that we can define nominal household savings as $y - C$. Since savings are held as money, bonds and shares we must have

$$\begin{aligned} y - C &= \frac{dD_m}{dt} + P_b\frac{dD_b}{dt} + P_s\frac{dD_s}{dt} \\ &= g_{D_m} D_m + P_b g_{D_b} D_b + P_s g_{D_s} D_s. \end{aligned} \tag{27}$$

We now define the change in household's real wealth. Divide equation (24) by P and differentiate with respect to time to get

$$\begin{aligned} \frac{d(V_h/P)}{dt} &= \frac{d(D_m/P)}{dt} + \frac{d(P_b D_b/P)}{dt} + \frac{d(P_s D_s/P)}{dt} \\ &= (g_{D_m} - g_P)\frac{D_m}{P} + (g_{P_b} + g_{D_b} - g_P)P_b D_b/P \\ &\quad + (g_{P_s} + g_{D_s} - g_P)\frac{P_s D_s}{P}. \end{aligned} \tag{28}$$

[3]The investment behaviour implied here is the standard Jongenson type of neoclassical function studied at length in an earlier chapter.

Now divide equation (27) by P and substitute into equation (28) to get

$$\frac{d(V_h/P)}{dt} + [y - g_P D_m + (g_{P_b} - g_P)P_b D_b$$

$$+(p_{P_s} - g_P)P_s D_s]/P - c \qquad (29)$$

where c is real consumption. Equation (29) simply states that the rate of change of household real wealth equals real saving out of real disposable income after capital gains.

We must now describe the household's portfolio holding, consumption and work decisions. We first describe household's demands for the three assets. We begin with bonds, move to the share market and finally to the demand for money.

The interest rate on bonds in $r(t)$. The after tax interest is $r(t)(1 - T)$. Given that the after tax discount rate is $(1 - T)i$ it follows that the after tax present (at time 0) value of interest payment at time t is, therefore,

$$(1 - T)r(t)\, e^{-(1-T)it}.$$

Define the present gross worth of the bond as the present worth of all its future after tax interest payments over its entire life (assumed to be infinity). This must be

$$k_b(0) = \int_0^\infty (1 - T)r(t)\, e^{-(1-T)it}\, dt. \qquad (30)$$

Assume that the interest payment is stationary i.e.

$$r(t) = r(0). \qquad (31)$$

We substitute this into equation (30) to realize

$$k_b(0) = \int_0^\infty (1 - T)r(0)e^{-(1-T)it}\, dt$$

$$= (1 - T)r(0) \int_0^\infty e^{-(1-T)it}\, dt$$

so that

$$k_b(0) = r/i. \qquad (32)$$

Now define the present net worth of the bond as its gross worth minus its price i.e.

$$n_b = k_b - P_b = r/i - P_b.$$

Now if $n_b > 0$ people would want to move into bonds so that P_b will rise. Similarly if $n_b < 0$ people would want to dispose off bonds. This excess supply would, then, lower the price. Equilibrium in the bond market would require[4] that

$$n_b = 0 \text{ i.e. } P_b = r/i. \qquad (33)$$

[4]Contrast this with equation (20) which is derived under the constraint that the net present worth of earnings from an entire unit of capital must be zero.

The way equation (33) is written it would appear that the tax rate does not affect the bond market. This is not quite true since T affects i. We will see this later in this chapter. Let us now look at the demand for shares.

Shares, like bonds, are for ever. At time t a share pays dividend $\delta(t)$ rupees per time period. By assumption capital income is taxed only once (before dividends are paid out) and none of it is retained. After tax dividend payment is worth

$$\delta(t)\, e^{-(1-T)it}.$$

Thus the present gross worth of a share is, therefore,

$$k_s(0) = \int_0^\infty \delta(t)\, e^{-(1-T)it}\, dt. \tag{34}$$

Let shareholders expect dividend payment to grow at the stationary rate g_δ so that

$$\delta(t) = \delta(0) \exp^{g_\delta t}. \tag{35}$$

Substituting in equation (34) we have

$$\begin{aligned} k_s(0) &= \int_0^\infty \delta(0) \exp\left(-[(1-T)i - g_\delta]t\right) dt \\ &= \delta(0)/[(1-T)i - g_\delta] \end{aligned} \tag{36}$$

(assuming that $(1 - T)i - g_\delta > 0$.)

Again define the present net worth of a share as

$$n_s = k_s - P_s = \frac{\delta}{[(1-T)i - g_\delta]} - P_s.$$

If $n_s > 0$ then households would want to move into shares which would, ceteris paribus, raise P_s. If $n_s < 0$ then households would want to move out of shares which would lower P_s. In share market equilibrium. therefore,

$$P_s = \frac{\delta}{[(1-T)i - g_\delta]}. \tag{37}$$

Now differentiate equation (12) with respect to time (for a fixed T) to get

$$g_\delta = g_s + g_P. \tag{38}$$

Substitute into equation (37), use the definition of ρ in equation (17) to write

$$P_s = \frac{\delta}{\rho}. \tag{39}$$

Hence the price of a share is a capitalization of its current dividend payment δ and the capitalization factor is $1/\rho$. (ρ as defined in equation (17) is the real rate of interest).

We work with a specific functional form of the demand for money

$$D_m = m[Y + rQ_b]\,[(1-T)i]^{\hat{\mu}} \tag{40}$$

with $m > 0$ and $\hat{\mu} < 0$.

The first square bracket captures the transactions demand for money whereas the second square bracket with $\hat{\mu}$ measures the speculative demand for money. Now since $(1 - T)i = \rho + g_P$ it follows that the demand for money varies inversely with the rate of inflation.

We can now look at the portfolio composition. Expressed as rupees per physical unit of asset per unit of time the after tax nominal return on an asset is the sum of its after tax earnings and its appreciation i.e. for money, bonds and shares we have

$$0 + 0 \tag{41}$$

$$(1 - T)r + \frac{dP_b}{dt} \tag{42}$$

$$\delta + \frac{dP_s}{dt}. \tag{43}$$

Divide by the prices 1, P_b, P_s and express the rates of after tax nominal return as the pure numbers per unit of time that is, $0 + 0$, $(1 - T)r/P_b + g_{P_b}$ and $\delta/P_s + g_{P_s}$ respectively. Finally we substract g_P to get real return. However we have been assuming that i and r are fixed. Hence from equation (33) we have

$$g_{P_b} = g_r - g_i = 0. \tag{44}$$

From equations (20) and (12) we realize that $P = \delta/\rho$. Hence from equation (39) we find that $P = P_s$. This must, of course, be true in equilibrium since output and capital are the same good-physically defined. Hence

$$g_P = g_{P_s}. \tag{45}$$

We can now use equations (33), (39), (44) and (45) to write the real after tax net rates of return on the three assets as

$$0 + 0 - g_P \text{ for money} \tag{46}$$

$$(1 - T)r/P_b + g_{P_b} - g_P = (1 - T)i - g_P = \rho \tag{47}$$

for bonds

$$\frac{\delta}{P_s} + g_{P_s} - g_P = \rho \tag{48}$$

for shares.

Bonds and shares have the same real net rate of return and are, in this sense, perfect substitutes. We now discuss the consumption behaviour of households.

For the households disposable income in the absence of capital gains is

$$y = (1 - T)(Y + rQ_b). \tag{49}$$

Assume

$$\alpha + \beta = 1. \tag{50}$$

We know from Euler's theorem that

$$W(\text{wage income}) + Z(\text{capital income}) = Y. \tag{51}$$

We now insert equation (51) into (49) and rewrite money disposable income before capital gains as

$$y = (1 - T)(W + Z + rQ_b). \tag{52}$$

After inserting equation (44) into (45) we can write equation (29) (except for real consumption c as)

$$[y - g_P(D_m + P_bD_b)].$$

Into this substitute for y from (52) to get real disposable income after capital gains as

$$[(1 - T)(W + Z + rQ_b) - g_P(D_m + P_bD_b)]/P. \tag{53}$$

Here $(1 - T)W/P$ is real disposable wage income whereas the rest is real disposable non-wage income. Let us suppose that the propensities to consume from these two sources of income are c_1 and c_2 respectively. Hence we write real consumption as

$$c = c_1(1 - T)W/P + c_2[(1 - T)(Z + rQ_b) - g_P(D_m + P_bD_b)]/P \tag{54}$$

with $\quad 0 < c_i < 1 \qquad i = 1, 2.$

The labour market in this model is characterized by unemployment. In fact there is an expectations augmented[5]. Phillips curve characterizing wage price behaviour in this market. The equation of the Phillips curve is

$$g_w = p(1 - \mu)\pi + \Phi g_P \tag{55}$$

with $\quad \Phi > 0, \pi < 0, p > 0.$

where p is a term capturing the inflationary potential in this market. μ, the rate of employment, is defined from the relation

$$L = \mu F \tag{56}$$

where F is the total available labour force. Clearly $\leqslant \mu \leqslant 1$. Φ and π are parameters. Ceteris paribus as μ goes up so does g_w. Once that leads to a change in the price level the Φg_P term takes over and the Phillips curve (defined in μ, g_w plane) shifts.

We now turn to a discussion of the behaviour of government.

Government

We first look at the balance sheet of the government. Since the government's stock of physical capital is rarely translated in the market, we choose to ignore such capital. The money and bonds issued by the government are its liabilities. Government nominal wealth, is therefore,

$$V_g = -M - P_bQ_b. \tag{57}$$

Government's (nominal) expense on the purchase of goods and services is G. It collects tax revenue and, further, pays interest on bonds. The nominal

[5]See for instance Phelps (1969) or Jha (1983).

deficit on the government's current expenditure account is covered by issuing money and bonds. Thus

$$G + rQ_b - R = \frac{dM}{dt} + P_b \frac{dQ_b}{dt}$$
$$= g_M M + P_b g_{Q_b} Q_b \tag{58}$$

where R is nominal tax revenue.

To get the change in government's real wealth we divide (57) by P and differentiate with respect to time to get

$$\frac{d(V_g/P)}{dt} = \frac{-d(M/P)}{dt} \frac{-d(P_b Q_b/P)}{dt} \tag{59}$$
$$= -(g_M - g_P)\frac{M}{P} - (g_{P_b} + g_{Q_b} - g_P)\frac{P_b Q_b}{P}.$$

We now multiply equation (58) by $(-1/P)$ and insert into equation (59) to get

$$\frac{d(V_g/P)}{dt} = -\left(\frac{g + rQ_b}{P} - R/P\right)$$
$$+ g_P \frac{M}{P} + (g_P - g_{P_b})\frac{P_b Q_b}{P} \tag{60}$$

where $g = G/P$ is real government expenditure. The term

$$\left(g + \frac{rQ_b}{P} - R/P\right)$$

is the real value of fiscal deficit by the government. The term $g_P \frac{M}{P}$ denotes the erosion in the real value of cash (and hence of a liability of the government) due to inflation. $g_P P_b Q_b/P$ denotes erosion of the real value of debt (due to bonds) whereas $g_{P_b} \frac{P_b Q_b}{P}$ denotes the appreciation in government's liability on bonds duc to an inflation in the price of bonds.

Finally we have government's tax revenue. We will make the simplifying assumption that tax revenue is a fixed fraction of gross household income i.e.

$$R = T(Y + rQ_b) \tag{61}$$

with $0 < T < 1.$

The Macro Dynamic Equilibrium

In this section we study the steady state of the system. We also discuss the role of fiscal and monetary policy in steady state. Moreover there is a discussion of the effects of government deficit on the real rate of interest.

By Walra's Law or by summing the three nominal budget constraints we get the nominal value of excess demand in the goods market[6] must equal the nominal value of excess supply in the money, bonds, and shares markets that is,

$$(c + I + g - X)P$$
$$= -\left(\frac{dD_m}{dt} - \frac{dM}{dt}\right) - P_b\left(\frac{dD_b}{dt} - \frac{dQ_b}{dt}\right)$$
$$-P_s\left(\frac{dD_s}{dt} - \frac{dQ_s}{dt}\right). \quad (62)$$

Hence for macroeconomic equilibrium we must have zero excess demands in the goods and money markets. Once this is achieved there will automatically be zero excess demand in the bond and shares markets. Why? Thus

$$X = c + I + g \quad (63)$$

and

$$M = D_m. \quad (64)$$

By differentiating equation (1) through (64) with respect to time or directly by intuition we can establish the following characteristics of steady state equilibrium.

$$g_c = g_x. \quad (65)$$

The rate of growth of real consumption is the same as the rate of growth of output. If this were not so the rate of investment would change which would, in turn, exert pressume on the rate of interest.

$$g_{D_b} = g_{Q_b}. \quad (66)$$

This ensures continuous clearing of the bond market

$$g_{D_m} = g_M. \quad (67)$$

This ensures continuous clearing of the money market

$$g_{D_s} = g_{Q_s}. \quad (68)$$

Thus the shares market is clearing continuously.

$$g_g = g_P. \quad (69)$$

The rate of growth of dividend equals the rate of inflation. This must be true since one share entitles the holder to one unit of capital and capital and output are the same commodity.

$$g_g = g_X. \quad (70)$$

The rate of growth of real government expenditure equals the rate of growth of output. If this were not so then the rate of growth of consumptions say, would change from its steady state rate which would then put

[6]We exclude the labour market excess supply/excess demand from the following analysis by assuming that the employment rate λ and the inflationary potential p are fixed.

pressure on the rate of interest. For analogous reasons we must have

$$g_I = g_X. \tag{71}$$

The rate of growth of the productivity of capital is the rate of growth of output minus the rate of growth of capital. Thus

$$g_s = g_X - g_K. \tag{72}$$

Since the rate of employment is constant we must have

$$g_L = g_F. \tag{73}$$

The money supply must be growing at the same rate as nominal national income that is,

$$g_M = g_Y. \tag{74}$$

Now from equation (8) $\qquad g_P = g_W + g_L - g_X.$

Substitute for g_w from equation (55) and use the definition of $g_L - g_X$ to write

$$g_P = \frac{p(1 - \lambda)^{\pi} - g_a/\alpha}{1 - \phi}. \tag{75}$$

We already know that

$$g_{P_b} = 0 \tag{76}$$

and that $\qquad g_{P_s} = g_P. \qquad (77)$

Moreover it must be true that

$$g_{Q_b} = g_Y. \tag{78}$$

Otherwise divergences in the rate of growth of Q_b from that of Y would put pressure on P_b.

Since a unit of output and a share are essentially the same thing it must be true that

$$q_{Q_s} = g_X. \tag{79}$$

Moreover

$$g_R = g_Y. \tag{80}$$

Moreover we have assumed that

$$g_i = 0 \tag{81}$$

and

$$g_\rho = 0. \tag{82}$$

Moreover

$$g_K = g_X. \tag{83}$$

Otherwise technical progress would be different from the purely neutral term a. Similarly

$$g_W = g_Y. \tag{84}$$

With a fixed λ the share of wage income in total income is constant. Hence also

$$g_Z = g_Y \tag{85}$$

with a fixed tax ratė T

$$g_Y = g_Y \tag{86}$$

i.e. the rate of growth of before tax income is the same as the rate of growth of after tax income.

By definition

$$g_Y = g_P + g_X. \tag{87}$$

From the production function we have

$$g_X = g_a + \alpha g_L + \beta g_K.$$

Now from equation (83) $g_K = g_X$. With a fixed λ, $g_L = g_F$. We also know that $\alpha + \beta = 1$ by assumption. Hence

$$g_X = g_a/\alpha + g_F. \tag{88}$$

Now from equation (7)

$w = \frac{\alpha XP}{L}\cdot$ Differentiating logarthmically with respect to time we have

$$g_W = g_X + g_P - g_L.$$

Now in steady state $g_L = g_F$. Using (88) then

$$g_w = \frac{p(1-\lambda)^{\pi} - \phi g_a/\alpha}{1-\phi}. \tag{89}$$

Using equations (75) and (89) then we must have

$$g_{w/P} = g_w - g_P = g_a/\alpha. \tag{90}$$

Steady state growth of real wage depends on rate of growth of a. Since this is a steady state relation thus is consistent with any λ. Hence the rate of unemployment consistent with fully anticipated inflation (the so called natural rate of unemployment) is not unique. As a matter of fact any rate of unemployment is potentially a natural rate of unemployment.

To find out the effects of inflation in steady state we use equation (4) and (77) to get

$$\frac{d(V_f/P)}{dt} = 0. \tag{91}$$

Firms do not issue, bonds so the real value of the firm's liability does not fall with increases in the rate of inflation. As a matter of fact since one share entitles one to one unit of capital (or output) and since in steady state $g_P = g_{P_s}$ it follows that firms in this story neither gain nor lose from inflation. This result would change if firms held government bonds (when firms would lose from inflation) or firms could issue bonds (when firms would, ceteris paribus, gain from inflation since the real value of this debt would decline).

Similarly from equations (76), (77) and (29) we get

$$\frac{d(V_h/P)}{dt} = (y - g_P(D_m + P_bD_b))/P - c. \tag{92}$$

Thus households lose from inflation. Apart from shares (whose price inflates at the same rate as the price of output) firms also hold bonds and money. Inflation erodes the real value of bonds and money.

Moreover using equations (60) and (76) we can write

$$\frac{d(V_g/P)}{dt} = -(g + rQ_b/P - R/P) + g_P(M/P + P_bQ_b/P). \tag{93}$$

Thus government gains from inflation. The first term on the right hand side is the real government deficit which falls with increases in P. The second term is the real value of government capital account liabilities which are falling in real value with a rise in inflation.

The result proved here that government wins from inflation whereas households lose and firms neither win nor lose—is quite straightforward and follows from the assumptions. The result would be different in firms and/or households could issue bonds or other debt whose real value would fall steadily with increases in the rate of inflation. We now discuss the determinants of the real rate of interest in steady state.

It has been one of the more important concerns of recent literature on fiscal policy that government current fiscal instruments have a profound impact on the allocation of resources. We demonistrate this proposition now. Use (23) and (63) to realize that the real rate of interest can be written as

$$\rho = \frac{(1 - T)\beta g_x X}{X - (c + g)}.$$

We want to substitute for real consumption and real government expenditure in the above relation. Into equation (54) insert (7) and (10) as also the equilibrium conditions $D_m = M$ and $D_b = Q_b$. We thus get c. To get g insert equation (61) into (58) and divide by P. Then substitute these into the above expression of P. Multiply and divide by $(1 - T)X$ and write PX as Y. Hence

$$\rho = \beta g x/A \tag{94}$$

where

$$A = 1 - (\alpha c_1 + \beta c_2) \frac{-(g_M - c_2g_P)M/Y + (g_{Q_b} - c_2g_P)P_bQ_b/Y}{1 - T} + (1 - c_2)rQ_b/Y.$$

Let us examine this expression for A rather carefully. With no government and no inflation all saving would be available for investment by firms so that $A = 1 - (\alpha c_1 + \beta c_2)$. The rate of interest would then depend simply on g_X. This is the classical result.

In our case however things are different. If $g_P = 0$ i.e. there is no inflation then the coefficients c_2g_P of M/Y and Q_b/Y would not have been there. Since they are there and are preceded by a negative sign we know that the negative capital gains from inflation reduce consumption or raise savings. In a similar vein had there been no government deficit $g_M = g_{Q_b} = 0$. With a deficit, however, we know that some savings are going just to finance government deficit. Thus the government deficit affects the real rate of interest.

The last term rQ_b/Y is the consequence of accumulated government debt. If the government had never had a deficit $Q_b = 0$ and this term would drop out.

It is important to note that both the current deficit and the accumulated value of government debt affect the real rate of interest. Hence these factors profoundly affect current choice of techniques and hence allocation of resources. Moreover a change in ρ affects the marginal rate of substitution between present and future consumption and hence government deficit/debt policy affects the intertemporal allocation of resources also.

This is a truly fundamental result in modern fiscal theory. We wish to explore its economic interpretation slightly. To do this we multiply both sides of equation (94) by $(1 - T)$ and insert real investment to get

$$(1 - T)A = I/X. \tag{94'}$$

Thus $(1 - T)A$ is simply the fraction of output invested in this economy with government current deficit and accumulated debt, and inflation.

Moreover realize from equation (94′) that both the before tax and the after tax nominal and real rates of interest are present in A. In its pre tax form the nominal rate of interest is present in the price of bonds i.e.

$$P_b = r/i.$$

To see where the after tax nominal interest fits in invoke equilibrium in the money market, divide both sides by Y and rearrange to get

$$(1 - T)i = [m(1 + rQ_b/Y)/(M/Y)]^{-1/\hat{\mu}}.$$

Let us call $\dfrac{(1 + rQ_b/Y)}{(M/Y)}$ as the bond money ratio. The higher a bond-money ratio the larger the proportion of government's deficit financed by bonds. Thus steady states with different bond-money ratios have different after tax nominal rates of interest.[7]

We relate this discussion to the real rate of interest by realizing that

$$(1 - T)i = \rho + g_s + g_P.$$

We thus realize that it is important to discover the effects of a change in g_P and T on ρ. There are two ways of doing this. When g_P changes the government deficit changes and hence the bond-money ratio changes. One

[7]Since $\hat{\mu} < 0$ a high bond-money ratio means a high after tax nominal rate of interest and a low bond-money ratio means a low after tax nominal rate of interest.

method keeps $1 + rQ_b/Y$ constant and allows M/Y to adjust. The other method keeps M/Y constant and allows $1 + rQ_b/Y$ to adjust. Similar comments hold for a change in T. We can then use straigthforward comparative static methods to assess the effects on ρ in both cases. However at the qualitative level not much can be said about the size of these derivatives. Numerical estimates have to be made.[8]

Policy Perturbations of the Keynesian and Monetarist Varieties

Suppose a steady state equilibrium satisfying conditions equations (62) through (89) exists. What must policy be to support this equilibrium state? We immediately realize that one characteristic must be that $g_M = g_{Q_b} = g_Y$.

Now since the M/Y and Q_b/Y ratios are constant it must be true that $g_A = 0$. Hence for this case the proof of stability given for the Solow one sector model in an earlier chapter will apply.

From this it is an easy step to show that $g_X = g_K$.

In this steady state equilibrium then output grows at the same rate as capital; money supply grows at the same rate as the quantity of bonds which grows at the same rate as nominal income. The price level inflates at the same rate as the price of shares. The nominal and real rates of interest, the tax rate, the rate of unemployment and the inflationary potential are all constant. Moreover there are no surprises.

In the literature such policy has been called accomodating. Why must we pursue non-accomodating policies? Keynesians may not like the rate of unemployment associated with the steady state whereas monetarists may complain about the inflationary potential of the economy. Let us look at non-accomodating policy of each variety.

A Keynesian might want to increase λ. To do this the policy maker along standard Keynesian lines will increase government purchases and the deficit. Thus instead of $g_M \equiv gQ_g = g_Y$ we will now have $g_M > g_Y$ and $g_{Q_b} > g_Y$. Since M/Y and Q_b/Y are growing, $g_A < 0$. But since ρ is inversely related to A it rises. Hence investment as a proportion of output will fall. This is the phenomenon of crowding out. But before this happens the increase in aggregate demand over the steady state level will increase the rate of employment.

In the bond market there is an excess supply of bonds (at the old P_b) as the government floats more debt to finance the increased deficit. This would tend to lower P_b. However in the money market there is also an excess supply since the government has printed more currency to finance part of its enlarged deficit. If people are unwilling to hold more money at the old P_b then they will switch to bonds whence P_b will rise on this count. The net effect on P_b is thus ambiguous.[9]

[8]Literally nothing of this variety has been attempted for India.

[9]Thus the proportion of deficit financed by money creation, among other things, becomes very important.

As a consequence events in the goods market might attain greater significance. The rise in government purchases first involves an unanticipated depletion of stocks of inventories. As excess demand persists employment starts to rise. However with higher λ wage inflation and then price inflation accelerates. This leads to further wage inflation and so on. If the system is stable it will settle down to a new steady state where once again $g_M = g_{Q_b} = g_Y$. This will have a higher wage, a lower A and, hence, a lower I/X, higher λ and higher steady state inflation.

Monetarist Policies. A monetarist may wish to lower the inflationary potential p. The policy prescription would be to lower government purchases and the deficit. Hence $g_M = g_{Q_b} = g_Y$ is replaced with $g_M < g_Y$ and $g_{Q_b} < g_Y$. Hence M/Y and Q_B/Y are falling which means $g_A > 0$ which means that the after tax real rate of interest, ρ, falls which means that I/X will rise. This is known as crowding in.

In the bond market the lowering of Q_b means that at the old P_b there is an excess demand for bonds which would put pressure on P_b to rise. In the money market, however, the reduction in M/Y will mean that at the old P_b there is an excess demand for money. Hence there will be a tendency here to move away from bonds into money. On this count P_b will fall. Hence the effect on P_b is ambiguous. Once again the proportion of the budget financed by money becomes important.

In the goods market the lower aggregate demand means that there is an unintended accumulation of inventories. As the slackness in demand persists the employment rate begins to fall. With increase in the rate of unemployment wage inflation and then price inflation tends to slacken. As price inflation slows so does wage inflation again and so on. If the system is stable we will settle to a new strady state where $g_M = g_{Q_b} = g_Y$. Here λ is lower and g_W and g_P are also lower. The real wage rate is higher and after tax real rate of interest is lower, I/X is higher. The inflationary pontential has heen reduced.

Is steady state possible in this system with zero inflation. The answer is no. With zero inflation $g_Y = g_X$ and $g_P = 0$. Hence there is no room for a government deficit i.e. $g_M = g_{Q_b} = 0$. With $g_X > 0$ it follows that the economy will contract. Steady state is not sustainable with zero inflation.

Conclusions

In this chapter we have studied a long run version of the dynamic fiscal policy model. We realize that current fiscal deficit (a flow) and the accumulated debt both have profound effects on the economy.

The analysis here can be extended in a number of directions e.g. having different tax rates for different incomes, introducing excise taxes in a multi commodity set up and so on. But most importantly a small macrodynamic model of this or similar variety needs to be tested on Indian data. We need to check the effects our fiscal policies have had.

17. Cost Benefit Analysis

In its most general form cost-benefit analysis refers to changes in the allocation of resources brought about by a project. Thus cost benefit analysis (or project evaluation, as it is sometimes called) is in principle a straightforward matter. One looks at the allocation of resources before and after the installation of the project. Given some norm of calculating social welfare one can compare social welfare in the two situations. If social welfare is higher after the project is installed then the project is worthwhile otherwise it is not.

While this is the most general method to follow, in practice cost benefit analysis is quite a complex matter. We will encounter and deal with some of these difficulties in some detail later in this chapter but some of them can be mentioned here as well. Let us suppose that we live in the simple world of the second optimality theorem of welfare economics. In this situation let us suppose that we are in perfectly competitive equilibrium and hence the allocation is Pareto optimal. We look at a project which is a marginal investment decision on the part of the government.

The output from this project can be easily priced and we know that this price will reflect the true social opportunity cost of the output. Similarly the inputs can be easily priced. If the project is going to produce output over a period of time and will also require inputs over a period of time we know that the real rate of interest (which in perfectly competitive equilibrium equals the marginal product of capital) will be the appropriate discount rate for discounting the stream of (anticipated) future benefits and costs. It is in this kind of situation that cost benefit analysis is a relatively straightforward matter.

In the real world, however, things are nowhere as simple. It is in such situations that cost benefit analysis becomes difficult and interesting. Consider the case of a malaria eradication programme in a poor country with imperfect and indeed, in some cases, non-existent markets. This programme clearly has profound external effects. Many lives are saved. The health of many people is maintained. Several industries and enterprises gain as a consequence. Many of these effects cannot be accurately measured since markets may not exist. It would be hard, indeed, to find a perfect market for the future health of the citizens of a poor country.

Even if markets exist it would be unrealistic to expect them to be perfect.

Tax distortions, quotas, regulations etc. have the effect of making prices depart from true social opportunity cost even if external effects are not present. The presence of import quotas and exchange regulations might indicate an "overvalued" exchange rate for instance. A related but distinct problem is that the project being considered might trigger off distortions in other sections of the economy.

Yet another set of problems arises if the project under consideration involves increasing returns to scale technolgy. In that case, clearly, marginal cost pricing would involve perpetual looses and the market profitability criterion would have to be broken down. Similarly there are further problems if two or more projects with increasing returns to scale technology compete for the same resources e.g. the same strip of land or the same funds.

When the project involves benefits and costs spread over a period of time additional complications arise. One set of problems relates to the fact that if there are distortions in the capital market the market rate of interest may not be the appropriate rate of discount. Moreover, it has been argued, that since the current generation benefits from the well being of future generations, the current generation will tend to under-save. When a member of the current generation saves more resources are, in principle, made available to all members of future generations. To that extent saving by the current generation is a public good. It follows, then, that since this aspect is not captured in the individual saver's benefits and costs it follows that there will be sub-optimal savings. In poor countries this problem is compounded by the fact that capital markets, where they exist, may give a rather inadequate framework to predict the future. Moreover with widespread poverty there might be an overwhelming desire to postpone or avoid saving. In other words the social rate of discount is lower than the private rate of discount. An additional problem is the treatment of the risk and uncertainty associated with future benefits and costs.

The theory of cost-benefit analysis vast and complex. A recent good survey is Dreze and Stern (1985). In this chapter we outline some of the important problems that are inherent in cost-benefit analysis. By no means is the analysis here exhaustive but it is suggestive of the kind of questions that have figured prominently in the literature.

What is a Good Decision Rule

We have outlined above a host of reasons why it might be difficult to measure accurately the benefits and costs from a project. We will postpone more elaborate discussions of these difficulties. In this section we will assume that benefits and costs have been accurately measured. We will then try to see what decision rules are available to society.

Suppose a project lasts for T-years. The benefits and costs in year t are B_t and C_t respectively. If r is the rate of discount then we can define the net present value of the project as

$$V = \sum_{t=0}^{T} \frac{(B_t - C_t)}{(1 + r)^t}. \qquad (1)$$

Some economists argue that if $V > 0$ the project should be undertaken clearly if $V < 0$ the project should not be undertaken. But even if $V > 0$ it does not automatically follow that the project should be undertaken. Clearly if the timings of a project is important then the project should be initiated at a time when V would be maximized. Additionally when funds are in short supply it makes eminent senses to rank projects according to their V's and then go down this list until funds are exhausted.

Criteria other than the net present value that have often been used are: (a) the benefit-cost ratio, and (b) the internal rate of return.

The benefit cost ratio is defined simply as the ratio of the present value of benefits to the present value of costs. Thus if B/C is the benefit cost ratio

$$\frac{B}{C} = \frac{B_t/(1 + r)^t}{C_t/(1 + r)^t}. \tag{2}$$

Thus $B/C \gtreqless 1$ as $V \gtreqless 0$.

The internal rate of return (IRR) is defined as that rate of discount which maket the net present value equal to zero. Hence if i is the internal rate of return then it must be true that

$$0 = \sum_{t=0}^{T} \frac{(B_t - C_t)}{(1 + i)^t}. \tag{3}$$

In principle it is hard to solve for i from equation (3). What we have is a polynomial of degree T and hence i may have as many as T solutions. The number of solutions depends on the number of times $B_t - C_t$ changes sign over time. In practice this problem may not be very serious. In the case of many projects initially $B_t - C_t < 0$ and later $B_t - C_t > 0$ till the end of the project. In such cases, therefore, i will be uniquely determined. Then if $i > r$ (where r is the social discount rate) then $V > 0$. Similarly if $i < r$ then $V < 0$. However if r varies from period to period then the IRR criterion is not very useful.

So far as B/C is concerned it has some inherent drawbacks since it neglects the scale of the project. Take an example. Project I has benefits and costs of magnitude Rs 400 and Rs 200 respectively. Corresponding magnitudes for project II are Rs 340 and Rs 160. Thus since $17/8 > 2$ project II would be preferred according to the B/C rule. However, it is clear that project I has a higher V.

The IRR has the further problem that it neglects the time profile of benefits and costs associated with the project. Consider a project which has looses for some time but large surpluses after a certain length of time. If the discount rate is low V might be high but as the discount rate rises future benefits get lower weightage and hence V falls. Through all this IRR remains unchanged.

The moral of the story so far is that B/C and IRR have some difficulties when it comes to the scale of a project and its optimal timing. The net present value criterion might also have some such difficulties if projects are lumpy and funds are limited. The project with the highest V might for instance, still have a lower V than two other projects combined and all three projects might be (financially) within the budget.

We see that choosing the appropriate criterion for social cost benefit analysis is no simple matter. But these difficulties pale into unsignificance when we consider the difficulties associated with measuring benefits and costs and choosing the "right" social rate of discount. To these we now turn.

The Social Rate of Discount

What is the "right" rate of discount to use for the stream of benefits and costs from a project? Suppose, we live in an economy of identical individuals. Suppose, further, that all markets are perfect and the project being considered is a marginal one i.e. it does not have any effect on the structure of costs and prices in the economy. In this economy suppose that each individual discounts the future at the real rate of interest r. Is the social rate of interest r? Is the social rate of discount the same as r in these circumstances?

At first sight the answer to this question would appear to be "yes". However this is the correct answer only under some further assumptions. In particular some value judgements will have to be made. The projects undertaken today have an effect on the resource/production position in the future. Decision on a project today will affect future generations either because the life span of a project is longer than the life span of a generation or because the structure of projects today affects the type and nature of projects that can be undertaken by future generations. Only if we neglect these effects can we claim that the social rate of discount is simply equal to the private rate of discount used by the current generation.

There is yet another reason why the private discount rate cannot be used as the social rate of discount. This is because even a perfect market today neglects the external effect that the welfare of future generations has on savings today. Suppose the society consists of n identical individuals with private rate of discount equal to the (perfect) real rate of interest r. Suppose the individual value one rupee transferred as assets to his inheritor as β Rs and 1 rupee transferred to the inhertors of others as α Rs. Suppose a proportion θ of his lifetime savings goes to his inhertors so that $(1 - \theta)$ goes to the inheritors of others. Hence the individual in formulating his optimal saving decision will equate the marginal cost of saving one rupee (which is 1 Re) to the private marginal benefit which $(\theta\beta + (1 - \theta)\alpha)(1 + r)$. Hence the private discount rate equals.

$$r = \frac{1}{\theta\beta + (1 - \theta)\alpha} - 1\cdot$$

The social benefit from saving one rupee is higher since the private saving of every individual has a beneficial effect on $(n - 1)$ individuals. The social benefits of one rupee saved are.

(i) private benefit of the saver

$$\theta\beta + (1 - \theta)\alpha$$

(*ii*) benefits to the current generation from the consumption of the savers' heirs i.e. $(n - 1)\theta\alpha$.

(*iii*) benefits to the current generation from their own heirs' consumption i.e. $(1 - \theta)\beta$

(*iv*) benefits to the current generation from the consumption of heirs other than those of the saver i.e. $(n - 2)(1 - \theta)\alpha$.

Total social benefit is, therefore, $\beta + (n - 1)\alpha$. Hence the social rate of discount r_s should be

$$r_s = \frac{1}{\beta + (n - 1)\alpha} - 1.$$

Only under very special circumstances is $r_s = r$. Usually $r_s < r$. By that taken it is also clear that savings will be less than optimal.

The analysis of the right social, rate of discount becomes even more complex if individual income distributional considerations become important The analysis here is indicative of the types of problems that arise even in the simplest case.

Evaluation of Costs and Benefits

The evaluation of costs and benefits is the next major problem to be considered. Even in a perfectly competitive economy it would not necessarily be appropriate to use market prices to evaluate the costs and benefits of a project. One would use market prices only if the projects was marginal in the sense that it did not effect market prices. On the other hand if the project is not marginal and if supply curves of inputs or/and the demand curve for the output of the project are elastic then the project itself will affect market prices. Thus, for instance, if the supply curve of inputs is upward sloping as the project starts producing it will raise input prices. Even in a perfect market such considerations will have to be borne in mind.

Things are, of course, much more difficult and challenging when markets do not exist or are distorted because of taxes, quotas etc. This is often the case in developing economies. When this is the case the project evaluator has to resort to shadow price. For any commodity, or service its shadow price is the "right" price (in the social price). This may vary greatly from the corresponding market price. We illustrate the concept of shadow price with a few examples. *Shadow Price of Labour*. Labour markets are often quite distorted. There might be involuntary unemployment so that at the going wage rate people are unable to find employment. In economies like ours the minimum wage paid in the urban/organized sector is higher than that prevailing in the rural/unorganized sector.

The project evaluator takes these distortions as a fact of life. He still has to determine the social opportunity cost of labour. Additional labour demanded by a project might come from three sources: workers previously employed elsewhere at the market wage rate, workers involuntarily unemployed and workers voluntarily unemployed. The shadow wage rate is a weighted average of the wage rate for each type of labour. For workers employed elsewhere the opport unitycost of using them in the project is the gross of tax wage (assuming they are being paid their marginal product) they were getting. For workers who are voluntarily unemployed it is the net of tax wage since they must be paid at least that much to induce them to work. The wage rate for involuntarily unemployed workers is a bit tricky. These workers are willing to work at less than the going wage rate but surely their opportunity cost of employment is greater than zero.[1] In practice several different numbers are often tried.

The Shadow Price of Foreign Exchange

Many projects directly or indirectly use tradeable inputs. Or the output of a project may be traded or this output may be an input in some other industry whose output is traded. It is important, then, for then project evaluator to have a good idea of the social opportunity cost of foreign exchange. If the economy under consideration is a small one (in the sense that it cannot affect world prices or interest rates) and there are no tariff or non-tariff restrictions on international trade in the country and we live in a world of fully flexible exchange rates then we can use the exchange rate itself as the appropriate opportunity cost of (that particular) foreign currency. In practice, however, there are many distortions in foreign trade so that shadow prices have to be used.

Let us take a simple case where the country is small and there is a common tariff (at rate t) on all imports. Thus all imports can be treated as a composite good and imports and exports can be denominated in terms of foreign exchange. The supply curve of foreign exchange from the sale of exports is upward sloping because given the world price of exports the higher the price (c) of foreign exchange the higher will be the price in domestic currency received from the sale of exports and the more will be produced for export. Imports mean a demand for foreign exchange and the price is equal to the international price plus the tariff. Hence the shadow price of foreign exchange (p_e) can be written as

$$p_e = e\frac{dX}{dG} - e(1+t)\frac{dM}{dG}$$

where dX/dG is the change in exports (X) as a consequence of change in the demand for foreign exchange by the project dM/dG is the corresponding change in imports.

This analysis can easily be extended to cover many imports with different tariff rates. Thus if there are n imports ($M_i(i = 1, \ldots, n)$) with n different tariff rates ($t_i(i = 1, \ldots, n)$ we can easily derive

$$p_e = e\frac{dX}{dG} - \sum_{i=1}^{n} e(1+t_i)\frac{dM_i}{dG}.$$

[1]A similar problem arise in the case of "disguised" unemployment in poor countries See Sen (1963), for instance.

The technique discussed above converts foreign prices into domestic prices. In the face of tariff distortions this will create wrong incentives. Thus with import tariffs and an overvalued exchange rate resources would be diverted to the export sector and there would be an incentive to economize on imports. Little and Mirrlees have advocated a system whereby all domestic prices are converted into foreign price equivalents. This raises problems when one comes to non-traded goods—say electricity. In this case they advocate going to an earlier stage of production—say the technology and equipment for power generation from thermal units. These goods are sold in the international market. While this logic, does take us some distance it cannot solve all our problems since certain goods are neither traded nor have traded goods as inputs. Primary factors of production e.g. labour fall in this category.

Shadow Value of Public Money

Many projects are not self financing. This may be because of economies of scale or because the project has benefits in the distant future or for some other reason. Currently however the deficit must be financed. One must also find out the opportunity cost of such financing since this financing is diverting resources from the private sector.

Marglin (1963) visualizes this problem in the following manner. Consider the financing of the deficit. This diverts resources from the private sector. Let us suppose that a fraction α of this would have been invested and $(1 - \alpha)$ consumed. We know from the last chapter that α depends on the method of financing e.g. money, bonds or taxes.

Currently a rupee's worth of consumption foregone is valued at one rupee. Let us take investment. Suppose the IRR on private investment is i_p. We might expect i_p to exceed the social rate of discount r because of corporate income tax etc. A rupee's worth of investment yields a perpetual stream of consumption of size i_p. Its present value is i_p/r. Hence the opportunity cost (η) of a rupee diverted from the private sector is

$$\eta = (1 - \alpha) + \frac{\alpha i_p}{r}.$$

We can easily visualize further complications in this story. We have been assuming that i_p is consumed. If part of i_p is invested it will yield a further income stream which will have to be considered in the formula for opportunity cost.

A general rule for evaluating projects when some of the revenue comes from public funds was developed by Feldstein (1972). He argues that if D_t is the deficit in year t then present net value should be defined as

$$V = \sum_{t=0}^{T} \frac{B_t - C_t - (\eta - 1)D_t}{(1 + r)^t}$$

η, as above, is the opportunity cost of public funds used in the project and $(\eta - 1)D_t$ is the additional opportunity cost incurred in the financing of the losses from the project over and above that incurred by a non-distortionary transfer of funds. It is clear that η and D_t may vary from one period to another.

Evaluation of Intangibles

A project often involves many intangible benefits and costs. The project evaluator must arrive at a monetary measure of these benefits. Let us study an example of this.

One of the major benefits of a transportation project is time saved. Suppose a road is to be widened so that traffic can move faster. How is one to measure the benefit of time saved? The opportunity cost of time saved is clearly the amount of money that the beneficiaries of the saved time will be willing to pay to have that saving. Saved time can be used for more work and/or leisure. The project evaluator uses different methods to evaluate the increases in these activities.

To the extent that the time saved is used for work and markets are perfectly competitive the appropriate monetary value to ascribe is the gross of tax wage rate. However a number of imperpections can arise. If a person's working hours are from 9 to 5 and he arrives at work at 8:30 there is not much he can do. The half hour saved must, of necessity, go to leisure. Moreover an employee may not be indifferent between the time saved and made available to his employer and the time that he can spend on his personal work. In that case one must arrive at a monetary value of the change in utility from saved time. In practice, however, that may be difficult to do and one usually has to use the wage rate.

When saved time becomes leisure then things get a bit problematic since neither saved time nor leisure are traded in the market place. A rational consumer would choose leisure and work so that

$$\begin{aligned} X &= MB_l - MB_t \\ &= W + MB_w - MB_t \end{aligned}$$

where X is the monetary value of a reduction in travelling time. W is the wage rate. MB_w (which is negative) is the marginal benefit from work and MB_t is the marginal benefit from time spent travelling. MB_t is again negative.

How does one estimate X? For example suppose there are two alternative methods of transport which differ in travel time and expense for the consumer. If the rupee costs of the two alternative methods of transport are competitively determined one can obtain the opportunity cost of travel time to the marginal consumer by observing the difference in money cost that exist to compensate for the differences in time cost of travel.

Similar problems arise in the treatment of other intrangibles such as the saving of lives, improvement in health etc.

Indirect Benefits and Costs

Projects sometimes have beneficial or harmful effects on the rest of the economy. These usually take the form of external effects. Clearly pecuniary externalities are not to be considered but physical externalities are important

Consider an irrigation project. This has a clear cut external effect. A new airport involves noise and changes in property values.

For each project a good project evaluator will have to catalogue the external effects and find out some method of estimating them. No general qualitative principles can be advanced.

Appendix

The Theory of Option Value

Suppose a forest is to be cut down and a township constructed on it. The forest will be lost forever. Should the theory of cost benefit be altered to accommodate this fact?

Indeed it must, particularly if there is reason to believe that we do not have enough information about the possible uses of this forest. Society realizes that these (yet unknown) options will no longer be available if the forest is destroyed. On this logic it may never be proper to cut down the forest. It is clear that a method must be found to be had from keeping the options alive. If such benefits are in some sense "high" enough the forest should not be cut down.

It is in this context that Henry (1974), Greenly, Walsh and Young (1981), Arrow and Fischer (1974) define an option value (for an individual) as an individual's willingness to pay for the assurance of selecting the presentation of an irreversible commitment until such time that sufficient information becomes available affecting the future option decision of selecting from among alternative uses. We may use the following model to better understand this concept. Consider a two period concept. Consider a two period model with the following specifications.

- u_i^t is the expected utility of the ith individual in period t.
- Y_i^t is the income of the ith individual in period t.
- $\bar{S}_i$ is the ith individual's consumer surplus from the use of the environmental resource
- e is the irreplacable environmental resource that is available
- e^* is the irreplacable environmental resource that is appropriated
- V_i is the option value of the ith individual
- C_i^t is the opportunity cost of retaining the environmental resource in period t.

Suppose that no new information is going to be available between periods 1 and 2 then it must be true that

$$u_i^1(Y_i^1 - S_i, e) + u_i^2(Y_i^2, e) = \sum_{i=1}^{2} u_i(Y_i^t, e).$$

The individual will be willing to pay an amount S_i in period 1 to have e, After paying S_i the individual will still receive the same expected utility as the situation in which the natural resource is not available. The individual will choose to preserve the natural environment rather than have it developed if $S_i > C_i^1$. Since, in this case, no new information is gained between the two periods if $S_i > C_i^1$ the natural resource is preserved once and for all.

Let us now assume that new information becomes available in period 2. We now want to know how much individual i would be willing to pay in period 1 to (*i*) enjoy the natural resource through period 1; and (*ii*) have the option of choosing under conditions of certainty in period 2 between development of the forest land or preservation of the natural resource. This idea is developed in the following equation

$$u_i^1(Y_i^1 - S_i^1 - V_i, e)$$
$$+ \max\left(u_i^2(Y_i^2, e), u_i^2(Y_i^2, e^*)\right) = \sum_{t=1}^{2} u_i^t(Y_i^t, e^*).$$

S_i and Y_i balance the above equation. In period 1 the individual will be willing to pay S_i^1 to enjoy the forest during period 1. In addition, he is willing to pay an amount V_i to choose in period 2, between preservation and development. The magnitude of V_i in period 1 depends on $u_i^2(e)$ and $u_i^2(e^*)$ in period 2 as they exist in period 1.

It sbould be clear that the existence of option value does not affect the decision making process so long as $S_i^1 > C_i^1$. Only when $S_i^1 < C_i^1$ in the first period is it necessary to consider option value. It then becomes necessary to consider the second period in making a choice in period 1.

18. Pricing in the Public Sector

In most societies public enterprises are important entities in the economy. This is certainly true of socialist economies and developing countries. It is also true of advanced capitalist societies such as USA and UK.

Whereas in advanced capitalist societies the rationale for a public sector usually involves considerations such as equity or natural monopoly[1] in our country the public sector has been given, special importance in the nation's industrial strategy. Whatever be the reason for the creation of public sector firms their existence has a profound impact on the economy.

An important problem that attends the public sector is the formulation of an appropriate price policy. Should public sector firms maximize or even earn profits? If the firm incurs a loss how is the deficit to be financed? Should the public undertaking indulge in price discrimination? These and several other important policy questions have to be answered.

In our own case given the importance of the public sector we have all come to realize that public sector prices are an important fiscal tool in the hands of the government. Ideally then direct and indirect taxes and public sector prices should be jointly determined by a welfare maximizing exercise. Some steps in this direction have been taken and will be discussed later in this chapter. But first we will attempt the partial equilibrium exercise of finding out the "best" price for a public sector firm assuming that the rest of the economy is already in first best optimum.

The plan of this chapter is as follows. In the next section we study public sector pricing as a partial equilibrium exercise. Then we bring in non-linear pricing we finally discuss the joint determination of taxes and public sector prices.

Linear Prices for the Public Sector

The formal similarity between indirect taxes and public sector prices overlooks the rather critical problem of the structure of public sector undertakings. These are quite à heterogenous, group. On the one hand we have say the Post and Telegraph department in India which is run pretty much like any other government department. On the other hand we have say,

[1]Utilities, for instance, are natural monopolies. A private sector firm operating a utility would, ceteris paribus, change a higher price and produce less than a public sector firm.

Renault, the French car manufacturing company which functions like any private corporation. Moreover, there are private companies which have the state as a large or even dominant shareholder. Hence it becomes important to define precisely the meaning of the term "public sector firm". This in itself is an important and controversial topic. It will be wise, therefore, to adopt a relatively straightforward definition. A public sector firm will be taken to be publicly owned but managed autonomously. Moreover the government defines both the objective function as well as the constraints, facing the enterprises. For example the government might stipulate a minimum rate of return on capital, minimum capacity utilization etc. and then control the funds that are available for investment in this enterprise.

Let us study the case, then, of a public undertaking whose operations are subject to a profit constraint. Initially we will assume that the private sector is perfectly competitive. Later we will allow pure profits in the private sector. Let there be just one public sector firm whose price is p_{n+1}. There are n private sector goods $X_1, \ldots, X_n$ (amounts are denoted by lower case letters) with prices $p_1, \ldots, p_n$. All individuals have identical utility functions $u(X_1, \ldots, X_n, X_{n+1}, L)$ where L is labour. Assuming that the only costs are labour costs and choosing labour as numeraire we can write the profits of the private sector as

$$\pi = \sum_{i=1}^{n} p_i x_i - G(x_1, \ldots, x_n) \tag{1}$$

where $G(\ )$ is labour requirement by the private sector). By assumption $\pi = 0$. The first order condition for profit maximization requires that

$$p_i = G_i \qquad i = 1, \ldots, n.$$

Let $H(x_{n+1})$ be the labour requirement of the public sector firm. Then society's labour constraint can be written as

$$G(x_1, \ldots, x_n) + H(x_{n+1}) - L = 0. \tag{2}$$

Let $V(p_1, \ldots, p_n, p_{n+1})$ be the indirect utility function that society attempts to maximize. The profit constraint before the public enterprise is

$$p_{n+1}x_{n+1} - H(x_{n+1}) + T \geqslant \pi_0 \tag{3}$$

where T is a pure (poll) subsidy paid by the government and π_0 is the stipulated minimum profit that the public enterprise must earn.

Setting up the Lagrangean we have

$$L = V(\ ) + \lambda[p_{n+1}x_{n+1} - H(\ ) - T]. \tag{4}$$

The first order condition for maximization with respect to p_{n+1} yields

$$0 = -\alpha x_{n+1} + \lambda \left[x_{n+1} + (p_{n+1} - H') \frac{\partial x_{n+1}}{\partial p_{n+1}} \right] \tag{5}$$

where α is the private marginal utility of income.

We should realize that T is free to vary so that we can as well have a lump sum tax to finance the deficit if any. Differentiating L with respect to T we have

$$-\alpha + \lambda = 0 \tag{6}$$

so that optimal price for the public sector is such that

$$p_{n+1} = H'(x_{n+1}). \tag{7}$$

This is a vindication of the commonsense result that price must equal marginal cost.

This pricing rule breaks down if costs are falling. With falling average (and marginal) costs when price equals marginal cost the firm will make a loss. To break even price must equal average cost and hence must be higher than marginal cost.

In practice however many public sector undertakings function so that there are many combinations of prices that will meet the profit constraint. So prices can depart from marginals costs. How should prices differ from marginal costs? There are two schools of thought on this. One school believes that the price should be as high as the market will bear i.e. we should follow the Ramsey rule and make prices very inversely with the elasticity of demand. The second school believes that prices should be proportional to marginal costs.

We can indicate the differences in the two approaches by studying a simple example of a two product public sector firm. p_{n+1} and p_{n+2} are the respective prices whereas x_{n+1} and x_{n+2} are the respective quantities of the two goods. The cost function is $H(x_{n+1}, x_{n+2})$. The Lagrangean is now

$$L = V(\ \ ) + \lambda[p_{n+1}x_{n+1} + p_{n+2}x_{n+2} - H(\ \ ) + T - \pi_0]. \tag{8}$$

The first order conditions for p_{n+1} and p_{n+2} are

$$-\alpha x_{n+1} + \lambda\left[(p_{n+1} - H_1)\frac{\partial x_{n+1}}{\partial p_{n+1}} + (p_{n+2} - H_2)\frac{\partial x_{n+2}}{\partial p_{n+1}} + x_{n+1}\right] = 0 \tag{9}$$

$$-\alpha x_{n+2} + \lambda(p_{n+1} - H_1)\frac{\delta x_{n+1}}{\delta p_{n+1}} + (p_{n+2} - H_2)\frac{\partial x_{n+2}}{\delta p_{n+2}} + x_{n+2}] = 0. \tag{10}$$

If we now consider the special case where demands are independent and there are no income effects then we can get for commodity x_{n+1}

$$\frac{p_{n+1} - H_1}{p_{n+1}}\left(\frac{-p_{n+1}}{x_{n+1}}\frac{\partial x_{n+1}}{\partial p_{n+1}}\right) = \frac{\lambda - \alpha}{\lambda} \tag{11}$$

which is a vindication of the Ramsey rule that prices should vary inversely with the elasticity of demand. Suppose the budget constraint is not binding because the lump sum tax can be used then $\lambda = \alpha$ and we are back to marginal cost pricing. Moreover with no lump sum taxes as profits reach π_0 $\lambda \to \infty$ so that

$$\frac{p_1 - H_1}{p_1}(\epsilon_1) = 1. \tag{12}$$

Where ϵ_1 is the elasticity of demand.

Now suppose the private sector earns a pure profit. To analyze this situation we follow the analysis of Munk (1978). We can now also introduce indirect taxation. We let $p_1, \ldots, p_n$ be the private sector producer prices and $q_1, \ldots, q_n$ be the corresponding consumer prices. We can then write per capita profits as

$$\pi = \sum_{i=1}^{n} p_i x_i - G(x_1, \ldots, x_n). \tag{13}$$

Let us suppose that this profit is taxed at the rate τ and the rest is distributed among the population as a lump sum subsidy. Thus the lump sum payment is $\pi(1 - \tau) = Y$. Now since supply functions are homogenous of degree zero in producer prices and demand functions are homogenous of degree zero in consumer prices it follows that this tax has the same effect as raising all consumer prices by a factor $1/1 - \tau$. Thus in any analysis of the optimal price tax mix this factor must be taken into account. We assume that τ is fixed and labour is not taxed. Suppose there are two public sector goods then we can write the individuals budget constraint as

$$p_{n+1}x_{n+1} + p_{n+2}x_{n+2} + \sum_{i=1}^{n} q_i x_i = L + (1 - \tau)\pi. \tag{14}$$

Hence the public sector budget constraint (on combining equation (13) and (14)) is

$$p_{n+1}x_{n+1} + p_{n+2}x_{n+2} - H(\;) + \sum_{i=1}^{n} (q_i - p_i)x_i + \tau\pi = 0 \tag{15}$$

that is tax revenue (from taxation of profits and private sector goods) plus revenue from the sale of public sector goods must meet the cost of operating the public sector. Society's indirect utility function is $V(p_{n+1}, p_{n+2}, q_1, \ldots, q_n, Y)$ so that we can write the Lagrangean for the public sector (on rearranging equation (15)) as

$$L = V(p_{n+1}, p_{n+2}, q_1, \ldots \, q_n) + \lambda[p_{n+1}x_{n+1} + p_{n+2}x_{n+2}$$
$$-H(\;) + \sum_{i=1}^{n} q_i x_i - G(\;) - (1 - \tau)\pi]. \tag{16}$$

The first order condition for choosing p_{n+1} is

$$\frac{\partial V}{\partial p_{n+1}} + \frac{\partial V}{\partial Y}\frac{\partial Y}{\partial p_{n+1}} + \lambda\Big[x_{n+1} + (p_{n+1} - H_1)\frac{\partial x_{n+1}}{\partial p_{n+1}}$$
$$+(p_{n+2} - H_2)\frac{\partial x_{n+2}}{\partial p_{n+1}} + \Sigma_i(q_i - G_i)\frac{\partial x_i}{\partial p_{n+1}} - (1 - \tau)\frac{\partial \pi}{\partial p_{n+1}}\Big] = 0. \tag{17}$$

Similarly for p_{n+2} we get

$$\frac{\partial V}{\partial p_{n+2}} + \frac{\partial V}{\partial Y}\frac{\partial Y}{\partial p_{n+2}} + \lambda\Big[x_{n+2} + (p_{n+1} - H_1)\frac{\partial x_{n+1}}{\partial p_{n+1}}$$
$$+(p_{n+2} - H_2)\frac{\partial x_{n+2}}{\partial p_{n+2}} + \Sigma_i(q_i - G_i)\frac{\partial x_i}{\partial p_{n+2}} - (1 - \tau)\frac{\partial \pi}{\partial p_{n+2}}\Big] = 0. \tag{18}$$

We can easily calculate

$$\frac{\partial \pi}{\partial p_{n+1}} = \sum_{i=1}^{n} (p_i - G_i)\frac{\partial x_i}{\partial p_{n+1}} + \sum_{i}\left(\sum_{i} x_j \frac{\partial p_j}{\partial x_i}\right)\frac{\partial x_i}{\partial p_{n+1}}. \tag{19}$$

For p_{n+2} we get

$$\frac{\partial \pi}{\partial p_{n+2}} = \sum_{i} (p_i - G_i)\frac{\partial x_i}{\partial p_{n+2}} + \sum_{i}\left(\sum_{j} x_j \frac{\partial p_j}{\partial x_i}\right)\frac{\partial x_i}{\partial p_{n+2}}. \tag{20}$$

We know from the condition of profit maximization that for the private sector commodities

$p_i = G_i$. So that we can replace $q_i - G_i$ by $q_i - p_i$.

From the Slutsky equation we note that

$$\frac{\partial x_{n+1}}{\partial p_{n+1}} = \left(\frac{\partial x_{n+1}}{\partial p_{n+1}}\right)_{u=\bar{u}} \frac{-\partial x_{n+1}}{\partial M}\left(x_{n+1} - \frac{\partial Y}{\partial p_{n+1}}\right) \tag{21}$$

where M is total income. We can write corresponding expressions for x_{n+2} and the private sector commodities. We can then collect the first order conditions to write

$$\sum_{k=1}^{2} (p_{n+k} - H_k)\left(-\frac{\partial x_{n+1}}{\partial p_{n+1}}\right)_{u=\bar{u}} + \sum_{i=1}^{n} (q_i - p_i)\left(\frac{-\partial x_i}{\partial p_{n+1}}\right)_{u=\bar{u}}$$

$$= \left[1 - \frac{\alpha}{\lambda} - \sum_{k=1}^{2} (p_{n+k} - H_k)\frac{\partial x_{n+1}}{\partial M} - \sum_{i=1}^{n} (q_i - p_i)\frac{\partial x_i}{\partial M}\right]\left(x_{n+1} - \frac{\partial Y}{\partial p_{n+1}}\right)$$

$$= \beta\left(x_{n+1} - \frac{\partial Y}{\partial p_{n+1}}\right). \tag{22}$$

One can write an analogous expression for x_{n+2}.

In the zero profit case one discovered that a tax on profits was equivalent to a uniform tax on all commodities. Now, however, in response to a tax the reduction of consumption along the compensated demand schedule is not the same for all commodities. There is an additional term because of profits. If we raise the price of x_{n+1} and find that profits are reduced by more than what would have been the case if the price of x_{n+2} had been raised then it follows that the price of x_{n+1} should be raised less than the price of x_{n+2}.

One can work out the case of an increase in the indirect tax rate in an analogous manner. The two cases are however fundamentally different, To see this consider the case where demands are independent, there are no income effects nor any joint production then the first order condition for a change in the price of the public sector product is reduced to the simple inverse elasticity formula. In the case of indirect tax, however, if we calculate $\frac{\partial \pi}{\partial q_i}$ and set $\frac{\partial L}{\partial q_i} = 0$ we can derive

$$\frac{q_i - p_i}{q_i} = \frac{1/\epsilon_i + (1-\tau)/\eta_i}{1/\gamma + (1-\tau)/\eta_i} \tag{23}$$

where $\gamma = 1 - \alpha/\lambda$

and η_i is the elasticity of supply of the ith commodity. Intutitively the difference between public sector prices and indirect taxes on private goods is the following. Under the assumptions made $\tau = 1$ for the public sector since all of the surplus is invested (more properly returned to the government). In the case of indirect tax on private goods, however, τ is less than unity and the supply elasticity becomes important. It also follows from equation (23) that goods with the lowest price elasticity of demand are taxed at the highest rate.

We have seen some reasons why the public sector prices may have to be different from marginal costs. Other reasons can easily be added on to this list. Thus if we are operating in a second best situation we would want prices to diverge from marginal cost. Similarly if we had redistributive as well as efficiency objectives then prices may have to diverge from marginal cost. We will explore this problem in detail later in this chapter.

Non-Linear Pricing

The analysis presented so far assumes that the public sector changes a single price. Let us now suppose that the public sector can discriminate among consumers with different incomes. In this analysis we follow Roberts (1978).

Consider an economy that is competitive apart from the presence of a single public utility which attempts to maximize some Social Welfare Function (SWF) subject to a profit constraint.

There are $n + 1$ goods in the economy: (*a* possibly composite) consumption good C which may be used as such or as an input for the production of X the n dimensional vector of goods supplied by the public utility. To produce a total output of X^* the public sector firm requires an input C^* of the consumption of good given by

$$C^* = m'X + F \tag{24}$$

F is a fixed cost and m is a vector of marginal costs appropriately defined.

There is a continuum of individuals in the economy—all individuals possessing identical, twice-differentiable and strictly concave utility functions given by

$$u = u(C, X) \tag{25}$$

where $u_c > 0$ and $u_x \gg 0$. Further all goods produced by the public utility are strictly normal that is,

$$\underline{n}(C, X) = u_{cx} - \frac{u_{cc}}{u_c} u_x{}^0 \gg 0. \tag{26}$$

Although individuals possess identical preferences, their behaviour differs because they have different levels of income y (the consumption good C is taken as numeraire). Let $f(y)$ be the proportion of the population with income y and let $\underline{y}$ and $\bar{y}$ be the lowest and highest incomes in the population, respectively. Thus

$$f(y) \geqslant 0 \quad \text{for all } y, \quad \text{and} \quad \int_{\underline{y}}^{\bar{y}} f(y)\, dy = 1. \tag{27}$$

The public utility's price schedule is given by $P(X)$: if an individual wishes to purchase a bundle X then must he pay an amount $P(X)$ to the firm. An individual with an income y chooses X so as to maximize equation (25) subject to

$$C + P(X) \leqslant y \tag{28}$$

and it must be the case that

$$u(c, X) \geqslant u(y, 0). \tag{29}$$

This last constraint captures the fact that the individual may, if he so wishes, leave the market and pay nothing to the public utility.

The utility has a (generalized) utilitarian objective given by

$$\overline{W} = \int_{\underline{y}}^{\bar{y}} W[u(y)]f(y)\, dy \tag{30}$$

where $u(y)$ is the utility of an individual with an income y. The generalized function W is introduced so that optimal price schedules may be computed under alternative redistributional objectives.

By appropriate choice of the function $P(X)$, the public utility wishes to maximize equation (30) subject to the constraint that profit is non-negative. This constraint is given by

$$\int_{\underline{y}}^{\bar{y}} \{P[X(y)] - m'X(y) - F\}f(y)\, dy \geqslant 0 \tag{31}$$

where $X(y)$ is the bundle of goods purchased by an individual with income y.

The utility wishes to maximize equation (30) subject to equation (31) and the constraint that individuals maximize (25) subject to equations (28) and (29). Instead of choosing the schedule $P(X)$ directly, we can think of the firm as choosing a set of two—part tariffs, a different two—part tariff being designed for individuals with different incomes. In fact, instead of choosing marginal prices and a licence fee for individuals with different incomes, the analysis is simplified if marginal prices and utilities are made the subject of choice. The two approaches are essentially equivalent: if $E(u, P)$ is the expenditure function corresponding to the utility function equation (25), that is,

$$E(u, P) = \min\,[C + P'X : u(C, X) \geqslant u] \tag{32}$$

and the licence fee $1(y)$ is given by

$$1(y) = y - E(u(y), P(y)) \tag{33}$$

where $u(y)$ is utility and $P(y)$ marginal prices. We note

$$E_u = 1/u_c; \quad E_P = X, \quad E_{PP} = X_P^C \tag{34}$$

where X_P^C is the Jacobian matrix of compensated demand derivatives. As the consumption good C is excluded from this matrix, E_{PP} can be taken as negative definite.

We now attempt to make the individual maximization constraint more amenable for analysis. First shift constraint equation (29) from individuals to the public utility, Utilities may be chosen subject to the constraint that

$$u(y) \geqslant u(y, 0). \tag{35}$$

In view of equation (29), this constraint must hold. Conversely equation (35) implies equation (29). We must now take care of the constraint that equation (25) is maximized subject to equation (28). First order conditions of maximization yield.

$$u_X - u_c P_X \leqslant 0 \tag{36}$$

with equality in the ith component if $x_i > 0$. Totally differentiating equation (25) with respect to y and making use of equation (36), we obtain an envelope condition

$$\frac{du}{dy} = u_c. \tag{37}$$

We may, however, write u_c as

$$u_c = V(u, P). \tag{38}$$

We also know that

$$V_u = \frac{u_{cc}}{u_c} + (u_{cX} - u_{cc}P)' E_{Pu}. \tag{39}$$

$$V_P = (u_{cX} - u_{cc}P)' E_{PP}. \tag{40}$$

Although individual utilities must be chosen subject to equation (27), it must also be the case that individuals are at a global maximum if X is lower in any argument for individuals with a higher income. Thus the constraint may be imposed that

$$\frac{dX}{dy} = \frac{d}{dy} E_P \geqslant 0.$$

We can show that equation (40) is, in fact, a necessary and sufficient condition for all individuals to be at a global maximum.

Finally $P(X(y))$ is given by

$$P(X(y)) = 1(y) + P(y)'X \tag{41}$$

so that utilizing equation (33) and (34), (31) becomes

$$\int_{\underline{y}}^{\bar{y}} (y - E(u, P) + (P - m')E_P(u, P) - F)f(y)\, dy \geqslant 0. \tag{42}$$

The firm must maximize equation (30) subject to equations (35), (37) (40) and (41). Introducing multipliers to take care of these constraints, we obtain the following maximand:

$$M = \int_{\underline{y}}^{\bar{y}} (\{W(u) + \lambda(y - E + (P - m)'E_P - F) + V(y)(u - u(y, 0))\}f(y) + \mu(y)\left(V - \frac{du}{dy}\right) + \xi(y)'\left(\frac{d}{dy}e_P\right) dy \tag{43}$$

u and P, are subject to choice and are to be viewed as functions of y. This looks, now, like a standard problem in the theory of optimal taxation. Applying the maximum principle to the variational problem, we obtain

$$N_1(u, P, y) = \{W^* + \lambda[-E_u + (P - m)'E_{Pu}] + V\}f + \mu\dot{V}_u + \dot{\mu} - \xi' E_{pu} = 0 \tag{44}$$

$$N_2(u, P, y) = \lambda f(P - m)'E_{PP} + \mu V_P - \dot{\xi}' E_{PP} = 0 \tag{45}$$

where a "dot" refers to differentiation with respect to y. We also have as transversality conditions.

$$\mu(\underline{y}) = \mu(\bar{y}) = 0$$
$$\xi(\underline{y}) = \xi(\bar{y}) = 0. \tag{46}$$

As marginal prices are subject to control, it is easy to modify the problem so as to incorporate explicit constraints on pricing schedules that may be chosen. For instance, if only linear schedules are to be admitted then it is easy to cope with the constraint.

$$\dot{P} = 0. \tag{47}$$

Similarly, if only quantity discounting is feasible, then, as goods are normal, one can impose the constraint.

$$\dot{P} \leqslant 0. \tag{48}$$

For the present analysis, it is useful to investigate the optimum schedule under the constraint that two different goods must be treated as a single good. Thus if the first two components of X are taken as these two goods, the pricing schedule, $P(X)$ must take the form.

$$P(X) = Q(x_1 + x_2, + x_3, \ldots, x_n) \tag{49}$$

for some function Q. This imposes the constraint.

$$P_1(y) = P_2(y) \text{ for all } y \tag{50}$$

on marginal prices. Incorporating this constraint, equation (43) becomes

$$M + \int_{\underline{y}}^{\bar{y}} \beta(y)(P_1(y) - P_2(y))\, dy. \tag{51}$$

Applying the maximum principle, equation (44) is unaffected. Equation (45) is now replaced by

$$N_2(u, P, y) = \beta(y)(-1, 1, 0, \ldots, 0)'. \tag{52}$$

For given u and y, equations (50) and (52) provide $n + 1$ equations in $n + 1$ unknowns.

The Price Schedule for a Single Good

We shall first investigate the form of the optimum pricing schedule when no extra constraints, are imposed. As $P = u_X/u_c$ substitution of equations (26) and (39) into equation (45) gives

$$[\lambda f(P - m)' + \mu n(C, X)' - \dot{\xi}']E_{PP} = 0. \tag{53}$$

But as E_{PP} is negative definite, we have

$$\lambda f(P - m)' + \mu n(C, X)' - \dot{\xi}' = 0. \tag{54}$$

Thus because no constraints are imposed upon the pricing schedule, gross elasticities may be ignored. Applying equations (26) and (49), equation (44) becomes

$$(W_u - \lambda E_u + V)f + [\lambda f(P - m) + \mu n(C, X) - \dot{\xi}']' E_{Pu}$$
$$+ \dot{\mu} + \mu \frac{u_{cc}}{u_c} = 0 \tag{55}$$

so that, applying equations (44) and (34)

$$\left(W_u - \frac{\lambda}{u_c} + V\right)f + \dot{\mu} + \mu \frac{u_{cc}}{u_c} = 0 \tag{56)}$$

equation (56) is a general first—order linear differential equation which is easily solved. Using equation (46) to eliminate the constant of integration we have

$$\mu(y) = \frac{1}{H(y)} \int_{\underline{y}}^{\bar{y}} \left[\frac{\lambda}{u_c} - V(Z) - W_u\right] H(Z) f(Z)\, dZ \tag{57}$$

where $H(y) = \exp\left[\int_{\underline{y}}^{\bar{y}} \frac{u_{cc}}{u_c}\, dZ\right].$ (58)

Thus, when individuals with different incomes are not bunched together, so that $x_i(y)$ is strictly increasing, equation (54) gives the optimum marginal price:

$$P_i(y) = m_i - \left\{\frac{\mu n_i}{\lambda f_i}\right\}. \tag{59}$$

The optimum distortion between marginal price and marginal cost depends upon four factors: μ, n_i, λ and f. As $\mu(\underline{y}) = \mu(\bar{y}) = 0$, we see that if individuals are not bunched together, individuals with the lowest and highest incomes should face undistorted marginal prices. Further, from equation (57), we see that if W_u is independent of y and $V(y) = 0$ for all y then, as $\mu(\bar{y}) = 0$, it must be the case that $\mu(y) = 0$ for all y. In this case marginal prices always equal marginal cost. This is not at all surprising if W^{*}_{uc} is independent of y, then the distribution of income is optimal and there is no need to introduce distortions into the system.

Equation (59) also has a ready interpretation for it states that the optimum distortion at a point on the pricing schedule where individuals with an income y are to be found is given by $\mu n_i/\lambda f \cdot \mu$ is a measure of the social value of giving a direct transfer to individuals with an income above y. The greater is μ the more one is willing to introduce a distortion by having a low marginal price which helps accomplish this transfer. μ/λ is a normalization of μ into an income measure. Finally n_i/f is a measure of the density of individuals around the point $X(y)$. With a low density the social value of introducing a distortion will be low. Thus one is more willing to introduce a distortion.

It can be shown that if an individual with income y^* is indifferent about participating in the market, i.e.,

$$u(y^*, D) = u\{y^* - P[X(y^*)], X(Y^*)\}$$

then individuals with a higher income will prefer participation and individuals with a lower income will strictly prefer non-participation. Thus, if there exist individuals who do not wish to participate in the market then these individuals will be given by the (connected) set $[\underline{y}, y^*]$. As $V(y) = 0$ if $y \geqslant y^*$, equation (57) becomes

$$\mu(y) = \frac{1}{H(y)}\left[\int_{\underline{y}}^{\bar{y}} \left(\frac{\lambda}{u_c} - W_u\right) H(Z)f(Z)\, dZ - L\right] \tag{60}$$

for all $y \geqslant y^*$. where

$$L = \int_{\underline{y}}^{y^*} V(Z)H(Z)f(Z)\, dZ \geqslant 0. \tag{61}$$

These suggest that it is useful to analyze two polar cases:

(*i*) *No Redistributional Objective*; *Some Individuals Excluded:* Then W_u is independent of y. Without loss of generality it may be assumed that $W_u = 1$. Applying equation (60)

$$\mu(y) = \frac{1}{H(y)}\left[\int_{\underline{y}}^{\bar{y}} \left(\frac{\lambda - 1}{u_c}\right) H(Z)f(Z)\, dZ - L\right] \tag{62}$$

so that if $L > 0$ then λ must exceed unity, recalling that $\mu(\bar{y}) = 0$, as $\lambda > 1$ and $\mu(\bar{y}) = 0$, we see that $\mu(y)$ must be strictly less than zero except at $\bar{y}$.

Inserting this result into equation (59), we obtain the result that with individuals excluded from the market, marginal prices should always exceed marginal cost except at the upper end point of the schedule. It may be mentioned that this result implies that there must be quantity discounts at the upper-end of the schedule.

The degree to which λ exceeds unity depends upon the social cost of having individuals excluded from the market. This has a straightforward interpretation: λ is the social value of funds to the public utility and the value reflects the fact that extra funds are of value because they can be passed on to the consumer and they enable a restructuring of the price schedule which permits more individuals to participate in the maket.

Finally a more detailed examination of the optimum schedule shows that X is a continuous function of y. With exclusion, it must therefore be the case that there exists individuals who purchase infinitesimal amounts of the good provided by the firm. This leads to the conclusion that

$$P(X) \to 0 \text{ as } X \to 0.$$

(*ii*) *Existence of a Redistributional Objective; No Exclusion:* It is commonly accepted that individuals with a higher income have a lower social marginal utility of income: in our terminology, W_u is a decreasing function of income.

If W_u is strictly declining and there is no distortion introduced by exclusion, i.e. $L = 0$, then from equations (60) and (46), $\mu(y)$ will be strictly negative except at the end-points where it will be zero. Thus, optimal marginal prices will exceed marginal cost except at both end points of the schedule (from 59).

Finally, putting together these two cases, we see from equation (60) that, except at the upper end of the schedule, marginal prices will exceed marginal cost when there is both a redistributional objective, and an exclusion effect, that is, $L > 0$.

This is about as far as one can go with the general analysis. To get more specific conclusions numerical computations have to be made.

Linear Taxation and Pricing with Redistribution

We now proceed to examine the problem of optimal linear pricing of the public sector output if the government also has redistributive objectives. The realization that indirect taxes and the price of a public sector good should be jointly determined dates back to the contribution of Diamond and Mirrlees (1971). Since then explicit formulae for the public sector price and the rates of indirect taxation have been derived. See, for instance, Feldstein (1972a, b, c) Munk (1978), Atkinson and Stizlitz (1980) and Murty (1983b).

The usual structure of these models is as follows. The public sector is embedded in a general equilibrium competitive framework which is basically the standard one period model with firms maximizing profits and households maximizing utility (defined over consumption and leisure). Hence one can derive explicit demand functions for private and public goods. Social welfare is visualized as an aggregate indirect utility function. This is maximized with respect to the price of the public sector commodity given an explicit reaction function of the government between public sector price and indirect taxes. This maximization is constrained by individual behavioural functions and an overall budgetary constraint.

Theoretical and empirical work using this approach has assumed Leontief type technology and hence fixed coefficients. This necessarily confines us, additionally, to the constant returns to scale case.

In a pioneering analysis Jha and Murty (1986) have extended this analysis to the flexible coefficients case and apply the results to the case of pricing of electricity in India. We discuss here the theoretical pricing model advanced by Jha and Murty.

Consider an economy having H individuals. There are $n + 1$ goods in the economy. The first n are private sector goods while the $n + 1$ 'st good is produced in the public sector, private sector production is defined by an input-output matrix A whence a_{ij} represents the amount of the ith commodity required as an intermediary input to produce a unit of the jth commodity. We define b as a $n \times 1$ vector representing the requirements of the public sector commodity as an intermediate input in the production of various private sector goods. The production function for the public sector good is

$$x_{n+1} = f(x_1, \ldots, x_n, L_{n+1}) \tag{63}$$

where L_{n+1} is labour input. The augmented input-output structure of the economy can be described by the matrix A^* where

$$A^* = \begin{pmatrix} A & X \\ b' & 0 \end{pmatrix}. \tag{64}$$

In the private sector input-output coefficients (the matrix A) are fixed so that for the private sector we must have

$$q' = p'A + p_{n+1}\, b' + Wl' \tag{65}$$

where p is consumer price, q is producer price and l labour input requirement vectors respectively. W is the (competitively determined) wage rate. Thus if t is the vector of indirect taxes we must have

$$p' = p_{n+1}b'(I - A)^{-1} + t'(I - A)^{-1} + Wl'(I - A)^{-1} \tag{66}$$

$$= p_{n+1}b'(I - A)^{-1} + t'^* + Wl'(I - A)^{-1} \tag{67}$$

where t^* is an $nx1$ vector of effective tax rates on private goods that take into account the taxes on direct and indirect requirements of various intermediary inputs that go into the production of a unit of the private sector good.

The hth individual has an indirect utility function $V^h(p,\ p_{n+1},\ Y^h)$ where Y^h is his income. Then the social welfare function can be written as $W(V^1, V^2,, \ldots, V^H)$. The government earns revenues from indirect taxes and public sector profits. The government's budget constraint can be written as

$$\sum_{i=1}^{n} t_i^* x_i + (P_{n+1} - m)x_{n+1} - F = 0 \tag{68}$$

where m and F are marginal and fixed costs respectively.

We form the Lagrangean for society's maximization problem

$$L = W(V^1, V^2, \ldots, V^H)$$
$$+ \lambda \left[\sum_{i=1}^{n} (t_i^* x_i) + (P_{n+1} - m)x_{n+1} \right] \tag{69}$$

where λ is an appropriate Lagrange multiplier. Differentiating L with respect to P_{n+1} we get

$$\frac{\partial L}{\partial P_{n+1}} = \sum_{i=1}^{n} \sum_{h=1}^{H} \frac{\partial W}{\partial V^h}\left(\frac{\partial V^h}{\partial P_{n+1}} + \frac{\partial V^h}{\partial P_i}\frac{\partial P_i}{\partial P_{n+1}}\right)$$
$$+ \lambda \left[\sum_{i=1}^{n} \left(t_i^* \frac{\partial x_i}{\partial P_{n+1}} + x_i \frac{\partial t_i}{\partial P_{n+1}} \right) \right.$$
$$+ (P_{n+1} - m)\frac{\partial x_{n+1}}{\partial P_{n+1}} + \left(1 - \left(\frac{\partial m}{\partial x_{n+1}}\frac{\partial x_{n+1}}{\partial P_{n+1}}\right.\right.$$
$$\left.\left.\left. + \sum_{i=1}^{n} \frac{\partial m}{\partial P_i}\frac{\partial P_i}{\partial P_{n+1}}\right)\right) x_{n+1} \right]. \tag{70}$$

In equation (70) we have assumed that change in P_{n+1} does not have any income effect. We know that

$$\frac{\partial V^h}{\partial P_i} = -\alpha^h x_i^h,\ i = 1, \ldots, n \tag{71}$$

where x_i^h is the consumption of the ith commodity by the hth individual and α^h is the marginal utility of his income. From Equation (68) we get

$$\frac{\partial P_i}{\partial P_{n+1}} = \frac{\partial t_i^*}{\partial P_{n+1}} + S_i,\ i = 1, \ldots, n$$

where $$S = b'(I - A)^{-1} \tag{72}$$

and $$\frac{\partial t_i^*}{\partial P_{n+1}} \leqslant 0.$$

Let β^h be the social marginal utility of income to the hth individual that is,

$$\beta^h = \frac{\partial W}{\partial V^h}\alpha^h.$$

We also define $b^h = \beta^h/\lambda$ as the marginal social valuation of the hth individual's income measured in terms of government revenue. Then

$$\frac{P_{n+1} - m(1 + e_{m,\, x_{n+1}})}{P_{n+1}} = \frac{(1 - \bar{b}\bar{R}) + (\bar{b}R_T - 1)q + \sum_{i=1}^{n} \frac{\partial m}{\partial P_i}\left(\frac{\partial t_i^*}{\partial P_{n+1}} + S_i\right)}{e_{p_{n+1}}} \tag{73}$$

where $\bar{b} = \frac{\Sigma b^h}{H}$, $R_i = \sum_{h=1}^{H} \frac{b^h x_i^h}{n\bar{b}\bar{x}}$, $i = 1, \ldots, n$

$$\bar{R} = \sum_{i=1}^{n} \frac{R_i x_i S_i}{x_{n+1}},\quad R_T = \frac{\sum_{i=1}^{n} R_i x_i \frac{\partial t_i^*}{\partial P_{n+1}}}{\sum_{i=1}^{n} x_i \frac{\partial t_i}{\partial P_{n+1}}}$$

$$q = \frac{\sum_{i=1}^{n} x_i \frac{\partial t_i}{\partial P_{n+1}}}{x_{n+1}},\quad e_{p_{n+1}} = \frac{\partial x_{n+1}}{\partial p_{n+1}} \frac{P_{n+1}}{x_{n+1}}$$

$$e_{m,\, x_{n+1}} = \frac{\partial m}{\partial x_{n+1}} \frac{x_{n+1}}{m}$$

or $$\frac{m}{P_{n+1}} = \frac{1 - \dfrac{(1 - \bar{b}\bar{R}) + (\bar{b}\bar{R}_T - 1) + \sum_{i=1}^{n} \frac{\partial m}{\partial P_i}\left(\frac{\partial t_i^*}{\partial P_{n+1}} + S_i\right)}{| e_{p_{n+1}} |}}{(1 + e_{m, x_{n+1}})} \tag{74}$$

We may regard R_i, $\bar{R}$ and R_T respectively as distributional characteristics of ith final consumption good, the public sector good and the indirect tax structure in the economy.

We may now relax the assumption of fixed coefficients in the public sector. To do this we have to visualize afresh the factors operating on the demand and supply side of the pricing of x_{n+1}.

To bring demand into the picture, assume that an aggregate utility function V is maximized realizing demand functions

$$x = x(P_x, P_{n+1}, W, Y) \tag{75}$$

$$x_{n+1} = x_{n+1}(P_x, P_{n+1}, W, Y) \tag{76}$$

$$L = L(P_x, P_{n+1}, W, Y) \tag{77}$$

where x is a vector of private goods, L is labour and $Y = WL + I_0$ is income for the economy as a whole, I_0 is non-wage income.

Define an expenditure function

$$\bar{e}(p_x, p_{n+1}, W, V) \tag{78}$$

so that compensated demand functions for x and x_{n+1} and supply of L are given by

$$x = \frac{\partial \bar{e}(\ )}{\partial p_x};\ x_{n+1} = \frac{\partial \bar{e}(\ )}{\partial P_{n+1}},\ L = \frac{\partial \bar{e}(\ )}{\partial W}.$$

Let $\frac{dA}{A} = \hat{A}$ for any variable Logarthmically differentiating equations (76), (77) and (78), we get

$$\hat{x} = E_{xx}\hat{P}_x + E_{xx_{n+1}}\hat{P}_{n+1} + E_{x_L}\hat{W} + \eta_x \frac{dV}{dY}\bar{e}_v \tag{79}$$

$$\hat{x}_{n+1} = E_{x_{n+1}x}\hat{P}_x + E_{x_{n+1}x_{n+1}}\hat{P}_{n+1} + E_{x_{n+1L}}\hat{W} + x_{n+1}\frac{\partial V}{dY}\bar{e}_v \tag{80}$$

$$\hat{L} = E_{xL}\hat{P}_x + E_{Lx_{n+1}}\hat{P}_{n+1} + E_{LL}\hat{W} + \eta_L \frac{dV}{dY}\bar{e}_v \tag{81}$$

where the E's are compensated elasticities and η's are income elasticities.

When labour supply is fixed $\hat{L} = \hat{W} = 0$. Then using the relation $E_{ij} = -E_{ii}$ we can write

$$(\eta_{x_{n+1}}\hat{x} - \eta_x\hat{x}_{n+1}) = (\eta_{x_{n+1}}E_{xx} + \eta_i E_{x_{n+1}x_{n+1}})(\hat{P}_n - \hat{P}_{n+1}). \tag{82}$$

But this is only a special case.

From the supply side let γ be a $nx1$ vector of unit costs or prices of private sector commodities associated with cost minimizing technologies (or prices of non-substitution theorem) without indirect taxes.

The gross price (P) is

$$P = \gamma(P, P_{n+1}, W) + t. \tag{82}$$

Let $A(\gamma)$ and $A(P)$ be the input-output matrices in the two price situations γ and P. Then the vector of social costs Γ of private sector good is

$$\Gamma' = mb'(\gamma)(I - A(\gamma)^{-1} + W(\gamma)1'(\gamma)(I - A(\gamma))^{-1}. \tag{83}$$

Moreover

$$P' = P_{n+1}b'(P)(I - A(P))^{-1} + W(P)l'(P)(I - A(P))^{-1} + t'(I - A(P))^{-1}. \quad (84)$$

Hence

$$P' - \Gamma' = (P_{n+1} - m)b'(P)\bar{A}(P) + t'\bar{A}(P) + m(b'(P)\bar{A}(P) - b'(\gamma)\bar{A}(\gamma)) + (W(P)l'(P) - W(\gamma)l'(\gamma)\bar{A}(\gamma)) \quad (85)$$

where $\bar{A}$ $(I - A)^{-1}$.
From equation (82) we have

$$\frac{\partial P_i}{\partial P_{n+1}} = \sum_{j=1}^{n} \frac{\partial \gamma_j}{\partial P_j} \frac{\partial P_j}{\partial P_{n+1}} + \frac{\partial \gamma_i}{\partial P_{n+1}} + \frac{\partial \gamma_i}{\partial W} \frac{\partial W}{\partial P_{n+1}} + \frac{\partial t_i}{\partial P_{n+1}}. \quad (86)$$

Let $\quad \dot{P} = \frac{\partial P}{\partial P_{n+1}}, \; \dot{W} = \frac{\partial W}{\partial P_{n+1}}, \; \dot{t} = \frac{\partial t}{\partial P_{n+1}}.$

We know that

$$\frac{\partial \gamma_i}{\partial P_j} = a_{ji}, j^{ith} \text{ element of } A$$

$$b = \frac{\partial \gamma}{\partial P_{n+1}} \quad \text{and} \quad 1 = \frac{\partial \gamma}{\partial W}.$$

Therefore we have

$$\dot{P}' = P'A(P) + b' + \dot{W}l'(P) + t'$$

$$\dot{P}' = b'(P)(I - A(P)^{-1} = \dot{W}l'(I - A(P))^{-1} + t'(I - A(P))^{-1} \quad (87)$$

$$\dot{P}_i' = G_i + \dot{W}l_i^* + t_i^*$$

where $G = b'(P)(I - A(P))^{-1}$

$l^* = l'(I - A(P))^{-1}$

$t^* = t'(I - A(P))^{-1}.$

Let $V^h(P, Y^h)$, $x^h(P, Y^h)$ and $L^h(P, Y^h)$ be respectively indirect untility function, demand function for x and labour supply of an individual h. The maximization of social welfare subject to the public sector budgetary constraint requires that

$$\sum_i \sum_h \frac{\partial W}{\partial V^h} \frac{\partial V^h}{\partial P_i} \frac{\partial P_i}{\partial P_{n+1}} + \sum_h \frac{\partial W}{\partial V^h} \frac{\partial V^h}{\partial Y^h} \frac{\partial Y^h}{\partial P_{n+1}} \quad (88)$$

$$+ \lambda \left[\sum_i \left(t_i^* \frac{\partial x_i}{\partial P_{n+1}} + x_i \frac{\partial t_i^*}{\partial P_{n+1}} + x_{n+1} + (P_{n+1} - m) \right) \frac{\partial x_{n+1}}{\partial P_{n+1}} \right] = 0.$$

Substituting equation (87) into equation (88) and rearranging we get

$$-\sum_i \sum_h \beta^h x_i^h \left(G_i + \frac{\partial t_i^*}{\partial P_{n+1}} + \dot{W} l_i^* \right) + \sum_h \beta^h \dot{Y}^h + \sum_i \left(t_i^* \frac{\partial x_i}{\partial P_{n+1}} + x_i \frac{\partial t_i^*}{\partial P_{n+1}} \right) + x_{n+1} + (P_{n+1} - m) \frac{\partial x_{n+1}}{\partial P_{n+1}} = 0. \quad (89)$$

We have supply and demand balancing equation for labour

$$\sum_i \sum_h x_i^h l_i^* = \sum_h L^h. \quad (90)$$

We also have

$$\dot{Y}^h = \dot{W} L^h + W \dot{L}^h + \dot{Y}^h. \quad (91)$$

Substituting equation (91) into equation (89) we get

$$-\sum_i \sum_h \beta^h x_i^h G_i / x_{n+1} - \sum_i \sum_h \beta^h x_i^h \frac{\partial t_i^*}{\partial P_{n+1}} / x_{n+1} + \sum_i x_i \frac{\partial t_i^*}{\partial P_{n+1}} / x_{n+1} + 1 + \frac{P_{n+1} - m}{P_{n+1}} (e_{P_{n+1}}) + \sum_h \beta^h (\dot{W} L^h + W \dot{L}^h + \dot{Y}^h) / x_{n+1} - \sum_i \sum_h \beta^h x_i^h l_i^* \dot{W} / x_{n+1} = 0. \quad (92)$$

We can now rewrite equation (92) as

$$\frac{P_{n+1} - m}{P_{n+1}} = \frac{(1 - \bar{b}\bar{R}) + q(\bar{b}R_T - 1) - (1 - k_1)k_2 + k_3}{(e_{P_{n+1}})} \quad (93)$$

where $k_1 = \dfrac{\sum_i \sum_h \beta^h x_i l_i^* W}{\sum_h \beta^h L^h \dot{W}}$

$$k_2 = \frac{\sum_h \beta^h \dot{W} L^h}{x_{n+1}} \text{ and}$$

$$k_3 = \frac{\sum_h \beta^h (\dot{L}^h W + \dot{Y}^h)}{x_{n+1}}$$

Equation (93) gives us the final form of the pricing equation to be estimated. Using a translog specification Jha and Murty estimate an equation like (93) for electricity in India. They find increasing returns to scale in electricity production so that working out the optimal price formulac for the flexible coefficients case is important as well as necessary.

Conclusions

In this chapter we studied some models of optimal pricing in the public sector. The careful reader can pick up many instances where theoretical advances have to be made. More importantly, however, a comprehensive study of optimal pricing for the Indian public sector has to be undertaken.

PART—IV

SOME PROBLEMS OF INDIAN PUBLIC FINANCE

19. An Overview of the Indian Public Sector

The roots of our public sector lie in the economic philosophy that the nation adopted soon after independence. The realization at that time was that the private sector could not be trusted (by itself) with the complex and multifacted problems caused by the rapid development of a poor society. The reasons why we needed a strong public sector are well known but it is worth our while to recount some of those reasons.

1. Investment in certain industries is of strategic importance. Thus one cannot trust the private sector with production of defence equipment or large scale infrastructural activities.

2. Many essential investments are lumpy in character so that gestation lags are likely to be long. In this case it would not be profitable for the private sector to invest.

3. We planned for a "socialistic" society where public operation and ownership would gradually replace private operation. Hence it would only be proper for the public sector to man the commanding heights of the economy.

4. The public sector was to be used for redistributing the gains of economic growth from rich to poor. Hence certain items of mass consumption had to be produced in the public sector. Moreover employment opportunities had to be increased rapidly and regional disparities had to be narrowed.

5. Last but not least, the public sector had to generate enough surplus for continued growth and health of the economy and the public sector.

The broad contours of the policy adopted were the following. An elaborate system of tariff and physical controls would protect the domestic market from foreign competition. Within the domestic economy the Industrial Policy Resolutions defined the industries in which the public sector was to be (*a*) the sole actor and (*b*) the dominant and relatively faster growing actor. The rest of the economy was left for free enterprise.

Today there is widespread disenchantment with this policy. The leftists have accused the public sector of essentially being an instrument designed to ensure the growth of capitalism in India. The public sector gave the private sector infrastructure and essential inputs at subsidized rates. The market was protected. The public sector financial corporations provided cheap finance and so on.

One the other hand there are those who argue that the public sector's performance has been dismal vis a vis the private sector. The public sector has been a drag on the economy because of mounting losses, industrial strife, low capacity utilization, poor quality control etc.

There is some evidence to support the view that the public sector his contributed to an escalation of costs in the economy. A recent NCAER study[1] brings out the evidence in both aggregate and sectoral industrial terms. At the aggregative level there is the serious and persistent shortfall of both actual output and capacity, utilization from the respective targeted amounts. At the sectoral level one notes serious shortfalls in the output of crucial industries and inordinate delays. In this connection the Table 19.1 for an organization as reputed as BHEL tells a succinct story.

TABLE 19.1 Project Costs

Project	*Original cost Rs. crores*	*Revised cost Rs, crores*
HEEP, Hārdwar	63.43	85.99 (Dec. 1966)
HEEP, Hyderabad	33.45	39.25 (Mar. 69)
Boiler Plant (Trichi)	27.39	25.01 (Sept. 1968)
Transformer Factory		
Jhansi	16.22	20.99
GFFP	22.40	32.20
SSTP	58.20	58.20
R&D	15.89	17.45
Phase II Expansion Boiler Plant (Trichi)	12.12	17.86
(New Units Under Completion (as on 31.3.82))		
Hydrosets Bhopal	6.42	7.05
Large Size TG sets (HEEP, Hardwar)		
Boiler Plant	43.08	50.35
Phase III Expansion	29.83	35.48
Boiler Plant, Rampet	21.59	32.02
Bowl Mills, Hyderabad	18.58	20.38

SOURCE: *NCAER (1983)*.

The cost implications of such behaviour are amply clear, and there would be no point in attempting to justify such recurrent mishaps in terms of the professed multifacted objectives that the public sector firms are supposed to have. Even if we discount the above evidence there is the very disturbing story of large, unwarranted and continuous accumulation of inventories of finished goods and raw materials at the (public) enterprise level, told by a number of Bureau of Public Enterprise publications.

[1]See NCAER (1983).

Before we get carried away by this kind of evidence we should note, two facts (*i*) the growth of the private sector has, in no sense of the term, been even and the public sector has played a crucial role in the expansion of the private sector; and (*ii*) we understand relatively little about the cost structure of Indian industries and hence much research is needed before a satisfactory policy conclusion can be arrived at.

That the development of the private sector has been highly uneven in terms of regions, performance or almost any other criterion will not come as a surprise to anyone, It has also been fairly well established emprically[2] that profitability in the private sector is linked to concentration in industry. We also know that anti-trust policy is no longer interested in removing monopoly but merely in controlling some of the more serious manifestations of monopoly. According to a recent study[3] about 77 percent of public funds earmarked for industrial financing have gone to the private sector. It is well known that most of these have gone to the larger industrial houses. A recent survey[4] of capacity utilization within the context of our industrial licencing system has found that in areas which yield larger profit margins there has been over utilization of capacity and, in others, gross under utilization of capacity. Such under utilization is more rampant in the private than the public sector. Thus, for instance, out of a sample of 131 central public sector units, 62 (47 percent) had a utilization rate of more than 75 percent. In the private sector only 24.54 percent of the private sector held licences were being utilized at 75 percent and above. It is difficult to escape the conclusion, then that the private sector is primarily responding to market incentives but such responses are not the best strategy for achieving greater social productivity. It would be self defeating for us to argue that a heavily capitalized public sector is inefficient and ignore the social costs of private oligopoly power.

In the face of an almost total absence of serious analytical work on the performance of the Indian public sector we will confine ourselves, in this chapter, to commenting on the aggregative data on the performance of the public sector. We will also study the performance of some sections of the public sector with particular reference to their pricing policies.[5]

INHERENT DIFFICULTIES WITH THE INTERPRETATION OF DATA

(*a*) Aggregative Ratios

A quick review of the statistical tables in the Annual Survey of Industries would suggest serious anomalies in the functioning of enterprises in the

[2]See Manju Pal (1981).

[3]See FICCI (1984).

[4]See S.K. Goyal (1983).

[5]It is clear that public enterprises have a host of other problems. Some key ones are (i) erratic infrastructural facilities, (ii) political interference in the day to day working of enterprises, (iii) insecurity of tenure of top management and rapid turnover at middle management levels; (iv) militant trade unions etc.

public and private sector of the Indian economy. Data pertaining to principal aggregates and structural ratios exhibit apparently wide gaps in the relative performance of enterprises in the two categories. For example, public sector units while accounting for roughly 70 percent of the total fixed assets in the factory sector (see Table 19.2) yielded only 30 percent of the total value added. The reverse is true for the private sector units.

Similarly, the official data on capital-output ratio (see Table 19.3) would reveal that in the aggregate profile the public sector required five times the fixed assets in comparison to the private sector to produce a single unit of value added. When productive capital and gross value of output is compared for the two sectors (2.5 : 1 for the public sector and 1 : 2 for the private sector) a somewhat identical impression is conveyed about the relative efficiency of the public sector.

Notwithstanding the numbers generated by these techno-empirical ratios, it is important to note that the real phenomenon may be quite different. To begin with, the valuations of both capital and output are suspect. As for capital, traditionally public enterprises have been established in sectors which require lumpy investments. This being one of the main raison d'etre for public sector units, a comparison of their capital-output ratio with that for private sector units may not be a true indicator of relative efficiency.

Furthermore, the fact that much of the capital formation especially in the private sector is due to depreciation funds, unrelated to technological changes, its comparison with the public sector to determine relative performance may be inappropriate. In fact, changes in technology and the vintage of equipment make the interpretation of aggregative data on capital and capital: output ratio difficult.

Depending on when the capital asset came into being and by how much it has been depreciated, the calculation for the capital: output ratio would be influenced. Longer established units would end up showing a better ratio as the capital base would be relatively small.

Non-tradeability of stocks, rather incomplete stock market for the public sector inhibits transmission of complete information through pricing. Therefore, in many ways one ends up comparing the non-comparables.

Besides, the above, the need to account for inflation using appropriate price index in each case makes the interpretation of the data more cumbersome.

Valuation of the gross output or value added by the public sector enterprises is yet another story. This is discussed at length in the section dealing with the pricing of public enterprises output.

(*b*) Profit/Loss Profile

Whatever the pricing practice, the profitability profile of the public enterprises has come to be viewed as the ultimate measure of the performacne at the public sector. Here again, one has to be careful in interpreting the data.

According to the latest survey *Public Enterprise Survey, 1982-83* issued by

TABLE 19.2 Principal Characteristics by Type of Ownership—All-India

(*Percentage distribution*)

Type of ownership	*Factories*	*Fixed capital*	*Productive capital*	*Employees*	*Employments*	*Total input*	*Gross output*	*Value added*
Wholly central Govt.	1.4	22.6	24.1	10.9	18.3	13.5	14.4	16.8
Wholly state/local Govt.	3.0	39.6	31.7	12.3	12.3	5.9	7.3	10.6
Central state/local Govt. jointly	0.2	0.7	0.6	0.5	0.6	0.3	0.3	0.4
Public sector	4.6	62.9	56.4	23.7	31.2	19.7	22.0	27.8
Central Govt. & private enterprises jointly	0.1	1.6	1.7	0.6	0.9	2.1	1.9	1.1
State/local Govt. and private enterprises jointly	1.5	3.8	3.9	4.4	3.3	4.1	4.0	3.4
Central, state/local Govt. & private enterprises jointly	0.1	1.3	1.4	0.8	1.5	1.7	1.7	1.4
Joint Sector	1.7	6.7	7.0	5.8	5.7	7.9	7.6	5.9
Wholly private enterprise	82.1	30.4	36.6	70.5	63.1	72.4	70.4	66.3
Unspecified	11.6	0.0	0.0	0.0	0.0	0.0	0.0	0.0
Total	100.0	100.0	100.0	100.0	100.0	100.0	100.0	100.0

SOURCE: *Annual Survey of Industries 1976-77.*

TABLE 19.3: Structural Ratios by Type of Ownership—All-India

Type of ownership	*Fixed capital per employee (Rs.)*	*Value added per employee (Rs.)*	*Fixed capital gross output ratio*	*Fixed capital value added ratio*	*Value added gross output ratio*	*Operating surplus gross output ratio*	*Operating surplus plus productive capital ratio*
Public sector	64382	12872	1.35	5.00	0.27	0.12	0.07
Joint sector	28352	11282	0.42	2.51	0.17	0.09	0.14
Private sector	10500	10338	0.20	1.02	0.20	0.11	0.30
Total	24319	10995	0.47	2.21	0.21	0.11	0.16

SOURCE: *Annual Survey of Industries, 1976-77*.

the Bureau of Public Enterprises, covering the performance of Central government enterprises, there are 110 profitmaking units, 81 loss making and two yielding neither profit nor loss. Thus, over 57 percent of the enterprises earned profits and nearly 43 percent incurred losses, with the net outcome of overall net pre-tax profit of Rs 1,545 crores.

A careful analysis of the lists of top ten enterprises in profit making and loss making groups would reveal that the interpretations is not unambiguous.

Of the ten profit making enterprises three are in the field of oil and natural gas accounting for 61 percent of the total profits. None of the remaining seven enterprises yielded more than 2.5 percent of the total profits. This concentration of profits in one industry where prices are administered would hardly be a measure of a wide spread dispersion and genuine profitability of the public sector.

Perhaps consistent with their relative share in the total investment, the top ten profit making enterprises account for over 75 percent of the total profits, with the remaining 100 enterprises contributing towards the total profit for no more than 25 percent.

Similarly, the data on losses incurred by the central public enterprises may not be reflective of the pure economic phenomenon. Here again, since most products or services rendered by ten loss making enterprises fall within the framework of administered prices, the reported loss may have to be read as a result of some conscious policy decision.

Enterprises producing Steel, Iron Ore, Fertilizers and Coal figure predominantly in the list of loss making enterprises. The ten enterprises in the list account for over 63 percent of the total loss incurred by central public sector units. Unlike profits, the distribution of loss among the top ten is evenly dispersed, though the remaining 71 units account for 37 percent of the total loss.

It is clear that while the respective lists of profit making and loss making enterprises simply emanate from units' revenue and costs data, the pricing policy for industries therein assumes added ramification.

TABLE 19.4 Top Ten Profit Making Enterprises (Profit Before Tax)

(Rs. in crores)

Sl. No.	*Name of enterprise*	*Pre-tax profit*	*Percentage to total pre-tax profit earned by profit-making enterprises*
1	2	3	4
1.	Oil and Natural Gas Commission	1182.87	46.94
2.	Oil India Ltd.	205.64	8.16
3.	Indian Oil Corporation Ltd.	150.08	5.96
4.	The State Trading Corpn. of India Ltd.	62.66	2.48
5.	The Minerals and Metals Trading Corpn. of India Ltd.	55.09	2.19
6.	Bharat Heavy Electricals Ltd.	53.64	2.13
7.	Indian Petro Chemicals Corpn. Ltd.	50.88	2.02
8.	Neyveli Lignite Corpn. Ltd.	47.44	1.88
9.	Bharat Earth Movers Ltd.	42.42	1.68
10.	Central Coalfields Ltd.	40.92	1.62
	Total	1891.64	75.06
	Total profit earned by profit making enterprises	2520.10	100.00

SOURCE: *BPE Annual Survey, 1982-83.*

TABLE 19.5 Top ten loss making enterprises

(Rs. in crores)

Sl No.	*Name of enterprise*	*Amount of loss 1982-83*	*Percentage to total loss of loss-making enterprises*
1	2	3	4
1.	Steel Authority of India Ltd.	(–) 105.77	10.85
2.	Delhi Transport Corporation	(–) 73.49	7.54
3.	Kundremukh Iron Ore Company Ltd.	(–) 66.31	6.80
4.	The Indian Iron & Steel Co. Ltd.	(–) 65.76	6.74
5.	The Fertilizer Corpn. of India Ltd.	(–) 65.72	6.74
6.	Hindustan Fertilizer Corpn. Ltd.	(–) 55.35	5.68
7.	Eastern Coalfields Ltd.	(–) 55.33	5.68
8.	Bharat Aluminium Co. Ltd.	(–) 52.83	5.42
9.	Heavy Engineering Corpn. Ltd.	(–) 47.48	4.87
10.	Hindustan Copper Ltd.	(–) 29.63	3.04
	Total	(–) 617.67	63.36
	Total loss incurred by loss making enterprises	(–) 974.73	100.00

SOURCE: *BPE Annual Survey, 1982-83.*

SIGNIFICANCE AND DEFICIENCIES OF PRICING PRACTICE IN SELECTIVE INDUSTRIES

In view of the evidence revealed by the profit/loss figures and several other means it is clear that pricing in the public sector has played a critical role in any assessment, according to prevalent norms, of the health of the public enterprises. There are two analytically separable but structurally linked propositions here viz., (*i*) *Ceteris paribus*, in the case of many public enterprises, pricing policy can almost dictate the pre-or post-tax rate of return to capital invested, and (*ii*) In the light of fact that there are no independent measures of what an appropriate cost structure should look like it is hard to evaluate the usefulness or otherwise of a given price for any public sector commodity. This last point deserves some explanation. In the stylized world of perfect competition with perfect capital markets we know that a competitive price will prevail and that, given the perfect security market, the "appropriate price" for coal can be compared to the "appropriate price" for computers. However when we move from this atmosphere to the arena in which public enterprises function we realise immediately the scope for a high degree of arbitrariness in defining both an appropriate level of costs and an appropriate price structure.

One of the widest gaps in our knowledge of the general equilibrium of the Indian public sector is in this area of a price structure for different commodities given our conditions. This is a long and extremely useful piece of work that is urgently required. Since our purpose in the present chapter is far less ambitious we focus our attention on the partial equilibrium exercise of critically assessing the pricing practices followed in a few specific industries viz. steel, coal, fertilizers, and petroleum.

(*a*) Steel

A wide variety of practices are followed in fixing prices in these industries and administrative control over these prices rests with different bodies e.g. the Joint Plant Committee, the Union Cabinet etc. Steel is an interesting case because, in principle, the market is fairly competitive and hence administered prices are largely moot. As a consequence the steel industry is subject to the pressures, over and above that of being largely in the public sector, of competition. As opposed to an industry such as petroleum then the steel industry displays large swings in fortune Tables 19.6-19.9 illustrate with time series data from 1970-71 to 1980-81 the performance of the Indian steel industry. There are a few interesting aspects to this story. The valued added to working capital ratio has not fluctuated very much around 1 : 2. At the same time the value added to sales ratio has showed a steady decline and the value of inventories has registered a sharp increase of almost 600 per-cent (not all of this can be explained by movements in the general price level). The first observation could be explained in part by the operation or commissioning of new plants with higher capital costs (and the inability to

TABLE 19.6 Performance of Steel Group of Enterprises H.S.L. 1154 Bokaro 1964 SAIL 1973

(Rs. in crores)

Year	*Equity*	*Loans*	*Total Investment*	*Depreciation*	*Free Reserves*	*Reserves specific*	*Capital Employed*	*Net Work*
1970-71	967.00	571.17	1538.17	484.30	0.34	16.72	1009.04	784.36
1971-72	1194.37	499.38	1693.75	551.16	0.37	18.28	1013.77	964.59
1972-73	1225.52	614.40	1839.92	624.46	0.34	22.52	1112.79	2239.12
1973-74	1325.99	679.21	2025.20	703.09	0.34	26.43	1297.35	2273.66
1974-75	1374.16	843.53	2217.69	780.04	0.65	49.89	1384.48	1135.75
1975-76	1458.49	1111.91	2570.40	848.46	0.68	43.08	1636.51	1246.47
1976-77	1584.72	1279.59	2864.31	1017.56	41.37	54.81	2005.72	1462.96
1977-78	2123.86	932.76	3056.62	1111.13	28.05	61.81	2133.01	2019.54
1978-79	2257.87	844.42	3102.29	1224.23	95.96	38.81	1950.12	2163.32
1979-80	2490.75	988.57	3479.32	1322.70	126.77	46.31	2116.63	2401.63
1980-81	2806.24	1326.18	4132.42	1441.27	73.57	56.41	2359.39	

SOURCE: *BPE Annual Report*.

ensure comparability of costs across plants because of the absence of a perfect stock market) but one is bound to suspect an escalation of unwarranted costs. The last two observations are partly mutually contradictory and could only be explained by recalling the custom of public sector units buying steel from public sector units thus increasing sales while faulty demand forecasting has led to a disturbing accumulation of inventories (perhaps of other varieties of steel). Even in profit making years the rate of return has not been very promising.

TABLE 19.7 Performance of the Steel Group of Enterprises

(Rs. in crores)

Year	*Working Capital*	*Investment*	*DRE*	*Inventories*	*Net profit (+)/ Net loss (−)*	*Value added*
1970-71	290.49	0.01	4.75	236.30	−5.41	
1971-72	323.90	1.16	7.07	282.13	−44.85	148.34
1972-73	332.39	84.14	10.15	327.66	−33.25	186.43
1973-74	469.05	103.69	14.20	408.52	−5.72	229.80
1974-75	495.63	109.55	13.60	522.37	36.59	315.52
1975-76	713.02	119.99	14.96	685.76	27.72	323.36
1976-77	819.83	136.88	15.99	755.68	66.50	510.25
1977-78	774.63	21.45	13.22	690.13	−3.98	442.74
1978-79	493.61	17.20	118.60	834.51	38.65	389.87
1979-80	592.25	17.71	116.40	1152.31	−3.50	415.59
1980-81	714.73	17.80	16.48	1333.74	−16.36	474.87

SOURCE: *BPE Annual Report.*

TABLE 19.8 Performance of Steel Group of Enterprises

Year	*Percentage of: Net Profit/ Equity*	*Gross Profit to capital employed*	*Net Profit to Net worth*	*Gross Sales to capital employed*	*Value added to sales*	*Total Gross Turnover Rs. crores*
1970-71	L	2.28	L	41.36		
1971-72	L	L	L	43.5	33.3	444.92
1972-73	L	L	L	53.6	30.8	604.64
1973-74	L	1.5	L	55.6	31.8	721.93
					Value added/ Capital Employed	
1974-75	2.7	4.8	3.2	76.4	22.8	1058.39
1975-76	1.9	3.9	2.2	55.4	19.8	906.07
1976-77	4.2	5.9	4.6	71.05	25.4	1425.03
1977-78	L	2.5	L	74.7	20.8	1593.40
1978-79	1.7	6.2	1.8	86.0	20.0	1676.64
1979-80	L	3.4	L	101.9	19.6	2155.98
1980-81	L	3.7	L		20.1	2880.63

SOURCE: *BPE Annual Number.*

TABLE 19.9 **Performance of Steel Group Internal Resources Generated**

Year	*Cost of Sales Rs crores*	*Ratio of Cost of Sales to turnover %*	*Depreciation (1970-71 not available)*	*Retained Profits*	*DRE written off*	*Total*
1970-71						
1971-72	690.55	110.2	68.73	−43.31		+25.42
1972-73	635.58	105.4	71.82	−27.80	.55	44.57
1973-74	727.65	100.72	79.68	− 4.15		75.53
1974-75	1021.06	96.48	83.94	36.59		120.53
1975-76	878.35	96.76	72.56	27.72		100.28
1976-77	1358.53	95.33	79.08	81.25		160.33
1977-78	1598.56	100.34	97.94	35.78		133.72
1978-79	1667.53	99.46	93.60	65.84	5.85	165.29
1979-80	1979.86		104.52	30.23	3.42	138.17
1980-81	2252.85		102.93	.58	1.97	105.48

SOURCE: *BPE Annual Number*.

The surmise that competitive pressures have affected the performance of the steel industry has a converse side-management of a sudden shortfall in the supply of steel. If such a supply shock does occur and the government is the dominant supplier it is clear that SAIL could operate like a near monopolist and set prices and quantities to improve, if not maximize, its rate of return. Herein lies the pitfall of pre-supposing that a competitive rule is always the best. No general plea for laissez faire should be swallowed. Instead the pricing policy in times of shortfalls and those of plenty must clearly have in mind a clear cut objective as to what such policy is supposed to attain. Needless to say that this clear enunciation of objectives will have to be complemented with a thorough understanding of how steel fits into the general equilibrium of the Indian public sector. Here input-output coefficients are not going to be of much help.

Two very broad guidelines can be offered. The steel industry should be able to survive competitive pressures and, indeed, ought to be compelled to do so. But, when it finds itself in a seller's market it can follow a system of administered prices provided that such prices are consistent with its own objectives and that the absence of market pressures does not lead to designing prices that are essentially a cover for inefficiency.

(*b*) Coal

From steel we move on to an intimately related industry—coal. The coal industry has almost consistently been in the red and follows a system of administered pricing. In finding the price for various varieties and grades of coal the Union Cabinet takes into account the importance of coal in our industrial framework and the sensitivity of other industries to increases in the price of coal. Almost invariably this has meant setting a price below the average cost of production. It hardly need be stated that the government, if it so desired, could change the pricing formula and earn a positive rate of profit and, given its dominat market position, be able to hide the inefficiencies, in the coal industry.

The reasons advanced for underpricing coal are the following (1) Coal is an important input into major industries and an increase in the price of coal would affect them and hence the economy. (2) This (cost push) inflationary impact of an increase in the price of coal is considered to be very significant. Because coal is a valuable input should not necessarily imply that it should be underpriced. We have to compare the inflationary and allocative implications of the deficit financing of the budget due to underpricing of coal with the allocative implications of the full cost pricing of coal to arrive at a sound judgement about this issue. Without such a comparison the case for underpricing is not above criticism.

Time series data on selected aspects of the performance of the coal industry are provided in Tables 19.10-19.13. Even if we discount the profit figures purely on the basis on the pricing formula we can detect inefficiencies,

TABLE 19.10 Performance of Coal Industry

(*Rs. crores*)

Year	*Total Investment*	*Equity*	*Loans*	*Reserves Free*	*Reserves Specific*	*Cumulative Depreciation*	*Net Worth*	*Capital Employed*
1973-74	308.53	186.09	122.44	0.74	8.85	76.18	140.89	206.96
1974-75	474.64	226.41	248.23	0.74	8.07	180.71	183.22	430.36
1975-76	920.86	535.90	384.96	—	8.08	212.07	299.66	708.15
1976-77	1040.15	472.17	567.98	5.66	—	150.59	267.21	618.71
1977-78	1155.53	564.53	591	2.43	4.78	209.12	228.76	732.26
1978-79	1512.55	681.78	830.77	7.82	—	275.56	143.23	757.34
1979-80	1935.05	887.47	1047.58	4.52	8.08	354.24	184.19	937.35
1980-81	2219.19	986.22	1232.87	109.93	5.61	428.38		1026.33

SOURCE: *BPR Annual Survey*

TABLE 19.11 Performance of Coal Industry

(*Rs. crores*)

Year	*Working capital*	*Investments*	*DRE*	*Net Profit*	*Value added*	*Inventories*	*Cost of Sales*
1973-74	60.53	0.31	2.70	—30.41	245.44	63.71	
1974-75	127.98	1.31	6.29	−71.82	342.96	122.01	452.21
1975-76	261.64	5.57	8.66	−32.08	498.39	187.68	616.68
1976-77	159.63	6.91	1.58	−45.49	354.05	189.75	594.78
1977-78	194.28	9.37	2.31	−100.00	360.02	165.10	757.06
1678-79	245.34	10.83	15.51	−217.07	510.84	177.46	777.31
1979-80	241.95	0.32	17.36	−104.04	737.28	244.74	970.86
1980-81	272.40	194.44	2.81	−27.53	1005.67	403.49	1206.16

SOURCE: *BPE Annual Survey*

TABLE 19.12 Performance of Coal Industry

(*Rs. crores*)

Year	*Internal Resources Depreciation*	*Generated Retained profits*	*Total*	*Gross Turnover*
1973-74	13.09	– 30.41	(–) 17.32	
1974-75	28.68	– 71.82	(–) 43.14	397.16
1975-76	33.71	– 32.08	1.63	584.60
1976-77	27.27	– 45.49	– 18.22	662.15
1977-78	36.13	–101.57	– 65.44	651.61
1978-79	52.30	–215.59	–163.29	619.59
1979-80	68.07	–101.93	– 33.86	859.29
1980-81	75.97	– 35.18	40.79	1100.37

SOURCE: *BPE Annual Survey.*

TABLE 19.13 Performance of Coal Industry

(*Percentage of*)

Year	*Net profit to Equity*	*Gross Profit to Capital Employed*	*Net Profit to net Worth*	*Gross Sales to Capital Employed*	*Cost of Sales to Turnover*
1973-74	L	L	L	135.4	
1974-75	L	L	L	100.1	115.05
1975-76	L	L	L	82.6	105.5
1976-77	L	L	L	89.1	
1977-78	L	L	L	89	
1978-79	L	L	L	71.9	
1979-80	L	L	L	89.9	
1980-81	L	10.3	L	105.5	

SOURCE: *BPE Annual Survey.*

TABLE 19.14 Performance of Coal Industry

Name of the Company	*Date of Incorporation*
1. Coal India Ltd. (Holding Co.)	1st November 1975
2. Eastern Coalfields Ltd.	-do-
3. Bharat Coking Coal Ltd.	-do-
4. Central Coalfields Ltd.	-do-
5. Western Coalfields Ltd.	-do-
6. Central Mining, Planning and Design Institute Ltd.	-do-
(Central Mining & Planning deleted in 1977-78 from A/cs.)	

SOURCE: *BPE Annual Survey.*

Note: Before this 3 enterprises were operating in Central Govt. Coal section. viz. Coal Mines Authority Ltd., National Coal Development Corpn. and Bharat Coking Coal Ltd.

because of the steady rise of inventories and the near steadiness of the value added to working capital ratio. This need hardly surprise us because if inflating administered prices can increase inefficiencies deflating these prices need not reduce these inefficiencies.

There are two reasons for justifying the loss situation in coal. Either ore is deliberately underpricing so that productivity can be increased. Implicit here is the thesis that the coal industry is badly managed and the pressures associated with a low price might stimulate productivity.

Or one could argue that coal is too vital an element of cost of its two major consumers. Here we see an element of arbitrariness that needs to be exposed. Isn't cost pricing coal and subsidising electricity production a viable alternative? After all if one is practising retention pricing in fertilizers thus assuring a plant of "satisfactory" rate of return and subsidising the farmers what prevents a similar logic from operating in ths coal industry[6]?

It needs to be mentioned that recurring losses can demoralize an enterprise and its management and can have long term implications for the progress of the industry. This is a matter that is serious enough to merit attention from researchers and administrators.

(*c*) Petroleum

Before discussing petroleum industry it may be useful to note yet another norm for pricing prevalent in the Indian public sector. This is the concept of retention pricing. Here the idea is the following. In the industry under consideration one tries to assess the cost of production of each individual plant. Then one assigns a "satisfactory" rate of capacity utilization say 80 percent and computes the cost of production if this target were achieved and maintained. In computing the price one allows a mark up (say 12 percent post-tax return) over the cost. Departures from planned capacity utilization evokes a penalty or incentive depending on under or over utilization of capacity. This is assuring profitability by design rather than by efficient functioning. In industries where this norm is practised (petroleum fertilizers etc.) there are plants of different vintages. Now, once again if there was a competitive stock market one could compared outputs (for pricing purposes) across different plants because the differences in technology and capital intensities would be reflected in the prices of the shares. In the absence of such a market how does one compare costs across plants of different vintages and arrive at a plant level price? Moreover there is the following incentive problem. The individual plant manager, who presumably knows his plant better than the inspecting team, can overstate his costs by hiding pertinent information. He can then profit from the pricing formula. The incentive implication of such pricing formulae penalize efficiency.

The petroleum industry is a case in point. In recent times in this industry we have attained the 12 percent post-tax return on norm because of this

[6]This does not mean that we condone retention pricing. We will come back to the later in this chapter.

TABLE 19.15 Performance of the Petroleum Industry in Public Sector

(Rs. in crores)

Year	*Equity*	*Loans*	*Total Investment*	*Cummulative Depreciative*	*Reserves*		*Net Worth*	*Capital Employed*	*Value Added*
					Free	*Specific*			
1970-71	220.26	179.48	399.74	109.25	122.78		322.64	444.01	
1971-72	226.36	168.19	394.55	137.27	171.35	4.72	374.30	458.96	
1972-73	228.32	150.66	378.98	171.21	201.49	6.13	407.09	426.60	477.88
1973-74	228.32	131.71	360.03	242.51	208.65	7.73	430.18	471.83	652.72
1974-75	239.66	189.35	429.01	413.38	216.73	30.23	435.26	524.37	275.25
1975-76	271.01	173.69	444.70	485.28	268.56	39.56	524.25	576.94	335.22
1976-77	375.14	273.77	648.91	540.18	374.64	18.12	726.10	800.83	429.72
1977-78	454.60	362.24	816.84	638.33	467.61	21.01	890.65	801.07	740.87
1978-79	466.84	426.37	893.21	603.88	605.26	23.32	1044.10	1347.51	779.84
1979-80	561.53	575.52	1137.05	749.01	721.35	14.40	1173.05	1683.94	871.01
1980-81	580.44	926.18	1506.22	957.98	835.57	28.86		2683.27	1009.01

SOURCE: *BEP Annual Survey.*

TABLE 19.16 Performance of the Petroleum Industry in Public Sector

(*Rs in crores*

Year	*Work Capital*	*Investments*	*DRE*	*Inventories*	*Net Profit*
1970-71	85.96	45.08	19.90	99.06	36.85
1971-72	93.21	48.74	22.35	117.09	49.87
1972-73	84.06	43.69	22.72	110.42	36.77
1973-74	134.77	44.84	6.79	233.09	42.11
1974-75	211.98	29.65	6.69	367.38	87.38
1975-76	190.06	23.80	9.21	401.23	69.22
1976-77	213.03	3.04	18.62	484.97	95.80
1977-78	181.43	3.04	31.56	556.10	129.02
1978-79	233.11	5.57	28.00	651.99	173.19
1979-80	514.50	5.57	24.99	1143.08	158.17
1980-81	1140.14	5.61	13.53	2061.64	156.96

SOURCE: *BPE Annual Survey.*

TABLE 19.17 Performance of the Petroleum Industry in Public Sector

Year	*Ratio of turnovers of Sales to Capital Employed %*	*Percentage of Net Profit to Equity*	*Net Profit to Net Worth*	*Gross Profit to Capital Employed*	*Value Added to Capital Employed*
1970-71	223.0	16.7	11.4	10.6	
1971-72	236	22.1	13.3	14.2	
1972-73	281.7	16.1	9.0	16.5	115.2
1973-74	331.2	18.4	9.8	14.6	149
1974-75	561.5	36.5	20.1	29.6	52.5
1975-76	638.4	26.1	13.2	25.9	58.1
1976-77	577.5	25.5	13.2	26.1	53.7
1977-78	731.9	28.4	14.5	32.5	92.5
	(Net Sales: Cap. Emp.)				
1978-79	471	37.1	16.6	21.8	57.9
1979-80	378.3	28.2	13.5	20.5	51.7
1980-81	331.2	27.1		14.2	37.6

SOURCE: *BPE Annual Survey.*

TABLE 19.18 Performance of the Petroleum Group

Year	*Cost of Sales Rs. crores*	*Ratio of Cost of Sales to Turnover* / *Total Sales Turnover*	*%*
1970-71			
1971-72	992.53	1048.71	94.6
1972-73	1138.56	1201.17	94.6
1973-74	1498.48	1562.81	96.1
1974-75	2802.27	2944.32	95.4
1975-76	3551.67	3683.07	96.4
1976-77	4423.98	4624.49	95.9
1977-78	5624.50	5862.99	95.9
1978-79	6122.16	6349.20	96.58
1979-80	7810.64	8082.42	96.63
1980-81	8740.18	10439.28	83.7

SOURCE: *BPE Annual Survey.*

TABLE 19.19 Performance of Petroleum Industry—Internal Resources Generated

(Rs. in crores)

Year	*Depreciation*	*Retained/ Ratios*	*DRE Written off*	*Total*
1972-73	27.54	28.98	15.06	71.58
1973-74	30.03	62.30		92.33
1974-75	55.58	85.71		141.29
1975-76	79.36	59.69		139.05
1976-77	95.02	73.82		168.84
1977-78	132.84	100.40		233.24
1978-79	126.23	139.35	54.67	320.25
1979-80	143.76	119.63	59.45	322.93
1980-81	224.64	118.25	57.25	400.14

SOURCE: *BPE Annual Survey.*

TABLE 19.20 Performance of the Petroleum Industry in the Public Sector

Name of the Undertaking	*Year of Incorporation*
1. O.N.G.C	1956
2. I.O.C. Ltd.	1959
3. Cochin Refineries Ltd.	1963
4. Madras Refineries Ltd.	1965
5. Hydrocarbon India Ltd.	1965
6. Lubrizol India Ltd.	1966
7. Indo-Burma Petroleum Ltd.	1971
8. Indian Oil Blending Ltd.	1974
9. Hindustan Petroleum Corpn. Ltd.	1974
10. Bharat Petroleum Corpn. Ltd.	1976
11. Caltex Oil Refining India Ltd.	1976

SOURCE: *BPE Annual Survey.*

pricing formula. Tables 19.15-19.20 give the details for the petroleum industry and Tables 19.21-19.25 for ONGC. In the first case the steady drop of value added to capital employed ratio and the build up of inventories leads us to suspect the presence of inefficiencies.

(*d*) Fertilizers

Another case in point is the Fertilizer Corporation of India. The retention price formula is used for individual plants which sell fertilizers to the FCI. The FCI then sells the fertilizers to farmers at a subsidized price. Data at the plant level was hard to get but the FCI data presented in Tables 19.26-19.30 do indicate the magnitude of this difficulty. The FCI has been in the

TABLE 19.21 Oil and Natural Gas Commission Incorporated in 1956

(*Rs. in lakhs*)

Year	Total Investment	Equity Capital	Long term loans	Reserves & Surplus		Depreciation cummulative	Net Worth	Capital Employed
				Free	Specific			
1968-69		12329.5		3559.5	119.6	3419	14356.1	17644.7
1969-70	20314	12434	7880.2	5314.6	146.0	3777.6	16030.5	19679.5
1970-71	21823	12710	9113	6237	177	4958	17026	15163.0
1971-72	22372	13320	9052	8114	209	6056	12958	17346.0
1972-73	22073	13515	8558	8884	247	7600	20186	18778.0
1973-74	21558	13515	8043	8388	287	11680	21279	22042.0
1974-75	20815	13515	7300	4136	346	23039	17048	14146.0
1975-76	28013	16725	11288	6597	1793	26456	22465	23517.0
1976-77	42064	24134	17930	9193	460	25434	31524	39420.0
1977-78	59505	32080	27425	13085	531	31783	42040	43515.0
1978-79	89321	46684	42637	18527	603	24598	48987	84107.0
1979-80	72834	33735	39099	22055	697	31337	53800	89289.0
1980-81	93566	34285	59281	24675	802	43146		114359.0

SOURCE: *BPE Annuel Survey*.

red since 1973-74 and the absolute magnitude of its value added has declined almost continuously since 1971-72. Not all of this can be explained by the rise in the cost of imports. The retention pricing formula used by the FCI must share the blame to some extent.

TABLE 19.22 Oil and Natural Gas Commission—Cost of Sales

(Rs. in lakhs)

Year	*Expenses on Production*	*Accretion in Stock*		*Depreciation Provision*	*DRE Written off*	*Total*
		Finished Goods	*Work in Progress*			
1968-69	809.0	−1.5	—	274.4	868.6	1953.5
1969-70	1024.2	−1.2	—	621.6	830.4	2475.0
1970-71	1174	−1	—	560	1004	2737
1971-72	1526	+2	—	828	1100	3456
1972-73	1817	—	—	864	1500	4181
1973-74	1997	—	—	923	2552	5472
1974-75	6410	—2	—	1187	1496	9091
1975-76	8639	—2	—	1894	2265	12796
1976-77	9370	+2	—	2843	2954	15169
1977-78	11766	2	—	5124	4622	21514
1978-79	15121	1		7426	5461	28009
1979-80	17001	−3		7612	5948	30558
1980-81	15894	4		14142	5719	35759

SOURCE: *BPE Annual Survey.*

TABLE 19.23 Oil and Natural Gas Commission

(Percentage of)

Year	*Working Capital*	*Investments*	*DRE*	*Net Profit to Equity*	*Gross Profit to Capital Employed*	*Net Profit to Net Worth*	*Sales of Capital Employed*
1968-69	4129	2382	1532.9	11.1	8.6	10.6	19.7
1969-70	4133.9	3169	1717.8	9,6	7.3	7.4	19.9
1970-71	4154	4296	1921	7.4	7.8	5.5	25.9
1971-72	4089	4609	2176	9.2	8.6	6.4	28.5
1972-73	4041	4122	2213	5.1	4.9	3.5	27.1
1973-74	5356	4173	624	18.1	12.2	11.5	37.0
1974-75	6733	4322	603	37.9	37.2	30.1	101.5
1975-76	8555	4584	857	14.6	17.0	10.9	71.5
1976-77	8731	2500	1803	15.8	11.6	12.1	50.1
1977-78	8828	2500	3125	16.1	17.0	12.3	66.5
1978-79	12381	2500	2775	21.8	12.2	14.8	45.0
1979-80	11337	2500	1990	16.4	14.6	10.3	48.5
1980-81	13771	2500	1323	13.6	8.2		

SOURCE: *BPR Annual Surrey.*

TABLE 19.24 Oil and Natural Gas Commission Internal Resources Generated

(*Rs. in lakhs*)

Year	*Depreciation*	*Retained Profit*	*Total*	*Net Profit/ Loss*	*Dividend Declared*	*Value of Inventories at the end of the year*	*Value Added*
1968-69				1293.1	—	3342.4	
1969-70	621.6	1900.8	2522.4	1070.4	—	3408.5	
1970-71	560			922	—	3359	
1971-72	828	2312	3140	1212	—	3391	
1972-73	864	2200	3064	700	—	3396	
1973-74	923	5000	5923	2448	—	3499	
1974-75	2683	5077	7760	5126	—	4699	
1975-76	4159	2441	6600	2441	—	8681	
1976-77	5797	2595	8392	3802	1207	10318	
1977-78	9746	3892	13638	5172	1280	9686	20394
1978-79	7426	12903	18329	7252	1810	12044	27287
1979-80	7512	9477	17089	5523	1994	15513	31752
1980-81	14142	8339	22481	4657	2037	22563	33596

SOURCE: *BPE Annual Survey*

TABLE 19.25 Oil and Natural Gas Commission

(*Rs. in lakhs*)

Year	*Total Gross Turnover*	*%age of Cost* of Sales to Net Turnover*	*Net Sales Turnover*	*Cost of Sales*
1968-69	3479.7	56.2	3479	
1969-70	3907.9	63.3	3908	2475
1970-71	3924.9	69.7	3924	
1971-72	4940	69.9	4940	3456.4
1972-73	5095	86.5	5092	4404
1973-74	8160	70.0	8154	5706
1974-75	14353	64.6	14353	9276
1975-76	16803	77.3	16803	12982
1976-77	19740	80.7	19740	15938
1977-78	28919	79.7	28919	23047
1978-79	37815	76.3	37816	24840
1979-80	43326	72.3	43326	27326
1980-81	45003	88.7	45003	35177

*Cost of Sales include Depreciation

SOURCE: *BPE Annual Survey.*

TABLE 19.26 Fertilizer Corporation of India Incorporated in 1961

(*Rs. in lakhs*)

Year	Total Investment	Equity Capital	Loans	Reserves and Surplus		Commulative Depreciation	Net Worth	Capital Employed
				Free Reserves	Specific			
1968-69				1654.6	—	6629.5	8842.3	14550.6
1969-70	20529.2	9655.1	10874.1	1663.6	—	7746.4	11237.4	13349.1
1970-71	22945.5	11555.1	11390.4	1564.8	99.9	8904.3	13071.2	17349.7
1971-72	25228.3	13753.1	11475.2	1733.8	91.0	9990.8	15407.3	15907.3
1972-73	34389	20306	14083	1752	74	11714	21614	11309
1973-74	43705	30107	13598	1618	66	13307	30720	10780
1974-75	59855	42646	17209	1609	—	15004	42904	15191
1975-76	82350	55175	27175	1633	—	16701	52995	17566
1976-77	110995	66275	44720	1478	—	19194	60685	33297
1977-78	129873	75058	54815	1056	1319	22257	62824	30048
1978-79	70894	37413	33481	939	—	8469	24319	2357
1979-80	82249	38481	43768	687	—	9906	19870	23537
1980-81	89990	39561	50429	522		13885		60879

SOURCE: *BPE Annual Survey*.

TABLE 19.27 Fertilizers Corporation of India Cost of Sales

(Rs. in lakhs)

Year	Expenses on Production	Accretion in Stock		Depreciation Provision	DRE Written off	Total
		Finished Goods	Work in Progress			
1968-69	3631.3	−326.2	2.1	842.2	38.6	4188.0
1969-70	5201.1	−482.2	3.0	1159.6	20.7	5902.2
1970-71	5916.6	162.8	−10.7	1182.0	20.7	7271.4
1971-72	7203.8	631.9	−10.8	1145.9	25.8	8996.6
1972-73	7527	109	6	1115	37	8794
1973-74	10195	−282	−10	1187	38	11128
1974-75	16243	—939	− 2	1550	126	16978
1975-76	18226	−670	6	1641	208	19411
1976-77	22573	133	−117	2360	212	25161
1977-78	28044	473	−110	3149	239	31795
1978-79	7807	136	40	496	6	8485
1979-80	8826	−402	−43	1503	19	9903
1980-81	11951	−1060	−45	4110	111	15067

SOURCE: *BPE Annual Survey.*

TABLE 19.28 Fertilizer Corporation of India

(Percentage of)

Year	Working Capital	Invest-ments	DRE	Net Profit to Equity	Gross Profit to Capital Employed	Net Profit to Net Worth	Sales to Capital Employed
1968-69	3191.0	—	87.4	5.6	4.7	4.6	33.5
1969-70	5942.2	—	81.3	0.3	4.1	0.3	39.7
1970-71	7468.2	2	115	0.5	3.0	0.4	44.9
1971-72	6623.6	2	267	1.2	3.1	1.2	74.9
1972-73	2567	2	444	0.1	2.3	0.1	91.1
1973-74	2348	2	1005	L	0.6	L	104.4
1974-75	1396	2	1351	L	1.3	L	113.0
1975-76	3841	2	1357	L	L	L	99.5
1976-77	5841	2	1329	L	L	L	68.8
1977-78	4742	2	1253	L	L	L	89.2
1978-79	—1854	1	579	L	L	L	336.0
1979-80	— 481	—	583	L	L	L	28.1
1980-81	2649	—	480	L	L	L	13.6

SOURCE: *BPE Annual Survey.*

TABLE 19.29 Fertilizer Corporation of India

(*Rs. in lakhs*)

Year	*Internal Depreciation*	*Resources Retained Profit*	*Generated Total*	*Net Profit/ Loss*	*Dividend Declared*	*Value of Inventories at the end of the Year*	*Value Added*
1968-69	842.2			402.5	—	2576.9	
1969-70	1159.6	44.1	1203.7	32.0	—	2920.2	
1970-71	1182.0			56.1	—	2801.8	
1971-72	1145.9	194.8	1340.7	169.0	—	2355.5	5209
1972-73	1115	55	1170	18	—	2554	5189
1973-74	1187	−96	1091	−134	—	2940	4416
1974-75	1676	−71	1605	−77	—	5256	5350
			Cash losses				
1975-76			607	−2456	—	6481	4223
1976-77			873	—3435	—	8188	5830
1977-78			3332	—6720	—	8755	7091
1978-79			1022	—1524	—	2315	1735
1979-80			3341	—4863	—	4159	1603
1980-81			5748	—9969	—	8907	2056

SOURCE: *BPE Annual Survey.*

TABLE 19.30 Fertilizer Corporation of India

(*Rs. in lakhs*)

Year	*Total Gross Turnover*	*%age of Cost of* Sales to Net Turnover*	*Net Sales Turnover*	*Cost of Sales*	*Exports*
1968-69	4879.1	85.7			1
1969-70	6579.9	89.1	6031	5379	16
1970-71	7801.8	92.8			15
1971-72	9501.7	94.5	8962.8	8470.1	204
1972-73	9166	93.6	8451	7909	70
1973-74	11253	101.1	11249	11383	3
1974-75	17173	100.3	17173	17244	20
1975-76	17474	114.0	17471	19927	17
1976-77	22922	115.0	22918	26363	5
1977-78	26816	125.1	26809	33529	5
1978-79	7920	123.6	7920	9335	8
1979-80	6611	180.8	6611	11602	—
1980-81	8337	229.2	8337	19015	—

*(Cost of Sales includes Depreciation)
SOURCE: *BPE Annual Survey*.

Conclusions

In this chapter we have attempted an overall apparaisal of the public sector in India. Thorough work is hampered by the absence of careful analytical understanding of the role of the public sector in India. In such conditions an overall survey cannot get much more sophisticated than what we have attempted here. The tables at the end of this book may help fill in some gaps.

20. India's Tax Structure

In this chapter we briefly want to take a look at the direct and indirect tax structure of India and evaluate its economic effects. Our tax structure is a varied and complex one with various levels of government imposing various kinds of taxes. A detailed study of the effects of all taxes is, therefore, likely to be voluminous and beyond the scope of the present work. In this chapter we want to comment on some of the more important constituents of our tax structure. Our limited ambition here is twofold (*a*) we want to investigate a framework for an integrated study of direct and indirect taxes, (*b*) we want to study some recent attempts to quantify the incidence of various indirect taxes[1] in India.

An Integrated Framework for the Study of Taxes

How should we study the effects of taxes? Ideally one realizes that (at the general equilibrium level) public sector prices and direct and indirect taxes are similar and to some extent substitutable) revenue gathering instruments in the hands of the government and hence should be studied (and applied) together. A full scale analysis covering these three fiscal instruments has not yet been attempted—even theoretically let alone empirically for the Indian case. Recently Murty (1984) has done pioneering work in this area. His work is tentative and can be extended but it stands out as a cogent attempt to come to grips with an important and difficult problem. We will study Murty's work in detail. What Murty is interested in is finding the social value of raising a rupee from alternative sources. In other words he compares the social value of raising a rupee (alternately) from direct taxes, indirect taxes and public sector prices.

Consider an economy having H individuals. There are $n_1 + n_2$ goods in the economy. The first n_1 goods are private sector goods and there are n_2 public sector goods in the economy. The production structure[2] of the economy is described by a matrix A^* where

[1]At no point in this book will we touch upon the important problem of tax avoidance and/or black money.

[2]Throughout fixed coefficients in production are assumed. This is the different from the pricing mechanism studied in Jha and Murty (1986) and discussed in an earlier chapter.

$$A^* = \begin{pmatrix} A & B \\ C & O \end{pmatrix} \tag{1}$$

where A is a square submatrix of order n_1. The elements of this matrix denote commodity input requirement of the private sector (of private sector goods). B is a matrix of order $n_2 \times n_1$ and each column of this matrix represents the requirement of a public sector commodity as an intermediate input in the production of various private sector commodities. C is order $n_1 \times n_2$ and each row of this matrix represents the requirements of various private sector commodities in the production of a unit of a public sector commodity.

We assume constant returns to scale and perfect competition in the private sector so that we can write the consumer price, q, in the private sector as

$$q' = p'A' + \pi'B' + wl' \tag{2}$$

where $p = q + t$ is the producer price vector with t as the vector of indirect tax rates, π is the vector of public sector prices, w is the wage rate of labour (the only primary factor of production) and l is the vector of unit labour requirements in the private sector. From equation (2) we can write

$$\begin{aligned} P' &= \pi'B(I - A')^{-1} + t'(I - A)^{-1} + wl'(I - A')^{-1} \\ &= \pi'B(I - A')^{-1} + t'^* + wl'(I - A')^{-1} \end{aligned} \tag{3}$$

where t^* is $n_2 \times 1$ vector of effective tax rates on private sector commodities that take into account the taxes on direct and indirect requirements of various intermediary inputs that go into the production of a unit of private sector good.

The hth individual has an indirect utility function $V^h(P, \pi, Y^h) h = 1, \ldots, H$ where Y^h is his income. P and π are prices of (final) private and public sector commodities. Social welfare is $W(V^1, V^2, \ldots, V^H)$.

We now discuss the budget of the public sector. We assume that the only sources of government revenue are direct and indirect taxes and public sector prices. We can then write the budget constraint of the public sector as

$$\begin{aligned} &\sum_{i=1}^{n_1} \overset{*}{t_i} x_i + \sum_{h=1}^{H} S^h(Y^h, G_Y) \\ &\qquad + \sum_{j=1}^{n_2} (\pi_j - m_j) x_j - \sum_{j=1}^{n_2} F_j = G \end{aligned} \tag{4}$$

where x_i is final consumption demand of ith private sector commodity,

x is final consumption demand of jth public sector commodity,

x_j is final consumption demand of jth public sector commodity,

m_j is marginal cost of jth public sector good,

F_j is fixed cost in jth public sector good,

S^h is an income tax function that shows the amount of income tax that individual h has to pay as a function of the individual's income and level of income tax revenue of the government

$$G_Y = \sum_{h=1}^{H} S^h(\quad) \text{ and}$$

G is total public sector revenue.

Murty conceives of the social cost of raising a rupee of government revenue as loss in welfare due to transferring a rupee of income from public to government through various sources of revenue for government budget. Thus if σ is the social cost of raising a rupee of government revenue than

$$\sigma = \frac{-\partial W}{\partial G}. \tag{5}$$

We make the simplifying assumption that the pattern of government spending is not related to the manner in which the government collects revenue. Then it is possible to compare σ from different sources i.e. direct tax (σ_D), indirect tax (σ_I) and public sector price (σ_P).

When all the public sector goods are intermediary goods the social welfare function taxes the special form

$$W(V^1(P, Y^1), \ldots, V^H(P, Y^H)).$$

We can then define

$$\sigma_P = -\partial W/\partial \pi_j \Big/ \frac{\partial G}{\partial \pi_j} \tag{6}$$

for raising a rupee of revenue by raising the price of the jth public sector good. We have

$$\frac{\partial W}{\partial \pi_j} = \sum_{i=1}^{n_1} \sum_{h=1}^{H} \frac{\partial W}{\partial V^h} \frac{\partial V^h}{\partial p_i} \frac{\partial p_i}{\partial \pi_j}, \tag{7}$$

$$j = 1, \ldots, n_2.$$

If α^h is thc marginal utility of income of the hth person we have from the property of indirect utility functions

$$\frac{\partial V^h}{\partial p_i} = -\alpha^h x_i. \tag{8}$$

If there are no indirect taxes in the private sector then

$$\frac{\partial p}{\partial \pi} - B'(I - A')^{-1} = D, \tag{9}$$

where D is an $n_2 \times n_1$ matrix. A typical element d_{ij} of D represents the direct and indirect input requirements of the jth public sector intermediary good to produce a unit of ith private sector good. We must then have

$$\frac{\partial p}{\partial \pi_j} = \alpha_j \text{ (}j\text{th column of } D). \tag{10}$$

Substituting equations (10) and (8) in (7), we get

$$\frac{\partial W}{\partial \pi_j} = \sum_{i=1}^{n_1} \sum_{h=1}^{H} \frac{\partial W}{\partial V^h} (-\alpha^h) x_i^h d_{ij}. \tag{11}$$

Let $\beta^h = \frac{\partial W}{\partial V^h} \alpha^h$ be the social marginal utility of income to individual h with government revenue being taken as the numeraire. Let $b^h = \beta^h/\mu$ where μ is the shadow price of government revenue. Hence we get,

$$\frac{-\partial W}{\partial \pi_j} = \sum_{h=1}^{H} \sum_{i=1}^{n_1} b^h x_i^h d_{ij}. \tag{12}$$

If public sector profits are the only source of government revenue it must be true from the public sector budget constraint that

$$\frac{\partial G}{\partial \pi_j} = x_j + (\pi_j - m_j) \frac{\partial x_j}{\partial \pi_j}$$

$$= x_j \left[1 + \frac{(\pi_j - m_j)}{\pi_j} e_j\right], \tag{13}$$

$$j = 1, \ldots, n_2$$

where e_j is the own price elasticity of demand of x_j. We must therefore, have

$$\sigma_{p_j} = -\partial W/\partial \pi_j / \frac{\partial G}{\partial \pi_j}$$

$$= \frac{\sum_{i=1}^{n_1} \sum_{h=1}^{H} b^h x_i^h d_{ij}}{x_j \left[1 + \left(\frac{\pi_j - m_j}{\pi_j}\right) e_j\right]}$$

$$= \frac{\bar{b} \sum_{i=1}^{n_1} \sum_{h=1}^{H} b^h x_i^h x_i d_{ij}}{\bar{b} n_1 \bar{x}_i x_j \left[1 + \left(\frac{\pi_j - m_j}{\pi_j}\right) e_j\right]} \tag{14}$$

with $\bar{b} = \sum_h \frac{b^h}{H}$ and $\bar{x}_i = \sum \frac{x_i^h}{H}$

$$= \frac{\bar{b} \sum_{i=1}^{n_1} R_i x_i d_{ij}}{x_j \left(1 + \left(\frac{\pi_j - m_j}{\pi_j}\right) e_j\right)} \tag{15}$$

where $R_i = \frac{\sum_{h=1}^{H} b^h x_i^h}{H \bar{b} \bar{x}_i}$, is

the distributional characteristic of ith private sector final consumption good.

Now $\sum_{i=1}^{n_1} x_i d_{ij} = x_j$ (total direct and indirect requirements of jth public sector commodity in the production of private sector goods is equal to the net supply in the economy). Hence

$$\sigma_{p_j} = \frac{\bar{b} R_j}{\left[1 + \frac{\pi_j - m_j}{\pi_j} e_j\right]}, \tag{16}$$

$$j = 1, \ldots, n_2$$

where,

$$\bar{R}_j = \sum_{i=1}^{n_1} \frac{R_i x_i d_{ij}}{x_j}$$

is the distributional characteristic of jth public sector intermediary[3] input.

From public sector prices we move to a system of indirect taxes. Let us suppose that indirect taxes are the only source of government revenue. The social welfare function is thus $W(V^1(p, Y'), \ldots, V^H(p, Y^H))$ and if indirect taxes are the only source of government revenue then $G = \sum_{i=1}^{n_1} t_i^* x_i$. Totally differentiating these two relations we have

$$dW = \sum_{i=1}^{n_1} \sum_{h=1}^{H} \frac{\partial W}{\partial V^h} \frac{\partial V^h}{\partial p_i} dp_i + \sum_{h=1}^{H} \frac{\partial W}{\partial V^h} \frac{\partial V^h}{\partial Y^h} dY^h \tag{17}$$

$$dG = \sum_{i=1}^{n_1} \frac{\partial G}{\partial t_i^*} dt_i^* + \sum_{i=1}^{n_1} \frac{\partial G}{\partial x_i} dx_i \tag{18}$$

$$= \sum_{i=1}^{n_1} x_i dt_i^* + \sum_{i=1}^{n_1} t_i^* dx_i.$$

Ignoring income effects we can write equation (17) as

$$dW = \sum_i \sum_h \frac{\partial W}{\partial V^h} \frac{\partial V^h}{\partial p_i} dp_i.$$

If, as assumed here, there is no public sector production we can write

$$dp_i = dt_i^* \tag{19}$$

so that

$$-dW = \sum_{i=1}^{n_1} \sum_{h=1}^{H} b^h x_i^h dt_i^*. \tag{20}$$

We can now use equations (18) and (20) to write

$$\sigma_I = -\frac{dW}{dG} = \frac{\sum_i \sum_h b^h x_i^h dt_i^*}{\sum_i x_i dt_i^* + \sum_i t_i^* dx_i}. \tag{21}$$

[3]If the public sector commodity is a pure consumer good then it can be shown by analogous reasoning that

$$P_j = \frac{R_j}{\left[1 + \left(\frac{\pi_j - m_j}{\pi_j}\right) e_j\right]}$$

where,

$$R_j = \frac{\sum_h b^h x_j^h}{H b \bar{x}_j}$$

is the distributional characteristic of jth public sector final consumption good.

Assuming that the effects of changes in indirect tan revenue due to changes in demand are negligible ($\Sigma t_i^* \, dx_i = 0$) in relation to changes in revenue due to changes in indirect tax rates we can write equation (21) as

$$\sigma_I = \frac{\sum_i \sum_h b^h x_i^h \, dt_i^*}{\sum_{i=1}^{n_1} x_i \, dt_i^*}$$

$$= \frac{\bar{b} \sum_i R_i \, x_i \, dt_i^*}{\sum_i x_i \, dt_i^*} \tag{22}$$

where,

$$R_i = \frac{\sum_{h=1}^{H} b^h x_i^h}{H \bar{b} \bar{x}_i}$$

is the distributional characteristic of ith consumption good. Define the distributional characteristic of indirect tax structure (R_I) as

$$R_I = \frac{\sum_i R_i x_i t_i^*}{\sum_i x_i \, dt_i^*}. \tag{23}$$

R_I is a weighted average of commodity specific R_i the weights being the proportion in which indirect tax revenue is raised through taxes on final consumption goods. Substituting equation (23) into equation (22) we have

$$\sigma_I = \bar{b} R_I \tag{24}$$

We finally move to income taxes. Again we consider them the only source of government revenue so that once again there is no public sector and producer prices equal consumer prices in the private sector. The social welfare function is now

$$W(V^1(p, y^1), \ldots, V^H(p, y^H))$$

where y^h is post-tax income of individual h. Since the only source of government revenue is direct taxes, the public sectors' budget constraint is

$$G = G_y = \sum_{h=1}^{H} S^h(Y^h, G_y) \tag{25}$$

The loss in social welfare due to government raising a rupee of revenue through income taxes can be defined as

$$\frac{-\partial W}{\partial G_y} = \sum_{h=1}^{H} \frac{\partial W}{\partial V^h} \frac{\partial V^h}{\partial y^h} \frac{\partial y^h}{\partial G_y}. \tag{26}$$

We know, however, that

$$\frac{\partial y^h}{\partial G_y} = \frac{-\partial S^h}{\partial G_y}. \tag{27}$$

Substituting equation (27) into (26) we get

$$\frac{\partial W}{\partial G_y} = \sum_h \frac{\partial W}{\partial V^h} \frac{\partial V^h}{\partial y^h} \frac{\partial S^h}{\partial G_y}$$

$$= \sum_h \beta^h \frac{\partial S^h}{\partial G_y}$$

$$= \sum_h b^h \frac{\partial S^h}{\partial G_y}. \tag{28}$$

From equation (25) we know that

$$\sum_h \frac{\partial S^h}{\partial G_y} = 1. \tag{29}$$

Hence the social cost of government raising a rupee of revenue through direct taxes can be defined as

$$\sigma_D = \frac{\partial W}{\partial G_y} = \bar{b} R_I \tag{30}$$

where $$R_I = \sum_h \frac{b^h}{\bar{b}} \frac{\partial S^h}{\partial G_y} \tag{31}$$

is the distributional characteristic of income tax structure in the economy. R_I is defined as the weighted average of social weights of income of different individuals, the weights being the proportions in which incremental income tax revenue is raised.

The essential weaknesses of Murty's model are the following.

(1) The comparison is an all or nothing one that is, when there are direct taxes there are no indirect taxes nor is there any public sector. The comparison is, then, not of incremental changes starting from the existing levels of direct taxes, indirect taxes and public sector prices.

(2) There is the critical assumption of zero income effects for indirect tax and public sector price charges.

(3) Fixed coefficients in production are another serious drawback.

There are many other difficulties with the model but the three mentioned above are potentially quite serious. These difficulties notwithstanding, Murty's paper remains the first (and to date best) attempt to provide an analytical framework to evaluate the economic effects of direct taxes, indirect taxes and public sector prices. Let us look at his empirical results.

To make this model operational the data requirements are (*a*) social weights on the income classes, (*b*) the distribution of final consumption goods among people in different income classes, (*c*) the distribution of public intermediary goods for their direct and indirect uses in the production of various final consumption goods, as determined by the existing production structure of the economy, (*d*) the structure or composition of demand for the final consumption goods, (*e*) direct (and derived) demand elasticities of public sector final consumption (and intermediate) goods, (*f*) the structure of indirect taxes, in the economy, (*g*) the structure of direct taxes in the economy and (*h*) the structure of production in the economy.

Murty's calculations are for the year 1973-74 and in some cases for 1974-75 and 1975-76. Murty uses the input-output tables of the CSO to describe the production structure of the economy. NSS data is used to form estimates of consumer demand and distributional characteristics of final consumption goods. Data released by the Directorate of Inspection gives detailed information on direct tax payments. For indirect taxes the effective rates calculated by Ahmad and Stern (1984) are used.

Murty empirically defines b^h as

$$b^h = \frac{\partial W}{\partial h^h} = \left(\frac{Y_m}{Y^h}\right)^e$$

where Y_m is a critical minimum income (taken alternatively as Rs 800 and Rs 1,200 per annum) and e is the elasticity of social marginal utility.

Murty is thus able to calculate the distributional weights reported in Table 20.1.

Then we move to a discussion of distributional characteristics (R_i) of private sector goods. Murty defines R_i as

$$R_i = \exp\left[-\eta_i e \sigma^2\right]$$

where η_i is income elasticity of demand. The income distribution is approximated by a lognormal probability distribution with variance σ^2. Murty estimates R_i for 18 commodities and these estimates are reported in Table 20.2.

Corresponding values for a representative case of public sector goods are reported in Table 20.3. Thus we are able to calculate the distributional characteristics of the indirect tax structure.

For direct taxes the distributional characteristic is approximated by the relation

$$R_D = \frac{\sum_{j=1}^{17} b_j W_j}{\Sigma S^h}$$

where $$W_j = \frac{x_j dt_j^*}{\Sigma x_j dt_j^*}.$$

We are now able to collate Murty's results. Tables 20.4, 20.5 and 20.6 describe the social cost of raising a rupee of government revenue by raising specific indirect taxes. Table 20.7 compares the social cost of raising a rupee (alternatively) by indirect (as a whole) taxes and direct taxes. Tables 20.8 and 20.9 give corresponding social cost for raising the price of some public sector goods. Broad conclusions that result from the study are as follows:

(*i*) Income taxes are more progressive than indirect taxes. In fact India's indirect tax structure is regressive.

(*ii*) This would imply that a welfare improving tax reform would be to increase income taxes (either the rates or bring more types of income (e.g. black income and agricultural income) in the tax net) and lower indirect taxes. Alternatively (or in conjunction with this) one could move from

TABLE 20.1 Sensitivity of Income Distributional Weights (b^s) and the Average of Income Distributional Weights ($\bar{h}$) with Respect to Elasticity of Social Marginal Utility (e) and Critical Minimum Income (I_m)

Capita Expenditure Class	I_m = *Rs. 800 per annum*				I_m = *Rs. 1,200 per annum*			
	$e = 0.5$	$e = 1$	$e = 2$	$e = 3$	$e = 0.5$	$e = 1$	$e = 2$	$e = 3$
(1)	(2)	(3)	(4)	(5)	(6)	(7)	(8)	(9)
0-13	2.981	8.889	79.014	702.358	3.651	13.333	177.769	2370.192
13-15	2.182	4.762	22.677	107.986	2.673	7.143	51.022	363.453
15-18	2.010	4.040	16.322	65.939	2.462	6.061	36.736	222.655
18-21	1.850	3.421	11.703	40.037	2.265	5.128	26.296	134.848
21-24	1.721	2.963	8.779	26.013	2.108	4.444	19.749	87.765
24-28	1,601	2.564	6.574	16.856	1.961	3.846	14.792	56.889
28-34	1.467	2.151	4.627	9.952	1.796	3.226	10.407	33.573
34-43	1.316	1.732	3.000	5.196	1.612	2.597	6.744	17.515
43-55	1.167	1.361	1.852	2.521	1.429	2.041	4.166	8.502
55-75	1.013	1.026	1.053	1.080	1.240	1.538	2.365	3.638
75-100	0.873	0.762	0.581	0.442	1.069	1.143	1.306	1.493
100-150	0.730	0.533	0.284	0.151	0.894	0.800	0.640	0.512
150-100	0.617	0.381	0.145	0.055	0.756	0.571	0.326	0.186
200	0.577	0.333	0.111	0.037	0.707	0.500	0.250	0.125
	1.155	1.453	2.730	6.986	1.430	2.178	6.139	23.567

SOURCE: Murty (1984).

TABLE 20.2 Sensitivity of Estimates of Distributional Characteristics for NSS Commodity Groups in the year 1973-74.

Commodity Group	*Distributional Characteristics* (R_I)			
	e = 0.5	*e = 1*	*e = 2*	*e = 3*
(1)	(2)	(3)	(4)	(5)
1. Foodgrains	0.945	0.891	0.782	0.638
2. Milk and milk products	0.823	0.668	0.441	0.262
3. Edible oil	0.870	0.757	0.570	0.392
4. Meat, fish and egg	0.854	0.735	0.547	0.384
5. Vegetables	0.888	0.792	0.631	0.479
6. Fruits and nuts	0.776	0.616	0.410	0.277
7. Sugar	0.868	0.748	0.544	0.356
8. Salt	0.955	0.913	0.824	0.660
9. Spices	0.913	0.834	0.689	0.536
10. Beverages and refreshments	0.760	0.596	0.394	0.258
11. Pan, tobacco and intoxicants	0.870	0.769	0.619	0.486
12. Fuel and light	1.253	1.144	0.959	0.775
13. Clothing	0.746	0.563	0.326	0.171
14. Footwear	0.719	0.522	0.283	0.138
15. Misc. goods and services	0.779	0.615	0.391	0.238
16. Durables	0.472	0.357	0.183	0.076
17. Rent	0.671	0.486	0.264	0.130
18. Electricity alone	0.838	0.728	0.503	0.301

SOURCE: Murty (1984).

TABLE 20.3 Estimates of Distributional Characteristics of Public Intermediary Inputs Fertilizers, Cement and Electricity in India

1. Elasticity of social marginal utility (e)	0.5	1.0	2.0	3.0
2. Fertilizers	0.905	0.826	0.690	0.540
3. Cement	0.630	0.464	0.262	0.137
4. Electricity	0.744	0.629	0.444	0.292

SOURCE: Murty (1984).

TABLE 20.4 Estimates of Loss in Welfare by Increasing the Prices of Various Final Consumption Goods by One Rupee Around the Point at which Price is Equal to Marginal Cost (P_1 = one)

Commodity	*e = 0.5*	*e = 1*	*e = 2*	*e = 3*
(1)	(2)	(3)	(4)	(5)
1. Foodgrains	1.351	1.941	4.801	15.036
2. Edible oils	1.244	1.649	3.500	9.238
3. Sugar	1.241	1.629	3.340	8.390
4. Fuel and light	1.792	2.491	5.887	18.264
5. Clothing	1.067	1.226	2.001	4.030
6. Electricity	1.526	1.586	3.088	7.094

SOURCE: Murty (1984).

TABLE 20.5 Estimates of Loss in Welfare by Increasing the Prices of Various Final Consumption Goods by One Rupee Around the Point at which Price-cost Mark up is 10 per cent ($/P_i\, m_i = 1.10$)

	Elasticity of Social Marginal Utility							
	e = .5		*e = 1*		*e = 2*		*e = 3*	
Commodity	*Rural*	*Urban*	*Rural*	*Urban*	*Rural*	*Urban*	*Rural*	*Urban*
(1)	(2)	(3)	(4)	(5)	(6)	(7)	(8)	(9)
1. Foodgrains	1.352	1.351	1.943	1.941	4.806	4.802	15.053	15.039
2. Edible oils	1.248	1.245	1.654	1.650	3.510	3.503	9.265	9.246
3. Sugar	1.246	1.242	1.635	1.630	33.353	3.343	8.423	8.398
4. Fuel and light	1.866	1.927	2.595	2.678	6.132	6.329	19.023	19.637
5. Clothing	1.073	1.147	1.233	1.318	2.013	2.007	4.054	4.333
6. Electricity	1.615	–	1.679	—	3.269	–	7.509	–

SOURCE: Murty (1984).

TABLE 20.6 Sensitivity of Loss in Welfare by Increasing the Prices of Final Consumption Goods by One Rupee with Respect to Price-cost Mark up (p_i/m_i)

	p_i/m_i			
	1.10		*1.15*	
Commodity	*Rural*	*Urban*	*Rural*	*Urban*
(1)	(2)	(3)	(4)	(5)
1. Foodgrains	4.806	4.802	4.809	4.802
2. Edible oils	3.510	3.503	3.515	3.505
3. Sugar	3.353	3.343	3.59	3.344
4. Fuel and light	6.132	6.329	6.244	6.543
5. Clothing	2.013	2.007	2.018	2.010

SOURCE: Murty (1984).

TABLE 20.7 Estimates of Distributional Characteristics of Income Taxes and Indirect Taxes in India

1. Elasticity of social marginal utility (e)	0.5	1.0	2.0	3.0
2. Indirect taxes	0.730	0.591	0.398	0.259
3. Income taxes	0.556	0.365	0.242	0.180

Note: Row (2) is estimated using the data relevant for the year 1973-74 while row (3) is estimated using the data of 1974-75.

SOURCE: Murty (1984).

TABLE 20.8 Estimates of Distributional Characteristics of Public Intermediary Inputs Fertilizers, Cement and Electricity in India

1. Elasticity of social marginal utility (e)	0.5	1.0	2.0	3.0
2. Fertilizers	0.905	0.826	0.690	0.540
3. Cement	0.630	0.464	0.262	0.137
4. Electricity	0.744	0.629	0.444	0.292

SOURCE: Murty (1984).

TABLE 20.9 Estimates of Loss in Welfare by Increasing the Prices of Public Sector Intermediary Goods by One Rupee Around the Point at Price is Equal to Marginal cost ($P_i = m_i$)

Commodity (1)	*e = 0.5* (2)	*e = 1.0* (3)	*e = 1.0* (4)	*e = 3.0* (5)
1. Fertilizers	1.294	1.799	4.236	12.726
2. Cement	0.901	1.011	1.608	3.287
3. Electricity	1.064	1.370	2.726	6.882

SOURCE: Murty (1984).

TABLE 20.9a Estimates of Loss in Welfare by Increasing the Prices of Public Sector Intermediary Goods by One Rupee Around the Point at Which Price-cost Mark up is 10 Percent ($P_i/m_i = 1.10$)

Commodity (1)	*e = 0.5* (2)	*e = 1.0* (3)	*e = 2.0* (4)	*e = 3.0* (5)
Fertilizers	1.561	2.171	5.111	15.354
Cement	1.085	1.397	2.779	7.016
Electricity	1.013	1.420	2.826	7.135

SOURCE: Murty (1984).

taxation of necessities to taxation of business. The quantitative importance of these results depends on society's strength of preperence for less inequality i.e. on *e*.

(*iii*) Necessities have higher distributional characteristics than luxuries.

(*iv*) For certain goods like foodgrains, edible oils, sugar, fuel and light, clothing and electricity it is appropriate to give a subsidy. In other words a subsidy will be welfare improving.

(*v*) Income taxes have the lowest welfare losses followed by profits from cement and textiles and then indirect taxes.

Existing Structure of Direct and Indirect Taxes

In this section we take a brief look at the existing structure of direct and indirect taxes in India. So far as direct taxes are concerned (and we first deal with them) we concentrate exclusively on the personal income tax.

In this area Anupam Gupta and P. Aggarwal have done important work and we take a brief look at their results. If the income tax structure of the economy is progressive then the distribution of post tax incomes should be less unequal than the distribution of pre tax incomes. Individuals constitute 85 to 95 percent of non-corporate assesses and also contribute that percentage of total direct taxes collected from personal incomes. There are some difficulties in the measurement of tax progressivity. What Gupta and Aggarwal do is to compute gross, assessed and net incomes for the population by deceles and also compute appropriate Lorenz ratios. Their results are presented in Tables 20.10 and 20.11. Because of a change in the method of derivation of assessed income from gross income one cannot compare the pre and post 1965-66 figures. Hence two sets of tables are necessary.

Certain broad conclusions can be drawn from the work of Gupta and Aggarwal. For all income groups salary constitutes the largest chunk of total personal income. This importance is much larger for the lower income groups and declines somewhat as incomes rises. Moreover the inequality in types of income other than salaries has grown slightly over the years. The upper income groups earn a disproportionately large amount of interest, rents, dividends etc. Thus the share of the top five percent of assesses in the total dividend income of individuals was 60 percent in 1965-66 and 55 percent in 1969-70 and 1974-75.

To further explore the redistributive (or otherwise) nature of the tax structure one can calculate differences in Lorenz Ratios as in Table 20.12. C is the Lorenz ratios of tax liabilities and t is defined as the "effective" tax rate in the manner of the last column of Table 20.12. Since Δ is positive it is safe to conclude that the personal income tax structure is progressive. But the very small magnitude of Δ suggests that the personal income tax structure is barely progressive. In fact it would be more accurate to call it a linear or proportional tax structure.

From direct taxes we now move to a discussion of the indirect tax structure of the Indian economy.

We have already spent some time on the indirect tax structure of the economy. We want to take a brief look at some aspects of the indirect tax structure left relatively untouched by us so far. In doing this we mainly follow the analysis of Chelliah and Lal (1978). In this work these authors study the incidence of indirect taxes for the year 1973-74 (the latest year for which detailed Annual Survey of Industries data is available).

We look at some of their results. In Table 20.13 we report total indirect taxes as percent total expenditure by various per capita groups.

Chelliah and Lal note that at this level of aggregation the burden of indirect taxation is fairly progressive with the higher expenditure groups paying a much larger proportion of their expenditure as indirect taxes than the less affluent households. This statement, though, is not complete since we do not know whether the rich also pay a higher proportion of their income as indirect taxes. Secondly, it is not immediately clear whether the

TABLE 20.10 Distribution of Assessed Income and Net Income of Individuals from 1953-54 to 1961-62

(Percent of total)

Percentage of Assessees		*1953-54*		*1954-55*		*1960-61*		*1961-62*	
		Assessed income	*Net income*	*Assessed income*	*Net income*	*Assessed income*	*Net income*	*Assessed income*	*Net income*
First	10%	2.56	3.40	2.84	3.11	3.89	4.43	3.54	4.00
Second	10%	3.49	4.28	3.54	4.26	4.38	5.02	4.27	4.98
Third	10%	4.06	5.32	4.45	4.92	4.38	5.02	4.37	4 98
Fourth	10%	4.92	5.96	5.00	5.93	4.69	5.15	4.68	5 08
Fifth	10%	4.92	5.96	5.00	5.93	6.55	7.39	6.51	7.41
Sixth	10%	5.35	6.56	5.53	6.42	6.55	7.40	6.50	7.44
Seventh	10%	7.93	9.38	8.07	9.33	8.07	8.81	7.97	8.66
Eighth	10%	9.39	10.88	9.44	10.44	10.26	11.20	10.22	11.19
Ninth	10%	14.55	16.06	14.48	16.28	14.76	13.68	14.84	13.70
Top	10%	42.83	32.19	41.64	32.88	36.46	31.90	37.10	32.60
Top	5%	31.46	21.03	30.68	21.30	25.76	18.79	26.21	19.25
Top	1%	15.38	7.89	15.37	7.63	10.74	5.75	10.93	5.96
Lorenz Ratio		0.494	0.402	0.479	0.320	0.422	0.355	0.430	0.375

SOURCE: A Gupta (1982).

TABLE 20.11 Distribution of Gross Income, Assessed and Net Income of Individuals from 1965-66 to 1975-76

(Percent of total)

Percentage of Assessees		*1965-66*			*1969-70*			*1974-75*			*1975-76*		
		Gross income	*Assessed income*	*Net income*	*Gross income*	*Assessed income*	*Net income*	*Gross income*	*Assessed income*	*Net income*	*Gross income*	*Assessed income*	*Net income*
First	10%	4.52	4.52	4.67	3.90	3.94	4.41	5.01	4.92	5,60	4.78	4.59	5.26
Second	10%	4.78	4.78	5.24	4.53	4.56	5.28	5.29	5.27	6.15	5.15	5.17	5.97
Third	10%	4.78	4.78	5.59	5.49	5.52	6.32	5.29	5.27	6.15	5.15	5.17	5.97
Fourth	10%	5.28	5.28	5.93	5.49	5.52	6.32	5.29	5.27	6.15	6.41	6.34	6.89
Fifth	10%	7.01	7.02	7.81	5.49	5.52	6.32	6.77	6.76	7.76	7.10	6.98	8.05
Sixth	10%	7.01	7.02	7.81	7.13	7.16	7.66	7.42	7.40	8.70	7.62	7.50	8.05
Seventh	10%	8.01	8.03	8.47	8.24	8.28	8.93	9.88	9.78	10.48	9.99	9.88	11.02
Eighth	10%	10.17	10.18	10.96	10.65	10.71	11.53	10.77	10.64	12.30	10.10	10.00	11.39
Ninth	20%	14.14	14.12	14.90	14.62	14.52	15.26	13.85	13.80	14.03	14.36	14.42	14.17
Top	10%	34.32	34.27	28.62	34.45	34.27	27.97	30.43	30.89	23.68	29.33	29.24	23.22
Top	5%	24.11	24.09	18.48	23.63	23.60	17.38	20.69	21.06	14.32	19.71	20.17	13.89
Top	1%	10.74	10.77	6.26	11.47	9.84	5.76	8.62	8.90	4.12	7.78	8.00	3.96
Lorenz Ratio		0.383	0.382	0.325	0.397	0.391	0.324	0.341	0.345	0.270	0.331	0.338	0.265

SOURCE: Gupta (1982).

TABLE 20.12 Lorenz Ratios and Estimates of Effective Progression

Year	*Lorenz ratio of assessed income* (L_1)	*Lorenz ratio of net income* (L_2)	*Change in Lorenz ratio* $\Delta = L_1 - L_2$	*Progression* $P = C - L = \frac{1-t}{t}\Delta$
1953-54	0.4936	0.4018	0.0918	0.4819
1954-55	0.4788	0.3902	0.0886	0.4034
1960-61	0.4222	0.3546	0.0677	0.4529
1961-62	0.4301	0.3749	0.0551	0.3689
1965-66	0.3816	0.3255	0.0561	0.4541
1969-70	0.3914	0.3245	0.0669	0.4111
1972-73	0.3666	0.2869	0.0797	0.4516
1974-75	0.3455	0.2699	0.0756	0.4285
1975-76	0.3382	0.2675	0.0707	0.4247

SOURCE: Gupta and Aggarwal (1982).

TABLE 20.13 Indirect Taxes as Percent or Total Expenditure and Total Cash Expenditure by Per Capita Expenditure Groups (1973-74)

Monthly per capita expenditure group (in rupees)	*Rural*		*Urban*		*All India*	
	Tax as percentage of total expenditure	*Tax as percentage of total cash expenditure*	*Tax as percentage of total cash expenditure*	*Tax as percentage of total cash expenditure*	*Tax as percentage of total expenditure*	*Tax as percentage of total expenditure*
0-15	2.91	4.55	3.63	4.44	2.96	4.56
15-28	3.33	5.25	6.31	6.79	3.63	5.46
28-43	4.45	7.27	7.36	7.93	4.89	7.41
43-55	6.18	10.32	9.66	10.31	6.85	10.31
55-75	6.71	11.40	11.86	12.70	7.92	11.82
75-100	10.02	16.43	14.80	15.85	11.40	16.21
100 and above	16.17	22.46	30.19	31.35	21.96	26.77
All households	8.03	12.87	17.96	19.03	10.54	14.96

SOURCE: Chelliah and Lal (1978).

result that Chelliah and Lal get is simply due to the particular ranges of expenditure groups chosen. In other words, if classification of tax burden had been done by different expenditure groups then the progressivity may not have been so unambiguous. From Murty's analysis already reported in this chapter we know that this is indeed the case.

In Table 20.14 the burden of indirect taxation as obligations to centre and state governments is detailed. The most important feature of this result is that the centre takes a much larger share of indirect taxes than the states and that this difference is more pronounced for the urban sector.

TABLE 20.14 Central and State Indirect Taxes as Percent of Consumer Expenditure by Per Capita Expenditure Groups (1973-74)

(in rupees)

	Monthly per capita expenditure groups							
	0-15	*15-28*	*28-43*	*43-55*	*55-75*	*75-100*	*100 and above*	*All house-holds*
(1)	(2)	(3)	(4)	(5)	(6)	(7)	(8)	(9)
Rural								
Central taxes	1.68	1.86	2.58	3.68	4.25	6.32	10.30	4.99
Central excise	1.42	1.50	2.01	2.92	3.27	4.85	7.87	3.85
Import duty	0.26	0.37	0.58	0.76	0.99	1.48	2.43	1.14
State taxes	1.23	1.47	1.86	2.50	2.46	3.70	5.87	3.04
Sales tax (including sales tax on motor spirit)	0.67	0.85	1.02	1.23	1.31	1.77	2.60	1.49
State excise	0.22	0.27	0.32	0.63	0.37	0.93	1.82	0.73
Others	0.34	0.35	0.53	0.64	0.78	1.00	1.44	0.83
All indirect taxes	2.91	3.33	4.45	6.18	6.71	10.02	16.17	8.03
Urban								
Central taxes	2.42	3.74	4.56	5.97	7.61	9.41	20.99	12.03
Central excise	2.42	3.11	3.75	4.94	6.25	7.77	16.78	9.73
Import duty	—	0.63	0.81	1.03	1.36	1.63	4.21	2.30
State taxes	1.21	2.57	2.80	4.69	3.25	5.40	9.20	5.93
Sales tax (including sales tax on motor spirit)	0.30	1.63	1.86	2.35	2.69	3.01	4.51	3.23
State excise	—	0.13	0.02	0.20	0.16	0.79	2.27	1.01
Others	0.91	0.82	0.92	1.14	1.41	1.60	2.41	1.69
All indirect taxes	3.63	6.31	7.36	9.66	11.86	14.80	30.19	17.96

(Contd.)

(1)	(2)	(3)	(4)	(5)	(6)	(7)	(8)	(9)
Rural and Urban								
Central taxes	1.72	2.05	2.88	4.13	5.04	7.21	14.71	6.77
Central excise	1.47	1.66	2 27	3.31	3.97	5.69	11.55	5.34
Import duty	0.24	0.39	0.61	0.81	1.07	1.52	3.16	1.43
State taxes	1.24	1.58	2.01	2.73	2.88	4.19	7.24	3.77
Sales tax (including sales tax on motor spirit)	0.65	0.93	1.16	1.44	1.63	2.13	3.39	1.93
State excise	0.21	0.25	0.27	0.54	0.32	0.89	2.01	0.80
Others	0.39	0.41	0.59	0.74	0.92	1.18	1.84	1.04
All indirect taxes	2.96	3.63	4.89	6.85	7.92	11.40	21.96	10.54

SOURCE: Chelliah and Lal (1978).

TABLE 20.14a Tax Burden as Percent of Consumer Expenditure on All Indirect Taxes According to Type of Goods

(in rupees)

	Monthly per capita expenditure groups							
	0-15	*15-28*	*28-43*	*43-55*	*55-75*	*75-100*	*100 and above*	*All households*
(1)	(2)	(3)	(4)	(5)	(6)	(7)	(8)	(9)
Rural								
1. Consumption goods	1.28	1.51	2.08	3.20	3.16	5.18	8.53	4.05
2. Intermediate goods	1.47	1.62	2.10	2.63	3.17	4.32	6.78	3.53
3. Capital goods partly capital goods and parts thereof	0.16	0.21	0.27	0.35	0.39	0.53	0.86	0.45
4. Total (all indirect taxes)	2.91	3.34	4.45	6.18	6.72	10.03	16.17	8.03
Urban								
1. Consumption goods	1.82	3.06	3.62	5.16	8.36	8.38	14.78	9.17
2. Intermediate goods	1.81	2.90	3.38	4.10	5.00	5.80	12.57	7.48
3. Capital goods, partly capital goods and parts thereof	—	0.35	0.36	0.40	0.50	0.62	2.84	1.31
4. Total (all indirect taxes)	3.63	6.31	7.36	9.66	11.86	14.80	30.19	17.96
Rural and Urban								
1. Consumption goods	1.32	1.66	2.31	3.58	3.91	6.10	11.11	5.34
2. Intermediate goods	1.47	1.75	2.30	2.91	3.59	4.75	9.17	4.53
3. Capital goods partly capital goods and parts thereof	0.16	0.22	0.28	0.36	0.42	0.55	1.68	0.67
4. Total (all indirect taxes)	2.95	3.63	4.89	6.85	7.92	11.40	21.96	10.54

SOURCE: Chelliah and Lal (1978).

Chelliah and Lal also estimate the burden of indirect taxation for different commodities by three broad categories of indirect taxes viz. central excise import duties and state taxes. The results are reported in Tables 20.15, 20.16 and 20.17 respectively. The major difference between these three tax categories is the following. In the case of central excise and import duties the burden falls heavily on intermediate goods. 55 percent of the incidence of central excise and 67 percent of the incidence of import duties are due to taxes on intermediate goods. In the case of state taxes consumer, goods are much more important than intermediate goods.

Conclusions

In this chapter we tried to do two things. We first tried to study a framework for evaluating direct and indirect taxes and public sector prices in India. We studied Murty's work in this area in some detail. We pointed out the many drawbacks of his analysis and also indicated that a framework was nevertheless necessary for evaluating taxes and public sector prices.

Secondly we provided a brief description of the direct and indirect tax structures of India.

TABLE 20.15 Burden of Central Excises as Percent of Consumer Expenditure According to Type of Goods

(in rupees)

	Monthly per capita expenditure groups							
	0-15	*15-28*	*28-43*	*43-55*	*55-75*	*75-100*	*100 and above*	*All households*
Rural								
1. Consumption goods	0.39	0.39	0.61	1.16	1.21	2.11	3.64	1.57
2. Intermediate goods	1.03	1.10	1.39	1.74	2.04	2.70	4.13	2.24
3. Capital goods, partly capital goods and parts thereof	—	0.01	0.01	0.02	0.02	0.04	0.10	0.04
4. Total central excise	1.42	1.50	2.01	2.92	3.27	4.85	7.87	3.85
Urban								
1. Consumption goods	0.61	1.13	1.51	2.25	3.03	3.91	7.00	4.28
2. Intermediate goods	1.81	1.96	2.22	2.67	3.19	3.76	8.70	5.04
3. Capital goods partly capital goods and parts thereof	—	0.02	0.02	0.02	0.03	0.10	1.08	0.41
4. Total central excise	2.42	3.11	3.75	4.94	6.25	7.77	16.78	9.73
Rural and Urban								
1. Consumption goods	0.41	0.46	0.74	1.37	1.63	2.62	5.03	2.25
2. Intermediate goods	1.06	1.19	1.52	1.92	2.31	3.01	6.01	2.95
3. Capital goods partly capital goods and parts thereof	—	0.01	0.01	0.02	0.03	0.06	0.51	0.14
4. Total central excise	1.47	1.66	2.27	3.31	3.97	5.69	11.55	5.31

—indicates negligible.

SOURCE: Chelliah and Lal (1978).

TABLE 20.16 Burden of Import Duties as Percent of Consumer Expenditure According to Type of Goods

(*in rupees*)

	Monthly per capita expenditure groups							
	0-15	*15-28*	*28-43*	*43-55*	*55-75*	*75-100*	*100 and above*	*All households*
Rural								
1. Consumption goods	0.02	0.04	0.11	0.16	0.24	0.34	0.56	0.25
2. Intermediate goods	0.23	0.30	0.42	0.52	0.67	1.01	1.65	0.79
3 Capital goods, partly capital goods and parts thereof	0.01	0.03	0.05	0.08	0.08	0.13	0.22	0.10
4. Total import duties	0.26	0.37	0.58	0.76	0.99	1.48	2.43	1.14
Urban								
1. Consumption goods	—	0.09	0.15	0.20	0.28	0.34	1.37	0.65
2. Intermediate goods	—	0.48	0.60	0.76	0.97	1.15	2.54	1.48
3. Capital goods, partly capital goods and parts thereof	—	0.06	0.06	0.07	0.11	0.14	0.30	0.17
4. Total import duties	—	0.63	0.31	1.03	1.36	1.63	4.21	2.30
Rural and Urban								
1. Consumption goods	0.02	0.04	0.12	0.17	0.25	0.34	0.90	0.35
2. Intermediate goods	0.21	0.32	0.44	0.56	0.73	1.05	2.02	0.96
3. Capital goods partly capital goods and parts thereof	0.01	0.03	0.05	0.08	0.09	0.13	0.25	0.12
4. Total import duties	0.24	0.39	0.61	0.81	1.07	1.52	3.17	1.43

—indicates negligible.

SOURCE: Chelliah and Lal (1978).

TABLE 20.17 Burden of State Taxes as Percent of Consumer Expenditure According to Type of Goods

(*in rupees*)

	Monthly per capita expenditure groups							
	0-15	*15-28*	*28-43*	*43-55*	*55-75*	*75-100*	*100 and above*	*All households*
Rural								
1. Consumption goods	0.87	1.08	1.36	1.38	1.71	2.73	4.33	2.23
2. Intermediate goods	0.21	0.22	0.29	0.37	0.46	0.61	1.00	0.50
3. Capital goods, partly capital goods and parts thereof	0.15	0.17	0.21	0.25	0.29	0.36	0.54	0.31
4. Total state taxes	1.23	1.47	1.86	2.50	2.46	3.70	5.87	3.04
Urban								
1. Consumption goods	1.21	1.84	1.96	2.71	3.05	4.13	6.41	4.24
2. Intermediate goods	—	0.46	0.56	0.67	0.84	0.89	1.33	0.96
3. Capital goods, partly capital goods and parts thereof	—	0.27	0.28	0.31	0.36	0.38	1.46	0.73
4. Total state taxes	1.21	2.57	2.80	3.69	4.25	5.40	9.20	5.93
Rural and Urban								
1. Consumption goods	0.89	1.16	1.45	2.04	2.03	3.14	5.18	2.74
2. Intermediate goods	0.20	0.24	0.34	0.43	0.55	0.69	1.14	0.62
3. Capital goods, partly capital goods and parts thereof	0.15	0.18	0.22	0.26	0.30	0.36	0.92	0.41
4. Total state taxes	1.24	1.58	2.01	2.73	2.88	4.19	7.24	3.77

—indicates negligible.

SOURCE: Chelliah and Lal (1978).

21. Centre-State Financial Relations

India has opted for a federal structure of government. This kind of arrangement can, in some sense of the term, be considered a compromise between two types of forces. On the one hand we have a system with several more or less autonomous units and a unitary form of government. The first arrangement satisfies needs of "regional autonomy" whereas the latter has the distinct advantage of providing a large market with unhampered flow of goods and factors of production. This clearly allows industries to reap advantages of economies of scale. In a planning context this would also mean that a unitary structure would be more conducive to the resolution of secondary uncertainty. In a large country the coordination of the steel producer's activities with those of the railways and the coal producer is going to be relatively easier than in a small country with limited resources and markets.

The fact that a federal structure is a compromise between two different notions of government means sometimes, that managing federal finance is a difficult and slightly delicate job. There is the distinct possibility that the structure of federal finance adopted may please neither those who support unitary government nor those who want more autonomy for states.[1] However the federal structure does indeed exist even if it is not able to strike the right balance between the various competing claims on it.

The government has broadly, but never exclusively, entrusted the task of guiding centre-state financial relations to a Finance Commission. The Constitution has laid down the following principles for the Finance Commission (under Article 280, clause 3):

> "It shall be the duty of the Finance Commission to make recommendations the President as to:
>
> (*a*) the distribution between the union and the states of the net proceeds of taxes which are to be, or may be, divided between them . . . and the allocation between the states of the respective shares of such proceeds.
>
> (*b*) the principles which should govern the grants-in-aid of the revenues of the states out of the consolidated fund of India;

[1]Thus some people want a strong centre whereas others make the equally insane remark that strong states mean a strong centre.

(*c*) the continuance or modification of the terms of any agreement entered into by the Government of India with the government of any state . . ., and

(*d*) any other matter referred to the commission by the President in the interest of sound finance".

One can, in general, visualise the problems of federal finance as falling in two groups. At the one level one has to sort out the difficult problem of the division of tax powers between centre and states and spell out clearly the responsibilities at both levels. Whereas a satisfactory answer to this question lays down the basic framework of centre-state relations there still remains the question of out-of-the-ordinary intervention by the centre. Such intervention can, in general, take three forms (*i*) to bring about a nationally acceptable solution when the autonomous action of concerned states may lead to non-efficient solutions. (The sharing of the waters of a river that flows through two or more states is a classic example of this problem), (*ii*) to reduce inequalities between the different regions of a country; (*iii*) to formulate guidelines for helping states at the time of natural disasters.

Having said this, however, we realise that the Finance Commission alone cannot (and should not) be permitted to solve the difficult problems faced by it. In particular, a harmonious, equitable and efficient delegation of financial powers between centre and states must be an integral part of the overall investment and planning objectives of the economy.

In retrospect it appears that the sentiments that guided the creation of the Finance Commission were not consistent with the guiding principles of planned economic development adopted by the policy makers. On the one hand planned economic development has invariably led to greater concentration of power with the centre and on the other, much greater access to financial resources for the centre. In many instances, it has been argued that in the case of a country like India such centralization is necessary. Such arguments would make some sense if one had the evidence that this centralization had indeed made a dent on the many serious problems facing the country. We know that the grave problems of hunger, unemployment, poverty, industrial stagnation, regional disparities have not been solved. In fact many of these problems have only been exacerbated. The rationale for such an overdose of centralization seems to be a very weak one. On can take this centralization phobia to rather extreme limits. Thus, for instance, although the draft Seventh Five-Year Plan got the approval of the National Development Council (of which the states are members) only recently it is supposed to be in operation since 1 April, 1985. Another very sobering realization is the fact that recently only about 43 percent of fiscal transfer to states has been effected through the Finance Commission. Institutions have been diluted in India but when things get stretched to such limits it becomes hard to talk about "objective criteria" for determining fiscal transfers to states.

This kind of idiosyncratic planning mechanism has resulted in many anomalies—particularly for centre-state financial relations. Thus states particularly less affluent states—have become more or less dependent on the centre for their finances. In the hope of acclerating the rate of industrial development the centre had invested heavily in the more affluent. But this industrial strategy has not paid off particularly for the weaker states. This has meant that they remain hopelessly dependent on the centre while the stronger states have resisted pressures for transfers to the weaker states.

Moreover since much of fiscal transfers to the states is in the form of loans, debt servicing has become a very important component (in some states the second largest component of non-plan expenditure) of expenditure. This naturally means that less is left for development purposes.

Next for every function allocated to the states there is a ministry or department in New Delhi. This arrangement has some justification. If the programme involves more than one state one needs a coordinating body to help in implementation. Such a body would also be more able to engage in research and development activities. However given that less than half the financial transfers from centre to states occur via the Finance Commission these departments/ministries have become a major force in determining transfer to states. Many a time such transfers are distinctly politically motivated.

This, of course, also means that the state governments effectively become less accountable to the people of the state and more to the coordinating departments/ministries. Apart from being arbitrary this is also undemocratic.

There is the further problem that states often take large overdrafts from the Reserve Bank of India. Some of these overdrafts (and the previously mentioned loans) get written off depending on political circumstances.

It becomes hard, then, to think of centre-state financial relations in India in purely theoretical/analytical terms. Since this is not a treatise on political economy we will confine ourselves to the formal part of this labyrinth—the Finance Commissions proper.

The Approach of the Finance Commissions

The First Finance Commission was asked to attend to its constitutional duties. It was further required to recommend grants-in-aid to states who had lost revenue because of the abolition of the export tax on jute (which had hitherto gone to the states). Moreover, it was asked to determine the amount of general purpose grants-in-aid which were to go to the states.

With the appointment of the Second Finance Commission the country had begun a much published drive toward industrialization with the implementation of the Second Five-Year Plan. The Second Finance Commission was then additionally asked to determine grants-in-aid to be paid to states (*i*) help them meet the requirements for the Second Five-Year Plan, and (*ii*) help them mobilize more resources in the long run. What should be noted here is that these additional clauses were added on only in the case of those states which were in need of funds.

The guidelines issued to the Third Finance Commission were the same as those issued to the second.

When the Fourth Finance Commission was appointed a major transformation was effected in that the commission was asked not merely to determine amounts of grants-in-aid but also some norms by which states could economise on their administrative expenditures.

Another major break that the Fourth Finance Commission made with the past was that the grants-in-aid were made independent of the ensuing plan. The Third Finance Commission had (unsuccessfully) tried to give 75 percent of their plan expenditure to the states as grants-in-aid. With the appointment of the Fourth Finance Commission it was felt that plan expenditures of the states should be handled by the Planning Commission.

The Fourth Finance Commission was further asked to scrutinize the revenue records and sources of the state governments and determine the committed (plan) expenditure and debt servicing of the states. It should be noted that different items on the revenue and expenditure accounts were sought to be scrutinized. But here lies the beginning of the approach that came to be known as the gap filling approach. Like the previous commissions this one was also asked to confine grants-in-aid to only those states that needed them.

In a major break with the past the Fifth Finance Commission was asked to determine the principles by which grants-in-aid were to be made. Previous commissions had confined themselves only to the amounts of the grants-in-aid. The consideration which the commission was asked to bear in mind in making recommendations were the following. First one the revenues available at base year rates of taxation. The expenditure to be covered included (*a*) administration, (*b*) interest charges, (*c*) upkeep of plan schemes, (*d*) transfer of funds to local bodies and aided institutions (*e*) other committed expenditure. The Commission was expected to fill in the gap between projected[2] revenues and expenditures but in doing so it was also asked to advise on better fiscal management and economy.

The Sixth Finance Commission was specially asked to keep in mind "provision for emoluments of government employees, teachers and local body employees as obtaining on a specified date as the Commission deem it proper in the light of the States' capacity and needs . . ." Additionally the commission was asked to keep in mind.

(*i*) the requirements of states which are backward in standards of general administration,

(*ii*) adequate maintenance and upkeep of assets and plan schemes and

(*iii*) the existing practice in regard to determination and distribution of Central assistance for financing state plans.

The Seventh and Eighth Finance Commissions had similar obligations.

Each of these Commissions have worked under severe constraints. Firstly in making its recommendation the Finance Commission takes the level of

[2]This finance commission was asked to forecast expenditure as well as revenues.

state revenue as that given by tax receipts of the last year of the previous plan. However, it has to make forecasts of revenue and receipts for each year of the next plan. There is an identification problem here in that the levels of receipts and expenses for the plan depend critically on the available finances. Hence, it will not be possible, in principle, to predict revenues and receipts without determining the amount and type (loan, grant etc.) of finance available to the States.

There are other difficulties with the method of forecast. We realise that non-plan expenditure of states comprises, in addition to the usual recurring expenditure of states, committed expenditure resulting from the past plans, interest payments resulting from the loan component of planning assistance provided for the past plans and discretionary expenditure plans (already mentioned above). All these elements have to forecasted. Given the identification problem already talked about above, we realise that such prediction is fairly ad hoc. Related to this is the difficulty that since no one knows what loans will be taken by the states during the plan period only those loans that are contracted starting from the base year of the plan are taken into account for determining interest payments. Hence there is an implicit bias in favour of those states that do some of their borrowing during the plan and against those states who contract for all or most of their loans during the base year of the plan. Similar comments apply to predicting nominal receipts/expenses. Inflation forecasting is purely ad hoc.

Another area of difficulty is in determining the amount of surplus to be left in non-plan revenue of deficit states. The Finance Commission has to predict the surplus and deficit of various states after taking into account the division of the two shared resources viz. national income tax and central excise duties. After this the grants-in-aid of those states that are in deficit or marginally in surplus are to be determined. The balance on a state's current account is extremely important as a source of finance for the state's plans. Thus the surplus—which is at least partly determined by the central governments' actions—is of vital importance in determining the size of the states' plans.

Those states which fail to generate sufficient surplus either go in for additional resource mobilisation (another method of harnessing resources) or turn again to the union government. Those states which have rather limited flexibility to collect resources through the first method invariably get increasingly dependent on the Central government. This has often turned out to be a vicious circle.

Another important problem in this area is the fact that states with greater flexibility in their revenue sources can get systematic benefits from the rules of the Finance Commission. As an example of this we can take the famous day meal scheme for school children instituted in Tamilnadu. The state government had enough resources to begin this programme on its own. Once the programme was begun it was counted as non-plan expenditure by the state. Subsequent finance commissions, then, used this expense as non-plan expenditure in determining the allocation to Tamilnadu.

One tends to suspect, then, that there are built in bases (intended or unintended) in favour of the more affluent states. Moreover over the years certain specific problems have arisen that have not been satisfactorily resolved by the Finance Commission. Thus the corporation tax—which was introduced in 1959—is not meant to be shared. One must remember, though, that the states played a major role in the evolution of the corporation tax and further that, over the years, the corporation tax has proved to be a fairly elastic source of revenue. This becomes particularly important in the face of the fact that the income tax whose receipts are shared with the states—has been virtually exhausted as a source of revenue. Both the Seventh and the Eighth Finance Commissions recommended that 85 percent of the receipts from the income tax be given back to the states. It is not possible to push further in this direction.

The other shared revenue is excise duties. They are certainly more elastic than income taxes. However in recent years one has experienced two problems with this source. One is that the central government takes up 11 percent of the collections as duties or cesses which are not to be shared with the states. Secondly, the central government has made it a habit to substitute increases in administered prices of public sector goods for increases in excise duties. The profits of the public sector are not shared with the states.

Having outlined some major difficulties in centre-state financial relations let us now move to a consideration of the actual working of the revenue sharing mechanisms. We first discuss sharing of tax revenue and then the disbursal of grants-in-aid.

Let us first look at the sharing of income tax receipts.

The first finance commission recommended 55 percent of the net yield from union excise duties on three taxable goods. The sharing of the proceeds from income tax could be expressed by the following equality.

$$Y_{s_i} = (55/100 \cdot Y)\left(80/100 \frac{n_i}{N} + \frac{20}{100}\frac{Y_i}{Y}\right) \tag{1}$$

where Y_{s_i} is share of ith state indivisible pool of income tax,

Y is total divisible net yield from income tax excluding the share of union territories,

Y_i is gross yield of income tax originating in ith state,

n_i is population of ith state

N is total population of all states.

In successive Finance Commissions this formula was altered as:

$$Y_{s_i} = (60/100Y)\left(90/100\frac{n_i}{N} + \frac{10}{100}\frac{Y_i}{Y}\right) \tag{2}$$

for the Second Finance Commission.

$$Y_{s_i} = (66.6/100Y)\left(\frac{80}{100}\frac{n_i}{N} + \frac{20}{100}\frac{Y_i}{Y}\right) \tag{3}$$

for the Third Finance Commission

$$Y_{s_i} = (75/100Y)\left(\frac{80}{100}\frac{n_i}{N} + \frac{20}{100}\frac{Y_i}{Y}\right) \tag{4}$$

for the Fourth Finance Commission

$$Y_{s_i} = \left(\frac{75}{100}Y\right)\left(\frac{90}{100}\frac{n_i}{N} + \frac{10}{100}\frac{Y_i}{Y}\right) \tag{5}$$

for the Fifth Finance Commission

$$Y_{s_i} = \left(\frac{80}{100}Y\right)\left(\frac{90}{100}\frac{n_i}{N} + \frac{10}{100}\frac{Y_i}{Y}\right) \tag{6}$$

for the Sixth Finance Commission

$$Y_{s_i} = \left(\frac{85}{100}Y\right)\left(\frac{90}{100}\frac{n_i}{N} + \frac{10}{100}\frac{Y_i}{Y}\right) \tag{7}$$

for the Seventh and Eighth Finance Commissions.

The successive Finance Commissions merely increased the share of states without affecting in any major way the distribution among the states. We must also remember that since 1959 (when the corporation tax was introduced) the states have been denied a share in it.

In determining the distribution of excise duties between centre and states two steps are involved. First the distribution between the centre and states (as a block) is determined. Then a different set of criteria is used to determine the distribution of the proceeds among the states. Table 21.1 illustrates the Finance Commissions' approach to the first problem. In the first column of Table 21.1, we list the particular finance commission we are talking about. In the second column we list the commodities on which excise duty was imposed and the proceeds shared with the states. The third column indicates the share of the proceeds going to the states. The fourth, fifth, sixth and seventh columns are the various criteria that have been used by the various finance commissions. The weights attached to the various criteria are shown in the columns.

We now come to the criteria used for distribution of proceeds among the states. The criteria used by successive finance commissions are as follows

$$Z_i = \left(\frac{40}{100}\cdot T_3\right)(\alpha_i \cdot 100) \tag{8}$$

for the First Finance Commission

$$Z_i = \left(\frac{25}{100}\cdot T_8\right)(\alpha_i \cdot 100) \tag{9}$$

for the Second Finance Commission

$$Z_i = \left(\frac{20}{100}T_{35}\right)(\alpha_i + \beta_i + \delta_i)\cdot 100 \tag{10}$$

TABLE 21.1 States' Share in the Net Yield From Union Excise Duties

Finance Commission	*Coverage (net yield from Union excise duties on)*	*States' share (percent)*	Criteria used for distribution among the states *Proportion of population of the state to the total population all states*	*Per capita income*	*Economic or social back-wardness*	*Other criteria*
(1)	(2)	(3)	(4)	(5)	(6)	(7)
First	Three commodities tobacco, matches and vegetable products.	40	100	—	—	—
Second	Eight commodities; tobacoo, matches, vegetable products, sugar, coffee, tea. paper and vegetable non-essentials.	25	29	—	—	10 percent used for adjustment
Third	All commodities on which Union excise duties collected in 1960-61 amounted to Rs 50 lakhs or more, (about 35).	20	Mainly on the basis of population along with relative financial weakness and economic backwardness as other factors.			
Fourth	All commodities excluding regulatory duties, special excise and earmarked cesses.	20	80	20 According to relative backwardness as indicated by seven[a] factors.		
Fifth	For 1969-70 to 1971-72 all types of Union excise duties excluding regulatory duties, special excises and duties and earmarked cesses; for 1972-73 and 1973-74 all types of Union excise duties including regulatory duties and earmarked cesses.	20	80	13.3 Distributed among only those states whose per capita income was below the all states average; in proportion to the shortfall of the state's per capita income from all states' average multiplied by the population of the concerned State		6.7 According to an integrated index of backwardness as indicated by six[a] factors.

(*Contd.*)

(1)	(2)	(3)	(4)	(5)	(6)	(7)
Sixth	For 1974-75 and 1975-76 all articles on which Union excise duties were levied excluding auxiliary duties of excise and cesses levied under special Acts and earmarked for special purposes.	20	75		25 According to the difference between a state's per capita income and that of the highest per capita income multiplied by the population of the concerned state.	
Seventh	Net proceeds from all Union excise duties collected on all commodities excluding the net proceeds of the duty on the generation of electricity.	40	25	25 Inverse ofper capita state domestic product	25 Percentage of poor or people below absolute poverty line as estimated by one of the members of the Commission.	25 According to a formula of revenue equalisation.[4]

Notes: (1) They include:

(*i*) relative financial weakness of the states
(*ii*) disparity in the levels of development reached
(*iii*) percentage of scheduled caste/tribe and other backward class population, etc.

(2) They include:

(*i*) per capita gross value of agricultural production
(*ii*) per capita value added by manufacture
(*iii*) percentage of workers to the total population
(*iv*) percentage of enrollment of children of school going age
(*v*) population per hospital bed
(*vi*) percentage of rural population
(*vii*) percentage of scheduled caste/tribe population.

(3) They include:

(*i*) percentage of scheduled tribe population
(*ii*) number of factory workers per lakh of population
(*iii*) net irrigated area per cultivator
(*iv*) length of railway lines and surfaced roads per 100 sq. km.
(*v*) percentage of children of school-going age not attending school
(*vi*) number of hospital beds per 1000 population.

(4) The percentage of the product of the different of the estimated per capita revenue potential (using Frank's index) of the state from that of Panjab and the population of each state in the total of these products for all states gives the share of each state in 25 percent component of the divisible pool of Union excise duties.

SOURCE: Compiled from the Reports of various Finance Commissions.

for the Third Finance Commission.

$$Z_i = \left(\frac{20}{100} T_a\right)\left(\frac{80}{100}\alpha_i + \frac{20}{100}\gamma_i\right) \tag{11}$$

for the Fourth Finance Commission

$$Z_i = \left(\frac{20}{100} T_a\right)\left(\frac{80}{100}\alpha_i + \frac{13.3}{100}(\bar{a} - a_i)\alpha_i + 6.7/100\rho_i\right) \tag{12}$$

for the Fifth Finance Commission

$$Z_i = \left(\frac{20}{100} u_a\right)\left(\frac{75}{100}\alpha_i + \frac{25}{100}(a - a_i)\alpha_i\right) \tag{13}$$

for the Sixth Finance Commission

$$Z_i = \left(\frac{40}{100} \cdot u_a\right)\left(\frac{25}{100}\alpha_i + \frac{25}{100}\frac{1}{a_i} + \frac{25}{100} \cdot \eta_i + \frac{25}{100} k_i\right) \tag{14}$$

for the Seventh Finance Commission

Z_i is share of *i*th state in divisible pool of union excise duties.
T_3 is net yield from union excise duties on three commodities.
T_8 is net yield from union excise duties on eight commodities.
T_{35} is net yield from union excise duties on 35 commodities.
T_a is net yield from union excise duties on all commodities.
α_i is percentage of scheduled caste/tribe and other backward class population with state.
β_i is relative financial weakness of *i*th state.
δ_i is relative backwardness of *i*th state as given by six indicators.
γ_i is relative backwardness of *i*th state as given by seven indicators.
ρ_i is relative disparity in the level of development reached by the *ith* state.
$\bar{a}$ is average per capita income of all states.
a_i is per capita income of *i*th state.
a is highest per capita income (of Panjab).
k_i is percentage of the product of the gap between the per capita estimated revenue of the *i*th state from the per capita revenue from Panjab.
η_i is the percentage of scheduled caste/tribe backward class of state *i* in the population below the absolute povery line in state *i*.

One sees in these equalities a tendency on the part of the Finance Commissions to be more equitable. The Eighth Finance Commission' formula was much like that of the Seventh Finance Commission's. One can see that the Seventh Finance Commission's formula is most comprehensive.

Some other minor taxes and duties are also shared between the centre and states. These include property tax, railway passenger fares, tax on agricultural property etc. The distribution of these proceeds is largely guided by constitutional and legal requirements.

Having discussed the sharing of tax revenue we can now move on to the question of grants-in-aid. When the approved expenditure of a state exceeds the anticipated revenue grants-in-aid are called for. Various finance commissions have talked of some objective criteria by which grants-in-aid are to be made.

In a federal system this objectivity is, in principle, feasible. If for instance we strive for equality in public services throughout the country then one can build up an objective calculus for making grants-in-aid. Thus if schooling, health care, police and fire services are very unevenly distributed throughout the country then one can think of grants-in-aid to the *i*th state as being a function of the gap between the standards of the best public services available in the country and those that obtain in the *i*th state. This kind of argument, of course, presumes two things. The first is that it is straightforward to quantify the quality of public services irrespective of the magnitude and nature of other central assistance to the state. Secondly, the assumption is that if we spend more on public services this will automatically improve. This is of course not a safe assumption to make.

In practice, however, grants-in-aid have generally gone to fill in the gap between expenses and receipts. To stress this point we cite an example of the Seventh Finance Commissions attempt to be guided by more objective criteria in recommending grants-in-aid.

The Seventh Finance Commission had thought of equality in per capita public services across different states as a good guide for grants-in-aid. The commission confined itself to very essential public services like general administration, police, jails and justice. The commission collected extensive data on the level and quality of these services. Then it recommended both revenue and capital grants of varying amounts to various states. Central ministries were asked to monitor the progress of these plans. The commission did not, however, measure the cost structure of providing these services in various states. Hence the recommendations of grants-in-aid were largely arbitrary. In practice grants-in-aid have essentially filled the gap between expense and revenues. Throughout the history of the Finance Commissions this principle has never really changed.

We now look at some indicators of the performance of the Finance Commissions. Tables 21.2 and 21.3 show the extent of fiscal centralization that has taken place over the years. One can easily see from them that the states (as a group) have become increasingly dependent on the centre. Given this picture then it becomes important to inquire about the relative importance of federal transfers to various states. Although it is possible to show that there has not been gross inequality in transfer to states one cannot escape the conclusion that some elements of inequality have crept into the picture. Tables 21.4 and 21.5 give us some idea of this.

Another point we have made is the arbitrary nature of the forecasts of revenue and expenses made by the Finance Commissions. Many reasons have been advanced for this. Among them are the arbitrary nature of the treatment of interest costs and problems in forecasting nominal values. One gets a good idea by looking at Tables 21.6 through 21.12 where the seriousness of the forecasting errors made by the various finance commissions is noted.

TABLE 21.2 Trends in Financial Centralization in the Indian Union

(As percent of total)

Year	*Tax Collections*		*Tax accruals*		*Revenue collections*		*Revenue accruals*		*Expenditure on revenue account*	
	States' share	*Central share*	*States' share*	*Central share*	*States share*	*Central share*	*States' share*	*Central share*	*States' share*	*Central share*
1950-51	35.4	64.6	43.0	57.0	38.1	61.9	47.5	52.5	50.9	49.1
1955-56	36.8	63.2	46.4	53.6	40.5	59.5	54.8	45.2	59.1	40.9
1960-61	33.7	66.3	45.9	54.1	34.1	65.9	56.1	43.9	57.1	42.9
1965-66	29.5	70.5	38.9	61.1	29.4	70.6	47.2	52.8	52.2	47.8
1970-71	32.5	67.5	48.4	51.6	30.6	69.4	53.4	46.6	55.0	45.0
1971-72	30.5	69.5	47.5	52.5	28.4	71.6	54.7	45.3	53.9	46.1
1972-73	30.0	70.0	46.5	53.5	28.1	71.9	53.9	46.1	54.4	45.6
1973-74	31.4	68.6	47.2	52.8	29.4	70.6	53.8	46.2	55.9	44.1
1974-75	31.4	68.6	44.7	55.3	30.2	69.8	50.9	49.1	52.9	47.1
1975-76	31.9	68.1	46.3	53.8	30.2	69.8	51.2	48.8	51.2	48.8

Note: States' share includes the shares of the Union Territories also.
SOURCE: Government of India, Ministry of Finance, Indian Economic Statistics—Public Finance (Annual).

TABLE 21.3 Fiscal Dependence of the States on the Central Government

Year	*Shared taxes and grants as a percentage of States' total revenue*	*Ratio of States' own revenues to their expenditures (in percent)*
1950-51	19.8	80.6
1955-56	26.0	68.5
1960-61	39.2	62.4
1965-66	37.8	61.1
1970-71	42.8	56.9
1971-72	48.1	52.0
1972-73	47.8	51.3
1973-74	45.3	53.4
1974-75	40.6	63.9
1975-76	41.1	68.1

Note: States' share includes the shares of the Union Territories also.

TABLE 21.4 Indices of Federal Transfers During Annual Plans

State	*Finance Commission transfers*	*Plan transfers*	*Total transfers*
Panjab	75.3	114.0	94.5
Haryana	62.9	140.0	98.9
Maharashtra	98.3	65.8	80.1
Gujarat	88.1	90.6	94.8
West Bengal	83.4	77.0	78.6
Assam	186.2	162.5	188.5
Tamil Nadu	94.5	88.9	92.8
Kerala	167.9	125.5	138.2
Karnataka	139.1	111.3	118.7
Andhra Pradesh	100.4	110.6	104.9
Orissa	211.1	116.6	149.6
Uttar Pradesh	76.7	86.4	80.2
Madhya Pradesh	77.5	102.1	89.6
Rajasthan	95.5	139.5	127.4
Jammu & Kashmir	279.8	398.9	112.4
Bihar	63.9	80.6	73.2
All States	100.0	100.0	100.0

Note: The States are arranged in descending order of per capita income averaged for the period 1967-68 to 1969-70 (estimated by CSO at State Prices).

TABLE 21.5 Indices of Federal Transfers During the Fourth Plan

State	*Finance Commission transfers*	*Plan transfers*	*Total transfers*
Panjab	85.0	115.0	115.3
Haryana	74.6	121.5	96.9
Gujarat	91.2	92.7	99.2
Maharashtra	101.6	76.6	100.3
West Bengal	105.9	76.7	93.2
Karnataka	88.1	91.2	88.4
Tamil Nadu	93.2	76.4	84.0
Kerala	114.0	127.2	110.4
Andhra Pradesh	99.2	85.4	93.7
Assam	141.7	203.0	171.0
Rajasthan	106.4	131.8	122.6
Orissa	140.2	113.3	124.0
Uttar Pradesh	90.1	92.5	86.8
Madhya Pradesh	87.9	97.2	89.5
Jammu & Kashmir	273.9	482.5	353.9
Bihar	99.2	92.0	86.9
All States	100.0	100.0	100.0

Note: The States are arranged according to descending order of per capita income averaged for the period 1970-71 to 1972-73 (estimated by CSO at State prices).

Conclusions

In this chapter we have studied some major problems affecting centre-state financial relations in India. The system is in serious need of careful reorganization. Moreover in the recent past severe strains of a political nature have been placed on centre-state financial relations.

Recently the Government of India has appointed the Sarkaria Commission to look into the various aspects of relations between the centre and the states. The Sarkaria Commission should look into some of the problems that we have discussed above. Moreover, recently there has been a drastic shift from the import-substitution/centralized control policies of earlier terms to more liberalized, decentralized policies. This of course has had and will continue to have serious implications for the finances of states. Thus import liberalization will mean reduced sales for state enterprises which will effect state revenues. The effects of such drastic change in the direction of economic policy will also have to be evaluated.

TABLE 21.6 Estimated and Actual Budgetary Gaps of State Governments During 1952-53 to 1956-57

(*Rs. crores*)

State	*First Finance Commission's estimation of budgetary gap after devolution of taxes*	*Actual budgetary gap*	*Extent of over estimation (+) or underestimation (−)*
Andhra Pradesh	Not estimated	−24.53	−24.53
Assam	−1.00	−26.03	−25.03
Bombay	—	−38.80	−38.38
Bihar	−2.48	−64.03	−61.55
Hyderabad	−1.20	− 10.78	− 9.58
Jammu & Kashmir	—	− 4.13	− 4.13
Madhya Bharat	−0.54	− 8.70	− 8.16
Madhya Pradesh	−1.50	−23.19	−21.69
Madras	—	−52.52	−52.52
Mysore	−0.40	−14.83	−14.43
Orissa	−1.72	−29.14	−27.42
PEPSU	−0.28	− 5.41	− 5.13
Panjab	−2.09	−15.08	−12.99
Rajasthan	−1.19	−11.11	− 9.92
Saurashtra	−0.40	−19.32	−18.92
Travancore-Cochin	−0.45	− 6.68	− 6.23
Uttar Pradesh	—	−38.52	−38.52
West Bengal	−0.80	−74.52	−73.72
Total for Part 'A' and Part 'B' States	−14.05	−466.32	−452.27

Notes: (1) The budgetary gaps estimated by the First Finance Commission include special financial need of some states for improving primary education facilities.

(2) Actual budgetary gaps refer to the four-year period 1952-53 to 1955-56. The data for 1956-57 are not available owing to reorganisation of states in 1956.

SOURCES: Compiled from the Reports of the First and Second Finance Commission and Reserve Bank of India Bulletins.

TABLE 21.7 Estimated and Actual Budgetary Gaps of State Governments During 1957-58 to 1961-62

(*Rs. crores*)

State	*Second Finance Commissions's estimation of non-plan budgetary gap after devolution of taxes*	*Actual budgetary gap*	*Extent of over-estimation (+) of under-estimation (−)*
Andhra Pradesh	−4.00	+14.07	+18.07
Assam	−4.05	− 0.20	+ 3.85
Bihar	−3.80	+16.36	+20.16
Bombay	—	− 4.88	− 4.88
Jammu & Kashmir	−3.00	+10.52*	+13.52
Kerala	−1.75	+11.73	+13.48
Madhya Pradesh	−3.00	+14.66	+17.66
Madras	—	− 3.13	− 3.13
Mysore	−6.00	+19.32	+25.32
Orissa	−3.35	−15.28	−12.93
Panjab	−2.25	+42.19	+44.44
Rajasthan	−2'50	+10.85	− 8.35
Uttar Pradesh	—	+12.62	+12.62
West Bengal	−3.00	+ 7.10	+10.10
Total of all reorganised States	−36.70	+128.30	+165.00

Note: *Budgetary gap refers to the four-year period from 1958-59 to 1961-62.

SOURCES: Compiled from the Report of the Second Finance Commission and the Reserve Bank of India Bulletins.

TABLE 21.8 Estimated and Actual Budgetary Gaps of State Governments During 1962-63 to 1965-66

(*Rs. crores*)

State	*Third Finance Commission's estimation of budgetary gap after devolution of taxes*	*Actual budgetary gap*	*Extent of over-estimation (+) of under estimation (−)*
Andhra Pradesh	− 9.50	+ 11.85	+ 21.35
Assam	− 6.00	− 26.05	− 20.05
Bihar	− 0.75	+ 46.04	+ 46.79
Gujarat	− 5.25	+ 16.88	+ 22.13
Haryana	Not estimated	Not estimated	Not estimated
Jammu & Kashmir	− 2.00	+218.00	+220.00
Kerala	− 6.25	− 7.30	− 1.05
Madhya Pradesh	− 3.00	+ 5.07	+ 8.07
Maharashtra	− 6.75	+ 7.25	+ 14.00
Mysore	−13.25	− 6.67	+ 6.58
Orissa	—	− 21.59	− 21.59
Panjab	—	+ 49.83	+ 49.83
Rajasthan	− 5.25	— 6.88	— 1.63
Tamil Nadu	− 3.00	− 9.35	− 6.35
Uttar Pradesh	—	+ 20.27	+ 20.27
West Bengal	—	+ 10.85	+ 10.85
Total	−61.00	+313.15	+374.15

SOURCES: Compiled from the Report of the Third Finance Commission and Reserve Bank of India Bulletins.

TABLE 21.9 Estimated and Actual Budgetary Gaps of State Governments During 1966-67 to 1968-69

(*Rs. crores*)

State	*Fourth Finance Commission's estimation of non-plan budgetary gap*		*Actual budgetary gap*	*Extent of over-estimation (+) or underestimation (−)*
	Before devolution of taxes	*After devolution of taxes*		
Andhra Pradesh	−702.73	− 36.10	− 37.69 (− 9.46)	− 1.59 (+ 25.64)
Assam	−144.96	− 82.60	− 76.84 (− 43.57)	+ 5.76 (+ 39.03)
Bihar	−108.21	+ 89.25	− 49.32 (− 22.82)	−138.57 (−112.07)
Gujarat	−113.55	+ 8.00	− 2.20 (+ 1.76)	− 10.20 (+ 9.76)
Jammu & Kashmir	− 66.10	− 32.85	+ 5.65 (+ 13.11)	+ 38.50 (+ 45.96)
Karnataka	−202.52	− 91.20	+ 46.08 (− 60.45)	+137.28 (+ 30.85)
Kerala	−188.61	−104.10	− 8.59 (+ 18.66)	+ 95.51 (+122.76)
Madhya Pradesh	−162.03	− 13.50	+ 29.24 (− 18.20)	+ 42.74 (− 4.70)
Maharashtra	− 44.72	+215.66	− 17.45 (− 15.29)	−233.11 (−230.95)
Nagaland	− 58.74	− 35.35	+ 12.46 (+ 0.83)	+ 47.81 (+ 36.18)
Orissa	−231.85	−145.90	− 10.88 (− 6.95)	+135.02 (+ 88.85)
Panjab	− 75.03	− 29.83	+ 78.43 (+ 22.54)	+107.26 (+ 52.37)
Rajasthan	−130.41	− 33.65	−174.46 (− 62.56)	−140.81 (− 28.91)
Tamil Nadu	−207.32	− 34.20	− 13.48 (+ 14.73)	+ 20.72 (+ 48.93)
Uttar Pradesh	−306.75	+ 79.02	+161.55 (+ 50.42)	+240.57 (+129.44)
West Bengal	−183.44	+ 13.97	− 78.10 (− 31.43)	− 92.07 (− 45.40)
Total	−2426.97	−173.72	−135.60 (−148.68)	− 38.12 (− 25.04)

Note: The Fourth Finance Commission was asked to recommend federal fiscal transfers for a five year period 1966-67 to 1970-71. However, the recommendations of the Commission were terminated at the end of the three-year period 1966-67 to 1968-69 owing to the termination of Annual Plans and the commencement of the Fourth Five-Year Plan. The actual budgetary gaps for these three years are shown in brackets.

SOURCES: Compiled from the Report of the Fourth Finance Commission and the Reserve Bank of India Bulletins.

TABLE 21.10 Estimated and Actual Budgetary Gaps of State Governments During 1969-70 to 1973-74

(*Rs. crores*)

State	*Fifth Finance Commission's estimation of non-plan budgetary gap after devolution of taxes*	*Actual budgetary gap*	*Extent of over-estimation (+) or underestimation (—)*
Andhra Pradesh	− 65.01	+ 23.58	+ 88.59
Assam	−101.97	−103.59	− 1.62
Bihar	−199.46	− 84.37	−283.83
Gujarat	+158.99	− 28.99	−187.98
Haryana	+ 79.88	+ 61.96	+141.84
Jammu & Kashmir	− 73.68	− 40.35	+ 33.35
Karnataka	− 17.99	+ 9.26	+ 27.25
Kerala	− 49.65	− 61.26	− 11.61
Madhya Pradesh	+ 15.09	+155.20	+170.29
Maharashtra	+419.29	−157.69	−576.98
Nagaland	− 77.95	+ 24.91	−102.86
Orissa	−104.67	− 90.21	+ 14.46
Panjab	+117.22	+106.74	+223.86
Rajasthan	− 51.49	−174.08	−122.59
Tamil Nadu	− 22.82	— 13.01	− 9.81
Uttar Pradesh	+280.87	+159.10	+439.97
West Bengal	− 72.62	— 91.45	− 18.87
Total	+632.95	−304.25	−932.20

SOURCES: Compiled from the Report of the Fifth Finance Commission and the Reserve Bank of India Bulletins.

TABLE 21.11 Estimated and Actual Budgetary Gaps of State Governments During 1973-74 to 1978-79

(*Rs. crores*)

State	*Forecast of budgetary gaps submitted by the state governments*	*Sixth Finance Commission's estimation of budgetary gaps*		*Actual budgetary gap*	*Extent of over estimation (+) or underestimation (—)*
		Before devolution of taxes	*After devolution of taxes*		
Andhra Pradesh	− 1329.23	− 776.01	−205.93	+ 395.50	+ 601.43
Assam	− 538.05	− 439.62	−254.53	+ 54.43	+ 308.96
Bihar	− 1086.74	− 844.72	−106.28	+ 383.56	+ 489.84
Gujarat	− 418.12	− 33.18	+335.46	+ 245.95	+ 581.41
Haryana	− 176.00	+ 102.69	+223.35	+ 85.61	+ 308.96
Himachal Pradesh	− 225.12	− 204.06	−160.96	− 10.00	+ 150.96
Jammu & Kashmir	− 347.27	− 232.28	−173.49	+ 282.36	+ 455.85
Karnataka	− 825.96	− 150.90	+232.74	− 63.62	− 296.36
Kerala	− 894.02	− 479.97	−208.93	+ 461.25	+ 670.18
Madhya Pradesh	− 945.10	− 433.39	+110.18	+ 472.77	+ 582.95
Maharashtra	− 812.29	+ 36.09	+748.42	+ 65.40	+ 813.82
Manipur	− 136.05	− 128.01	−114.53	+ 35.19	+ 149.72
Maghalaya	− 104.63	− 87.52	− 74.67	+ 33.25	+ 107.92
Nagaland	− 150.76	− 135.67	−128.84	+ 15.51	+ 144.35
Orissa	− 750.96	− 577.32	−304.73	+ 810.49	+1115.22
Panjab	− 58.20	− 172.51	+341.48	+ 112.31	− 453.79
Rajasthan	− 647.62	− 563.92	−230.53	+ 17.69	− 248.22
Tamil Nadu	− 889.91	− 354.04	+184.53	− 91.52	− 276.05
Tripura	− 191.58	− 132.19	−112.50	+ 19.48	− 131.98
Uttar Pradesh	− 3856.21	−1349.05	−198.83	− 527.71	+ 726.54
West Bengal	− 1292.40	− 822.93	−234.86	+ 138.24	+ 373.10
Total	−15676.27	−7433.49	−333.45	+3991.60	+4325.05

SOURCES: Compiled from the Report of the Sixth Finance Commission and Reserve Bank of India Bulletins.

TABLE 21.12 Estimated Budgetary Gaps of State Governments During 1979-80 to 1983-84

(*Rs. crores*)

State	*Forecast of budgetary gaps submitted by the state governments*	*Seventh Finance Commission's estimation of budgetary gaps*		*Difference between State's forecast and Finance Commission's estimation before devolution of taxes*
		Before devolution of taxes	*After devolution of taxes*	
Andhra Pradesh	− 2652.47	− 579.72	+ 923.18	−2072.68
Assam	− 1113.38	− 410.12	+ 86.82	− 703.26
Bihar	− 3552.14	− 1057.23	+ 1092.32	−2494.91
Gujarat	− 842.39	+ 164.12	+ 1127.99	+1006.51
Haryana	+ 228.51	+ 370.06	+ 678.63	− 141.55
Himachal Pradesh	− 489.21	− 317.33	− 207.07	− 171.88
Jammu & Kashmir	+ 1009.98	− 358.61	− 199.56	−1368.59
Karnataka	− 1742.55	+ 1.15	+ 1006.15	+1743.70
Kerala	− 2021.22	− 531.11	+ 235.05	−1490.11
Madhya Pradesh	− 2072.16	− 422.63	+ 1111.25	− 624.79
Maharashtra	− 1376.37	+ 1290.70	+ 3004.75	+2667.07
Manipur	− 294.80	− 134.08	− 146.32	− 110.72
Meghalaya	− 245.89	− 129.29	− 92.61	− 116.60
Nagaland	− 384.79	− 236.26	− 218.35	− 148.53
Orissa	− 1816.99	− 952.19	− 136.92	− 864.80
Panjab	− 642.55	+ 389.97	+ 809.50	+1032.52
Rajasthan	− 2115.46	− 663.24	+ 220.28	−1452.22
Sikkim	− 35.51	+ 36.20	+ 35.72	+ 71.71
Tamil Nadu	− 2362.97	− 849.00	+ 627.39	−1513.97
Tripura	− 304.58	− 196.23	− 136.70	− 108.35
Uttar Pradesh	− 6213.50	− 1258.16	+ 1943.86	−4954.64
West Bengal	− 3046.13	− 857.23	+ 715.27	−2188.90
Total	−32086.57	−40115.47	+12409.19	+8028.80

SOURCES: Report of the Seventh Finance Commission, Government of India, New Delhi 1972.

Bibliography

AARON, H.J. (1975), "Cautionary notes on the experiment", in *Work Incentives and Income Guarantees*, J.A. Pechman and P.M. Timpane (eds.), Brookings Institution, Washington DC.

——— (ed.) (1976), *Inflation and the Income Tax*, Brookings Institution, Washington DC.

AARON H.J. and M.C. MCGUIRE (1969), "Efficiency and equity in the optimal supply of a public good", *Review of Economic and Statistics*, 51, 31-39.

——— and ——— (1970) "Public goods and income distribution", *Econometrica*, 38, 907-920.

ABEL, A. (1978), *Investment and the Value of Capital*, Garland Publishing Company, Boston.

ABBOTT, M. and O. ASHENFELTER (1976), "Labour supply, commodity demand and the allocation of time", *Review of Economic Studies*, 43, 389-412.

AHAMAD and N.H. STERN (1982), "Indirect Taxes and Prices in India. The Calculation of Effective Tax Rates using Input-Output Methods", Discussion Paper, University of Warwick.

——— and ——— (1984), "Effective Taxes and Tax Reform in India," *Journal of Public Economics*.

AHSAN, S.M. (1974), "Progression and risk-taking", *Oxford Economic Papers*, 26, 318-328.

AHSAN, S.M. (1976), "Taxation in a two-period temporal model of consumption and portfolio allocation", *Journal of Public Economics*, 5, 337-352.

AKERLOF, G.A. (1978), "The economics of 'tagging", *American Economic Review*, 68. 8-19.

ALLAIS, M. (1948), "Le problem de la coordination des transports et la theorie economique", *Revue Economique Politique*, 58, 212-271.

ALLEN, F. (1979), M. PHIL. Thesis, University of Oxford.

ALLINGHAM, M.G. (1972), "The measurement of inequality", *Journal of Economic Theory*, 5, 163-169.

ALLINGHAM, M.G. and A. SANDMO (1972), "Income tax evasion: a theoretical analysis", *Journal of Public Economics*, 1, 323-338.

ALT, J. and A. CHRYSTAL (1977), "Endogenous government behaviour", University of Essex Discussion Paper.

ANDO, A. and F. MODIGLIANI (1963), "The 'life cycle' hypothesis of saving: aggregate Annual Survey of Industries, detailed tables 1973-74 data, Government of India implications and tests", *American Economic Review*, 53, 55-84.

Annual Survey of Industries, detailed tables 1973-74, Government of India.

ARNOTT, R. and J.E. STIGLIZ (1980), "Aggregate land rents, aggregate transport costs and expenditure on public goods", *Quarterly Journal of Economics*, 97.

ARROW, K.J. (1952), *Social Choice and Individual Values*, John Wiley, New York (2nd edn 1963).

——— (1962), "The economic implications of learning by doing", *Review of Economic Studies*, 29, 155-173.

ARROW, K.J. (1965), *Aspects of the Theory of Risk-Bearing*, Yrjo Johnssonin Saatio, Helsinki.

——— (1970a), *Essays in the Theory of Risk-Bearing*, North Holland, Amsterdam.

——— (1970b), "The organisation of economic activity: issues pertinent to the choice of market versus non-market allocation" in *Public Expenditure and Policy Analysis*, R.H. Haveman and J. Margolis (eds), Markham, Chicago.

——— (1971a), "Equality in public expenditure", *Quarterly Journal of Economics*, 85, 409-415.

——— (1971b), "Political and economic evaluation of social effects and externalities" in *Frontiers of Quantitative Economics*, M.D. Intriligator (ed.), North-Holland, Amsterdam.

——— (1973), "Some ordinalist-ultilitarian notes on Rawl's theory of justice", *Journal of Philosophy*, 70, 245-263.

——— (1977), "The Property Rights Doctrine", Discussion Paper, Harvard University.

ARROW, K.J. and F.H. HAHN (1971), *General Competitive Analysis*, Oliver and Boyd, Arrow, K.J. (1977) "The Property Rights Doctrine", Discussion paper, Harvard University.

ARROW. K.J. and M. KURZ (1970). *Public Investment, the Role of Return and Optimal Fiscal Policy*, Johns Hopkins University Press.

ARROW, K.J. and K.C. LIND (1970), "Uncertainty and the evaluation of public investment decisions", *American Economic Review*, 60, 364-378.

ASHENFELTER, O. and J. HECKMAN (1973), "Estimating labor-supply functions" in *Income Maintenance and Labor Supply*, G.G. Cain and H.W. Watts (eds), Rand McNally, Chicago.

——— and ——— (1974), "The estimation of income and substitution effects in a model of family labor supply", *Econometrica*, 42, 73-85.

ASHWORTH, J. and D.T. ULPH (1977), "On the structure of family labour supply decisions", *Economic Journal*, 84, 267-288.

ATKINSON, A.B. (1969), *Poverty in Britain and the Reform of Social Security*, Cambridge University Press, London.

——— (1970), "On the measurement of inequality", *Journal of Economic Theory*, 2, 244-263.

——— (1971), "Capital taxes, the redistribution of wealth and individual savings", *Review of Economic Studies*, 38, 209-228.

——— (1972), "Maxi-min and optimal income taxation", paper presented at the Budapest Meeting of the Econometric Society.

——— (1973), "How progressive should income tax be?" in *Essays in Modern Economics*, M. Parkin and A.R. Nobay (eds), Longman, London.

——— (1975a), "La 'maxi-min' et l'imposition optimale des revenus", Cahiers du Seminaire d'Econometrie, Nr 16.

——— (1975b), *The Economics of Inequality*, Oxford University Press, Oxford.

——— (1976), "The income tax treatment of charitable contributions" in *Public and Urban Economics*, R.E. Grieson (ed.), Lexington Books, Lexington, Mass.

——— (1977a), "Housing allowances, income maintenance and income taxation" in *The Economics of Public Services*, M.S. Feldstein and R.P. Inman (eds), Macmillan, London.

ATKINSON, A.B. (1977b), "Optimal taxation and the direct versus indirect tax controversy", *Canadian Journal of Economics*, 10, 590-606.

——— (1979), "Horizontal equity and the distribution of the tax burden" in *The Economics of Taxation*, H.J. Aaron and M.J. Bosking (eds), Brookings Institution, Washington DC.

——— (1980), "The distribution of income and the taxation of inheritance" in *Essays in Honour of James Meade*, G.M. Heal and G.A. Hughes (eds), Allen and Unwin, London.

ATKINSON, A.B. and A.J. HARRISON (1978), *Distribution of Personal Wealth in Britain*, Cambridge University Press. London.

ATKINSON, A.B. and A. SANDMO (1977), "The welfare implications of personal income and consumption taxes", University College London Discussion Series, revised 1979.

ATKINSON, A.B. and N.H. STERN (1974), "Pigou, taxation and public goods", *Review of Economic Studies*, 41, 119-128.

ATKINSON, A.B. and N.H. STERN (1979), "On labour supply and commodity demands", SSRC Programme on Taxation, Incentives and the Distribution of Income, Discussion Paper.

ATKINSON, A.B. and J.E. STIGLITZ (1969), "A New view of technological change", *Economic Journal*, 79, 573-578.

——— and ——— (1972), "The structure of indirect taxation and economic efficiency", *Journal of Public Economics*, 1, 97-119.

——— and ——— (1976), "The design of tax structure: direct versus indirect taxation", *Journal of Public Economic*, 6, 55-75, Atkinson, A.B. and J. Stiglitz (1980), *Lectures on Public Economics*, McGraw Hill.

AVERCH, H. and L.L. JOHNSON (1962), "Behaviour of the firm under regulatory constraint", *American Economic Review*, 52, 1052-1069.

BAILEY, E.E. (1973), *Economic Theory of Regulatory Constraint*, Lexington Books, Lexington, Massachusetts.

BALASKO, Y. (1978), "Economic equilibrium and catastrophe theory an introduction", *Econometrica*, 46, 557-569.

BALLENTINE, J.G. (1977), "Non-profit-maximising behaviour and the short run incidence of the corporation income tax", *Journal of Public Economics*, 7, 135-146.

BALLENTINE, J.G. and I. ERIS (1975), "On the general equilibrium analysis of tax incidence", *Journal of Political Economy*, 83, 633-644.

BARLOW, R., and H.R. BRAZER and J.N. MORGAN (1966), *Economic Behavior of the Affluent*, Brookings Institution, Washington, DC.

BARLOW, R. and G.R. SPARKS (1964), "A note on progression and leisure", *American Economic Review*, 54, 372-377.

BARNA, T. (1945), *Redistribution of Income Through Public Finance in 1937*, Oxford University Press, Oxford.

BARR, N.A., S.R. JAMES and A.R. PREST (1977), *Self-Assessment for Income Tax*, Heinemann, London.

BARRO, R.J. (1974), "Are government bonds net wealth?", *Journal of Political Economy*, 82, 1095-1117.

BARRO, R.J. and H.I. GROSSMAN (1976), *Money, Employment and Inflation*, Cambridge University, London.

BARRY, B.M. (1970), *Sociologists, Economists and Democracy*, Collier Macmillan, London.

BAUMOL, W.J. (1958), "On the theory of oligopoly", *Economica*, 25, 187-198.

——— (1967), "Macroeconomics of unbalanced growth: the anatomy of urban crisis", *American Economic Review*, 57, 415-426.

BAUMOL, W.J. and D.F. BRADFORD (1970), "Optimal Departures from Marginal Cost Pricing", *American Economic Review*, 60, 265-283.

BAUMOL, W.J. and A.K. KLEVORICK (1970), "Input choices and rate of return regulation: an overview of the discussion", *Bell Journal of Economics*, 1, 162-190.

BAUMOL, W.J. and W.E. OATES (1975), *The Theory of Environmental Policy*, Prentice-Hall, Englewood Cliffs, NJ.

BECKER, G.S. (1965), "A theory of the allocation of time", *Economic Journal*, 75, 493-517.

——— (1974), "A theory of social interactions", *Journal of Political Economy*, 82, 1063-1093.

BEN-PORATH, Y. (1975), "The years of plenty and the years of famine: a political business cycle", *Kyklos*, 28, 410-413.

BERGLAS, E. (1976), "Distribution of tastes and skills and the provision of local public goods", *Journal of Public Economics*, 6, 409-423.

BERGSON, A. (1972), "Optimal pricing for a public enterprise", *Quarterly Journal of Economics*, 86, 519-544.

BERGSTROM, T.C. and R.P. GOODMAN (1973), "Private demands for public goods", *American Economic Review*, 63, 280-296.

BEVAN, D.L. (1974), "Savings, inheritance and economic growth", unpublished paper, Oxford University.

BHATIA, K.B. (1979), "Corporate taxation, retained earnings and capital formation", *Journal of Public Economics*, 11, 123-134.

BIERWAG, G.O. and M.A. GROVE (1967), "Portfolio selection and taxation", *Oxford Economic Papers*, 19, 215-220.

BIERWAG, G.O. M.A. GROVE and C. KHANG (1969), "National debt in a neoclassical growth model: comment", *American Economic Review*, 59, 205-210.

BISCHOFF, C.W. (1969), "Hypothesis testing and the demand for capital goods", *Review of Economics and Statistics*, 51, 354-368.

——— (1971), "The effect of alternative lag distributions" in *Tax Incentives and Capital Spending*, G. Fromm (ed.), North-Holland, Amsterdam.

BISHOP, R.L. (1968), "The effects of specific and ad valorem taxes", *Quarterly Journal of Economics*, 82, 198-218.

BLACK, D. (1948), "On the rationale of group decision-making", *Journal of Political Economy*, 56, 23-34.

——— (1958), *The Theory of Committees and Elections*, Cambridge University Press, Cambridge.

BLINDER, A.S. (1973), "A model of inherited wealth", *Quarterly Journal of Economics*, 87, 608-626.

———(1975), "Distribution effects and the aggregate consumption function", *Journal of Political Economy*, 83, 447-475.

BLINDER, A. and R. SOLOW (1974), "Analytical foundations of fiscal policy, "in *The Economics of Public Finance*, Brookings.

BLISS, C.J. (1975), *Capital Theory and the Distribution of Income*, North-Holland, Amsterdam.

BLUM, W.J. and H. KALVEN (1963), *The Uneasy Case for Progressive Taxation*, University of Chicago Press and Phoenix Books, London.

BOADWAY, R. (1979), Public Sector Economics, *Winthrop*.

——— (1977), "Dynamic Tax Incidence", mimeo Queen's University.

BOADWAY, R.W. and N. BRUCE (1979), "Depreciation and interest deductions and the effect of the corporation income tax on investment", *Journal of Public Economics*, 11, 93-105.

BOHM, P. (1971), "An approach to the problem of estimating the demand for public goods", *Swedish Journal of Economics*, 73, 55-56.

——— (1972), "Estimating demand for public goods: an experiment", *European Economic Review*, 3, 111-130.

BOITEUX, M. (1956), "Sur la gestion des monopoles publics astreints a l' equiblire budgetaire", *Econometrica*, 24, 22-40.

——— (1971), "On the management of public monopolies subject to budgetary constraints" (translation of Boiteux, 1956), *Journal of Economic Theory*, 3, 218-240.

BORCHERDING, T.E. (ed.) (1971), *Budgets and Bureaucrats*, Duke University Press, Durham, North Carolina.

BORCHERDING, T.E. and R.T. Deacon (1972), "The demand for the services of non-federal governments", *American Economic Review*, 62, 842-853.

Bos, D. (1978), "Cost of living indices and public prices", *Economica*, 45, 59-69.

Bos, D. (1985), "*Public Sector Pricing*" in M. Aeldstein and A Awrbach eds Handbook of Public Economics, North Holland.

BOSKIN, M.J. (1967), "The negative income tax and the supply of work effort, *National Tax Journal*, 20, 353-367.

——— (1973a), "Local government tax and product competition and the optimal provision of public goods", *Journal of Political Economy*, 81, 203-210.

——— (1973b), "The economics of labor supply" in *Income Maintenance and Labour Supply*, G.G. Cain and H.W. Watts (eds), Rand McNally, Chicago.

——— (1975a), "Efficiency aspects of the differential tax treatment of market and household economic activity", *Journal of Public Economics*, 4, 1-25.

——— (1975b), "Notes on the tax treatment of human capital" in Conference of Tax Research 1975, Department of the Treasury, Washington DC.

——— (1977), "Social security and retirement decisions", *Economic Inquiry*, 15, 1-25.

——— (1978), "Taxation, saving. and the rate of interests", *Journal of Political Economy*, 86, S3-S27.

BOSKIN, M.J. and M.D. HURD (1978), "The effect of social security on early retirement", *Journal of Public Economics*, 10, 361-377.

BOSKIN, M.J. and L.J. LAU (1978), "Taxation, and aggregate factor supply, preliminary estimates" in Compendium of Tax Research 1978, Department of the Treasury, Washington DC.

BOSKIN M.J. and E. SHESHINSKI (1978), "Optimal income redistribution when individual welfare depends on relative income", *Quarterly Journal of Economics*, 92, 589-602.

BOSSONS, J. (1965), "A comprehensive tax base as a tax reform goal", *Journal of Law and Economics*, 8, 327-363.

BOSWORTH, B. (1975), "The stock market and the economy", *Brookings Papers on Economic Activity*, 257-290.

BOWEN, H.R. (1943), "The interpretation of voting in the allocation of economic resources", *Quarterly Journal of Economics*, 58, 27-48.

BOWEN, W.G., R.G. DAVIS and D.H. KOPF (1960), "The public debt: a burden on future generations?", *American Economic Review*, 50, 701-706.

BRADFORD, D.F. (1978), "The case for personal consumption tax", paper presented to Brookings Conference.

BRADFORD, D.F. and W.F. OATES (1971a), "Towards a predictive theory of intergovernmental grants", *American Economic Review*, Papers and Proceedings, 61, 440-448.

——— and ——— (1971b), "The analysis of revenue-sharing in a new approach to collective fiscal decisions", *Quarterly Journal of Economics*, 85, 416-439.

BRADFORD, D.F. and H.S. ROSEN (1976), "The Optimal Taxation of commodities and income".

BRAINARD, W.C. and J. TOBIN (1977), "Asset Markets and the cost of Capital", in *Economic Progress, Private Values and Public Policy* eds, Richard Nelson and B. Belassa, North Holland, American Economic Review, Papers and Proceedings, 66, 94-101.

BREAK, G.F. (1957), "Income taxes and incentives to work: an empirical study", *American Economic Review*, 47, 529-549.

——— (1974), "The incidence and economic effects of taxation" in *The Economics of Public Finance*, A. Blinder et al., Brookings Institution, Washington DC.

BREMS, H. (1983), *Fiscal Theory*, Lexington Books.

BRECHLING, F.P.R. (1975), *Investment and Employment Decisions*, Manchester University Press, Manchester.

BRENNAN, G. (1976), "The distributional implications of public goods", *Econometrica*, 44, 391-399.

BRENNAN, G. and J.M. BUCHANAN (1977), "Towards a tax constitution for Leviathan", *Journal of Public Economics*, 8, 255-274.

——— and ——— (1978), "Tax instruments as constraints on the disposition of public revenues", *Journal of Public Economics*, 9, 301-318.

BRETON, A. (1974), *The Economic Theory of Representative Government*, Macmillan, London.

BRITTAIN, J.A. (1966), *Corporate Dividend Policy*, Brookings Institution, Washington DC.

——— (1972), *The Payroll Tax for Social Security*. Brookings Institution, Washington DC.

BROOME, J. (1975), "An important theorem on income tax", *Review of Economic Studies*, 42, 649-652.

BROWN, C.V. and E. LEVIN (1974), "The effects of income taxation on overtime", *Economic Journal*, 84, 833-848.

BROWN, C.V., E. LEVIN and D.T. ULPH (1976), "Estimate of labour hours supplied by married male workers in Great Britain", *Scottish Journal of Political Economy*, 23, 261-277.

BROWN, E.C. (1948), "Business income taxation and investment incentives" in Income, Employment and Public Policy, *Essays in Honor of Alvin H. Hansen*, L.A. Metzler et al., (eds), Norton, New York.

BROWING, E.K. (1971), "Incentive and disincentive experimentation for income maintenance policy purposes: note", *American Economic Review*, 61, 709-712.

BRUNO, M. (1972), "Market distributions and gradual reform", *Review of Economic Studies*, 39, 373-383.

——— (1976), "Equality, Complementarity and the incidence of public expenditures", *Journal of Economics*, 6, 395-407.

BRYSON, A. and Y. HO (1975), *Applied Optunal Control*, Wiley.

BUCHANAN, J.M. (1958), *Public Principles of Public Debt*, Irwin, Homewood, Illinois.

——— (1960), *Fiscal Theory and Political Economy*, University of North Carolina Press, Chapel Hill, North Carolina.

——— (1965), "An economic theory of clubs", *Economica*, 32, 1-14.

——— (1968), *The Demand and Supply of Public Goods*, Rand McNally, Chicago.

——— (1969), "External diseconomies, corrective taxes and market structure", *American Economic Review*, 59, 174-177.

BUCHANAN, J.M. (1970), *The Public Finances* (3rd edn), Irwin, Homewood, Illinois.

——— (1972), "Toward analysis of closed behavioural systems" in *Theory of Public Choice*, J.M. Buchanan and R.D. Tollison (eds), University of Michigan Press, Ann Arbor, Michigan.

——— (1976a), "Barro on the Ricardian equivalence theorem", *Journal of Political Economy*, 84, 337-342.

——— (1976b), "A Hobbesian interpretation of the Rawlsian difference principle", *Kyklos*, 29, 5-25.

BUCHANAN, J.M. and C.J. Ooetz (1972), "Efficiency Limits of fearal mobility: an assessment of the Tobout Model", *Journal of Public Economics*, Vol. 1, 25-43.

BUCHANAN and R. WAGNER (1970), "An efficiency basis for federal fiscal equalization", in J. Margolis (ed.), *The Analysis of Public Output*, Columbia University Press.

BUCHANAN, J.M. and M.Z. KAFOGLIS (1963), "A note on public goods supply", *American Economic Review*, 53, 403-414.

BUCHANAN, J.M. and G. TULLOCK (1962), *The Calculus of Consent*, University of Michigan Press, Ann. Arbor, Michigen.

BUCTER, W. and J. TOBIN (1976), "Long Run Effects of Fiscal and Monetary Policy on Aggregate Demand", in *Monetarism: Studies in Monetary Economics*, ed. J.L. Stein, North Holland, Bureau of Public Enterprises, Government of India, Annual Surveys various issues.

Bureau of Public Enterprises, Government of India, Annual Surveys, various issues.

BURMEISTER, E. and A.R. DOBELL (1970), *Mathematical Theories of Economic Growth*, CollierMacmillan, New York.

BURTLESS, G. and J.A. HAUSMAN (1978), "The effect of taxation on labor supply: evaluating the Gary negative income tax experiment", *Journal of Political Economy*, 86, 1103-1130.

CAGAN, P. (1956), "The Monetary Dynamics of Hyperinflation", in M. Friedman ed. *Studies in the Quantity* Theory of Money, University of Chicago Press.

CAIN, G.G. and M.D. DOOLEY (1976), "Estimation of a model of labor supply, fertility, and wages of married women", *Journal of Political Economy*, 84, S179-199.

CAIN, G.G. and H.W. WATTS (eds) (1973), *Income Maintenance and Labour Supply*, Rand McNally, Chicago.

CALVO, G. (1977), "Some Notes, on Time Inconsistency and Rewels Maximin Criterion," *Econometricee.*

CARTTER, A.M. (1955), *The Redistribution of Income in Postwar Britain*, Yale University Press, New Haven Connecticut.

CARVER, T.N. (1904), "The minimum sacrifice theory of taxation", *Political Science Quarterly*, 19, 66-79.

CASS, D. (1965), "Optimum growth in an aggregative model of capital accumulation", *Review of Economic Studies*, 32, 233-240.

CASS, D. and J.E. STIGLITZ (1970), "The structure of investor preferences and asset returns, and separability in portfolio allocation", *Journal of Economic Theory*, 2, 122-160.

——— and ——— (1972), "Risk aversion and wealth effects on portfolios with many assets", *Review of Economic Studies*, 39, 331-354.

CAVES, R.E. and R.W. JONES (1977), World Trade and Payments, Little, Brown, Boston, United States", *Revue Economique*, 25, 635-671.

Central Statistical Office (1979), "The effects of taxes and benefits on household income 1977, Central Statistical Organization, Government of India, various issues of National Accounts Statistics, *Economic Trends*, 303, 97-130.

CHELLIAH, R. and R. LAL (1978), *The Incidence of Indirect Taxes in India*, NIPFP.

CHELLIAH R. et. al (1981), *Trends and Issues in Indian Federal Finance*, NIPFP.

Central Statistical Organisation, Government of India, various issues of National Accounts Statistics.

CHIPMAN, J.S. (1974), "The welfare ranking of Pareto distributions," *Journal of Economic Theory*, 9, 275-282.

CLARKE, E.H. (1971), "Multipart pricing of public goods", *Public Choice*, 11, 17-33.

——— (1972), "Multipart pricing of public goods: an example" in *public prices for public products*, S. Mushkin (ed.), Urban Institute, Washington DC.

COASE, R. (1960), "The Problem of Social Cost", *Journal of Law and Economics*.

COEN, R.M. (1971), "The effect of cash flow on the speed of adjustment" in *Tax Incentives and Capital Spending*, G. Fromm (ed.), North-Holland, Amsterdam.

COEN, R.M. and B.G. HICKMAN (1970), "Constrained joint estimation of factor demand and production functions", *Review of Economics and Statistics*, 52, 287-310.

COLM, G. and H. TARASOV (1940), Who Pays the Taxes? Temporary National Economic Committee, Monograph 3, Washington DC.

COLWYN COMMITTEE (1927), Report of Committee on National Debt and Taxation, HMSO, London.

CONLISK, J. (1977), "An exploratory model of the size distribution of income", *Economic Inquiry*, 15, 345-366.

COOPER, G. (1952), "Taxation and incentive in mobilization", *Quarterly Journal of Economics*, 66, 43-66.

COOTER, R. (1978), "Optimal Tax Schedules and Tates: Mirrlees and Ramsey", *American Economic Review*.

COOTNER, R. and E. HELPMAN (1974), "Optimal Income taxation for transfer payments", *Quarterly Journal of Economics*, 88, 656-670.

CORLETT, W.J. and D.C. HAGUE (1953), "Complementarity and the excess burden of taxation", *Review of Economic Studies*, 21, 21-30.

DALTON, H. (1954), *Principles of Public Finance*, Routledge and Kegan Paul, London.

DANZIGER, L. (1976), "A graphic representation of the Nash and Lindahl equilibria in an economy with a public good", *Journal of Public Economics*, 6, 295-307.

DASGUPTA, P.S. and J.E. STIGLITZ (1972), "On optimal taxation and public production", *Review of Economic Studies*, 39, 87-103.

——— and ——— (1974), EBenefit-cost analysis and trade policies", *Journal of Political Economy*, 82, 1-33.

DAVID, M. (1968), *Alternative Approaches to Capital Gains Taxation*, Brookings Institution, Washington DC.

DAVID, P.A. and J.L. SCADDING (1974), "Private savings: ultrarationality, aggregation and 'Dension's Law'", *Journal of Political Economy*, 82, 225-249.

DAVIDSON, J.E.H., D.F. HÉNDRAY, F. SRBA and S. YEO (1978), Econometric modelling of the aggregate time-series relationship between consumers' expenditure and income in the United Kingdom", *Economic Journal*, 88, 661-692.

DAVIDS, O.A. and A.B. WHINSTON (1967), "Piecemeal policy in the theory of second best", *Review of Economic Studies*, 34, 323-331.

DE GRAAFF, T. (1957), *Theoretical Welfare Economics*, Cambridge University Press.

DEATON, A.S. (1977), "Equity, efficiency and the structure of indirect taxation", *Journal of Public Economics*, 8, 299-312.

——— (1978), "Optimal taxes and the structure of preferences", mimeo, University of Bristol, 1978.

——— (1979), "The distance function in consumer behaviour with applications to index numbers and optimal taxation", *Review of Economic Studies*.

DEBREU, G. (1959), *Theory of Value*, John Wiley, New York.

——— (1976), "Regular differentiable economics", *American Economic Review*, 66, 280-287.

DIAMOND, P.A. (1965), "National debt in a neoclassical growth model", *American Economic Review*, 55, 1125-1150.

DIAMOND, P.A. (1968), "Negative taxes and the poverty problem: a review article", *National Tax Journal*, 31, 288-303.

——— (1970), "Incidence of an interest income tax", *Journal of Economic Theory*, 2, 211-224.

——— (1973a), "Consumption externalities and imperfect competitive pricing", *Bell Journal of Economics*, 4, 526-538.

——— (1973b), "Tamation and public production in a growth setting" in *Models of Economic Growth*, J.A. Mirrlees and N.H. Stern (eds), Macmillan, London.

——— (1975a), "Inflation and the comprehensive tax base", *Journal of Public Economics*, 4, 277-244.

——— (1975b), "A many person Ramsey tax rule", *Journal of Public Economics*, 4, 335-342.

——— (1978), "Tax incidence in a two good models, *Journal of Public Economics*, 9, 283-299.

DIAMOND, P.A. and D.L. MCFADDEN (1974), "Some uses of the expenditure function in public finance", *Journal of Public Economics*, 3, 3-21.

DIAMOND, P.A. and J.A. MIRRLEES (1971), "Optimal taxation and public production I: production efficiency and II: tax rules", *American Economic Review*, 61, 8-27 and 261-278.

——— and ——— (1973), "Aggregate production with consumption externalities", *Quarterly Journal of Economics*, 87, 1-24.

DIAMOND, P.A. and J.E. STIGLITZ (1974), "Increases in risk and in risk aversion", *Journal of Economic Theory*, 8, 337-360.

DIAMOND, P.A. and M. YAARI (1972), "Implications of the theory of rationing for consumer choice under uncertainty", *American Economic Review*, 62, 333-343.

DIEWERT, W.E. (1974), "Applications of duality theory" in *Frontiers of Quantitative Economics*, M.D. Intriligator and D. Kendrick (eds), North-Holland, Amsterdam.

——— (1978), "*Optimal tax perturbations*", *Journal of Public Economics*, 10, 139-177.

——— (1979), "Duality Approaches to Microeconomic Theory" in *Handbook of Mathematical Economic*, K.J. Arrow and M. Intriligator (eds), North-Holland, Amsterdam.

DIXIT, A.K. (1970), "On the optimum structure of commodity taxes", *American Economic Review*, 60, 295-301.

——— (1975), "Welfare effects of tax and price changes", *Journal of Public Economics*, 4, 103-123.

——— (1976a), *Optimization in Economic Theory*, Oxford University Press, Oxford, London.

——— (1976b), *The Theory of Equilibrium Growth*, Oxford University Press, Oxford.

——— (1976c), "Public finance in a Keynesian temporary equilibrium", *Journal of Economic Theory*, 12, 242-258.

DIXIT, A.K. (1979), "The role of investment in entry-deterrence", Warwick Economic Research Paper 140.

DIXIT A.K. and K.J. MUNK (1977), "Welfare effects of tax and price changes: a correction", *Journal of Public Economics*, 79, 417-423.

DIXIT, A.K. and J.E. STIGLITZ (1977), "Monopolistic competition and optimum product diversity", *American Economic Review*, 67, 297-308.

DOBB, M (1969), *Welfare Economics and economics of socialism*, Cambridge University Press.

——— (1960), *Essay on Economic Growth and Planning*, London.

——— (1967), *Papers on capitalism, Development and Planning*, London.

DODGE, D.A. (1975), "Impact of tax, transfer, and expenditure policies of government on the distribution of personal income in Canada", *Review of Income and Wealth*, 21, 1-52.

DOMAR, E.D. and R.A. Musgrave (1944), "Proportional income taxation and risk-taking", *Quarterly Journal of Economics*, 58, 388-422.

DORFMAN, R. (1975), "Note on a common mistake in welfare economics", *Journal of Political Economy*, 83, 863-864.

DOUGLAS, P.H. (1934), *The Theory of Wages*, Macmillan, New York.

DOWNS, A. (1957), *An Economic Theory of Democracy*, Harper and Row, New York.

DREZE, J.H. (1964), "Some postwar contributions of French economists to theory and public policy", *American Economic Review*, 54 (Supplement).

DREZE, J.H., J. NASKOLD-GABSZEWICZ and A. POSTLEWAITE (1977), "Disadvantageous monopolies and disadvantageous endowments", *Journal of Economic Theory*, 16, 116-121.

DREZE, J.H. and F. MODIGLIANI (1972), "Consumption decisions under uncertainty", *Journal of Economic Theory*, 5, 308-335.

DREZE, J.H. and D. DE LA VALLEE POUSSIN (1971), "A tatonnement process for public goods", *Review of Economic Studies*, 38, 133-150.

DUE, J.F. (1963), *Government Finance* (3rd edn), Irwin, Homewood, Illinois.

DUE, J.F. and A.F. FRIEDLAENDER (1973), *Government Finance* (5th edn), Irwin, Homewood, Illinois.

EATWELL, J.L. (1971), "On the proposed reform of corporation tax", *Bulletin of the Oxford University Institute of Economics and Statistics*, 33, 267-274.

EDGEWORTH, F.Y. (1897), "The pure theory of taxation", *Economic Journal*, 7, 46-70, 226-238 and 550-571 (reprinted in Edgeworth, 1925).

——— (1925), *Papers Relating to Political Economy*, Volume II, Royal Economic Society, Macmillan, London.

EISNER, R. and M.I. NADIRI (1968), "Investment behaviour and neo-classical theory", *Review of Economics and Statistics*, 50, 369-382.

EISNERL R. and R. STROTZ (1963), "Determinants of business investment" in Impacts of Monetary Policy: A series of *Research Studies Prepared for the Commission of Money and Credit, D.B.* Suits et al., Prentice-Hall, Englewood Cliffs, New Jersey.

EKELUND, R.B. (1973), "Public economics at the Ecole des Ponts et Chaussees: 1830-1850", *Journal of Public Economics*, 2, 241-256.

EKERN, S. (1971), "Taxation, political risk and portfolio selection" *Economica*, 38, 421-430.

EKERN, S. and R. WILSON (1974), "On the theory of the firm in an economy with incomplete markets", *Bell Journal of Economics and Management Science*, 5, 171-180.

ELLICKSON, B. (1973), "A generalization of the pure theory of public goods", *American Economic Review*, 63, 417-432.

FAIR, R.C. (1971), "The optimal distribution of income", *Quarterly Journal of Economics*, 85, 551-579.

FARQUHARSON, R. (1969), *Theory of Voting, Yale University* Press, New Haven, Connecticut.

FARRELL, M.J. (1958), "In defence of public-utility price theory", *Oxford Economic Papers*, 10, 109-123; amended version in R. Turvey (ed) (1968), Public Enterprise, Penguin Harmondsworth.

FELDSTEIN, M.S. (1969), "The effects of taxation on risk-taking", *Journal of Political Economy*, 77, 755-764.

——— (1970a), "Inflation, specification bias, and the impact of interest rates", *Journal of Political Economy*, 78, 1325-1339.

——— (1970b), "Corporate taxation and dividend behaviour", *Review of Economic Studies*, 37, 57-72.

FELDSTEIN, M.S. (1972a), "Distributional equity and the optimal structure of public prices", *American Economic Review*, 62, 32-36.

——— (1972b), "Equity and efficiency in public sector pricing: the optimal two-part tariff", *Quarterly Journal of Economics*, 86, 175-187.

——— (1973a), "Tax incentives, corporate saving and capital accumulation in the United States", *Journal of Public Economics*, 2, 159-171.

——— (1973b), "On the optimal progressivity of the income tax", *Journal of Public Economics*, 2, 357-376.

——— (1974a), "Social security, induced retirement and aggregate capital accumulation", *Journal of Political Economy*, 82, 905-926.

——— (1974b), "Tax incidence in a growing economy with variable factor supply", *Quarterly Journal of Economics*, 88, 551-573.

——— (1974c), "Incidence of a capital income tax in a growing economy with variable savings rates", *Review of Economic Studies*, 41, 505-513.

——— (1976a), "Social Security and saving: the extended life cycle theory", *American Economic Review*, Papers and Proceedings, 66, 77-86.

——— (1976b), "Personal taxation and portfolio composition: an econometric analysis", *Econometrica*, 44, 631-650.

——— (1976c), "Perceived wealth in bonds and social security, a comment", *Journal of Political Economy*, 84, 331-336.

——— (1977), "Social security and private savings: international evidence in an extended life cycle model" in *The Economics of Public Services*, M.S. Feldstein and R.P. Inman (eds), Macmillan, London.

——— (1978a), "The rate of return, taxation and personal savings", *Economic Journal*, 88, 482-487.

——— (1978b), "The welfare cost of capital income taxation", *Journal of Political Economy*, 86, S29-51.

FELDSTEIN, M. (ed.) 1983, *Behavioural Simulation Methods in Tax Policy Analysis*, NBER.

FELDSTEIN, M.S. and J.S. FLEMMING (1971), "Tax policy, corporate saving and investment behaviour in Britain", *Review of Economic Studies*, 38, 415-434.

FELDSTEIN, M.S., J.R. GREEN and E. SHESHINSKI (1978), "Corporate financial policy and taxation in a growing economy", *Journal of Political Economy.*

FELDSTEIN, M.S. and R.O. INMAN (eds) (1977), *The Economics of Public Services*, Macmillan", London.

FELDSTEIN, M.S. and A. PELLECHIO (1977), "Social security and household wealth accumulation", NBER Paper No. 206.

FELDSTEIN, M.S. and S.C. Tsiang (1968), "The interest rate, taxation, and the personal savings incentives", *Quarterly Journal of Economics*, 82, 419-434.

FELDSTEIN, M.S. and S. YITZHAKI (1978), "The effects of the capital gains tax on the selling and switching of common stock", *Journal of Public Economics*, 9, 17-36.

FERBER, R. and W.Z. HIRSCH (1978), "Social experimentation and economic policy: a survey", *Journal of Economic Literature*, 16, 1379-1414.

FERGUSON, J.M. (1964), *Public Debt and Future Generations*, University of North Carolina Press, Chapel Hill, North Carolina.

Finance Commission, Government of India, Various Reports.

FISHER, F.M. (1971), "Discussion" in *Tax Incentives and Capital Spending*, *G. Fromm* (ed.), North-Holland, Amsterdam.

FISHER, I. (1937), "Income in theory and income taxation in practice", *Econometrica*, 5, 1-55.

FLATTERS, F., V. HENDERSON and P. MIESZKOWSKI (1974), "Public goods, efficiencv, and regional fiscal equalisation", *Journal of Public Economics*, 3, 99-112.

FOGELMAN, F., M. QUINZII and R. GUESNERIE (1978), "Dynamic Processes for tax reform theory", *Journal of Economic Theory*, 17, 200-226.

FOLEY, D.K. (1967), "Resource allocation and the public sector," *Yale Economic Essays*, 7, 45-98.

——— (1970), "Lindahl's solution and the core of an economy with public goods", *Econometrica*, 38, 66-72.

——— (1978), "State expenditure from a Marxist perspective," *Journal of Public Economics*, 9, 221-238.

FOSTER, E. and H. SONNENSCHEIN (1970), "Price distribution and economic welfare", *Econometrica* 38, 281-297.

FRANZEN, P., K. LOVGREN and I. ROSENBERG (1975), Redistribution effects of taxes and public expenditures in Sweeden", *Swedish Journal of Economics*, 77, 31-55.

FREY, B.S. (1976), "Taxation in fiscal exchange-a comment, *Journal of Public Economics*, 6, 31-35.

——— (1978), "Politico-economic models and cycles", *Journal of Public Economics*, 9, 203-220.

FREY, B.S. and F. SCHNEIDER (1978a), "A politico-economic model of the United Kingdom", *Economic Journal*, 88, 243-253.

——— and ——— (1978b), "An econometric model with an endogenous government sector", *Public choice*.

——— and ——— (1978c), "An empirical study of politico-economic interaction in the United States", *Review of Economics and Statistics*, 60, 174-183.

FRIEDLAENDER, A.F. (1967), "Indirect taxes and relative prices", *Quarterly Journal of Economics*, 81, 125-139.

FRIEDMAN, M. (1952), "The 'welfare' effects of an income tax and an excise tax", *Journal of Political Economy*, 60, 25-33.

——— (1957), *A Theory of the Consumption Function*, Princeton University Press, Princeton, New Jersey.

FRISCH, R. (1939), "The Dupuit taxation theorem", *Econometrica*, 7, 145-150.

FROMM, G. and P. TAUBMAN (1973), *Public Economic Theory and Policy*, Macmillan, New York.

FULLERTON, D., J.B. SHOVEN and J. WHALLEY (1978), "General equilibrium analysis of U.S. taxation policy" in Compendium of Tax Research 1978, Department of the Treasury, Washington DC. Fullerton, D:, J.B. Slioven and J. Whalley (1983), "Replacing the U.S. Income Tax with a Progressive Consumption Tax, "*Journal of Public Economics*, Vol. 20, pp. 3-23.

GARNIER, LE MARQUIS (ed.) (1822), *Introduction to Recherches sur le Nature et les Causes de la Richesse de Nations, Agasse*, Paris.

GEVERS, L. and S. PROOST (1978), "Some effects of taxation and collective goods in postwar America: a tentative appraisal", *Journal of Public Economics*, 9, 115-137.

GIBBARD, A. (1973), "Manipulation of voting schemes: a general result" *Econometrica*, 41, 587-601.

GILLESPIE, W.I. (1965), "Effect of public expenditure on the distribution of Income" in *Essays in Fiscal Federalism*, R.A. Musgrave (ed.), Brookings Institution, Washington DC.

——— (1976), On the redistribution of income in Canada", *Canadian Tax Journal*, 24, 419-450.

GODFREY, L. (1975), Theoretical and Empirical Aspects of the Effects of Taxation on the Supply of Labour, OLCD, Paris.

GOETZ, C.G. (1977), "*Fiscal illusion in state and local finance*" *in Budgets and bureaucrats*, T.E. Borcherding (ed.), Duke University Press, Durham, North Carolina.

GOLDMAN, M.B., H.E. LELAND and D.S. SIBLEY (1977), "Optimal non-uniform prices", Bell Laboratories Discussion Paper.

GOLLADAY, F.L. and R.H. HAVEMAN (1977), *The Economic Impacts of Tax-Transfer Policy*, Academic Press, New York.

GOODE, R. (1949), "The Income tax and the supply of labour", *Journal of Political Economy*, 57, 428-437.

———(1964), *The Individual Income Tax*, Brookings Institution, Washington DC (2nd edn 1976).

——— (1977), "The economic definition of income" in *Comprehensive Income Taxation*, J.A. Pechman (ed.), Brookings Institution, Washington DC.

GORDON, D.M. (1972), "Taxation of the poor and the normative theory of tax incidence", *American Economic Review*, Papers and Proceedings, 62, 319-328.

GORDEON, R.J. (1967), "The incidence of the corporation income tax in U.S. Manufacturing 1925-62", *American Economic Review*, 57, 731-758.

GORDON, S. (1976), "The new contractarians", *Journal of Political Economy*, 84, 573-590.

GORMAN, W.M. (1976), "Tricks with utility functions" in *Essays in Economic Analysis*, M.J. Artis and A.R. Nobay (eds), Cambridge University Press, London.

GRAAFF, J. DE V. (1957), *Theoretical Welfare Economics*, Cambridge University Press, London.

GRANDMONT, J.N. (1977), "Temporary general equilibrium theory", *Econometrica*, 45, 535-572.

GRAVELLE, H.S.E. (1976), "Public enterprises under rate of return financial targets", *Manchester School*, 44, 1-16.

GREEN, H.A.J. (1961), "The social optimum in the presence of monopoly and taxation", *Review of Economic Studies*, 29, 66-78.

——— (1976), *Consumer Theory* (end edn), Macmillan, London.

GREEN, J.J.E. KOHLBERG and J.J. LAFFONT (1977a), "Characterisation of satisfactory mechanisms for the revelation of preferences for public goods", *Econometrica*, 45, 427-438.

GREEN, J.E. KOHLBERG and J.J. LAFFONT (1976), "Partial equilibrium approach to the free-rider problem", *Journal of Public Economics*, 6, 375-394.

GREEN J. and J.J. LAFFONT (1977b), "On the revelation of preferences for public goods", *Journal of Public Economics*, 8, 79-93.

——— and ——— (1979), *Individual Incentives in Public Decision-Making*, North-Holland Amsterdam.

GREEN, J. and E. SHESHINSKI (1976), "Direct versus indirect remedies for externalities", *Journal of Political Economy*, 84, 797-808.

——— and ——— (1978), "Optimal capital-gains taxation under limited information", *Journal of Political Economy*, 86, 1143-1158.

GRIESON, R.E. (1975), "The incidence of Profits taxes in a neoclassical growth model", *Journal of Public Economics*, 4, 75-85.

GRONAU, R. (1973), "The effect of children on the housewife's value of time", *Journal of Political Economy*, 81, S168-199.

GROSSMAN, S.J. and J.E. Stiglitz (1976), "Information and competitive price systems", *American Economic Review*, Papers and Proceedings, 66, 246-253.

——— and ——— (1977), "On value maximisation and alternative objective of the firm", *Journal of Finance*, 32, 389-402.

GROVES, T. (1970), Ph.D. dissertation, University of California, Berkeley.

——— (1973), "Incentives in teams", *Econometrica*, 41, 617-631.

GROVES, T. and J. LEDYARD (1977), "Optimal allocation of public goods: a solution to the 'freerider' problem", *Econometrica*, 45, 783-809.

GROVES, T. and M. LOEB (1975), "Incentives and public inputs", *Journal of Public Economics*, 4, Gupta, D. and S. Gupta (1985), *Inflation, Taxation and the Incentive to Invest*, Radiant Publishers, 211-226.

GUESNERIE, R. (1975), "Public production and taxation in a simple second best model", *Journal of Economic Theory*, 10, 127-156.

——— (1977), "On the direction of tax reform", *Journal of Public Economics*, 7, 179-202.

——— (1978), "General statements on second-best Pareto Optimality", *Journal of Mathematical Economics*.

HAHN, F.H. (1965), "On two-sector growth models", *Review of Economic Studies*, 32, 339-346.

——— (1966), "Equilibrium dynamics with heterogeneous capital goods", *Quarterly Journal of Economics*, 80, 633-646.

——— (1973), "On optimum taxation", *Journal of Economic Theory*, 6, 96-106.

——— (1977), "Keynesian economics and general equilibrium theory: reflections on some current debates", in *The Microeconomic Foundations of Microeconomics*, G.C. Harcourt (ed.), Macmillan, London.

HAHN, F.H. and R.C.O. MATTHEWS (1964), "The theory of economic growth: a survey", *Economic Journal*, 74, 779-902.

HAKANSSON, N.H. (1970), "Optimal investment and consumption strategies under risk for a class of utility functions", *Econometrica*, 38, 587-607.

HALL, R.E. (1969), "Consumption taxes versus income taxes: implications for economic growth", Proceedings of the 61st National Tax Conference, National Tax Association, Columbus, Ohio.

——— (1973), "Wages, income and hours of work in the US labour force" in *Income Maintenance and Labour Supply*, G.G. Cain and H.W. Watts (eds), Rand McNally, Chicago.

——— (1975), "Effects of the experimental negative income tax on labour supply" in *Work Incentives and Income Guarantees*, J.A. Pechman and P.M. Timpane (eds), Brookings Institution, Washington DC.

——— (1977), "Investment, interest rates, and the effects of stabilization policies", *Brookings Economic* Papers, 61-103.

HALL, R.E. and D.W. JORGENSON (1967), "Tax policy and investment behaviour", *American Economic Review*, 57, 391-414.

——— and ——— (1969), "Reply and further results", *American Economic Review*, 59, 388-401.

——— and ——— (1971), "Application of the theory of optimum capital accumulation" in *Tax Incentives and Capital Spending*, G. Formm (ed.), North-Holland, Amsterdam.

HAMADA, K. (1972), "Lifetime equity and dynamic efficiency on the balanced growth path", *Journal of Public Economics*, 1, 379-396.

HANNAWAY, J. (1979), unpublished paper, Columbia University.

HANOCH, G. and M. HONIG (1978), "The labor supply curve under income maintenance programs", *Journal of Public Economics*, 9, 1-16.

HANSEN, B. (1958), *The Economic Theory of Fiscal Policy*, Allen and Unwin, London.

HARBERGER, A.C. (1962), "The incidence of the corporation income tax", *Journal of Political Economy*, 70, 215-240.

——— (1964), "Taxation, resource allocation, and welfare" in *The Role of Direct and Indirect Taxes in the Federal Revenue System*. J. Due (ed), Princeton University Press, Princeton, New Jersey.

——— (1968), "Taxation: Corporation Income taxes" in *International Encyclopedia of the Social Sciences*, D.L. Sills (ed.), Macmillan, New York.

——— (1974), "The corporation income tax: an empirical appraisal" in *Taxation and Welfare*, Little, Brown, Boston.

HARBERGER, A.C. and N. BRUCE (1976), "The incidence and efficiency effects of taxes on income from capital: a reply", *Journal of Political Economy*, 84, 1285-1292.

HARCOURT, G.C. (1972), *Some Cambridge Controversies in the Theory of Capital*, Cambridge University Press, London.

——— (ed.) (1977), *The Microeconomic Foundations of Microeconomics*, Macmillan, London.

HARRIS, R.G. (1975), "A note on convex-concave demand systems", Queens University Discussion Paper No. 197.

HARVIS, J. and M. TODANO (1971), "Migration, Unemployment and Development, of Two Sector Analysis", *American Economic Review*.

HARRIS, R.G. and J.G. MACKINNON (1979), "Computing optimal tax equiliboia", *Journal of Public Economic*, 11, 197-212.

HARRIS, R.G. and M. TOWNSEND, (1978), "Equilibrium under Uncertainty, Multi Agent Statistical Decision Theory", mimeo, Carnegie-Mellon University.

HARSANYI, J.C. (1955), Cardinal welfare, individualistic ethics and inter-personal comparisons of utility", *Journal of Political Economy*, 73, 309-321.

HART, O.D. (1975), "Some negative results on the existence of comparative statics results in portfolio theory", *Review of Economic Studies*, 42, 615-621.

——— (1977), "Take over bids and stock market equilibrium", *Journal of Economic Theory*, 16, 53-83.

HATTA, T. (1977), "A theory of piecemeal policy recommendations", *Review of Economic Studies*, 44, 1-21.

HAUSMAN, J.A. and D.A. WISE (1977), "Social experimentation, truncated distributions, and efficient estimation", *Econometrica*, 45, 919-938.

HEAD, J.G. (1962), "Public goods and public policy", *Public Finance*, 17, 197-219.

——— (1966), "A note on progression and leisure: comment", *American Economic Review*, 56, 172-179.

HEAD, J.G. and C.S. SHOUP (1969), "Public goods, private goods and ambiguous goods", *Economic Journal*, 79, 567-572.

HEADY, C. and P. Mitra (1977), "The computation of optimum linear taxation", University College London Discussion Papers in Public Economics, 1.

HEAL, G.M. (1973), *The Theory of Economic Planning*, North-Holland, Amsterdam.

HECKMAN, J.J. (1974), "Shadow prices market wages and labour supply", *Econometrica*, 52, 679-694.

——— (1978), "A partial survey of recent research on the labour supply of women", *American Economic Review*, Papers and Proceedings, 68, 200-207.

——— (1979), "Sample selection bias as a specification error", *Econometrica*, 47, 153-161.

Heller, W. (1966), *New Dimensions of Political Economy*, Harvard University Press Cambridge, Massachusetts.

HELLER, W.P. and K. SHELL (1974), "On optimal taxation with costly administration", *American Economic Review*, Papers and Proceedings, 64, 338-345.

HELLIWELL, J.F. (1972), "Book review of Fromm (1971)", *Journal of Public Economics*, 1, 159-161.

——— (ed.) (1976), *Aggregative Investment: Selected Readings*, Penguin, Harmondsworth.

HEMMING, R.C.L. (1977), "The effect of state and private pensions on retirement behaviour and personal capital accumulation", *Review of Economic Studies*, 44, 169-172.

HICKS, J.R. (1939), *Value and Capital*, Oxford University Press, London.

——— (1962), "*Liquidity*", Economic Journal, 72, 787-802.

——— (1965), *Capital and Growth*, Oxford University Press, Oxford.

HICKS, J.R. (1939), "*The Foundations of Welfare*", *Economic Journal.*

HICKS, U.K. (1947), *Public Finance*, Nisbet, London.

HILDENBRAND, W. and A.P. KIRMAN (1976), *Introduction to Equilibrium Analysis*, North-Holland, Amsterdam.

HINICH, M.J., J.O. LEDYARD and P.C. ORDENSHOOK (1972), "Nonvoting and the existence of equilibrium under Majority rule", *Journal of Economic Theory*, 4, 144-153.

HIRSCHMAN, A.O. (1970), *Exit, Voice and Loyalty*, Harvard University Press, Cambridge, Massachusetts.

HMSO (1971), Value-Added Tax, Cmnd 4621, London, HMSO.

HOCHMAN, H.M. and J.D. RODGERS (1969), "Pareto optimal redistributions", *American Economic Review*, 59, 542-557.

HOFFMAN, R.F. (1972), "Disaggregation and calculations of the welfare cost of tax", *Journal of Political Economy*, 80, 409-417.

HOLLAND, DANIEL M. (1969), "The effect of taxation on effort: some results for business executives" in National Tax Association, Proceedings of the Sixty-Second Annual Conference, September 1969.

——— (1977), "Effect of taxation on incentives of higher income groups" in Fiscal Policy and Labour supply, Institute for Fiscal Studies, London.

HOTELLING, H. (1929), "Stability in competition", *Economic Journal*, 39, 41-57.

——— (1938), "The general welfare in relation of problems of taxation and a railway and utility rates", *Econometrica*, 6, 242-269.

HOUTHAKKER, H.S. (1960), "Additive preferences", *Econometrica*, 28, 244-257.

HU, S.C. (1980), "Demand for Dunable Goods and the consumer lifetime Allocation Process when capital Markets are Imperfect", *Econometrica*.

HURWICZ, L. (1972), "On informationally decentralised systems" in *Decision and Organisation*, R. Radner and C.B. McGuire (eds), North Holland, Amsterdam.

INADA, K. (1963), "On a two-sector model of economic growth: comments and a generalisation", *Review of Economic Studies*, 30, 119-127.

INMAN, R.P. (1978), "Testing political economy's 'As if' proposition: is the median income voter really decisive?", *Public Choice*, 33.

INTRILIGATOR, M.D. (1971), *Mathematical Optimization and Economic Theory*, Prentice-Hall, Englewood Cliffs, New Jersey.

ITSUMI, Y. (1974), "Distributional effects of linear income tax schedules", *Review of Economic Studies*, 41, 371-382.

JAFFEE, D.M. and T. RUSSELL (1976), "Symposium, The economics of information: imperfect information, uncertainty and credit rationing", *Quarterly Journal of Economics*, 90, 651-666.

JAKOBSSON, U. (1976), "On the measurement of the degree of progression", *Journal of Public Economics*, 5, 161-168.

JESSOP, B. (1977), "Recent theories of the capitalist state", *Cambridge Journal of Economics*, 1, 353-373.

JHA, R. (1979), Linear Maximum Taxatation for Intra and Inter-Generational Justice, Working Paper, Williams College.

——— (1986), Optimal labour Supply and the Accumulation of Human and Financial Capital with Capital Market Imperfections, *Indian Economic Review*, Vol. 21.

——— and U. Lachler (1981), Optimal Taxation and Public Production in a Dynamic Harris-Todaro World, *Journal of Development Economics*.

——— and ——— (1983), Inflation and Economic Growth in a Competitive Economy with Exhaustible Resources, *Journal of Economic Behaviour and Organisation*.

JHA and M.N. MURTY (1986), "Distributional Equity and Optimal Structure of Prices for the Public Electricity supply in India: The Flexible Coefficients Case", *Energy Economics* (forthcoming).

JOHANSEN, L. (1960), *A Multi-Sectoral Study of Economic Growth*, North-Holland, Amsterdam.

——— (1965), *Public Economics*, North-Holland, Amsterdam.

——— (1977), "The theory of public goods: misplaced emphasis?" *Journal of Public Economics*, 7, 147-152.

——— (1978), *Lectures on Macroeconomic Planning*, Volume 2, North-Holland, Amsterdam.

JOHANSON, H.G. (1956), "General equilibrium analysis of excise taxes, comment", *American Economic Review*, 46, 151-156.

——— (1959), "International trade, income distribution and the offer curve", *Manchester School*, 27, 241-260.

JOHNSON, H.G. and P.M. MIESZKOWSKI (1970), 'The effects of unionization on the distribution of income: a general equilibrium approach", *Quarterly Journal of Economics*, 84, 539-561.

JOHNSON, S.B. and T. MAYER (1962), "Ab extension of Sidgwick's equity principle", *Quarterly Journal of Economics*, 76, 454-463.

JONES, H.G. (1975), *An Introduction to Modern Theories of Economic Growth*, Nelson, London.

JONES, R.W. (1965), "The structure of simple general equilibrium models", *Journal of Political Economy*, 73, 557-572.

——— (1971a), "Distortions in factor markets and the general equilibrium model of production", *Journal of Political Economy*, 79, 437-459.

——— (1971b), "A three-factor model in theory, trade and history" in *Trade, Balance of Payments and Growth*, J. Bhagwati et al. (eds). North-Holland, Amsterdam.

JORDAN, J. (1971), "Investment under uncertainty", University of Minnesota, Memio.

JORGENSON, D.W. (1963), "Capital theory and investment behaviour", *American Economic Review*, 53, 247-259.

——— (1971), "Economic studies of investment behaviour: a survey", *Journal of Economic Literature*, 9, 1111-1147.

——— (1972), "Investment behaviour and the production functions", *Bell Journal of Economics*, 3, 220-251.

JORGENSON, D.W. and J.A. STEPHENSON (1967), "Investment behaviour in U.S. Manufacturing 1947-1960", *Econometrica*, 35, 169-220.

JUNANKAR, P.N. (1972), *Investment: Theories and Evidence*, Macmillan, London.

KADANE, J.B. (1975), "Statistical problems of merged data files", Office of Tax Analysis Paper 6.

KAIZUKA, K. (1965), "Public goods and decentralization of productions, *Review of Economics and Statistics*, 47, 118-120.

KALDOR, N. (1955), *An Expenditure Tax*, Allen and Unwin, London.

——— (1956), "Alternative theories of distribution", *Review of Economic Studies*, 23, 83-100.

——— (1966), "Marginal productivity and the macroeconomic theories of distribution", *Review of Economic Studies*, 33, 309-320.

KALDOR, N. (1939), "Welfare Productions and Interpersonal Comparisons of utility", *Economic Journal.*

KALDOR, N. WITH J.A. MIRRLESS (1962), "A new model of economic growth", *Review of Economic Studies*, 29, 174-192.

KALECKI, M. (1937), "A theory of commodity, income and capital taxation", *Economic Journal*, 47, 444-450.

KAY, J.A. (1977), "Inflation accounting: a review article", *Economic Journal*, 87, 300-311.

——— (1978), "A lifetime expenditure tax", unpublished paper, St John's College, Oxford.

KAY, J.A. and M.A. KING (1978), The British Tax System, *Oxford University Press*, London.

KELLY, J.S. (1980), *Arrow Impossibility Theorems*, New York.

KENNEDY, C. (1964), "Induced bias in innovation and the theory of distribution", *Economic Journal*, 74, 541-547.

KENNEDY, W. (1913), *English Taxation 1640-1799*, Bell, London.

KESSELMAN, J.R. (1973), "A Comprehensive approach to income maintenance: SWIFT", *Journal of Public Economics*, 2, 59-88.

——— (1976), "Tax effects on job search, training and work effort", *Journal of Public Economics*, 6, 255-272.

KEYNES, J. (1936), The General Theory of Employment, Interest and Money London, Lange, O. (1938), *On the Economic Theory of Socialism*, University of Minnesota Press.

KING, M.A. (1972), "Taxation and investment incentives in a vintage investment model", *Journal of Public Economics*, 1, 121-147.

——— (1974), "Taxation and the cost of capital", *Review of Economic Studies*, 41, 21-35.

——— (1975), "Taxation, corporate financial policy and the cost of capital, —a comment", *Journal of Public Economics*, 4, 271-279.

——— (1977), *Public Policy and the Corporation*, Chapman and Hill, London.

KLEVORICK, A.K. and G.H. KRAMER (1973), "Social choice on pollution management: the Genossenschaften", *Journal of Public Economics*, 2, 101-146.

KOLM, S-CH. (1968), Prix Publics Optimaux, CNRS, Paris.

——— (1969), "The optimal production of social justice" in *Public Eco*, J. Margolis and H. Guitton (eds), Macmillan, London.

——— (1971), L'Etat et le systeme des prix, I: La Valeur Publique II: Prix publics optimaux, III: La theorie des contraintes de valeur et ses applications, Dunod, Paris.

KRAMER, G.H. (1973), "On a class of equilibrium conditions for majority rule", *Econometrica*, 41, 285-297.

——— (1977a), "A dynamical model of political equilibrium", *Journal of Economic Theory*, 16, 310-334.

——— (1977b), "Theories of political processes" in *Frontiers of Quantitative Economics III*, M.D. Intriligator (ed.), North-Holland, Amsterdam.

KRAMER, G.H. and A.K. KLEVORICK (1974), "Existence of a 'local" co-operative equilibrium in a class of voting games", *Review of Economic Studies*, 41, 539-547.

KRAUSS, M.B. (1971), "General equilibrium aspects of Canada's white paper on tax reform", *Canadian Journal of Economics*, 4, 256-263.

——— (1972), "Differential tax incidence: large versus small tax changes", *Journal of Political Economy*, 80, 193-197.

KRAUSS, M.B. and H.G. JOHNSON (1972), "The theory of tax incidence: a diagrammatic analysis", *Economica*, 39, 357-382.

KRZYZANIAK, M. (1967), "Long-run burden of general tax on profits in a neoclassical world", *Public Finance*, 22, 472-491.

KRZYZANIAK, M. and R.A. MUSGRAVE (1963), *The Shifting of the Corporation Income Tax*, Johns Hopkins Press, Baltimore.

KUHN, H.W. (1968), "Simplicial approximations of fixed points", *Proceedings of the National Academy of Sciences*, 61, 1238-1242.

——— (1976), "How to compute economic equilibria by pivotal methods" in *Computing Equilibria: How and Why*, *J. Los* and M.W. Los (eds), North-Holland, Amsterdam.

KURZ, M. (1974), "Experimental approach to the determination of the demand for public goods", *Journal of Public Economics*, 3, 329-348.

LANCASTER, K.J. (1966), "A new approach to consumer theory", *Journal of Political Economy*, 74, 132-157.

LAU, L.J., E. SHESHINSKI and J.E. STIGLITZ (1978), "Efficiency in the optimum supply of public goods", *Econometrica*, 46, 269-284.

LEITMAN, G. (1966), *An Introduction to Optimal Control*, McGraw-Hill, New York.

LELAND, H.E. (1974), "Production theory and the stock market", *Bell Journal of Economics and Management Science*, 5, 125-144.

LERNER, A.P. (1944), *The Economics of Control*, Macmillan, New York.

——— (1948), "The burden of the National Debt" in *Income, Employment and Public Policy: Essays in Honor of Alvin H. Hansen*, L.A. Metzler et al. (eds.), Norton, New York.

——— (1959), "Consumption loan interest and money", *Journal of Political Economy*, 67, 523-525.

LEUTHOLD, J.H. (1968), "An empirical study of formula income transfers and the work decision of the poor", *Journal of Human Resources*, 3, 312-323.

LEVHARI, D. and T.N. SRINIVASAN (1969), "Optimal savings under uncertainty", *Review of Economic Studies*, 36, 153-164.

LEVITT, M. (1964), "Comparison of the equilibrium labor supply under proportional and progressive taxation", *Journal of Political Economy*, 72, 496-497.

LEWIS, W.A. (1941), "The two-part tariff", *Economica*, 8, 249-270.

LINDAHL, E. (1919), "Positive Losung, Die Gerechtigkeit der Besteuerung" translated as "Just taxation—a positive solution" *in Classics in the Theory of Public Finance*, R.A. Musgrave and A.T. Peacock (eds), Macmillan, London.

LIPSEY, R.G. and K. LANCASTER (1956-57), The General Theory of Second Best", *Review of Economic Studies*, 24, 11-32.

LITTLE, I.M.D. (1951), "Direct versus indirect taxes", *Economic Journal*, 61, 577-584.

LITTLE, I.M.D. and J.A. MIRRLEES (1974), *Project Appraisal and Planning for Developing Countries*, Heinemann, London.

LIVIATAN, N. (1966), "Multiperiod future consumption as an aggregate", *American Economic Review*, 56, 828-840.

LLUCH, C., A.A. POWELL and R.A. WILLIAMS (1977), *Patterns in Household Demand and Saving*, Oxford University Press, New York.

LODIN, S.O. (1976), Progressive Utgiftsskatt-ett alternative?, Statens Offentliga Utredringa, Stockholm.

LOISTL, O. (1976), "The erroneous approximation of expected utility by means of a Taylor's series expansion, analytic and computational results", *American Economic Review*, 66, 904-910.

LOVELL, M.C. (1978), "Spending for education: the exercise of public choice", *Review of Economics and Statistics*, 680, 487-495.

LUCAS, R.E. (1967), "Adjustment costs and the theory of supply", *Journal of Political Economy*, 75, 321-335.

——— (1976), "Econometric policy evaluation: a critique" in *The Phillips Curve and Labor Markets*, K. Brunner and A.H. Meltzer (eds), North-Holland, Amsterdam.

LUCE R.D. and P. SUPPES (1965), "Preference utility and sulyeitive Probability," in R.D. Luce, R.R. Bush and E. Gallanter (eds) *Hand-book of Mathematical Psychology*, John Wiley.

McCULLOCH, J.R. (1845), *A Treatise on the Principles and Practical Influence of Taxation and the Funding System*, (Scottish Economic Society edn, 1975, ed. D.P. O'Brien, Scottish Academic Press, Edinburgh).

McFADDEN, D. (1975, 1976), "The revealed preferences of a government of bureaucracy", *Bell Journal of Economics*, 6, 401-416, 7, 55-72.

McGUIRE, M.C. (1974), "Group segregation and optimal jurisdictions", *Journal of Political Economy*, 82, 112-132.

McLURE, C.E. JR. (1969), "The inter-regional incidence of general regional taxes, *Public Finance*, 24, 457-483.

——— (1970), "Taxation, substitution, and industrial location", *Journal of Political Economy*, 78, 112-132.

——— (1971), "The theory of tax incidence with imperfect factor mobility", *Finanzarchiv*, 30, 27-48.

——— (1974), "A diagrammatic exposition of the Harberger model with one immobile factor", *Journal of Political Economy*, 82, 56-82.

——— (1975), "General equilibrium incidence analysis: the Harberger model after ten years", *Journal of Public Economics*, 4, 125-161.

McLure, C.E. and W.R. Thirsk (1975), "A simplified exposition of the Harberger model I: The incidence", *National Tax Journal*, 28, 1-27.

MacRae, D.C. (1977), "A Political model of the business cycle", *Journal of Political Economy*, 85, 239-263.

Magee, S.P. (1971), "Factor market distortions, production, distribution and the pure theory of international trade", *Quarterly Journal of Economics*, 85, 623-643.

——— (1973), "Factor market distortions, production and trade: a survey", *Oxford Economic Papers*, 25, 1-43.

——— (1976), *International Trade and Distortions in Factor Markets*, Marcel Dekker, New York.

Malinvaud, E. (1971a), "Procedures for the determination of a program of collective consumption", *European Economic Review*, 2, 187-217.

——— (1971b), "A planning approach of the public good problem", *Swedish Journal of Economics*, 11, 96-112.

——— (1972), *Lectures on Microeconomic Theory*, North-Holland, Amsterdam.

——— (1977), *The Theory of Unemployment Reconsidered*, Basil Blackwell, Oxford.

Marglin, S.A. (1975), "What to bosses do?-Part II", *Review of Radical Political Economics*.

Marglin, S.A. (1984), *Growth, Distribution and Prices, Neoclassical, New-Marxian and Neo-Keynesian Approaches to the study of capetalian*, *Harvard University Press*.

Markowitz, H.M. (1959), *Portfolio Secection Efficient Diversification of Investments*, John Wiley, New York.

Marris, R. (1964), *The Economic Theory of "Managerial" Capitalism* Macmillan, London.

Mayston, D.J. (1975), "Optimal licensing in public sector tariff structures" in *Contemporary Issues in Economics*, M. Parkin and A.R. Nobay (eds), Manchester University Press, Manchester.

Meade, J.E. (1951), *Balance of Payments*, Oxford University Press, Oxford.

——— (1955), *Trade and Welfare*: Mathematical Supplement, Oxford University Press, Oxford.

——— (1958), (1959), "Is the National Debt burden?", *Oxford Economic Papers*, 10, 163-183; 11, 109-110.

——— (1961), *A Neo-Classical Theory of Economic Growth*, Allen and Unwin, London.

——— (1964), *Efficiency, Equality and the Ownership of Property*, Allen and Unwin, London.

——— (1966), "Life-cycle savings, inheritance and economic growth", *Review of Economic Studies*, 33, 61-78.

——— (1975), *The Intelligent Radical's Guide to Economic Policy*, Allen and Unwin, London.

——— (1976), *The Just Economy*, Allen and Unwin, London.

——— (1978), *The Structure and Reform of Direct Taxation*, Allen and Unwin, London.

MEADE, J.E. and J.M. FLEMING (1944), "Price and Output policy of state enterprise", *Economic Journal*, 54, 321-339.

MEADE, J.E. and F.H. HAHN (1965), "The rate of profit in a growing economy", *Economic Journal*, 75, 445-448.

MERTON, R.C. (1978), "Investment under uncertainty", Mimeo MIT Manglin, S.C.

METCALF, C.E. (1973), "Making inferences from controlled income maintenance experiments", *American Economic Review*, 63, 478-483.

——— (1974), "Predicting the effects of permanent programs from a limited duration experiment", *Journal of Human Resources*, 9, 530-555.

METCALFE, J.E. and I. STEEDMAN (1971), "Some effects of taxation in a linear model of production", *Manchester School*, 39, 171-185.

METZLER, L.A. (1951), "Taxes and subsidies in Leontief's input-output model", *Quarterly Journal of Economics*, 65, 433-438.

MIESZKOWSKI, P.M. (1966), "The comparative efficiency of tariffs and other tax-subsidy schemes as a means of obtaining revenue or protecting domestic production", *Journal of Political Economy*, 74, 587-599.

——— (1967), "On the theory of tax incidence", *Journal of Political Economy*, 75, 250-262.

——— (1969), "Tax incidence theory: the effects of taxes on the distribution of income", *Journal of Economic Literature*, 7, 1103-1124.

——— (1972), "The property tax: an excise tax or a profits tax?", *Journal of Public Economics*, 1, 73-96.

——— (1977), "The cash flow version of an expenditure tax", Office of Tax Analysis Paper 26.

MILLERON, J.C. (1968). "L'approche per dualite dans la theorie des effects externes et des consommations collectives", INSEE.

——— (1972), "Theory of value with public goods: a survey article", *Journal of Economic Theory*, 5, 419-477.

MINARIK, J.E. (1977), "The yield of a comprehensive income tax" in *Comprehensive Income Taxation*, J.A. Pechman (ed.), Brookings Institution, Washington DC.

MIRRLEES, J.A. (1971), "An exploration in the theory of optimum income taxation", *Review of Economic Studies*, 38, 175-208.

——— (1972a), "On producer taxation", *Review of Economic Studies*, 39, 105-111.

——— (1972b), "Population policy and the taxation of family size", *Journal of Public Economics*, 1, 169-198.

——— (1973), "Introduction", in *Models of Economic Growth*, J.A. Mirrless and W.H. Stern (eds), Macmillan, London.

——— (1975), "Optimal commodity taxation in a two-class economy", *Journal of Public Economics*, 4, 27-33.

——— (1976), "Optimal tax theory: a synthesis", *Journal of Public Economics*, 6, 327-358.

——— (1977), "Labour supply behaviour and optimal taxes" in *Fiscal Policy and Labour Supply*, Institute for Fiscal Studies, London.

——— (1979), "The theory of optimal taxation" in *Handbook of Mathematical Economics*, K. Mishan, E.J. (1963), "How to make a burden of the public debt", *Journal of Political Economy*, 71, 529-542.

———1971, "The post war literature on externalities: an interpretive essay", *Journal of Economic Literature*, 9, 1-28.

MITRA, P.K. (1975), "Taxation and intergenerational equity", mimeo, University College, London.

MODIGLIANI, F. (1961), "Long-run implications of alternative fiscal policies and the burden of the national debt", *Economic Journal*, 71, 730-755.

——— (1975), "The life cycle hypothesis twenty years later" in *Current Economic Problems*, M. Parking and A.R. Nobay (eds), Cambridge University Press, Cambridge.

MODIGLIANI, F. and R. BRUMBERG (1955), "Utility analysis and the consumption function: an interpretation of cross-section data" in *Post Keynesian Economics*, K.K. Kurihara (ed.), Allen and Unwin, London.

MODIGLIANI, F. and M.H. MILLER (1958), "The cost of capital, corporation finance, and the theory of investment", *American Economic Review*, 48, 261-297.

MOSSIN J. (1968), "Taxation and risk-taking: an expected utility approach", *Economica*, 35, 74-82.

MUELLBAUER, J.N.J. (1975), "Aggregation, income distribution and consumer demand", *Review of Economic Studies*, 42, 525-543.

——— (1976), "Community preferences and the representative consumer", *Econometrica*, 44, 979-999.

MUELLER, D.C. (1976), "Public choice: a survey", *Journal of Economic Literature*, 14, 396-433.

MUENCH, T.J. (1972), "The core and the Lindahl equilibrium of an economy with a public good: an example", *Journal of Economic Theory*, 4, 241-255.

MUNK, K.J. (1975), "Optimal public sector pricing taking the distributional aspects into consideration", Aarhus Discussion Paper.

——— (1978), "Optimal taxation and pure profit", *Scandinavian Journal of Economics*, 80, 1-19.

MUNNELL, A.H. (1976), "Private pensions and saving: new evidence", *Journal of Political Economy*, 84, 1013-1032.

MURTY, M.N. and P. NAYAK (1982), "Pollution Abatement and Externalities", *Indian Economic Review*.

MURTY, M.N. (1983a), "Efficiency and distributional equity and optimal structure of prices for public electricity supply in India", Working Paper No. E/86/83, Institute of Economic Growth, Delhi.

——— (1983a), "Distributional equity, indirect taxation and optimal structure of price for a public sector commodity", mimeo.

——— (1984), "Distributional equity, government revenue and price and tax policies in India, mimeo.

MUSGRAVE, R.A. (1953a), "General equilibrium aspects of incidence theory", *American Economic Review*, 43, 504-517.

——— (1953b), "On incidence", *Journal of Political Economy*, 61, 306-323.

——— (1959), *The Theory of Public Finance*, McGraw-Hill, New York.

——— (1964), "Estimating the distribution of the tax burden" in *Income Redistribution and the Statistical Foundations of Economic Policy*, C. Clark and G. Stuvel (eds), Bowes and Bowes, London.

——— (1969), *Fiscal Systems, Yale University* Press, London.

——— (1976), "ET, OT and SBI, *Journal of Public Economics*, 6, 3-16.

MUSGRAVE, R.A., J.J. CARROLL, L.D. COOK and L. FRANE, (1951), "Distribution of tax payments by income groups: a case study for 1948", *National Tax Journal*, 4, 1-53.

MUSGRAVE, R.A. and P.B. MUSGRAVE (1976), *Public Finance in Theory and Practice*, 2nd edn, McGraw-Hill, New York.

MUSGRAVE, R.A. and TUN THIN (1948), "Income tax progression 1929-1948", *Journal of Political Economy*, 56, 498-514.

MUSSA, M. (1974), "Tariffs and the distribution of income", *Journal of Political Economy*, 32, 1191-1203.

KUTH, R. (1966), "Household production and consumer demand functions", *Econometrica*, 34, 699-708.

NADIRI, M.I. and S. ROSEN (1969), "Interrelated factor demand functions", *American Economic Review*, 59, 457-471.

National Economic and Social Council (1975), Income Distribution: A preliminary Report, Prl 4575, The Stationary Office, Dublin.

NEARY, J.P. (1976), B. Phil. Thesis, University of Oxford.

——— (1978), "Dynamic stability and the theory of factor-market' distortions", *American Economic Review*, 68, 671-682.

NEGISHI, T. (1967), "The perceived demand curve in the theory of Second Best", *Review of Economic Studies*, 34, 315-321.

NEWBERY, D.M.G. and J.E. STIGLITZ (1979), "Pareto inferior trade", Oxford University Discussion Paper.

NG. Y. (1979), *Introduction to Modern Welfare Economics*, McMillan.

NG. Y. and M. WEISSER (1974), "Optimal pricing with a budget constraint-the case of the two-part tariff", *Review of Economic Studies*, 41, 337-345.

NICHOLSON, J.L. (1964), *Redistribution of Income in the United Kingdom in 1959, 1957 and 1953*, Bowes and Bowes, Cambridge.

NICKELL, S.J. (1978), *The Investment Decisions of Firms*, J. Nisbet, Welwyn Garden City.

NISKANEN, W.A. Jr. (1971), *Bureaucracy and Representative Government*, Aldine, Chicago.

NORDHAUS, W.D. (1975), "The political business cycle", *Review of Economic Studies*, 42, 169-190.

NORICK, R. (1974), *Anarchy, State and Utopia*, Basil Blackwell, Oxford.

OATES, W.E. (1972), *Fiscal Federalism*, Harcourt Brace Jovanovich, New York.

O'CONNOR, J. (1973), *The Fiscal Crisis of the State*, St. Martin's Press, New York.

OKUN, A.M. (1975), *Equality and Efficiency*, Brookings Institution, Washington DC.

OLSON, M. (1965), *The Logic of Collective Action*, Harv ard University Press, Cambridge, Massachusetts.

ORCUTT, G.H. and A.G. ORCUTT (1968), "Incentive and disincentive experimentation for income maintenance policy purposes", *American Economic Review*, 58, 754-772.

ORDOVER, J.A. (1976), "Distributive justice and optimal taxation of wealth and wages for intragenerational lifetime justice: some steady-state cases, *American Economic Review*, 65, 660-673.

——— and E.S. PHELPS (1979), "The concept of optimal taxation in an over-lapping generations model of capital and wealth", Journal of Public Economics, 12, 1-26.

ORDOVER, J. and R. WILLIG, (1979), "The Role of Information in Designing Socially Optimal Policies Toward Externalities, *Journal of Public Economics*.

PANZAR, J.C. and R.D. WILLING (1976), "Vindication of a 'Common mistake' in welfare economics", *Journal of Political Economy*, 84, 1361–1363.

PASSINETTI, L.L. (1962), "Rate of profit and income distribution in relation to the rate of economic growth", *Review of Economic Studies*, 29, 267-279.

PATTANAIK, P.K. (1971), *Voting and Collective Choice*, Cambridge University Press, Cambridge.

PAULY, M.V. (1967), "Clubs, Commonality, and the Core", *Economica*, 34, 314-324.

——— (1970a), "Optimality, 'public' goods and local government: a general theoretical analysis", *Journal of Political Economy*, 78, 572-585.

——— (1970b), "Cores and clubs", Public Choice, 9, 53-65.

PEACOCK, A.T. (1974), "The treatment of government expenditure in studies of income distribution" in *Public Finance and Stabilisation Policy*, W.L. Smith and J.M. Ertson (eds), North-Holland, Amsterdam.

PEACOCK, A.T. and J. WISEMAN (1967), *The Growth of Public Expenditure* in the United Kingdom, 2nd edn, Allen and Unwin, London.

PECHMAN, J.A. (1965), "Financing state and local government", Proceedings of a Symposium Federal Taxation, *American Bankers' Association*, New York.

PECHMAN, J.A. and B.A. OKNER (1972), "Individual income tax erosion by income classes" in joint Economic Committee, The Economics of Federal Subsidy Programs, U.S. Congress, Washington DC.

——— and ——— (1974), Who Bears the Tax Burden?, Brookings Institution, Washington DC.

PECHMAN, J.A. and P.M. TIMPANE (eds) (1975), *Work Incentives and Income Guarantees*, Brookings Institution, Washington DC.

PENCAVEL, J. (1979), "Constant-Utility Index Numbers of Real Wages", *American Economic Review*, 69, 240-243.

PESTIEAU, P.M. (1974), "Optimal taxation and discount rate for public investment in a growth setting", *Journal of Public Economics*, 3, 217-235.

PESTIEAU, P. and U. POSSEN (1978), "Optimum growth and Distribution Policies", *Journal of Public Economics*.

PHELPS, E.S. (1973), "The taxation of wage income for economic justice", *Quarterly Journal of Economics*, 87, 331-354.

——— (1977), "Linear 'maximin' taxation of wage and property income on a 'maximin' growth path", in *Economic Progress, Private Values and Public Policy*, B. Balassa and R. Nelson (eds), North-Holland, Amsterdam.

PHELPS, E.S. (1961), "The golden rule of Accumulation: a fable for growthmen", *American Economic Review*, Vol. 51, 638-43.

——— (1976), "Recent Developments in Welfare Economics: Justice et Equite", in M. Intsilligation, (ed.) *Frontiers of Quantitative Economics*, North Holland.

——— and J. RILEY (1976), "Rawalsian Growth: Dynamic Programming of Wages and Wealth for Intergenerational Justice", *Review of Economic Studies*.

PHELPS, E.S. and K. SHELL (1969), "Public debt, taxation, and capital intensiveness", *Journal of Economic Theory*, 1, 330-346.

PIGOU, A.C. (1947), *A Study in Public Finance* (3rd edn), Macmillan, London.

PLOTT, C.R. (1967), "A notion of equilibrium and its possibility under majority rule", *American Economic Review*, 57, 787-806.

POLINSKY, A.M. (1973), "A note on the measurement of incidence", *Public Finance Quarterly*, 1, 219-230.

——— (1974), "Imperfect capital markets, intertemporal redistribution and progressive taxation", in *Redistribution Through Public Choice*, H.M. Hochman and G.E. Peterson (eds), Columbia University Press, New York.

POMMEREHNE, W.W. (1978), "Institutional approaches to public expenditure: empirical evidence from Swiss municipalities", *Journal of Public Economics*, 9, 255-280.

POMMEREHENE, W.W. and B.S. FREY (1976), "Two approaches to estimating public expenditures", *Public Finance Quarterly*, 4, 395-407.

POMMEREHNE, W.W. and F. SCHNEIDER (1978), "Fiscal illusion, political institutions, and local public spending", *Kyklos*, 31, 381-408.

PRATT, J.W. (1964), "Risk aversion in the small and in the large", *Econometrica*, 32, 122-136.

PREST, A.R. (1955), "Statistical calculations of tax burdens", *Economica*, 22, 234-245.

——— (1968), "The budget and interpersonal distribution", *Public Finance*, 23, 80-98.

——— (1975), *Public Finance in Theory and Practice* (5th edn), Weidenfeld and Nicolson, London.

PROJECTOR, D.S. and G.S. WEISS (1966), Survey of Financial Characteristics of Consumers, Board of Governors of the Federal Reserve System, Washington DC.

QUINN, J.F. (1977), "Microeconomic determinants of early retirement: a cross-sectional view of white married men", *Journal of Human Resources*, 12, 329-346.

RAMSEY, F.P. (1927), "A contribution to the theory of taxation", *Economic Journal*, 37, 47-61.

RAWLS, J. (1971), *A Theory of Justice*, Harvard University Press, Cambridge, Massachusetts.

——— (1973), Reply to Alexander and Musgrave", *Quarterly Journal of Economics*, 87, 633-655.

——— (1974), Concepts of distributional equity: some reasons for the maximin criterion", *American Economic Review*, Papers and Proceedings, 64, 141-146.

RAY, R. (1986a). "Sensitivity of "optimal" commodity tax-rates to alternative demand functional forms: an econometric case study of India", "*Journal of Public Economics*.

——— (1986b), "On setting the indirect tax rate using the Ramsey approach: evidence from Indian budget data", *Journal of Quantitative Economics*.

——— (1985), "On calculating the optimal indirect tax rate: an alternative to social welfare maximization", *Economics Letters*.

RAYNER, A.C. (1969), "On the identification of the supply of working hours", *Oxford Economic Papers*, 21, 293-298.

REDDAWAY, W.B. (1970), Effects of the Selective Employment Tax, First Report, The Distributive Trades, HMSO, London.

REES, A. and H.W. WATTS (1975), "An overview of the labor supply results" in *Work Incentives and Income Guarantees*, J.A. Pechman and P.M. Timpane, Brookings Institution, Washington DC.

REES, R. (1968), "Second best rules for public enterprise pricing", *Economica*, 35, 260-273.

——— (1976), *Public Enterprise Economics*, Weidenfeld and Nicolson, London.

Reserve Bank of India Bulletins, various issues.

REYNOLDS, M. and E. SMOLENSKY (1976), *Public Expenditures, Taxes and the Distribution of Income*, *Academic* Press, New York.

RICHTER, D.K. (1978), "Existence and computation of a Tiebout general equilibrium", *Econometrica*, 46, 779-805.

RICHTER, M.K. (1960), "Cardinal utility, portfolio selection and taxation", *Review of Economic Studies*, 27, 152-166.

ROBBINS, L. (1930), "On the elasticity of demand for income in terms of effort", *Economica*, 10, 123-129.

——— (1938), "Interpersonal comparisons of utility: a comment", *Economic Journal*, 48, 635-641.

ROBERTS, D.J. (1973), "Existence of Lindahl equilibrium with a measure space of consumers", *Journal of Economic Theory*, 6, 355-381.

——— (1974a), "A note on returns to group size and the core with public goods", *Journal of Economic Theory*, 9, 350-356.

——— (1974b), "The Lindahl solution for economies with public goods", *Journal of Public Economics*, 3, 23-42.

——— (1976), "The incentives for correct revelation of price-taking behaviour in large exchange economies", *Econometrica*, 44, 115-128.

ROBERTS, D.J. and H. SONNENSCHEIN (1977), "On the foundations of the theory of monopolistic competition", *Econometrica*, 45, 101-113.

ROBERTS, K.W.S. (1977), "Welfare consideration of nonlinear pricing", *Economic Journal*, 89, 66-83.

ROBERTS, M.J. (1971), "Portfolio models and the impact of taxation on investment: a reconsideration", Harvard Discussion Paper.

ROBERTSON, D.H. (1927), "The Colwyn Committee, the income tax and the price level", *Economic Journal*, 37, 566-581.

ROMER, T. (1975), "Individual welfare, majority voting and the properties of a linear income tax", *Journal of Public Economics*, 4, 163-185.

ROMER, T. and H. ROSENTHAL (1977), "Bureaucrats vs voters", unpublished paper, Carnegie-Mellon.

——— and ——— (1979), "The elusive median voter", *Journal of Public Economics*, 12, 143-170.

ROSEN, H.S. (1976a), "Taxes in a labor supply model with joint wage-hours determination", *Econometrica*, 44, 485-507.

——— (1976b), "Tax illusion and the labor supply of married women", *Review of Economics and Statistics*, 58, 167-172.

ROSSE, P.H. (1975), "A critical review of the analysis of nonlabour force responses" in *work incentives and Income Guarantees*, J.A. Pechman and P.M. Timpane (eds), Brookings Institution, Washington DC.

ROTHSCHILD, M. (1971), "On the cost of adjustment", *Quarterly Journal of Economics*, 85, 622.

ROTHSCHILD, M. and J.E. STIGLITZ (1970), "Increasing risk I: A definition". *Journal of Economic Theory*, 2, 225-243.

——— and ——— (1971), "Increasing risk II: Its economic consequences", *Journal of Economic Theory*, 3, 66-84.

——— and ——— (1976), "Equilibrium in competitive insurance markets", Quarterly *Journal of Economics*, 90, 629-650.

RUBINFELD, D.L. (1977), "Voting in a local school election: a micro analysis", *Review of Economics and Statistics*, 59, 30-42.

RUSSELL, T. (1974), "The effect of improvements in the consumer loan market", *Journal of Economic Theory*, 9, 327-339.

SABINE, B.E.V. (1966), *A History of Income Tax*, Allen and Unwin, London.

SADKA, E. (1976), "On income distribution, incentive effects and optimal income taxation", *Review of Economic Studies*, 43, 261-268.

——— (1977), "A theorem on uniform taxation", *Journal of Public Economics*, 7, 387-391.

SAMUEL, LORD (1919), "The taxation of the various classes of the people", *Journal of the Royal Statistical Society*, 82, 143-182.

SAMUELSON, P.A. (1947), *Foundations of Economic Analysis*, Harvard University Press, Cambridge, Massachusetts.

——— (1951), Unpublished memorandum for the US Treasury.

——— (1954), "The pure theory of public expenditure", *Review of Economics and Statistics*, 36, 387-389.

——— (1955), Diagrammatic expositions of a theory of public expenditure", *Review of Economics and Statistics*, 37, 350-356.

——— (1956), "Social indifference curves", *Quarterly Journal of Economics*, 70, 1-22.

——— (1958a), "An exact consumption-loan model of interest with or without the social contrivance of money", *Journal of Political Economy*, 66, 467-482.

——— (1958b), "Aspects of public expenditure theories", *Review of Economics and Statistics*, 40, 332-338.

——— (1964a), "Discussion" in *American Economic Review*, Papers and Proceedings, 54, 93-96.

——— (1964b), "Tax deductibility of economic depreciation to insure invariant valuations", *Journal of Political Economy*, 72, 604-606.

——— (1965), "A theory of induced innovation along Kennedy-Weizsacker lines", *Review of Economics and Statistics*, 47, 343-356.

——— (1969), "Pure theory of public expenditures and taxation" in *Public Economics*, J. Margolis and H. Guitton (eds.), Macmillan, London.

——— (1975), "Optimum social security in a life-cycle growth model", *International Economic Review*, 16, 539-544.

SAMUELSON, P.A. and F. MODIGLIANI (1966), "The Pasinetti paradox in neoclassical and more general models", *Review of Economic Studies*, 33, 269-303.

SANDMO, A. (1969), "Capital, risk, consumption, and portfolio choice", *Econometrica*, 37, 586-599.

——— (1970), "The effect of uncertainty on saving decisions", *Review of Economic Studies*, 37, 353-360.

——— (1972), "Optimality rules for the provision of collective factors of production", *Journal of Public Economics*, 1, 149-157.

——— (1973), "Public goods and the technology of cosumption", *Review of Economic Studies*, 40, 517-528.

——— (1974a), "A note on the structure of optimal taxation", *American Economic Review*, 68, 701-706.

——— (1974b), "Investment incentives and the corporate income tax", *Journal of Political Economy*, 82, 287-302.

——— (1975), "Optimal taxation in the presence of externalities", *Swedish Journal of Economics*, 77, 86-98.

——— (1976a), "Direct versus indirect Pigovian taxation", *European Economic Review*, 7, 337-349.

——— (1976b), "Optimal taxation—an introduction to the literature", *Journal of Public Economics*, 6, 37-54.

SATO, R. and R.F. HOFFMAN (1974), "Tax incidence in a growing economy", *in Public Finance and Stabilisation Policy*, W.L. Smith and J.M. Culbertson (eds), North-Holland, Amsterdam.

SATTERTHWAITE, M.A. (1975), "Strategy-proofness and Arrow's conditions", *Journal of Economic Theory*, 10, 187-217.

SAWERS, L. and H.M. WACHTEL (1975), "Theory of the state, government tax and purchasing policy, and income distribution", *Review of Income and Wealth*, 21, 111-124.

SCARF, H.E. (1967), "On the computation of equilibrium prices", in *Ten Economic Studies in the Tradition of Irving Fisher*, John Wiley, New York.

——— (1969), "An Examply of an algorithm for calculating general equilibrium prices", *American Economic Review*, 59, 667-669.

SCARF, H.E. With the Collaboration of T. HANSEN (1973), *The Computation of Economic Equilibria*, Yale University Press, New Have, Connecticut.

SCHMOLDERS, G. (1977), "Attitudes to taxation and their effects on work effort" in *Fiscal Policy and Labour Supply*, Institute for Fiscal Studies, London.

SCHUMPETER, J.A. (1954), *Capitalism, Socialism and democracy*, Harper, New York.

SCITOVSKY, T. (1976), *The Joyless Economy*, Oxford University Press, New York.

SEADE, J.K. (1977), "On the shape of optimal tax schedules", *Journal of Public Economics*, 7, 203-236.

——— (1979), "Optimal nonlinear policies for non-utilitarian motives", Warwick Economic Research Paper.

SEN, A.K. (1966), "Labour allocation in-cooperative enterprise", *Review of Economic Studies*, 33, 361-371.

——— (1970a), "Interpersonal aggregation and partial comparability", *Econometrica*, 38, 393-409.

——— (1970b), *Collective choice and Social Welfare, Holden-Day*, San Francisco.

——— (1973), *On Economic Inequality*, Oxford University Press, Oxford.

——— (1973a), "Social choice theory: are-examination", *Econometrica*, 45, 53-89.

——— (1977b), "On weights and measures: informational constraints in social welfare analysis", *Econometrica*, 45, 1539-1572.

SEN, A.K. (ed.) (1970), *Growth Theory*, Pengiun Books.

——— (1970), The Impossibility of a Paretian Liberal", *Journal of Political Economy*.

——— (1979), Personal Utilities and Public Judgements of What's wrong with Welfare Economics, *Economic Journal*.

SHAPLEY, L.S. (1973), "Lets block 'block", *Econometrica*, 41, 1201-1202.

SHAPLEY, L.S. and M. SHUBIK (1977), "An example of a trading economy with three competitive equilibria", *Journal of Political Economy*, 85, 873-875.

SHEPHARD, R.W. (1944), "A mathematical theory of the incidence of taxation", *Econometrica*, 12, 1-18.

SHESHINSKI, E. (1971a), "Welfare aspects of a regulatory constraint: note", *American Economic Review*, 61, 175-178.

——— (1971b), "On the theory of optimal income taxation", HIER Discussion Paper No. 172.

——— (1972), "The optimal linear income tax", *Review of Economic Studies*, 39, 297-302.

——— (1976), "Income taxation and capital accumulation", *Quarterly Journal of Economics*, 90, 138-149.

——— (1977), "The supply of communal goods and revenue sharing", in *The Economics of Public Services*, M.S. Feldstein and R.P. Inman (eds), Macmillan, London.

SHORROCKS, A.F. (1975), "On stochastic models of size distributions", *Review of Economic Studies*, 42, 631-641.

——— (1979), "The structure of intergenerational transfers between families", *Econometrica*, 46, (in Press).

SHOUP, C.S. (1969), *Public Finance*, Weidenfeld and Nicolson, London.

SHOVEN, J.B. (1974), "A proof of the existence of a general equilibrium with ad valorem commodity taxes", *Journal of Economic Theory*, 8, 1-25.

——— (1976), "The incidence and efficiency effects of taxes on income from capital", *Journal of Political Economy*, 84, 1261-1284.

SHOVEN, J.B. and J. WHALLEY (1972), "A general equilibrium calculation of the effects of differential taxation of income from capital in the U.S.", *Journal of Public Economics*, 1, 281-321.

——— and ——— (1973), "General equilibrium with taxes: a computational procedure and an existence proof", *Review of Economic Studies*, 60, 475-490.

——— and ——— (1977), "Equal yield tax alternatives: general equilibrium computational technique", *Journal of Public Economics*, 8, 211-224.

SHUBIK, M. (1970), "Voting, or a price system in a competitive market structure", *American Political Science Review*, 64, 179-181.

SIDGWICK, H. (1883), *Principles of Political Economy*, Macmillan, London.

SIMONS, H.C. (1938), *Personal Income Taxation*, University of Chicago Press, Chicago.

SLUTSKY, S.M. (1975), "Abstentions and majority equilibrium", *Journal of Economic Theory*, 11, 292-304.

——— (1977), "A voting model for the allocation of public goods: existence of an equilibrium", *Journal of Economic Theory*, 14, 299-325.

SMITH, ADAM (1976), *An Inquiry into the Nature and Causes of the Wealth of Nations*, E. Cannan (ed.), Methuen, London, 1904.

SODERSTROM, H. (1976), "Production and Investment under Adjustment costs: A Survey", *Zetscfrift fur Nationalokonomee.*

SCITOVSKY, T. (1941), "A Note on Welfare Propositions in Economics", *Review of Economic Studies.*

SOLOW, R.M. (1956), "A contribution to the theory of economic growth", *Quarterly Journal of Economics*, 70, 65-94.

——— (1961), "Note on Uzawa's two-sector model of economic growth", *Review of Economic Studies*, 29, 48-50.

——— (1970), *Growth Theory: An Exposition*, Clarendon Press, Oxford.

——— (1971), "Some implications of alternative criteria for the firm", in *The Corporate Economy*, R. Marris and A. Wood (eds), Macmillan, London.

SPENCE, M. (1973), "Job market signaling", *Quarterly Journal of Economics*, 87, 355-379.

——— (1977), 'Non-linear prices and welfare", *Journal of Public Economics*, 8, 1-18.

STARRETT, D.A. (1972), "Fundamental non-convexities in the theory of externalities", *Journal of Economic Theory*, 3, 180-199.

——— (1974), "On the nature of externalities", IMSSS Technical Report 129, Stanford University.

STERN, N.H. (1976), "On the specification of models of optimum income taxation", *Journal of Public Economics*, 6, 123-162.

——— (1977), "*Optimum taxation with errors in administration*", University of Oxford (unpublished).

STIGLER, G.J. (1967), "Imperfections in the capital market", *Journal of Political Economy*, 75, 287-292.

——— (1970), "Director's law of public income redistribution", *Journal of Law and Economics*, 13, 1-10.

——— (1974), "Free riders and collective action", *Bell Journal of Economics*, 5, 359-365.

——— (1975), *The Citizen and the State*, University of Chicago Press, Chicago.

STIGLITZ, J.E. (1969a), "A re-examination of the Modigliani-Miller theorem", *American Economic Review*, 29, 784-793.

——— (1969b), "Distribution of income and wealth among individuals", *Econometrica*, 37, 382-397.

——— (1969c), "The effects of income, wealth and capital gains taxation on risk-taking", *Quarterly Journal of Economics*, 83, 262-283.

——— (1970a), "Factor price equalization in a dynamic economy", *Journal of Political Economy*, 78, 456-488.

——— (1970b), "A consumption-oriented theory of the demand for financial assets and the term structure of interest rates", *Review of Economic Studies*, 37, 321-351.

——— (1972), "Theory of Finance", *Bell Journal of Economics and Management Science*, 3, 458-482.

——— (1973), "Taxation, corporate financial policy, and the cost of capital", *Journal of Public Economics*, 2, 1-34.

——— (1974a), "On the irrelevance of corporate financial policy", *American Economic Review*, 64, 851-866.

——— (1974b), "The demand for education in public and private school systems", *Journal of Public Economics*, 3, 349-385.

——— (1974c), "Growth with exhaustible natural resources: the competitive economy", *Review of Economic Studies*, 41, 139-152.

——— (1975a), "The theory of 'screening'", education, and the distribution of income", *American Economic Review*, 65, 283-300.

——— (1975b), "Information and economic analysis", in *Current Economic Problems*, M. Parking and A.R. Nobay (eds), Cambridge University Press, Cambridge.

——— (1976a), "The corporation tax", *Journal of Public Economics*, 5, 303-311.

——— (1976b), "Estate taxes, growth and redistribution", in *Public and Urban Economics*, R.B. Grieson (ed.), "Simple formulate for optimal income taxation and the measurement of inequality", mimeo.

——— (1977), "The theory of local public goods", in *The Economics of Public Services*, M.S. Feldstein and R.P. Inman (eds), Macmillan, London.

——— (1978a), "Notes on estate taxes, redistribution and the concept of balanced growth path incidence", *Journal of Political Economy*, 86, S137-150.

——— (1978b), "Equality, taxation and inheritance", in *Personal Income Distribution*, W. Krelle and A.F. Shorrocks (eds), North-Holland, Amsterdam.

——— (1979), "Local public goods and matching", unpublished, Oxford University.

——— (1980), *Information and Economic Analysis*, Oxford University Press, Oxford.

STIGLITZ, J.E. and M.J. BOSKING (1977), "Some lessons from the new public finance", *American Economic Review*, 67, 295-301.

STIGLITZ, J.E. and P.S. DASGUPTA (1971), "Differential taxation, public goods, and economic efficiency", *Review of Economic Studies*, 38, 151-174.

STIGLITZ, J.E. and A. WEISS (1979), "Theory of credit rationing", unpublished discussion paper, Bell Laboratories.

STONE, J.R.N. (1954), "Linear Expenditure Systems and Demand Analysis", *Economic Journal*, 64, 511-527.

——— (1964), "Private saving in Britain, past, present and future", *Manchester School*, 32, 79-112.

STRUMPEL, B. (1969), "The contribution of survey research to public finance", in *Quantitative Analysis in Public Finance*, A.T. Peacock (ed.), Praeger, New York.

SUMNER, M.T. (1975), "Neutrality of corporate taxation, or on not accounting for inflation", *Manchester School*, 43, 353-361.

THIMMAIAH, G. (1982), *A Critique of the Finance Commission*, Wheeler.

THOMPSON, E.A. (1967), "Debt instruments in macroeconomic and capital theory", *American Economic Review*, 57, 1196-1210.

TIDEMAN, T.N. and G. TULLOCK (1976), "A new and superior process for making social choices", *Journal of Political Economy*, 84, 1145-1159.

TIEBOUT, C.M. (1956), "A pure theory of local expenditures", *Journal of Political Economy*, 64, 416-424.

TOBIN, J. (1955), "A dynamic aggregative model", *Journal of Political Economy*, 63, 103-115.

——— (1958), "Liquidity preference as behaviour towards risk", *Review of Economic Studies*, 25, 65-86.

——— (1965), "The burden of the public debt: A review article", *Journal of Finance*, 20, 679-682.

——— (1967), "Life cycle saving and balanced growth", in *Ten Economic Studies in the Tradition of Irving Fisher*, John Wiley, New York.

——— (1970), "On limiting the domain of inequality", *Journal of Law and Economics*, 13, 263-277.

TOWNSEND, P.B. (1968), "The difficulties of negative income tax", in *Social Services for All?* Part Four, Fabina Society, London.

TULKENS, H. (1978), "Dynamic processes for public goods: an institution-oriented survey", *Journal of Public Economics*, 9, 163-201.

TULLOCK, G. (1970), "A simple algebraic logrolling, model", *American Economic Review*, 60, 419-426.

TURNOVSKY, S.J. (1977), *Macroeconomic Analysis and Stabilisation Policy*, Cambridge University Press.

——— (1978), "Macroeconomic Dynamics and Growth in a Monetary Economy", *Journal of Money, Credit and Banking*, Vol. 10, pp. 1-26.

——— (1980), "Monetary and Fiscal Policies in a Long Run Macroeconomic Model", *Economic Record*, Vol. 56, pp. 158-170.

TURVEY, R. (ed.) (1968), *Public Enterprise*, Penguin, Harmondsworth.

——— (1971), *Economic Analysis and Public Enterprises*, Allen and Unwin, London.

ULPH, D.T. (1976), "Income distribution and public goods", mimeo.

——— (1978), "On the optimal distribution of income and educational expenditure", *Journal of Economic Theory*, 19, 492-512.

——— (1977), "On labor supply and the measurement of inequality", mimeo.

——— (1979), "Income distribution and public goods", *Econometrica*, 47.

US Department of Health, Education and Welfare (1973), Summary Report: New Jersey Graduated Work Incentive Experiment, Government Printing Office, Washington DC.

US Treasury (1977), Blueprints for Basic Tax Reform, Government Printing Office, Washington DC.

USHER, D. (1977), "The welfare economics of the socialisation of commo dities", *Journal of Public Economics*, 8, 151-168.

UZAWA, H. (1961), "On a two-sector model of economic growth", *Review of Economic Studies*, 29, 40-47.

VANDENDORPE, A.L. and A.F. FRIEDLAENDER (1976), "Differential incidence in the presence of initial distorting taxes", *Journal of Public Economic*, 6, 205-229.

VARIAN, H.R. (1978), Microeconomic Analysis, Norton, New York.

——— (1960), "Utility, strategy and social decision rules", *Quarterly Journal of Economics*, 74, 507-535.

——— (1961), "Counterspeculation, auctions and competitive sealed tenders", *Journal of Finance*, 16, 8-37.

VINER, J. (1920), "Who paid for the War?" *Journal of Political Economy*, 28, 46-76.

WALES, T.J. and A.D. WOODLAND (1979), "Labor Supply and progressive taxes", *Review of Economic Studies*, 46, 83-95.

WALKER, D. (1955), "The direct-indirect tax problem: Fifteen years of controversy", *Public Finance*, 10, 153-176.

WALTERS, A.A. (1967), "How to make a benefit of the burden of national debt", *National Tax Journal*, 20, 316-318.

WAN, H.Y. (1971), *Economic Growth*, Harcourt Brace Jovanovich, New York.

WATTS, H.W. et al. (1974), "The labor-supply response of husbands", *Journal of Human Resources*, 9, 181-200.

WATTS, H.W. and A. REES (eds) (1977), *The New Jersey Income Maintenance Experiment*: Volume 2–Labor Supply Resources, Academic Press, New York.

WEISBORD, B.A. (1968), "Income redistribution effects and benefit-cost analysis", in *Problems in Public Expenditure Analysis*, S.B. Chase (ed.), Brookings Institution, Washington DC.

WEITZMAN, M.L. (1974), "Prices vs quantities", *Review of Economic Studies*, 41, 477-491.

——— (1977), "Is the price system or rationing more effective in getting a commodity to those who need it most? *Bell Journal of Economics*, 8, 157-524.

VON WEIZSACKER, C.C. (1966), "Tentative Notes on a two sector Model with Induced Technical Progress", *Review of Economic Studies*, 33, 245-251.

WELLS, P. (1955), "General Equilibrium Analysis of Excise Taxes", *American Economic Review*, 45, 345-359.

WESSON, J. (1972), "On the distribution of personal incomes", *Review of Economic Studies*, 39, 77-86.

WESTHOFF, F. (1977), "Existence of equilibria in economies with a local public good", *Journal of Economic Theory*, 14, 84-112.

WHALLEY, J. (1975), "A general equilibrium assessment of the 1973 UK Tax Reform", *Econometrica*, 42, 139-161.

——— (1977), "The U.K. tax system 1968-1970: some fixed point induations of its economic impact", *Econometrica*, 45, 1837-1858.

——— and J.R. PIGGOTT (1977), "General equilibrium investigations of U.K. tax-subsidy policy: a progress report", *Analysis*, M.J. Arts and A.R. Nobay (eds) AITE, 1976.

WHEATCROFT, G.S.A. (1969), "Inequality in Britain's tax structure", *Lloyds Bank Review*, 93, 11-26.

WILLIAMS, A. (1966), "The optimal provision of public goods in a system of local government", *Journal of Political Economy*, 74, 18-33.

WILLIG, R.D. (1978), "Pareto-superion non-linear outlay schedules", *Bell Journal of Economics*, 9, 56-69.

WILSON, R.B. (1969), "An axiomatic model of logrolling", *American Economic Review*, 59, 331-341.

——— (1970), "The game-theoretic structure of Arrow's general possibility theorem", *Journal of Economic Theory*, 2, 14-20.

YAARI, M.E. (1964), "On the consumer's lifetime allocation process", *International Economic Review*, 5, 304-317.

——— (1965), "Uncertain lifetime life insurance and the theory of the consumer", *Review of Economic Studies*, 32, 137-150.

ZECKHAUSER, R. (1977), "Taxes in fantasy, or Most any tax on labor can turn out to help the laborers", *Journal of Public Economic*, 8, 133-150.

STATISTICAL APPENDIX

In this appendix we provide three sets of data relating to the Indian public sector. The first set is drawn from National Account Statistics, the second from the Annual Survey of Industries and the third from some assorted publications.

LIST OF TABLES

Set. I from National Accounts Statistics

1.14 Gross Capital Formation of Public Sector by Industry of Use (Percentage) 1970–1 to 1980–1.
1.15 Gross Domestic Capital Formation by Industry of Use at Current prices: 1970–1 to 1980–1.
1.16 Gross Domestic Capital Formation by Industry of use at 1970–1 prices: 1970–1 to 1980–1.
1.17 Gross Domestic Capital Formation by Industry of Use (Percent): 1970–1 to 1980–1.
1.18 Public Sectors Gross Domestic Capital Formation by Industry of Use (Percentage): 1970–1 to 1980–1.
1.19 Sources and Users of Gross Savings and Investment at current prices.
1.20 Price Index for NDP by Industry 1970–1 = 100: 1960–1 to 1980–1.
1.21 Price Index for GDCF: 1970–1 = 100: 1960–1 to 1980–1.
1.22 Price Index for GDCF in Public Sector by Industry of Use—1970–1 = 100: 1970–1 to 1980–1.
1.23 Employment in the Organised Sector: 1960–1 to 1980–81.

Accounts for the National Economy

(*Sub-Heads for Data*)

INDUSTRY

1. Agriculture, Forestry and Fishing.
2. Mining and Duarrying.
3. Manufacturing.
4. Construction.
5. Electricity, Gas, and Water Supply.
6. Transport, Storage, and Communication.
7. Trade, Hotels and Restaurants.
8. Banking and Insurance.
9. Public Administration and Defence.
10. Other Services.

*This includes Real Estate and Ownership of Dwellings.

SOURCE: National Accounts Statistics. Jan. 1981 and Feb. 1983.

TABLE 1.1 Net Domestic Product Originating in Public and Private Sectors at (Current Prices) 1960-61 to 1980–81.

(*Rs. Millions.*)

Year	*Net Domestic Product From*			*Relative Share in NDP*	
	Public Sector	*Private Sector*	*Total*	*Public Sector*	*Private Sector*
1960-61	14220	119130	133350	10.66	89.34
1961-62	16020	124830	140850	11.37	88.63
1962-63	18360	130670	149030	12.32	87.68
1963-64	21330	149560	170890	12.48	87.52
1964-65	23810	177670	201480	11.82	88.18
1965-66	27430	180580	208010	13.19	86.81
1966-67	30680	210100	240780	12.74	87.26
1967-68	34650	248470	283120	12.24	87.76
1968-69	39390	249230	288620	13.65	86.35
1969-70	44710	274060	318770	14.03	85.97
1970-71	50070	295120	345190	14.51	85.49
1971-72	56210	312430	368640	15.25	84.75
1972-73	62140	343580	405720	15.32	84.68
1973-74	72280	455210	507490	14.24	85.76
1974-75	95260	502110	597370	15.95	84.05
1975-76	113740	509500	623240	18.25	81.75
1976-77	133790	536080	669870	19.97	80.03
1977-78	145260	612430	757690	19.17	80.83
1978-79	161360	651430	812790	19.86	80.14
1979-80	184580	697610	882190	20.92	79.08
1980-81	214480	847610	1062090	20.19	79.81

SOURCE: National Accounts Statistics Oct. 1976—Jan. 1981. Feb. 1983.

TABLE 1.2 Net Domestic Product From Public Sector at Factor Cost by Industry (at Current Prices)

(*Rs. Millions*)

Industry/Department	*1960-61*	*1961-62*	*1962-63*	*1963-64*	*1964-65*	*1965-66*	*1966-67*	*1967-68*	*1968-69*	*1969-70*
Agriculture	300	410	430	540	620	800	910	990	1150	1130
Departmental Enterprises	300	410	430	530	610	750	870	930	1090	1080
Non-Departmental Enterprises	00	00	00	10	10	20	40	60	60	50
Forestry*	480	520	570	620	660	770	810	880	960	1020
Mining and Quarrying**	160	130	240	280	210	330	530	640	700	800
Manufacturing	820	970	1250	1740	2100	2360	2550	2950	3460	4370
Departmental Enterprises	580	640	670	800	1050	1140	1160	1200	1330	1420
Non-Departmental Enterprises	240	330	580	940	1050	1220	1390	1750	2130	2950
Construction	430	470	540	530	620	800	850	1040	1220	1260
Departmental Enterprises	240	250	280	350	330	490	480	640	690	720
Non-Departmental Enterprises	10	20	30	50	50	50	50	40	30	40
Administrative Departments	180	200	230	230	240	260	320	360	500	500
Electricity, Gas. . .	450	530	620	760	890	1040	1240	1480	1820	2230
Administrative Departments	—	—	—	—	—	—	—	—	—	—
Departmental Enterprises	100	110	110	160	120	130	200	220	170	1340
Non-Departmental Enterprises	350	420	510	600	770	910	1040	1260	1650	1890
Transport	3740	4180	4670	5250	5520	6160	6770	7120	8350	8920
Administrative Departments	20	20	20	30	30	40	40	50	50	60
Departmental Enterprises	3500	3860	4280	4810	4990	5540	6020	6170	7260	7720
Non-Departmental Enterprises	220	300	370	410	500	580	710	900	1040	1140
Trade, Hotel & Restaurant**	50	50	80	70	120	220	340	300	460	700
Departmental Enterprises	—	—	—	—	—	—	—	—	—	—
Non-Departmental Enterprises	50	50	80	70	120	220	340	300	460	700
Banking and Insurance	620	710	960	1040	1210	1550	1550	1840	2080	2880
Departmental Enterprises	20	30	30	40	40	50	50	60	60	70
Non-Departmental Enterprises	600	680	930	1000	1170	1500	1500	1780	2020	2820
Public Administration	5380	5930	6680	7780	8900	9890	11040	12520	13700	15030

TABLE 1.2 (*Contd.*)

Industry/Department	*1960-61*	*1961-62*	*1962-63*	*1963-64*	*1964-65*	*1965-66*	*1966-67*	*1967-68*	*1968-69*	*1969-70*
Other Services	1790	2120	2320	2620	2960	3510	4090	4890	5490	6370
Administrative Departments	1770	2100	2300	2590	2910	3480	4060	4870	5450	6340
Non-Departmental Enterprises	20	20	20	30	50	30	30	20	40	30
Total Public Sector	14220	16020	18360	21330	23810	27430	30680	34650	39390	44710
Administrative Department	7350	8250	9230	10630	12080	13670	15460	17800	19700	21930
Departmental Enterprises	5220	5820	6370	7310	7800	8900	9590	10100	11560	12370
Non-Departmental Enterprises (Departmental)	1650	1950	2760	3390	3930	4860	5630	6750	8130	10410
Departmental Enterprises	360	220	180	190	400	330	730	730		
Non-Departmental Enterprises	2070	2400	2660	2710	3630	4860	6580	7600		
Transport, Storage and Communications.	9490	10370	10670	10810	13510	16470	21070	22180		
Administrative Departments.	60	60	60	70	00	00	00	00		
Departmental Enterprises	8160	8930	8780	8430	10780	13210	16730	17580		
Non-Departmental Enterprises	1270	1380	1830	2310	2730	3260	4340	4600		
Trade, Hotels and Restaurants	840	1290	1450	1810	2260	4070	5090	6090		
Departmental Enterprises	00	00	00	00	00	00	00	70		
Non-Departmental Enterprises	840	1290	1450	1810	2260	4070	5090	6020		
Banking and Insurance	4220	5110	5870	7690	10190	13270	16210	18210		
Departmental Enterprises	90	100	110	120	130	200	220	230		
Non-Departmental Enterprises	4130	5010	5760	7570	10060	13070	15990	17980		
Public Administration and Defence	16350	18310	19760	22210	28560	32370	34530	36940		
Other Services	6880	7740	8570	9720	11370	13390	15600	17140		
Administrative Departments	6860	7720	8540	9600	11260	13260	15400	16880		
Agriculture	1400	1620	1950	2060	2500	2790	3130	3710		
Departmental Enterprises	1350	1570	1880	1970	2360	2620	2900	3470		
Non-Departmental Enterprises	50	50	70	90	140	170	230	240		

TABLE 1.2 *(Contd)*

Industry/Department	*1960-61*	*1961-62*	*1962-63*	*1963-64*	*1964-65*	*1965-66*	*1966-67*	*1967-68*	*1968-69*	*1969-70*
Forestry*	1070	1250	1420	1660	2010	2310	2740	3040		
Mining and Quarrying**	780	560	850	2530	4530	6220	7000	6620		
Manufacturing	5060	5500	6730	8290	12920	14150	16820	17890		
Departmental Enterprises	1520	1660	2060	2060	2570	3370	3080	3520		
Non-Departmental Enterprises	3540	3840	4670	6230	10350	10780	13740	14370		
Construction	1330	1580	1730	2250	2970	3060	3740	4440		
Departmental Enterprises	750	850	920	1160	1400	1630	2000	2410		
Non-Departmental Enterprises	60	110	160	270	470	310	490	650		
Administrative Departments	520	620	650	820	1100	1120	1250	1380		
Electricity, Gas and Watter Supply	2650	2880	3140	3250	4440	5640	7860	3000		
Administrative Department	220	260	300	350	410	450	550	670		
Non-Departmental Enterprises	20	20	30	120	110	130	200	260		
Total Public Sector	50070	56210	62140	72280	95260	113740	133790	145260		
Administrative Departments	24010	26970	29310	33050	41330	47200	51730	55870		
Departmental Enterprises	13300	14580	15350	15590	19650	23670	28400	31050		
Non-Departmental Enterprises	12760	14660	17480	23640	34280	42870	53660	58340		
Agriculture	4380	4710	5740							
Departmental Enterprises	3980	4270	5070							
Non-Departmental Enterprises	400	440	670							
Forestry	3490	3780	4240							
Mining and Quarrying	7440	11590	13330							
Manufacturing	20400	23340	26760							
Departmental Enterprises	3240	3650	4040							
Non-Departmental Enterprises	17160	19690	22720							
Construction	5140	7310	8860							
Departmental Enterprises	2680	4000	4680							
Non-Departmental Enterprises	920	1000	870							
Administrative Departments	1540	2310	3310							
Electricity, Gas and Water Supply	11310	12900	13720							
Administrative Departments	840	880	1030							
Departmental Enterprises	810	740	820							

TABLE 1.2 *(Contd.)*

Industry/Department	*1960-61*	*1961-62*	*1962-63*	*1963-64*	*1964-65*	*1965-66*	*1966-67*	*1967-68*	*1968-69*	*1969-70*
Non-Departmental Enterprises	9660	11280	11870							
Transport, Storage and Communications	23230	24380	25530							
Administrative Departments	00	00	00							
Departmental Enterprises	18140	19240	19730							
Non-Departmental Enterprises	5090	5140	5800							
Trade, Hotels and Restaurants	6060	7020	7720							
Departmental Enterprises	60	80	260							
Non-Departmental Enterprises	6000	6940	7460							
Banking and Insurance	20000	22510	28840							
Departmental Enterprises	250	290	270							
Non-Departmental Enterprises	19750	22220	28570							
Public Administration and Defence	40720	45890	54150							
Other services	19190	21150	25590							
Administrative Departments	18840	20670	25030							
Non-Departmental Enterprises	350	480	560							
Total Public Sector	161360	184580	214480							
Administrative Departments	61940	69750	83520							
Departmental Enterprises	32650	36050	39110							
Non-Departmental Enterprises	66770	78780	91850							

Notes: *Departmental Enterprises only.
**Non-Departmental Enterprises.

SOURCE: National Accounts Statistics Oct. 1976—Jan. 1981—Feb. 1983

TABLE 1.3 Net Domestic Product from Public Sector at Factor Cost by Industry

(Rs. in Millions at 1970-71 Prices)

Industry	*1960-61*	*1961-62*	*1962-63*	*1963-64*	*1964-65*	*1965-66*	*1966-67*	*1967-68*	*1968-69*	*1969-70*
Agriculture	1550	1027	1852	1900	1871	2022	1827	1852	2143	2115
Mining	265	217	367	415	301	496	706	758	750	805
Manufacturing	1289	1523	1910	2496	2879	3146	3079	3392	3906	4633
Construction	764	823	930	1063	950	1137	1111	1244	1411	1345
Electricity	728	881	1000	1240	1318	1531	1574	1811	2090	2317
Transport	6077	6519	6954	7683	7718	8383	8557	8458	9075	9508
Trade	91	92	144	119	181	309	413	328	517	761
Banking	1039	1213	1555	1594	1753	2158	2105	2411	2751	3735
Administration	7690	8180	9250	10300	11421	10571	12490	13010	13850	15080
Services	2981	3353	3555	3783	3882	4230	4482	4878	5189	5558
	22474	23828	27517	30593	32274	33953	36344	38142	41681	45857

Industry	*1970-71*	*1971-72*	*1972-73*	*1973-74*	*1974-75*	*1975-76*	*1976-77*	*1977-78*	*1978-79*	*1979-80*	*1980-81*
Agriculture	2470	2751	2743	2411	2650	3551	3729	4192	4902	4502	4797
Mining	780	547	813	2196	2836	3403	3508	3098	3269	4091	4309
Manufacturing	5060	5133	5900	6411	7866	8363	9741	9901	10907	10663	10868
Construction	1330	1456	1497	1721	1994	1883	2159	2457	2675	3526	3700
Electricity	2650	2846	3013	2987	3328	3890	4580	4771	5586	5679	5791
Transport	9490	9919	9829	9129	9834	11664	13511	13615	13162	13490	13544
Trade	840	1210	1233	1295	1251	2177	2703	3068	3108	2946	2671
Banking	4220	4841	5196	6073	6879	8220	9502	10214	11043	11326	13099
Administration	16350	17849	18629	19800	20860	22380	23699	25350	28190	31460	35939
Services	6880	7249	7529	7701	7729	8342	8611	8632	8990	9377	10130
	50070	53801	56382	59724	65227	73853	81743	85298	91832	97060	104848

SOURCE: Table 1.2—Calculated from values at Current Prices by using Sectoral Implicit Price Deflators for the National Economy.

TABLE 1.4 Industrial Origin of Gross Domestic Product from Public Sector at Factor Cost

(*Rs. Million Current Prices*)

Industry	*1970-71*	*1971-72*	*1972-73*	*1973-74*	*1974-75*	*1975-76*	*1976-77*	*1977-78*	*1978-79*	*1979-80*	*1980-81*
Agriculture[1]	2490	2890	3390	3760	4570	5190	5980	6860	8020	8660	1019
Mining	1180	1300	1660	3890	5420	7450	8730	8960	9930	14300	1724
Manufacturing	6580	7140	8570	10510	15110	16610	19610	21190	24110	28240	3240
Construction	1350	1520	1740	2290	3050	3090	3830	4580	5300	7510	9100
Electricity[2]	3610	3970	4300	4500	5890	7420	9870	11290	13800	15780	1708
Transport[3]	10950	11890	12590	12950	15630	19000	23980	25290	26940	28760	3124
Trade[4]	890	1340	1510	1890	2370	4240	5260	6260	6230	7200	791
Banking[5]	4290	5200	5980	7820	10340	13430	16390	18410	20230	22760	2913
Administration[6]	16350	18310	19760	22210	28560	32370	34530	36940	40720	45890	54150
Services	6880	7740	8570	9720	11370	13400	15610	17150	19210	21180	2562
Total Public Sector	54560	61370	68070	79540	102310	122200	143790	156930	174490	200280	23406
NAP SECTOR (11-1)	52070	58480	64680	75780	97740	117010	137810	150070	166470	191620	22387

SOURCE: National Accounts Statistics, Jan. 1981, Feb. 1983.

Notes: [1]Agriculture includes Forestry.

[2]Electricity, Gas and Water Supply.

[3]The Figures for Transport include Communications.

[4]Trade, Hotels and Restaurants.

[5]Banking and Insurance.

[6]Public Administration and Defence.

TABLE 1.5 Industrial Origin of Gross Value Added in Public Sector

(*Percent*)

Industry	*1970-71*	*1971-72*	*1972-73*	*1973-74*	*1974-75*	*1975-76*	*1976-77*	*1977-78*	*1978-79*	*1979-80*	*1980-81*
Agriculture	4.56	4.71	4.98	4.73	4.47	4.25	4.16	4.37	4.59	4.32	4.35
Mining	2.16	2.12	2.44	4.89	5.30	6.10	6.07	5.71	5.69	7.14	7.36
Manufacturing	12.06	11.64	12.59	13.21	14.77	13.59	13.64	15.50	13.82	14.10	13.84
Construction	2.46	2.59	2.56	2.88	2.98	2.53	2.66	2.92	3.04	3.75	3.89
Electricity	6.62	6.47	6.32	5.66	5.76	6.07	6.86	7.19	7.91	7.88	7.30
Transport	20.07	19.37	18.49	16.28	15.28	15.55	16.68	16.11	15.44	14.36	13.35
Trade	1.63	2.18	2.22	2.38	2.32	3.47	3.66	3.99	3.57	3.59	3.78
Banking	7.86	8.47	8.78	9.83	10.11	10.99	11.40	11.73	11.59	11.36	12.44
Administration	29.97	29.84	29.03	27.92	27.91	26.49	24.01	23.54	23.34	22.91	23.13
Services	12.61	12.61	12.59	12.22	11.11	10.96	10.86	10.93	11.01	10.57	10.94
P.E. Sector											
Total	100.00	100.00	100.00	100.00	100.00	100.00	100.00	100.00	100.00	100.00	100.00
NAPE Sector (11-1)	95.44	95.29	95.02	95.27	95.53	95.75	95.84	95.63	95.41	95.68	95.65

Note: Calculated on the basis of Table 1.4

TABLE 1.6 Industrial Origin of GDP of Public Sector at Factor Cost at 1970-71 Prices

(Rs. Millions)

Industry	*1970-71*	*1971-72*	*1972-73*	*1973-74*	*1974-75*	*1975-76*	*1976-77*	*1977-78*	*1978-79*	*1979-80*	*1980-81*
Agriculture	2490	2770	3080	3210	3640	3940	4290	4740	5420	5430	6070
Mining	1180	1230	1530	2620	2530	3120	3410	3380	3510	4200	4480
Manufacturing	6580	6860	7730	7890	8480	8410	9590	10320	10730	10850	11040
Construction	1340	1540	1620	2010	2200	2110	2560	3040	3490	4910	5770
Electricity	3610	3880	4060	4180	4360	4960	5480	5700	6340	6420	6830
Transport	10950	11430	12130	12140	12520	14030	15720	16350	16750	17440	18430
Trade	890	1050	1230	1760	1360	1660	1720	1820	1810	1800	1890
Banking	4290	4740	5210	5730	5130	6100	6750	7710	9110	8970	10140
Public Admn.	16350	17850	18630	19800	20860	22380	23700	25350	28190	31460	35940
Services	6880	7550	8080	8660	8310	9260	10720	11770	13300	14520	17010
Public Sector Total	54560	58900	63300	68000	69390	75970	83940	90180	98650	106000	117600
NAP Sector (11-1) total	52070	56130	60220	64790	65750	72030	79650	85440	93230	100570	115300

NAP: Non-Agriculture Public Sector.

SOURCE: National Account Statistics—Jan. 1981—Feb. 1983.

TABLE 1.7 Industrial Origin of GDP from Public Sector

(Percent)

Industry	*1970-71*	*1971-72*	*1972-73*	*1973-74*	*1974-75*	*1975-76*	*1976-77*	*1977-78*	*1978-79*	*1979-80*	*1980-81*
Agriculture	4.56	4.70	4.87	4.72	5.24	5.19	5.11	5.26	5.49	5.12	5.16
Mining	2.16	2.09	2.42	3.85	3.65	4.11	4.06	3.75	3.56	3.96	3.81
Manufacturing	12.06	11.65	12.21	11.60	11.22	11.07	11.42	11.44	10.88	10.23	9.39
Construction	2.46	2.61	2.56	2.96	3.17	2.78	3.05	3.37	3.54	4.63	4.91
Electricity	6.62	6.59	6.41	6.15	6.28	6.53	6.53	6.32	6.43	6.05	5.81
Transport	20.07	19.40	19.16	17.85	18.04	18.47	18.73	18.13	16.98	16.45	15.67
Trade	1.63	1.78	1.95	2.59	1.96	2.18	2.05	2.02	1.83	1.70	1.61
Banking	7.86	8.05	8.23	8.43	6.39	8.03	8.04	8.55	9.23	8.46	8.62
Administration	29.97	30.31	29.43	29.12	30.06	29.46	28.23	28.11	28.57	29.68	30.56
Services	12.61	12.82	12.76	12.73	11.98	12.19	12.77	13.05	13.48	13.70	14.46
Public Sector	100.0	100.00	100.00	100.00	100.00	100.00	100.00	100.00	100.00	100.00	100.00
NAP SECTOR (11-1)	95.44	95.30	95.13	95.28	94.76	94.81	94.89	94.74	94.51	94.88	94.84

Note: NAP: Non-Agriculture Public Sector.

SOURCE: Calculated on the basis of Table 1.6.

TABLE 1.8 Industrial Origin of Gross Domestic Product at Factor Cost to Nation

(*Rs. Million at Current Prices*)

Industry	*1970-71*	*1971-72*	*1972-73*	*1973-74*	*1974-75*	*1975-76*	*1976-77*	*1977-78*	*1978-79*	*1979-80*	*1980-81*
Agriculture[1]	174240	180830	199350	267880	290450	278450	284930	326500	335440	343690	426400
Mining	3780	3960	4270	4870	6950	8840	10110	11170	12150	15150	17620
Manufacturing	52230	57490	63750	75720	98580	103750	115200	128560	147860	169890	196990
Construction	19520	21420	23160	24050	26370	32930	39080	45400	46740	46580	54840
Electricity[2]	4190	4560	4910	5250	6750	8350	10950	12490	14900	17010	18770
Transport[3]	18690	20230	22320	24900	31340	35240	41600	45440	52910	57490	64180
Trade[4]	40430	43920	48610	60250	81050	92080	95970	109760	117450	139410	178310
Banking[5]	21140	23600	26110	30100	35230	41180	47240	52460	58470	65480	74900
Administration[6]	16350	18310	19760	22210	28560	32370	34530	36940	40720	45890	54150
Services[7]	16790	18410	20170	22490	27350	30510	35030	38540	43080	48110	56550
Total Public Sector	367360	392630	432410	537720	632630	663700	714640	807260	869720	948700	114271
NNA Sector (11-1)	193120	211800	233060	269840	342180	385250	429710	480760	534280	605010	71631

NNA Sector—National—Non-Agricultural Sector.

Notes: [1]Agriculture includes Forestry and Fishing.
[2]Electricity, Gas and Water Supply.
[3]Transport and Communications.
[4]Trade, Hotels and Restaurant.
[6]Banking and Insurance and Ownership of Dwellings have been clubbed together.
[6]Public Administration and Defence.
[7]Other Services.

SOURCE: National Accounts Statistics—Jan. 1981—Feb. 1983.

TABLE 1.9 Industrial Origin of Gross Domestic Product at Factor Cost in Nation

(*Rs. Million at 1970-71 Prices*)

Industry	*1970-71*	*1971-72*	*1972-73*	*1973-74*	*1974-75*	*1975-76*	*1976-77*	*1977-78*	*1978-79*	*1979-80*	*1980-81*
Agriculture	174240	173390	162840	174830	171690	193490	180980	202710	213320	181920	204540
Mining	3780	3850	4060	4120	4300	4800	4890	5120	5230	5270	5470
Manufacturing	52230	53670	55900	58610	59900	61280	66680	71080	78950	77530	79740
Construction	19520	19740	20050	18390	17710	20270	22560	25130	24330	22470	22900
Electricity	4190	4510	4720	4850	5070	5770	6380	6630	7370	7470	7910
Transport	18690	19450	20770	21420	23250	25290	26960	28000	30070	31910	33920
Trade	40430	41220	41380	43130	45090	49320	51030	55390	60360	58610	61810
Banking	21140	22210	23030	23490	23230	25010	27250	28990	31460	31630	32220
Administration	16350	17850	18630	19800	20860	22380	23700	25350	28190	31460	35940
Services	16790	17240	17720	17820	18600	19010	19340	19680	20180	21330	22390
Total	367300	373130	369100	386460	389700	426620	429860	468080	494460	469600	506820
N.N.A. Sector (11-1)	193120	199740	206260	211630	218010	233130	248880	265370	281140	287680	302300

Notes: NNA = National Non-Agriculture Sector.
SOURCE: National Accounts Statistics Jan. 1981, Feb. 1983.

TABLE 1.10 Share of Industrial Origin of GDP of Public Sector in Nation

(Percent at 1970-71 prices)

Industry	*1970-71*	*1971-72*	*1972-73*	*1973-74*	*1974-75*	*1975-76*	*1976-77*	*1977-78*	*1978-79*	*1979-80*	*1980-81*
Agriculture	1.43	1.60	1.89	1.84	2.12	2.04	2.37	2.34	2.54	2.982	2.97
Mining	31.22	31.95	37.68	63.59	58.84	65.00	68.47	66.01	67.11	79.70	81.90
Manufacturing	12.60	12.78	13.83	13.46	14.16	13.72	14.38	14.52	13.59	13.99	13.84
Construction	6.86	7.80	8.08	10.93	12.42	10.41	11.35	12.10	14.34	21.85	25.20
Electricity	86.16	86.03	86.02	86.19	86.00	85.96	85.90	85.97	84.87	85.94	86.35
Transport	58.59	58.77	58.40	56.68	53.85	55.48	58.31	58.39	55.70	54.65	54.33
Trade	2.20	2.55	2.97	4.08	3.02	3.37	3.37	3.29	3.00	3.07	3.06
Banking	20.29	21.34	22.62	24.39	22.08	24.39	24.77	26.59	28.95	28.36	31.46
Administration	100.00	100.00	100.00	100.00	100.00	100.00	100.00	100.00	100.00	100.00	100.00
Services	40.98	43.79	45.60	48.60	44.68	48.71	55.43	59.81	65.90	68.07	75.97
Total Share of P.E. Sector.	14.85	15.79	17.15	17.60	17.81	17.81	19.53	19.26	19.95	22.57	23.20
Share of NAPE Sector in NNA Sector	26.96	28.10	29.20	30.61	30.16	30.90	32.00	32.20	33.16	34.96	36.89

Note: Calculated on the basis of Tables 1.6 and 1.9.

TABLE 1.11 Net Domestic Capital Formation Originating in Public and Private Sectors (at Current Prices) 1960-61 to 1980-81

(Rs. Millions)

Year	*Net Domestic Capital Formation*			*Relative Shares in NDCF*	
	Public Sector	*Private Sector*	*Total*	*Public Sector*	*Private Sector*
1960-61	10210	7870	18080	56.47	43.53
1961-62	10380	5880	16260	63.84	36.16
1962-63	13060	6780	19840	65.83	34.17
1963-64	15010	7640	22650	66.27	33.73
1964-65	17140	9090	26230	65.35	34.65
1965-66	19670	11940	31610	62.23	37.77
1966-67	18530	21820	40350	45.92	54.08
1967-68	19990	17770	37760	52.94	47.06
1968-69	18100	16170	34270	52.82	47.18
1969-70	18460	25240	43700	42.24	57.76
1970-71	23240	26360	49600	46.85	53.15
1971-72	26490	29280	55770	47.50	52.50
1972-73	30140	23830	53970	55.85	44.15
1973-74	40880	46730	87610	46.66	53.34
1974-75	49590	48210	97800	50.51	49.29
1975-76	68310	38520	106830	63.94	36.06
1976-77	75130	45350	120480	62.36	37.64
1977-78	62830	67950	130780	48.04	51.96
1978-79	83360	97640	181000	46.06	53.94
1979-80	102050	78220	180270	56.61	43.39
1980-81	116930	107310	224240	52.16	47.84

SOURCE: National Accounts Statistics Oct. 1976. Jan. 1981 and Feb. 1983.

TABLE 1.12 Gross Capital Formation in Public Sector by Industry of Use

(*Rs. in Million at Current Prices*)

Industry	*1970-71*	*1971-72*	*1972-73*	*1973-74*	*1974-75*	*1975-76*	*1976-77*	*1977-78*	*1978-79*	*1979-80*	*1980-81*
Agriculture	3480	4040	5250	5880	6140	7450	10570	12580	14520	16860	19200
Mining	840	970	1480	2100	2760	5190	6590	6310	6260	8040	11640
Manufacturing	4360	5590	6780	10210	14960	14450	17370	16070	18700	26560	30990
Construction	30	150	40	420	1040	630	440	960	1210	1070	2570
Electricity	6400	6540	6830	7270	9430	14570	15680	18570	20760	25020	27330
Transport	5110	5870	7960	7290	9190	11210	10270	10710	12900	14920	18680
Trade	1990	1480	(—)1820	2230	3110	11920	11710	(−)1820	4640	1850	(−)2570
Banking	170	290	270	460	350	370	490	490	700	680	1100
Administration	4710	5910	8030	10760	8000	9160	9390	7970	13440	18610	22710
Services	640	810	1250	1520	1660	1820	2630	2660	3360	4140	4860
P.E. Sector total	27730	31650	36070	48140	56640	76770	85140	74500	96490	117750	136510
NAPE Sector	24250	27610	30820	42260	50500	69320	74570	61920	81970	100890	117310
(11-1)	50500	69320	74570	61920							

SOURCE: National Accounts Statistics Jan. 1981—Feb. 1983.

TABLE 1.13 Gross Domestic Capital Formation in Public Sector by Industry of Use at 1970-71 Prices

(*Rs. in Millions*)

Industry	*1970-71*	*1971-72*	*1972-73*	*1973-74*	*1974-75*	*1975-76*	*1976-77*	*1977-78*	*1978-79*	*1979-80*	*1980-81*
Agriculture	3480	3690	4360	4320	3720	4240	5850	6720	7130	7190	7120
Mining	840	900	1290	1650	1680	2930	3900	3710	3360	3730	4840
Manufacturing	4360	5220	5930	8070	8890	8220	10530	9320	10160	12240	12580
Construction	30	140	40	330	620	360	280	550	660	490	1030
Electricity, Gas and Water Supply	6400	6250	6210	5960	6170	9020	9060	10250	10710	11260	11270
Transport Storage and Communication	5110	5490	6900	5970	6110	6190	6190	6290	7050	7230	8480
Trade, Hotels & Restaurant	1990	1400	−1570	1610	1800	6890	6630(−)	970	2490	840(−)	990
Banking and Insurance	170	270	230	190	230	210	290	290	300	310	460
Public Administration and Defence	4710	5510	6930	8160	4940	5230	5190	4250	6510	7930	8490
Services	640	740	1030	1120	1010	1040	1460	1430	1670	1790	1850
Public Sector Total	27730	29570	31350	37380	35170	44330	49380	41840	50120	53010	55200
NAP Sector (11-1)	24250	25880	26990	33060	31450	40090	43530	35120	42990	45820	48010

SOURCE: National Account Statistics—Jan. 1981 and Feb. 1983.

Notes: Banking and Insurances includes Real Estate and Ownership of Dwellings NAP Sector is Non-Agricultural Public Sector.

TABLE 1.14 Gross Capital Formation of Public Sector by Industry of Use

(*Percent*)

Industry	*1970-71*	*1971-72*	*1972-73*	*1973-74*	*1974-75*	*1975-76*	*1976-77*	*1977-78*	*1978-79*	*1979-80*	*1980-81*
Agriculture	12.55	12.48	13.91	11.56	10.58	9.56	11.84	16.06	14.23	13.56	13.02
Mining	3.03	3.04	4.11	4.41	4.78	6.61	7.90	8.87	6.70	7.03	8.77
Manufacturing	15.72	17.65	18.92	21.59	25.28	18.54	21.32	22.27	20.27	23.09	22.79
Construction	0.11	0.47	0.13	0.88	1.76	0.81	0.57	1.31	1.32	0.92	1.86
Electricity	23.08	21.15	19.81	15.94	17.54	20.35	18.35	24.50	21.37	21.24	20.42
Transport	18.43	18.43	22.01	15.97	17.37	13.96	12.53	15.03	14.07	13.64	15.36
Trade	7.18	4.74(−)	5.01	4.31	5.12	15.54	13.43 (−)	2.32	4.96	1.58 (−)	1.79
Banking	0.61	0.91	0.73	0.51	0.65	0.47	0.59	0.69	0.76	0.58	0.83
Administration	16.98	18.63	22.11	21.83	14.05	11.80	10.51	10.16	12.99	14.96	15.38
Services	2.31	2.50	3.28	3.00	2.87	2.35	2.96	3.42	3.33	3.38	3.35
Public Sector											
Total	100.00	100.00	100.00	100.00	100.00	100.00	100.00	100.00	100.00	100.00	100.00
Share of NAP Sector (11-1)	87.45	87.52	86.09	88.44	89.42	90.44	88.16	83.94	85.77	86.44	86.98

Note: Calculated on the basis of Table 1.13.

TABLE 1.15 Gross Domestic Capital Formation by Industry of Use in National Economy

(Rs. in Millions at Current Prices)

Industry	*1970-71*	*1971-72*	*1972-73*	*1973-74*	*1974-75*	*1975-76*	*1976-77*	*1977-78*	*1978-79*	*1979-80*	*1980-81*
1. Agriculture	13650	14660	17260	21290	20450	22250	34150	37490	49190	46110	59390
2. Mining	920	1500	1310	2300	3370	6410	7860	7540	6190	8500	12700
3. Manufacturing	19760	21430	18980	32270	46880	41300	34740	44600	65810	77740	88860
4. Construction	1090	1570	1480	2010	2390	2400	3640	4940	3690	4030	6110
5. Electricity	6500	6660	6900	7070	9560	14690	15750	19630	22440	25720	29240
6. Transport	8140	9060	11300	12140	14150	15040	15010	17060	19910	23140	29300
7. Trade	6020	6900	3100	11750	10620	18590	18220	10820	21720	13750	17790
8. Banking	9960	10950	10750	16300	15690	15400	23650	26770	31410	25140	33690
9. Public Admn.	4710	5910	8030	10760	8000	9160	9390	7970	13440	18610	22710
10. Services	1020	1120	1550	1950	1950	2050	2840	3530	4130	4040	5070
11. Total	71770	79760	80660	117840	133060	147290	165250	180350	237930	246780	304860
12. NNA Sector (11-1)	58120	65100	63400	96550	112610	125040	131100	142860	188740	200670	245470

SOURCE: National Accounts Statistics Jan. 1981—Feb. 1983.

TABLE 1.16 Gross Domestic Capital Formation by Industry of Use in National Economy

(Rs. In Million at 1970-71 Prices)

Industry	1970-71	1971-72	1972-73	1973-74	1974-75	1975-76	1976-77	1977-78	1978-79	1979-80	1980-81
1. Agriculture	13650	13910	15130	15940	12960	12780	18790	19910	24630	20200	23620
2. Mining	920	1430	1170	1850	2140	3540	4450	4320	3240	3630	4830
3. Manufacturing	19760	20290	16600	24500	27910	23530	19550	24550	34290	34830	34840
4. Construction	1090	1480	1300	1550	1550	1430	2020	2650	1900	1870	2370
5. Electricity	6500	6370	6270	5800	6270	8760	9100	10840	11570	11570	12060
6. Transport	8140	8450	9840	9950	9220	8910	8870	9830	10560	10510	12240
7. Trade	6020	6630	2810	8950	6330	10680	10140	6070	11330	5920	6820
8. Banking	9960	10340	9330	12480	9510	8200	12380	13800	14580	9920	11660
9. Administration	4710	5510	6930	8160	4930	5230	5190	4250	6510	7930	8490
10. Services	1020	1060	1370	1540	1220	1160	1600	1950	2080	1760	1970
11. Total	71770	75470	70750	90720	82050	84220	92090	98170	120690	108140	118900
12. NNA Sector Total (11-1)	58120	61560	55620	74780	69090	71440	73300	78260	96060	87940	95280

SOURCE: National Accounts Statistics Jan. 1981. Feb. 1983.

TABLE 1.17 Gross Domestic Capital Formation by Industry of Use in Nation

(Percent)

Industry	*1970-71*	*1971-72*	*1972-73*	*1973-74*	*1974-75*	*1975-76*	*1976-77*	*1977-78*	*1978-79*	*1979-80*	*1980-81*
1. Agriculture	19.02	18.43	21.39	17.57	15.79	15.17	20.40	20.28	20.17	18.68	19.86
2. Mining	1.28	1.89	1.65	2.04	2.61	4.20	4.83	4.40	3.47	3.36	4.06
3. Manufacturing	27.53	26.88	23.46	27.01	34.01	27.94	21.23	25.00	28.08	32.21	29.30
4. Construction	1.52	1.96	1.84	1.71	1.88	1.70	2.19	2.70	1.56	1.73	1.99
5. Electricity	9.06	8.44	8.86	6.39	7.64	10.40	9.88	11.04	9.47	10.70	10.14
6. Transport	11.34	11.20	13.91	10.97	11.24	10.58	9.63	10.01	8.64	9.72	10.29
7. Trade	8.39	8.79	3.97	9.86	7.71	12.68	11.01	6.18	9.28	5.47	5.74
8. Banking	13.88	13.70	13.19	13.76	11.59	9.74	13.44	14.06	11.94	9.17	9.81
9. Administration	6.56	7.30	9.79	8.99	6.02	6.21	5.64	4.33	5.66	7.33	7.14
10. Services	1.42	1.41	1.94	1.70	1.48	1 38	1.74	1.99	1.70	1.63	1.66
11. Total	100.00	100.00	100.00	100.00	100.00	100.00	100.00	100.00	100.00	100.00	100.00
12. NNA Sector Total (11-1)	80.98	81.57	78.61	82.43	84.21	84.83	79.60	79.72	79.83	81.32	80.14

Note: Calculated on the basis of Table 16.

TABLE 1.18 Share of Public Sector Gross Capital Formation by Industry of the Nation

(*Percent*)

Industry	*1970-71*	*1971-72*	*1972-73*	*1973-74*	*1974-75*	*1975-76*	*1976-77*	*1977-78*	*1978-79*	*1979-80*	*1980-81*
1. Agriculture	25.49	26.53	28.82	27.10	28.70	33.17	31.13	33.75	28.95	35.59	30.44
2. Mining	91.30	62.94	110.26	89.19	78.50	82.77	87.64	85.88	79.25	102.75	100.21
3. Manufacturing	22.06	25.73	35.72	32.94	31.85	34.93	53.86	37.96	29.63	35.14	36.11
4. Construction	2.75	9.46	3.08	21.29	40.00	25.17	13.86	20.75	34.74	26.20	43.45
5. Electricity	98.46	98.12	99.04	102.76	98.41	102.97	99.56	94.55	92.57	97.32	93.45
6. Transport	62.78	64.50	70.72	60.00	66.27	69.47	69.79	63.98	66.76	68.79	69.20
7. Trade	33.06	21.12(—)	55.87	17.99	28.44	64.51	65.38	−15.98	21.98	14.19	−14.51
8. Banking	1.71	2.61	2.47	1.52	2.42	2.56	2.34	2.10	2.61	3.12	3.94
9. Administration	100.00	100.00	100.00	100.00	100.00	100.00	100.00	100.00	100.00	100.00	100.00
10. Services	62.75	69.81	75.18	72.73	82.79	89.66	91.25	73.33	80.29	101.76	93.91
11. Share of Public Sector	38.64	39.18	44.31	41.20	42.86	52.63	53.62	42.62	41.05	49.02	46.42
12. Share of NAPE Sector	41.72	42.04	48.53	44.21	45.52	56.12	59.39	44.88	44.11	52.10	50.39

Note: Calculated on the basis of Tables 13 and 16.

TABLE 1.19 Sources and Users of Gross Savings and Investment in Nation[1]

(Rs. in Million at Current Prices)

Sources	*1970-71*	*1971-72*	*1972-73*	*1973-74*	*1974-75*	*1975-76*	*1976-77*	*1977-78*	*1978-79*	*1979-80*	*1980-81*
					Gross Savings						
Administration[2]	5760	5300	5150	9370	14750	20940	20590	19890	23430	23890	19190
Public enterprise[3]	6770	7480	8170	8700	12010	12450	20550	20660	22620	23960	25520
(Share)	(9.43)	(9.38)	(10.13)	(7.38)	(9.03)	(8.45)	(12.44)	(11.46)	(9.50)	(9.70)	(8.39)
Public Sector	19910	21690	23280	27780	35930	35470	37700	41970	49140	58640	69650
Households	35390	40510	41090	68070	63840	79600	99500	112480	141460	134490	166500
Foreign[4]	3940	4870	2970	3920	6530	(−)1170	(−)13090	(−)14650	1280	5800	24000
					Gross Investment[1]						
Administration[2]	5810	7400	10140	13250	10800	12210	13060	11820	18200	25430	30880
Public Enterprises	21920	24250	25930	34890	45840	64560	72070	62680	78290	92320	105630
(Share)	(30.54)	(30.40)	(32.15)	(29.61)	(35.45)	(48.83)	(43.61)	(34.75)	(32.90)	(37.41)	(34.65)
Private Sector	44040	41810	44590	69700	76420	70520	80120	105850	141440	129030	168350
Households	00	00	00	00	00	00	00	00	00	00	00
Foreign[3]	00	00	00	00	00	00	00	00	00	00	00
Gross Savings Investment	71770	79760	80660	117840	133060	147290	165250	180350	237930	246780	304860

SOURCE: National Accounts Statistics: Feb. 1983 and Jan. 1981.

Gross Savings

Notes: [1]Net Domestic Savings figures are converted into Gross Domestic Savings by adding Aggregate Capital Consumption Gross Domestic Capital Formation minus Net hiflow of Capital from Abroad is equal to Gross Domestic Savings. Gross Savings and Investment Equality requires adding Net hiflows of Capital from abroad to Gross Domestic Savings.

[2]Gross Savings of Administration are separated from Government Sector by subtracting Gross Savings Originating from Departmental and Non-departmental Enterprises.

[3]Public Enterprises Sector includes Departmental and Non-departmental.

[4]Refers to Net hiflow of Capital from abroad which is treated as source of Gross Savings.

Gross Investment

[1]Gross Investment is identical with GDCF [2]Gross Investment of Administration is equal to Gross Capital Formations.

[3]Net hiflow of capital is treated as source of Gross Savings.

(Figures in parentheses refer to percentages for the Public Sector)

TABLE 1.20 Price Index for NDP 1970-71 = 100 By Industry

Industry	*1960-61*	*1961-62*	*1962-63*	*1963-64*	*1964-65*	*1965-66*	*1966-67*	*1967-68*	*1968-69*	*1969-70*	*1970-71*
Agriculture	50.32	51.39	54.01	61.06	68.43	77.66	94.15	100.99	98.45	101.66	100.00
Mining	60.36	59.92	63.63	67.41	69.82	70.83	75.00	84.38	93.29	99.42	100.00
Manufacturing	63.61	63.70	65.44	69.72	72.94	75.01	82.83	86.98	88.59	94.32	100.00
Construction	56.31	57.11	58.08	59.29	65.28	70.34	76.52	83.63	86.44	93.66	100.00
Electricity	61.82	60.16	61.97	61.27	67.54	67.92	78.76	81.71	87.08	96.23	100.00
Transport	61.54	64.12	67.16	68.33	71.52	73.48	79.12	84.18	92.01	93.82	100.00
Trade	54.81	54.61	55.66	58.71	66.47	71.28	82.35	91.59	88.94	91.98	100.00
Banking	59.68	58.54	61.72	65.26	69.04	71.82	73.63	76.32	75.62	77.10	100.00
Public Administration	69.96	72.49	72.22	75.53	77.93	84.10	88.39	96.23	98.92	99.67	100.00
Services	60.04	63.23	65.26	69.25	76.25	82.98	91.26	100.25	105.83	114.60	100.00
	54.74	55.92	58.25	63.49	69.41	76.10	87.61	94.56	94.17	98.01	100.00

Industry	*1971-72*	*1972-73*	*1973-74*	*1974-75*	*1975-76*	*1976-77*	*1977-78*	*1978-79*	*1979-80*	*1980-81*
Agriculture	104.31	122.85	154.30	170.19	143.62	157.42	161.01	160.56	188.57	208.04
Mining	102.41	104.58	115.19	159.74	182.78	199.53	213.66	227.60	283.30	309.32
Manufacturing	107.14	114.07	129.30	164.25	169.19	172.68	180.69	187.04	218.88	246.22
Construction	108.54	115.55	130.76	148.96	162.47	173.20	180.68	192.12	207.31	239.46
Electricity	101.19	104.23	108.79	133.43	144.99	171.62	188.64	202.46	227.14	236.92
Transport	104.55	108.56	118.41	137.38	141.20	155.95	162.91	176.48	180.73	188.50
Trade	106.62	117.58	139.82	180.59	186.98	188.34	198.53	194.97	238.32	289.04
Banking	105.56	112.98	126.62	148.14	161.43	170.60	178.79	181.11	198.75	220.16
Public Administration	102.58	106.07	112.17	136.91	144.64	145.70	145.72	145.45	145.87	150.67
Services	106.78	113.83	126.22	147.10	160.51	181.17	195.87	213.46	225.56	252.61
	105.24	117.59	140.79	163.11	155.21	165.99	172.03	175.00	201.05	224.05

SOURCE: National Accounts Statistics: Various issues from Oct. 1976.

TABLE 1.21 Price Index Number for GDCF 1970-71 = 100

Industry	*1960-61*	*1961-62*	*1962-63*	*1963-64*	*1964-65*	*1965-66*	*1966-67*	*1967-68*	*1968-69*	*1969-70*	*1970-71*
Agriculture	53.18	57.14	53.24	62.86	62.71	65.25	78.39	89.00	89.68	95.18	100.00
Mining	57.14	60.29	60.67	72.07	69.28	82.09	82.20	90.20	106.25	95.68	100.00
Manufacturing	59.76	56.91	67.76	59.23	68.42	73.88	91.82	88.84	101.23	88.33	100.00
Construction	44.95	51.85	38.68	62.92	60.20	66.35	72.89	89.20	73.15	90.12	100.00
Electricity	61.62	64.29	68.36	69.56	71.94	77.34	83.69	91.61	89.17	92.45	100.00
Transport	62.48	62.41	63.02	68.27	70.22	74.36	80.71	85.06	90.22	89.80	100.00
Trade	46.67	100.00	60.78	60.42	61.59		72.01	103.08	85.65	93.79	100.00
Banking	53.58	55.94	54.51	64.86	64.32	68.63	70.09	85.62	86.66	95.08	100.00
Administration	57.92	62.37	63.86	66.16	68.27	73.27	76.68	83.75	84.82	93.47	100.00
Services	51.91	53.64	41.95	67.32	62.89	70.00	73.51	86.86	89.19	91.97	100.00
Total	56.25	58.89	60.65	64.29	66.92	71.15	81.45	88.19	90.97	92.29	100.00

Industry	*1971-72*	*1972-73*	*1973-74*	*1974-75*	*1975-76*	*1976-77*	*1977-78*	*1978-79*	*1979-80*	*1980-81*
Agriculture	105.39	114.08	133.56	157.79	174.10	181.75	188.30	199.72	228.27	251.44
Mining	104.90	111.97	124.32	157.48	181.07	176.63	174.54	191.05	234.16	262.94
Manufacturing	105.62	114.34	131.71	167.97	175.52	177.70	181.67	191.92	223.20	255.05
Construction	106.08	113.84	129.68	154.19	167.83	180.20	186.42	194.21	215.51	257.81
Electricity	104.55	110.05	121.90	152.47	167.69	173.08	181.09	193.95	222.30	242.45
Transport	107.22	114.84	122.01	153.47	168.80	169.22	173.55	188.54	220.17	239.38
Trade	104.07	110.32	131.28	167.77	174.06	179.68	178.25	191.70	232.26	260.85
Banking	105.90	115.32	130.61	164.98	187.80	191.03	193.99	215.43	253.43	288.94
Administration	107.26	115.87	131.86	161.94	175.14	180.92	187.53	206.45	234.68	267.49
Services	105.66	113.14	126.62	159.84	176.72	177.50	181.03	198.56	229.55	257.36
Total	105.68	114.01	129.89	162.17	174.89	179.44	183.71	197.14	228.20	256.40

SOURCE: National Accounts Statistics, Various issues from Oct. 1976.

TABLE 1.22 Price Index Number for G.D.C.F. in Public Sector by Industry of Use: 1970-71 = 100

Industry	*1970-71*	*1971-72*	*1972-73*	*1973-74*	*1974-75*	*1975-76*	*1976-77*	*1977-78*	*1978-79*	*1979-80*	*1980-81*
Agriculture	100	109.49	120.41	136.11	165.05	175.71	180.68	187.20	203.65	234.49	267.04
Mining	100	107.78	114.73	127.27	162.28	177.13	168.97	170.08	186.31	215.55	240.50
Manufacturing	100	107.09	114.33	126.52	168.28	175.79	167.83	172.42	184.06	216.99	246.34
Construction	100	107.14	100.00	127.27	167.74	175.00	157.14	174.55	183.33	218.37	249.51
Electricity	100	104.64	109.98	121.98	152.84	161.53	173.07	181.17	193.84	222.20	242.50
Transport	100	107.71	115.36	122.11	150.41	181.10	165.91	170.27	182.98	206.36	220.28
Trade	100	105.71	115.92	138.51	172.78	173.00	176.62	187.63	186.35	220.24	259.60
Banking	100	107.41	117.39	292.11	152.11	176.19	165.52	168.96	184.21	219.35	239.13
Administration	100	107.26	115.87	131.86	161.94	175.14	180.92	187.53	206.45	234.68	267.49
Services	100	109.46	121.36	135.71	164.36	175.00	180.14	186.01	201.20	231.28	262.70
Total Public Sector	100	107.03	115.05	128.78	161.04	173.18	173.02	178.06	192.52	222.13	247.30

TABLE 1.23 Trends in Employment in the Organised Sector : 1961 to 1981

End of March	*Lakh numbers*			*% Share in total employment*		*% Increase over previous year*		
	Public Sector	*Private Sector*	*Total*	*Public Sector*	*Private Sector*	*Public Sector*	*Private Sector*	*Total*
1961	70.50	50.40	120.90	58	42	—	—	—
1962	74.17	51.60	125.77	59	41	5.20	2.38	4.03
1963	79.53	54.50	134.03	59	41	7.23	5.62	6.57
1964	84.54	57.80	142.34	59	41	6.30	6.05	6.20
1965	89.57	60.40	149.97	60	40	5.95	4.50	5.36
1966	93.78	68.10	161.88	58	42	4.70	12.75	7.94
1967	96.34	66.80	163.14	59	41	2.73	(−) 1.91	0.78
1968	98.02	65.20	163.22	60	60	1.74	(−) 2.39	0.05
1969	100.95	65.30	166.25	61	39	2.99	0.15	1.86
1970	103.74	66.80	170.54	61	39	2.76	2.30	2.58
1971	107.31	67.42	174.73	61	39	3.44	0.93	2.46
1972	112.09	67.69	179.78	62	38	4.45	0.40	2.89
1973	119.71	68.49	188.20	64	36	6.80	1.18	4.68
1974	124.80	67.94	192.74	65	35	4.25	(−) 0.80	2.41
1975	128.88	68.08	196.96	65	35	3.27	0.21	2.19
1976	133.22	68.44	201.66	66	34	3.37	0.53	2.39
1977	137.66	68.67	206.33	67	33	3.33	0.34	2.32
1978	142.00	70.43	212.43	67	33	3.15	2.56	2.96
1979	146.76	72.08	218.84	67	33	3.35	2.34	3.02
1980	150.78	72.27	223.05	68	32	2.74	0.26	1.92
1981	154.84	73.95	228.79	68	32	2.69	2.32	2.57

Note: 1. Data before 1966 are not comparable to those after 1966. Organised Sector covers all the Enterprises in the Public Sector and only the Non-agricultural Establishments in the Private Sector employing 25 or more workers from 1961 to 1965 and 10 or more workers from 1966 onwards.

2. The National Industrial Classification has been introduced w.e.f. 1st April 1975 and hence the figures from 1975 onwards are not comparable with those for earlier years. The data prior to March 1975 are based on Standard Industrial Classification.

SOURCE: *Economic Survey*, 1977, 1982.

Set. II from Annual Survey of Industries: 1975-76 to 1978-79

Tables

TABLE 2.1 Principal Characteristics by Type of Ownership—All India

Type of Ownership	*Factories Number*	*Fixed Capital Rs. lakhs*	*Productive Capital Rs. lakhs*	*Employee Number*	*Emolument Rs. lakhs*	*Output Rs. lakhs*	*Value Adds. Rs. lakhs.*
Wholly Central Government	1093	296380	456290	692949	60865	399832	99253
Wholly State/Local Government	2395	508280	590537	780362	42264	219198	66550
Central and State/Local Government jointly	256	4702	7027	16918	945	7993	1904
Public Sector	3744	809362	1053862	1490229	104074	627023	167707
Central Government and Private Enterprises jointly.	126	14411	29207	33998	3053	48168	6547
State/Local Government and Private	1093	47582	71816	261138	10461	118294	22542
Enterprises jointly Central, State/Local Government and Private Enterprise jointly	88	17337	21451	35929	3487	38136	5333
Joint Sector	1307	79330	122474	331065	17001	204598	34422
Wholly Private Enterprises	60539	492289	843083	4532962	223770	2150618	434561
Unspecified	6115	21929	23773	36489	1451	4406	1978
Total	71705	1402910	2043192	6380745	346296	2986645	638668

SOURCE: *Annual Survey of Industries* 1975-76.

TABLE 2.2 Principal Characteristics by Type of Ownership—All India

(Percentage Distribution)

Type of ownership	*Factories*	*Fixed Capital*	*Productive Capital*	*Employed*	*Emoluments*	*Output*	*Value Add*
Wholly Central Government	1.52	21.13	22.33	10.86	17.58	13.39	15.54
Wholly State/Local Government	3.34	36.23	28.90	12.23	12.20	7.34	10.42
Central and State/Local Government jointly	0.36	0.34	0.35	0.27	0.27	0.26	0.30
Public Sector	5.22	57.70	51.58	23.36	30.05	20.99	26.26
Central Government and Private Enterprises jointly	0.18	1.03	1.43	0.53	0.88	1.61	1.02
State/Local Government and Private Enterprises jointly	1.52	3.39	3.51	4.09	3.02	3.96	3.53
Central, State/Local Government and Private Enterprises jointly	0 12	1.23	1.05	0.57	1.01	1.28	0.84
Joint Sector	1.82	5.65	5.99	5.19	4.91	6.85	5.39
Wholly Private Enterprises	84.43	35.09	41.27	71.04	64.62	72.01	68.00
Unspecified	8.53	1.56	1.16	0.41	0.42	0.15	0.00
Total	100.00	100.00	100.00	100.00	00.00	100.00	100.00

SOURCE: *Annual Survey of Industries* 1975-76.

TABLE 2.3 Structural Ratios by Type of Ownership—All India

Type of Ownership	*Fixed Capital Per Employee Rs.*	*Value Added Per Employee Rs.*	*Fixed Capital/ Output Ratio*	*Fixed Capital Value Added*	*Value Added Output Ratio*	*Operating Surplus/ Output*	*Operating Surplus Productive Capital*
Public Sector	54311	11254	1.29	4.83	0.27	0.10	0.06
Joint Sector	23962	10397	0.39	2.30	0.17	0.09	0.14
Private Sector	10860	9587	0.23	1.13	0.20	0.10	0.25
Total	21987	10009	0.47	2.20	0.21	0.10	0.14

SOURCE: *Annual Survey of Industries* 1975-76.

TABLE 2.4 Principal Characteristics by Type of Organisation—All India

Type of Organisation	*Factories (Number)*	*Fixed Capital (Rs. lakhs)*	*Productive Capital (Rs. lakhs)*	*Employee (Number)*	*Emolument (Rs. lakhs)*	*Output (Rs. lakhs)*	*Value Added (Rs. lakhs.)*
1. Individual Proprietorship	11811	8186	14095	278230	4834	49710	8246
2. Partnership	36231	63164	125518	1259795	27553	505317	59648
Public Limited Company	5142	590534	964434	2589381	195123	1590175	375996
Private Limited Company	7817	80006	132088	832837	38831	380018	76195
Public Corporation	1310	501725	583518	671926	41811	235744	66317
3. Corporation Sector	14269	1172265	1680040	4094144	275765	2205937	518508
4. Cooperative Society	1398	45038	59819	221625	5901	87353	9510
5. Others	1930	92421	140170	501910	30836	135050	40936
6. Unspecified	6066	21836	23550	25041	1407	3278	1820
Total	71705	1402910	2043192	6380745	346296	2986645	638668

SOURCE: *Annual Surrey of Industries* 1975-76.

TABLE 2.5 Principal Characteristics by Types of Organisation—All India

(Percentage distribution)

Type of Organisation	*Factories*	*Fixed Capital*	*Productive Capital*	*Employees*	*Emoluments*	*Output*	*Value Added*
Individual Proprietorship	16.47	0.58	0.69	4.36	1.40	1.67	1.29
Partnership	50.53	4.50	6.14	19.75	7.96	16.92	9.34
Public Limited Company	7.17	42.10	47.20	40.58	56.35	53.24	58.87
Private Limited Company	10.90	5.70	6.47	13.05	11.21	12.73	11.93
Public Corporation	1.83	35.76	28.56	10.53	12.07	7.89	10.39
Corporate Sector	19.90	83.56	82.23	64.16	79.63	73.86	81.19
Co-operative Society	1.95	3.21	2.93	3.47	1.70	2.92	1.49
Others	2.69	6.59	6.86	7.87	8.90	4.52	6.41
Unspecified	8.46	1.56	1.15	0.39	0.41	0.11	0.28
Total	100.00	100.00	100.00	100.00	100.00	100.00	100.00

SOURCE: *Annual Survey of Industries* 1975-76.

TABLE 2.6 Structural Ratios by Type of Organisation—All India

Type of Organisation	*Fixed Capital Per Employee (Rs.)*	*Value Added Per Employee (Rs.)*	*Capital Output Ratio*	*Capital Value Added Ratio*	*Value Added Output Ratio*	*Operating Surplus Output Ratio*	*Operating Surplus Productive Capital Ratio*
Individual Proprietorship	2942	2964	0.16	0.99	0.17	0.07	0.24
Partnership	5014	4735	0.12	1.05	0.12	0.06	0.26
Public Limited Company	22806	14521	0.37	1.57	0.24	0.11	0.19
Private Limited Company	9606	9149	0.21	1.05	0.20	0.10	0.28
Public Corporation	74670	9870	2.13	7.57	0.20	0.10	0.04
Corporate Sector	28633	12665	0.53	2.26	0.24	0.11	0.14
Co-operative Sector	20322	4291	0.52	4.74	0.11	0.04	0.06
Others	18414	8156	0.68	2.26	0.30	0.07	0.07
Unspecified	87201	7268	6.66	12.00	0.56	0.13	0.02
Total	21937	10009	0.47	2.20	0.21	0.10	0.14

SOURCE: *Annual Survey of Industries* 1975-76.

TABLE 2.7 Principal Characteristics by Type of Ownership—All India

Type of Ownership	*Factories No.*	*Fixed Capital (Rs. lakhs)*	*Productive Capital (Rs. lakhs)*	*Employees No.*	*Emoluments (Rs. lakhs)*	*Total Input (Rs. lakhs)*	*Gross Output (Rs. lakhs)*	*Value Added (Rs. lakhs)*
Wholly Central Government	1110	365093	559510	726120	66568	346907	490723	123067
Wholly State/Local Government	2405	639371	737415	819574	44570	151095	247787	77141
Central & State/Local Government jointly	198	11893	15254	32934	2150	8021	12076	2987
Public Sector	3713	1016357	1312179	1578628	113288	506023	750586	203195
Central Government and Private Enterprises jointly	120	25294	38682	35454	3439	52983	64204	8228
State/Local Government and Private Enterprises jointly	1181	62003	91269	293212	11957	104575	135461	24708
Central State/Local Government and Private Enterprises jointly	107	21312	31614	54406	5387	45052	57348	10281
Joint Sector	1408	108609	161565	383072	20783	202610	257013	43217
Wholly Private Enterprises	66725	491999	850117	4685591	229545	1862046	2400823	484409
Unspecified	9431	91	200	1959	54	384	643	249
Total	81277	1617056	2324061	6649250	363670	2571063	3409065	731070

SOURCE: *Annual Survey of Industries* 1976-77.

Table 2.8 Principal Characteristics by Type of Ownership—All India

(Percentage distribution)

Type of Ownership	*Factories*	*Fixed Capital*	*Productive Capital*	*Employees*	*Emoluments*	*Total Input*	*Gross Output*	*Value Added*
Wholly Central Government	1.4	22.6	44.1	10.9	18.3	13.5	14.4	16.8
Wholly State/Local Government	3.0	39.6	31.7	12.3	12.3	5.9	7.3	10.6
Central State/Local Govt. jointly	0.2	0.7	0.6	0.5	0.6	0.3	0.3	0.4
Public Sector	4.6	62.9	56.4	23.7	31.2	19.7	22.0	27.8
Central Government and Private Enterprises jointly	0.1	1.6	1.7	0.6	0.9	2.1	11 9	1.1
State/Local Government and Private Enterprises jointly	1.5	3.8	3.9	4.4	3.3	4.1	4.0	3.4
Central, State/Local Government and Private Enterprises jointly	0.1	1.3	1.4	0.8	1.5	1.7	1.7	1.4
Joint Sector	1.7	6.7	7.0	5.8	5.7	7.9	7.6	5.9
Wholly Private Enterprises	82.1	30.4	36.6	70.5	63.1	72.4	70.4	66.3
Unspecified	11.6	0.0	0.0	0 0	0.0	0.0	0.0	0.0
Total	100.00	100.00	100.00	100.00	100.00	100.00	100.00	100.00

SOURCE: *Annual Survey of Industries* 1976-77.

TABLE 2.9 Structure Ratios by Type of Ownership—All India

Type of Ownership	*Fixed Capital Per Employee (Rs.)*	*Value Added Per Employee (Rs.)*	*Fixed Capital Gross Output Ratio*	*Fixed Capital Value Added Ratio*	*Value Added Gross Output Ratio*	*Operating Surplus Gross Output Ratio*	*Operating Surplus Productivity Capital Ratio*
Public Sector	64382	12872	1.35	5.00	0.27	0.12	0.07
Joint Sector	28352	11282	0.42	2.51	0.17	0.09	0.14
Private Sector	10500	10338	0.20	1.02	0.20	0.11	0.30
Total	24319	10955	0.47	2.21	0.21	0.11	0.16

SOURCE: *Annual Survey of Industries* 1976-77.

TABLE 2.10 Principal Characteristics by Type of Organisation—All India

Type of Organisation	*Faciores (number)*	*Fixed Capital (Rs. lakhs)*	*Productive Capital (Rs. lakhs)*	*Employees (number)*	*Emoluments (Rs. lakhs)*	*Total Input (Rs. lakhs)*	*Gross Output (Rs. lakhs)*	*Value Added (Rs. lakhs)*
Individual Proprietorship	24024	9230	16069	343195	6195	47372	59239	10914
Partnership	38803	61582	121463	1328408	29838	491450	568503	70186
Public Limited Company	5592	679031	1084206	2683260	201273	1339385	1826123	427633
Private Limited Company	7975	80520	131687	815952	38350	319404	403625	75046
Public Corporation	1398	457144	552250	595614	40090	170484	268676	81315
Corporate Sector	14965	1216695	1768143	4094826	279713	1829273	2498424	583994
Co-operative Society	1544	40970	56354	241857	6550	73646	87303	9926
Others	1896	288543	361956	640241	41361	129060	195301	56022
Unspecified	45	36	76	723	13	262	295	28
Total	81277	1617056	2324061	6649250	363670	2571063	3409065	731070

SOURCE: *Annual Survey of Industries* 1976-77.

TABLE 2.11 Principal Characteristics by Type of Organisation—All India

(Percentage distribution)

Type of Organisation	*Factories*	*Fixed Capital*	*Productive Capital*	*Employees*	*Emoluments*	*Total Input*	*Gross Output*	*Value Added*
Individual Properietorship	29.6	0.6	0.7	5.2	1.7	1.9	1.7	1.5
Partnership	47.7	3.8	5.2	20.0	8.2	19.1	16.7	9.6
Public Limited	6.9	42.0	46.6	40.3	55.3	52.1	53.6	58.5
Private Limited	9.8	5.0	5.7	12.3	10.6	12.4	11.8	10.3
Public Corporation	1.7	28.3	23.8	9.0	11.0	6.5	7.9	11.1
Corporate Sector	18.4	75.2	76.1	61.6	76.9	71.1	73.3	79.9
Co-operative society	1.9	2.5	2.4	3.6	1.8	2.9	2.6	1.3
Others	2.3	17.8	15.6	9.6	11.4	5.0	5.7	7.7
Unspecified	0.1	0.0	0.0	0.0	0.0	0.0	0.0	0.0
Total	100.00	100.00	100.00	100.00	100.00	100.00	100.00	100.00

SOURCE: *Annual Survey of Industries* 1976-77.

TABLE 2.12 Structural Ratios by Type of Organisation—All India

Type of Organisation	*Fixed Capital Per Employee (Rs.)*	*Value Added Per Employee (Rs.)*	*Fixed Capital Gross Output Ratio*	*Fixed Capital Value Added Ratio*	*Value Added Gross Output Ratio*	*Operating Surplus Gross Output Ratio*	*Operating Surplus Productive Capital Ratio*
Individual Proprietorship	2689	3180	0.16	0.85	0.41	0.08	0.29
Partnership	4636	5283	0.11	0.88	0.12	0.07	0.33
Public Limited Company	25306	15937	0.37	1.59	0.23	0.12	0.21
Private Limited Company	9868	9197	0.20	1.07	0.19	0.09	0.28
Public Corporation	76752	13652	1.70	5.62	0.30	0.15	0.07
Corporate Sector	29713	14262	0.49	2.08	0.23	0.12	0.17
Co-operative Society	16940	4104	0.47	4.13	0.11	0.04	0.06
Others	45068	8750	1.48	5.15	0.29	0.08	0.04
Unspecified	4979	3873	0.12	1.29	0.10	0.05	0.20
Total	24319	10995	0.47	2.21	0.21	0.11	0.16

SOURCE: *Annual Survey of Industries* 1976-77.

TABLE 2.13 Principal Characteristics by Type of Ownership—All India

Type of Ownership	*Factories (number)*	*Fixed Capital (number)*	*Productive Capital (Rs. lakhs)*	*Employees (number)*	*Emoluments (Rs. lakhs)*	*Total Input (Rs. lakhs)*	*Gross Output (Rs. lakhs)*	*Value Added (Rs. lakhs)*
Wholly Central Government	1087	421117	601170	760648	72919	413304	556467	118862
Wholly State/Local Government	2515	846977	976370	922590	56875	165333	287084	98118
Central and State/Local Government Jointly.	263	2768	4831	20557	1233	7216	9169	1742
Public Sector	3865	1270862	1582371	1703795	131027	585853	852720	218722
Central Government and Private Enterprises jointly.	110	20502	32838	33579	3014	31554	44695	10628
State/Local Government, and Priavet Enterprises jointly	1357	82808	109017	323255	13969	116030	148470	23784
Central, State/Local Government and Private Enterprises jointly	91	14004	20035	43399	4802	44596	53263	7270
Joint Sector	1558	117314	161890	400213	21785	192180	246418	41682
Wholly Private Enterprises	71436	557955	947264	4987034	266714	2173053	2785624	551971
Unspecified	8065	260	395	2440	105	1019	1271	219
Total	84924	1946391	2691920	7093382	419631	2952105	3886033	812594

SOURCE: *Annual Survey of Industries* 1977-78.

TABLE 2.14 Structural Ratios by Type of Ownership—All India

Type of Ownership	*Fixed Capital Per Employee (Rs.)*	*Value Added Per Employee (Rs.)*	*Fixed Capital Gross Output Ratio*	*Fixed Capital Value Added Ratio*	*Value Added Gross Output Ratio*	*Emoluments Value Added Ratio*	*Operating Surplus Productive Capital Ratio*
Public sector	74590	12837	1.49	5.81	0.26	0.60	0.06
Joint sector	29313	10415	0.48	2.81	0.17	0.52	0.12
Private sector	11188	11068	0.20	1.01	0.20	0.48	0.30
Total	27440	11456	0.50	2.40	0.21	0.52	0.15

SOURCE: *Annual Survey of Industries* 1977-78.

TABLE 2.15 Principal Characteristics by Type of Organisation—All India

Type of Organisation	*Factories (number)*	*Fixed Capital (Rs. lakhs)*	*Productive Capital (Rs. lakhs)*	*Employees (number)*	*Emoluments (Rs. lakhs)*	*Total Input (Rs. lakhs)*	*Gross Output (Rs. lakhs)*	*Value Added (Rs. lakhs)*
Individual Properietorship	23629	10971	17645	373878	3571	56158	69486	12159
Partnership	41266	71514	141299	1459903	35707	594441	683518	80968
Public Limited Company	5974	764996	1164663	2771858	226960	1493169	2017900	45915
Private Limited Company	8579	89548	146190	846624	43583	378340	476434	87900
Public Corporations	1535	565794	687994	671702	19836	215803	331974	95234
Corporate Sector	16088	1420338	1998847	4290184	320399	2087312	2826308	642288
Co-operative Society	1858	45450	62222	264720	7289	84568	102101	13314
Others	1989	398009	471712	703005	48793	128828	203677	63750
Unspecified	100	109	186	1692	72	798	943	134
Total	84924	1946391	2691920	7093382	419631	2952105	3886033	812594

SOURCE: *Annual Survey of Industries* 1977-78.

TABLE 2.16 Principal Characteristics by Type of Organisation—All India

(Percentage distribution)

Type of Organisation	*Factories*	*Fixed Capital*	*Productive Capital*	*Employees*	*Emoluments*	*Total Input*	*Gross Output*	*Value Added*
Individual Proprietorship	27.8	0.6	0.7	5.3	1.8	1.9	1.8	1.5
Partnership	48.6	3.7	5.2	20.6	8.5	20.1	17.6	10.0
Public Limited Company	7.0	39.3	43.3	39.1	54.1	50.6	51.9	56.5
Private Limited Company	10.1	4.6	5.4	11.9	10.4	12.8	12.3	10.8
Public Corporation	1.8	29.1	25.6	9.5	11.9	7.3	8.5	11.7
Corporate Sector	18.9	73.0	74.3	60.5	76.4	70.7	72.7	79.0
Co-operative Society	2.2	2.3	2.3	3.7	1.7	2.9	2.6	1.6
Others	2.4	20.4	17.5	9.9	11.6	4.4	5.3	7.9
Unspecified	0.1	0.0	0.0	0.0	0.0	0.0	0.0	0.0
Total:	100.0	100.0	100.0	100.0	100.0	100.0	100.0	100.0

SOURCE: *Annual Survey of Industries* 1977-78.

TABLE 2.17 Structural Ratios by the Type of Organisation—All India

Type of Organisation	*Fixed Capital Per Employee (Rs.)*	*Value Added Per Employee (Rs.)*	*Fixed Capital Gross Output Ratio*	*Fixed Capital Value Added Ratio*	*Value Added Gross Output Ratio*	*Emoluments Value Added Ratio*	*Operating Surplus Productive Capital Ratio*
Individual Proprietorship	2934	3252	0.16	0.90	0.17	0.61	0.27
Partnership	2899	5545	0.10	0.88	0.12	0.44	0.32
Public Limited Company	27599	16575	0.38	1.67	0.23	0.49	0.20
Private Limited Company	10577	10382	0.19	1.02	0.18	0.50	0.30
Public Corporation	84233	14178	1.70	5.94	0.29	0.52	0.07
Corporate Sector	33107	14971	0.50	2.21	0.23	0.50	0.16
Co-operative Society	17169	5029	0.45	3.41	0.13	0.55	0.10
Others	56615	9068	1.95	6.24	0.31	0.77	0.03
Unspecified	6442	7920	0.12	0.81	0.14	0.54	0.33
Total	27440	11456	0.50	2.40	0.21	0.52	0.15

SOURCE: *Annual Survey of Industries* 1977-78.

TABLE 2.18 Principal Characteristics by Type of Ownership—All India

Type of Ownership	*Factories* (*number*)	*Fixed Capital* (*Rs. lakhs*)	*Productive Capital* (*Rs. lakhs*)	*Employee* (*number*)	*Emoluments* (*Rs. lakhs*)	*Gross Output* (*Rs. lakhs*)	*Value Added* (*Rs. lakhs*)
Wholly Central Government	1177	526669	754150	810397	80735	583691	124045
Wholly State/Local Government	3846	1015220	1152822	1036132	63832	415782	140978
Central/state/local Government jointly	395	25722	42335	89771	6363	57923	16374
Public Sector	5418	1567611	1949377	1936300	150930	1057396	281397
Central Government and Private Enterprises jointly	321	34681	63059	109166	10520	148046	27130
State/local Government and Private Enterprises jointly	1064	87631	120187	262910	15500	186184	29577
Joint Sector	1385	126312	183246	372076	26020	334230	56707
Wholly Private Enterprises	70921	594641	1008633	4939631	284214	3042514	617230
Unspecified	10353	29	63	102	8	239	62
Total	88077	2288593	3141319	7248109	461172	4434379	9553696

SOURCE: *Annual Survey of Industries* 1978-79.

TABLE 2.19 Principal Characteristics by Type of Ownership—All India

(Percentage distribution)

Type of Ownership	*Factories*	*Fixed Capital*	*Productive Capital*	*Employees*	*Emoluments*	*Gross Output*	*Value Added*
Wholly Central Government	1.3	23.0	24.0	11.2	17.5	13.2	13.0
Wholly State/Local Government	4.4	44.4	36.7	14.3	13.8	9.4	14.8
Central and State/Local Government jointly	0 4	1.1	1.4	1.2	1.4	1.3	1.7
Public Sector	6.1	68.5	62.1	26.7	32.7	23.9	29.5
Central Government and Private Enterprises jointly	0.4	1.7	2.0	1.5	2.3	3.2	2.8
State/Local Government and Private Enterprises jointly	1.2	3.8	3.8	3.6	3.4	4.2	3.1
Joint sector	1.6	5.5	5.8	5.1	5.7	7.5	5.9
Wholly Private Enterprises	80.5	26.0	32.1	68.2	61.6	68.6	64.6
Unspecified	11.8	—	—	—	—	—	—
Total	100.0	100.0	100.0	100.0	100.0	100.0	100.0

SOURCE: *Annual Survey of Industries* 1978-79.

TABLE 2.20 Structural Ratios by Type of Ownership—All India

Type of Ownership	*Fixed Capital Per Employee (Rs.)*	*Value Added Per Employee (Rs.)*	*Fixed Capital Gross Output Ratio*	*Fixed Capital Value Added Ratio*	*Value Added Gross Output Ratio*	*Emoluments Value Added Ratio*	*Operating Surplus Productive Capital Ratio*
Public Sector	80959	14533	1.48	5.57	0.27	0.54	0.07
Joint Sector	33948	15241	0.38	2.23	0.17	0.46	0.17
Private Sector	12039	12496	0.20	0.96	0.20	0.46	0.33
All Establishment	31575	13181	5.02	2.40	0.22	0.48	0.16

SOURCE: *Annual Survey of Industries* 1978-79.

TABLE 2.21 Principal Characteristics by Type of Organisation—All India

Type of Organisation	*Factories (number)*	*Fixed Capital (Rs. lakhs)*	*Productive Capital (Rs. lakhs)*	*Employees (number)*	*Emolument (Rs. lakhs)*	*Gross Output (Rs. lakhs)*	*Value Added (Rs. lakhs)*
Individual Proprietorship	26660	12326	23163	410262	6719	83872	14026
Partnership	40431	94626	185688	1534254	45239	778233	100691
Public Limited Company	7515	805696	1262326	2829092	248790	2320825	530614
Private Limited Company	8367	101491	179959	855867	50336	558645	108244
Public Corporation	1676	577691	683432	655894	46000	304695	95894
Corporate Sector	17558	1484378	2125717	4340853	345126	3184165	734752
Co-operative Society	1758	51798	68451	240918	9114	112844	10480
Others	1670	644964	738300	712792	54974	275265	89447
Total	88077	2288593	3141319	7938109	461172	4434379	955396

SOURCE: *Annual Survey of Industries* 1978-79

TABLE 2.22 Principal Characteristics by Type of Organisation—All India

(Percentage distribution)

Types of Organisation	*Factories*	*Fixed Capital*	*Productive Capital*	*Employees*	*Emoluments*	*Gross Output*	*Value Added*
Individual Proprietorship	30.3	0.5	0.7	5.7	1.5	1.9	1.5
Partnership	45.9	4.1	5.9	21.2	9.8	17.5	10.5
Public Limited Company	8.5	35.2	40.2	39.0	53.9	52.3	55.5
Private Limited Company	9.5	4.4	5.7	11.8	10.9	12.6	11.8
Public Corporations	1.9	25.3	21.8	9.1	10.0	6.9	10.1
Corporations Sector	19.9	64.9	67.7	59.9	74.8	71.8	76.9
Co-operative Society	2.0	2.3	2.2	3.4	2.0	2.6	1.7
Others	1.9	28.2	23.5	9.8	11.9	6.2	9.4
Total	100.0	100.0	100.0	100.0	100.0	100.0	100.0

SOURCE: *Annual Survey of Industries* 1978-79

TABLE 2.23 Structural Ratios by Type of Organisation—All India

Type of Organisation	*Fixed Capital Per Employee (Rs.)*	*Value Added Per Employee (Rs.)*	*Fixed Capital Gross Output Ratio*	*Fixed Capital Value Added Ratio*	*Value Added Gross Output Ratio*	*Emolument Value Added Ratio*	*Operating Surplus Productive Capital Ratio*
Individual Proprietorship	3004	3419	0.15	0.88	0.17	0.48	0.32
Partnership	6168	6563	0.12	0.94	0.13	0.45	0.30
Public Limited Company	28479	18756	0.35	1.52	0.23	0.47	0.22
Private Limited Company	11858	12647	0.18	0.94	0.19	0.47	0.32
Public Corporation	83077	14620	1.89	6.02	0.31	0.48	0.07
Corporate Sector	34207	16926	0.47	2.02	0.23	0.47	0.18
Co-operative Society	20724	6593	0.46	3.14	0.15	0.55	0.11
Others	90484	12549	2.31	7.21	0.32	0.61	0.05
All Establishment	31575	13181	0.52	2.40	0.22	0.48	0.16

SOURCE: *Annual Survey of Industries* 1978-79.

TABLE 2.24 Principal Characteristics of Public Sector Units by Type of Ownership 1975-79

Type of Ownership	*Fixed Capital Per Employee*	*Value Added Per Employee*	*Fixed Capital Output Ratio*	*Fixed Capital to Value Added*	*Value Added to Value Ratio*	*Emoluments to Value Added*
1975-76						
1. Wholly Central Government (1975-76)	0.43	0.143	0.741	2.986	0.248	0.613
2. Wholly State/Local Government	0.65	0.085	2.32	7.637	0.303	0.635
3. Central and State/Local Government jointly	0.27	0.113	0.588	2.469	0.238	0.496
1976-77						
1. Wholly Central Government	0.50	0.17	0.743	2.97	0.25	0.54
2. Wholly State/Local Government	0.78	0.09	2.58	8.29	0.31	0.57
3. Central and State/Local Government jointly	0.36	0.09	0.985	3.98	0.25	0.72
1977-78						
1. Wholly Central Government	0.55	0.156	0.757	3.54	0.213	0.613
2. Wholly State/Local Government	0.92	0.106	2.95	8.632	0.34	0.58
3. Central and State/Local Government jointly	0.14	0.85	0.30	1.589	0.19	0.71
1978-79						
1. Wholly Central Government	0.65	0.153	0.902	4.25	0.213	0.650
2. Wholly State/Local Government	0.98	0.136	2.44	7.20	0.339	0.453
3. Central and State/Local Government jointly	0.29	0.182	0.44	1.57	0.283	0.389

SOURCE: Computed from Annual Survey of Industries: *1975-76, 1976-77, 1977-78, 1978-79*

Set. III Some Salient Features of the Public Sector as reported in UCAER study, "*Public Sector Growth and Performance*" (*1983*).

Table

3.1 Capital Stock and Output Growth in the Public, Sector (at Current and 1970-71 Prices): 1960-61 to 1979-80.

3.2 Growth of Resources in the Public Sector (at Current Prices) 1969-61 to 1979-80.

3.3 Share of Non-departmental Undertakings in Specific Direct and Indirect Taxes (%): 1960-61 to 1979-80.

TABLE 3.1 Capital Stock and Output Growth in the Public Sector

(*Rs. Crores at 1970-71 prices.*)

Year	*Capital Stock*	*Public Sector NDP at Factor Cost*	*Average Capital–Output Ratio**
1960-61	15423	2581	5.98
1961-62	17185	2845	6.04
1962-63	19340	3214	6.02
1963-64	21674	3349	6.47
1964-65	24236	3431	7.06
1965-66	26999	3614	7.47
1966-67	29272	3572	8.19
1967-68	31572	3698	8.54
1968-69	33610	4222	7.96
1969-70	35572	4605	7.72
1970-71	37896	5007	7.57
1971-72	40402	5395	7.49
1972-73	43046	5778	7.45
1973-74	46193	6179	7.48
1974-75	49250	6460	7.62
1975-76	53158	7071	7,52
1976-77	57358	7834	7.32
1977-78	60771	8392	7.24
1978-79	64965	9123	7.12
1979-80	69245	9602	7.21

*Interpret with caution because of Administered Prices.

SOURCE: *Capital Stock*

SOURCE: Derived from National Accounts Statistics, CSO.

1. Uma Datta Roy Chaudhuri, Industrial Breakdown of Capital Stock in India, ***The Journal of Income and Wealth***, Oct. 1976, p. 158
2. J.L. Kapoor and R.N. Khera, Estimates of Wealth in the Public Sector, ***The Journal of Income and Wealth***, October 1976, p. 168

TABLE 3.2 Growth of Resources in the Public Sector

(Rs. crores at Current Prices.)

Year	Departmental Undertakings			Non Departmental Undertakings.			
	Interest	Profit and Dividends.	Total	Surplus	Indirect taxes (–)	Subsidies	Total
1960-61	91	96	187	42	13	1	54
1965-66	177	146	323	205	132	8	329
1970-71	299	158	457	503	490	39	954
1975-76	468	177	645	1669	1213	393	2489
1979-80	713	368	1081	3387	2351	1210	4528

SOURCE: *C.S.O. National Accounts Statistics.*

TABLE 3.3 Share of Non-Departmental Undertakings in Specific Direct and Indirect Taxes

Percentages)

Year	Corporation Tax.	Excise Duties	Subsidies	Net Indirect Taxes.
1960-61	9.9	2.8	1.1	1.3
1961-62	6.4	3.9	1.8	1.8
1962-63	8.1	5.0	2.1	2.4
1963-64	8.4	7.2	1.4	3.4
1964-65	7.3	8.8	2.7	4.1
1965-66	9.2	13.2	4.2	6.2
1966-67	9.4	17.0	2.4	8.1
1967-68	14.1	18.1	3.9	8.9
1968-69	14.7	19.7	3.5	9.8
1969-70	11.6	24.9	12.9	11.8
1970-71	16.5	27.3	11.6	12.8
1971-72	20.6	24.4	7.6	12.8
1972-73	20.8	25.7	8.3	13.3
1973-74	25.7	27.2	9.6	13.8
1974-75	32.9	27.6	9.6	13.8
1975-76	47.8	28.9	35.1	10.6
1976-77	55.7	30.4	51.2	7.8
1977-78	46.4	37.4	45.6	11.6
1978-79	34.8	37.1	35.4	13.1
1979-80	38.5	35.8	49.9	9.4

SOURCE: *C.S.O. National Accounts Statistics.*

Index